Computers and Management

In a Changing Society

Computers and Management

In a Changing Society

Third Edition

Donald H. Sanders
M. J. Neeley School of Business
Texas Christian University

Stanley J. Birkin
College of Business Administration
University of South Florida

McGraw-Hill Book Company

New York St. Louis San Francisco Auckland Bogotá Hamburg
Johannesburg London Madrid Mexico Montreal New Delhi Panama
Paris São Paulo Singapore Sydney Tokyo Toronto

This book was set in Times Roman by Black Dot, Inc. (ECU).
The editors were Charles E. Stewart and James B. Armstrong;
the production supervisor was Dominick Petrellese.
New drawings were done by J & R Services, Inc.
The cover was designed by Mark Rubin.
R. R. Donnelley & Sons Company was printer and binder.

COMPUTERS AND MANAGEMENT
In a Changing Society

Copyright © 1980, 1974, 1970 by McGraw-Hill, Inc. All rights reserved. Printed in the United States of America. No part of this publication may be reproduced, stored in a retrieval system, or transmitted, in any form or by any means, electronic, mechanical, photocopying, recording, or otherwise, without the prior written permission of the publisher.

1234567890 DODO 89876543210

Library of Congress Cataloging in Publication Data

Sanders, Donald H comp.
Computers and management.

Includes index.
1. Business—Data processing. 2. Management information systems. I. Birkin, Stanley J., joint author. III. Title.
HF5548.2.S22 1980 658.4'03 79-22490
ISBN 0-07-054627-4

A.T.I.C.
658.403
S215c3

To my mother, Irene.
D.H.S.

To my parents, Arthur and Sarah.
S.J.B.

Contents

2

THE INFORMATION REVOLUTION

3

COMPUTER IMPLICATIONS FOR ORGANIZATIONS AND INDIVIDUALS

4

PLANNING FOR COMPUTERIZATION

5

THE COMPUTER'S IMPACT ON PLANNING AND ORGANIZATIONAL STRUCTURE

6

STAFFING IMPLICATIONS OF COMPUTER USAGE

7

CONTROL AND THE COMPUTER

8
COMPUTERS IN NOT-FOR-PROFIT ORGANIZATIONS

Preface

Computers continue to play an ever-increasing role both in our everyday lives and in organizations of all types. Within these organizations the impact of computerization results in tremendous change and presents management in many situations with one of the most difficult of all contemporary challenges.

Colleges are now focusing much attention on the computer through courses in business administration and in the social and behavioral sciences. This increased attention is justified, since students destined to become managers in tomorrow's organizations will find themselves working in an environment significantly affected by the use of computer-based information systems. This is the case both in the business community and in the not-for-profit sector.

In order to prepare for a successful working relationship with these computerized information systems, present and potential managers must (1) learn about the computer—what is is, what it can and cannot do, and how it operates—and (2) acquire an understanding of the managerial and social implications of computer usage.

Many introductory data processing courses emphasize the first of these needs; they employ textbooks and/or manuals which are technically oriented and which are designed to provide the necessary grasp of hardware and programming concepts. Such courses are valuable and needed. However, they often do not deal with the broad impact that computers have had, are having, and may be expected to have on managers and on the environment in which managers work.

The purpose of this book is to provide the broad managerial orientation which is needed. More specifically, this volume (1) explains why knowledge of information processing is required (and in so doing introduces readers to some basic information processing concepts); (2) points out the managerial implications of computer usage to many whose data processing preparation is not likely to be extensive; (3) discusses some of the ways in which computers may possibly influence the society in which managers live and work; and (4) provides, in a single source, *relevant readings* taken from leading publications and written by respected authorities.

TEXT ORGANIZATION

In *Chapter 1,* the subject of management information is examined. The data processing steps necessary to produce such information are identified; the need for (and the importance of) management information is presented; and the desired properties of quality information are discussed. The concluding pages of the chapter are devoted to a study of the evolution of information processing.

Chapter 2 focuses attention on the information processing revolution which is now under way. Topics treated in this chapter include (1) the technological, social, and economic changes that provide the setting for sweeping informational changes and (2) the new management information systems being developed to enable administrators to cope with rapid environmental change. This chapter explains, in part, why future managers must have knowledge of information processing.

Chapter 3 is an orientation chapter which presents a broad-brush treatment of the implications of computer usage for management and society. Also included are analyses of the potential benefits of computers and a discussion of the negative implications of computerization. *Chapters 4 through 7* examine the problems and issues related to the areas of planning, organizing, staffing, and controlling.

Chapter 8, the final chapter, considers the use and impact of computers in not-for-profit organizations such as those in the fields of health, law, government, and social services. Even though many facets of computer usage are standard across all areas, these nonprofit organizations merit special attention because of their relatively new use of computers and because of the significance of the implications for society as a whole.

CHANGES IN THIS EDITION

This edition contains a significant number of changes. Among the more important changes are:

- The expansion and updating of the treatment given to important contemporary topics such as data-base systems and MIS applications.

- The replacement of the majority of the readings found in the second edition with more current articles.
- The development and inclusion of new cases replacing most of those in the second edition. (These cases can be used as starting points for discussion of the text material in the chapters.)
- The addition of an *entirely new chapter,* "Computers in Not-for-Profit Organizations," which focuses on the usage of computers in these types of organizations.

USE OF THIS BOOK

Computers and Management requires no mathematical or data processing background and is designed to be used (1) in introductory data processing courses (it will supplement the programming books and manuals used in technically oriented courses and can be used as a readings book regardless of the course orientation); (2) in basic management courses, where it will serve to impress upon management students the importance of the computer as a managerial tool; (3) in introductory systems-analysis courses, where it will expose potential analysts to the effects which their proposed systems changes are likely to have on managers and on the managerial environment; and (4) in business and not-for-profit organizations where managers will find in this volume a concise presentation of current trends and future expectations in the area of business information systems.

It would be inappropriate to conclude these opening remarks without acknowledging the contributions of those publishers and authors who have granted permission for their materials to be used as readings in this book. Their individual contributions are mentioned in the body of the book.

Donald H. Sanders
Stanley J. Birkin

Computers and Management
In a Changing Society

Chapter 1

Management Information: Introductory Concepts

Just under 30 years ago, the first general-purpose computer was installed at the U.S. Bureau of the Census. At the time, it was considered little more than a scientific curiosity, and its future use was projected to be limited to a few applications, mostly scientific and statistical in nature. This was a time when the data processing world was preoccupied with tabulating card systems. Few individuals were able to envision the ultimate growth and impact of the computer industry and computer usage in organizations. In a special report in *Dun's Review,* it has been projected that by 1985 there may be as many as a half a million computers installed in the United States.[1] In other words, there will be one computer for every business with over 50 employees. Furthermore, as an industry, the information system business is expected to grow at an annual rate exceeding 20 percent for the next decade, reaching the $82 billion level by 1985.[2]

The whirlwindlike growth of computer usage in many types of organizations

[1]"Management and the Computer," *Dun's Review,* July 1977, p. 65.

[2]Edward W. Pullen and Robert G. Simko, "Our Changing Industry," *Datamation,* January 1977, p. 55.

has created tremendous change in methods and procedures, in information collection and dissemination techniques, in management control processes, and in decision-making activities. As with any type of organizational change, it was to be expected that there would be some resistance by employees against the seemingly endless encroachment of the computer into almost all areas of activity. But unlike the earlier major epic change eras of mechanization and automation, computerization affected primarily the administrative task itself. Never before has the process of management been so influenced by changes in the functional areas of planning, organizing, staffing, and controlling.[3] The background and training of many managerial personnel was for the most part inadequate for the task of understanding and meeting the needs of the highly technological computer world. Consequently, most organizations developed a specialized group of computer professionals who were responsible for the design and development of computerized systems. The only problem was that many of these computer professionals lacked experience and understanding of the various business and managerial activities. The result was that in many organizations there developed a significant gap in communication between management and the computer/data processing departments. Managers lacking a clear understanding of the potential and capabilities of the computer were unable to direct the proper design and development of the newer information systems. In many cases, the computer/data processing departments filled this void by developing data processing systems which were not "user-oriented." The presence and significance of this communications gap has been somewhat alleviated during the past decade. It is quite common nowadays for data processing personnel to be required to have a business-related background in areas such as finance, accounting, and management. In turn, companies now frequently look for some computer-related experience as a requirement for their management trainees. Schools of business and other academic areas focusing on public administration, health care administration, etc., often include some

[3]Whether the resulting change has occurred because of computers and computer usage or has been made possible through the capabilities of computers is an issue which will be explored in Chapter 5.

"My computer doesn't understand me."

exposure to the computer in their curricula at both graduate and undergraduate levels. This brings us to the topic of the scope and objective of this book.

PURPOSE AND ORGANIZATION

The basic objective of this book is to enable the reader to gain an insight into the broad impact resulting from the use of computers in contemporary organizations. Specifically, we shall examine these impacts in the light of their effect on managers and their work and on the techniques and processes that are used in decision making. In addition, the book will introduce the reader to the capabilities and limitations of computers as they are used in the design and development of modern information systems. The technical coverage of computer hardware and software concepts is limited to those essential areas that are necessary for the reader to gain a fuller understanding of the impact of computer usage. A more comprehensive study of these topics, which is beyond the scope of this book, is to be found in a number of other books.[4]

The material in this book is organized into broad topical areas. In each chapter there are presentations of the major concepts, issues, and developments in the respective area. These are followed by a series of selected readings from the literature, chosen on the basis of interest, content, and clarity of presentation. These readings are intended to supplement and/or expand on the text matter. In addition, they frequently provide alternative and contrasting viewpoints on specific issues. More important, they introduce the reader to publications which are recommended sources of information, both now and for the future.

In Chapter 2 we shall examine the information revolution now under way by looking at (1) the technical, social, and economic developments that provide the setting for sweeping changes in information requirements and availability and (2) the new developments in management information systems designed to enable administrators to cope with these rapid environmental changes.

Chapter 3 is an orientation chapter which presents a broad-brush treatment of computer usage implications for management. Included is an analysis of the problems of adaptation associated with the information revolution and an examination of some of the major social issues, such as privacy, security, and individualism. *Chapters 4 through 7 focus on the problems and issues associated with the areas of planning, staffing, organizing, and controlling* the computer-related activities within organizations. *The final chapter takes a look at the use and impact of computers in nonprofit organizations,* such as those involved with health, law, government, education, the military, and social services. Even though many facets of computer usage are standard across all areas, these nonprofit organizations merit special attention today because of (1) the increased and relatively new involvement of computers in many of these areas

[4]An orientation to the stored program computer—what it is, what it can and cannot do, how it operates, and how it is programmed—may be found in Chapters 5 through 12 of Donald H. Sanders, *Computers in Business: An Introduction,* 4th ed., McGraw-Hill Book Company, New York, 1979.

and (2) the significance of the implications for society as a whole resulting from these developments.

In the remaining pages of this chapter, we shall examine more closely a very important subject, that of *management information.* We shall then summarize briefly the highlights of the *evolutionary development of information processing* before proceeding to Chapter 2 to explore the "information revolution."

INFORMATION CONCEPTS

Three elements fundamental to human activities are information, energy, and materials. All these elements are necessary to provide the physical things which humans need—i.e., food, clothing, shelter, and transportation. In addition to supporting physical production, however, information is also the substance of all human intellectual activity; it is basic to education, government, literature, the conduct of business, and the maintenance and expansion of our store of knowledge. The harnessing of energy brought about the industrial revolution; the attempt to harness and transform information is bringing about another revolution at the present time.[5]

Information Defined

The word *data* is the plural of *datum,* which means *fact.* Data, then, are facts, unevaluated messages, or informational raw materials, but they are not information, except in a constricted and detailed sense. Data are independent entities and are unlimited in number. Although often considered to be numerical values, data may also be defined to include nonnumerical perceptions and observations made by human beings and machines.

As used in this text, the term *information* is generally considered to designate data arranged in ordered and useful form. Thus, *information* will usually be thought of as relevant knowledge, produced as output of processing operations and acquired to provide insight in order to (1) achieve specific purposes or (2) enhance understanding.[6] From this definition, we see that information is the result of a transformation process. Just as raw materials are transformed into finished products by a manufacturing process (Figure 1-1*a*), so, too, are raw data transformed into information by the data processing operation (Figure 1-1*b*). The products produced by the manufacturing process have little

[5]This information revolution is the subject of the next chapter. An indication of the scope and importance of information is found in the estimate of the director of the President's Office of Telecommunications Policy that during 1975 "more than 50 percent of the US labor force and more than 50 percent of the gross national product were expected to be devoted to the production, processing, or distribution of information . . ." See "Washington Info" *Infosystems,* January 1976, p. 14.

[6]The above definition emphasizes management information in what might be termed the "formal" sense. Of course, managers also receive information from overheard conversations, from the actions rather than the words of others, and from other informal sources. In this informal sense, the manager processes the input data mentally and stores in his memory the information output for possible future use.

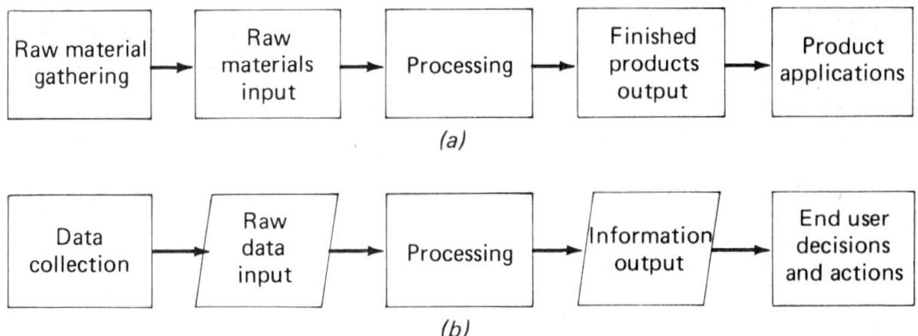

Figure 1-1 Transformation processes.

utility until they are properly applied; similarly, the information produced by data processing is of little value unless it supports meaningful end-user decisions and actions.

The purpose of data processing is to evaluate and bring order to data and place them in proper perspective or context so that meaningful information will be produced. The primary distinction between data and information, therefore, is that while all information consists of data, not all data produce specific and meaningful information that will reduce uncertainty and lead to greater insight and better decisions.

Sources of Data

The input data used to produce information originate from internal and external sources. *Internal sources* consist of individuals and departments located within an organization. These sources may furnish facts on a regular and planned basis (i.e., on a formal basis) to support decisions if the potential user is aware that the facts are available. Internal data gathered on a formal basis typically relate to events that have already happened; they often represent feedback to managers of the effectiveness and accuracy of earlier plans. Once the need for the data is established (and the value of supplying it is deemed to be worth the cost), a systematic data-gathering procedure is designed to produce the facts.[7] Of course, in addition to these planned data-gathering activities, data may also be received from internal sources on an informal basis through casual contacts and discussions.

External, or *environmental,* sources are the generators and distributors of data located outside the organization. These sources include such categories as customers, suppliers, competitors, business publications, industry associations, and government agencies. Such sources provide the organization with environmental and/or competitive data that may give managers important clues on what is likely to happen. Government agencies, for example, furnish businesses with a wealth of environmental statistics—such as per capita income, total consumer

[7]Not infrequently, a procedure for gathering and processing data continues to be followed after the need for the information no longer exists.

expenditures, and population-growth estimates—which are valuable for planning purposes.

Data Processing

All data processing, whether it is done by hand or by the latest electronic methods, consists of *input, manipulation,* and *output* operations.

Input Activities Data must be *originated* or captured in some form for processing. Data may be initially recorded on paper *source documents* such as sales tickets or deposit slips, and they then may be converted into a machine-usable form for processing. Alternatively, they may be initially captured directly in a paperless machine-usable form.

Manipulative Operations One or more of the following operations may then need to be performed on the gathered data:

Classifying. Identifying and arranging items with like characteristics into groups or classes is called *classifying.* Sales data taken from a sales ticket may be classified by product sold, location of sales point, customer, sales clerk, or any other classification that the processing cycle may require. Classifying is usually done by a shortened, predetermined method of abbreviation known as *coding.* The three types of code used are *numeric* (e.g., your Social Security number), *alphabetic* (grades A, B, and C), and *alphanumeric* (an automobile license plate stamped CSN-1763).

Sorting. After the data are classified, it is usually necessary to arrange or rearrange them in a predetermined sequence to facilitate processing. This arranging procedure is called *sorting.* Sorting is done by number as well as by letter. Sales invoices may be sorted by invoice number or by customer name. Numeric sorting usually requires less time than alphabetic sorting in machine-based processing systems and is therefore generally used.

Calculating. Arithmetic manipulation of the data is known as *calculating.* In the calculation of an employee's pay, for example, the total of hours worked, multiplied by the hourly wage rate, would give the taxable gross earnings. Payroll deductions such as taxes and insurance are then computed and subtracted from gross earnings to leave net or take-home earnings.

Summarizing. To be of value data must often be condensed or sifted so that the resulting output reports will be concise and effective. Reducing masses of data to a more usable form is called *summarizing.* Sales managers may be interested only in the total sales of a particular store. Thus, it would be wasteful in time and resources if they were given a report that broke sales down by department, product, and sales clerk.

Output/Records-Management Activities Once the data have been transformed into information, one or more of the following activities may be required:

Communicating. The information, in a usable form, must be *communicated* to the user. Output information may be in the form of a vital printed report, but output can also be in the form of a gas bill on a punched card or an updated reel of magnetic tape.

Storing. Placing similar data into files for future reference is *storing.* Obviously, facts should be stored only if the value of having them in the future exceeds the storage cost. Storage may take a variety of forms. Storage *media* that are frequently used include paper documents, microfilm, magnetizable media and devices, and punched paper media.

Retrieving. Recovering stored data and/or information when needed is the *retrieving* step. Retrieval methods range from searches made by file clerks to the use of quick-responding inquiry terminals that are connected directly (i.e., they are *online*) to a computer. The computer, in turn, is connected directly to a mass-storage device that contains the information.

Reproducing. It is sometimes necessary or desirable to copy or duplicate data. This operation is known as data *reproduction* and may be done by hand or by machine.

These, then, are the basic steps in data processing. Figure 1-2 presents these steps and indicates some of the ways in which they are accomplished. The means of performing the steps vary, according to whether *manual, electromechanical,* or *electronic* processing methods are used. Many businesses find that the best solution to their processing requirements is to use a combination of methods; e.g., manual methods may be used for small-volume jobs, while computers may be used for large-volume tasks.

The above brief remarks on the sources of data and the nature of data processing now make it possible to expand Figure 1-1*b*. In Figure 1-3 we see that data input is divided into sources and that data processing is broken down into operational steps. The solid lines represent the possible communication of data and information in a single processing cycle; the dashed lines represent the feedback communication required to obtain additional data and recycle the data base for future processing.

NEED FOR MANAGEMENT INFORMATION

Information is needed in virtually every field of human thought and action. At a personal level, if you always had high-quality information you could take better advantage of your future career opportunities and you would be better equipped to make other personal decisions.

But besides being essential to individuals who use it to achieve personal ends, information is also needed by managers in organizations. Managers at all levels must perform such basic management tasks or functions as *planning, organizing, staffing,* and *controlling.*[8] The success of any business is determined

[8]Information is also needed to meet demands originating from the environment in which the business operates. Reports of various kinds are required by government bodies. In one extreme example, a farm-products firm handled 173 different federal forms in a single year. Various reports were sent in at different intervals ranging from daily to annually. A final total of 37,683 reports, involving 48,285 man-hours of work, was submitted! In addition, dues reports are prepared for labor unions, financial reports are expected by creditors and stockholders, and market and product information may be desired by customers and suppliers of raw materials.

STEPS IN THE DATA PROCESSING OPERATION

Processing Methods	Originating-Recording	Classifying	Sorting	Calculating	Summarizing	Communicating	Storing	Retrieving	Reproducing
Manual Methods	Human observation; handwritten records; pegboards	Hand posting; pegboards	Hand posting; pegboards; edge-notched cards	Human brain	Pegboards; hand calculations	Written reports; hand-carried messages; telephone	Paper in files, journals, ledgers, etc.	File clerk; bookkeeper	Clerical; carbon paper
Manual with Machine Assistance	Typewriter; cash register; manual	Cash register; bookkeeping machine	Mechanical collators	Adding machines; calculators; cash registers	Accounting machines; adding machines; cash registers	Documents prepared by machines; message conveyors	Motorized rotary files; microfilm		Xerox machines; duplicators; addressing machines
Electro-mechanical Punched Card Methods	Prepunched cards; key-punched cards; mark-sensed cards; manual	Determined by card field design; sorter; collator	Card sorter	Accounting machines (tabulators); calculating punch		Printed documents; interpreter	Trays of cards	Manual tray movement	Reproducing punch
Electronic Methods	Magnetic tape encoder; magnetic and optical character readers; card and tape punches; on-line terminals; manual; key-to-disk encoder	Determined by systems design; computer	Computer sorting	Computer		Online data transmission; printed output; visual display; voice output	Magnetizable media and devices; punched media; computer; microfilm	Online inquiry with direct-access devices; manual movement of storage media to computer	Multiple copies from printers; microfilm copies

Figure 1-2 Tools and techniques for data processing.

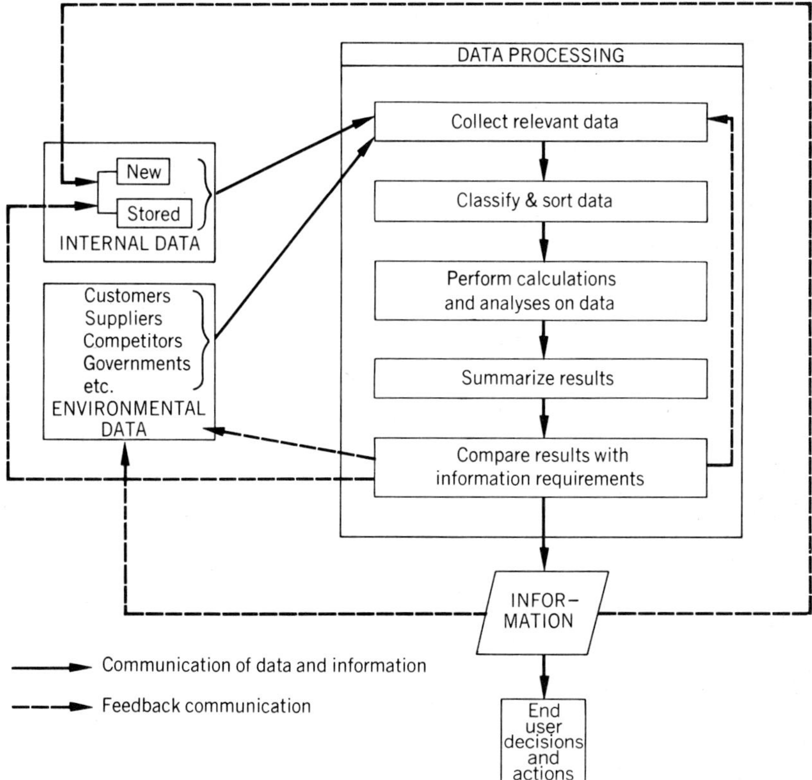

Figure 1-3

by how well its executives perform these activities. And how well these functions are carried out is dependent, in part, upon how well the information needs of managers are being met. Why is this? It is because each function involves decision making, and decision making must be supported by quality information. If a manager's information is of poor quality, the decisions that are made will probably suffer and the business (at best) will not achieve the success it might otherwise have had.

In summary, as shown in Figure 1-4, quality information in the hands of those who can effectively use it will support good decisions; good decisions will lead to effective performance of managerial activities; and effective managerial performance will lead to successful attainment of organizational goals. Thus, information is the bonding agent that holds an organization together.

What Information Is Needed?

What information does the manager need to manage effectively? A common need basic to all managers is an understanding of the purpose of the organization, i.e., its policies, its programs, its plans, and its goals. But beyond these basic informational requirements, the question of what information is

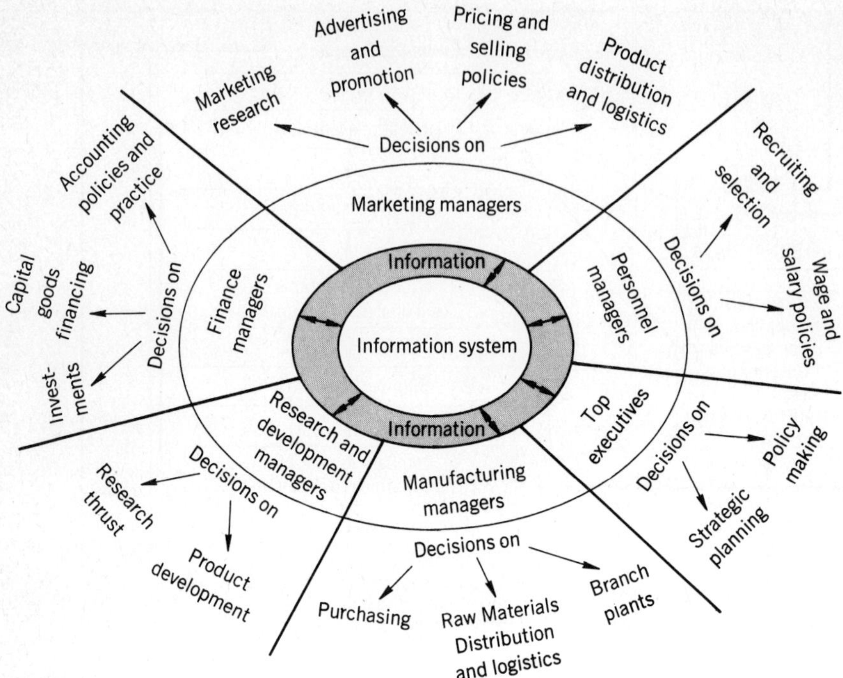

Figure 1-4

needed can only be answered in broad, general terms because individual managers differ in the ways in which they view information, in their analytical approaches in using it, and in their conceptual organization of relevant facts. An additional factor that complicates the subject of the information needed by managers is the organizational level of the managerial job. Managers at the lower operating levels need information to help them make the day-to-day operating decisions. At the top levels, however, information is needed to support long-range planning and policy decisions.

In Figure 1-5*a* we see that at the lower managerial levels more time is generally spent in performing control activities (e.g., checking to make sure that production schedules are being met), while at the upper levels more time is spent on planning (e.g., determining the location and specifications of a new production plant). Figure 1-5*b* shows that although lower-level managers need detailed information relating to daily operations of specific departments, top executives are best served with information that summarizes trends and indicates exceptions to what was expected. A final generalization is that the higher one is in the management hierarchy, the more one needs and is likely to use information obtained from external sources (see Figure 1-5*c*). A supervisor uses internally generated feedback information to control production processes, but a president studying the feasibility of a new plant needs information about customer product acceptance, pollution control, local tax structures, competitive

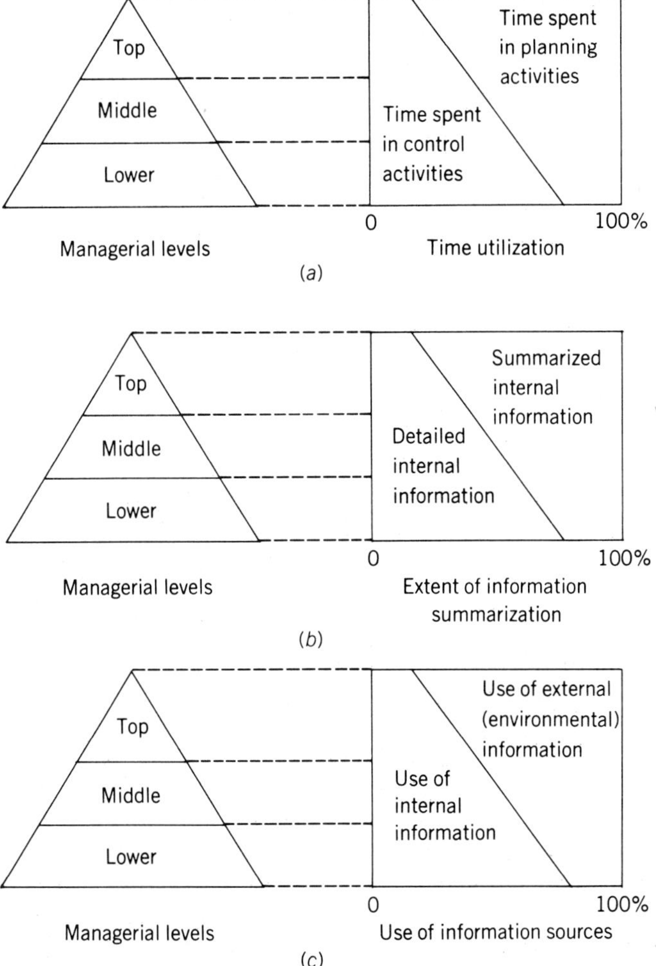

Figure 1-5

reactions, availability of labor and suppliers, etc., and this information is environmental in nature.

In summary, the types of decisions made by managers vary, and so information needs also vary. Thus, it is unlikely that we shall soon see (if, indeed, we ever do) an information system that is uniformly suitable and desirable for all managers in an organization.

Desired Properties of Management Information

As a general rule, the more information serves to reduce the element of uncertainty in decision making, the greater is its value. But information is one of the basic resources available to managers and, like other resources, it is usually not free. It is therefore necessary that the cost of acquiring the resource be compared with the value to be obtained from its availability. Just as it would be economically foolish for an organization to spend $100 to mine $75 worth of coal, so, too, would it be unsound to produce information costing $100 if this information did not lead to actions that yielded a net return. In other words, information should be prepared if (1) its cost is less than the additional *tangible revenues* produced by its use, (2) it serves to reduce *tangible expenses* by a more than proportionate amount, or (3) it provides such *intangible benefits* as greater insight, faster reaction time, better customer service, etc., which the information *user* considers to be worth the costs involved.

You should keep these brief comments on information economics in mind as we look at the desirability of information that possesses the characteristics of *accuracy, timeliness, completeness, conciseness,* and *relevancy.* Up to a certain point, information that possesses these properties may be expected to be more valuable than information lacking one or more of these characteristics.

Accuracy Accuracy may be defined as the ratio of correct information to the total amount of information produced over a period of time. If, for example, 1,000 items of information are produced and 950 of these items give a correct report of the actual situation, then the level of accuracy is 0.95. Whether or not this level is high enough depends upon the information being produced. Fifty incorrect bank balances in a mailing of 1,000 bank statements would hardly be acceptable to depositors or to the bank. On the other hand, if physical inventory records kept on large quantities of inexpensive parts achieve an accuracy level of 0.95, this might be acceptable. In the case of bank statements, greater accuracy *must* be obtained; in the case of the parts inventory, greater accuracy *could* be obtained, but the additional value to managers of having more accurate inventory information might be less than the additional costs required. Inaccuracies are the result of *human errors* and/or *machine malfunctions.* Human error (in system design, machine operation, the preparation of input data, and other ways) is the primary cause of inaccuracy.

Timeliness Timeliness is another important information characteristic. It is of little consolation to a manager to know that information that arrived too late to be of use was accurate. Accuracy alone is not enough. How fast must be the *response time* of the information system? Unfortunately, it is once again impossible to give an answer which will satisfy all situations. In the case of *regular reports,* an immediate response time following each transaction would involve a steady outpouring of documents. The result might well be a costly avalanche of paper that would bury managers. Thus, a compromise is often required. The response time should be short enough so that the information does not lose its freshness and value, but it should be long enough to reduce volume (and costs) and reveal important trends that signal the need for action (see Figure 1-6). The most appropriate information interval is therefore a matter which must be determined by each organization. However, as we shall see in the next chapter, new quick-response computer-based systems have been developed to give end users immediate access to the "time critical" information they need

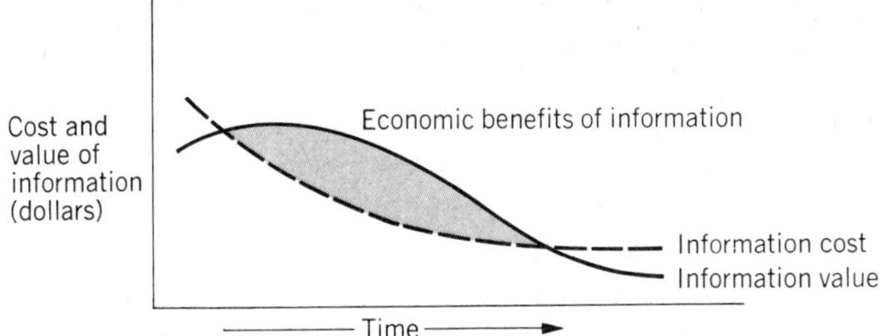

Figure 1-6 Relationship between information cost and value over time.

to make operating decisions between regular reporting periods and/or to provide them with prompt answers to nonrecurring questions that are not available from regular reports.

Completeness Most managers faced with a decision to make have been frustrated at some time by having supporting information that is accurate, timely—and *incomplete.* An example of the consequences of failure to consolidate related pieces of information occurred at Pearl Harbor in 1941. Historians tell us that data available, in bits and pieces and at scattered points, if integrated, would have signaled the danger of a Japanese attack. Better integration of the facts available at scattered points in a business for the purpose of furnishing managers with more complete information is a goal of information systems designers, as we shall see in the next chapter.

Conciseness Many information systems have been designed on the assumption that lack of completeness is the most critical problem facing managers. This assumption has led designers to employ an ineffective shotgun approach, peppering managers with more information than they can possibly use. Important information, along with relatively useless data, is often buried in stacks of detailed reports. Managers are then faced with the problem of extracting those items of information that they need. Concise information that summarizes (perhaps through the use of tables and charts) the relevant data and that points out areas of exception to normal or planned activities is what is often needed by—but less often supplied to—today's managers.

Relevancy Relevant information is "need-to-know" information that leads to action or provides new knowledge and understanding. Reports that were once valuable but are no longer relevant should be discontinued.

INFORMATION IMPROVEMENT AND COMPUTER PROCESSING

As long as an important resource is supplied to us when and where we need it, in the right quantity and quality and at a reasonable cost, we tend to take the resource for granted. It is often only when the supply, quality, and/or cost of the resource deteriorates that we recognize its importance. So it is with management information. Several weaknesses have been encountered with earlier information systems that have often prevented users from receiving information that possessed the desirable properties discussed in the preceding section. And as pressures to improve the quality of management information have built, managers have often turned to computer usage for relief. Included among the weaknesses that have contributed to information improvement efforts are:

1 *Difficulties in handling increased workloads.* Processing capability in many firms has been strained by (*a*) the growth in the size, complexity, and multinational scope of the firm; (*b*) the increased requirements for data from external sources such as local, state, and federal governmental agencies; and (*c*) the demands of managers for more kinds of information.[9] Fortunately, the greater the volume of data that must be processed, the more economical computer processing becomes, relative to other processing methods.

2 *Failures to supply accurate information.* If a processing system has gone beyond the capacity for which it was originally planned, inaccuracies will begin to appear and the control of organizational activities will suffer. Computer processing, however, will be quite accurate *if* the tasks to be performed have been properly prepared.

3 *Failures to supply timely information.* Meaningful information is timely information, but with an increase in volume, there is often a reduction in the speed of processing. Managers demand timely information. Unfortunately, although they may receive information about areas of virtual certainty in short order, information that reduces the element of uncertainty is often delayed until such time as it is merely collaborative. Thus, many businesses have turned to the use of computers to speed up their processing.

4 *Increases in costs.* The increasing labor and materials costs associated with a non–computer processing operation have often caused managers to look to computer usage for economic relief. For example, when compared with other alternatives, the use of computers may make it possible for certain costs to be reduced while the level of processing activity remains stable. Figure 1-7 gives a general idea of the cost relationships between computer processing methods and alternative methods. The curves show the average cost of processing a typical document or record using different processing approaches. Point A shows the breakeven cost position between manual and computer processing at a volume of A'. When volume is less than A', it would be more economical to use manual methods than a computer. Points B and C show other breakeven positions. Of course, the cost curves in Figure 1-7 do not remain constant. Each increase in clerical labor rates and the cost of clerical office supplies, for example, shifts the manual method curves upward, while each new hardware innovation may serve to reduce computer costs and thus shift the computer curve downward. The net result has been to make computer processing methods more attractive at lower processing volumes (see Figure 1-8).

[9]One drug company recently reported that it was required to furnish the federal government with 200,000 pages of data at a cost of $15 million, and a banking authority reports that if the more than 26 billion checks that were written and processed in the United States in a recent year were placed in a stack, the pile would extend over 1,500 miles into space.

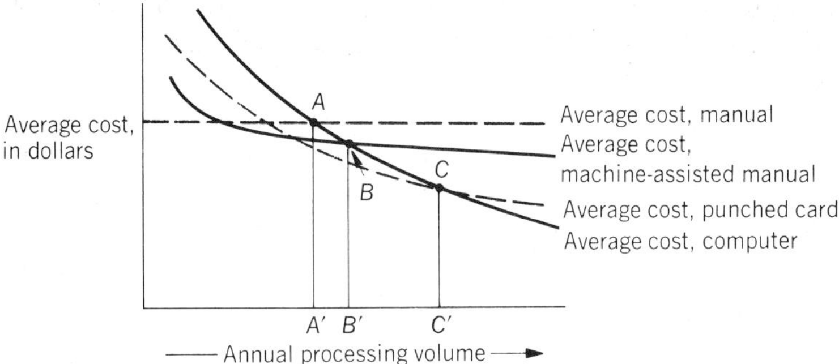

Figure 1-7 Average cost relationships.

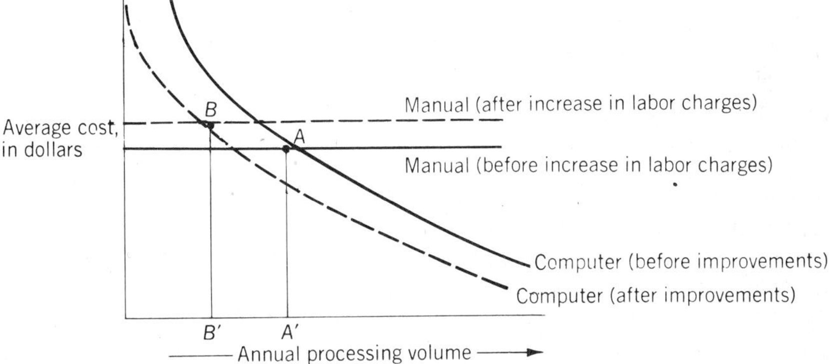

Figure 1-8 A'=Breakeven volume prior to shifts. B'=Breakeven volume after shifts.

EVOLUTION OF INFORMATION PROCESSING

Earlier in the chapter (in Figure 1-2), we classified processing methods into *manual, machine-assisted manual, electromechanical punched card,* and *electronic computer* categories. In the remaining pages of this chapter, let us use these categories to look briefly at the history of information processing.

The Manual Stage

For centuries, people lived on earth without keeping records. But as social organizations such as tribes began to form, adjustments became necessary. The complexities of tribal life required that more details be remembered. Methods of counting, based on the biological fact that people have fingers, were thus developed. However, the limited number of digits, combined with the need to remember more facts, posed problems. For example, if a shepherd were tending a large tribal flock and if he had a short memory, how was he to keep control of his inventory? Problems bring solutions, and the shepherd's solution might have been to let a stone, a stick, a scratch on a rock, or a knot in a string represent each sheep in the flock.

As tribes grew into nations, trade and commerce developed. Stones and sticks, however, were not satisfactory for early traders. In 3500 B.C., the ancient Babylonian merchants were keeping records on clay tablets.

Manual record-keeping techniques continued to develop through the centuries, with such innovations as record audits (the Greeks) and banking systems and budgets (the Romans). In the United States, in the 20 years following the Civil War, the main tools of data processing were pencils, pens, rulers, work sheets (for classifying, calculating, and summarizing), journals (for storing), and ledgers (for storing and communicating).

The volume of business and government processing during this period was expanding rapidly, and, as might be expected, such complete reliance upon manual methods resulted in information that was relatively inaccurate and often late. To the consternation of the Census Bureau, for example, the 1880 census was not finished until it was almost time to begin the 1890 count! In spite of accuracy and timeliness limitations, however, *manual processing methods have the following advantages:* (1) information is in a humanly readable form; (2) changes and corrections are easily accomplished; (3) no minimum economic processing volume is generally required; and (4) manual methods are easily adapted to changing conditions.

Machine-Assisted Manual Development

The evolution of machine-assisted manual processing methods has gone through several phases. In the *first phase,* machines were produced which improved the performance of a *single* processing step. In 1642, for example, the first mechanical calculating machine was developed by Blaise Pascal, a brilliant young Frenchman. And in the 1880s, the typewriter was introduced as a recording aid that improved legibility and doubled writing speeds.

In the *second phase* of machine-assisted methods, equipment was invented which could *combine* certain processing steps in a single operation. Machines that calculate and print the results were first produced around 1890. They combine calculating, summarizing, and recording steps and produce a printed tape record suitable for storing data. After World War I, accounting machines designed for special purposes (e.g., billing, retail sales, etc.) began to appear. These machines also combine steps and often contain several adding *registers* or *counters* to permit the accumulation of totals (calculation and summarization) for different classifications. For example, the supermarket cash register has separate registers to sort and total the day's sales of health items, hardware, meats, produce, and groceries.

A *third phase* has emerged in recent years. Equipment manufacturers have taken steps to ensure that small calculators and accounting machines are not made obsolete by the computer. Features of these machines are being combined with features taken from computers to create new electronic pocket-size and desk-size hardware. Many of these new calculators (computers?) have data-storage capability and can be programmed to perform processing steps in sequence just like computers. However, programmable calculators cannot yet match the speed and versatility of a computer in processing, storing, and retrieving both alphabetic and numeric data.

When compared with the manual processing of the late 1800s, machine-assisted manual methods have the advantages of greater speed and accuracy. However, a higher processing volume is generally required to justify equipment costs, there is some reduction in the flexibility of the processing techniques, and it is relatively more difficult to (1) correct or change data once they have entered the processing system and (2) implement changes in machine-assisted procedures.

Electromechanical Punched Card Development

Punched card methods have been in *widespread* business use only since the 1930s, but the history of the punched card dates back to about the end of the American Revolution when a French weaver named Jacquard used them to control his looms.

Although punched cards continued to be used in process control, it was not until the use of manual methods resulted in the problem of completing the 1880 census count that they began to be considered as a medium for data processing. The inventor of modern punched card techniques was Dr. Herman Hollerith, a statistician. He was hired by the Census Bureau as a special agent to help find a solution to the census problem. In 1887, Hollerith developed his machine-readable card concept and designed a device known as the "census machine." Tabulating time with Hollerith's methods was only one-eighth of that previously required, and so his techniques were adopted for use in the 1890 count. Although the population had increased from 50 to 63 million people in the decade after 1880, the 1890 count was completed in less than 3 years. (Of course, this would be considered intolerably slow by today's standards,[10] but the alternative in 1890 would have been to continue the count beyond 1900 and violate the constitutional provision that congressional seats be reapportioned every 10 years on the basis of census data.)

Following the 1890 census, Hollerith converted his equipment to business use and set up freight statistics systems for two railroads. In 1896 he founded the Tabulating Machine Company to make and sell his invention. Later, this firm merged with others to form what is now known as International Business Machines Corporation (IBM).

Punched card processing is based on a simple idea: Input data are initially recorded in a coded form by punching holes into cards, and these cards are then fed into machines that perform processing steps—e.g., sorting, calculating, and summarizing.

Computer Development

In 1833, Charles Babbage, Lucasian Professor of Mathematics at Cambridge University in England, proposed a machine, which he named the *analytical*

[10]The 1950 census, using punched card equipment, took about 2 years to produce; the 1970 census yielded figures in a few months.

engine. Babbage was an eccentric and colorful individual who spent much of his life in a vain attempt to build his machine.[11] Babbage's dream—to many of his contemporaries it was "Babbage's folly"—would have incorporated a punched card input; a memory unit, or *store;* an arithmetic unit, or *mill;* automatic printout; sequential program control; and 20-place accuracy. In short, Babbage had designed a machine that was a prototype computer and that was a hundred years ahead of its time. Babbage died in 1871, and little progress was made until 1937.

Beginning in 1937, Harvard professor Howard Aiken set out to build an automatic calculating machine that would combine established technology with the punched cards of Hollerith. With the help of graduate students and IBM engineers, the project was completed in 1944. The completed device was known as the Mark I digital computer. (A *digital* computer is one that essentially does counting operations.) Internal operations were controlled automatically with electromagnetic relays; arithmetic counters were mechanical. The Mark I was thus not an *electronic* computer but was rather an *electromechanical* one. In many respects the Mark I was the realization of Babbage's dream. Appropriately, this "medieval" machine is now on display at Harvard University.

The first *electronic* digital computer to be put into full operation was built as a secret wartime project between 1939 and 1946 at the University of Pennsylvania's Moore School of Electrical Engineering. The team of J. Presper Eckert, Jr., and John W. Mauchly was responsible for its construction. However, as was later determined by a federal judge in an important patent suit, Eckert and Mauchly did not invent the automatic electronic digital computer themselves, but instead derived that subject matter from a Dr. John Vincent Atanasoff. (Atanasoff was a professor of physics and mathematics at Iowa State College and did his most important computer work between 1935 and 1942, at which time he stopped work on his prototype and left Iowa State to work at the Naval Ordnance Laboratory.)

Vacuum tubes (19,000 of them!) were used in place of relays in the Eckert-Mauchly machine. This computer was called "ENIAC" and could do 300 multiplications per second (making it 300 times faster than any other device of the day).[12] Operating instructions for ENIAC were not stored internally; rather, they were fed through externally located plugboards and switches. In 1959, ENIAC was placed in the Smithsonian Institution.

In 1946, in collaboration with H. H. Goldstine and A. W. Burks, John von Neumann, a mathematical genius and member of the Institute for Advanced

[11]He was also something of a literary critic. In "The Vision of Sin," Tennyson wrote: "Every moment dies a man/Every moment one is born." Babbage wrote Tennyson and pointed out to the poet that since the population of the world was increasing, it would be more accurate to have the verse read: "Every moment dies a man, Every moment one and one-sixteenth is born." What he lacked in aesthetic taste he compensated for with mathematical precision!

[12]William Shanks, an Englishman, spent 20 years of his life computing π to 707 decimal places. In 1949, ENIAC computed π to 2,000 places in just over 70 hours and showed that Shanks had made an error in the 528th decimal place. Fortunately, Shanks was spared the knowledge that he had been both slow and inaccurate, for he preceded ENIAC by 100 years.

Study in Princeton, New Jersey, suggested in a paper that (1) *binary* numbering systems be used in building computers and (2) computer *instructions* as well as the data being manipulated could be stored internally in the machine. These suggestions became a basic part of the philosophy of computer design. The binary numbering system is represented by only two digits (0 and 1) rather than the 10 digits (0 to 9) of the familiar decimal system. Since electronic components are typically in one of two conditions (on or off, conducting or not conducting, magnetized or not magnetized), the binary concept facilitated equipment design.

Although these design concepts came too late to be incorporated in ENIAC, Mauchly, Eckert, and others at the University of Pennsylvania set out to build a machine with stored program capability. This machine—the EDVAC—was not completed until several years later. To the EDSAC, finished in 1949 at Cambridge University, must go the distinction of being the first *stored program electronic* computer.

One reason for the delay in EDVAC was that Eckert and Mauchly founded their own company in 1946 and began to work on the UNIVAC. In 1949, Remington Rand acquired the Eckert-Mauchly Computer Corporation, and in early 1951, the first UNIVAC-I became operational at the Census Bureau. In 1963, it, too, was retired to the Smithsonian Institution—a historical relic after just 12 years! The first computer acquired for data processing and record keeping by a *business organization* was another UNIVAC-I, which was installed in 1954 at General Electric's Appliance Park in Louisville, Kentucky.

In the period from 1954 to 1959, many businesses acquired computers for data processing purposes, even though these *first-generation* machines had been designed for scientific uses. Managers generally considered the computer to be an accounting tool, and the first applications were designed to process routine tasks such as payrolls and customer billing. Unfortunately, in most cases, little or no attempt was made to modify and redesign existing accounting procedures in order to produce more effective managerial information. The potential of the computer was consistently underestimated; more than a few were acquired for no other reason than prestige.

But we should not judge the early users of electronic data processing too harshly. They were pioneering in the use of a new tool not designed specifically for their needs; they had to staff their computer installations with a new breed of workers; and they initially had to cope with the necessity of preparing programs in a tedious machine language. In spite of these obstacles, the computer was found to be a fast, accurate, and untiring processor of mountains of paper.

The computers of the *second generation* were introduced around 1959 to 1960 and were made smaller, faster, and with greater computing capacity. The vacuum tube, with its relatively short life, gave way to compact *solid state* components such as diodes and transistors. Unlike earlier computers, some second-generation machines were designed from the beginning with business processing requirements in mind.

In 1964, IBM ushered in the *third generation* of computing hardware when it announced its System/360 family of computers. And during the early 1970s, several manufacturers introduced new equipment lines. For example, IBM announced the first models of its System/370 line of computers. These machines continued the trend toward miniaturization of circuit components. Further improvements in speed, cost, and storage capacity were realized. In the next chapter we shall look in more detail at some of the recent developments in computer technology.

The Computer Industry In 1950 the developers of the first computers agreed that 8 or 10 of these machines would satisfy the entire demand for such devices for years to come. Of course, we now know that this was a monumental forecasting blunder; in fact, it must go down in history as one of the worst market estimates of all time! By 1956 over 600 general-purpose computer systems (worth about $350 million) had been installed by organizations in the United States; today, such general-purpose installations are numbered in the hundreds of thousands (and this does not count the tens of thousands of very small computers that individuals have recently installed in their homes).[13] Thus, the theme of a recent computer conference—"Computers . . . by the millions, for the millions"—now characterizes the size and scope of the computer industry.

There are several dozen *computer manufacturers,* many of whom specialize in scientific, process control, and/or very small general-purpose machines. In terms of the estimated revenues received in 1976 from data processing products and services, the seven largest firms are listed in Figure 1-9.[14] Of these largest companies, most were initially business machine manufacturers (IBM, Burroughs Corporation, Sperry UNIVAC, and NCR Corporation), or they manufactured electronic controls (Honeywell). Exceptions are Control Data Corporation and Digital Equipment Corporation, which were founded to produce computers. As you can see in Figure 1-9, the industry leader is IBM, with at least 50 percent of the entire industry market. In spite of the economic health of the computer industry as a whole, however, more than a few firms were unable to compete profitably in certain segments of the market in the 1970s. Some of the more notable "dropouts" were General Electric, Xerox, and RCA. There have also been numerous antitrust suits and countersuits in the 1970s involving various manufacturers (particularly IBM) and the federal government.

[13]Nobody knows the exact number or present value of these computer systems because many computer manufacturers do not officially release installation data. And since there are disagreements in present estimates, it is not surprising that there are large variances in future expectations. For example, the president of one of the large computer industry firms puts the estimate of the installed value of general purpose systems in 1980 at more than $90 *billion.* But an expert at a leading consulting firm places the figure in 1981 at "only" $70 to $75 billion. In either case, the numbers are huge and there are no immediate signs of market saturation in the computer industry.

[14]Revenue is heavily concentrated in only a few firms in the computer industry. The seven firms in Figure 1-9 probably account for nearly 80 percent of the data processing revenues received by all United States companies. For more information on the top 50 companies, see Oscar H. Rothenbuecher, "The Top 50 U.S. Companies in the Data Processing Industry," *Datamation,* June, 1977, pp. 61–74.

Figure 1-9 Estimated Revenues from Data Processing Products and Services

Company	1975 revenue (in billions)	1976 revenue (in billions)	Percentage increase
IBM	$11.12	$12.72	14
Burroughs Corporation	1.45	1.63	13
Honeywell	1.32	1.43	8
Sperry UNIVAC	1.30	1.43	11
Control Data Corporation	1.22	1.33	9
NCR Corporation	.96	1.10	15
Digital Equipment Corp.	.53	.74	38
Totals	$17.90	$20.38	14

Source: Adapted from Oscar H. Rothenbuecher, "The Top 50 U. S. Companies in the Data Processing Industry," *Datamation,* June, 1977, pp. 61–74.

Computer Size Categories Although the first computers were all large enough to store grain in, today's machines vary in size from very large to those that are smaller than this book. Thus, in terms of relative computing power and cost, today's systems may be classified as *micro-sized, mini-sized, small, medium,* or *large.*

A *microprocessor* is assembled from tens of thousands of tiny transistors, resistors, and other electronic components to perform the arithmetic and logic functions of a computer. The typical microprocessor is fabricated on a single tiny chip of silicon and is combined with other elements that provide input/output connections, storage, and control to form a complete *microcomputer* on a board that may be smaller than this page. Microcomputers are general-purpose processors that may perform the same operations and use the same program instructions as much larger computers. They began to appear in quantity in 1973. Although they are relatively slow in operation and have relatively limited data-handling capabilities, these computers are being used in a rapidly expanding number of applications. Perhaps their most common use at this writing is to provide control and intelligence functions for some of the peripheral devices used with larger computer systems. They are also very popular with hobbyists; as noted earlier, tens of thousands of them have been purchased by individuals for their personal use and entertainment. Microcomputers range in price from a few hundred to a few thousand dollars, depending on the type and number of input/output devices used and on the amount of storage capacity obtained.

Minicomputers are small machines, but there is no clear-cut distinction between the largest microcomputers and the smallest minis, on the one hand, or between the larger minis and small-scale business systems, on the other. As a rough guide, however, minicomputers typically cost between $2,500 and $25,000, usually weigh less than 50 pounds, and may be plugged into any standard electrical outlet. Minicomputers perform the same arithmetic and logic functions, use several of the same programming languages, and have many of the same circuitry features as larger computers. Although they are general-purpose devices, some are used for special or dedicated purposes such as controlling a machine tool or a process. Others are (1) used for business data processing purposes, (2) connected to larger computers to act as input/output (I/O) and message-switching devices, (3) used in school systems for educational purposes, and (4) used in laboratories for scientific computation purposes. The versatility of minicomputers, combined with their low cost, accounts for their rapid acceptance.

Small business computers come in a bewildering range of models and capabilities. Some are desk-sized, are designed specifically to meet the data processing requirements of small businesses, and are similar in basic capabilities to minicomputers; some are the punched card–oriented successors to electromechanical punched card installations; and some are the smallest models of a line of computers that includes a number of medium-sized and very large processors. These small members of a "family" of computers typically use magnetic tapes (resembling large sound recording tapes) and magnetic disks (resembling large phonograph records) as data-storage media. They are generally faster than desk-sized models and card processors, have greater internal data-storage capacity, and are thus more expensive. (Desk-sized processors and card-oriented systems typically sell for $20,000 to $80,000; the smallest models of computer families typically sell for $70,000 to $200,000.)

Medium-sized computers may sell for $200,000 to $1 million, and *larger systems* exceed this price range. In return for higher prices, users receive faster processing speeds, greater storage capacity, wider selection of optional equipment from which to choose, and a lower cost-per-calculation figure.[15]

REVIEW AND DISCUSSION QUESTIONS

1 (*a*) What is management information? (*b*) What is the difference between data and information? (*c*) Compare the manufacturing process with the information-producing process.
2 Identify and explain the sources of business data.
3 (*a*) Identify and explain the basic data processing steps. (*b*) What processing methods may be used to perform these steps?
4 "Beyond certain basic informational requirements the question of what information is needed by managers can only be answered in broad, general terms." Discuss this statement.
5 (*a*) Why does the organizational level of the managerial job affect the information needed? (*b*) How do informational needs differ?

[15]This assumes that the volume of work is sufficient to keep a large machine occupied. If a man can compute the answer to a multiplication problem in 1 minute, and there are 125 million such problems to be solved, the total cost to do the calculations manually would exceed $10 million. The UNIVAC I (which in terms of computing power is a very small machine by today's standards) could have done the job for $4,300. However, a large machine today that rents for over $100,000 per month could do the job for less than $4.

6 Identify and discuss the desired properties of management information.
7 What factors have focused attention on the need for management information improvement in recent years?
8 The figure below shows the typical total-cost relationships between computer processing methods and alternative methods. (*a*) Discuss the meanings of points *A*, *B*, and *C* in the figure. (*b*) "The total cost for computer processing may exceed that for other methods when the processing volume is small." Discuss this statement. (*c*) Discuss the meanings of *A*′, B′, and *C*′ in the figure.

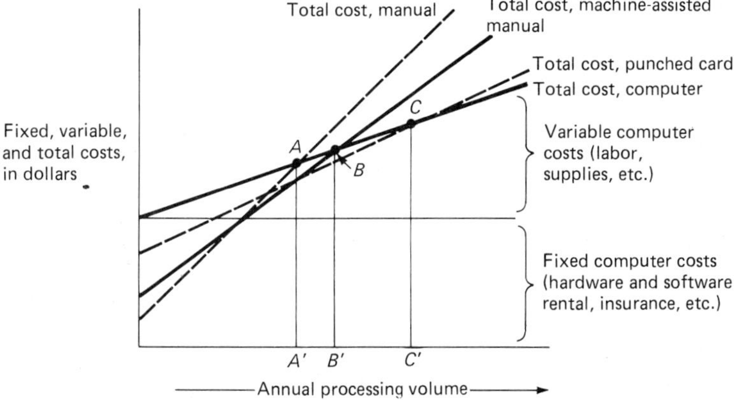

Figure 1-9 Estimated revenues from data processing products and services.

9 What are the advantages and limitations of manual data processing methods?
10 What are some of the differences between second- and third-generation computers?
11 What are some of the major trends in computer systems and computer usage? Describe your projections as to the capabilities of the next "generation" of computer equipment.
12 After a survey of a computer center available to you, identify: (*a*) The hardware generation of the equipment, (*b*) the approximate purchase price and/or leasing cost of the equipment, (*c*) the name of the firms providing the equipment, program, and supplies to the center, (*d*) the size category of the center's computer (or computers), (*e*) an organization chart showing the functional and administrative divisions within the center, and (*f*) the services provided to the users of the center.

Chapter 1 Readings

INTRODUCTION TO READINGS 1 THROUGH 3

1 Advances in computer technology in recent years have led to a wide variety of systems, and in many cases managers have had little to say in the development of these decision support systems. In this article, Steven L. Alter reports his findings from a study of 56 systems and pinpoints areas in which effective managers use information systems.

2 Five assumptions commonly made by designers of management information systems are identified by Professor Ackoff. In this article, he points out that these assumptions (*a*) are usually false and (*b*) have led to major deficiencies in many designed systems. After examining each of these five assumptions, he outlines a design procedure which avoids these assumptions.

3 Only too frequently, the lack of communication between managers and the data processing department has resulted in the development of information systems that have failed to meet expectations. In this article, William S. Anderson gives some practical advice on how to close the gap between systems anticipation and systems performance.

Reading 1

How Effective Managers Use Information Systems

Steven L. Alter

What can managers realistically expect from computers, other than a pile of reports a foot deep dumped on their desks every other week?

Everyone knows, for instance, that computers are great at listing receivables. But what about all the promises and all the speculations over the past few decades about the role of the computer in management? While there have been advances in basic information retrieval, processing, and display technologies, my recent study of 56 computerized decision support systems confirms the common wisdom that very few management functions have actually been automated to date, and all indications are that most cannot be.

Instead, my findings show what other researchers have reported: applications are being developed and used to *support* the manager responsible for making and implementing decisions, rather than to *replace* him. In other words,

Reprinted from *Harvard Business Review,* November–December 1976. Reprinted by permission from *Harvard Business Review.* Copyright © 1976 by the president and fellows of Harvard College; all rights reserved.
Mr. Alter is on the faculty of the Business School of the University of Southern California.

people in a growing number of organizations are using what are often called decision support systems to improve their managerial effectiveness.

Unfortunately my research also bore out the fact that while more and more practical applications are being developed for the use of decision makers, three sizable stumbling blocks still stand in the way of others who might benefit from them.

First, managers and computer users in many organizations are familiar with only a few of the types of systems now in use. As a result, different types of innovative systems have often been conceived and nurtured by internal or external "entrepreneurs," *not* by the system users or their superiors.

Second, and closely related to my first finding, these entrepreneurs tend to concentrate on technical characteristics. Too often, this myopia means that they fail to anticipate the ways in which such systems can be used to increase the effectiveness of individuals in organizations.

Finally, highly innovative systems—the very ones management should find most useful—run a high risk of never being implemented, especially when the impetus for change comes from a source other than the potential user.

Quite simply, my purpose in this article is to discuss, without getting into the technology involved, the high potential of a variety of decision support systems, the challenges and risks they pose to managers and implementers, and a wide range of strategies to meet these challenges and risks.

TYPES OF DECISION SUPPORT SYSTEMS

While there are many ways to categorize computer systems, a practical one is to compare them in terms of what the user does with them:

- Retrieves isolated data items.
- Uses as a mechanism for ad hoc analysis of data files.
- Obtains prespecified aggregations of data in the form of standard reports.
- Estimates the consequences of proposed decisions.
- Proposes decisions.
- Makes decisions.

As Figure 1 indicates, EDP reporting systems usually perform only the third function in this list of operations, which I have organized along a dimension from "data-orientation" to "model-orientation." Hence, unlike the EDP user who receives standard reports on a periodic basis, the decision support system user typically initiates each instance of system usage, either directly or through a staff intermediary.

Although decision-oriented reporting systems often grow out of standard EDP systems, I will concentrate on seven distinct types, briefly describing one example of each type.

Incidentally, it is interesting to note that external consultants developed the

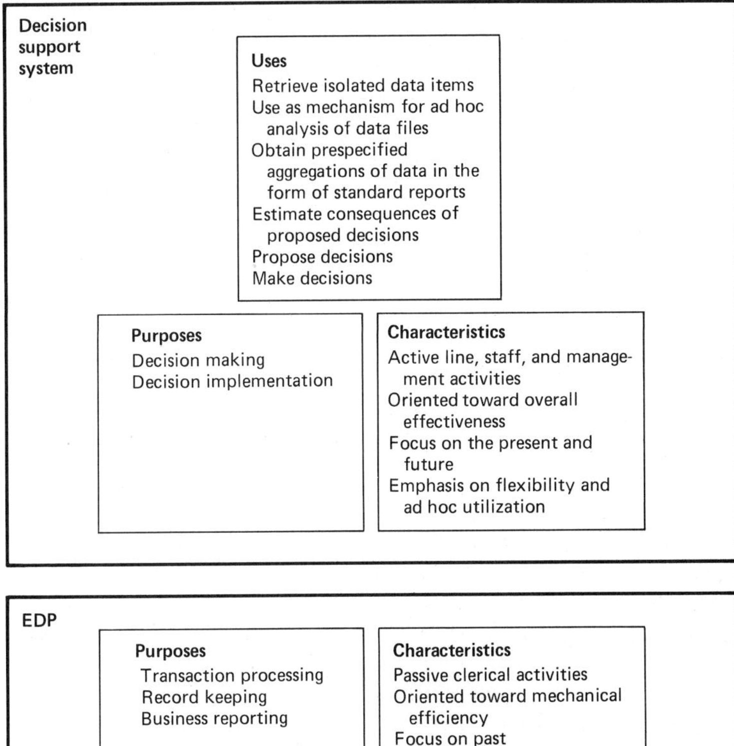

Figure 1 Comparison of uses, purposes, and characteristics of EDP systems versus decision support systems.

systems cited in my second, fifth, and seventh examples, while those of the first, third, and sixth were the creations of people acting as internal entrepreneurs through staff roles; only the fourth system was developed on direct assignment by the user. This same pattern of initiation of innovative systems by people other than the users was present in many of the 56 systems.

1 *Retrieval Only—A Shop Floor Information System*

In order to help production foremen improve the percentage yield on a newly developed 50-stage process for manufacturing micro-circuits, the management of one company has installed an on-line, shop floor information system. Operators submit daily piecework reports, which include yield, release date, identification of the person who does the work, and so on. The foremen then juggle this information to obtain productivity data by operation, operator, machine, and lot.

Thus they are able to use the system in a number of ways. They can monitor work flow, pinpoint yield problems, and settle day-to-day questions such as who worked on which lot when, and which operators are ahead of or behind schedule, or below standards. The foremen have 13 standard commands by which they can retrieve the data stored in the system and display them on a cathode ray tube terminal. The commands permit them to tailor reports to their needs.

2 *Retrieval and Analysis—A Portfolio Analysis System*

Before advising clients or making authorized trading decisions, the portfolio managers at a bank I studied used an on-line system to analyze individual portfolios. The managers can bypass time-consuming manual methods and obtain up-to-date and clearly organized portfolio information in either graphic or tabular form.

Depending on the situation, a manager can inspect both individual portfolios and groups of portfolios from different viewpoints—for example, rank them in different ways, obtain breakdowns by industry or risk level, and so on. With this kind of flexibility, the bank's portfolio managers make more effective use of a vast amount of information, most of which had existed prior to the system but had been accessible only through tedious manual analysis.

3 *Multiple Data Bases Plus Analysis—Sales Information Systems*

Greater flexibility was also the reason that two consumer products companies and one manufacturing company I looked at developed sales information systems which are quite similar. Standard EDP functions were too inflexible to produce ad hoc sales analysis reports in a timely and cost-effective manner for those in the companies' marketing and planning areas. In each case, information extracted from the EDP systems is now maintained separately in order to have it handy and, in two instances, to be able to analyze it in conjunction with externally purchased proprietary data bases and models.

Basically, each system is a vehicle by which a staff man or group tries to help decision makers. Their modus operandi is incremental: identify a problem; bring the current system and existing expertise to bear on it; develop a solution in the form of an analysis or additional system module; and incorporate the results into an expanded version of the system.

4 *Evaluating Decisions Using an Accounting Model—A Source-and-Application-of-Funds Budget*

To expedite operational decision making and financial planning over a two-year horizon, an insurance company is using an on-line, source-and-application-of-funds budget system. Inputs are projections of future business levels in various lines of insurance and investment areas, plus assumptions concerning important numbers such as future money-market rates. The output is a projected overall cash flow by month.

An investment committee uses the model to allocate funds across investment areas and to minimize the amount of cash left idle in banks. The committee compares projected cash flows based on different allocation decisions; the decisions that it actually adopts are those that produce adequate projected cash flows and that are acceptable to the various groups in the company.

Actually, the system is an accounting definition of the company. There is no question about the accuracy of the relationships in the model, so the only way projected results can be in error is if estimates of business activity levels or money market rates are incorrect.

5 *Evaluating Decisions Using a Simulation Model—A Marketing Decision System*

In order to provide a more rational basis for repetitive marketing decisions, a consumer products company uses a model that relates levels of advertising promotions, and pricing to levels of sales for a particular brand. The model was developed in a team setting by reconciling an analysis of historical brand information with an individual's subjective feelings concerning the effects on sales of various levels and types of advertising and other marketing actions.

The model was validated by tracking its accuracy in predicting sales based on the competitive actions that were taken. Unlike the accounting model I just mentioned, this is a simulation model in which some of the most important relationships are estimates at best. For instance, there simply is no rule by which it is possible to predict sales with certainty based on advertising levels. In fact, this was the heart of the issue in developing the model.

Even though it has turned out to be useful for prediction, much of the value of the model lies in the company's improved understanding of the market environment.

6 *Proposing Decisions—Optimization of Raw Materials Usage*

Another consumer products company, faced with short-run supply problems for many of its raw materials, has developed an optimization model to solve the mathematical puzzle of choosing and balancing among various product recipes.

The inputs to the model include a series of different recipes for many products, short-run supply levels for raw materials, and production requirements for finished products. The output is the choice of recipes that maximizes production using existing supplies. When the short-run supply situation shifts, the model can be revised and a new set of recipes chosen.

The system has had a major impact on the way managers view allocation policy. Initially, they considered allocating scarce raw materials to products by setting priorities among products. The model showed that it was more advantageous to start with production requirements and then allocate scarce resources by optimizing the mix of product recipes.

7 *Making Decisions—An Insurance Renewal Rate System*

As an outgrowth of an overhaul of its group insurance information system, an insurance company has developed a system to eliminate part of the clerical burden associated with renewal underwriting and to help assure that rate calculations are consistent and accurate.

Instead of calculating renewal rates by hand, underwriters fill out coded input sheets for the system, which calculates a renewal rate based on a series of standard statistical and actuarial assumptions. Since these assumptions might or might not apply to a particular policy, the underwriters review documentation accompanying the policies and decide whether the standard calculations are applicable. If they are not, the coding sheet is modified in an appropriate manner and resubmitted.

In effect, the system makes the decision in completely standard situations, while the underwriter decides whether the situation is standard and, if not, what adjustments are required. As a result, the underwriters can concentrate on the substance of their jobs rather than the related clerical chores.

Spectrum of Possibilities

These seven systems represent a wide range of approaches in supporting decisions. The first one helps production foremen by simply providing rapid access to historical information such as who worked on what lot, and when the work was done. But the foremen must decide what should be done once they have the information. At the other extreme, the system supporting the underwriters virtually makes the decision in some cases. Between the two extremes, analysis systems and model-oriented systems help people organize information and also facilitate and formalize the evaluation of proposed decisions.

Although managers in most large companies have used budgeting or planning systems similar to the source-and-application-of-funds model I mentioned, the spectrum of possibilities for other kinds of decision support systems is surprisingly wide. Obviously, some of these systems are of no particular use in many settings. Still, their variety suggests that most companies should have a number of genuine opportunities for applying the concept of computer-based support for decision making.

MOTIVES OF MANAGERS

What do decision support systems do that actually helps their users? What is their real impact? In my survey, answers to these questions proved elusive in many cases, since the users valued the systems for reasons that were completely different from initial ideas of what the systems were to accomplish. In fact, a wide range of purposes exists for these systems. While many decision support systems share the goals of standard EDP systems, they go further and address other managerial concerns such as improving interpersonal communication, facilitating problem solving, fostering individual learning, and increasing organizational control.

Such systems can affect interpersonal communication in two ways: by providing individuals with tools for persuasion and by providing organizations with a vocabulary and a discipline which facilitates negotiations across subunit boundaries.

Tools of Persuasion

Standard texts on systems analysis totally overlook the personal use of decision support systems as tools of persuasion. But consider the following "offensive" (persuading someone else to do something) uses to which various companies have put these systems:

- The manager of a chemical plant was attempting to meet output goals (quantities by product) that were being set by a marketing group. Unfortunately, the group was setting goals without much consideration of raw material shortages under which the plant was operating. The plant had been using a model to calculate production mixes.

  At one point, it occurred to the plant manager that he could use this model to investigate whether marketing was setting goals that resulted in poor plant utilization and made him appear inefficient. As he ran the model under a series of different production mix goals, it became clear that this was the case, and he used the results to persuade marketing to change his plant's production mix.
- A data retrieval and manipulation system first received wide exposure in a transportation company when a number of the company's top executives used it to develop a good quantitative rationale for a proposed merger. With the system, it was possible to explore and manipulate a large data base of information on the industry.

  Although the merger was not approved, management thought that the system helped it put up a good fight.
- The management of a shipping company found that a system it used in consolidating and fine-tuning strategic investment plans also helped it negotiate with banks. The banks and other sources of financing seemed to be uniformly impressed by the careful computer-based analysis on which management based its financing requests. The resulting edge in credibility was small, but, in management's opinion, noticeable.

Now that we have seen illustrations of the offensive tools of persuasion, let us turn to examples of the "defensive" (persuading someone that the user has done a good job) uses of these systems:

- When asked whether he ever made direct use of a case tracking system, the head of an adjudication group in a government regulatory agency said that he remembered only one instance. This was when he spent a lunch hour generating a report to make his group's recent performance appear as favorable as possible, in spite of some unfortunate delays and problems that made the standard report look bad.

• The new president of a large conglomerate used a one-year budgeting model to learn about the budgeting choices that existed, as well as to help him discount what people in various areas claimed concerning their own budgetary needs.

• The class scheduler of a training school for a company's service personnel had found his job frustrating because it was always difficult to justify the budget on explicit grounds.

With a model that generated optimal training schedules, the scheduler could protect himself very easily by saying: "Using these assumptions concerning attrition, acceptable peak-time shortfalls, and other considerations, this is the best budget. If you (the budget cutter) would like me to change these assumptions, I would be glad to generate a new budget. What level of shortfall do you suggest?" Thus the system not only helped the scheduler make decisions, but also helped him defend them.

• Many people suspected that a new product venture in a consumer company might not be worthwhile. but no one knew exactly why. When a risk analysis was carried out with a model, the reason became clear: the venture had a very substantial downside risk. In addition to sealing the decision, the analysis provided an understandable response to the people who had proposed the venture.

A cynic might contend that the people in these situations were taking advantage of or abusing the systems. A more practical conclusion is that these systems simply serve to improve managers' effectiveness in their organizations by helping them communicate with other people. My point is that much of the benefit of many of the decision support systems in my sample was of this sort.

Aids to Communication

Decision support systems also help managers negotiate across organizational units by standardizing the mechanics of the process and by providing a common conceptual basis for decision making.

During my survey, managers frequently commented that consistent definitions and formats are important aids to communication, especially between people in different organizational units such as divisions or departments. In a number of instances, the development of these definitions and formats was a lengthy and sometimes arduous task that was accomplished gradually over the course of several years, but which was also considered one of the main contributions of the systems.

For example, one of the purposes of some of the model-oriented systems in my sample was to estimate beforehand the overall result of decisions various people were considering separately, by filtering these decisions through a single model. In these cases, the system became an implicit arbiter between differing goals of various departments. Instead of arguing from their own divergent viewpoints, marketing, production, and financial people could use the model to demonstrate the effect of one group's proposals on another group's actions and on the total outcome. As a result, issues were clarified and the negotiation process expedited.

The production foremen I mentioned earlier noted the same kind of facilitation. It helped them in work-scheduling discussions and problem investigations by providing immediate access to "objective" information about "who did what, when, and how well on any production lot in the shop."

Value to User

Although the implementers of a number of the successful systems I studied found it necessary to go through the motions of presenting a cost/benefit rationale which attributed a dollar value to personal effectiveness, they didn't believe these numbers any more than anyone else did. Management usually decided to proceed on the basis that the proposed system seemed to make sense and would likely have a beneficial impact on the way people interacted and/or made decisions.

Monetary savings are obviously a very important and worthwhile rationale for developing computer systems, but it should be clear at this point that the EDP-style assumption that systems should always be justified in these terms does not suffice in the area of decision support systems.

Equally obvious, there is a definite danger in developing a system simply because someone thinks it makes sense, especially if that someone is not the direct user of the system. In fact, the systems I cited as my first, second, and fifth examples began this way and encountered resistance until they were repositioned as something that users would want in order to become more effective.

Again, the general problem here is a common tendency for technical people to concentrate on the "technical beauty" of a system or idea and to assume that nontechnical people will somehow see the light and will be able to figure out how to use the system in solving business problems. This sort of overoptimism was present in the history of almost every unsuccessful system in the sample.

The message is clear: try to take advantage of the creativity of technical experts but be sure that it is channeled toward real problems. The challenge, of course, is how to accomplish both of these goals. There are a number of ways, which I shall now discuss.

PATTERNS OF DEVELOPMENT

Despite the common wisdom that the needs of users must be considered in developing systems and that users should participate actively in implementing them, the users did not initiate 31 of the 56 systems I studied and did not participate actively in the development of 38 of the 56.

The results, illustrated in Figure 2, are not surprising. Intended users neither initiated nor played an active role in implementing 11 of the 15 systems that suffered significant implementation problems. Conversely, there were

Figure 2 Systems Resisted by Users

	Few or none of the intended users involved in implementing system	**All or most of the intended users helped implement system**
Intended users did not initiate	11 of 25 systems	0 of 6 systems
Intended users helped initiate	2 of 13 systems	2 of 12 systems

relatively few such problems in 27 of the 31 systems in which the users had a hand in initiating and/or played an active role in implementing.

But it would be wrong to infer from these findings that systems should be avoided totally, if intended users neither initiate them nor play an active role in their implementation. For one thing, 14 of the 25 systems I studied in which this was the pattern were ultimately successful. More important, many of the genuinely innovative systems in my sample, including 5 of the 7 that I described earlier, exhibited this pattern.

On the other hand, many of the systems initiated by users do little more than mechanize existing practices. While such mechanization can be very beneficial, and while I'm certainly not suggesting that major innovations must come from outside sources, the real challenge is to be able to use insights regardless of their source.

One way to do this is to devise an implementation strategy to encourage user involvement and participation throughout the development of the systems, regardless of who originated the concept. Examples of successful strategies follow.

Impose Gracefully Marketing and production managers in a decentralized company did not relish the extra work (format changes and data submission requirements) needed for a yearly budgeting system, which top management was installing. Initially, they were especially unenthusiastic because they thought the system would not really help them.

So at every stage the designers made a point of developing subsystems to provide these middle managers with sales and materials usage information that had never been available. This quid pro quo worked well; instead of seeing the system as a total imposition, the managers saw it as an opportunity for them to take part in something which would be beneficial to them.

Run a Dog and Pony Show Central planning personnel in two companies designed systems for budgeting and financial analysis. In one company, the system never caught on, despite lengthy training demonstrations for divisional staff and other potential users. These individuals seemed enthusiastic about the system's possibilities but never really used it unless corporate planning people did all the work for them.

In contrast, the training program for the system in the other company fostered immediate and active involvement. In order to attend the workshops, people were required to bring their own financial analysis problems. They learned to use the system by working on these problems. When the workshops ended, many users were enthusiastic; not only did they know how to use the system, but they had also proved to themselves that it could help them.

Use a Prototype Two ever-present dangers in developing a system are creating a large, expensive one that solves the wrong problem or creating one that some people in the organization cannot live with. Either can happen, not only when the system is designed without consulting the user and affected parties, but also when there is no one having enough experience with the particular kind of system under consideration to clearly visualize its strengths and weaknesses before it is built.

Implementers of a number of systems in my sample avoided these traps by building small prototypes, which gave the users something specific to react to. As a result, the large-scale version could be developed with a realistic notion of both what was needed and what would fly in the organization. A similar approach, also successful, was simply to build systems in small pieces that could be used, changed, or discarded easily.

Hook the User with the Responsibility Each new module or application developed as an outgrowth of one of the three sales information systems I mentioned earlier goes through three stages. The first stage consists of general, uncommitted discussions of any current problem areas with which user groups are concerned. Following research by the management science staff, the second stage is a brief formal problem statement written in conjunction with the user group. In addition to describing the problem, this statement goes over the methodology and resources that will be required to respond to it. The third stage is a formal request for authorization of out-of-pocket expenses.

Sell the System In one of the companies I studied, a marketing analysis group used a direct selling procedure to convince people of the merits of a sales forecasting system. The pitch was very simple: they compared manual monthly forecasts for one year with the system's forecasts. The system's forecasts proved to be more accurate in ten months out of twelve, with less error overall than the manual ones. The system was adopted.

In another company, management had a real-time system installed for monitoring the largely automatic production of an inexpensive consumer item in order to minimize material loss due to creeping maladjustments in machine settings. During the initial installation, the implementation team discovered suspected, but previously unsubstantiated, cheating by piecework employees; more pieces were leaving many machines than were entering them. Discreet hints were dropped that the monitor had to be checked because it was registering "impossible" results. The employees were sold on the new system: they knew very well that it worked.

FUNDAMENTAL CHANGES

Despite extensive experience with EDP, many organizations have used no more than one or two of the seven types of decision support systems I have illustrated here.

One reason for this is that justifying such systems can be difficult: quantifying the impact of replacing ten clerks with one computer is one thing, while quantifying the impact of improved individual effectiveness of line personnel is quite a different thing. Another reason is that implementation can be tricky: many of the ideas come from people other than the users.

Nevertheless, developing a decision support system makes sense when it becomes clear that a fundamental change may be needed in the way decisions are reached and implemented. Often, the process of defining the system is every bit as valuable as the system produced.

My final point is that the concept of decision support systems itself can help managers in understanding the role of computers in their organizations. As the name implies, data processing systems systematize and expedite the mechanics of carrying on business activities by processing masses of data automatically. On the other hand, the decision-oriented extensions of these systems help people make and communicate decisions concerning administrative and/or competitive tactics and strategy.

The decision support systems I have discussed go one step further. Instead of starting as extensions of existing data processing systems, many decision support systems are built from scratch for the sole purpose of improving or expediting a decision-making process. The underlying philosophy is that the use of computers to help people make and communicate decisions is every bit as legitimate and worthwhile as the use of computers to process masses of data.

There is evidence that this viewpoint has caught on to a certain degree and is becoming more widely accepted. The implication is not that all organizations should get on the bandwagon, but rather that managers should be aware of the opportunities and challenges in this area and should attempt to assess whether their organizations should move in this direction.

READING 1 DISCUSSION QUESTIONS

1 Which types of decision support systems described in this article seem to have the best chance of succeeding in an organization? Why?

2 What are the major justifications for installing the types of decision support systems described?

3 What types and forms of resistance would you anticipate encountering when these types of systems are being implemented?

Reading 2

Management Misinformation Systems

Russell L. Ackoff

The growing preoccupation of operations researchers and management scientists with Management Information Systems (MIS's) is apparent. In fact, for some the design of such systems has almost become synonymous with operations research or management science. Enthusiasm for such systems is understandable: it involves the researcher in a romantic relationship with the most glamorous instrument of our time, the computer. Such enthusiasm is understandable but, nevertheless, some of the excesses to which it has led are not excusable.

Contrary to the impression produced by the growing literature, few computerized management information systems have been put into operation. Of those I have seen that have been implemented, most have not matched expectations and some have been outright failures. I believe that these near- and far-misses could have been avoided if certain false (and usually implicit) assumptions on which many such systems have been erected had not been made.

There seem to be five common and erroneous assumptions underlying the design of most MIS's, each of which I will consider. After doing so I will outline an MIS design procedure which avoids these assumptions.

GIVE THEM MORE

Most MIS's are designed on the assumption that the critical deficiency under which most managers operate is the *lack of relevant information.* I do not deny that most managers lack a good deal of information that they should have, but I do deny that this is the most important informational deficiency from which they suffer. It seems to me that they suffer most from an *overabundance of irrelevant information.*

This is not a play on words. The consequences of changing the emphasis of an MIS from supplying relevant information to eliminating irrelevant information are considerable. If one is preoccupied with supplying relevant information, attention is almost exclusively given to the generation, storage, and retrieval of information: hence emphasis is placed on constructing data banks, coding, indexing, updating files, access languages, and so on. The ideal which has emerged from this orientation is an infinite pool of data into which a manager can reach to pull out any information he wants. If, on the other hand, one sees the manager's information problem primarily, but not exclusively, as one that arises out of an overabundance of irrelevant information, most of which was not

Reprinted from *Management Science* (Application Series), vol. 14, no. 4, pp. B-147–B-156, December 1967. Reprinted by permission from The Institute of Management Sciences, Providence, R.I. Russell L. Ackoff is a professor at the Wharton School of the University of Pennsylvania.

asked for, then the two most important functions of an information system become *filtration* (or evaluation) and *condensation.* The literature on MIS's seldom refers to these functions, let alone considers how to carry them out.

My experience indicates that most managers receive much more data (if not information) than they can possibly absorb even if they spend all of their time trying to do so. Hence they already suffer from an information overload. They must spend a great deal of time separating the relevant from the irrelevant and searching for the kernels in the relevant documents. For example, I have found that I receive an average of forty-three hours of unsolicited reading material each week. The solicited material is usually half again this amount.

I have seen a daily stock status report that consists of approximately six hundred pages of computer print-out. The report is circulated daily across managers' desks. I've also seen requests for major capital expenditures that come in book size, several of which are distributed to managers each week. It is not uncommon for many managers to receive an average of one journal a day or more. One could go on and on.

Unless the information overload to which managers are subjected is reduced, any additional information made available by an MIS cannot be expected to be used effectively.

Even relevant documents have too much redundancy. Most documents can be considerably condensed without loss of content. My point here is best made, perhaps, by describing an experiment that a few of my colleagues and I conducted on the OR [operations research] literature several years ago. By using a panel of well-known experts we identified four OR articles that all members of the panel considered to be "above average," and four articles that were considered to be "below average." The authors of the eight articles were asked to prepare "objective" examinations (duration 30 minutes) plus answers for graduate students who were assigned the articles for reading. (The authors were not informed about the experiment.) Then several experienced writers were asked to reduce each article to 2/3 and 1/3 of its original length only by eliminating words. They also prepared a brief abstract of each article. Those who did the condensing did not see the examinations to be given to the students.

A group of graduate students who had not previously read the articles was then selected. Each one was given four articles randomly selected, each of which was in one of its four versions: 100%, 67%, 33%, or abstract. Each version of each article was read by two students. All were given the same examinations. The average scores on the examinations were then compared.

For the above-average articles there was no significant difference between average test scores for the 100%, 67%, and 33% versions, but there was a significant decrease in average test scores for those who had read only the abstract. For the below-average articles there was no difference in average test scores among those who had read the 100%, 67%, and 33% versions, but there was a significant *increase* in average test scores of those who had read only the abstract.

The sample used was obviously too small for general conclusions but the results strongly indicate the extent to which even good writing can be condensed without loss of information. I refrain from drawing the obvious conclusion about bad writing.

It seems clear that condensation as well as filtration, performed mechanically or otherwise, should be an essential part of an MIS, and that such a system should be capable of handling much, if not all, of the unsolicited as well as solicited information that a manager receives.

THE MANAGER NEEDS THE INFORMATION THAT HE WANTS

Most MIS designers "determine" what information is needed by asking managers what information they would like to have. This is based on the assumption that managers know what information they need and want it.

For a manager to know what information he needs he must be aware of each type of decision he should make (as well as does) and he must have an adequate model of each. These conditions are seldom satisfied. Most managers have some conception of at least some of the types of decisions they must make. Their conceptions, however, are likely to be deficient in a very critical way, a way that follows from an important principle of scientific economy: the less we understand a phenomenon, the more variables we require to explain it. Hence, the manager who does not understand the phenomenon he controls plays it "safe" and, with respect to information, wants "everything." The MIS designer, who has even less understanding of the relevant phenomenon than the manager, tries to provide even more than everything. He thereby increases what is already an overload of irrelevant information.

For example, market researchers in a major oil company once asked their marketing managers what variables they thought were relevant in estimating the sales volume of future service stations. Almost seventy variables were identified. The market researchers then added about half again this many variables and performed a large multiple linear regression analysis of sales of existing stations against these variables and found about thirty-five to be statistically significant. A forecasting equation was based on this analysis. An OR team subsequently constructed a model based on only one of these variables, traffic flow, which predicted sales better than the thirty-five variable regression equation. The team went on to *explain* sales at service stations in terms of the customers' perception of the amount of time lost by stopping for service. The relevance of all but a few of the variables used by the market researchers could be explained by their effect on such perception.

The moral is simple: one cannot specify what information is required for decision making until an explanatory model of the decision process and the system involved has been constructed and tested. Information systems are subsystems of control systems. They cannot be designed adequately without taking control into account. Furthermore, whatever else regression analyses can yield, they cannot yield understanding and explanation of phenomena. They describe and, at best, predict.

GIVE A MANAGER THE INFORMATION HE NEEDS AND HIS DECISION MAKING WILL IMPROVE

It is frequently assumed that if a manager is provided with the information he needs, he will then have no problem in using it effectively. The history of OR stands to the contrary. For example, give most managers an initial tableau of a typical "real" mathematical programming, sequencing, or network problem and see how close they come to an optimal solution. If their experience and judgment have any value they may not do badly, but they will seldom do very well. In most management problems there are too many possibilities to expect experience, judgment, or intuition to provide good guesses, even with perfect information.

Furthermore, when several probabilities are involved in a problem the unguided mind of even a manager has difficulty in aggregating them in a valid way. We all know many simple problems in probability in which untutored intuition usually does very badly (e.g., What are the correct odds that 2 of 25 people selected at random will have their birthdays on the same day of the year?). For example, very few of the results obtained by queuing theory, when arrivals and service are probabilistic, are obvious to managers; nor are the results of risk analysis where the managers' own subjective estimates of probabilities are used.

The moral: it is necessary to determine how well managers can use needed information. When because of the complexity of the decision process, they can't use it well, they should be provided with either decision rules or performance feed-back so that they can identify and learn from their mistakes. More on this point later.

MORE COMMUNICATION MEANS BETTER PERFORMANCE

One characteristic of most MIS's which I have seen is that they provide managers with better current information about what other managers and their departments and divisions are doing. Underlying this provision is the belief that better interdepartmental communication enables managers to coordinate their decisions more effectively and hence improves the organization's overall performance. Not only is this not necessarily so, but it seldom is so. One would hardly expect two competing companies to become more cooperative because the information each acquires about the other is improved. This analogy is not as far-fetched as one might first suppose. For example, consider the following very much simplified version of a situation I once ran into. The simplification of the case does not affect any of its essential characteristics.

A department store has two "line" operations: buying and selling. Each function is performed by a separate department. The Purchasing Department primarily controls one variable: how much of each item is bought. The Merchandising Department controls the price at which it is sold. Typically, the measure of performance applied to the Purchasing Department was the turnover rate of inventory. The measure applied to the Merchandising Department was gross sales; this department sought to maximize the number of items sold times their price.

Now by examining a single item let us consider what happens in this system. The merchandising manager, using his knowledge of competition and consumption, set a price which he judged would maximize gross sales. In doing so he utilized price-demand curves for each type of item. For each price the curves show the expected sales and values on an upper and lower confidence band as well. (See Figure 1.) When instructing the Purchasing Department how many items to make available, the merchandising manager quite naturally used the value on the upper confidence curve. This minimized the chances of his running short which, if it occurred, would hurt his performance. It also maximized the chances of being over-stocked, but this was not his concern, only the purchasing manager's. Say, therefore, that the merchandising manager initially selected price P_1 and requested that amount Q_1 be made available by the Purchasing Department.

In this company the purchasing manager also had access to the price-demand curves. He knew the merchandising manager always ordered optimistically. Therefore, using the same curve he read over from Q_1 to the upper limit and down to the expected value from which he obtained Q_2, the quantity he actually intended to make available. He did not intend to pay for the merchandising manager's optimism. If merchandising ran out of stock, it was not his worry. Now the merchandising manager was informed about what the purchasing manager had done so he adjusted his price to P_2. The purchasing manager in turn was told that the merchandising manager had made this readjustment so he planned to make only Q_3 available. If this process—made

Figure 1 Price-demand curve.

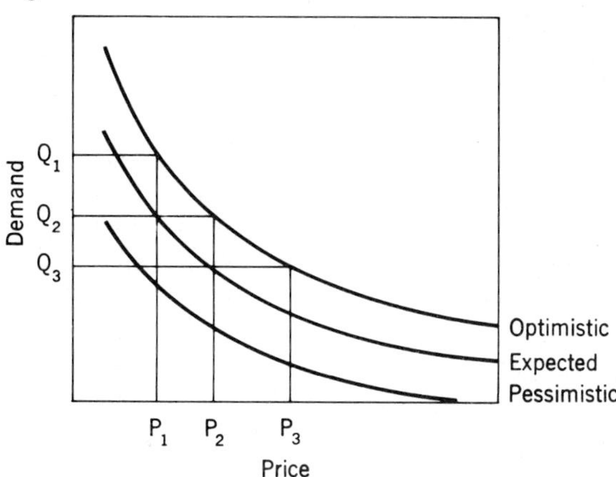

possible only by perfect communication between departments—had been allowed to continue, nothing would have been bought and nothing would have been sold. This outcome was avoided by prohibiting communication between departments and forcing each to guess what the other was doing.

I have obviously caricatured the situation in order to make the point clear: when organizational units have inappropriate measures of performance which put them in conflict with each other, as is often the case, communication between them may hurt organizational performance, not help it. Organizational structure and performance measurement must be taken into account before opening the flood gates and permitting the free flow of information between parts of the organization. (A more rigorous discussion of organizational structure and the relationship of communication to it can be found in "Systems Theory from an Operations Research Point of View.")[1]

A MANAGER DOES NOT HAVE TO UNDERSTAND HOW AN INFORMATION SYSTEM WORKS, ONLY HOW TO USE IT

Most MIS designers seek to make their systems as innocuous and unobtrusive as possible to managers lest they become frightened. The designers try to provide managers with very easy access to the system and assure them that they need to know nothing more about it. The designers usually succeed in keeping managers ignorant in this regard. This leaves managers unable to evaluate the MIS as a whole. It often makes them afraid to even try to do so lest they display their ignorance publicly. In failing to evaluate their MIS, managers delegate much of the control of the organization to the system's designers and operators, who may have many virtues, but managerial competence is seldom among them.

Let me cite a case in point. A Chairman of a Board of a medium-sized company asked for help on the following problem. One of his larger (decentralized) divisions had installed a computerized production-inventory control and manufacturing-manager information system about a year earlier. It had acquired about $2,000,000 worth of equipment to do so. The Board Chairman had just received a request from the Division for permission to replace the original equipment with newly announced equipment which would cost several times the original amount. An extensive "justification" for doing so was provided with the request. The Chairman wanted to know whether the request was really justified. He admitted to complete incompetence in this connection.

A meeting was arranged at the Division at which I was subjected to an extended and detailed briefing. The system was large but relatively simple. At the heart of it was a reorder point for each item and a maximum allowable stock level. Reorder quantities took lead-time as well as the allowable maximum into account. The computer kept track of stock, ordered items when required and

[1]S. S. Sengupta and R. L. Ackoff, "Systems Theory from an Operations Research Point of View," *IEEE Transactions on Systems Science and Cybernetics,* vol. 1, November 1965, pp. 9–13.

generated numerous reports on both the state of the system it controlled and its own "actions."

When the briefing was over I was asked if I had any questions. I did. First I asked if, when the system had been installed, there had been many parts whose stock level exceeded the maximum amount possible under the new system. I was told there were many. I asked for a list of about thirty and for some graph paper. Both were provided. With the help of the system designer and volumes of old daily reports I began to plot the stock level of the first listed item over time. When this item reached the maximum "allowable" stock level it had been reordered. The system designer was surprised and said that by sheer "luck" I had found one of the few errors made by the system. Continued plotting showed that because of repeated premature reordering the item had never gone much below the maximum stock level. Clearly the program was confusing the maximum allowable stock level and the reorder point. This turned out to be the case in more than half of the items on the list.

Next I asked if they had many paired parts, ones that were only used with each other; for example, matched nuts and bolts. They had many. A list was produced and we began checking the previous day's withdrawals. For more than half of the pairs the differences in the numbers reordered as withdrawn were very large. No explanation was provided.

Before the day was out it was possible to show by some quick and dirty calculations that the new computerized system was costing the company almost $150,000 per month more than the hand system which it had replaced, most of this in excess inventories.

The recommendation was that the system be redesigned as quickly as possible and that the new equipment not be authorized for the time being.

The questions asked of the system had been obvious and simple ones. Managers should have been able to ask them but—and this is the point—they felt themselves incompetent to do so. They would not have allowed a hand-operated system to get so far out of their control.

No MIS should ever be installed unless the managers for whom it is intended are trained to evaluate and hence control it rather than be controlled by it.

A SUGGESTED PROCEDURE FOR DESIGNING AN MIS

The erroneous assumptions I have tried to reveal in the preceding discussion can, I believe, be avoided by an appropriate design procedure. One is briefly outlined here.

1 Analysis of the Decision System Each (or at least each important) type of managerial decision required by the organization under study should be identified and the relationships between them should be determined and flow-charted. Note that this is *not* necessarily the same thing as determining what decisions *are* made. For example, in one company I found that make-or-buy decisions concerning parts were made only at the time when a part was introduced into stock and was never subsequently reviewed. For some items this decision had gone unreviewed for as many as twenty years. Obviously, such decisions should be made more often; in some cases, every time an order is placed in order to take account of current shop loading, underused shifts, delivery times from suppliers, and so on.

Decision-flow analyses are usually self-adjusting. They often reveal important decisions that are being made by default (e.g., the make-buy decision referred to above); and they disclose interdependent decisions that are being made independently. Decision-flow charts frequently suggest changes in managerial responsibility, organizational structure, and measure of performance which can correct the types of deficiencies cited.

Decision analyses can be conducted with varying degrees of detail, that is, they may be anywhere from coarse to fine grained. How much detail one should become involved with depends on the amount of time and resources that are available for the analysis. Although practical considerations frequently restrict initial analyses to a particular organizational function, it is preferable to perform a coarse analysis of all of an organization's managerial functions rather than a fine analysis of one or a subset of functions. It is easier to introduce finer information into an integrated information system than it is to combine fine subsystems into one integrated system.

2 An Analysis of Information Requirements Managerial decisions can be classified into three types:

a Decisions for which adequate models are available or can be constructed and from which optimal (or near optimal) solutions can be derived. In such cases the decision process itself should be incorporated into the information system thereby converting it (at least partially) to a control system. A decision model identifies what information is required and hence what information is relevant.

b Decisions for which adequate models can be constructed but from which optimal solutions cannot be extracted. Here some kind of heuristic or search procedure should be provided even if it consists of no more than computerized trial and error. A simulation of the model will, as a minimum, permit comparison of proposed alternative solutions. Here too the model specified what information is required.

c Decisions for which adequate models cannot be constructed. Research is required here to determine what information is relevant. If decision making cannot be delayed for the completion of such research or the decision's effect is not large enough to justify the cost of research, then judgment must be used to "guess" what information is relevant. It may be possible to make explicit the implicit model used by the decision maker and treat it as a model of type *(b)*.

In each of these three types of situation it is necessary to provide feedback by comparing actual decision outcomes with those predicted by the model or decision maker. Each decision that is made, along with its predicted outcome, should be an essential input to a management control system. I shall return to this point below.

3 Aggregation of Decisions Decisions with the same or largely overlapping informational requirements should be grouped together as a single managers' task. This will reduce the information a manager requires to do his job and is likely to increase his understanding of it. This may require a reorganization of the system. Even if such a reorganization cannot be implemented completely, what can be done is likely to improve performance significantly and reduce the information loaded on managers.

4 Design of Information Processing Now the procedure for collecting, storing, retrieving, and treating information can be designed. Since there is a voluminous literature on this subject, I shall leave it at this except for one point. Such a system must not only be able to answer questions addressed to it; it should also be able to answer questions that have not been asked by reporting any deviations from expectations. An extensive exception-reporting system is required.

5 Design of Control of the Control System It must be assumed that the system that is being designed will be deficient in many and significant ways. Therefore it is necessary to identify the ways in which it may be deficient, to design procedures for detecting its deficiencies, and for correcting the system so as to remove or reduce them. Hence the system should be designed to be flexible and adaptive. This is little more than a platitude, but it has a not-so-obvious implication. No completely computerized system can be as flexible and adaptive as can a man-machine system. This is illustrated by a concluding example of a system that is being developed and is partially in operation. (See Figure 2.)

The company involved has its market divided into approximately two hundred marketing areas. A model for each has been constructed as is "in" the computer. On the basis of competitive intelligence supplied to the service marketing manager by marketing researchers and information specialists, he and his staff make policy decisions for each area each month. Their tentative decisions are fed into the computer, which yields a forecast of expected performance. Changes are made until the expectations match what is desired. In this way they arrive at "final" decisions. At the end of the month the computer compares the actual performance of each area with what was predicted. If a deviation exceeds what could be expected by chance, the company's OR Group then seeks the reason for the deviation, performing as much research as is required to find it. If the cause is found to be permanent the computerized model

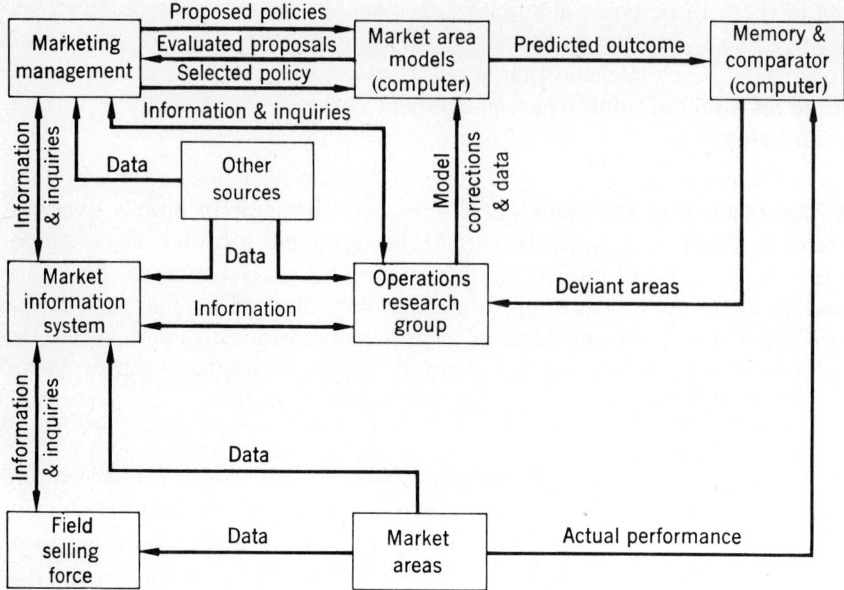

Figure 2 Simplified diagram of a market-area control system.

is adjusted appropriately. The result is an adaptive man-machine system whose precision and generality is continuously increasing with use.

Finally it should be noted that in carrying out the design steps enumerated above, three groups should collaborate: information systems specialists, operations researchers, *and managers*. The participation of managers in the design of a system that is to serve them assures their ability to evaluate its performance by comparing its output with what was predicted. Managers who are not willing to invest some of their time in this process are not likely to use a management control system well, and their system, in turn, is likely to abuse them.

READING 2 DISCUSSION QUESTIONS

1 Identify and discuss the five assumptions which have often produced "management misinformation systems."

2 Discuss the five steps in the suggested procedure for designing an MIS.

Reading 3

The Expectation Gap

William S. Anderson

Desire often overcomes reason in the development of management information systems and an expectation gap develops. The following define the expectations gap more precisely:

- From the viewpoint of top management, it's the difference between what management expects from a new or improved information system and what that system finally delivers.
- From the viewpoint of the systems professional, it's the difference between the guidance and participation he expected from his top management and what he actually got.

I'm not aware of any company or any organization which is immune to this problem. That's rather surprising—especially in view of the sophistication of today's information processing industry.

Consider management's dilemma: Too often, the information management need is either not available when it's needed, or its accuracy is questionable, or it conflicts with other information.

Few business managers today question the importance—indeed the necessity—of good Management Information Systems. Instead, they look upon such systems as the nerve center of the entire enterprise. The difficulty is that when management looks at this nerve center, it sometimes concludes that the organization is on the verge of a nervous breakdown.

When serious information gaps exist, management has no recourse but to muddle through. It scrapes together what information it can, largely by brute force. It adds a dash of experience and a touch of intuition, and then makes the decisions that have to be made. Usually a heavy price is paid for that kind of haphazard, seat-of-the-pants management.

No doubt every generation of management believes it faces the most difficult problems in the history of business. Management today *is* more challenging than ever before. As one writer said recently, "For top executives, the world has never looked as hostile or bewildering as it does today."

Consider the view from the front office today: The economic outlook is uncertain in virtually every industry. Business management is asking itself, "What will inflation do to my costs and prices later this year, next year, or five years from now?" To compound the problem, competition in most industries is cutthroat, interest rates are rising, capital investments are lagging, the dollar is wobbling around, the administration's economic policies are less than encourag-

Reprinted from the *Journal of Systems Management,* June 1978, pp. 6–10. Reprinted by permission of the author. Mr. Anderson is chairman of NCR Corporation.

ing, and the stock market is a disaster area. Meanwhile, the political situation around the world seems to be getting worse rather than better.

And heavy pressures are faced by management in non-commercial fields as well. Schools, hospitals and government agencies share with business the challenge of balancing their ever-rising costs with the revenues available to them. In all of these fields, the systems professional is squarely in the middle. He is being asked to accomplish more and more—even as the pressure increases on his budget for doing so. Thus, the expectations gap continues to widen—at the very time when the interests of everyone dictate that it should be narrowing.

CAUSES OF THE EXPECTATION GAP

It seems to me that most of the expectations gap can be attributed to four basic factors:

- The first of these factors is the very human tendency to let our expectations be dictated by desire rather than by reason. Too often the systems professional promises too much. An information system promoted as a money-saver and efficiency-improver develops an insatiable appetite. Hardware, software and personnel multiply at an ominous rate. And when the rumblings of pending disaster eventually reach management's ears, there is a sudden fear that an information-processing monster has been spawned. Alarms are sounded, tables are pounded, and management understandably wonders why everything costs more than was expected. Naturally no one remembers that the payroll is processed right on schedule every week, or that in scores of other ways the systems people are doing a remarkable job.
- After over-anticipation, perhaps the next biggest cause of the expectations gap is a lingering misunderstanding by top management of what the computer is, and what it can accomplish. Although the computer industry is now a quarter of a century old, there are still those who view the computer as a kind of bionic Moses. They think it is capable of leading any company or organization to a promised land of milk and honey, where systems problems no longer exist. These are the same managers who believe the computer can relieve them of the need for intelligent decision-making, and who cherish the illusion that the computer can resolve any problem and do any job well. Those of us who have been on the EDP firing line for many years know better.
- Third, top management frequently does not give systems problems the attention they deserve. What is the result? Often systems development takes a do-it-yourself direction. Each department in an organization clamors for the system it wants, rather than the system the organization as a whole needs. As James Matheson of Stanford Research Institute said, "People tend to gather the information they know how to gather, rather than what is important."

Especially disturbing is the appalling lack of long-range planning in the higher echelons of many organizations. The questions, "What are we trying to do, what information do we therefore need, and when and how do we get that information?" are rarely asked. Even when those questions are raised, critical decisions are frequently made by top management without meaningful participation by the systems professionals. The result is that the systems manager, who will have to implement the project, is placed in a difficult reactive role, rather than a creative and cooperative role.

Still worse is a climate in which top management shuns all involvement in systems planning and development. Like an unwanted stepchild, the systems management function is shunted off to some remote office with the comment, "You handle it." The wages of this particular sin is that frequently the computer—instead of the chief executive—winds up running the organization.

• But what about the systems professional? He too is responsible for part of the expectations gap. It is unfortunate but true that many systems professionals suffer from a serious occupational disease. I'm referring to their tendency to be systems specialists first, and businessmen only in a secondary way.

There's validity in the complaint that many systems professionals see the trees more clearly than they see the forest. There are still not enough systems professionals who can help solve the critical management problems faced by their organizations. Usually this is due to inadequate understanding of those problems. Many systems managers lack cost-awareness; they are sometimes only vaguely aware of their company's objectives, or how the company's assets are being used to achieve those objectives. And sometimes they float so far above the battle that they are incapable of converting management concepts into systems realities.

In varying degrees all these complaints have validity. The challenge to the systems profession, and to top management in every organization is to do something about them.

NARROWING THE EXPECTATIONS GAP

At NCR we do have a systems expectations gap—despite the fact that we are in the systems business. But we are trying to make sure that the shoemaker's children are as well shod as his customers' children. The point I stress the most to our internal systems people is this: To come closer to top management's expectations, the systems professional has to become a generalist as well as a specialist. By this I mean that he has to find out what management is trying to do, what information is therefore needed, and when and how that information should be supplied.

To gain this broader perspective, the systems professional must learn how the business or organization really functions—all the way from purchasing to customer billing. That demands a working knowledge of the requirements of all divisions and departments, not just those that generate a lot of paper. The systems professional should also study in intimate detail how the organization is structured—to develop, produce and distribute its products or services. He also needs some degree of empathy with the chief executive. As one example, he must understand his company's competitive environment, and all the other factors that tend to keep the chief executive awake at night.

He ought to cultivate that depth of knowledge and understanding on a continuing basis. Information requirements are constantly changing as the organization itself changes and as external factors change.

It used to be much easier. The systems professional could wait for others to come to him with their changing information requirements. I don't believe many systems professionals enjoy that luxury today. If a systems specialist wants to be really good, his knowledge of his organization must rival that of top management. And that is a staggering challenge. It requires constant study and probing, and periodic reexamination of the current and long-term objectives of the organization.

It's important to remember that the artificial boundaries of a company's organizational chart may not have too much bearing on the flow of information which management requires. I think the systems professional is in greater danger if he allows his thinking to be boxed in by structural boundaries.

It is a demanding job to be both a specialist in one of the world's most demanding professions, and at the same time be a business generalist. It requires men and women of exceptional ability and drive. The dean of the Wharton Management School summed it up well, when he said that the systems profession today needs "a new breed of Renaissance people, who combine technical expertise with the management function and organization."

DON'T PROMISE TOO MUCH

Another guideline I've suggested to our own systems people is to avoid promising too much, too soon. One of the great temptations in systems development and implementation is to bite off more than we can chew. At NCR we are very much aware of that problem, because excessive promises get us as a supplier in trouble, just as they do the systems professional. We are already on the side of the systems people; we want them to succeed because that is the only way that we can succeed. So we are going to do our best to help in the implementation of a new system. However, we are not workers of miracles. Nor is any other computer supplier a worker of miracles.

I'm not suggesting, of course, that a systems professional should be hesitant or faint-hearted. Indeed, a career in systems management is not for the timid. What I *am* suggesting is that ambitious plans need to be tempered with common sense. So I tell our systems people not to overdo it. To be selective. To tackle first things first. Then, as we get better and better, we can also get fancier.

Because of explosive technology in the computer systems industry, the systems professional also requires long-range technical vision. He is the person best qualified in most organizations to keep abreast of what is happening in the computer systems industry. He should be a company's early warning system, constantly scanning the horizon for new developments which can impact on his organization. What wasn't practical yesterday may well be practical today.

AVOID TECHNICAL OVERKILL

My next suggestion to help reduce the expectations gap is to constantly urge our systems people to avoid overdependence on hardware or software or mere techniques. In other words, I advise them to steer clear of technical overkill.

This is a problem in our own company—after all, we can get the data processing equipment wholesale!

I often remind our systems people that their success will be measured not by how much hardware they operate, not by the volume of their data throughput, but by whether their systems are generating timely, accurate information on which intelligent management decisions can be based.

There have been many cases where the computer industry has oversold its customers. It has said to them, in effect, "If you just buy enough hardware and enough software all of your systems problems will be solved." I strongly disagree with that approach. Cost/performance. That's what it's all about. But how often do we measure the systems management function by the hard standard of cost/performance? The answer, I suspect, is not as often as we should.

However this is changing. Under today's intense cost pressures, top management is casting an increasingly critical eye toward the systems function. So the systems professional faces a double challenge: He has to develop, implement and operate good systems and he has to do it at the lowest possible cost.

Periodically we ought to ask ourselves whether a task should be performed at all; or, if it should be, whether or not it should be done on a computer. Beautiful solutions to non-problems may be aesthetically pleasing to a systems professional. But I assure you they are poison in the Executive Office. The truth is that most organizations can generate certain kinds of systems improvements without involving the computer at all. As one example, not long ago we launched a corporate-wide effort at NCR to get rid of redundant forms and reports, and to improve our document distribution in general. That program didn't involve spending a single dollar for additional computer hardware or software. Yet it has saved us hundreds of thousands of dollars. And our systems people tell me it was one of the most interesting and rewarding projects they ever carried out.

There is one additional precaution I try to instill in our own systems professionals. I tell them that if they find themselves on the wrong road, I hope they will recognize that fact, and then have the courage and good sense to turn back. Perhaps the most beguiling of all temptations in systems development is to charge ahead with an ill-conceived project, even though danger signals are popping up all over the place.

Any chief executive is subject to unpleasant little surprises all the time. They come with the job. It is the unpleasant big surprises that cause heads to roll. So I urge our own people to be their own best critics. I ask them to research thoroughly the full implications of every system change, to make sure that their unpleasant little surprises do not turn into my unpleasant big surprises.

ATTRACTING TOP MANAGEMENT INVOLVEMENT

It's unfortunate but true that in most organizations, the visibility of the systems group is more negative than positive. A report is late or inaccurate. A project is behind schedule. A top manager cannot get the information he needs, or he has to wait a month for it—when he needs it now. The trouble is that all the work that is done flawlessly gets little or no visibility. For that reason systems people tend to become known for their failures, rather than for their more frequent successes. I'm convinced this is usually a bad rap. But the situation will never correct itself until systems professionals do a better job of selling themselves to top management. And that requires better communications.

Let's assume the systems manager has become a good enough generalist to develop a comprehensive plan for the future direction of the organization's management information system. No matter how good the plan is, it will not reach top management through some mysterious process of osmosis. The systems manager should present his proposals to management himself. He must make sure that management understands what he is currently doing, and what he could be doing. Then he must get the necessary decisions on where the available resources will be allocated.

At NCR, senior management of the Information Systems function meets with numbers of top management every quarter. This is a long enough period to enable our systems group to make meaningful progress. Yet it's not so frequent that it imposes on the time of those involved. Incidentally, these meetings usually last no more than an hour. The purpose is not to spread out, for everyone's examination and criticism, all the nuts and bolts of existing or proposed systems. Instead, it is to explain their general design, their purpose, how much they will cost, and what contribution they will make to conducting NCR's business more effectively and profitably. In the case of projects already approved, we simply get a report on their progress.

In most companies, top management is two or three layers removed from the systems group. Or maybe top management has the reputation of being unapproachable. How, then does the systems group surmount these communications barriers? It's usually not all that difficult. Typically, any organization's data processing budget represents a very respectable figure. And I've never met a company president who is not interested in where big chunks of money are going. If you are a systems professional, and you aren't getting through, send the top man a brief memo, proposing a regular reporting and review schedule. Remind him of how much money your group is spending. Be sure to point out the conflicting demands being made on your available resources—demands that only the chief executive can either approve, reject or modify.

By bringing your story directly to his attention, you will indicate that you are a responsible employee and that you are taking the initiative to improve the cost/performance of your operation. You'll also be making it clear that you recognize where the ultimate decisions are made.

PRESENTATION, THE KEY TO SUCCESS

Two steps should precede such an action, however. One is to work closely with the key managers you serve—in order to get their input in developing your presentation. And of course you want to be sure that when you go to the top, you can present a well-thought-out plan.

If new systems are proposed, it's essential to cover the business functions that are to be served, how data is to be captured, how and when it will be processed and reported, what general files are involved, and perhaps most important, project schedules, costs and anticipated benefits. Above all, I would urge you not to dump your systems problems into the lap of management. You are being paid to develop solutions to problems, not to create problems.

I think most chief executives today view the systems manager not as the top EDP man in the organization, but rather as the manager in charge of EDP. So if you want to establish creditability, you must talk the language of management—not the jargon of the computer room.

Recently one of our divisional vice presidents told me that he would serve as an intermediary between the manager of his systems development group and myself. I told him that if his systems manager was not capable of reporting directly to me, then he had the wrong man in the job.

One added thought on communicating with top management: It's helpful to do so in the presence of all the upper management people who will be affected by a systems development. This will provide not only the necessary give and take; it will also give the systems professional the visibility he needs to accomplish his goal. It also brings the upper management group into the decision-making process.

DEVELOPING BETTER INFORMATION SYSTEMS

Fortunately, the people who have been moving up the management ladder in recent years are more systems knowledgeable than their predecessors. That has created a favorable climate for constructive systems change. But in any organization there is a pressing need for continuous rethinking—by top management—of the information requirements of their organization. Not just the requirements of today, but what they will be five or even 10 years from now.

The chief executive is vital to this process. He sets the basic course of the organization. He determines how and when that course will change. And more important than anything else, it is the chief executive who can make things happen.

The company whose chief executive is future-minded, who helps set systems objectives and determines priorities is fortunate indeed. As a computer systems supplier, NCR has found that when top management is actively involved in the development of a new system, the chances for its success rise correspondingly. But heaven help the organization whose chief executive establishes arbitrary systems goals or implementation timetables without researching their full implications—in terms of cost, internal disruption and possible eventual failure. "Full speed ahead and damn the torpedoes" may be a good strategy in war, but it is ruinous in systems development.

I strongly believe that top management must also take the lead in building respect throughout the organization for the professionalism of the systems function. This means giving systems professionals adequate authority, and the status required to operate effectively across organizational boundaries. It also requires a level of remuneration that reflects the contribution which systems professionals make to the profitability of the enterprise. Pats on the back are always welcome, of course, but the most effective thank-you note is what shows up in the paycheck.

SUMMARY

I've touched on a few aspects of the expectations gap with which we all live daily. I've scarcely mentioned the dazzling array of new information processing tools which are now available to the systems designer. With more versatile mainframes, with new microprocessor-driven data terminals, with powerful new minicomputers and improved communications systems, we have today an unparalleled opportunity to vigorously attack the expectations gap with technology as well as intellectually. Many more technological tools will be forthcoming. However, I suspect that over the next several years it will be creative systems development, rather than technology per se, which will spearhead most information processing advances.

The systems expectations gap will never be completely eliminated. Anticipation will always tend to outrun performance. It seems to me, therefore, that our ultimate objective lies somewhere in the middle ground—in other words, to control the expectations gap. I think this can be accomplished. But it will take more than the efforts of systems professionals. And it will take more than the efforts of top management. What it will take is systems professionals and top management working more closely together—and supported by the computer systems supplier.

If we set achievable systems goals, if we develop workable plans, and if we then follow through on those plans, there is every reason to believe the systems expectations gap *can* be controlled. That will represent a tremendous contribution—to the future success of your organization and to your own career as well.

READING 3 DISCUSSION QUESTIONS

1 Describe some of the ways by which organizations can narrow the *expectation gap* in the development of information systems in their organizations.
2 What are some of the major reasons for the *gap* that exists between systems performance and systems expectations?

SUMMARY OF CHAPTER 1

Future managers must prepare for successful working relationships with computerized information processing systems. The primary purpose of this book is to provide an insight into the broad impact which computers have had, are having, and may be expected to have on managers and on the environment in which managers work.

Management information is relevant knowledge, produced as output of data processing operations and acquired to achieve specific purposes. It is basic to the conduct of business; it is needed by managers to support the decisions which must be made if organizational goals are to be achieved. Although the information needed by managers can only be described in broad general terms because individual managers differ in the ways in which they view and use information, it is possible to identify the desirable properties of management information. In addition, as Steven Alter has emphasized, managers need to be trained to use their information systems effectively. To be of value, information should be accurate, timely, complete, concise, and relevant. In seeking to design systems which provide these characteristics, however, designers should not build upon the false assumptions identified by Professor Ackoff in his article. Nor should they ignore costs in an attempt to obtain unnecessary accuracy or unwarranted shorter information periods. Otherwise, what may result is an *expectation gap* between systems expectations and systems performance, as described by William S. Anderson.

The processing methods used to produce management information have evolved from manual to electronic techniques. Each processing method has its place in data processing. Mechanical tools have been developed to extend man's capabilities in performing specific steps. Later mechanical and electromechanical devices enabled man to combine some steps in one operation. The computer, with its ability to store and act upon its own instructions, made possible automatic communication between processing steps. Several generations of commercial computers have been produced since 1951. Although there have been a number of business failures in the computer industry, the industry as a whole is growing at an impressive rate.

Chapter 2

The Information Revolution

History records, in a relatively unfavorable light, periods such as the Dark Ages, which followed the fall of the Roman Empire, when European political and religious leaders reduced the tempo of change. But it can hardly be said today that the tempo of change has diminished. Rather, we are now living in a time when revolutionary technological, social, and economic changes are taking place more quickly than ever before in history. Not surprisingly, these changes are threatening to sweep aside many of the current (and sometimes comfortable) practices followed by business organizations. Thus, the managerial techniques that were adequate in the past may not continue to be effective in our rapidly changing environment. For managers working in such an environment, the risks of failure and the rewards of success are probably higher than they have ever been. In fact, a basic challenge to managers in the next few years will be to foresee and manage (and not be swept along by) the changes facing their organizations.

Of course, if rapidly changing conditions are to be controlled, leaders must have high-quality information for decision making. Thus, in the following pages of this chapter we will first briefly consider the *revolutionary environmental changes* with which decision makers must contend. We will then examine the *revolutionary developments in computer technology* and in *management information systems* that can produce the better information that managers must now have.

REVOLUTIONARY ENVIRONMENTAL CHANGES

We are witnessing today rapid *technological* changes that are taking place on a broad front. These changes, in turn, are often accompanied by pervasive *social* and *economic* changes—and problems. Let us now look more closely at some of these changes that will affect your future.

Scientific and Technological Changes

The ancient Greeks were obsessed with several dreams. One of these was the Promethean dream of stealing fire from the gods; another was the dream of soaring away from Earth and beyond the planets. Of course, these ancient dreams remained unrealized for thousands of years. Yet in a span of less than 40 years, both dreams have now been achieved. The fires of atomic furnaces have been ignited, humans have moved out into space, and their machines have traveled beyond the planets.[1] In addition, microbiologists have learned how to combine bits of genetic material from one organism with the genes of another species, and this recombinant DNA research has rekindled the ancient dream of learning the divine secrets of the creation of life itself.

Such scientific breakthroughs have encouraged further acceleration and expansion of the *scope* of scientific inquiry.[2] In addition, there has also been great acceleration in the *speed* with which new knowledge is put to use. Before World War I, there was an average wait of 33 years between the time a thing was invented and the time it was actually applied. But microprocessors on single tiny chips were developed in the early 1970s and are now being used in games, household appliances, automobiles, and traffic lights (to name just a few applications).

Social and Economic Changes

A wave of social and economic changes often follows in the wake of new technological developments. For example, a new technological development may create the opportunity in business to improve on a production process or to do something that was previously not possible. When such a development occurs, there will usually be those who will seek to take advantage of the new opportunity, even though changes in the ways individuals and groups are organized may then be necessary. And these newly organized groups may then compete for economic resources with established units. Thus, gains achieved by new groups in utilizing the new technology may create problems and economic

[1]Without computers (and without the microelectronic circuits made possible by the research conducted by military and space agencies and by computer manufacturers) much, if not most, of the technological progress of the past decade would not have been possible. Certainly, without the nearly 200 computers that were part of the NASA Apollo System, men could not have journeyed to the Moon.

[2]Although they may seem unbelievable, consider the following facts: Half the total scientific research ever conducted in the United States has been done in the past 10 years; about 90 percent of all the scientists and engineers ever formally trained are alive today; and the output of scientific information is doubling about every 8 to 10 years.

losses for those that are using older tools and techniques. The development of the automobile, for example, created a new industry and millions of new jobs, but buggy manufacturing organizations were virtually eliminated and their employees were displaced; automobiles have increased individual mobility and suburbs have sprung up, but many older central cities are in decay and their public transportation facilities have deteriorated; and automobiles have been responsible for the construction of convenient new shopping centers, but urban streets are congested, the air is polluted, and the world's oil reserves are being depleted at a rapid rate. In short, as the development of the automobile has illustrated, both positive and negative social and economic effects may be expected when significant technological changes occur.

Managerial Implications of These Changes

The managerial implications of rapid scientific, social, and economic changes are clear—managers must be prepared to make continual adjustments to their business plans. They must make more and better decisions about new products and existing products because of their shorter profitable life span; they must make decisions about product prices, new markets, and channels of distribution; they must be prepared to make decisions in the face of increasingly aggressive foreign and domestic competition; and they must decide on how to finance the necessary resources. Furthermore, these decisions may often involve greater risk and be valid only within a time span that is constantly shrinking. Thus, as reaction time diminishes, opportunities for profitable action are lost because preoccupied managers fail to reach out and grasp them (Figure 2-1).

In addition to facing pressures of a competitive nature, managers must also recognize the social effects of their decisions—i.e., they cannot take actions to utilize the latest technology without at the same time considering the possible effects of such actions on social organizations, existing production systems, and

Figure 2-1

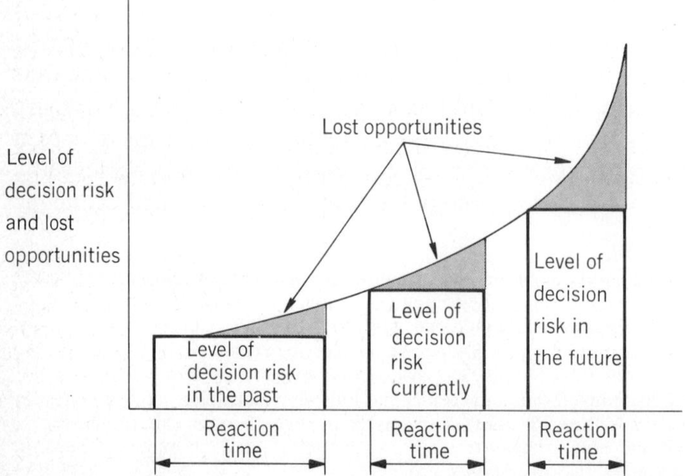

human skills and feelings. To compete profitably in the future, and to take a responsible role in seeking solutions to the social ills which exist in the environment in which they live and work, managers will require information of the highest possible quality. The computer, which is undergoing rapid technological improvement, is a tool that can provide the needed information.

REVOLUTION IN COMPUTER TECHNOLOGY

The computer is a tool that is *contributing* to advances in virtually all fields. Computer-hardware technology is also benefiting from new discoveries in the fields of electronics and physics. Computer *hardware* consists of all the machines that make up a functioning computer system. Basically, these machines accept data input, store data, perform calculations and other processing steps, and prepare information output.

Hardware alone, however, is merely one or more boxes of electronic parts that represent an expense; an equally important (perhaps more important) consideration in the effective use of computers is the *software.* Software is the name give to the multitude of instructions, i.e., the name give to *programs* and *routines,* that have been written to cause the hardware to function in a desired way. Let us now briefly look at the technological advances in computer hardware and software.

Hardware Developments

Hardware technological development has been incredibly rapid, as may be seen by an examination of the factors of (1) *size,* (2) *speed,* (3) *cost,* (4) *information storage capacity,* and (5) *reliability.* And as Figure 2-2 shows, the past trends in these factors are likely to continue through the 1980s.

Size Second-generation computers were much smaller than their predecessors because transistors and other smaller components were substituted for tubes. And as you can see in Figure 2-2, this size reduction continues today. It is now possible, through *large-scale integration* (LSI) of electronic circuits, to pack billions of *circuits* into a cubic foot of space. Furthermore, each circuit contains a number of separate components. Since 1965, in fact, the average number of components per advanced integrated circuit has doubled each year. Thus, by the time you read this sentence LSI chips may contain the equivalent of 1 million components.[3]

[3]As the president of a company that produces LSI chips has noted, "An individual integrated circuit on a chip perhaps a quarter of an inch square now can embrace more electronic elements than the most complex piece of electronic equipment that could be built in 1950. Today's microcomputer, at a cost of perhaps $300, has more computing capacity than the first large electronic computer, ENIAC. It is 20 times faster, has a larger memory, is thousands of times more reliable, consumes the power of a light bulb rather than that of a locomotive, occupies 1/30,000 the volume and costs 1/10,000 as much." See Robert N. Noyce, "Microelectronics," *Scientific American,* September 1977, pp. 63–69.

"Renfrew is totally devoted to data processing. He's the one eating microchips-and-dip."

Has the end to the feasible size reduction of computer circuitry been reached? Hardly. The boards of today will become the tiny chips of tomorrow. One scientist has speculated that by about the early 1980s it may be possible to achieve the packing density currently obtained on a square inch *throughout a cubic inch* of material. The density of electronic components would then be "about a fourth the density of nerve cells in the human brain."[4] Thus, it is expected that in the 1980s central processors with the power of today's large computers will occupy the space of a shoebox!

Speed Circuit miniaturization has brought increased speed of operation to the latest computers. Why is this? It is because size reduction means shorter distances for electric pulses to travel, and thus processor speed has increased.

Early computer speed was expressed in *milliseconds* (thousandths of a second); second-generation speed was measured in *microseconds* (millionths of a second); third- and fourth-generation hardware has internal operating speeds measured in *nanoseconds* (billionths of a second). Since circuit speeds are likely to increase by five times between 1975 and 1985, future machines may have speeds measured in *picoseconds* (trillionths of a second).[5]

Cost A significant cause of the growth in the number of computer installations is the dramatic reduction in the cost of performing a specific number

[4]F. G. Heath, "Large-Scale Integration in Electronics," *Scientific American,* February 1970, p. 22.

[5]Such speeds are difficult to comprehend. A space ship traveling toward the Moon at 100,000 miles per hour would move less than 2 *inches* in 1 microsecond; it would move only the length of 10 fat germs in a nanosecond. More antiseptically speaking, there are as many nanoseconds in one second as there are seconds in thirty years, or as many nanoseconds in a minute as there are minutes in 1,100 *centuries.* Electricity travels about 1 foot per nanosecond, and this fact imposes an ultimate limit to internal computer speed.

Hardware Development Factors	1950	1960	1970	1975	1980s
Size Factor:					
Number of circuits per cubic foot	1,000	100,000	10 million	1 billion	Many billions
Speed Factor:					
Time to execute an instruction in the central processor	300 microseconds	5 microseconds	80 nanoseconds	25 nanoseconds	5 nanoseconds or less
Cost Factors:					
Cost (in dollars) to process 1 million basic computer instructions	28	1	0.02	0.001	Less than 0.001
Cost (in cents) to provide storage for one binary number in the central processor	261.	85.	5.	.1	Less than .05
Storage Capacity Factors:					
Primary storage capacity (in characters) of the central processor	20,000	120,000	1 million	10 million	Much greater than 10 million
Characters of secondary online storage	—	20 million	Over 100 billion	Virtually unlimited	Virtually unlimited
Reliability Factor:					
Mean (average) time between failures of some central processors	Hours	Tens of hours	Hundreds of hours	Thousands of hours	Tens of thousands of hours (years)

Figure 2-2 Summary of hardware developments.

of operations (see Figure 2-2). If automobile costs and technological improvements had changed at a rate comparable with computer hardware over the last 15 years, you would now be able to buy a self-steering car for $20 that could attain speeds up to 500 mph and could travel the entire length of California on one gallon of gas. Nor does it appear that the end is in sight in computational cost reduction. The cost of certain basic components will continue to decline while their speed and performance increase.

Information Storage Capacity Information may be stored for use by a computer in a number of ways. The central processing unit (CPU) of the computer holds data and the instructions needed to manipulate the data internally in its *primary storage,* or *main memory,* section. Figure 2-2 summarizes the trend in primary storage capacity. Perhaps even more impressive has been the improvement in mass *external online* (or *secondary*) storage devices (see Figure 2-2). These devices are connected directly to—i.e., they are *online* to—the CPU, and they serve as *reference libraries* by accepting data directly from and returning data directly to the CPU without human intervention. Of course, data which the computer may use are also stored outside the CPU in the form of punched cards and magnetic tape, but these facts are *offline,* since the CPU does not have direct and unassisted access to them.

Reliability The reliability of hardware has improved substantially with the substitution of long-life solid state components for the early vacuum tubes. Much of the research effort directed toward achieving greater reliability has been sponsored by the United States government for space and missile programs. For example, scientists have been working on self-repairing computers that would remain in operation during unmanned space missions lasting many years. The self-repairing concept essentially involves partitioning the computer into functional blocks and building identical components into each block. Some of the parts are used for processing immediately: others serve as standby spares. A failure occurring in one component or subsystem would be detected by a status-sensing device, and the faulty part would be electronically and automatically replaced with a spare.

The down-to-earth benefits of increased reliability are great: for example, self-repairing computers could be incorporated into the intensive-care monitoring and control systems of hospitals, where a failure could result in a death. And they would be especially beneficial in those computerized navigational systems that are used to bring aircraft in safely in zero-visibility conditions. If those sections of future earthbound computers with a reduced number of standby spares were replaced during periodic preventive maintenance, the mean (average) time between failures would probably be measured in years rather than in weeks or months. Although completely self-repairing *commercial* computers are still on the drawing boards because of the additional cost of redundant spare parts, this obstacle will likely be overcome in the not-too-distant future as LSI circuit technology produces lower costs.[6]

At the present time, better accessibility of the circuitry enables technicians to get to the problem and quickly effect a repair. Computer circuit boards can be promptly replaced, and equipment *downtime* can be kept to a minimum. It is possible for a malfunctioning computer to be linked to another "diagnostic" computer in order to determine the cause of the problem. For example, NCR Corporation's V-8560 processor has a remote diagnostic capability that permits engineers at an NCR division in San Diego to check out any such processor installed anywhere in the United States. Also, *self-diagnostic* or fault-location features are being built into equipment to help on-site technicians minimize downtime.

Software Developments

Software is the general name given to all the programs and routines associated with the use of computer hardware. Unfortunately, when compared with the tremendous hardware advances, the developments in the software area seem less impressive. Furthermore, as anticipated hardware improvements are realized, an overwhelming proportion of the problems experienced in utilizing the computer to produce managerial information will be traceable to software difficulties. Today, in fact, the production of good software is a costly and time-consuming process that generally determines the speed with which computer-based projects are completed. As a result, the investment in programming and systems personnel and in the software they create now far exceeds the investment in hardware in most installations. And as Figure 2-3 shows, this trend will undoubtedly continue, because hardware production is automated, while increasingly complex software is still generally written on an artisan basis.

Yet there have been significant gains in the development of software. The three basic software categories are (1) *translation programs,* (2) *applications programs,* and (3) *operating-system programs.* Let us look at the developments in each of these categories.

Translation Programs In the early 1950s, users had to translate problem-solving instructions into special machine codes for each computer. Such instructions typically consisted of strings of numbers (sometimes in a binary form), which were quite tedious to prepare. In addition to remembering dozens of operation code numbers (21 might mean add), the employee performing the task of instructing the computer (a *programmer*) was also required to keep track of the locations in the central processor where the instructions and data items

[6]One current example of this trend toward much greater reliability is found in the primary storage section of Digital Equipment Corporation's PDP 11/60 minicomputer. This semiconductor memory has an error correction code feature that produces a calculated mean-time-between-failure in excess of 20,000 hours.

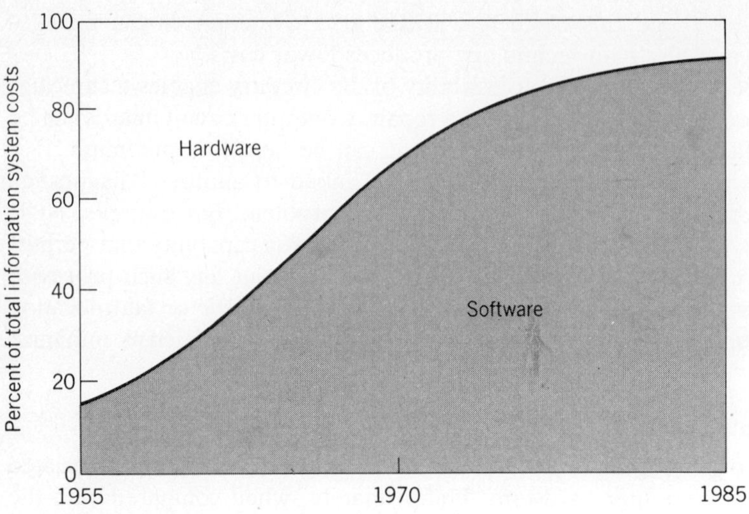

Figure 2-3 Total cost trends for information systems.

were stored. Initial program coding often took many months; checking instructions to locate errors was about as difficult as writing the instructions in the first place; and modifying programs was often a nightmare.

To ease the programmer's burden, a compromise approach between people and machine was developed which resulted in the introduction of special coding *languages* that save time and are more convenient to use. In using these languages, the programmer writes instructions in a form that is easier to understand—e.g., the programmer may print the word "ADD" or use the plus symbol rather than use the number 21. Unfortunately, this code is not in the machine's language, and so it does not directly understand the orders. How, then, can the machine execute instructions if they are in a language that it cannot understand? Just as an American and a German can communicate if one of them uses a translating dictionary, so, too, can the programmer and computer communicate if a separate translation program is employed. Briefly, this translating program is loaded into the computer, where it controls the translation procedure. The instructions written by the programmer (called the *source program*) are then fed into the computer, where they are translated. The result of this operation is a set of machine instructions (called the *object program*) that may then be used to control the processing of problem data (see Figure 2-4).

Almost all problem-solving programs prepared today are first written in languages preferred by programmers and are then translated by special software into the equivalent machine language codes. Continuing efforts are being made to produce software that will permit easier human/machine communication. For example, efforts are being made to develop software that will give the ultimate users of the processed information the ability to prepare programs in languages that are more familiar to them.

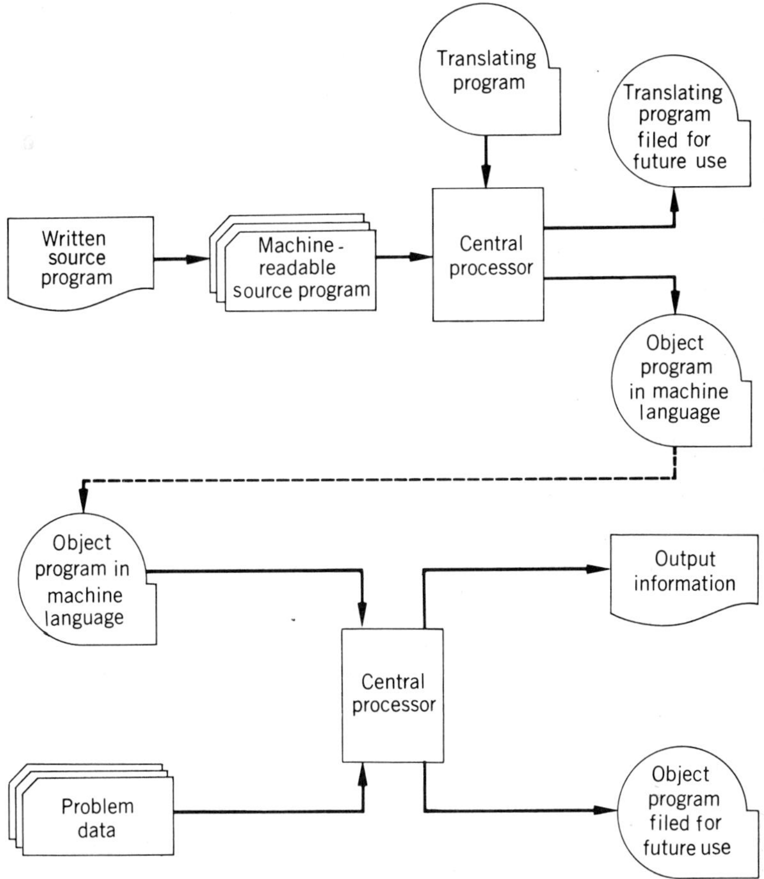

Figure 2-4 Program translation process.

Application Programs The programs written for the purpose of solving particular processing jobs also come under the heading of software. These programs are commonly prepared by each using organization to process such applications as payroll, inventory control, and other tasks. Many applications programs must, of course, be prepared by users to process tasks that are unique to their particular needs. In the past, however, much programmer time has been spent in duplicating programs prepared in other companies. Recognizing the wastefulness of such duplication, equipment manufacturers and independent software companies have prepared generalized *applications packages* (or *packaged programs*) for widely used applications. Retail stores, for example, sell on credit and thus maintain credit records and perform billing operations. Since many retail firms employ essentially the same accounting procedures in such cases, a billing and accounts-receivable application package may often be purchased by a retailer from an outside source and used with good results. But although a packaged program prepared by an excellent programmer specialist

"Am I familiar with FORTRAN? I may be—what's his first name?"

may be implemented more quickly and may be more efficient and less expensive than a run-of-the-mill program prepared by the user, there is also the possibility that an available package may not fit the needs of the user without extensive modification—a potentially difficult task for user programmers who may be unfamiliar with the package.

Operating-System Programs As the name implies, the *Operating System* (OS) was initially a set of programs prepared by equipment manufacturers and users to assist the computer operator. It is the function of the operator to load data input devices with cards and tapes, to set switches on the computer console, to start the processing run, and to prepare and unload output devices. It should not be the operator's job, however, to waste time (both human and machine) doing things that the computer could do more quickly and reliably. Housekeeping duties such as loading and unloading input and output equipment, clearing central processor storage locations between jobs, and loading into storage the next job program and data from the jobs stacked up in a waiting queue are now controlled by the software. Shifting control to specially prepared operating programs thus reduced the operator's work, cut down on the programmer's drudgery (by eliminating the need to rewrite certain input and output instructions for each program), provided relatively nonstop operation, and therefore speeded up the amount of processing that could be accomplished. The name given to the software that aids in performing the housekeeping duties just described is the input/output control system (IOCS)—an important segment of a modern operating system.

The objective of current operating systems is still to operate the computer with a minimum of idle time and in the most efficient and economical way during the execution of application and translation programs. But the operating software is now vastly more complex. More sophisticated software has been required to keep faster and more powerful hardware occupied. An example is the development of *multiprogramming,* the name given to the *interleaved* execution of two or more different and independent programs by the same computer.[7]

Multiprogramming *is not* generally defined to mean that the computer is executing instructions from several programs at the *same instant* in time;[8] instead, multiprogramming *does* mean that there are a number of programs stored in primary and/or online storage and that a portion of one is executed, then a segment of another, and so on. The processor switches from one program to another almost instantaneously. Since internal operating speeds of CPUs are much faster than are the means of getting data into and out of the processor, the CPU can allocate time to several programs instead of remaining idle while one is bringing in data or printing out information. With multiprogramming, it is therefore possible for several user stations to share the time of the CPU. This *timesharing* feature may permit more efficient use of the capacity of the processor.

In recent years, operating-system development (and specialized hardware) has also made possible the widespread[9] introduction of computers with *virtual storage* capability. Prior to this development, the size of an application program was effectively limited by the size of the computer's primary storage section. This was because the complete program was typically held in primary storage during its entire execution. If the program size did not exceed the limited primary storage capacity, then there was no problem; if, on the other hand, the task required several thousand instructions, then the programmer might be forced to write two or more programs to complete the job. With virtual storage capability, however, the computer can divide total programs into small sequences of instructions called *pages.* Then only those program pages that are actually required at a particular time in the processing need be in primary storage. The remaining segments may be kept temporarily in online storage, from which they can be rapidly retrieved as needed (see Figure 2-5). Thus, from the programmer's point of view, the effective (or "virtual") size of the available primary storage may appear to be unlimited.

The incorporation of multiprogramming and virtual storage capabilities into the OS has, of course, complicated matters. For example, software must keep track of the locations in primary and secondary storage of each of the several

[7]If you are mechanically inclined, you may know that the automobile distributor head rotates, makes electrical contact with, and zaps a pulse of electricity to each spark plug in one revolution. Similarly, the computer may allocate a small amount, or *slice,* of time—say, 150 milliseconds per second—to each program being executed. Fifteen-hundredths of a second may not seem like much time to you, but that is enough to calculate the amounts owed to hundreds of employees for a given pay period. The result of such speed is that each user has the illusion that he or she has the undivided attention of the computer.

[8]The term *multiprocessing* is used to describe interconnected computer configurations or computers with multiple arithmetic-logic units that have the ability to *simultaneously* execute several programs.

[9]The virtual storage concept was being used in the 1950s in Europe, and Burroughs Corporation introduced the concept in the United States in 1962. But *widespread* acceptance of virtual storage did not occur until IBM announced its intention to employ the technique 10 years later.

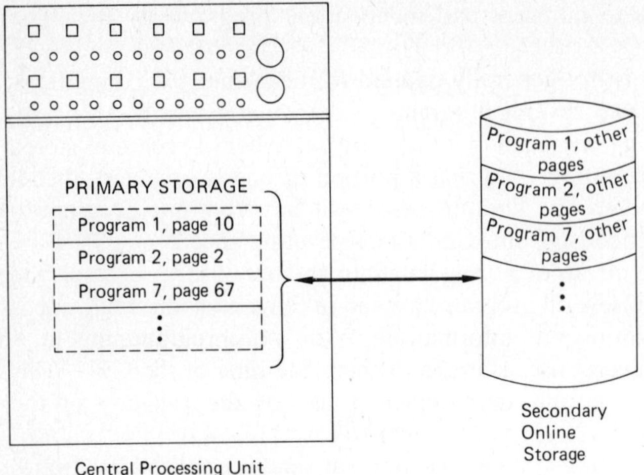

Figure 2-5 Virtual storage capability.

programs and program segments, must remember at what point it should return to an interrupted program, and must, perhaps, assign job priorities to the several tasks waiting to be completed. The operating systems of many of today's computers are, in short, integrated collections of processing programs and a master control program that are expected to perform the *scheduling, control, loading,* and *program call-up* functions described below:

1 The *scheduling* function involves the selection of jobs to be run on a priority basis from a table or list of jobs to be processed. Available storage space and the most suitable peripheral hardware to use is allocated to the job or jobs being processed. Whenever possible, jobs are selected to balance input/output and processing requirements. They are added to and deleted from the job table as required.

2 The *control* function consists of a number of activities, including (*a*) the control of input and output housekeeping operations, (*b*) the proper handling, shifting, and protection of data, instructions, and intermediate processing results when a high-priority program interrupts the processing of a lower-priority program, (*c*) the timing of each job processed and the allocation of processor time to user stations, and (*d*) the communication of error and control messages to human operators.

3 The *loading* function includes reading in and assigning storage locations to object programs and data. Checks are also made to prevent the loading and processing of incorrect files.

4 The *program call-up* function emphasizes the overall control of the OS master program (referred to by such names as *monitor, executive routine,* and *supervisor*) over other software elements, including *translating programs, service programs,* or *utility routines* (for loading programs, clearing storage, sorting and merging data, diagnostic testing of new programs, etc.), and the installation's stored file of *applications programs.* The monitor integrates this assorted software into a single consistent system. The system monitor generally remains in primary storage, where it may occupy 25 to 60 percent of the available space; in installations with online storage capability, many of the other programs and routines are kept online and are called up and temporarily stored in the CPU as needed.

Figure 2-6 summarizes the relationship existing between the hardware and software categories discussed previously.

Technological advances in computer hardware and software have both contributed to, and been stimulated by, a dynamic environment. And as we will see in the next section, managers have sought to implement computer-oriented management information systems that will enable them to cope with rapidly changing conditions.

DEVELOPMENTS IN MANAGEMENT INFORMATION SYSTEMS

Traditional information systems have often been found wanting because they do not provide information with the desired properties mentioned in Chapter 1—that is, the information they produce may be too costly and is not (1) timely, (2) properly integrated, (3) concise, (4) available in the proper format, or (5) relevant. To reduce the difficulties experienced with traditional approaches, new computer-oriented management information system concepts have been developed (and are now emerging).

An MIS Orientation

What is a Management Information System (MIS)? Strangely enough, it is not easy to pin down these innocent-looking words, for they are defined in dozens of different ways, and the definitions vary in scope and breadth.[10] At one extreme, a particular MIS could be defined as an all-encompassing system that immediately provides all managers in an organization with any and all needed information. Obviously, this definition would make it impossible for such a system to ever be realized. And at the other extreme, an MIS could be defined as any system that provides information to a manager—without specifying the nature or quality of the information. Of course, this latter system would be easy to attain; in fact, every firm or organization has one. Not surprisingly, the definitions used by most authorities to describe the MIS concept fall somewhere between these extremes.

For our purposes, a *management information system* may be defined as a network of computer-based data processing procedures developed in an organization and *integrated as necessary* with other manual, mechanical, and/or electronic procedures for the purpose of providing timely and effective information to support decision making and other necessary management

[10]Systems specialists even have difficulty agreeing on the definition of the word *systems*. At one meeting of these specialists, definitions offered ranged from "helping administrators ease decision-making when faced with multidirectional functional alternatives" to "presenting a synthesis of a very diverse network of homogeneous complexities." As *The New York Times* dryly reported, "Jargon came into its own that day."

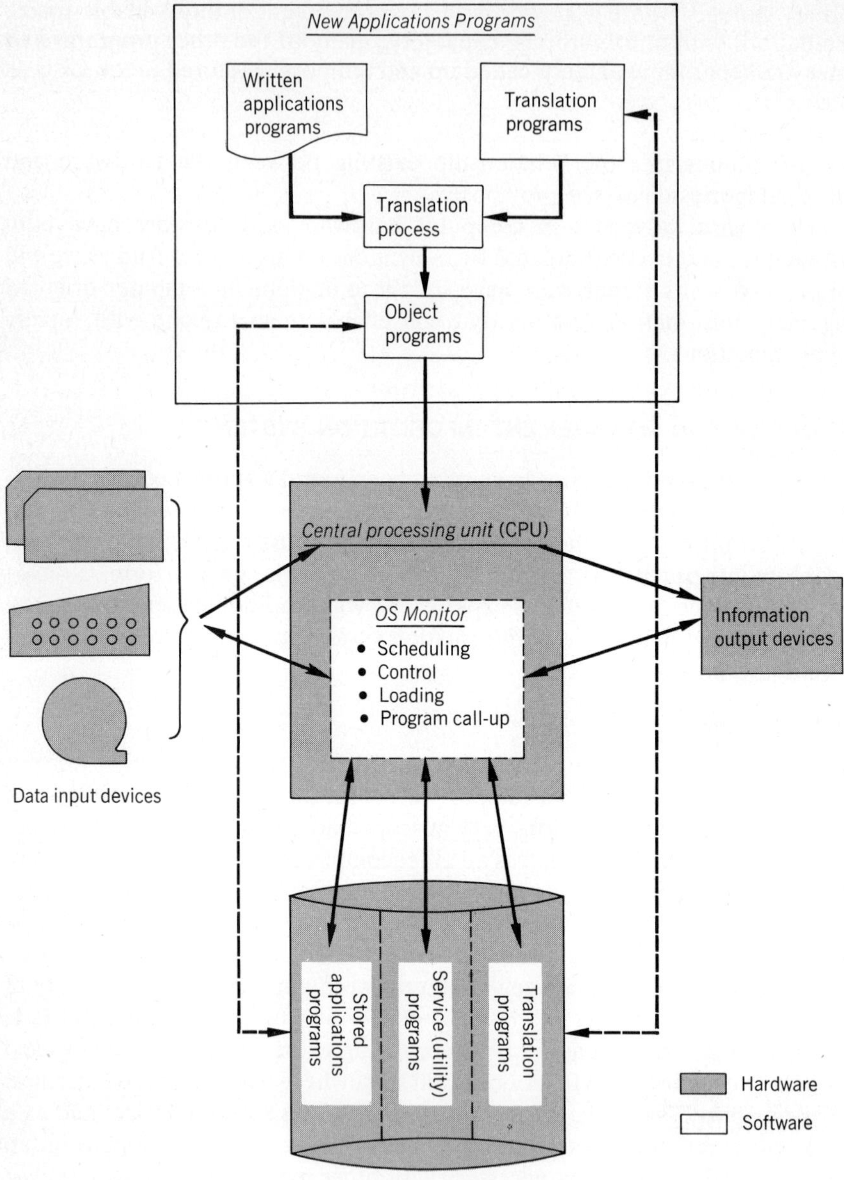
New Applications Programs
Written applications programs
Translation programs
Translation process
Object programs
Central processing unit (CPU)
OS Monitor
• Scheduling
• Control
• Loading
• Program call-up
Information output devices
Data input devices
Stored applications programs
Service (utility) programs
Translation programs
Hardware
Software
Operating system elements

Figure 2-6

functions. The phrase "computer-based" used in this definition might not be an absolute requirement in an MIS of a very small concern. But since an MIS is expected to produce information that is more timely and more complete than that produced by a traditional information system, a system possessing these capabilities is generally not feasible in larger organizations unless a computer is employed. Also, the phrase "data processing procedure" refers to a related group of data processing steps, or *methods* (usually involving a number of people in one or more departments), which have been established to perform a recurring processing operation. Figure 2-7 illustrates these definitions in the narrow context of information needed by personnel managers. Each line represents a procedure (consisting of a series of steps, or methods, indicated by the squares) that is directed toward achieving the objective of more effective personnel management. Each procedure produces needed information, and several procedures cut across departmental lines. This personnel information system is, of course, only one of several information-producing activities in a business.[11]

[11]Some writers treat the entire business as a single *system* and the component parts of the business as *subsystems*. In this case our personnel system would be labeled a subsystem within the overall business system. We have no quarrel with this treatment, since the difference is primarily one of semantics. Some also treat the entire business as a single information system. If total integration were possible, a single system would result from our definition. It should be pointed out, however, that the degree to which information systems (or subsystems) can and should be integrated is rather controversial at this time.

Figure 2-7 Personnel information system.

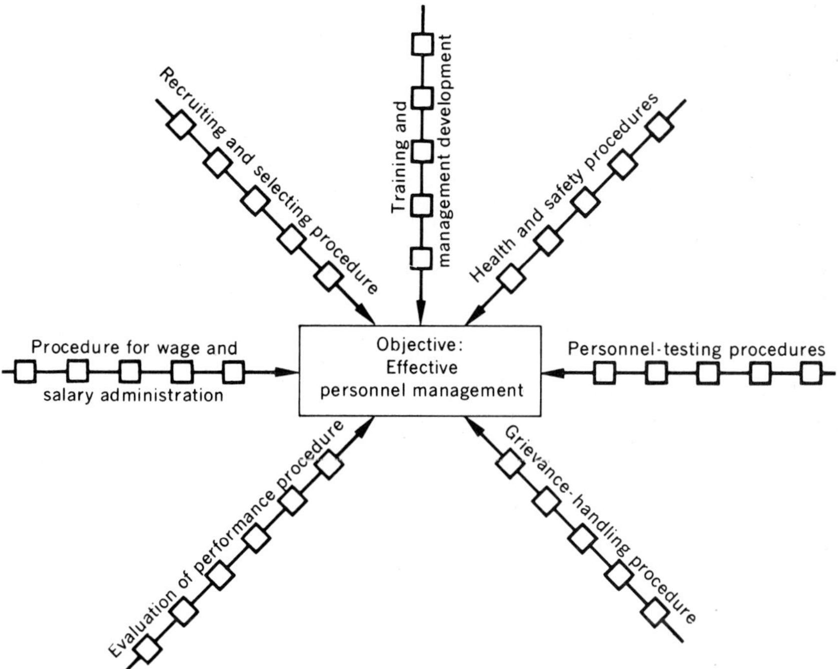

Running a business is a complicated process which, in larger organizations, takes place on at least three levels. As we saw in Figure 1-5, top executives plan and make policy decisions of *strategic* importance. These strategic decisions are then used by middle-level managers, who devise the *tactics* to allocate resources and establish controls to implement the top-level plans. And finally, lower-level *operating* managers make the necessary day-to-day scheduling and control decisions to accomplish specific tasks. Figure 2-8 shows some of the representative tasks performed and the information flows needed to support decision making. Generally speaking, the information needed by managers who occupy different levels and who have different responsibilities is obtained from a collection of management information systems (or subsystems). These systems

Figure 2-8 An MIS orientation.

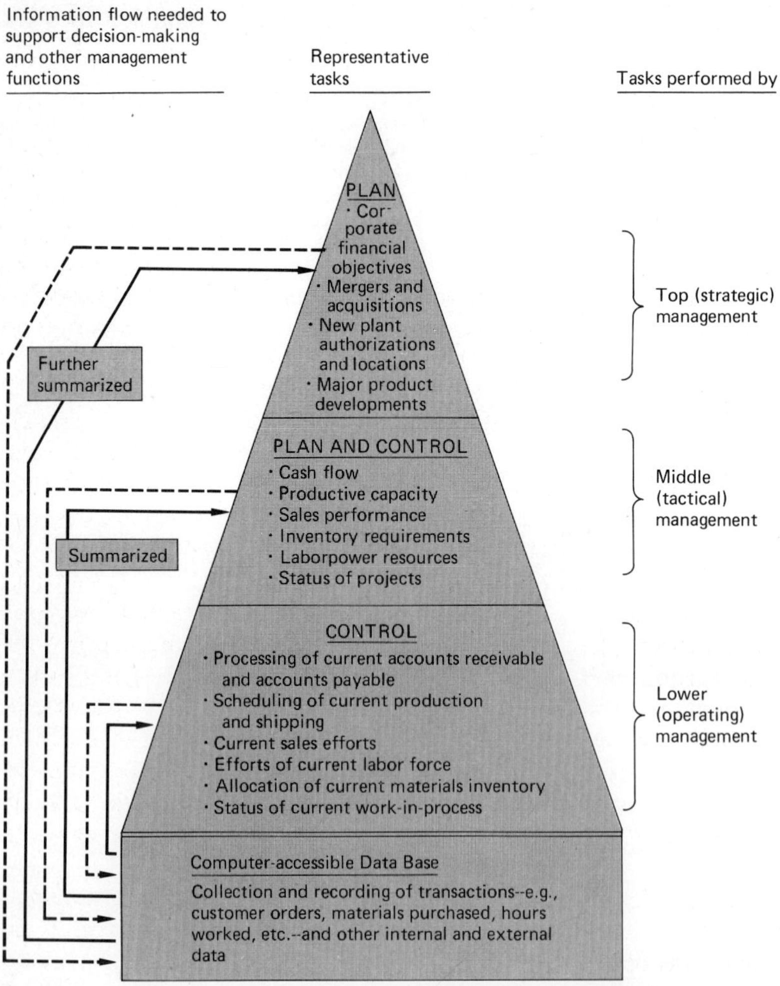

may be tied together very closely; more often, however, they are more loosely coupled.

Although the development of new information systems is a challenging assignment, many organizations have now adopted an MIS orientation and are moving toward the implementation of new systems utilizing concepts that are *quicker responding* and *broader in scope* than those employed with traditional systems. Let us now look at systems possessing these characteristics.

Quick-Response Systems

Quick-response systems, as the name implies, have been developed to increase the timeliness, effectiveness, and availability of information. They may allow users to react more rapidly to changing conditions, reduce waste in the use of time and other resources, and permit quick follow-up on creative ideas. They may also be described by a bewildering variety of Computerese terms, which we will try to cut through by examining the concepts of (1) *online processing,* (2) *real time processing,* (3) *timesharing and remote computing services,* and (4) *distributed processing networks.*

Online Processing The term "online" is used in different ways. We have seen that a peripheral machine connected directly to and capable of unassisted communication with the central processor is said to be an online device. Online also describes the status of a person who is communicating directly with (i.e., having *direct access* to) the central processor without the use of media such as punched cards or magnetic tape. Finally, online refers to a *method of processing data.* However, before looking at the concept of *online processing,* we should pause to describe the characteristics of the *batch processing* approach.

Perhaps an illustration will best explain batch processing (it is also called *serial* or *sequential* processing). Let us trace the activities that follow Zelda Zilch's credit purchase of a zither in a department store. The sales slip for this *transaction* is routed to the accounting office, where it and others are collected for several days until a large batch accumulates. The data on the slips may be recorded on a machine input medium such as punched cards. The cards are then sorted by customer name or charge-account number into the proper sequence for processing. Processing consists of adding the item description and price of all the recent transactions to the customer's other purchases for the month. Thus, a customer accounts-receivable master file, perhaps in the form of magnetic tape, must be updated to reflect the additional charges. The sequence in which the new transactions are sorted is an ordered one and corresponds to the sequence on the master file. Figure 2-9 illustrates this batch processing procedure. At the end of the accounting period, the master file is used to prepare the customer statements.

Other files are periodically updated in a similar fashion. A *file,* then, is a collection of related records and items treated as a unit. In our example, the zither purchase was one *item* on Zelda's bill; Zelda's bill would represent one

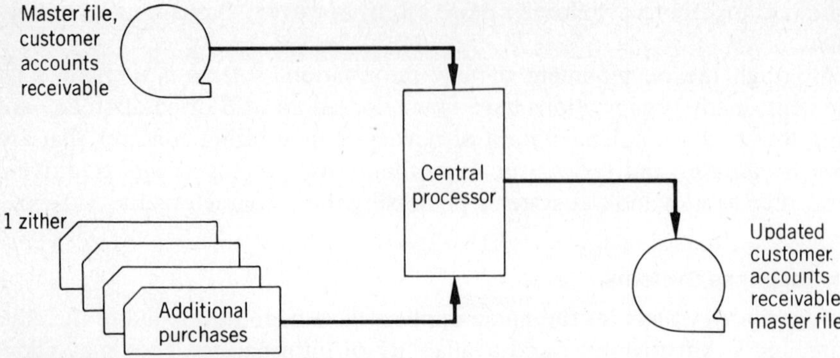

Figure 2-9 Batch processing.

charge-account *record;* and the purchase records of all credit customers would comprise the accounts-receivable *file*. Furthermore, a set of integrated files may be organized into a *data base* (see Figure 2-10).

Batches may be collected at a central computer site or at other locations. One *other* location might be a small business that is a client of a computer service center; another might be a branch office of a large firm. In either case, batches may be collected and converted into the appropriate input medium. These ordered transactions may then be sent to the computer center through the mail, by messenger, or by the use of *remote batch processing stations* which often employ telephone circuits to transmit data directly into the central computer system. Depending on the type of user and the nature of the input data, the central computer may (1) update online files, (2) process the data and transmit the output information back by mail or messenger, or (3) process the data and transmit the output information back to a printer at the remote station.

The *advantages of batch processing* are that it is (1) economical when a large volume of data must be processed and (2) the most appropriate method for those applications (e.g., payroll) where the delay caused by accumulating data into batches does not reduce the value of the information. However, the *limitations of batch processing* are that it (1) requires sorting prior to processing, (2) reduces

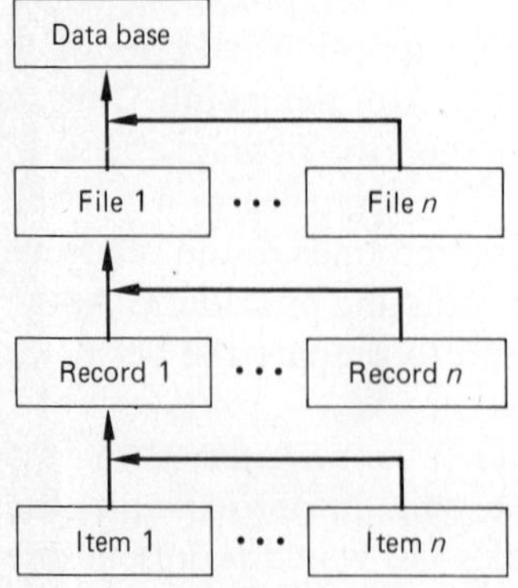

Figure 2-10 Data hierarchy.

timeliness in some cases, and (3) requires sequential file organization—and this may prove to be a handicap if the current status of a record near the end of a file needs to be determined.

Online processing has been developed for certain uses as an answer to the batch processing deficiencies noted above. In contrast to batching, online (or *direct access* or *random*) processing permits transaction data to be fed under CPU control directly into secondary online storage devices from the point of origin without first being sorted. These data may be keyed in by the use of a terminal, or they may be produced by a variety of other data-collection and transaction-recording devices. Information contained in any record is accessible to the user without the necessity of a sequential search of the file and within a fraction of a second after the inquiry message has been transmitted. Thus, online processing systems may feature *random* and rapid input of transactions and immediate and *direct access* to record contents as needed (see Figure 2-11).

Online processing and direct access to records *require unique hardware and software.* For example, the capacity of the primary storage unit of the CPU must be adequate to (1) handle the complex online operating-system control program and (2) serve a variety of other storage uses. Also, since many online users may have access to stored records, software security provisions are necessary to (1) prevent confidential information from falling into unauthorized hands and (2) prevent deliberate or accidental tampering with data and program files. Finally, data transmission facilities must be provided to communicate with online terminals located in the next room, on the next block, or thousands of miles away.

The speed of processing *needed* by a business varies with the particular application. As we have seen, batch processing is appropriate for many jobs. Ontime processing, although quicker responding than traditional methods, may involve different degrees of quickness in the needed response. For example, a system may combine immediate online access to records for inquiry purposes with *periodic* (perhaps daily) transaction input and batch updating of records from a central collecting source. Such a system would meet many needs and would be simpler and less expensive than a real time system (described next) that requires that all input, output, and record updating be done immediately through online terminals.

Real Time Processing The words "real time" represent a semantic bucket of worms—you can choose from dozens of definitions that have surfaced. The consensus, however, is that a real time processing operation is (1) in a parallel

Figure 2-11 Online processing.

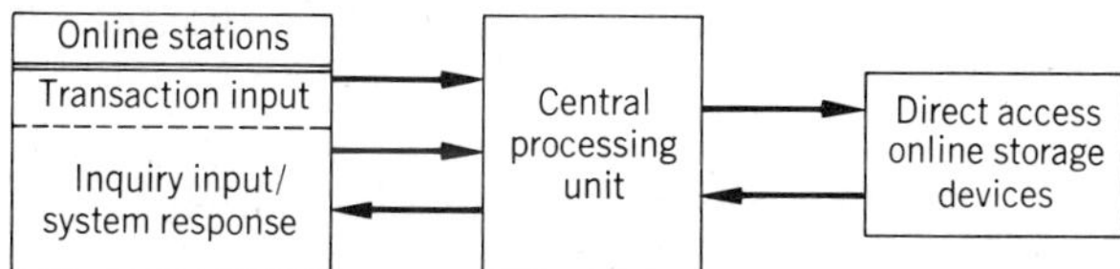

time relationship with an ongoing activity and (2) producing information quickly enough to be useful in controlling this current live and dynamic activity. Thus, we shall use the words "real time" to describe an online processing system with severe time limitations.

Since real time processing requires immediate rather than periodic transaction input from all input-originating terminals, many remote stations may be tied directly by high-speed communications equipment into one or more central processors. Several stations may be operating simultaneously, files may be updated each minute, and inquiries may be answered by instant access to up-to-the minute records.

Among the examples of real time processing are the systems designed to keep track of the availability of motel and hotel rooms, the systems that provide for immediate updating of customer records in savings banks, and the reservation systems used by airlines to control the inventory of available seats. In the airline systems, central computers receive transaction data and inquiries from remote terminals located at hundreds of reservation and ticket sales desks across the nation. In seconds, a customer may request and receive information about flights and available seats. If a reservation is made, the transaction is fed into the computer immediately and the inventory of available seats is reduced. The reverse, of course, occurs in the event of a cancellation. What if a flight is fully booked? If the customer desires to be placed on a waiting list, data such as customer name and telephone number are maintained by the computer. If cancellations occur, waiting-list customers are notified by agents. In addition, the reservation systems of competing airlines are tied together to provide an exchange of information on seat availability. Thus, an agent for any of the participating companies may sell space on *any* of the airlines if the system shows it is available.

Real time processing is required and cooperation is necessary among airlines because of the perishability of the service sold—when an airplane takes off, vacant seats have no value until the next landing. It would be a mistake, however, to assume that real time processing should be universally applied to all data processing applications. A quick-response system can be designed to fit the needs of the business. As you have seen earlier, some applications should be processed on a lower-priority or "background" basis using batch methods, some can be online with only periodic updating of files, and some can utilize real time methods.

Timesharing and Remote Computing Services "Timesharing" is a term used to describe a processing system with a number of independent, relatively low-speed, online, *simultaneously usable* stations. Each station provides direct access to the central processor. The speed of the system and the use of miltiprogramming allow the central processor to switch from one using station to another and to do a part of each job in the allocated "time slice" until the work is completed. The speed is frequently such that the user has the illusion that no one else is using the computer.

There are various types of timesharing systems. One type is the "in-house" installation that is designed for, owned by, and used exclusively in, a *single organization.* The number of such dedicated systems is growing rapidly. For example, timesharing systems utilizing minicomputers are popular with managers and engineers who must solve problems that are too large for calculators, but may not be large enough to receive a high priority at the organization's large computer center.

Another type of timesharing system was established a number of years ago by commercial *remote computing services* (RCS) to provide computer resources to *many different client organizations* seeking to process a broad range of business and scientific jobs. Many RCS firms (sometimes referred to as *service bureaus*) will do custom batch processing and will assume the responsibility for (1) analyzing the client's needs, (2) preparing computer programs to perform the needed processing, and (3) converting the client's input data into machine-acceptable form.[12] However, when the timesharing facilities for RCS firms are used, the control of the processing generally remains with the using business. Transactions are initiated from, and output is delivered to, the premises of the user at electronic speeds. The subscriber pays for the processing service in much the same way he or she pays for telephone service: There is an initial installation charge; there are certain basic monthly charges; and perhaps largest of all, there are transaction charges (like long-distance calls), which vary according to usage. These variable charges are generally based on the time the terminal is connected to the central processing system and/or on the seconds of CPU time used.

In addition to providing raw computing power to timesharing clients—a service that may be vulnerable to the purchase and use by clients of the new, low-cost processors discussed in Chapter 1—many RCS organizations also offer a library of specialized applications programs that are designed to meet the needs of a particular industry. Customers then need only supply the input data and access these online programs to obtain the needed output information. (Some of these RCS firms are now branching into a new service area by selling these specialized programs to clients who have decided to acquire their own small computers.)

Distributed Processing Networks In earlier paragraphs we have used the word "timesharing" because it is commonly applied to the interleaved use of the time of a computer. When *one* or *two* processors handle the workload of several outlying terminals, then the term "timesharing" is probably still appropriately descriptive. But when *many* dispersed or *distributed* independent computer systems are connected by a communications network, and when messages, processing tasks, programs, data, and other information-processing resources are transmitted between processors and terminals, then the term "timesharing" may no longer be adequate. Such a distributed computer-communications

[12]For example, Automatic Data Processing, Inc., with revenues of about $200 million per year, does the payrolls for about 400 banks and 30,000 other firms.

network is similar in some respects to public utilities such as telephone and electric companies—e.g., electric power plants are geographically dispersed and the energy resources generated are transmitted through a coordinating regional network or grid to the places where the energy resources are needed. (In the past, in fact, timeshared networks were called *information utilities* and computing *utilities*.)

The term "distributed processing network" is now frequently used to describe this extension of timesharing, which may result in a large number of computers and significant software resources being shared among a large number of users. Distributed processing networks, like smaller timesharing systems, may be for the use of a *single* organization or for *many* organizations. Figure 2-12, for example, shows the worldwide distributed network that Hewlett-Packard Company has developed for its own internal use. This network, with more than 130 computers located at 94 sites, links manufacturing facilities and sales offices with the company's central computer center in California. Although overall control of the network is maintained by the California center, division computers operate autonomously to process local jobs.[13]

[13] Other examples of single organization distributed processing networks are the *OCTOPUS* system, which connects 1,000 researchers at the University of California with 5 very large computers, and *Eastern Airlines' network,* which links 5 large computers in Miami and Charlotte, North Carolina, with over 2,700 ticket agent, flight operations, and internal business operations terminals. And other networks used by multiple organizations are the *ARPA net,* which connects over 30 universities and research institutions throughout the United States and Europe with 50 processors ranging in size from minicomputers to giant number crunchers, and the *General Electric network* which uses over 100 computers to serve over 100,000 users in more than 20 countries.

Figure 2-12 Hewlett-Packard Company distributed processing network.

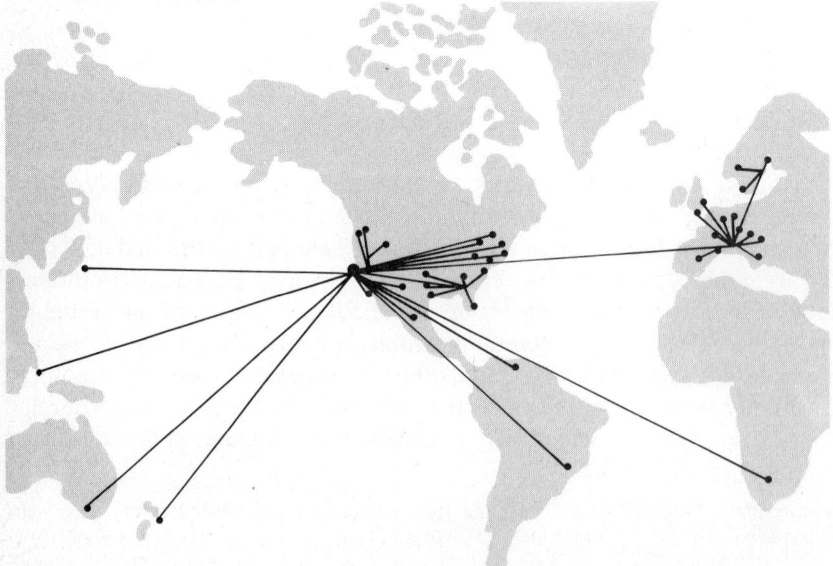

As you might expect, there are both advantages and disadvantages at present to the sharing of computing resources. Some of the *advantages of resource sharing* using timesharing and distributed processing systems are that (1) central processor idle time may be reduced, (2) sophisticated computers and a growing library of applications programs may be immediately available to end users whenever needed, (3) skilled professionals (either in-house or in the employ of RCS firms) may be available to help users develop their own specialized applications, (4) the possible availability of multiple processors in the system permits peak load sharing and provides backup facilities in the event of equipment failure, and (5) managers may be able to react more rapidly to new developments, and they may be able to *interact* with the system in order to seek solutions to unusual problems.

Unfortunately, however, some of the *possible limitations of resource sharing* at present are that (1) the reliability and cost of the data communications facilities used, and the cost and quality of the computing service received, may be disappointing in some cases, (2) input/output terminals are often rather slow and inefficient when compared with the equipment used with batch processing, and (3) provisions for protecting the confidentiality and integrity of user programs and data files maintained in online storage are generally ineffective against a skilled penetrator.

The quick-response-system concepts that we have now considered are improving the timeliness, effectiveness, and availability of information. In addition, many of these emerging quick-response systems are taking a *broader data-base approach* to the needs of organizations by attempting to provide better integration of information-producing activities. In the following section we shall briefly examine this trend.

"Henderson here has some terrific ideas on controlling our communications costs."

Data-Base Systems

Better integration of information-producing activities can lead to information that is more complete and relevant. Traditionally, data processing activities have been organized by departments and by applications. Many computers were originally installed to process a large-volume job. Other applications, treated independently, followed, but it soon became clear that this approach was unsatisfactory. Each application program typically operated on data files that had been created specifically for it, but since basic data were often defined and organized in different ways for each application, these facts could not be easily integrated with the data used in other programs run by the organization. Thus, data were often expensively duplicated (with an increase in the possibility of error) because it was impossible to combine these facts in meaningful ways. For example, a great deal of redundant data on a bank customer (home address, age, credit rating, etc.) might be contained in separate checking account, savings account, automobile loan, and home mortgage files. And integrating file data would be difficult because Charlie Brown, account number 1234, in one file became Charles M. Brown, account number 5678, in another.

Dissatisfied with such conditions, some organizations began looking for ways to consolidate activities using a data-base approach. Although there are some differences of opinion about what constitutes a data-base system, the most prevalent view is that such systems are designed around a centralized and integrated shared data file (or *data base*) that emphasizes the *independence* of programs and data. This data base is located in directly accessible online storage, and data transactions are introduced into the system only once. These data are now a neutral resource with respect to any particular program, and specific data elements are readily available as needed to all authorized applications and users of the data base. All data-base records that transactions affect may be updated at the time of input. Of course, the data-base concept requires that input data be commonly defined and consistently organized and presented throughout the business. And this requirement, in turn, calls for rigid input discipline; it also means that someone in the organization must be given the overall authority to standardize (and approve any necessary changes to) data with company-wide usefulness.[14]

Why the interest in data-base systems? One reason is that a data-base system, combined with *data-base management software* that will organize, process, and present the necessary data elements, will enable managers to search, probe, and query file contents in order to extract answers to nonrecurring and unplanned questions that are not available in regular reports. These questions might initially be vague and/or poorly defined, but managers can "browse" through the data base until they have the needed information. In short, the data management software will "manage" the stored data items and

[14]Several authorities believe that although a closely integrated system might not now be planned, it is important for firms to begin now to achieve this standardization so that at a later time they will have the *option* of introducing broader systems.

assemble the needed items from a common data base in response to the queries of managers who are not programming specialists. In the past, if managers wished to have a special report prepared using information stored in the data base, they would probably communicate their needs to a programmer, who, when time permitted, would write one or more programs to prepare the report. The availability of data-base management software[15], however, offers the user a much faster alternative communications path (see Figure 2-13).

Perhaps an illustration of the possible use of a data-base system is in order here. Suppose, for example, a personnel manager of a large multinational corporation has just received an urgent request to send an employee to a foreign country to effect an emergency repair of a hydraulic pump that the company stopped making 6 years ago. The employee needed must be a mechanical engineer, must have knowledge of the particular pump (and therefore, let us assume, must have been with the corporation for at least 8 years), must be able to speak French, and must be willing to accept an overseas assignment. Obviously, there is not likely to be a report available that will have the names of engineers with just these characteristics. However, the records on each employee in the corporate personnel file stored in the data base do contain information on educational background, date of employment, work experience, and language capability. Although in the past it might have been necessary for the manager to request that a time-consuming program be prepared that would locate employees who match the requirements, with data-base management

[15]Data management software can be purchased or rented from a computer vendor or a software house. Among the most popular of the over 2,000 software packages now in use are IBM's "Information Management System," Informatics' "Mark IV," Honeywell's "Integrated Data Store," and CinCom Systems' "Total."

Figure 2-13 A data-base system.

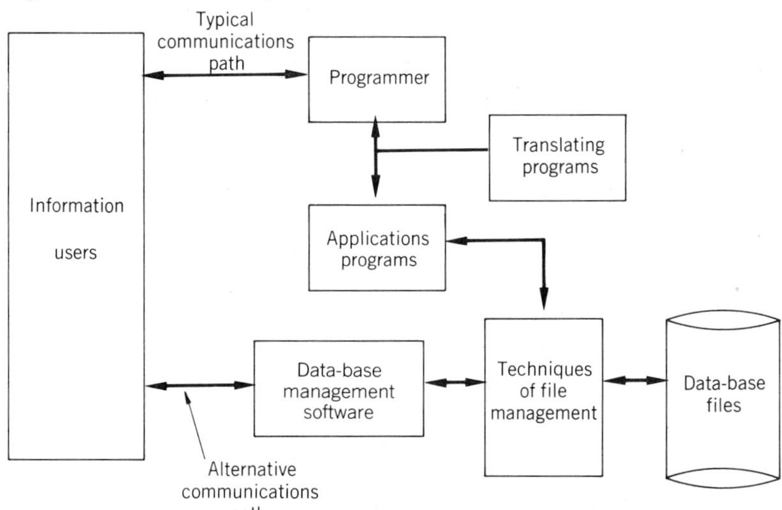

software it is now possible for the manager to use an online terminal to search through the personnel file and sort out the records of French-speaking mechanical engineers with 8 or more years of company experience. Armed with such information, obtained in a few minutes, the manager can then contact the employees named to fill the overseas assignment.

In addition to having direct access to data generated *within* the organization, a decision maker may also have *externally produced* data readily available for use. Data suppliers may make external data available to users in several ways. In the least restrictive form, data may be *sold outright* by vendors on some medium such as magnetic tape, and buyers may then incorporate these facts in their data bases in almost any way they choose. Economic statistics and United States census data, for example, may be purchased on tapes from government agencies for use in this way. Some remote computing services offer financial and marketing data on a *rental basis* to subscribers; users then access these facts from online terminals and pay for the resources used according to the pricing scheme employed by the supplier.[16] Finally, a user may buy special reports prepared from a data base owned by an outside supplier.

In summary, as you have probably anticipated, *there are both benefits and limitations* at present *to the use of data-base systems.* Among the *possible benefits* are (1) fewer applications programs and lengthy regular reports containing reference data may be needed when managers can directly access the data base, (2) better integration (and less duplication) of data originating at different points is feasible, (3) faster preparation of information to support nonrecurring tasks and changing conditions is possible, (4) savings in the cost of developing new applications, and in data entry and data storage costs, may be possible, and (5) fewer errors (and thus an increase in data integrity) may result when several records may be updated simultaneously.

But some of the *possible limitations are* (1) more complex and expensive hardware and software are needed; (2) a lengthy conversion period may be needed, higher personnel training costs may be incurred, and more sophisticated skills are needed by those responsible for the data-base system; (3) people may be reluctant to adapt to significant changes in established data processing procedures; and (4) sensitive data in online storage might find its way into unauthorized hands, and hardware or software failures might result in the destruction of vital data base contents.

REVIEW AND DISCUSSION QUESTIONS

1 Discuss this statement: "The basic challenge to the leaders of today is to foresee and manage (and not be swept along by) the flood of changes facing their organizations, and to do this within a democratic framework, for the benefit of society."

[16]Several RCS suppliers, for example, offer a COMPUSTAT data bank that contains annual and quarterly sales and earnings figures on about 2,700 companies, and Data Resources, Inc., offers online data banks dealing with thousands of different economic variables from regional, national, and international sources. For further information on other data vendors, see Joel W. Darrow, "Financial Data Banks: A Guide for the Perplexed," *Computer Decisions,* January 1975, pp. 47–48 ff., and Laton McCartney, "Data for Rent," *Datamation,* July 1977, pp. 167–168.

2 Why does a technological change simultaneously create new opportunities and problems?
3 (*a*) What changes have taken place in computer hardware? (*b*) In computer software?
4 (*a*) What are the three basic software categories? (*b*) Discuss the developments in each of these categories.
5 What functions are performed by operating systems?
6 What is the purpose and orientation of an MIS? (Hint: See Figure 2-8.)
7 (*a*) Why have quick-response systems been developed? (*b*) What are the advantages of such systems? (*c*) What is the distinction between online processing and real time processing?
8 (*a*) What is batch processing? (*b*) How does it differ from online processing? (*c*) What are the advantages and disadvantages of batch processing?
9 "Online processing and direct access to records require unique hardware and software." Discuss this statement.
10 (*a*) What is meant by *timesharing?* (*b*) What is a *distributed processing network?* (*c*) What do you think the long-term implications of distributed computer networks will be? (*d*) What are the advantages and limitations of resource sharing?
11 Identify and discuss the data-base approach to information systems design.
12 (*a*) Will data-base management software have any effect on applications programmers? (*b*) Defend your answer to 12(*a*).
13 "Difficult problems and challenges face individuals and organizations as they attempt to adapt to changes brought about by the information revolution." Discuss this statement from the viewpoint of (*a*) a systems designer, (*b*) a law enforcement officer, (*c*) a civil liberties advocate, (*d*) a spy or saboteur, (*e*) a junior business executive, (*f*) a college student, (*g*) a competitor of IBM, (*h*) a telephone company executive, (*i*) a bookkeeping machine operator, (*j*) an individual with social security number 350-26-5840, (*k*) a politician, and (*l*) a postal worker.

Chapter 2 Readings

INTRODUCTION TO READINGS 4 THROUGH 7

4 To achieve successful information systems, William Ainsworth suggests that data processing personnel must subordinate themselves to the users who ultimately will make the system work or not. In this article he emphasizes that data processing people still look upon the purchase of a computer as being the establishment of an information system and warns that a lack of understanding on both sides still remains one of the primary causes of user resistance.

5 George E. Mueller describes the continued dependency that corporations have on their computer systems as each year more and more business functions and activities are transferred to the computer. In this article, he challenges a common notion that information systems problems can all be solved by adding to computer complexes. He proposes that data processing machines of the future may well emphasize much more their ability to process data bases in an efficient manner.

6 In this article, Martin J. Shio takes a new look at MIS systems by describing some of the major obstacles that hinder their progress. He also proposes procedures to overcome and/or remove the barriers to effective MIS development.

7 Science fiction writers for many years have portrayed computers as having the ability to communicate with humans by using spoken language. In this article, John R. Hansen describes some of the advances in voice communication with machines and describes the major areas of application.

Reading 4

The Primacy of the User (Part 1)

William Ainsworth

The subject of "user involvement" in systems development and installation is certainly not a new and unique one and, in fact, has appeared in the literature and lecture agendas many times in recent years. Why, then, do I choose to comment further and ask that you take time to evaluate my thoughts on this well-worn topic? Perhaps it is because I recognize that the problem still exists to a degree and is still deserving of further analysis, and also, perhaps, because I believe the solution to the problem lies in an approach somewhat opposite to

Reprinted from *Infosystems,* April 1977, pp. 46–48. Reprinted by permission from Hitchcock Publishing Company, Wheaton, Ill. 60187. Copyright © 1977, Hitchcock Publishing Company. William Ainsworth is a principal with Peat, Marwick, Mitchell & Co.

that proposed in past discussions. The problem of lack of user involvement has traditionally been treated by a positive action on the part of DP personnel, an approach which sounds outwardly commendable but which seems to have met with significant rebuff. I propose that the solution lies in another direction, a negative approach, if you will, whereby the DP people subordinate themselves to the user and refuse to act independently of them.

The ultimate objective of both DP and user is a successful system installation. "Success" must, however, be defined from the point of view of both, and experience shows that the criteria of each may be quite different. To illustrate, consider a manufacturing control system which was installed about four years ago at great expense to the company and is still functioning today. This is a system which by DP measurement standards can be considered a rousing success. It accomplishes functions which would typically be present only on a larger machine. It has online, real time inventory control, purchasing, shop floor control and inquiry capability. It has a requirement planning subsystem and a series of other specialized functions. From the point of view of the key users of the system, it is quite unsuccessful. Since it was installed over four years ago, inventory has gone up, customer service has gone down, personnel in using departments have increased, and overall business volume has decreased.

This system was designed by data processing personnel and it is not really responsive to the actual demands of the business. It does respond to the business as it should be, but not as it really is. In addition, it is technically so complex that in order to supply all these functions on limited hardware it has the rigidity of Gibraltar. As real life situations develop and as the business changes, the system cannot cope and gets more and more out of date. Why is the system so unsuccessful? There are no cost savings, no integrated information and technical complexity dictated that the system cannot expand. It is rigorous and inflexible, and there are too many detail reports.

This system was designed as a general system for several divisions of a multidivisional company. It was designed with a minimum amount of user interface and almost no user control. It has failed, and the investment of several million dollars which the company has made has been wasted. A new system is being designed with almost total user control and incorporating the following:

1 A system to present management with the controls needed to run the business.

2 Limited detail reporting. Extensive exception reporting.

3 A less complex and more usable system without any real time functions except inquiry.

4 An implementation schedule built upon user availability and a reduced data processing staff.

5 A series of short-term goals which result in improvements to the present system.

The concept that the DP department staff subordinate itself to the user may be distasteful to some, but I suggest you hear me out. Computers and DP departments play an important role in the total functioning of a modern enterprise, but they too must withstand the scrutiny of return on investment logic. Computers and systems must be addressed as one tool among many used by a company to generate or assure profit, directly or indirectly.

The purpose of a computer system is perhaps best discussed in an historical context. Computers originally started as a device to speed up calculations. As such, input information was well defined and output was very objective in nature. The extension of computers into commercial areas, particularly manufacturing, resulted in a far more complex and subjective environment; no longer an engineer-to-programmer contact, but now involving many people of varying skills and intelligence. By this extension, the purpose of the computer system has undergone a change. Where its original purpose was to solve a problem, it has now become the key to control within an organization. Its ability to store and manipulate data, and the speed with which it can do so, has made it an indispensable tool. The purpose of the computer system has thus changed from being the problem solver to that of being the prime source of information, coordination and control within an organization.

This change of purpose has led to a change in general management and DP attitudes. In many companies which have data processing applications, particularly those with large information systems or large manufacturing systems, the attitude of management has taken a path from infatuation through antipathy and finally to disillusionment with data processing. Some of this is due to the cost and pure financial considerations of DP, but much of it is due to the changed purpose of a computer system. The DP people still look upon the purpose of the system as being the system itself. In the extreme case they feel that a sophisticated system of programs is its own justification for existence. This leads them to base their commitments to management upon the belief that a computer system is a series of programs which perform functions. The program development is quantifiable, it can be broken down into phases and modules, and time, money and resources calculated against these.

The plan is then presented to management in a logical form and, after acceptance, development is started with management's enthusiastic participation. As the project goes along, schedules begin to slip, conflicts develop, new requirements appear and suddenly a new schedule has to be developed and presented to management. This is greeted with less enthusiasm, but approval is given and work proceeds. Any successive iterations are greeted with less enthusiasm and more hostility until finally, when the system starts to process data and the usual problems of missing functions, bad data, no procedures, etc., begin to appear, total management disillusionment sets in. The talk is then: "Where has all the money gone, and why has all the effort been invested for this?" Strong consideration is even given to throwing out the system and going back to the old ways. While the above process does not occur in all instances, as you well know, it is prevalent enough to be of significant concern. It is time then that data processing personnel started to look at the causes and think about solutions to these problems. It is time that they rejected the pride of authorship security blanket which causes systems to be designed and written which are not really matched to the realities of their business. The computer is a great tool, but we have failed in many cases to apply it correctly and must now consider how we can reverse that trend. The best place to start would probably be to look at the fellow on the other side of the fence: *THE USER!*

The user is very difficult to define. He runs the full range of skills and intelligence levels which make up the human race. It is this range which is at the very core of the problems DP people must face. We have all encountered the situation of working with the dynamic, progressive, aggressive user who wants only to get things done, and we related very well to him. Unfortunately, to DP people he is a rare individual. The type most often encountered is the old-time line manager who doesn't like computers, figures what he has been doing for 20 years is good enough and thinks changes will be forced upon him just because some computer guy says so. As a result of this, over the years the data processing people have divided the users into two groups: the good guys and the bad guys. They must now step back from this black/white attitude and take a thoughtful look at the people they are dealing with and why they react as they do.

Consider again the changed purpose of the computer system. It is the prime source of information, coordination and control within an organization. The system supplies the information which allows the user to coordinate the activities of the company and exercise control over its operations. The element most often missed by DP people is that it is the user, and only the user, who makes the system work. He needs the information; he uses it.

It would be useful at this point to catalog the user according to the type of information he needs and how he uses it. The information requirements within a company can be considered as being a pyramid which corresponds to the organization chart. As you go up the pyramid, the volume of information required decreases and the frequency with which it is required also decreases. However, the type of information required becomes more complex as you go up the pyramid, since management requires that information from many areas of operation be integrated in order to do their job properly. This fact, despite all its implications, is perhaps the most neglected aspect of computer systems development. Too much work is done on the line function operations and too little on the management requirements. This is caused by the lack of sufficient user involvement at all levels, and the result is systems which, from a middle and top management outlook, are technical and detailed exercises in line functions.

There is not sufficient time here to review in detail all of the requirements which a user can impose on a computer system. Those imposed by the line user are generally well known in any event, but we should discuss what management can gain from a computer system. Perhaps the most important aspect of management information is that it is integrated information; that is, it supplies the manager with a clear presentation of the overall operation of the company and of the operation of his department with respect to the company.

The following guiding principles are offered to the data processing fraternity for application in the development of systems designs:

1 The system must be designed to meet management goals and objectives. The goals and objectives must be satisfied at all levels of the company's management.

2 Organizational responsibilities and their informational needs must be identified and provided for in the system concept. The organizational responsibilities should correspond to systems functions and elements.

3 The system should provide various levels of management within the company the necessary elements of information for control. This implies summary information for top levels of management and more detailed information concerning quantities and qualitative data for managements directly responsible for operations.

4 The data processing and information systems should be developed to a level of sophistication consistent with the company's present and future requirements. This guideline prevents overdesign for the sake of state-of-the-art reasoning and assures that the system will be user-oriented—accepted, understood and supported by them.

There is little need to discuss what the line people require from a computer system in any great detail. We have all designed and implemented systems which satisfy line requirements as we see them. It would be appropriate to talk a little about user resistance, however, as this is most often encountered in line personnel. There have been very few systems which have been installed without significant user resistance on some level. The reasons for this are many, but the following are perhaps the most predominant: lack of understanding, job security and human nature.

The first two can perhaps be considered a product of human nature. It is human nature to resist change and rebel at the unfamiliar. Combine this with the first two reasons and the problem becomes quite severe. Lack of understanding, however, is the primary cause of user resistance, and this has been, in many respects, fostered and encouraged by DP attitudes. Like any other profession, they have created their own language which has excluded outsiders from their conversations. They have applied a mystique to the computer in the eyes of the user, and they seem to be unable to describe their own product so as to make their service understandable to the man they expect to use it and pay for it. They expect the user to describe all his functions, but they do not seem to appreciate the value or need to return the favor. Additionally, often the first reaction of a data processing staff person to a user who is resistant is the assumption that he is incompetent. A man who has held a position for years and who has advanced in his field is not usually an incompetent. A man cannot be expected to support a systems effort he does not understand. DP is also looked at as a direct job threat by many a line user. This is an unfortunate situation, as it has been shown that a computer system usually creates jobs, or at worst merely changes the function of the present staff. I think we are unfairly tied to the concept of automation as being a mechanical or electronic replacement of manual labor. Nevertheless, we must learn to cope with resistance caused by job security fears.

In summing up the idea of the user, we see that we have someone who is very complex. He is set in his ways, fearful for his job and, in many cases, does not understand what a system is intended to do. He is also the key to the successful system, the source of information and often the man who pays the bills. In order to emphasize the latter aspects of his role, we must learn to deal with and eliminate the former. This can only be done by a significant change in outlook and a realignment of roles and responsibilities in the systems implementation.

READING 4 DISCUSSION QUESTIONS

1 "To achieve successful infosystems installation, DP people must subordinate themselves to the user. The user is the source of information, and often, the man who pays the bills." Discuss this statement.
2 Given the limited training that most managers have in the data processing and computer areas, is the *primacy of the user* a realistic premise on which to develop an information system?

Reading 5

Beyond the Computer Age

George E. Mueller

The most significant trend of the past two decades has been the growing dependence of world business upon the computer. Each year corporations commit more and more of their basic business functions to computers. In fact, few companies could operate at all today without their computers, and most are eager to assign still more functions to them. Serene in their assumption that the computer is omnipotent, they "know" from experience that all they need do is add to their computer complexes and make them operate faster.

But they are wrong. In fact, it would not be an exaggeration to say that the computer era as we know it today is coming to an end. A large part of my company's business involves programming computers of many types and manufacture, and it is evident from our experience that these machines are laboring mightily—and inefficiently—just to perform the functions assigned to them today. And unless we halt what appears to be an inexorable trend to automate more and more business functions, we simply will not be able to afford the larger and faster versions of today's computers that will be required to perform the desired tasks. But since expanded processing capability is essential

Reprinted, by permission of the publisher, from *Management Review,* May 1977, Copyright © 1977 by AMACOM, a division of American Management Associations. All rights reserved. Mr. Mueller is chairman and president, System Development Corporation.

to coping with tomorrow's complex society, it is not too farfetched to say that most of today's computers eventually will be replaced by quite different machines—devices that will make today's number-crunching computing systems as obsolete as the hand-cranked adding machine.

This transformation will be brought about by what is prosaically referred to in the data processing systems industry as data base management. Functionally, the management and utilization of a common data base is quite simple and straightforward, requiring only that common data used by various departments in a corporation be kept current so that users can have access to it for their own specific needs. This chore involves a huge amount of data that has to be located, extracted, and disseminated fast enough so that it doesn't slow the using departments; however, no really complex processing is needed.

Since data base management is so straightforward, why then will it be beyond the capability of our present computers? The truth is that although today's computers are wonderfully efficient at performing complex mathematical calculations, they are woefully *deficient* at all the mundane operations of storing, sorting, and fetching—all tasks that are required in data base management and that constitute 90 percent of what we ask computers to do today. Even though the computer industry has gone through three generations of development, it has designed machines optimized for only 10 percent of the workload.

Furthermore, the disparity between workload and capability will grow wider in the years ahead. As processing becomes an ever more pervasive part of our everyday lives, the new applications will have little need for complex arithmetic calculations. Rather, they will have a simple primary need—to query a data base and get a specific answer as quickly and cheaply as possible. Simple as that may be, it will present virtually insurmountable problems for the computers we have today.

HOW COMPUTERS "GREW"

To appreciate the reasons for this anomaly, an understanding of why computers have evolved as they have is required. Early computers were mainly designed to do complex arithmetic calculations. They were asked to do simpler data manipulation operations as well, but since it was hard enough to sell one computer, much less two, in those days, designers naturally structured their machines for the more difficult task. As a result, computer architecture became optimized for such necessary esoterics as floating point computation and double precision arithmetic. Each subsequent generation of computers followed this path, leading to the enormously complex adding machines of today.

It is obvious that inverting complex 30 by 30 matrices, running sophisticated computational programs, and processing all the data redundancy needed for number-crunching uses up a great deal of computer time. Moreover, the executive routines, the operating systems, and the memory configurations are carefully tailored to meet the requirements of complex arithmetic calculations.

They perform these functions very well, too, but that very excellence has made their application to data base management functions a difficult and inefficient task. The result, even in this age of microminiaturization, has been large banks of computers and storage devices in order to fulfill an organization's *total* processing needs. Adding a new data base access function today involves a contest between the programmer and the computer. Since the computer's architecture is so structured and inflexible, the computer invariably wins such a contest. The programmer must resort to convoluted paths, using excessive time and storage, just to enable his company to keep track of inventory.

Even though a business is willing to invest in all the extra processing equipment needed for "brute force" processing of data base inquiries, it will find that it is severely limited by yet another factor—input/output. Computer designers never envisioned that businesses would want to tie in direct-access terminals throughout the using departments. Although the use of remote terminals is just beginning to proliferate, computer input/output structures are already proving inadequate even for the relatively few terminals and peripheral devices being used.

Our present-day computers can still satisfy the requirements generated by users of a common data base. The solution may be inefficient and expensive, but we have not yet gone completely beyond their capabilities. It is the future—and the not-too-distant future, at that—that concerns me.

As we move toward a paperless society, the demands for efficient and reliable storage and retrieval will become even more acute. When we abandon the crutch of the ubiquitous computer printout, more and more of our records will be relegated to electronic storage.

Even if a paperless society is far off in the future, applications dependent upon efficient data base management systems are appearing almost every day. Banks are turning to electronic funds transfer (when a customer makes a purchase, his file must be searched and modified with minimum delay). Businesses are linking their manufacturing plants and their sales offices over phone lines, and all share a common data base (when a customer wants to know if an item is in stock or when he can take delivery, the file for that part must be searched and perhaps modified quickly). In addition, pressures are steadily mounting for a common data base for maintaining records needed by various government agencies, and the incipient explosion of the word-processing market may well double electronic storage and processing requirements before 1980.

We simply won't be able to meet these growing demands by making our number-crunching computers bigger and faster. For both technical and economic reasons, we are nearing the end of the line on *that* brute force approach. The magnitude of the data base management role is reaching such proportions that a radically different approach is essential.

There is no question that an entirely new type of processor will be developed in the next five to ten years, and that this new machine will be optimized for data base management functions. Probably, out of habit, we'll still call it a computer, but it will be very different from the computers we know today. With the lower hardware costs resulting from *large-scale integration* devices, we will no longer be economically required to force-fit a number-crunching computer to data base management functions that will so predominate. The small percentage of the tasks requiring complicated calculations will be handled by stripped-down versions of today's computers.

Although the new architecture will be strikingly different from that used in today's computers, it will not be too expensive to develop. In effect, the new architecture will eliminate much of the overhead and many of the cataloging functions that now use so much computer time; it will also substitute an instruction set optimized for the information storage functions of addressing, sorting, fetching, list-processing, and the like.

An essential feature of the new architecture will be effective utilization of mass storage. Today's computers are quite wasteful of mass memory for two principal reasons.

First, the file systems cannot efficiently accommodate large, frequently used files and tables—exactly the storage organizations required for efficient data base management. Also, access for such large files necessitates either a large amount of unused disk space or an inordinately long time to access a given file. Neither alternative is efficient; thus an entirely new approach is needed to permit automatic compaction of data, yet still enable total regeneration and immediate access of the complete file without delay.

Second, efficient mass memory utilization requires the elimination of redundancies. Today's computer systems store huge amounts of redundant data—including all the blank space—simply because the computer architecture is such that data cannot be recovered in a usable form unless they are recorded in a pre-set file format. Hence, since it is now very inefficient to use the central processing unit for multiple fetching and reformatting of common data for different applications, files are maintained on disks for each application, even though much common data are maintained from file to file.

Another major change that will be required to effectively implement a responsive data base system affects the system access provisions. Even in today's "simplest" time-sharing systems, a trained programmer is needed to enter and retrieve data efficiently. Languages, such as BASIC, have helped somewhat for simple programs, but operators must still be trained, and the programs they write are generally extremely inefficient in terms of number of fetches, mass-memory allocation, and so on.

The new system architecture must allow for the fact that tomorrow's systems will be used by clerks, not programmers. Ideally, a clerk should be able to enter a request in free-form English without resorting to special key words, mnemonics, or special symbols. The system should not require that the clerk spell correctly, or even enter the request in any structured order. In effect, the system should respond to the clerk just as if it were another person.

Another necessary major area of development will be the storage medium itself. There is no doubt that we cannot afford to rely on electromechanical devices, such as disks and magnetic tapes, much longer. Not only will storage requirements grow tremendously, but fail-safe operation also will be extremely important. As we move toward a paperless society, more and more essential records will be stored exclusively on these devices. Electromechanical devices are, inherently, subject to breakdown, an eventuality that would at best disrupt the system and at worst cause these essential records to be irrevocably lost. Unless we are willing to pay the stiff price of completely redundant storage of all records, it appears to me that these electromechanical storage media must be replaced by some kind of cost-effective, solid-state mass memories.

Fortunately, we are on the verge of a breakthrough in memories. The work on electron-beam, laser, and super-cooled memories is extremely promising, and cost-effective, solid-state mass storage and archival capability seem certain to be fully developed within the next five years. When that happens, both the processing capability and the storage capability will be available to build spectacularly different and larger data base management systems.

Finally, we need to develop an entirely new input/output structure—one that is designed specifically for shared access of the data base by a large number of users. Here, the protection of the data will be a major concern. The system structure will have to be designed to protect the stored data from being accessed or modified by an unauthorized user. The basic techniques exist today; they need only be synthesized in a fundamental input-output system design optimized for efficient storage and retrieval by authorized users throughout the company.

TOMORROW'S SYSTEM

What will such a system look like? Well, we can safely predict that a typical system will be quite large, with geographically dispersed elements probably linked by voice-grade communications links. The processing elements will undoubtedly be distributed with intelligent terminals accessing a common data base.

The system will be designed so that clerks will be able to enter data and access the data base using free-form English commands. The intelligent terminals will probably provide cues on the display screen (or perhaps audibly) so that even relatively unskilled operators will be sure to enter all needed commands and will be alerted when they have made input errors. Initially, there will probably be printers at each terminal, but as we move closer to a paperless society, the requested data will simply be displayed to the operator. For example, a clerk will ask, "What is the status of Part #123456?", and the system will display some such answer as, "572 units are in inventory in Moline." Or, in the same transaction, the clerk could order the part using his terminal, and the system would automatically transmit the instruction to Moline and modify the data base records accordingly.

There's nothing particularly new in this entire flow—except that it will be done simply and efficiently because the machine is designed specifically for data base access. Since the complexity of today's number-crunching computers will not be needed, the data base processing and storage equipment can be much more compact and less expensive. We won't need supercomputers operating a million instructions per second. The peripherals and I/O equipment can be much more efficient. We can take advantage of the remarkable breakthroughs in size and cost of computer modules we're beginning to see today. I estimate that we'll be able to store and process at least a bibliography of all the literature in the United States, using a system no larger than a conventional office desk. Today, if anyone even attempted such a Gargantuan task, he would probably need a roomful of computers at least.

How will we get to these first truly effective systems? The path will be the same as it was for the computer. The first of the new machines will be developed to meet government needs, then business needs, and, finally, the needs of the huge consumer market.

Why the government first? The more readily available funding is one reason, of course, but another prime reason is the enormous data base inherent in modern government operations. Moreover, the size of this data base is greatly influenced by the widespread duplication of data. IRS data are duplicated by census data, which are duplicated by security data, *ad infinitum.* This duplication is becoming prohibitively expensive, and it is a problem for which a centralized data base management system is an ideal solution. Certainly, storage costs alone could be cut in half.

Business is sure to benefit directly and quickly once system architectures are defined and hardware is developed for the government market. As in the evolution of computers, the normal course of free enterprise will quickly stimulate manufacturers to adapt systems for the needs of large businesses first, then for smaller and smaller businesses, until the systems are as pervasive as computers are today. The process may occur even more quickly than did the proliferation of computers, since the new machines will be designed for the primary processing needs of business and will be operable by untrained personnel.

I am quite confident in my prediction that we are about to witness the end of the computer age. All the classic elements leading to a major new development exist:

- We certainly have a need, for without a new processing approach, government and business alike will be severely hampered.
- The need is urgent: the capabilities of present computers will be inadequate within a very few years, and increased efficiency is the fundamental goal underlying the development.
- Since much of the required technology exists and need only be integrated into a different system design, the development is technically and economically possible.

READING 5 DISCUSSION QUESTIONS

1 The author suggests that today's technology is not suitable for many of the tasks that computers are expected to perform. In what ways may this be the case?

2 Are there current developments that are underway in computer configurations that support the author's theses concerning the future?

Reading 6

New Look at MIS

Martin J. Shio

Information has of late come to be recognized by many organizations as an important resource which managers rely on to do their work properly just as they rely on money, material, and labor. Information just as any other resource has to be acquired and managed properly for it to be productive. At least every organization has some form of an information system. In the early sixties we saw a swift growth in the use of management information systems by many organizations. This was made necessary by the growth in business in general, which resulted in increasing corporate complexity, moves towards diversification and decentralization. All this meant a growing need for improved management information. This growing need of information led to many managers turning to MIS as a panacea for many of their organization's problems.

Many organizations use the MIS concept without knowing what it is. MIS describes systems which range from preparation of an inventory report showing updated ending balances to the simulation of how new products will fare in complex market environment. Many confuse MIS with other concepts such as electronic data processing.

Dearden[1] suggests that most of the common MIS notions are understood differently by people in organizations and he admits difficulty in defining MIS. A recent survey defined MIS as: "A system for providing information to all levels of management to assist in the decision making process and it is not necessarily computerized."[2]

MISs do not just happen, they are uniquely constructed to fit the enterprise they are to serve, they take years to develop and are costly. One executive replied to the question, "Why have an MIS" by saying: "We have an MIS primarily to help us to manage better and not only to save clerical costs."

MIS has been able to improve the decision making capability of many managers. Despite these reported successes some writers have expressed disappointment and in some cases indignation at the lack of progress made in

[1]J. Dearden, "MIS is a Mirage," *Harvard Business Review,* Jan./Feb. 1973.
[2]M. J. Shio, "An Analytical Study of MIS Developments in the U.K." Unpublished dissertation (1976).

Reprinted from the *Journal of Systems Management*, May 1977, pp. 38–40. Reprinted by permission from the Association for Systems Management, Cleveland, Ohio 44138. Mr. Shio is a lecturer in information systems and management at the Institute of Development Management, Mzumbe, Tanzania.

MIS. I feel that MIS has been partially successful rather than a total failure. My feeling is that MIS has partially failed to provide top management the information they require to carry out their functions, while it has been quite successful at the operational management level and partially successful at the middle management level. Often users have had inflated expectations of what MIS can do and as a result, despite what MIS has achieved it still has been considered unsuccessful. The general agreement is that there has been a partial success and that MIS has more to give.

OBSTACLES TO MIS

If MIS has made significant contributions to better management information and promises a greater contribution in the future, why haven't systems people been able to exploit this potential? The following are the main hindering factors to the development of MIS:

1 *Lack of proper objectives and goals for many MIS projects.* Too many MIS projects are embarked upon by organizations without clear objectives and goals, which leads them into not being able to design and implement a good MIS. With a lack of objectives many organizations have failed to coordinate their information systems, which is essential for the proper working of MIS. The result is that the uncoordinated efforts of the different departments end up being wasted.

2 *Lack of management participation and development.* There has been a general lack of top management participation and involvement in many MIS projects. Too many MIS projects are left to project leaders who neither have the authority nor know much about the management process. Some managers, in order to appear that they are involved, delegate the participation to one of their assistants. The thing these managers fail to realize is that they are the ones going to use the information, and not the assistants. The main reason for this lack of management participation is basically the fact that many of the managers find themselves in a dilemma. On the one hand there are those enthusiasts who believe an MIS can do everything, while there are those who think that MIS should be abandoned. Most managers are then caught in the middle of these views and they find it difficult to make a decision one way or the other. As a result they either do not commit themselves or they delegate the work to a junior person who predictably fails to attain the expected results.

3 *Control measures and evaluative criteria are inadequate or absent.* Lack of control is a direct result of lack of management involvement and results in a lack of proper MIS objectives. Many organizations that have control measures have found them dysfunctional to the MIS development. For example, tight controls have put pressure on MIS executives, forcing them only to seek short cuts.

4 *False assumptions are used in designing MIS.* MIS information analysts must make many assumptions, some of which hold while others do not. False assumptions often lead to improperly defined system objectives.

5 *Inability of many system designers to identify information needs for managers.* It is very difficult to determine the information needs for managers. Because managers, by the nature of some of their decisions, cannot determine their own information needs. System designers, not being sure what information the managers actually require, go ahead and design systems they hope will satisfy the managers. Sometimes systems designers are able to determine the information needs of the operating management and they try to apply those needs to all the other management levels, which is of little use.

6 *Lack of flexibility in many MIS.* Some MISs fail the test of time when the environment they were designed for changes. Any MIS requires a degree of flexibility to meet changing and diverse information needs of managers.

7 *Poor implementation program.* Just as a good MIS design program is required, a good implementation program is also of high priority. Many well-designed MISs have failed because of lack of proper implementation programs. When considering implementation, a number of issues are involved, such as how should MIS be implemented? Also connected with the implementation program is the fact that there is a tendency for many organizations to try to implement MIS through the same techniques and people as used for data processing.

8 *Too much emphasis is placed on technical aspects while placing relatively little emphasis on human factors.* Many MISs have been designed around only technical factors giving little or no consideration at all to the humans who will use the system. Many good technically designed systems have failed to work because the designers have failed to recognize this important man/machine relationship.

REMOVING OBSTACLES

Having seen the reasons for the poor success in MIS, what then do we do with these problems? Are these problems too numerous for anything to be done? Have we come to the end of the management information dream? A lot has been written on improving MIS but has not contributed much because it has been too general to be of any use to any individual organization. Some organizations have even taken suggestions and applied them to their organizations only to find they don't work. There is no reason why certain rules that have worked in one organization should be applicable in another organization. An MIS is so unique to each organization that much of the design and implementation techniques will greatly vary from organization to organization.

Instead of suggesting rules for designing and implementing MIS, I have taken the problems organizations are now facing with their management information system and suggested how these problems can be solved. These are only suggestions and each individual organization's problems will have to be taken on their own merits. The following are some of the suggested ways of improving MIS.

I *Set up clear objectives and goals for MIS.* As we saw earlier one of the main causes for the poor MIS success was a lack of clear objectives and goals.

The clarity of goals and objectives is essential for a proper MIS and these objectives should be in line with the overall organizational goals. Organizational goals are not easy to identify. The best way to go about this is to find out what the overall objectives and goals of the organization are, in terms of the firm's future direction and growth, and see how MIS is expected to contribute to the achievement of these objectives. In doing this it is easy for the analyst and the managers to set up attainable goals for the MIS. This will ensure a good start because each of the parties concerned will then know what he can expect from each other in terms of the MIS.

II *Ensure proper top management and other user involvement.* Another important aspect for an MIS to be successful is for the user management (including top management) to participate in the design, approval and continual review of the MIS. Management involvement is necessary in setting the goals of any MIS, since they are going to be the users of the output. Furthermore the involvement should not be pseudo-involvement or what others have called "involvement by representation."

III *Clearly identify the information requirements of the managers.* The aim of any MIS is to provide the various management levels with the needed information to improve their decision making capability. As indicated earlier many MISs have failed to meet the managers' information requirements because their information needs have not been clearly identified in the first place. The success of MIS depends largely on the ability of designers and managers to determine information needs and to design a unique system to meet these information requirements. In determining the information requirements top management has to be able to perform their strategic planning functions and will need information relating to the environment such as intelligence on threats, opportunities, risks and also information relating to the future. Middle management on the other hand, will require information that is more internal and historical. The operational managers are more concerned with precise and exact information such as production schedules, production costs, inventory reports and much more non-monetary information. Unless this distinction is recognized it will be difficult to design a good MIS. What is required is a new effort by systems designers to define this information diversity and to design systems that meet the information requirements. The two commonly used methods for determining information requirements are data analysis and decision analysis.

IV *Need for a proper control system.* Any MIS needs a system to control design costs. There should also be a good cost/benefit analysis carried out to ensure that what is being done is within agreed lines. One of the major benefits of an MIS is improved decision-making resulting from improved information. This is definitely very difficult to quantify, if not impossible.

V *Set up a good implementation program.* Good design work can be thwarted by a poor implementation program. My observation has been that many of the MIS problems have been more with implementation rather than with design. To improve implementation:

A Avoid implementing too much in too short a time. Any MIS should be implemented in a piecemeal approach. Axelrod refers to this approach as "moving the mountain one teaspoonful at a time." By doing this the system designer will be in a better position to anticipate the problems associated with implementation and he can, through this learning process, be able to implement the subsequent pieces without much trouble. The information analyst will also be able to gain the user's confidence by taking this evolutionary approach.

B Organizations should recognize the difference between the implementation of MIS and other systems such as data processing. MIS is different from these other systems in many respects and no attempt should be made to implement them in a similar fashion.

VI *MIS should be designed as a sociotechnical system.* It is worth noting that a work organization has social and psychological properties of its own that are independent of technology. This sociotechnical view of MIS emphasizes that both the technical and the human aspects of the system should be given due consideration. It realizes that optional technical solutions may result in an unsatisfactory job environment for the manager and the other workers. Human factors such as people's attitudes, aspirations, enthusiasm and job satisfaction should be considered. It is by doing this that we can realize the technical advantages of MIS.

VII *Design decision support models into the MIS.* Accepting that MIS has as one of its aims improved managerial decisions we should then do all we can to improve the manager's decision making capability. One way to do this is by integrating into the MIS decision support models. The aim of the decision support models is really to help the manager by reducing uncertainty. The models will depend on the level of management activity that will use them, ranging from simulation models to be used by top management to optimization models which will be common at the operational level management. Many organizations have been using decision support models on an ad hoc basis rather than making it an integrated part of the MIS. Other organizations have now started to make decision support models an integral part of the MIS. A cost/benefit analysis should be carried out before an organization decides on how they will handle the decision support models.

These improvements should result in better MIS. However, these suggestions should not be taken as a panacea but should be carefully applied to the varying nature of organizations.

READING 6 DISCUSSION QUESTIONS

1 What are some of the major obstacles that hinder the development of *successful* management information systems?

2 Describe ways of overcoming these obstacles. Which ones do you consider would be most effective?

Reading 7

The Computer Gets a Voice

John R. Hansen

Using the human voice to communicate with the computer was virtually unheard of seven years ago. Today, voice is used both for computer input and output. Mention input/output and we normally think of such peripheral devices as keyboard/CRT, disks, mag tapes or even punched cards. But talking to the computer to enter information and listening to receive information are working systems in specialized applications, and the future looks bright.

These are two distinct capabilities, however, and are not usually tied to the same computer. This means that both talking and listening have not been combined in the same computer, but there are definite applications for such systems in the future. Meanwhile, voice recognition systems are used to input information, especially in hands-busy applications where it is slow or inconvenient to use a keyboard. And voice response systems are used to output information either through a loud speaker or telephone. Applications using each type are expanding.

COMPUTERIZED MONEY TRACKING

For example, the Bank of America (B of A) in San Francisco now offers a computerized money tracking system with voice response. Called Bank of America Tracking System (BAMTRAC), the service is directed to middle-size and large industrial companies, thrift institutions, non-bank investment firms, insurance companies and other non-banking financial institutions. The aim of the system is to help companies track cash flow in accounts established with B of A and other banks.

Using the system, the customer communicates with the computer by standard Touch Tone® telephone and the response is a synthesized voice from a VOTRAX voice synthesizer developed by Vocal Interface Div., Federal Screw Works, Troy, MI.

VOICE RESPONSE BANKING

BAMTRAC reports, collects and transfers deposits and balances from local banks throughout the country into a concentrated corporate account. Customers can get information any time of day or night over the phone. The system organizes a company's total balances and deposits from the previous day into a daily report available at 9 a.m. EST. The overnight reporting saves time and

Reprinted from *Infosystems,* August 1977, pp. 50–53. Reprinted by permission from Hitchcock Publishing Company, Wheaton, Ill. 60187. Copyright © 1977, Hitchcock Publishing Company. Mr. Hansen is a senior editor with *Infosystems.*

reduces the expense of multiple phone calls, Telex® wires and manual processing. Daily reports can be programmed to meet a customer's specific needs.

Another voice system based on the Vocal Interface synthesizer is being used to train blind persons for jobs with governmental agencies. Called Projects with Industry, the program is being developed jointly by Arkansas Enterprises for the Blind and the Federal Civil Service Commission. Together they train and employ the blind as information specialists in Civil Service job information centers across the country.

According to D. C. MacFarland, director, Office for the Blind and Visually Handicapped, Dept. of Health, Education, and Welfare, a significant part of the program has been the development of a six-month testing and demonstration effort involving the voice synthesizer.

Both sighted and blind information specialists use the computer terminal with voice response to retrieve stored information from the Civil Service's new computer center in Macon, GA. The program demonstrates that blind information specialists already on the job will be able to continue their employment when the Civil Service eventually computerizes all its job information. "It will also open a variety of other jobs of a computer-related nature both within the Civil Service Commission and other federal departments and agencies," MacFarland says.

Use of voice response in banking for consumers is another relatively new application. One such system was recently announced by Periphonics Corp., an affiliate of Exxon Enterprises, Inc. Called Bank-From-Home, the system affords consumers direct access to account status and complete control of their various financial transactions such as paying bills and transferring funds, according to Periphonics. The system uses the company's VoicePac 2000 audio response capability and the standard 12-button Touch Tone® phone as the input device.

Periphonics' President, J. H. Pyle, views the capability as "a viable approach to educating the consumer to the social benefits of Electronic Funds Transfer Systems (EFTS). This is achieved through the use of an already accepted terminal—the telephone," says Pyle. "We view Bank-From-Home as a springboard for entry into other EFTS programs."

Voice response is also used as part of a communication service supplied by Rapidata, Inc., Fairfield, NJ. The service is called Rapidvoice and is available on a nationwide, toll-free basis, according to the company. Subscribers using the service access the Rapidata computers containing the customer's data base through the standard pushbutton phone. Data is keyed in through the pushbutton keypad and instructions and output are by voice response, similar to the systems described previously.

In a typical application, salesmen or customers can contact Rapidvoice and place an order using product codes. They will receive instant verification of inventory status and price. The entered information is consolidated and transmitted to the shipping location for further processing.

Voice recognition on the other side of the computer, the input side, is a different story. Here, the voice can be used to enter data directly or to control a function. One of the voice data entry applications is in the quality control area. In a paper entitled, "Effective Quality Control Through Voice Data Entry," Reinold T. Belle, marketing manager, data entry systems, Threshold Technology, Inc., Delran, NJ, describes the use of voice recognition in quality control. Belle says that the present price of minicomputers makes them highly practical for quality control (QC) operations but that capturing and entering the QC data is a problem. "Hands-busy quality control applications where numeric and visual defect data is captured require somewhere between 30 and 50 percent of the inspector's time," Belle notes. "Additionally, many gauge measurements are compared against known factors to determine that the inspected item is within company standards, lengthening the inspection time."

Only after the information is entered can the results be finalized and decisions made "in those critical areas requiring attention that affect company production and profits."

"Most of the input methods available today are only faster means of old techniques," Belle explains. And placing a keyboard at the inspection source is no help—it only compounds the problem. He says that QC personnel would be required to develop new skills, understanding and motivation which would detract from their day-to-day inspection operation.

Obviously, voice data entry is the answer. He says it is possible to combine the inspector's normal work requirements with the simultaneous entry of data that he measures and observes. He goes on to explain how it's done. "With a voice data entry system, an inspector wearing a small microphone and having both hands free can follow a checklist appearing on a visual display in front of him and describe the physical measurement or condition verbally." The verbal information is transmitted directly into the central minicomputer. Results: cost savings by improving the efficiency of the inspectors and improvements in production quality from inspection reports that are both timely and accurate.

PROMPTING THE INSPECTOR

In one application Belle describes, the system prompts the inspector through the inspection sequence and indicates the measurement to be taken and the nominal value in the sample currently being inspected. As each dimensional entry is entered by voice and verified visually, it is compared by the computer to the predetermined standards. If a particular measurement is outside acceptable limits, an audio/visual indication of the unacceptable condition is provided so that the operator can alert the proper people of the situation.

After describing other inspection applications and listing other uses, Belle notes that the results of initial operating systems installed by Threshold Technology in the early 1970s indicate that a factory worker with minimal training can use a speech recognition system quite successfully. He says that recognition accuracies obtained were equal to or superior to keying accuracies obtained from the same personnel.

"Since the cost of a voice data entry terminal is competitive with the cost of intelligent terminals used in conventional data entry systems, speech recognition systems can be used in a very broad area of industrial applications," Belle concludes.

Using the voice to control a function is exemplified by applications in voice-controlled sortation systems. One example is the well-known system installed by Threshold at a United Parcel Service distribution center in Southern California. The installation includes 42 Threshold voice input terminals linked to a single Threshold 550 central processor. Using the system, an operator speaks a destination code into a wireless microphone as packages are unloaded on the center's arrival docks. The code becomes a command for a conveyor system which distributes each parcel to the proper outgoing truck dock.

VOICE CONTROL

Using the voice data input for control purposes is the name of the game for Centigram Corp., a new company in Sunnyvale, CA, headed by George Glaser. Centigram is entering the picture through the OEM market, offering a 16-word, microprocessor-based evaluation device for $3,875, ready to plug in and talk to. Glaser says the unit handles command-type input like "left," "right," "down," etc., including numbers. He says the unit can be applied to sortation systems and quality control applications and that the significant thing is the low price—even lower for production quantities, because he doesn't expect OEMs to buy the power supply in the evaluation unit. He expects them to buy only the speech electronics.

Looking to the future of voice recognition systems, Marvin B. Herscher, Threshold's executive vice president, told *Infosystems* that there has been no substantial growth in the industry over the past year but that "things are just beginning to happen now. We have a lot of trial systems people are experimenting with and they're just beginning to come back now with larger reorders. I believe over the next year or two we'll see substantial growth."

But how soon will we see a voice recognition system on the input and a voice response on the output of the same computer? "There are very definite applications like that," Herscher explains. "We showed off a system at the NCC to attract attention which showed the concept for inventory applications.

"In this particular system, we had a voice recognition system activated by a radio transmitter. It, in turn, sent a signal to a little calculator which could be carried around and display whatever was spoken, like 'one,' 'two,' 'three,' etc."

Herscher explains that this could be the predecessor to a completely alphanumeric display system where inventory information like part numbers and quantity could be entered by voice as the operator walked along an aisle. "Or it could have voice response where you'd get immediate verification tied in with a computer on-line. And if there are any mistakes in inventory, it checks you while you're still on the floor."

READING 7 DISCUSSION QUESTIONS

1 Critics of some of the more recent input/output devices such as voice response systems claim that they are essentially gimmicks that are *not* cost beneficial. Discuss this statement.
2 Project yourself 20 years ahead in time. What areas of application do you foresee for voice response systems—both input and output?

Case A

Computer Models: "Black Box" or Management-Oriented?

Michael C. Luecke

To meet the challenge of an increasingly complex business environment, modern companies are developing computer models in growing numbers. This recent trend has been inevitable for two reasons: (1) the constantly improving methods of management science, with greater reliance on sophisticated quantitative techniques; and (2) the rapidly increasing speed and capacity of large computers which make the new methods feasible. Consequently, models are finding new applications in nearly every facet of business in which management decisions are based primarily upon quantifiable or generated data—i.e., where rational analysis can replace intuition.

New probability techniques like risk analysis, for example, permit management to use simulation models which automatically take the consequences of risk—or uncertainty—into account for various uncertain input data. Older methods like linear programming are enjoying a resurgence of popularity outside the traditional areas of application such as production; "optimization" models are now feasible for solving a broad spectrum of business problems. Sensitivity analysis, which provides management with quick answers to critical "What if?" questions (e.g., optimistic and pessimistic variations of key input parameters), is often incorporated in simulation models. A time-shared computer terminal is commonly used to achieve an "interaction" between manager and computer in sensitivity analysis. Large "on-line" corporate models are also emerging in greater numbers.

Why, then, do so many "good" computer models meet a premature death—on a shelf—through lack of use or interest? Too often the answer lies not with the technical design of the model itself but with the "black box" image the model gives to the decision maker. Shelving a technically sound model—or not using it to fullest advantage—is particularly tragic when one considers the important role such models can play in the decision-making process, not to mention the considerable time and expense normally required to develop these models.

Reprinted by permission of *Management Adviser,* January–February 1973, pp. 17–24. Copyright © 1973 by the American Institute of Certified Public Accountants, Inc. Michael Luecke is senior financial analyst for CIBA-GEIGY, Basel, Switzerland.

The purpose of this article is to: (1) shed some light on the common pitfalls which prevent most companies from getting the payoff they should from computer models; (2) present some guidelines on how to develop a successful model; and (3) illustrate the guidelines with a case study.

WHY MODELS FAIL

If a manager cannot understand a computer model, naturally he will not have full confidence in it. The obvious result: the manager will be reluctant to use the model for important decision-making. It is crucial, therefore, that future models shrug off the "black box" image so that they will be more readily—even enthusiastically—accepted *and used* by management.

Is it any wonder that management is slow to embrace any decision-making tool which is often delivered to them with one or more of the following characteristics:

- Explanations are in technical jargon and computerese.
- Printouts appear in cluttered, cryptic format difficult to interpret.
- Only a specialist can use the model.
- Input data must be translated in terms of the model's abstract or inflexible input format.
- Modifications are difficult when changes are necessary.
- Documentation is poor—no single person "understands" the entire model.
- Fictitious or unrealistic input data were used during the test phase.
- The model is more sophisticated (and complicated) than necessary.

Despite the technical competence of the model builders, most models being developed contain several of the negative characteristics listed, at least to some degree.[1] In other words, these models are not management oriented. But whose fault is the "black box" image—the model builders' or management's? The blame can usually be shared by both.

GUIDELINES FOR THE MODEL BUILDER

Although usually a specialist, the model builder can easily overcome most of the major problems by following these guidelines:

Jargon. Ordinary English can replace much of the technical jargon to convey the basic ideas to management. For instance, why should management be less impressed by the term "external factors" than "exogenous variables"?

Printout. A model is often judged by the appearance of its printout. Clear, well-organized output "report" formats—without the cryptic abbreviations—require very little additional computer coding. Computer graphics are also easy to program if a plotter is available. The payoff: the printout is suitable for presentation, and nearly any manager in the company can interpret the results!

[1]Schrieber, Albert N., *Corporate Simulation Models,* University of Washington, Seattle, 1970.

Use. The model should always be programed with the user in mind. The user instruction manual should be comprehensive, including examples, so that a nontechnical person can easily use the model. User seminars may be given to supplement training. Depending upon the model's application, it can be catalogued on disk or tape in the computer library, accessible to numerous authorized users.

Input. The model's input data should be in a flexible form which is familiar to the user. For example, if sales volume is always expressed in pounds companywide, why use tons for the model input?

Modifications. The model should always be programed in building blocks, or "modules," using submodels and subroutines as much as possible. The modular approach permits enormous advantages in flexibility and also cuts total development time. In addition, any data subject to change should be programed as input to the model. As an extreme (but actual) example, one large model did not handle the "date" as input—i.e., the model had to be "re-programed" each new day the model was run! Finally, a generalized model is much more versatile (and useful) than a model developed for one narrow application.

Documentation. The computer program should be well documented *as it is developed,* and kept up-to-date as revisions and personnel turnovers occur.

Testing. Depending on the type of model, it should be tested using "live" input data, if possible. Otherwise, validate the model with realistic test data submitted by management.

Sophistication. Keep the model as basic and simple as possible. Unnecessary sophistication, however impressive, will only hinder development and may cause problems later.

Remember that the finished product, while meeting management's technical requirements, must nevertheless be "sold" to management. Some of the most vital elements of this "marketing" job include: (1) correct "packaging" (e.g., easy-to-understand printouts and documentation); and (2) good "promotion" (e.g., nontechnical, dynamic presentation). In short, deliver the model with management's perspective clearly in mind.

GUIDELINES FOR MANAGEMENT

What steps can management take to ensure that it gets a useful product from the model builders? First, management should *actively* participate in the model's design phase, giving the model builders a clear definition of its requirements. Management participation is especially important if the model is a "top-down" type; interaction and feedback are essential. Management should never delegate "carte blanche" responsibility for the model's overall design to a specialist. Second, management should try to keep informed on the new quantitative methods, learning at least the basic concepts and terminology. This learning process is not just going "halfway" with the specialists—it is a necessary part of executive development. Finally, management must realize that models, particularly corporate models, usually require several man-years by highly qualified (and expensive) specialists to develop and implement. Total development cost can easily exceed $100,000 for a single model—and this is precisely the reason that the end result should not be a "black box" on a shelf.

Shortly after its merger in 1970, CIBA-GEIGY's Basel, Switzerland, headquarters began an improved formal planning program for its extensive multinational operations. As a part of this program, management recognized the great need for a tailormade, sophisticated capital investment simulation model to assist in project evaluation, capital budgeting, and investment strategy decisions. Both risk analysis and sensitivity analysis were desired as methods; both internal rate of return (DCF) and Net Present Value were preferred as the primary yardsticks of financial performance. Since capital investment decision making was decentralized, the model would need to be universal in scope for implementation and use by subsidiaries around the world. Although standard investment procedures had been established, the model would have to be versatile enough to accommodate the various local tax laws, depreciation methods, investment grants, etc. In addition, management wanted a model that would be easy to use and interpret—i.e., no "black box."

DESIGNING THE MODEL

The author was assigned the challenging task of building the model to management's requirements within one year's time. It was decided very early in the design stage to follow the "modular" approach so that four different versions of the basic model could be easily assembled and implemented as "packages," depending on the user's application and/or hardware capability:

- Sensitivity model, using time-shared terminal
- Sensitivity model, using printer and computer graphics
- Risk model, with computer graphics
- Risk model, without computer graphics

Due to its modular design, individual subroutines of the different versions could be programed and debugged independently, speeding the total development time. In fact, the sensitivity models were already operational while the final subroutines of risk analysis were still being debugged.

WHAT THE MODEL CAN DO

It was decided to make the model as flexible and general as possible to ensure maximum use. Some of the model's major capabilities include:

- Acceptance of nearly any type or size of investment project.
- Flexible handling of a wide variety of input data (up to 75 different types of variables).
- The various input data can be input on a quarterly, yearly, or constant basis over the life of the investment.
- Options include: five economic indexes (e.g., inflation); three methods of depreciation; two tax methods.

• Up to 67 key input parameters can be varied singly or in any combination in sensitivity analysis.

• The eight most "risky" input parameters can assume a wide range of alternative values, with corresponding probability weights in risk analysis. (The model is flexible enough to treat these parameters as mutually independent or interdependent in the Monte Carlo simulation.)

• Sensitivity and risk analysis can be used together to test "shifts" in critical input parameters.

A general flow chart of the basic model is shown in Figure 1.

USING THE MODEL

Management can submit all relevant input data associated with an investment project by filling in a specially designed questionnaire. This questionnaire is "keyed" to card layout sheets for easy keypunching of input data. The model is programed to automatically print out all the input data involved, in labeled format, along with the final results. In other words, management knows *exactly* what input data the computer processed, lending greater credibility to the results.

A user instruction manual was written in step-by-step fashion and filled with examples. Although sophisticated, the model is simple to use and interpret—even a secretary can run the model and get the correct result. User seminars have proved helpful. The model is now being implemented worldwide.

The basic output results from a *single* sensitivity run of a typical investment project are illustrated in Figure 2. The "report" format is suitable for presentation and is extremely easy to interpret. The various yardsticks of performance are printed out in the top table; a "pro forma" income statement with net cash flows from the entire project is pointed out in the lower table.

A computer-generated graph of the cumulative net cash flows over the life of the investment is shown in Figure 3 for the single sensitivity run. The cumulative flows are plotted in two curves: undiscounted and discounted at cost of capital. The dramatic effect of a 10 percent rate over an 11-year horizon is illustrated.

A graphical summary of a *complete set* of sensitivity runs is displayed in Figure 4. This example shows the results of a "classical" sensitivity analysis—i.e., only *one* input variable is changed for each run. CIBA-GEIGY executives favor this graph due to its simplicity in identifying the critical input variables in the sensitivity analysis. Those variables whose curves are most horizontal or "flat" are most sensitive to change; conversely, those variables whose curves are most vertical or "steep" are least sensitive to change. The non-linear relationships inherent in sensitivity analysis are clearly evident.

The basic output results of risk analysis are depicted in Figure 5. It is interesting to note that this sample risk analysis and the sample sensitivity analysis shown previously were generated from *the same investment project.* The great advantage of risk analysis in capital investment studies is apparent. In risk analysis, the computer makes hundreds of different DCF calculations (itera-

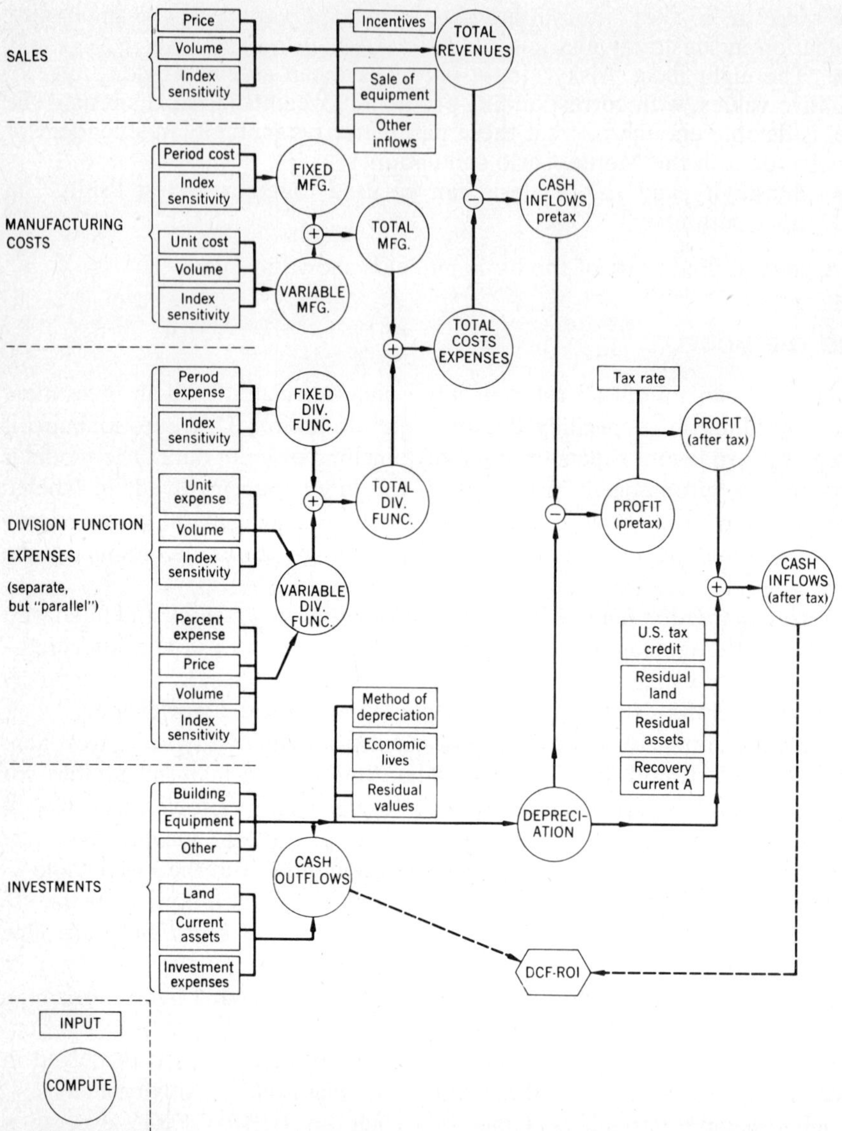

Figure 1 General flow chart of model.

tions), each based on a random selection of the eight "risky" input variables—according to their probabilities, or chances, or occurrence. (The selection process is like spinning a roulette wheel—i.e., Monte Carlo simulation.) An internal rate of return on investment (DCF-ROI) and net present value (not shown) are computed for each random *combination,* or set, of input data involved. The output result of risk analysis is a probability distribution ("Risk

CIBA-GEIGY
PRIVATE
DATA

CAPITAL INVESTMENT
SIMULATION MODEL

PROJECT: DEMONSTRATION RUN
DATE: JULY 4, 1971
CURRENCY: LIRA

OUTPUT DATA

Summary of profitability analysis	**Run no. 0**
Internal rate of return on investment (after taxes)	16%
Net present value (000) (after tax) at cost of capital of 10.00%	3368.
Profitability index (after tax)	152.
Pay-back time & date (after tax) at cost of capital of 10.00%	27 QUARTERS/1979, QUARTER 3
Pay-back time & date (after tax) undiscounted	21 QUARTERS/1978, QUARTER 1
Maximum net cumulative cash outflow (000) & date (after-tax, undiscount.)	−6248./1973, QUARTER 4
Breakeven date (total revenues = total expenses) (before-tax, st.-line)	1974, QUARTER 1
Return on sales (before tax, st.-line)	53.5%

Figure 2 Output results from single sensitivity run.

CIBA-GEIGY PRIVATE DATA

CAPITAL INVESTMENT SIMULATION MODEL

PROJECT: DEMONSTRATION RUN
DATE: JULY 4, 1971
CURRENCY: LIRA

OUTPUT DATA

ANNUAL PERFORMANCE				**Run No. 0**		
Year	**Total revenues (000)**	**Total expenses (000)**	**Profit (pre-tax)(1) (000)**	**Net cash flows (2) (000) discounted:**		
				at 16%	**at 10.0%**	**at 0%**
1971	0.	700.	−700.	−5620.	−5189.	−4590.
1972	200.	1072.	−872.	−1038.	−1023.	−1000.
1973	983.	1585.	−602.	−597.	−620.	−658.
1974	3039.	1828.	1211.	739.	816.	951.
1975	4040.	2001.	2040.	1035.	1216.	1562.
1976	3974.	1794.	2180.	870.	1091.	1548.
1977	4002.	1368.	2634.	986.	1319.	2068.
1978	4039.	1589.	2450.	766.	1094.	1896.
1979	5553.	1343.	4210.	1070.	1631.	3123.
1980	3788.	1202.	2587.	575.	936.	1980.
1981	3029.	881.	2149.	411.	714.	1669.
1982	1325.	442.	883.	732.	1383.	3682.
TOTAL	33973.	15803.	18170.	−73.	3368.	12229.

(1) Using straight-line depreciation
(2) Using declining-bal (after-tax)

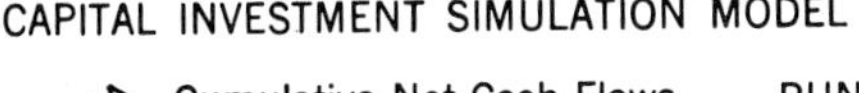

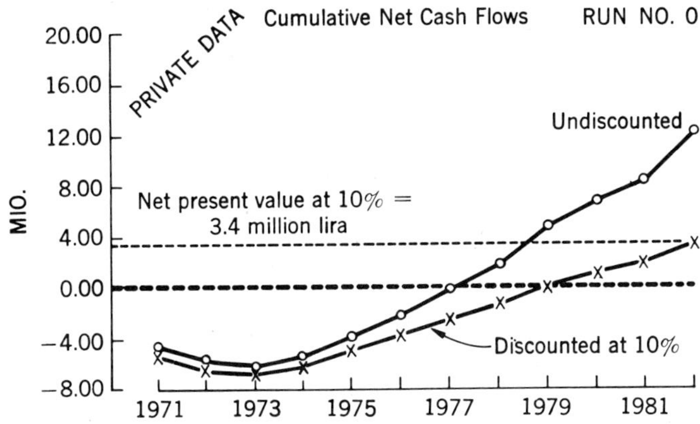

Figure 3 Computer graphics for sensitivity run.

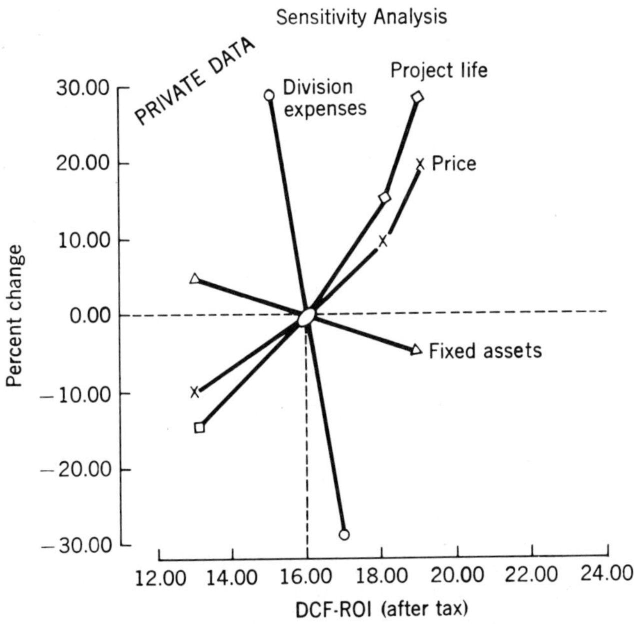

Figure 4 Graphical summary for set of sensitivity runs.

Profile") of all the possible outcomes (i.e., return-on-investment results). The cumulative "Risk Profile" (graph, upper left, Figure 5) gives management *a clear picture of the risks* associated with each possible return on investment (i.e., the chance of exceeding a given return). The ordinary "Risk Profile" (graph, upper right, Figure 5) is the probability distribution and the basis for the

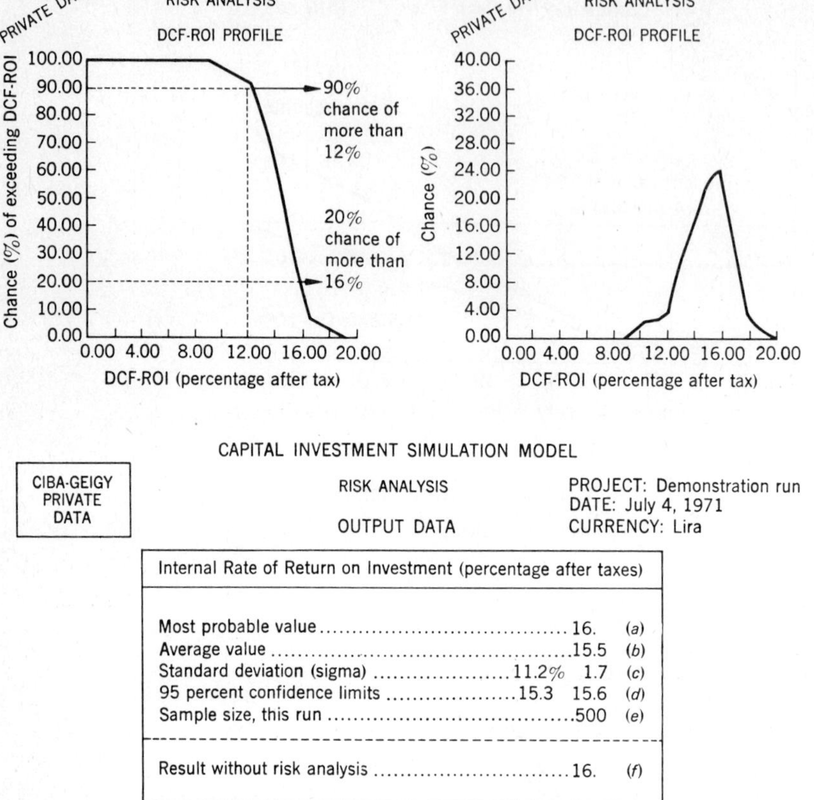

CAPITAL INVESTMENT SIMULATION MODEL

CIBA-GEIGY PRIVATE DATA

RISK ANALYSIS

OUTPUT DATA

PROJECT: Demonstration run
DATE: July 4, 1971
CURRENCY: Lira

Internal Rate of Return on Investment (percentage after taxes)			
Most probable value		16.	(*a*)
Average value		15.5	(*b*)
Standard deviation (sigma)	11.2%	1.7	(*c*)
95 percent confidence limits	15.3	15.6	(*d*)
Sample size, this run		500	(*e*)
Result without risk analysis		16.	(*f*)

(*a*) Mode.

(*b*) Arithmetic mean ("expected value" of this analysis).

(*c*) ⅔ of all values fall within + & − one sigma of the average, if the distribution is normal (Gaussian).

(*d*) 95 % sure that "true" average value lies within these limits, if distribution of means is normal (Gaussian).

(*e*) Total of iterations by computer.

(*f*) With all input data fixed (i.e., deterministic rather than probabilistic analysis).

Figure 5 Computer risk analysis results.

cumulative "Risk Profile." This distribution is approximately normal or bell shaped in this case.

The table shown in the lower half of Figure 5 contains the various statistical calculations of the risk analysis results. In this case, 500 iterations were performed, and the risk profiles shown reflect a graphical summary of the 500 different return-on-investment calculations. The main statistical measures are: (1) the average value ("Expected Value") of the 500 results; and (2) the statistical variation ("Standard Deviation") of the 500 results. Basically, the greater the standard deviation, the greater the degree of risk associated with the project.

Sensitivity analysis, on the other hand, does not explicitly take risk into account and can only give management a rough idea of "optimistic" and "pessimistic" outcomes. For high-risk investment projects, risk analysis will often give the decision maker a dramatically improved picture of the odds of making a high return—or a low return. Another benefit of risk-based decision making is that management can rank numerous alternative investment proposals according to *degree of risk* as well as return on investment.

There is no doubt that computer models will be developed in increasing numbers, and that a manager is more than willing to use a model as a decision-making tool—if he has confidence in the model and can understand it. Otherwise, there is a good chance that the model will eventually become a "black box" on a shelf. It has been demonstrated that a management-oriented model can be developed by following a few common-sense guidelines. The model builder is not solely responsible for developing a successful model—management must play an active role. The end result will be a model which is not only technically sound, but effectively used.

CASE A DISCUSSION QUESTION

What difficulties, if any, would you anticipate in "selling" this model to a "typical" manager?

SUMMARY OF CHAPTER 2

Technological changes are occurring rapidly today and are creating new opportunities and problems. Rapid reductions in size and cost (and significant increases in speed and storage capacity) of computer hardware, combined with advances in computer software, are contributing to the development of quicker-responding and more integrated MIS concepts to meet the informational need of decision makers.

Quick-response systems utilizing online processing techniques enable managers to react more rapidly and to reduce waste in the use of economic resources. In some cases immediate updating of records from all online transaction-originating terminals is required, and so a real time system must be installed. "Timesharing" is a term that describes a quick-response system with a number of online, simultaneously usable terminals that are connected to the central processor. A *distributed processing network* is an extension of the original timesharing concept that may result in a large number of computers and significant software resources being shared among a large group of users.

Many quick-response systems are taking a broader approach to the needs of organizations by attempting to provide better integration of information-producing activities. *Data-base systems,* utilizing data-base management software, are being designed to help managers find answers to nonrecurring questions.

The development of these advanced technology data processing systems has not been without its problems; one serious concern is the involvement of the *user* in the design and development of systems, which was emphasized by William Ainsworth. Another, as detailed by George E. Mueller, is a growing concern that today's current technological *marvels* will be unable to meet future information processing needs. Martin J. Shio also has shown some of the obstacles that prevent the development of effective information systems.

The greatest challenge for management is to take advantage of the developments that continue to occur. Newer technologies such as *voice response systems* provide a potential for much more efficient methods of performing activities. Whether managers will react favorably to such types of developments will depend upon how well their introduction is handled. In the next chapter, we shall examine some of the social and managerial implications of computers and their use.

Chapter 3

Computer Implications for Organizations and Individuals

The purpose of this chapter is to provide a broad orientation to the implications of computer usage in our changing society. Earlier it was observed that the computer is an agent of change—an agent that influences and also introduces change to both organizations and individuals. Many activities in our everyday work and private lives are affected directly or indirectly by the use of computers. The majority of these effects are beneficial and are welcomed, while others present challenges to existing and well-accepted procedures and are therefore resisted. In this chapter, we shall look at (1) *the types of organizations that are affected by computers,* (2) *the potential benefits for organizations and individuals resulting from computer use,* and (3) *the negative impacts that computer usage may have for individuals and organizations in our changing society.*[1].

TYPES OF ORGANIZATIONS AFFECTED BY COMPUTERS

Organizations using computers are likely to be engaged in processing operations that have one or more of the following characteristics: (1) a large volume of input data, (2) repetitive processing tasks, (3) the need for speed in processing

[1]For more information on this general topic, see Donald H. Sanders, *Computers in Society,* 2d. ed., McGraw-Hill Book Company, New York, 1977.

and retrieval, (4) the need for a high degree of accuracy, and (5) processing complexities that require or encourage computer usage.

The types of organizations affected by computers may be classified into *economic* and *public* categories. Economic organizations include those engaged in financing, marketing, producing, and servicing activities that involve private decision making. Public organizations, on the other hand, include those engaged in government, law enforcement, public health, education, and other social activities that involve public policy decisions. In the following sections let us briefly examine some of the effects of computers on these types of organizations.

Economic Organizations

Economic organizations that have large volumes of data to process in repetitive fashion include financial institutions such as banks and insurance companies, marketing organizations such as retail department store chains, and extractive enterprises such as oil companies that may produce in one country and sell on credit to customers in other countries. Quick responding and accurate information systems are needed by such economic organizations as airlines and other transportation and travel-oriented concerns. And private research laboratories must often deal with complexities that require computer usage.

Computers are used in economic organizations to improve the quality of, and accelerate the flow of, information, to thus speed up and improve the performance of planning, decision making, and control activities, and to thereby improve efficiency and raise the level of productivity in the organization. Since, during the last decade, the overall increases in productivity in United States industries has trailed those of many other industrial nations, the need for greater computer usage is recognized by many decision makers in economic organizations.

Certain economic organizations may also be affected by computer usage in the following ways:

1 *Through the organization's use of electronic funds transfer systems (EFTS).* Originally labeled the "cashless society" and then the "less-check society," the EFTS concept is dependent on computers and may permit (*a*) the electronic transfer of money among financial institutions and economic organizations on a national scale, (*b*) the use of automated clearing houses that electronically handle the settlement of transactions among banks and the Federal Reserve System, (*c*) the electronic transfer of preauthorized payroll and bill payments by organizations and individuals, (*d*) the electronic authorization for immediate cash and credit transactions—e.g., between a bank customer drawing on funds in a checking or savings account and a merchant at a point-of-sale location, and (*e*) the installation at convenient locations in banks and remote sites of electronic terminals that enable customers to withdraw and deposit cash, open new accounts, and receive other financial services. Although at this writing legal and regulatory confusion exists and the future scope of EFTS cannot be determined, it is obvious that (*f*) *commercial banks* are interested in EFTS as a means of improving the efficiency of their operations and of preserving their dominant position in the payments system, (*g*) *other thrift institutions* (credit unions, savings banks, etc.) view EFTS both as a commercial banking competitive threat and as an opportunity to play a larger future role in the nation's payment system, (*h*) *small retailers see* EFTS as a means of reducing bad check losses and of safely increasing credit sales, (*i*) *large retailers* may view EFTS as a threat to their own private credit card business, and (*j*) *national credit card organizations* see themselves as a vital part of any system issuing national *debit* cards (a debit card allows holders to make purchases or obtain cash electronically from their funds on deposit). In short, organizations and individuals have a stake in the ways that computers can influence how "money" is transmitted and accounted for.

2 *Through the organization's use of the Universal Product Code (UPC).* The grocery industry has selected a standard 10-digit code to represent every type of product sold in supermarkets. The code is represented by a rectangle of light and dark bars printed on the product by the manufacturer. An automated check stand scans the UPC symbol and transmits the data to a computer that looks up the price, possibly updates inventory and sales records, and forwards price and description information back to the check stand. Grocery retailing organizations expect that the new check-out equipment and the use of the UPC will increase supermarket efficiency and provide customers with faster and more accurate service.

3 *Through the organization's ability to change the employment situation.* The use of computers has created hundreds of thousands of new jobs in economic organizations, and many of these employees are currently working in challenging and satisfying positions. However, greater efficiency and productivity in some organizations also either has eliminated the need for certain jobs or has modified the content of remaining jobs. In some cases, displaced individuals have found it difficult to find suitable new employment, and in other cases the remaining jobs have become less fulfilling.

4 *Through the threat to the organization's security.* There are organizations whose very existence has been threatened by computer system control problems. They have failed to design adequate controls to prevent theft, fraud, espionage, sabotage, accidental erasure of vital records, and/or physical destruction (e.g., through fire or flood) of important files. In one reported case, for example, an organization received a long-distance call from a computer operator who had failed to report for work. The operator was calling from a European city with disturbing news: he claimed to have the only tape of a vital master file and announced that he would return it only when the organization had deposited a large amount in a numbered Swiss bank account. His claim was quickly checked, found to be correct, and the ransom was reluctantly paid. Other organizations have been equally vulnerable. The subject of security will be considered again later.

5 *Through the organization's ability to compete.* Many small hardware- and software-producing organizations have gone bankrupt trying to compete in the computer industry itself; larger organizations such as RCA, General Electric, and Xerox have lost hundreds of millions of dollars in futile competitive efforts; and IBM, the industry giant, is currently defending itself against numerous antitrust suits at a cost of millions of dollars. In addition, software producers have been unable to use patents to protect their products from competitive copying. And finally, organizations with limited computing capabilities may be less able to compete against those that have greater resources, with the result that computers may contribute to a greater concentration of economic and social power. A wealthy law firm, for example, with a terminal connected to an expensive legal data retrieval service[2] may provide to its large and powerful corporate clients legal services not available to the less affluent clients of smaller law firms.

6 *Through the organization's use of computers across national boundaries.* International airlines have reservation systems that cross many national boundaries; international news agencies have worldwide information and retrieval networks; stock quotation services have expanded to provide their customers with up-to-the-minute quotations from the major securities exchanges in the free world; and engineering, extracting, and manufacturing organizations link multinational facilities by computer/communications networks for planning and control purposes. Such broad networks may be expected to improve decision making and efficiency for the multinational organizations, but they may also increase the tension among nations and the companies that operate within their boundaries. Nations claim sovereignty over the types of changes that occur within their borders, but rapid cultural, social, and economic changes may result from the operations within their jurisdiction of powerful multinational corporations using global technology. Organizations may thus find that computer usage has brought them into greater conflict with national governments.

7 *Through the organization's need to protect individual privacy.* Existing and proposed laws require that some organizations handle and use computerized information about people in such a way as not to invade their privacy. These laws may differ in every state in which an organization operates, and complying with them may be expensive.

Public Organizations

Many of the public concerns of modern nations have become so intertwined with computer technology that they are virtually inseparable. For example, government agencies such as the Internal Revenue Service and the Social Security Administration have such large volumes of data to process in repetitive fashion that they must use computers; law enforcement agencies, public hospitals, and government space and missile laboratories need the quick-responding and accurate information systems made possible by computers; and the large size of many public organizations encourages computer usage as a means of dealing with complexities brought about by size.

Of course, in the past some socially beneficial organizations such as hospitals, law enforcement agencies, schools, and welfare offices were not as successful as larger economic and public enterprises in using computers because (1) they were often rather small in size and lacked the necessary personnel and

[2]In one such service, the minimum cost is $36,000 per year on a long-term contract basis. See Milton R. Wessel, *Freedom's Edge: The Computer Threat to Society,* Addison-Wesley Publishing Company, Reading, Mass., 1974, pp. 85–90.

financial resources, and (2) they were often governed by regulations which specified what data were to be gathered and processed and what interaction with other similar organizations was to be allowed.

Today such constraints are less restrictive. Many social service organizations are growing in size to meet increasing demands for their services, and this growth makes it possible to justify computer usage as a means of reducing costs and/or improving services. Also, of course, the cost of computing power has been significantly reduced in recent years. (The greater availability of computing power may, in fact, have been a major *contributing force* leading to the development of new programs and to the growth of many existing services provided by public organizations.) Finally, increased cooperation between some governmental agencies and other social service organizations is resulting in the development of standardized data-base information systems that can be jointly used by similar organizations in a county, a state, or nationwide.

In addition to the above developments, *computers may affect certain public organizations in the following selected ways:*

1 *Through their support of scientific decision-making techniques.* In a historical sense, a number of relatively new scientific agencies such as the National Aeronautics and Space Administration and the Atomic Energy Commission have been added in government; professional scientists have been included in some public policy decisions and have been consulted by government officials in the policy-making process; and computerized information systems and data banks for gathering, analyzing, storing, and retrieving information have been implemented in public organizations. One result of these trends is that the computer-based decision-making tools used to tackle scientific and industrial management problems have been applied in the attempt to solve public problems at the federal, state, and local levels. The state of California, for example, has called on aerospace firms to conduct systems studies on such problems as police protection and waste management. It should be noted, however, that the decision-making techniques developed for military, space, and industrial applications have not always been appropriate for the social problems to which they have been applied. In some cases, precise computer-generated analyses of the behavior of complex humanistic systems have simply not been relevant to the real-world social, political, and economic problems that face individuals and groups.[3]

2 *Through their use in the election process.* Computers may be used in the election process in several ways, and they may thus have a direct impact on the composition of government bodies. How? I'm glad you asked. *Prior to election day,* a state has to define the boundaries of its congressional districts according to the latest census. The political party in power in a state is essentially free to

[3]For more information on the limitations of using scientific tools to solve social problems, see Ida R. Hoos, "Can Systems Analysis Solve Social Problems?" *Datamation,* pp. 82–83ff, June 1974; and C. C. Gotlieb and A. Borodin, *Social Issues in Computing,* Academic Press, New York, 1973, pp. 126–137.

draw up district boundaries in *any way,* so long as each district contains about the same population. For decades, state political leaders have used this opportunity to arrange new boundaries so as to benefit their own candidates and parties at the expense of their opponents. Thus, this process—called "gerrymandering"—isn't new, but the computer has greatly increased the potential for such finagling. In addition to population data, the computer can also store and process data on registered voters and party strength. Thus, the use of the computer permits the party in power to process more data than was previously possible, in order to create more sophisticated gerrymanders. In Indiana, for example, one district that had been L-shaped with only 8 corners became, with the computer's help, a district with 24 corners; furthermore, a black community that usually votes Democratic was removed from this district and added to an ultrasafe Republican sector so as to deny these votes to the Democratic incumbent in the district. (Needless to say, in Indiana the Republicans were defining the boundaries; in some other states the Democrats have had the advantage.) The point is, however, that skillful gerrymandering with the help of a computer "can easily convert one party's majority at the polls into the other party's majority in a legislative or congressional delegation."[4] Also prior to the election, a candidate's staff may compile data on voters, including such variables as age, sex, party affiliation, economic status, issues of interest, ethnic background, etc. These data may then be processed by computers programmed to prepare lists of probable supporters for voter registration and fund-raising drives and to compose "individualized" letters appealing to the particular interests of the voter. This "marketing" of the candidate like a bar of soap is not necessarily undesirable if information gathered about the views of the voters on important issues helps the candidate do a better job of explaining his or her position to them. The net result may be better communication between the candidate and the electorate. However, if individualized letters are used to promise one thing to one type of voter, and another (perhaps contradictory) thing to voters from different economic and ethnic backgrounds, then the computer has been used to deceive and manipulate the voters. Computers are also used *on election day* to predict the outcome of contests on the basis of early returns from key districts, and they are used *after the polls close* to count the votes. As we will see later, present computer systems cannot be considered totally secure. Thus computerized vote counts, like manual tabulations, could conceivably be altered either accidentally or deliberately. In a primary election some time ago in Washington, D.C., for example, it was finally discovered that a test tape that was used earlier in a system shakedown had been accidentally included with the live voting results, had been counted without incident, and had become part of the vote tally!

3 *Through their impact on government operations.* Computers are being used in government planning, decision making, and controlling applications at the federal, state, and local levels. In some cases, those government agencies with well-organized and sophisticated computer resources have gained power at the expense of other government organizations. If there is a disparity, for example, between the use of computers by a legislative branch and an executive

[4]Robert W. Dietsch, "The Remarkable Resurgence of Gerry's Gambit," *Saturday Review,* June 3, 1972, p. 42.

department, and if, as is likely, the department has a data processing advantage, the legislators may be required to use either less timely and incomplete data or interpreted and filtered information obtained from the department itself in order to pass judgment on a departmental proposal or budget.

4 *Through their impact on health care services.* Computers are being applied to help solve some of the existing problems in health care systems. Certain tests and tasks that highly trained and expensive personnel have traditionally performed have been turned over to computers in an attempt to control costs; and certain procedures for collecting and analyzing large amounts of complex data have been followed by computer programs in order to obtain accurate diagnoses and improve the effectiveness and quality of health care.

5 *Through their impact on educational programs.* Computers may be used in educational programs by teachers to plan for individualized instruction, and by students to obtain immediate feedback of successes and failures in achieving learning objectives.

BENEFITS TO INDIVIDUALS IN ORGANIZATIONS

Both *administrators* and *employees* are the beneficiaries of their organizations' use of computers.

Administrators

High-level executives have, in some cases, been able to use better and more timely information in order to reassume some of the decision-making powers previously delegated to subordinates. In other cases, executives have, with a greater feeling of confidence in their ability to monitor performance through computer-produced reports, delegated additional authority to subordinates. However, the primary role of top executives lies in formulating objectives and policies and planning and guiding overall organizational strategy. Computer-based systems should, through the use of improved simulation techniques, help remove some of the uncertainties from the usually unique and ill-structured problems that top administrators face. But substantial changes in the top executive role have not occurred, nor are they expected in the near future.

A most important role of *lower-level supervisors* is to provide face-to-face communication, direction, and leadership to operating employees. But these administrators have, in the past, been caught in a squeeze between rising personnel and materials costs on the one hand and the need to maintain cost controls and remain within budget limits on the other. Computer usage has benefited administrators in business and government, and in school systems, hospitals, and other social service organizations, by permitting them to (*a*) schedule operations more efficiently, (*b*) maintain better control over economic resources, and (*c*) cope with a generally increasing level of paperwork. By relieving supervisors of many of their clerical duties, computers have thus made it possible for them to give more attention to the important personnel administration aspects of their work.

Administrators occupying *middle-level positions* in an organization,[5] like all managers, must perform the activities of planning, organizing, staffing, and controlling. As a result of computer information systems, some middle managers no longer need to spend as much time in controlling, because the computer can take over many of the clerical control activities—e.g., it can signal with a triggered report whenever actual performance varies from what was planned. Time saved in controlling has enabled some middle-level administrators to devote more attention to planning and directing the work of subordinates. More accurate and timely organizationwide information supplied by the computer has given some administrators the opportunity to spend more time identifying problems, recognizing opportunities, and planning alternate courses of action. In this respect, then, their jobs have become more challenging and more nearly resemble those of chief executives. With more time to devote to departmental employee matters, improved morale may be expected; furthermore, the more timely information that is now available to some middle managers puts them in a position to be able to react more rapidly to external changes.

Employees

Programmers, systems analysts, and *computer operations personnel* whose jobs depend on the use of computers; *operations researchers* using the techniques of linear programming, simulation, etc.; *scientists* conducting research into complex problem areas that could not be considered without computers; *design engineers* and *architects* using computer models to predict the effect of stresses on different structural configurations; *lawyers* using legal data banks to locate precedent cases in order to better serve clients; *sales personnel* who receive more timely information about customers and product inventories and who are able to promise more efficient handling of sales orders in order to serve their customers better and thus improve their own sales performance; *teachers* who have been able to devote more time to giving students individual attention because record-keeping and grading chores have been reduced and because computer-assisted instruction techniques have reduced the time-consuming routine drill work; *clerical employees* whose job duties have changed from routine, repetitive operations to more varied and appealing tasks—all these individuals are among the beneficiaries of the use of computers in organizations. Computer information systems have furnished them with well-paying jobs, and/or the systems have replaced routine procedures with more challenging and rewarding opportunities to use their creative abilities.

BENEFITS TO INDIVIDUALS IN PRIVATE LIFE

Private individuals receive benefits from the ways in which both *economic* and *public* organizations use computers.

[5]*Middle managers* may be defined as those who are above the lowest level of supervision and below the highest level of a self-contained operating organization. Thus, the term "middle manager" is rather nebulous and is applied to a number of levels in many organizations. The difficulties of generalizing about such a wide range of positions should be recognized.

Benefits from Economic Organizations

Most of us have probably been disturbed by the way prices have increased for many of the goods and services that we buy. However, what we may perhaps fail to realize is that, to the extent that economic organizations have avoided waste and improved efficiency and productivity through the use of computers, the prices we now pay may be less than they would otherwise have been. Edmund Berkeley, editor of *Computers and People,* has estimated, for example, that "the use of computers on a large scale has made prices lower by 10 to 30 percent and often much more, than they would be without computers."[6]

In addition to possibly having an impact on the prices we pay *to* economic organizations, computers may also play a role in improving the quality of the services we receive *from* them. Computer processing techniques, for example, make possible the shortening of customer waiting lines at airline ticket offices and at the reservation desks of hotels, motels, and car-rental agencies; the use of credit cards as a convenient means of handling purchase transactions; and the efficient control of inventory in retail outlets so that popular items are reordered in time to avoid many of the out-of-stock situations that frustrate consumers.

Some other benefits which private individuals may receive from economic organizations as a result of computer usage are:

1 *The possible benefits of EFTS.* We saw previously that financial and retailing institutions are very interested in the use of electronic funds transfer systems (EFTS). But how can these systems benefit individuals? Although EFTS are still in the formative stages and the fully developed version(s) will be shaped by intense competition and government regulation, their general shape is clear enough for us to identify certain advantages for individuals. In a *checkless payment system,* for example, authorized credits to specified individuals from an employer, pension fund, etc., are recorded on magnetic tape along with the name of the recipient's bank and his or her bank account number. The tape is delivered to the paying organization's bank. This bank sorts out its own customers, deposits the payment amounts to their accounts, and then transfers the remaining names to an *automated clearing house* (ACH) facility. An ACH computer sorts the remaining names according to their banks and then notifies these banks of the amounts to be deposited in the specified accounts. A benefit of this EFTS approach is that it eliminates the fear of theft of checks. Millions of people are now receiving direct-deposit Social Security payments in lieu of mailed checks. As one recipient living on Chicago's South Side has noted, "It's better for (the check) to be in the bank than to take the chance of having it in your mailbox."[7] Another way in which EFTS may benefit individuals will involve the use of terminals conveniently located anywhere that substantial numbers of nontrivial financial transactions occur. Point-of-sale *cash terminal systems,* for example, have been tested and found to be technologically feasible. When such systems are fully developed, you might present your plastic "currency" or "debit" card (which uses, perhaps, a magnetic stripe to supply the

[6]Edmund C. Berkeley, "How Do Computers Affect People?," *Computers and People,* April 1975, p. 6.

[7]*Wall Street Journal,* November 18, 1975, p. 15.

necessary account information) to make a request at a store's terminal for an electronic transfer of funds to pay for a purchase. The terminal would then send a message to your bank asking for approval of the transfer. If your account has the necessary funds (or if you are eligible for sufficient credit), the bank's computer would (*a*) send a message approving the transaction to the merchant's terminal, and (*b*) see to the transfer of the payment funds to the merchant's account. This EFTS approach would give individuals the benefits associated with completing transactions for cash (speed, lack of "red tape," etc.) without the possible dangers associated with carrying large amounts of cash. Of course, you and the merchant may use different banks and so one or more ACH facilities would be used in the transaction to switch and process messages. Fully developed cash terminal systems will depend on a strong national network of ACHs. But a National Automated Clearing House Association (NACHA) has been formed, and other ACH facilities are being developed throughout the nation.

2 *The possible benefits of UPC.* For the reasons mentioned previously, merchants selling products coded with UPC symbols expect to receive benefits. But individuals may also find that a UPC system (*a*) reduces their waiting time and gives them faster service at checkout counters, (*b*) reduces the chances for human error at checkouts, and (*c*) provides them with an *itemized* sales receipt rather than just a tape with a column of numbers.

3 *The possible recreational benefits.* Some organizations are using computers for the sole purpose of amusing and entertaining individuals. For example, the computer of Recreational Computer Systems, Inc., Atlanta, Georgia, is used for just this purpose. In one application, image enhancement technology developed for the Mariner spacecraft project has been used to convert a small customer photograph into a 12- by 12-inch mosaic of computer printer characters as shown in Figure 3-1. In addition to those organizations that are using computers to entertain customers, there are other concerns that are manufacturing sophisticated games containing microprocessors that may be attached to television sets.

Benefits from Public Organizations

Private individuals benefit from computer usage directly and indirectly through *government* environmental planning and the control of pollution and through improved weather forecasting, more effective urban planning, and more efficient law enforcement and fire-fighting techniques. In one Kansas City application, for example, a computer stores the names and addresses of 400 invalids online so that when a fire alarm is received, a dispatcher can use a visual display terminal to see if an invalid lives at the address. If so, fire fighters en route are notified and given the invalid's location in the building so that precious time is not lost searching through smoke-filled rooms.

Individuals also gain from the use of computers in public and private *health care facilities* to provide (1) faster and more thorough approaches to medical history preparation and analysis, (2) faster and more thorough testing to detect and identify disease, (3) more accurate methods of physiological monitoring, (4) better control of lab test results, and (5) better control of pharmacy services.

The use of computer-assisted instruction in *educational institutions* may be more effective with some students than traditional classroom methods. Computers may also take over routine tasks so that teachers are able to devote more attention to individual instruction. Of course, computers in education should be used to provide insight and not merely numbers. Better insight is achieved when more realistic problems can be assigned to those high school and college students who have access to computers. Since they are relieved of having to spend hours on tedious computations, freshmen civil engineering students can now work on the highway cloverleaf intersection problems that were formerly assigned to seniors.

POSSIBLE NEGATIVE IMPLICATIONS OF BUSINESS COMPUTER USAGE

It should be apparent by now that computer systems have taken on increasingly responsible tasks in many organizations and are now performing vital functions in our society. Thus, it is essential that in the data processing steps performed by business computers *vital and relevant data are not lost or stolen, errors are not introduced into the data, and data are not stored, retrieved, modified, or communicated without proper authorization.* In other words, we emphasize that

Figure 3-1

it is essential that the interrelated issues of *data integrity, data security,* and *personal privacy* be given careful consideration in the design and use of business computer systems. Unfortunately, however, some businesses have used questionable data processing practices that have tended to ignore some of these issues and that have thus had adverse effects on the private lives of individuals.

Data Integrity Issues

The data processing steps that must be carried out properly if data integrity is to be maintained are *originating-recording, classifying, sorting,* and *calculating.* Let's now look at some of the possible ways in which the insensitive and/or thoughtless performance of these steps may lead to undesirable social results.

Data originating-recording matters A staggering volume of information of a highly personal nature has been (and is being) gathered and recorded by businesses (e.g., credit bureaus, insurance companies, etc.) as well as by governmental agencies. One fear arising from this development is that an unscrupulous person could be tempted by existing technology and the availability of mounds of computer-accessible data on individuals to misuse the data in ways not originally intended. Facts about age, sex, income, marital status, health, spending habits, lifestyle, etc., could be analyzed in a trial-and-error fashion just to see what might happen. In summary, as Frank T. Cary, chairman of the board of IBM, has observed:

> In the past you had to be famous or infamous to have a dossier. Today there can be a dossier on anyone. Information systems, with a seemingly limitless capacity for storing and sorting information, have made it practical to record and transfer a wealth of data on just about anyone. The result is that we now retain too much information. The ambiguous and unverified are retained along with legitimate data. . . . One way of preventing misuse of personal information is to discourage its collection in the first place.[8]

In addition to the widespread general concern about the seemingly uncontrolled collection of personal information on individuals, some more specific problems associated with the originating-recording step are:

1 *Gathering data without a valid need to know.* When he was Vice President, Gerald Ford wrote that it was the responsibility of all who use computers to "assure that information is not fed into the computer unless it is relevant. Even if it is relevant, there is still a need for discretion. A determination must be made if the social harm done from some data outweighs its usefulness."[9]

2 *Using gathered data in ways not originally intended.* It was brought out

[8]Quoted by Hanna Shields and Mae Churchill in "The Fraudulent War on Crime," *The Nation,* Dec. 21, 1974, p. 655.

[9]Gerald R. Ford, "Individual Privacy and Databanks," *The Internal Auditor,* July–August 1974, p. 14.

during the Watergate scandal that the Nixon administration had tried to obtain printouts from IRS computers in order to possibly use the tax information against its political opponents. Although abuses of this magnitude have not been reported in business, any temptation to use personal data gathered for some legitimate purpose in ways not originally planned or approved should be resisted.

3 *Gathering inaccurate and incomplete data.* More "computer errors" may be attributed to inaccurate and incomplete data input than to either hardware failure or incorrect software. *Unintentional mistakes* in filling out input forms, keying records, coding accounts, etc., are common enough in any record-keeping system. But the consequences may be more serious in a computer-based system because there may be fewer individuals to catch errors and the speed with which inaccurate information is made available to system users may be much faster than the speed with which errors are detected and corrected. The author, for example, had a check to a major oil company "bounce" because that particular check had been encoded with an incorrect account number by a clerk at his bank. Although in time the bank wrote letters of apology and a new check was issued to the oil company, there is still the possibility that in some credit bureau data bank there may be a negative entry in his dossier that has not been corrected. In another example, a keypunching mistake resulted in an electric bill (and subsequent warnings about nonpayment) being sent to the wrong address. You have probably already guessed the outcome: One cold night the electricity was cut off as a result of a computer-prepared disconnect message, and the household was without power until the error could be corrected. Additional problems can result from cases of *mistaken identity*. Good, bad, and indifferent input data prepared by grantors of credit usually find their way into credit bureau data banks. If your name is not keyed correctly, if your address has changed, if you have a common name, or if you are not consistent in the way you use your first name and initials, you may be confused with some other individual (and with your luck it would be a "deadbeat" rather than a millionaire). Thus, as Robert L. Patrick has observed: "Despite all the programming done by all the clearing-houses to date, these mistaken identities do occur, they are troublesome, and they are one of the primary reasons why credit reporting agencies treat individuals unfairly."[10] Unfortunately, in addition to the unintentional mistakes that occur in credit bureau input data, *deliberate* errors have also been introduced into these data banks that are so important to individuals. "In one credit bureau, investigators have admitted to falsifying computer input data because they feel their case loads are too heavy to allow them time to gather all the details called for by the system."[11]

4 *Problems of confusion and bewilderment associated with data gathering.* There have been several verified cases of frustrated individuals actually firing bullets into computers. And the number of such incidents would probably be much larger if individuals, confused and bewildered by computer data input procedures, had followed their initial impulses. A significant cause of this confusion, of course, is that people affected by an information system are often

[10]Robert L. Patrick, "Privacy, People, and Credit Services," *Datamation,* January 1974, p. 49.

[11]Frederic G. Withington, "Five Generations of Computers," *Harvard Business Review,* July–August 1974, p. 107.

ɔt informed of what the system does or how it works. And the result of this confusion may be the belief on the part of individuals that they have been tricked or deceived by the system. Credit application forms, for example, may not indicate that the supplied data are going to be entered into third-party data banks and used in rather secretive ways. Innocent errors in filling out one form may be considered as highly suspicious discrepancies in a consolidated data bank. Another potential source of confusion lies in the pricing of products in supermarkets using scanning equipment to read UPC symbols. As originally designed, the UPC system would save time and money for stores by eliminating the need to mark the price on *each* item; rather, a *single* price would be posted on the shelf containing the item. (The computer, of course, would store the current prices of all products in the store for checkout purposes.) However, consumers are concerned about price confusion that may result in their knowing less and paying more. At this writing legislation has been introduced in Congress and in dozens of state and local governments to require that the price be stamped on every item. Individuals may also find it confusing to operate the computer input devices that are replacing more familiar forms and procedures. Automated voting systems, for example, have confused voters and have produced questionable tallies. Finally, people have been bewildered by the use of the deposit slips with magnetically encoded account numbers that banks supply to customers. It is reported that in at least one case a man distributed his encoded deposit slips about the lobby of a bank, where they were used by bewildered depositors who wrote their names and account numbers on the slips. Since the names and handwritten numbers were ignored by the bank's MICR equipment, however, the deposits were credited to the account number encoded on the slips. The following morning our resourceful swindler closed out his $67,000 account and proceeded on his way.

Classification-sorting matters Classifying and sorting input data according to some commonly defined and consistently organized coding scheme can lead to more *standardized* information systems. And the standardization now taking place in organizations may result in economies and increased efficiency. But standardization may also lead to unwanted *depersonalization.* As an individual comes in contact with an increasing number of computer systems, the use of numerical codes for identification purposes may also be expected to increase. Although individuals may understand that their being treated as numbers can lead to standardized and efficient computer usage by organizations, they may wish that it were not so. Instead of being numerically coded and molded to meet the computer's needs, they might prefer that the computer systems be designed so that they would be treated as persons rather than as numbers. *This is not likely to happen.* Depersonalization is something that individuals are likely to have to submit to more often in the future. Of course, as standardization spreads, individuals may need to remember fewer code numbers—e.g., their Social Security numbers may be substituted for several different codes. In fact, the Social Security number is now being used as the personal identifier in a number of large data systems. The Internal Revenue Service, the U.S. Army, colleges and universities, state driver's license departments, insurance companies, banks, credit bureaus—these and many other organizations may know you as 353-27-4765. The threat of an eventual "universal identifier," of course, is that the separate data records you have established for particular purposes can easily be consolidated through the use of the common number, and the combined data can be merged into a large personal dossier.

In addition to treating individuals as numbers, standardized procedures, once established, tend to become inflexible.[12] Thus, if an individual's needs do not conform to the "norms" of the system, there may be difficulty in getting the system to deal properly with the exception. This tendency to try to force everyone into the same mold may naturally give the individual a feeling of helplessness in trying to cope with a cold, impersonal, and remote organization. A Mr. D'Unger, for example, wrote several organizations asking them to spell his name correctly. He received several replies, all telling him that it was impossible because of the equipment employed by the systems. A computer expert then looked into the matter and found that the line printers involved had the apostrophe available, but the systems did not bother to use it.

System miscalculations Miscalculations are primarily due to human errors in preparing input data, in designing and preparing programs, and in operating the hardware. Thus, when the computer itself is blamed for some foul-up, it is frequently being used as a convenient "scapegoat" to cover up human error, carelessness, or indifference. Or, perhaps, it is being used to add credibility to false claims. For example, the Allen Piano and Organ Company of Phoenix, Arizona, advertised on a radio broadcast that its computer had made a mistake and as a result the firm was overstocked with furniture which it was now offering at bargain prices. When a local computer professional, on behalf of the Association for Computing Machinery, contacted the firm and offered to repair any malfunctioning computer hardware free of charge, he found that the company did not have a computer and did not use any computing service!

Of course, the unfortunate fact remains that people may believe such false advertising because they are aware of computer system miscalculations that actually have occurred. Since we have already seen some examples of business system miscalculations in Chapter 3, we need not belabor the point here. But perhaps it might be appropriate to conclude this section with a few pitiful examples of nonbusiness computer system "atrocities" that have had a negative impact on individuals.

1 A New York City employee failed to get his check for three pay periods after a computer payroll system was installed. Finally, after the employee had initiated legal action against the City, a program bug was discovered, removed, and Mr. Void was at last paid.

[12]This tendency toward inflexibility is *not* an inherent flaw of computer usage. Actually, computerized systems can make individual treatment possible and can cater to individuality for less cost than manual systems. But uniform and rigid treatment costs even less to provide and is thus the approach too often used by systems designers.

2 Individuals have been arrested for "stealing" their own cars. The sequence of events goes something like this: The car is stolen, the theft is reported to a law enforcement data bank, the car is recovered (perhaps in another jurisdiction) and returned to its owner, the recovery is not entered into the data bank, and the owner is then picked up while driving the recovered property. Since the arrest may also be entered into the data bank, but the final disposition may not be, the owner may wind up with an arrest record for "grand theft-auto." If you do not think this can be serious, you should consider the plight of the ex-Marine from Illinois who has been jailed several times for desertion because of incorrect information stored in the FBI's computerized National Crime Information Center.

Data Security Issues

In addition to the need to maintain data integrity, businesses must also maintain the security of the data if adverse effects are to be eliminated. In other words, the data processing steps of *summarizing, communicating, storing, retrieving,* and *reproducing* must also be controlled if negative consequences for organizations and for people are to be avoided. It does not help an organization if its secret product data that fall into the hands of a competitor are accurate. And it does not help much for people to know that the information is *not secured* and protected against theft, fraud, accidental or malicious scrutiny, manipulation, and/or destruction.

Problems with the security of information systems existed before and during the time that computers first began to replace file cabinets. But the vulnerability of computer systems has increased substantially in recent years, and so the security issue has become much more important. Early computers were generally located in self-contained installations, were accessible to a relatively small number of specialists, and were employed to process batches of data in a single stream. As computer systems increased in number and became more sophisticated, however, multiprogramming and multiprocessing concepts became available, many more individuals had access to information systems, the use of shared resources and jointly used data became common, and remote access to direct interaction with a distant computer became a routine operation for even casual users. Such an environment has obviously increased the difficulty of maintaining security. But in addition to the security difficulties caused by easy systems access by many people, the vulnerability of systems has also increased because (1) the information to be found in a relatively complete and up-to-date data bank may be of sufficient value to provide the incentive for outsiders to seek access to it, and (2) an increased number of individuals has now been trained in computer science and in the skills required to program, penetrate, and manipulate computer systems.[13]

Since the security of computer systems was recognized as a significant

[13]For example, a few years ago, as a part of their rehabilitation programs to provide inmates with marketable skills, several penitentiaries began offering courses in computer programming. For one example of such a program, see Derek Reveron, "Computer Enterprise Behind Prison Walls Wins Outside Clients," *The Wall Street Journal,* October 19, 1977, pp. 1ff.

problem only in recent years, the computer hardware in general use today was not designed with security provisions in mind. Thus, the security provisions that do exist are found in the software and in the organizational policies, administrative procedures, and data processing controls that may exist in the particular system.

When it comes to security, existing *software* is indeed soft. Clever individuals have had no difficulty in breaking through the security provisions of those computer operating system programs that they have sought to penetrate. In fact, a favorite activity of some bright students on college campuses has been to successfully infiltrate the college computer system. For example, two students—one a theology major—at little Southern Missionary College in Collegedale, Tennessee, "broke through" the file-security system used in the Hewlett-Packard 2000 series timeshared computers and devised programs that decoded protected files.

Whether the invaders be theology majors who covet their neighbor's files for the challenge presented, or whether they be thieves, criminal manipulators, saboteurs, or spies, they have found that the computer center of an organization may be its nerve center, that it usually contains sensitive information, and that it is often vulnerable to attack. Without adequate computer security provisions, a business, as we have seen, may be exposed to danger through theft, through careless handling of records, through espionage, and/or through sabotage. But a lack of control over data security has also led to *undesirable consequences for individuals in society.*

Individuals as well as organizations *lose* money to the computer thief. In one instance a computer was used to send out phony invoices to individuals. The thief knew that some people pay authentic-looking bills automatically, without questioning their validity. When a phony bill was questioned, however, the thief would merely send back a form letter saying, "Sorry. Our computer made an error." In another instance, bank customers have found that several times a year small errors in favor of the bank have occurred in their statements. Some customers have complained, but since the losses are small, most people probably have not bothered. At this writing, the bank in question does not know what is happening. It is estimated, however, that the mysterious thief may be realizing about $300,000 each year from individuals. A person's finances could also become fouled up as a result of the penetration of an EFTS by an enemy or an unethical competitor. Invalid charges from organizations selected by the penetrator—e.g., insurance companies, utilities, department stores—could be entered against the individual's accounts. At best, the resulting mess would probably involve long delays and great *inconvenience* to straighten out; at worst, it could result in financial ruin.

Finally, our society expects that confidential data on individuals be preserved and used only by authorized persons for approved purposes. But a lack of control over data security can lead to the invasion of an individual's legitimate *right to privacy*. Since this is the subject of the next section, we will not dwell on it here. It should be pointed out here, however, that the majority of computer systems installed in the nation today are *not* secure enough to meet the personal data confidentiality conditions required by existing laws; nor are they secure enough to protect the privacy rights which existing laws give to individuals.

The Privacy Issue

As every man goes through life, he fills in a number of forms for the record, each containing a number of questions. There are thus hundreds of little threads radiating from each man, millions of threads in all. If these threads were suddenly to become visible, people would lose all ability to move.

Alexander Solzhenitsyn

As we have emphasized, both data integrity and security are needed to protect an individual's legitimate *right to privacy*—i.e., to protect the right of an individual to limit the access to personal and often sensitive information to persons authorized to use it in the individual's best interests.

For years, private and public organizations have been building separate files containing "threads" of information about those with whom they come in contact. We know that the use of these files has led to past abuses of individuals' legitimate right to keep to themselves (or to have kept on a confidential basis) those facts, beliefs, thoughts, and feelings that they do not wish to divulge publicly. But many of these older files are incomplete and poorly maintained. Thus, the value of their contents may be such that unauthorized persons have little incentive to snoop. But as we saw in the last chapter, *the development of computer data banks has changed the situation*. Up-to-date personal information files stored on readily accessible media and devices in large consolidated data banks may now be worthy targets for unscrupulous persons. Thoughtful opponents of consolidated data banks are therefore concerned about the threat that they might eventually present to an individual. The concern is perhaps best summarized in a *Saturday Review* cartoon which shows a distressed executive listening to a telephone message. The message is: "This is the Computer Data Bank. Leave $100,000 in small bills in Locker 287 at the Port Authority Bus Terminal or I'll print out your complete dossier and send it to your wife."

There are several possible negative implications of business computer usage that are linked to the subject of individual privacy. The following examples and speculations should be sufficient to demonstrate how a computer system or network could be used for *surveillance activities,* for *list-compiling abuses,* and for the creation of a *climate that can restrict individual freedom.*

EFTS surveillance possibilities Although the EFTS being designed and implemented by banks and other financial institutions are not intended for surveillance, they may be easily adapted to this purpose in the future. If all your nontrivial financial transactions were normally to be processed through EFTS computers, a *daily record* of much of *what* you do and *where* you do it could be prepared. Thus, the situation illustrated in a *New Yorker* magazine cartoon of a husband and wife trying to decide what movie to see and the wife asking her husband, "What would look good on our dossier?" could become less amusing and more possible in the future. Furthermore, if you were to decide to use cash for a transaction that you wished to keep private, the cash acquisition might be quite conspicuous (and suspicious?). In 1971, a group of computer, communication, and surveillance experts was gathered and given the following hypothetical problem: As advisers to the head of the KGB (the Russian Secret Police), they were to design an *unobtrusive* surveillance system to monitor the activities of all citizens and visitors inside the U.S.S.R. As Paul Armer testified in congressional hearings:

> That exercise . . . was only a two-day effort. I am sure we could add some bells and whistles to increase its effectiveness somewhat. But the fact remains that this group decided that if you wanted to build an unobtrusive system for surveillance, you couldn't do much better than an EFTS.[14]

Of course, EFTS proponents in the financial community maintain that adequate laws can be passed to prevent surveillance abuse. But critics are not so sure. They point out that existing check authorization systems, and systems such as BankAmericard, Master Charge, and American Express, can "flag" individual accounts so that if a "flagged" individual tries to cash a check or make a purchase someone (police perhaps?) can be notified of the individual's exact location. And they are fearful that future operators of EFTS networks would be unable to resist the pressures from government organizations to allow the EFTS to be used for surveillance purposes.

List-compiling abuses Mailing lists giving details about individuals are regularly compiled and sold by both private and public organizations. State auto licensing agencies, for example, sell lists to auto equipment suppliers. There is probably not much harm in this if it results only in your receiving literature that tries to persuade you to buy seat covers a few weeks after you have registered your new car. But what about the case of the computer dating service that sold its list of female clients to a publishing organization that printed and sold through local newsstands lists of "Girls Who Want Dates"? Try and tell one of those girls that her privacy hasn't been invaded!

1 At this time, thousands of bank, employment agency, and credit company employees have access to law-enforcement and other data-gathering networks that contain information on millions of people. It is possible that employees without any real "need to know" may while away the time browsing through the records of friends and acquaintances just to see what they can uncover.

[14]See Paul Armer, "Computer Technology and Surveillance," *Computers and People,* September 1975, p. 11.

2 In at least one state, insurance companies have access to records containing the name, Social Security number, and diagnosis of patients hospitalized for psychiatric treatment.

3 Most categories of personal information gathered for legitimate research purposes by reputable social and behavioral scientists do not enjoy any statutory protection. Thus, sensitive personal information gathered by well-intentioned researchers may be obtained through a subpoena issued by a court, legislative committee, or other government body and put into data banks for future use. If the researchers, who may have assured the respondents that their replies would be kept in strictest confidence, refuse to honor the subpoena and turn over the data, they may be cited for contempt and be made to suffer the consequences. Given that alternative, the data are generally surrendered.

The awareness of such facts and such uses of large computerized data banks tends to have a sobering effect on individuals—it tends to restrict their freedom, and it tends to have a chilling effect on their actions even when the data are accurate, even when the use of the data is authorized by law, and even when controls on the use of the data are imposed. You may agree, for example, that credit bureau data banks play important roles in a modern society, but you may also resent being listed in an unsecured system that makes your financial records available to thousands of people; you may be in favor of mental health departments keeping records on psychiatric patients, but you may question the wisdom of possibly recommending to disturbed friends that they seek professional help because their records might then fall into the hands of an insurance industry data network; and you may believe that a market researcher (or a university professor) should conduct a study that requires the gathering and analyzing of personal data, but you may not feel free to personally participate in that study. In short, you may now tend to behave differently (and less freely) than you once would have because of your increasing awareness that what you say and do may become part of some computer record.[15]

REVIEW AND DISCUSSION QUESTIONS

1 How may business computer usage benefit nonbusiness organizations?
2 (*a*) How can computer usage result in greater operating efficiency in a business? (*b*) How may greater efficiency benefit individuals in society?
3 "Computers can play a role in improving the quality of the products we receive from businesses." Discuss this statement.
4 How may computer-using firms provide better service to customers?
5 (*a*) What are the possible benefits of EFTS for individuals? (*b*) What are the possible benefits of UPC?
6 "Some businesses have used questionable data processing practices that have had adverse effects on the private lives and records of individuals." Discuss this statement.

[15]If you think that the privacy issue has been exaggerated here, see Robert E. Smith, "Take the Privacy Initiative," *Computer Decisions*, January 1977, pp. 35–36; and "Striking Back at the Super Snoops," *Time*, July 18, 1977, pp. 15ff.

7 (*a*) How may a lack of control over data originating-recording lead to undesirable social results? (*b*) How may computer system classifying and sorting practices lead to the same results?

8 What are the primary causes of computer system miscalculations?

9 How may a lack of control over data security lead to undesirable consequences for individuals in society?

10 Why has the creation of integrated computer data banks increased the possible threat to an individual's right to privacy?

11 How may a computer system be used (*a*) for surveillance and (*b*) to create a climate that can restrict individual freedom?

12 (*a*) How have top-level administrators benefited from computer usage? (*b*) How have middle-level administrators benefited? (*c*) Lower-level supervisors?

13 Identify employees of organizations who have benefited from computer usage and explain how they have helped.

14 How have individuals in private life been helped by computer systems?

Chapter 3 Readings

INTRODUCTION TO READINGS 8 THROUGH 10

8 Problems faced by managers who are either using or supervising data processing continue to change as advances in hardware and software develop. In this article, Gilbert H. Hoxie and Donald M. Shea describe, from a consultant's point of view, how today's executives are finding it increasingly more difficult to stay on top of and resolve the broad spectrum of issues.

9 The impact of computerized systems on the employees in an organization is explored in this article by the authors, Theodor D. Sterling and Kenneth Laudon. They emphasize that the effects of systems flaws on people are nonresponsiveness, harassment, drops in performance or service, and in some cases even frank exploitation.

10 Business continues to look for ways to hasten the transmission and delivery of important messages while reducing the costs of mail service. It appears certain that computerized mail systems will become common in the future, and in this article Frederick.W. Miller describes some of the recent developments and advancements that have been made in electronic mail.

Reading 8

Ten Hot Buttons Facing Management

Gilbert H. Hoxie
Donald M. Shea

The job of managing information systems and processing is getting bigger and tougher. The top information resource executive is finding that it is becoming more difficult to stay on top of and to resolve the strategically and tactically broadening spectrum of issues.

So we said one year ago when we defined ten of these issues, with an attentive ear to the concerns of management and an eye to the broader strategic perspective of the issues. Since then, we and our colleagues have tracked and sharpened these and other emerging hot buttons in the course of our information systems consulting practice and are now ready to report on some significant shifts and trends among the "top ten" as viewed by the managers we serve. Each issue is described below in our clients' own words with our comments as consultants.

Reprinted from *INFOSYSTEMS,* September 1977, pp. 60–100. Reprinted by permission from Hitchcock Publishing Company, Wheaton, Ill. 60187, Copyright ©, 1977, Hitchcock Publishing Company. The authors are associates with the *Information Services* unit of Booz, Allen & Hamilton, Inc., Los Angeles.

1 DISTRIBUTED PROCESSING: TECHNOLOGY

> We started into distributed processing cautiously, concentrating on our 'gut' accounting applications at the regional level. We selected a mini manufacturer with good accounting software packages, but their terminals were stone-age so we got those from another vendor. Next, the regional manufacturing guys went distributed, but we found that the software packages to support them required yet another hardware vendor. Still, the boxes themselves were cheap enough . . . but then we found that the communications protocols differed and we couldn't share the same data network with the accounting systems . . . well, to make a long story short, I'm now dealing with four different hardware and software vendors, and nobody can tell me how to tie this !$†! show together!—vp-MIS (recently "retired")
>
> A major criterion for selecting our distributed processors was how rich a software library existed. How were we to know that they couldn't all work on the same machine at the same time? For example, if we want to use a data base system, we have to run in pure batch mode. Or if we want to do interactive data entry and editing, we can't be communicating on a network at the same time. And this one takes the cake: any real-time application program has to be written in Assembly language!—regional materials manager

Amid the hoopla about $10 microprocessors and end-users doing their own thing, it's easy for managers to lose sight of practical considerations regarding the current state of distributed technology. Too often, concentration on the apparent relative costs of deployment alternatives has masked a tacit assumption of equal *risks.* And the vendors are not about to highlight these risks in their sales pitches.

In fact, the present state of distributed hardware and software technology poses questions for careful scrutiny in several areas.

- *Compatibility*—Mini vendors and their systems-house "retailers" have tended to develop and market hardware and software bundled together in application-specific "packages" offering limited flexibility for new application development. Moreover, vendors lack complete application libraries, and the bundled systems are often incompatible between vendors. In too many cases, the result has been separate processors, different software disciplines and parallel data networks to support single location application needs.
- *Flexibility and ease of use*—Technical software development is still fairly primitive in many cases, with limited capability operating systems, programming languages or DBMS tools. In addition, elements of existing software libraries often require a "stand-alone" processing mode, forcing serial scheduling of the hardware resource. Finally, many of the distributed processors are at about the second generation mainframe level in terms of ease of operation.
- *Reliability*—Vendor equipment maintenance and software support can be spotty, especially in remote areas.
- *Security*—Physical security of hardware and vital corporate information is obviously compounded in a distributed environment, and in addition, software tools to limit access to information are often inadequate.

These present technical problems are the points of potential vulnerability in the distributed environment of today, and they are expected to linger for at least two years. Distributed technology decisions, therefore, require planning mechanisms that anticipate these risks. Otherwise, management will soon face data integrity and systems integration problems as distributed information moves up the corporate "tree."

2 DISTRIBUTED PROCESSING: HUMAN RESOURCES

> Things looked pretty rosy when we planned our distributed set-up. We were going to have the best of both worlds: tight central control to assure overall standards, but local autonomy to guarantee responsiveness. Well, it isn't working out quite that way. First, most of my best systems guys didn't want to go to the sticks, so I helped our offices hire locally . . . and then I discovered that it didn't matter if the new guys turned out to be turkeys, because district management didn't know DP and couldn't tell the difference anyway. But it sure mattered to my control. I've got the halt leading the blind out there, and somehow I'm supposed to stay on top of it all, keep costs in line and assure that when we need to close the corporate books all the numbers add up and mean the same thing. I'm not trying to duck my responsibilities, but I'm finding it impossible to effectively monitor the activities of fifteen guys at fifteen different locations.—director, corporate MIS

As the first distributed strategies have been implemented, however, the "growing pains" that accompany most significant shifts in business methods have surfaced in the form of management and control problems—problems that many DP managers thought they had mitigated in the 1960s and early 1970s through centralization.

By substituting reasonable access for direct control of hardware, DP managers were able to pool human management and technical talent to gain some measure of control over DP activities in terms of design quality, adherence to standards, operating controls and cost justifications. Of course, this required new formal procedures to assure user involvement in projects. And, as DP functions were consolidated, key executives were assigned at the corporate level where DP benefits and demands gained increased visibility.

Now, as hardware and applications are being redistributed, so must the DP management function and its reporting relationship be redeveloped. Our central control mechanisms no longer apply, however, and most companies haven't yet worked out where to draw the line—in short, we find that many managers and professionals are uncertain of their proper role in a distributed environment.

The results, in some cases, look distressingly familiar to those of us who lived through the conversions and hybrid systems that immediately preceded centralization operations, fully integrated systems and data bases. Poor design and documentation, increasing maintenance demands, spotty data integrity and operations control, and limited career mobility for DP professionals—these are some of the old DP problems that have begun to resurface in many outposts of distributed processing today. The real challenge to successful distributed processing, therefore, is not minimizing hardware/telecommunication costs but matching management and human resources to the desired distribution mix.

3 EDUCATION AND ROLE OF USERS

> Two years ago, we got the marketing vp's attention—boy, did we get it! He carved out a full week of his time and led us through his concept of an integrated order entry, production scheduling and delivery commitment system. We pitched right in and figured out what kind of terminals and DBMS were required and then built it and made it work. Only one problem: The order clerks don't understand it; the production manager can't respond fast enough; and the customers don't really care all that much about committed delivery dates that far ahead. We've spent the past six months stripping the system back pretty much to what we had before! With that level of user involvement, where did we go wrong?—director, MIS

Computer applications used to be built on the premise that users should take a somewhat "stand-offish" stance with respect to DP. That is, DP generally would identify automation opportunities, users would supply "specifications," systems would build the application, and the users would send in input and receive output.

Now, much of that process has changed—trends toward decentralized management are imposing greater independence and accountability on user-managers.

This growth in user involvement has been a mixed blessing—the positive side we have been clamoring for for years: greater user accountability (and, presumably, thoughtfulness) for the integrity and value of their computer systems. We believed (and continue to do so) that user involvement is a guarantee of system success.

However, the opposite has often been the case: user-managers generally lack full awareness of both the potential and the limitations of computer systems—sometimes they try to change too much too fast; more often, they hit the symptoms and overlook the cause. Whichever excess occurs (and generally it's one or the other), we still wind up with unsatisfactory results and only the bleak consolation that systems can blame (or at least share the blame with) the user. Furthermore, this scenario is being acted out more frequently and with deteriorating results, especially for organizations moving into distributed data processing (as pointed out in Hot Button No. 2).

Clearly, user involvement itself is not the culprit; but if it is to work, it must be informed user involvement—the systems profession's equivalent of the legal profession's informed consent and mental competence. This implies a substantially raised level of users' systems competence.

All this, of course, requires training and, in many cases, staffing additions in the users' organizations. But few DP organizations are geared to provide intensive entry-level through systems management training and practice programs for users—after all, how can one quickly *train* users in skills that typically take years of full-time programmer-analyst–project leader training and experience to develop? We believe this conflict between the present need and the time required to develop the skills will require systems and users to continue to work closely together during a lengthy training/doing transition period until user systems management competence is developed.

4 GROWING REGULATION

> I've just reviewed my current cost allocation by project, and discovered that the !?†/$ federal government is my third-biggest user!—VP, I-S

For many companies, the government has in fact become a major user of DP services. Increasing federal, state and local government regulation and reporting requirements imposed on nearly every industry are filtered down to the data processing systems that support company operations. Also, certain federal agencies could influence data base and communications architectures. For example:

- EEO—personnel and payroll systems now need to be able to report employment and compensation by ethnic origin and gender.
- FTC—requiring historical account of product pricing moves (among others).
- ERISA—mandating stricter accounting and new programs for pension plans.
- OSHA—requiring some companies to maintain detailed statistics on work- and product-related injuries.
- FDA—imposing strict (and varying) standards on product traceability.
- FCC—"non-decisions" (such as those related to Telpak, WATS and Computer Communications Inquiry I), generating a period of confusion, uncertainty, reversals, deferrals, and reconsiderations.
- Privacy—posing a specter of liability without clear guidelines.

Short of mounting a rebellion, systems managers can do little but try to anticipate, plan and budget for their "government-user's" requirements or impact on systems architectures. However, DP should account for the resources used to meet government needs; perhaps top management would get excited enough to organize an industry-wide lobby to get the Feds to back off. Ah well, we also believe in Santa Claus.

5 ELECTRONIC OFFICE

> We've started to meet with our administrative systems people on what each of us is doing for (to?) our office-types. So far, all we've accomplished is to identify our conflicts; as things are now going, each group of offices is likely to wind up with a combination of word-processing minis, distributed data processing minis, facsimile

devices, transaction terminals connected to our central computer, timesharing terminals connected to a service bureau and electronic mail terminals connected to each other! And I'd be surprised that any of these boxes will yield meaningful cost reductions or other benefits. This is the office of the future?—director, systems development

Last year we initially surfaced what the coming merger of word processing, data processing and telecommunications implied. At that time, we recommended that data processing systems managers get involved at least to help chart a course of action and define the roles and responsibilities of the players.

A few leading edge (some say "bleeding" edge) users have stepped into the arena, and their experiences have helped sharpen our perception of what the electronic office can be. For example: electronic mail, terminal editing of dictation transcriptions, round-robin memo "teleconferencing,"rapid proposal report generation, direct access to computer reports—the list goes on and on. Most importantly, top management is becoming aware of two key potential benefits:

- Improved quality of analysis, writing, and information.
- Improved productivity of managers and others.

To date, however, the few pioneer systems have to be regarded as experimental—their value is primarily in defining the remaining potential rather than in realized benefits. But that's as it must be—the first thousand telephone users didn't have many people to talk to, either. The point to remember is that the electronic office will happen: the pressures from top management, users, vendors and technology guarantee it. But it won't happen overnight. We can hasten it and ease the birth pains by looking ahead *now* and coordinating our current word processing, data processing, distributed processing and telecommunications developmental activities so they will fit together comfortably in the electronic office.

6 INTERORGANIZATIONAL NETWORKS

I'm working toward integrating our information networks across the company . . . It's an ambitious job, and I figure we're still at least three years away from a single data network. But over the last few months, I'm beginning to hear the top guys talk about the need to hook into industrywide data bases . . . I think getting our own act together is going to be tough enough without having to worry about what everyone else is doing . . . —manager, technical services.

At present, only a few businesses and government bodies, such as the airlines, banks, securities firms, utilities and law enforcement agencies, have felt it necessary to develop interorganizational networks to support the exchange of critical data on an interactive basis. In the face of decreasing material and capital, and increasing regulation and costs, however, some top executives are beginning to discover that their external information exchanges (to and from suppliers, buyers, regulatory bodies and capital markets) often equal or exceed their internal volumes and costs.

Serious discussions of interorganizational networks are presently underway in most major industries and, in some instances, ambitious plans are being drawn up. The first shared networks will involve discrete transactions such as orders or shipments. But more ambitious networks will eventually encompass the whole cycle of demand, production, distribution, billing and payment (through EFT), in addition to providing data base inquiry access for planning purposes.

Our experience with these interorganizational network movements points up imposing technical, economic, regulatory, operational and competitive issues. But most of these will slowly be overcome. And one critical step systems managers can take today is to analyze existing and planned internal systems in terms of segregating communications processing and external input/output steps from internal processing and storage functions. This will reduce (but not eliminate) exposure to application changes as firms move to plug into "foreign" networks.

No matter how carefully DP managers plan for inter-organization information sharing needs, there will undoubtedly be many incompatibilities between organizations with large investments in their own networks.

7 INFORMATION POLICY

> My CEO tells me that he's tired of refereeing the battles between the corporate DP group, the distributed centers, the users, the office services guys, the regulators . . . he says we've got to get someone in charge of all our information resources, and he says we've got to have a comprehensive corporate information policy. I understand his concern—things do seem to be getting out of control—but I'm not sure how to formulate, much less implement, such a policy . . . —director, systems.

This topic can most properly be described as a top management hot button beginning to be felt at the systems management level. Last year, we coined the term "Information Resource Management" (IRM) to describe an organization approach that encompassed all corporate information resources—and that would hopefully grease the skids for a synergistic blending of information communications and processing units and avoid the collision course that many companies are currently embarked upon. A corporate information policy is the cornerstone, the basic building block of the IRM charter.

What should an information policy contain? At minimum, it should cover the following broad subjects:

- *Scope of IRM*—A charter of services and resources to be managed or coordinated by the IRM unit, typically encompassing DP, systems, word processing, telecommunications and internal mail.
- *Responsibility*—A definition of where the responsibility lies for such

IRM tasks as planning, budgeting, development, operation, maintenance, purchasing, training and control.

• *Data collection and retention*—Guidelines on what information is (or is not) to be collected and stored, and what types of data bases are needed, how they are to be maintained, and standards for company-wide data base compatibility and physical data security.

• *Data control and dissemination*—Policies covering the "ownership," definition, creation, update, control, use of, and access to information, including both external (outside of the company) and internal dissemination, and special privacy protection requirements.

Increasingly, top management is coming to view company information as a company resource, and, as with other resources (raw materials, manpower, etc.), they want to assure quality, sufficiency, dependable access and economy—they don't want duplication or surplus. Top management has begun to realize that these objectives for corporate information may be in jeopardy largely because of the issues and problems we discussed in the first six topics. They want information controlled like other corporate resources, and the first necessary step in that direction is a clear and comprehensive statement of information policy.

8 SYSTEMS PRODUCTIVITY

> I think our computer operations department has become pretty efficient and reliable. But systems—that's another story! Less than 10 percent of our projects get done on time, and then only because we rob staff from less critical jobs to bail us out of a crisis. My systems manager tells me he has tried all the new tricks—on-line programming, structured programming, data base—but nothing seems to help. And I'm hearing rumors that some of the user departments are planning to staff and manage their own projects.—vp, I-S

> Who's running this show: The computer? Or me?—CEO

Computers are involved in virtually all business activities being planned or implemented today in nearly all industries. And, let's face it, the time to build computer support systems is lengthening at the same time that project estimating is subject to greater uncertainties. Conventional wisdom cites five causes:

- Shifting user requirements.
- Growing application complexity.
- Conflicts with existing applications and data bases.
- Declining analyst/programmer professionalism.
- Missing performance measurement criteria.

These are all valid points (in fact, performance measurement was one of last year's "hot buttons"), but we think they mask the most potent reason: most systems managers don't really believe their area can be managed very much better. This smugness and complacency about planning and managing carries over into the implementation of the productivity improvement tools systems managers have attempted to install over the years. The analysts and programmers sense the prevailing attitude and, as a result, nobody in the department really tries to make new tools or procedures work; and so, of course, they don't.

We suspect that many users have become aware of this situation, and that awareness may be why they are beginning to take on responsibility for their own systems—they believe that they aren't tied to old, ineffective methods.

There's no question about it; systems productivity can be improved. But, the first step isn't to buy a lot of tools; instead we need to develop our system managers' skills and confidence—that "can-do" attitude—and then embark on a well-structured productivity improvement program. Perhaps most importantly, though, we need to assure that the program isn't torpedoed by analysts and programmers who may seek to ride out just another management wave so they can slip back into their old comfortable (and ineffectual) ways of working.

9 IBM COPIES

> I like the cost-performance advantage offered by Amdahl, Control Data and Itel in their IBM 370 copies, but our technical guys tell me that IBM could obsolete us overnight and we'd be stuck like a dinosaur in a tar pit, sinking further and further behind IBM's latest hardware and software . . . —director, information systems

The first returns are in and it seems clear that IBM hasn't knocked off the 370 "knock-off" companies, nor have they obsoleted their hardware and software, nor have they wiped out the cost-performance differential—in short, all the easy reasons for not evaluating the 370 copies are reduced in significance, leaving medium and scale IBM mainframe users (or potential users) with real opportunities requiring real analysis.

Last year, speculation was rife about IBM's next generation, providing a convenient excuse to postpone major mainframe decisions. Now the issues can be drawn more clearly, and the merits of IBM versus IBM-compatibility can be evaluated rationally. As we see it, the four big issues for most IBM customers are:

What level of service can the IBM "copycat" provide?

- Equipment reliability.
- Scheduled preventive maintenance.
- Machine-down recover or backup.
- Spare parts availability.

How bad is it *really* to be several months behind IBM's software releases?

- Delay in latest features, versus
- Debugging new releases.

Do any of the purchase/lease/rental options with the IBM copy vendor satisfy my financial constraints?

What is the true risk of being locked into a "state of the art" that might soon be obsoleted?

- By IBM
- Or by another, cheaper 370 "knock-off"

Of course, there are additional but more conjectural risks—IBM might do "something" to its system control programs or hardware (perhaps "Selectable Units" are the opening wedge) that would freeze users on current releases or peripherals (but wouldn't it also impact those *real* 370 users?); or one of the compatible manufacturers might drop out of the business (but the machine doesn't stop working overnight—talk to some existing RCA Spectra users). Present risks notwithstanding, the concept of IBM copies looks as though it is here to stay and is a hardware alternative that demands evaluation by hardware configuration planners.

10 CAREER PATHS

> I've got a staff rotation policy to make sure that nobody gets stuck on maintenance forever, but maintenance is still increasing as a percent of my total work. And I've been losing one or two of my top systems people every year because I can't offer enough new development work, let alone state of the art. These guys and gals are trained professionals, and they represent a real loss to the company not to mention my affirmative action program. Meanwhile, I've got pressures from the users to transfer some systems talent to them, and I've tried to make marriages between my people and the people in marketing, accounting, manufacturing . . . but my salary scale in systems is way out of whack with theirs—I simply have to pay more money for comparable first and second line managers—and I'm being left with a group of high priced, underutilized people who can see the handwriting on the wall . . .
> —manager, MIS

In attempting to attract and keep top professionals, DP managers are getting squeezed between two slowly accelerating counterpressures. Managements have been talking for some time about adjustments in pay scales and titles to permit more fluid movement between systems and other staff and line positions, but too little has been implemented in this admittedly difficult area.

Compounding the problem is the inevitable growth of maintenance as a percent of systems activity, as the installed base of systems grows. Our client experience indicates that over the past five years, the ratio of overall maintenance to development work has flip-flopped from about 40 percent to 60 percent to about 60 percent to 40 percent.

Caught in a box where they can't market their talent within the company or provide sufficient motivation within their shop, DP managers are looking for answers to stem the loss of senior professionals, especially minorities and women, trained in systems disciplines. One answer that we touched upon last year seems to be proving helpful to a few forward looking companies, and that is the information resource management (IRM) concept. Although by no means a panacea, companies that have begun to move toward an organizational union of data processing, telecommunications and office systems are reaping the by-product benefits of more flexible positioning and mobile advancement of qualified systems-trained professionals.

IN CONCLUSION

One word of caution—our contacts with information resource managers over the past year have left us with an uneasy feeling—distributed processing and other "NOW" issues appear to be absorbing the talent that should be taking a balanced approach to planning all three to five year application and resource needs. Failure to look ahead each year merely strews time-bombs about the landscape.

For example, we believe that many of the hot button issues which now concern top information systems managers would not have heated up had these managers engaged in strategic planning one or two years ago. The lack of credible long-range strategy and planning in most systems organizations raises serious questions about whether or not these companies can successfully negotiate the technological, management and business changes ahead. Managers must make time to generate and execute such plans, or the accelerating pace of business and technological changes ahead will overwhelm their ability to react.

READING 8 DISCUSSION QUESTIONS

1 How do these *ten hot buttons* affect managers at all levels of the organizations?
2 Which of the buttons do you consider to be the most serious and challenging ones to the organization as a whole? Are there others that were not included?

Reading 9

Humanizing Information Systems

Theodor D. Sterling
Kenneth Laudon

Large scale computing systems have revolutionized the management of most, if not all, means by which goods and services are produced, or information is accumulated. Such systems interact with organizational, historical, and political pressures and goals to shape the internal structure of industrial, governmental, and other organizations. And not least, they also shape the way in which organizations interact with individuals.

By any criteria of management performance, computerization of a system makes possible almost unlimited control over its details, making the computer then the ideal management tool. But the cost of the control is high. Therefore, the questions have been asked whether large computerized systems can be developed by anyone except governments and large corporations, and whether or not such organizations will use such systems mainly for antihuman purposes.

During active proliferation of new and revised management procedures, designers of information systems cannot help but also be organizational designers as well. They cannot avoid changing organizations. But which way will the changes go? Norbert Wiener pointed out many years ago that intelligent understanding of a machine mode of control may be delayed until long after this control has been exercised (*The Human Use of Human Beings,* Doubleday, New York, 1954). Thus there exists widespread concern about the ultimate effect of management information systems on the quality of life of their end users (and also of many of their participants).

In this article, we have explored two areas to examine critically the humane qualities of Management Information Systems (MIS's): (1) criteria that may humanize information systems, and (2) development of an interface mechanism between end user and system—called "the Computer Ombudsman." The two areas are not unrelated.

Design and implementation criteria for MIS's to make them less harsh and more amenable to human tastes have been discussed in a number of meetings sponsored by the Canadian Information Processing Society (CIPS) and ACM. A proposed set of guidelines for humanizing information systems has resulted (see accompanying table).

The criteria as summarized in the guidelines almost speak for themselves. Possible exceptions are D.1. and E.3. There is a complex opposition of

Reprinted with permission of *Datamation* ® magazine, © copyright by Technical Publishing Company, a division of Dun-Donnelly Publishing Corporation, a Dun & Bradstreet company, 1978—all rights reserved.
Professor Sterling is chairman of the Computing Science Department at Simon Fraser University, Burnaby, Canada. Dr. Laudon is an associate professor of sociology at John Jay College of Criminal Justice (City University of New York).

procedures ensuring privacy to those supporting humanization. We can see this immediately if we ask what a system would need to know about an end user in order to assure that it can meet criteria A.5., B.1., B.2., C.1., C.3., and E.2. (and hence criterion D.1.). E.3. may be the most controversial and certainly the most difficult criterion to implement. More than any of the other criteria, it requires clear definitions of the sources of gain for any method of benefit or loss calculation.

Here is a deceptively simple example. If technology replaces the telephone operator, are ultimate cost savings to be limited to the quasi-public telephone utility, or are costs to the larger society to be included? What are the "costs" to society of losing a large number of relatively interesting (or humane type) jobs requiring relatively little technical skill and primarily filled by women, either prior to marriage or after raising a family?

In developing humanizing criteria, we had to rely largely upon anecdotal evidence of the effects of system malfunctions or of design features perceived as dehumanizing. Substantive data of the effect of systems on participants, end users, complainants, citizens, or just bystanders, now come from studies of actual incidents, or from information gathering schemes especially designed to probe relevant systems features.

THE COMPUTER OMBUDSMAN

One such major study was undertaken in 1973, using as a vehicle the Vancouver Ombudsman Committee. Information obtained through this Ombudsman Committee indeed justifies a concern that large scale management information systems fall short of the criteria by which their human qualities may be judged. DP experts may differ in how much they are concerned with humane qualities of systems, especially if to implement humanizing features would require increases in systems overhead and decreases in its efficiency. Yet it may be exceedingly beneficial to discuss openly features that determine the quality of life of various classes of people who are affected by systems of management.

The Computer Ombudsman Service (COS) was established in 1973, after a year's study, by a special interest group of CIPS, with the cooperation of the Consumer Association of Canada (CAC) and the Law Reform Commission. The service became effective officially in 1974, with its headquarters at Simon Fraser University.

The COS is staffed by members of Vancouver CIPS (who occupy various levels of management in industry or government), with a sprinkling of academics. Cases accepted for study by COS are investigated by one of the ombudsmen. A number of investigations have also been initiated by the committee. These investigations were generated by commonly recurring observations. The CAC serves as a screening mechanism for most cases that might be viewed as consumer complaints. But cases have also been referred by private and public organizations as a result of public knowledge about the Ombudsman Service. (And there has been relatively little publicity.)

Cases that are accepted by the Ombudsman Service are characterized by three criteria:

1 They are not trivial.
2 Solutions for them have not been built into a system.
3 Possible solutions may be accomplished through expert knowledge of systems operations.

The primary purposes of the Ombudsman Service are to investigate features related to humanizing/dehumanizing dimensions of existing computer based information systems, and the ability of those systems to respond to humanizing efforts. Thus the Ombudsman is primarily a fact finding venture, and not a complaint department. However, it is true that most of the cases accepted for investigation by the Ombudsman have been resolved in the process of fact finding procedures.

It should be pointed out that only a relatively small number of cases were processed by the Ombudsman Service. The load has averaged approximately two cases a month. That number underestimates the actual number of problems that may exist or may be perceived to exist.

One limitation in the number of cases that come to the attention of the Vancouver Ombudsman Committee is imposed by the prescreening mechanism that has been established through CAC. Only those cases are passed on that clearly deal with a computer related problem not yet completely investigated. Problems for which solution models have been established subsequently may be resolved by CAC staff.

More important, however, may be the relatively small number of substantive problems that are recognized in the first place as computer or system caused. After all, modern systems have been designed with some care, and the effort has especially been made to eliminate simple sources of errors taught by experience with "manual" predecessors of computerized procedures. The results may have been an overall reduction in numbers of errors or problems.

On the other hand, those errors that occur now may be of infinitely greater complexity. They may have as their source combinations of rare events, each of which may occur with a very low probability; however, they do appear when the total number of transactions in a system become very large. Those same rare events or combinations of them will then occur with almost complete certainty. Two errors that are independent of each other, each of which may occur no more often than one time in 1,000, will combine no more often than one time in 1,000,000. But for a system that averages 100,000 transactions a month, such rare errors would occur with almost complete certainty at least once a year.

As a consequence, only relatively complex cases come to the attention of the Ombudsman. But, at the same time, the implications of cases and studies we discuss here reflect strikingly upon criteria for humanizing information systems.

In studying system flaws and their effects on end users and participants, we found it useful to classify our cases according to criteria of nonresponsiveness, harassment, decrease of performance or service, and frank exploitation.

Criteria for Humanizing Management Information Systems

A. Procedures for dealing with users

1. The language of a system should be easy to understand.
2 Transactions with a system should be courteous.
3 A system should be quick to react.
4 A system should respond quickly to users (if it is unable to resolve its intended procedure).
5 A system should relieve the users of unnecessary chores.
6 A system should provide for human information interface.
7 A system should include provisions for corrections.
8 Management should be held responsible for mismanagement.

B. Procedures for dealing with exceptions

1 A system should recognize as much as possible that it deals with different classes of individuals.
2 A system should recognize that special conditions might occur that could require special actions by it.
3 A system must allow for alternatives in input and processing.
4 A system should give individuals choices on how to deal with it.
5 A procedure must exist to override the system.

C. Action of the system with respect to information

1 There should be provisions to permit individuals to inspect information about themselves.
2 There should be provisions to correct errors.
3 There should be provisions for evaluating information stored in the system.
4 There should be provisions for individuals to add information that they consider important.
5 It should be made known in general what information is stored in systems and what use will be made of that information.

D. The problem of privacy

1 In the design of a system, all procedures should be evaluated with respect to both privacy and humanization requirements.
2 The decision to merge information from different files and systems should never occur automatically. Whenever information from one file is made available to another file, it should be examined first for its implications for privacy and humanization.

E. Guidelines for system design having a bearing on ethics

1 A system should not trick or deceive.
2 A system should assist participants and users and not manipulate them.
3 A system should not eliminate opportunities for employment without a careful examination of consequences to other available jobs.
4 System designers should not participate in the creation or maintenance of secret data banks.
5 A system should treat with consideration all individuals who come in contact with it.

NONRESPONSIVENESS

A complaint heard very often is that the "computer" does not reply to inquiries, especially concerning possible errors. Our observation would bear this out. In many instances of errors, system replies to end users were slow, and in most cases nonexistent. Yet in no instance was the "system" unaware of the existence of a problem or of an error! There was always some level of management that knew of it, usually within the data processing segment.

Case A received tax notices addressed to the previous tenant of a house (who also owned the property). The new tenant returned these notices with the information that the previous tenant no longer resided at that address. When tax notices kept coming, the new tenant sent a number of letters to the tax bureau, again with the information that the previous tenant had moved. However, tax notices did not stop coming, nor was there ever any reply received from the tax office.

On investigation, the Ombudsman found that the existing rules stipulated that in cases of an unknown residence of a taxpayer, the post office was to attempt to forward mail to a new address if such an address existed. The obliging new tenant had returned the notices to the tax office rather than to the post office so that the letter could proceed with further search. No one in the provincial or municipal dp center in fact knew about that rule or had any authority to reply to messages, nor was there anyone there with authority to stop sending notices to the last known address of the taxpayer.

Case B was a customer of a large department chain who through mysterious circumstances found himself in possession of two separate accounts. For almost a year, he thought this was just a matter of confusion of bills or of his own records. When he discovered he was billed under two separate accounts he so notified the company, but received no replies.

On investigating, the Ombudsman found that the source of these two accounts was of considerable concern to dp management. However, because of the time that had passed, and because of the load of day-to-day dp work, it was simply not possible to track the source of the error. Occasionally half-hearted attempts were made to investigate how the customer's two accounts had come about. In the meantime, no action was taken either to reply to him or to eliminate the wrong account.

Both examples are clearly violations of criteria A. 3,4,7, and C. 2,3 (see table). In the two cases, and in fact in all cases of error investigated by the Ombudsman, some level of the system was aware that an error had occurred. No action was taken because no provision for action existed at the level of the dp management structure involved with a particular type of error. Inquiries remained unanswered, either because there was no horizontal communication between the different vertical management structures that handle different parts of the organization's responsibilities (as in Case A), or because dp management was unwilling to take action until the source of the error had been discovered (as in Case B).

HARASSMENT

Case B is also an example par excellence of harassment due to faulty intrasystem communications. Although the customer received no answer to inquiries concerning two account numbers, he was notified first by letter and then in person that his account was delinquent, and was subsequently threatened with action by a collection agency and damage to his credit standing.

Another instance of harassment is *Case C*. This individual had his wallet stolen in 1971. The credit cards that were in the wallet had been used by the thief to establish an alias. The thief was apprehended for armed robbery in 1972, and the wallet, including the credit cards but not the money, was returned. In 1976, the former victim was stopped for a minor traffic violation and was required to go through lengthy clearing procedures. He found out that his name was on a list of possible aliases used by a dangerous known criminal.

This example from the Vancouver Ombudsman files luckily had no more serious consequences than momentary embarrassment. But under similar circumstances, a man was killed by a Florida state trooper who mistook his car for a stolen vehicle after checking with the state's crime computer. The victim's 1975 car license plate bore the same number issued for the stolen vehicle in 1971, but which was still in the state's active stolen vehicle data base.

These examples are related to inadequate horizontal communications between vertical management structures. Upon inquiry the Royal Canadian Mounted Police agreed that there was really no need to keep this particular alias alive as the criminal in question had been apprehended and all identifications had been returned to the former victim. The RCMP, the Florida State Police, and the store's billing systems clearly failed on criteria A.7, B.1,2, C.2,3, and D.1,2, (although for different reasons).

The concept of harassment is of course relative. What harasses one individual may not harass another. Under a very broad definition, harassment may be any action taken by a system that could lead to damage or loss. (The action need not *actually* lead to damage or loss; the fact that such possibility exists may be felt harassing by many individuals.)

One such class of harassment (albeit relatively trivial), and that also demonstrates the problems that arise from poorly designed systems, is the lag between billing and mailing dates of bills for many major credit organizations.

After receiving a number of inquiries (not necessarily cases handled by the Ombudsman) about bills having been received too late to permit payment of obligations to avoid interest, members of Vancouver CIPS were asked to keep envelopes in which they received computerized bills and mark on them the

Time Lags in Days between Billing Date, Postmark Date, and Date Bills Are Received

Time intervals	Dept. stores	Oil companies	Credit services
Average time lags between billing date and postmark date	7.12	3.65	5.4
Average time lags between postmark date to date received	10.53	8.35	8.85
Range of billing date to postmark date	4–20	1–19	1–10
Range of postmark date to date received	6–24	4–20	3–13

billing date as well as the date on which the bills had been received. (The mailing date was given by the metered postage mark.) Replies were analyzed by type of credit industry (only major credit companies were included—the three major department chains in Canada, the banks that handled *Bank Americard* accounts [named *Chargex* in Canada], and major oil companies).

The delays between billing date and mailing date are given in the accompanying table. While the average periods of time lag between billing date and date at which a customer may receive a bill for different categories of accounts may range from 8 to 10 days, individual instances of delay actually range from 3 to 24 days. As most credit accounts are explicit in counting time from billing date during which customers can satisfy their obligations (the usual time period to settle an account is 25 days from billing date), the delay in mailing bills may result in unnecessary problems to organizations advancing the credit, and to the customer who may be confused about his obligations. Also, in general, a third of the customers received bills so late that it was not physically possible for them to settle their accounts within the specified grace period.

(Our time estimates may not hold exactly for the U.S., but the differences probably are small. The U.S. postal system seems to be more efficient than the Canadian so that the delay caused by mail handling would be less for U.S. than Canadian customers. Billing procedures for *Chargex* and the Canadian offices of the major oil companies seem to have been imported from U.S. sources. Nevertheless, it might be important to repeat the same survey for comparable U.S. companies.)

While the billing lag study addresses itself to perhaps trivial matters from the system design perspective, it exemplifies rather well problems created both by centralizing large scale operations and by increasing the number of transactions according to the capabilities of computers. Clearly it is not too difficult for a good system to spew out so many bills a day that the mechanical operations to stuff them into envelopes and mail all of them takes three weeks.

We have classified the billing example under "harassment" because potentially an end user of the system stands in danger of taking a financial loss. On inquiry by the Ombudsman with all companies involved in the study, it was claimed that any interest accrued when a customer complained for reasons of delayed mailing of bills would be wiped from the records. However, this still required customers to be aware that they were being billed late, and to write to the billing agency. Relatively few would do so. A recent study found that while 20% of clients of a particular organization had a legitimate complaint, fewer than 1% actually complained. The most important obstacles to complaints were ignorance of whom to address the complaint to, followed by distrust of the effectiveness of complaining. But even to correct for the registered complaints may have led to unnecessary expenses and loss to the billing agency itself.

While inquiring into this billing lag, the Ombudsman encountered a great deal of waffling. Not a single one of the companies involved would admit that there was a time lag between printing and mailing of bills, although none of them denied it. None of the companies indicated that they would deal with that

"I wrote to the FBI for my personal file. They say they never heard of me and I should stop bothering them."

© DATAMATION ●

problem or try to correct it. Their unwillingness to face up to systems flaws, however, may have additional undesirable consequences.

The failure of the industry to deal with its own problems may result in corrective legislation. In the present instance, the Ministry of Consumer Affairs of British Columbia has brought in a bill stipulating that a customer must have at least 15 days from receipt of his bill to satisfy his account. While this bill is bad on a number of counts and is opposed by COS, it may still be required unless industry takes the initiative in investigating and correcting such system design flaws itself.

DECREASE IN PERFORMANCE OF SERVICE

We use as a pragmatic criterion that a decrease in performance or service has occurred when the system, after a reorganization, gives less service to an end user than it had previously. From this point of view, the failure of the post office to deliver mail twice a day or six days a week is such a decrease service of the postal system. We also count as decrease in performance of service an increase in cost without accompanying improvement in service or an increase in the amount of work or effort required by participants or end users, not resulting in improvement in system's performance.

An example of such decrease in performance came from a study of the Vancouver Resource Board. There was an attempt by the Province of British Columbia to combine all its health and welfare services. After the system was installed (and continued on without improvement for almost a year), approximately one third of the communications with the system were erroneous. Approximately one third of the checks mailed to the clients of the system had to be manually recomputed and redone. The combined welfare organizations with computerized management systems apparently resulted in decreased performance of service to clients (and to lower echelons of management). Other but similar systems failures have been reported by the *New York Times* (March 17, 1975) which estimates that on a national level twice as many eligible welfare clients are denied assistance than the number of ineligibles who receive it.

But instances of decrease in performance of service are not limited to welfare systems. One instance involved the switch from a bimonthly to monthly mailing of alimony checks from an escrow account when the responsibility to write and mail these checks is transferred from the courts to a computerized banking service (*Denver Post,* April 13, 1976). What are we to call the recent credit organizations that now only send a summary of purchases rather than copies of the original purchases (*Chargex,* 1976)? While the inconvenience to the credit holder of the service may be trivial, the fact remains that he gets less service without an accompanying decrease in cost.

Similarly the large error rate of various systems may be viewed as a decrease in performance or service. For instance, in New York State's criminal justice system, over 20% of the summary criminal rap sheets contain substantial errors of facts (not all of which are computer related). Yet these reports are used by police, prosecutors, and judges to determine the fate of arrested persons. Despite ten years of previous experience, this particular agency has not systematically redressed the origins of these errors or investigated the consequences for arrested persons (*New York Times,* Oct. 24, 1975). In this sense, too, the failure of bills to be mailed in sufficient time to give customers notice when payment is due is a decrease in the system's performance as well as a system flaw.

EXPLOITATION

There is a design strategy that accounts for a large number of dehumanizing practices in management systems. In order to increase the efficiency of an enterprise, end-users and participants in the systems are treated as unpaid components whose time, effort, and intelligence do not appear in the cost accounting. It is precisely this kind of exploitation of human intelligence and labor that computerized systems ought to do away with. But do they?

In the example of the Vancouver Resource Board, employees of lower management strata were required no fewer than three times to prepare the same input, listing information from each client record. Apparently no attempt was made to save previous files, or to develop an editing system or an adequate data base. And such practice of creating unnecessary work has not been limited to the Vancouver Resource Board. Very often when errors occur, lower level staff are required to redo tasks that easily could have been saved them. These examples not only violate criterion A.5, but even more so, criterion E.5, which requires that employees of a system be treated with the same consideration shown to others.

One related practice of many universities is a procedure by which students who add or drop courses after registration still perform many of the clerical functions for manual record keeping of enrollment. Students are usually required to fill out forms in multiples which they carry around to departments, faculty, and registrar offices. While such procedures become almost completely redundant once the registration of a student is computerized, they are continued in many schools. Although the work done by each student may be small, the total amount of labor performed by the approximately one fourth of all students who add or drop courses during each semester is enormous, and yet the amount of additional work by the computerized registration system may be next to nothing.

Another sort of exploitation is the selling of names. The COS bought a list of names and addresses of senior Canadian citizens for the Vancouver area (freely on sale) and asked each person on the list if he knew that his name was being used in this manner. Almost without exception, all individuals queried bitterly resented finding their names on a list offered for sale. (The purchaser of such a list should also have some resentment because a high percentage of the names failed to be accurate.)

SUMMARY CONCLUSIONS

As a result of experience with the Canadian Computer Ombudsman Service and our examination of the criteria needed to humanize information systems, we note the following trends which dp managers should be alerted to. There exist:

1 A diminution of opportunities for individuals to negotiate with a bureaucracy, and thereby a diminishing of the humane qualities of the systems with which they deal.

2 A decline in the ability of the system to fulfill an intended service function.

3 Little horizontal communication between components of a management system where control functions primarily exert themselves vertically. As a consequence (*a*) communications between end users and participants and other points of the system become difficult, and (*b*) individuals may be harassed by one part of the system that accepts incorrect output from another part for further actions.

4 Obscuring where the authority for decisions actually exists, to protect the *privacy of incompetence.*

5 Exploitation of the labor of lower level managers, workers, and end users in ways that do not show up in the total accounting of system expenditure, in order to patch system flaws, or to bridge difficult horizontal communications between system components.

Yes, it is true that computerized management technology is relatively new, that the development of that technology is expensive, that errors are unavoidable, that large numbers of transactions made possible through computerization will multiply the probability that makes for difficulties, and that time is needed eventually to cure all ills, including those inflicted by hasty systems design. However, it is also true that time by itself will not cure errors, and that the dp community may be faced with the choice of investigating and correcting its own ills—or, failing to do so, have these ills become a running sore of an otherwise vigorous and innovating profession.

READING 9 DISCUSSION QUESTIONS

1 "The effects of system flaws on people are nonresponsiveness, harassment, drop in performance or service, and even frank exploitation." Discuss this statement
2 How realistic is the concept of implementing or using an ombudsman service in an organization? What reactions do you anticipate from managers at various levels and in different departments?

Reading 10

Electronic Mail Comes of Age

Frederick W. Miller

Transmitting written messages by electricity is as old as the telegraph; that pioneer system helped railroads open the western US to an influx of population more than 125 years ago. Invented in 1837, the telegraph was first used to send a message on May 24, 1844, from Baltimore to Washington, DC, a distance of 40 miles.

Now, the greatly acclaimed method for telegraphing messages at higher speeds and lower costs is called "electronic mail," and it's based on the same principle as the telegraph—sending a message a long distance by electricity.

Reprinted from *Infosystems,* November 1977, pp. 56–64. Reprinted by permission from Hitchcock Publishing Company, Wheaton, Ill. 60187. Copyright © 1977, Hitchcock Publishing Company. Mr. Miller is a senior editor for *Infosystems.*

In today's business/industrial community, electronic mail is being used by a few firms, and is under study by many others. The topic requires some definition, but many would agree there is a single definition and several implementations of it.

Electronic mail is a system in which "information must be transmitted in electronic form . . . what differs are the types of messages sent by each system, the scope of the delivery system and the justification used to develop the system," according to International Resource Development Inc., a market research and product planning firm in New Canaan, CT.

This broad definition includes such services as Telegram, Mailgram, and TWX/Telex by Western Union; message switching services offered by various nationwide timesharing services; intra-office electronic networks such as that at Citibank in New York City; or a computer-based network at the Wharton School of Business at the Univ. of Pennsylvania in Philadelphia; and the highly touted and renowned ARPANET developed by Bolt, Beranek & Newman, Cambridge, MA.

Two overriding principles—speed and cost—are key to any electronic mail system. Many business people are seeking ways to hasten the transmission and delivery of important messages within their companies and also to reduce the cost of mail sent through the US postal service. Many firms already are using extensive telecommunications networks to transmit data in both centralized and decentralized DP networks. Others have extensive teletype-style networks for hardcopy communications.

AN ECONOMIC IDEAL

With the advent of high-speed (under one minute per page) facsimile transceivers and communicating word processing typewriters, the prognosticators are looking for a growth in the use of electronic mail employing these two types of equipment. An economical idea—possibly 10 or more years in the future—is a desk-to-desk electronic mail system that operates much like today's nationwide telephone network.

Electronic mail got a big push in 1971–72 when Western Union (WU) introduced Mailgram as a joint venture with the Post Office for the overnight delivery of business messages. WU's Robert McCarthy, assistant vice president, sales and marketing, Mailgram, said the name "electronic mail" is a registered trade mark of Western Union but is generally ignored by others and therefore widely used to describe all forms of electronic message and mail transmission. "We didn't know what we had (in Mailgram) until somebody coined the word 'electronic mail,'" McCarthy said.

Mailgram service has grown at an average rate of 25 percent a year and now businesses send between 22 million and 25 million Mailgram messages a year, McCarthy noted. He sees continued growth of the service and feels Mailgram service "will be put into place as one of the priority options" for sending important communications not only between business enterprises, but between businesses and consumers (homeowners). He said a Mailgram has higher response and reading time ratios than other forms of letters, notices and other traditional forms of communications.

Western Union, which may in the long-range future offer electronic mailbox and least-cost message routing services, also offers users "Stored Mailgram Services" for frequently used text material and mailing lists at a minimum monthly cost of $340 including special CRT-type terminal; and "Infocom," a shared communications network that has many of the advantages of a private network and costs $1,200 a month, which provides the user with 26 hours of usage.

McCarthy said Western Union has a "number of services (for electronic mail) available at customer option," including those mentioned.

Facsimile (fax), which is the electronic transmission of text and/or graphic materials, is one form of electronic mail, but observers point out that as much is spent on facsimile equipment to send messages as is spent on the cost of sending the message over standard telephone lines on a dial-up basis. This would tend to defeat the cost-reduced advantages of other systems. The use of facsimile, often called the forerunner of tomorrow's electronic mail systems, was discussed in detail in the September 1977 issue of INFOSYSTEMS magazine.

A LIMITING FACTOR

Although fax is widely used and new equipment that operates at higher speeds is now available, observers feel growth in its use is still limited by the incompatibility of different firms' machines, and the unknown and unmonitored cost of sending fax via telephone lines.

At least two companies, Graphic Scanning Inc. and Datapost, are offering fax communications services. Graphic Scanning Inc., Englewood, NJ, is an FCC-regulated store and forward fax delivery service that went into operation in 1975. The firm established its own network to handle the traffic.

Input to the firm's Graphnet is via dial-up TWX or Telex terminals, and output is facsimile, which is used to telephone the message to the recipient. A copy also is sent by mail. Graphic Scanning has about 110 delivery points across the US to speed these messages, which include tracers on shipments, job offers, product recalls and others.

Graphnet and its Faxgram competes with Western Union's Telegram, costs subscribers one dollar per month and then $2.23 per Faxgram.

The other firm, Datapost, an electronic facsimile service provided by TDX Telecommunications Inc., Houston, TX, receives messages and mail via telecopier/facsimile at its Chicago distribution center, sorts and packages the messages by zip code, then hands them to the US Postal Service for next-day delivery to 25 major cities as priority mail. Datapost is an unregulated mail/communications service. The firm said transmission to the distribution center by 3 pm one day "virtually assures next business day delivery in most large cities."

Datapost has a minimum monthly fee of $210, which equals 200 messages at

$1.05 each. Datapost officials, at introduction of their service in mid-June this year, acknowledged that Western Union's Mailgram is its prime competitor for this next-day, high-impact mail service.

HERE COMES THE MINI

The heart of many future electronic mail systems and networks is likely to be a minicomputer, used either as a central store-and-forward device that transforms it into an "electronic mailbox," or as the processing unit of a manager's workstation that includes electronic transmission as one of its functions.

Computer-based mail systems got their start several years ago when timesharing service firms used a technique to store messages centrally that could be retrieved from any terminal that could call into the timesharing service.

Allen J. Rose, vice president–technical director and co-founder, Scientific Time Sharing Corp., Bethesda, MD, said his co-founders used the electronic mail technique to maintain daily contact with one another as they traveled around the country and built the business.

Rose admits the system was a contributor in the firm's success in the early 1970s. Electronic mail is now offered as a regular "product" by STSC under the name "Mailbox." Minimum cost is $100 a month.

Other timesharing services, including Bowne Time Sharing, New York, a text processing/document processing service, provide a similar electronic mail service but only to subscribers to the computer-based text processing service, a spokesman said.

A variation of the electronic mailbox is that used at Wharton School of Business, Philadelphia. Based on Digital's DECSystems 10 large-scale minicomputer, the mail system includes more than 110 terminals for students and faculty member homes.

"This is the standard mode of communication within the department (of decision sciences)," said Prof. David N. Ness, vice dean of the Wharton School and associate professor of decision sciences. He said 11 kinds of mail—return receipt, classified response, etc.—are handled by the system. Mail can be read any of six ways, including printing it on a hard-copy terminal or filing it in electronic file folders set up with the computer system.

For the faculty members who don't have computer terminals, or don't want them, a hardcopy message is automatically generated and delivered. "We don't want to coerce people into using the computer," Prof. Ness said.

His general comment about what has been learned since the system went into operation after March, 1974, was: "We learned it (electronic mail) is really different from other means of communications."

He said the system proved especially useful one recent weekend when a critical payroll and budget problem for one person was solved in less than 24 hours using electronic mail. Regular internal office mail would not have solved the same problem for several days, partly because some of the principal players in the drama were not going to be in their offices during that time, Ness explained. One course in the Wharton School, Decisions Systems (DS-2), makes heavy use of the electronic mail system for faculty-to-student communications involving task group assignments, Ness said.

Communicating word processors, and similar devices, are predicted to become important modes in future electronic mail networks, mainly because of their ability to "capture" words and messages, have them edited and then transmitted to single or multiple locations electronically.

Electronic mail is considered a "hot button" among users concerned with rising costs and slowing speeds of mail and messages in the business community. The future of electronic mail depends not only on cost-effective terminals and low-cost satellite-type transmission network, but on secretaries, managers and other users adapting themselves to this new methodology.

"The expectation of instantaneous contact fostered by the telephone is an important psychological factor influencing the growth of electronic mail," according to International Resource Development, the consulting firm.

READING 10 DISCUSSION QUESTIONS

1 "Business is looking for ways to hasten the transmission and delivery of important messages while reducing the cost of mail service." Given the relatively high cost of computer equipment, how realistic and cost efficient is electronic mail?
2 Looking ahead 20 years, project areas of application for electronic mail systems.

CASE B

The Computer Impact: An Optimistic Outlook

One hundred years from now, historians will consider the development of computer technology to be a major contribution of our time. But they may also conclude in future decades that computers were machines that we had not yet learned how to use. Oh, these later historians may admit that we had developed some effective data processing, but if today's optimists are correct, historians may also write that we had only begun to realize the computer's potential in more important areas—i.e., in those areas which improve the quality of life and the well-being of people themselves. For optimistic forecasters believe that *greater freedom and individuality,* and a *more human and personalized society,* will result from future computer applications.

GREATER FREEDOM AND INDIVIDUALITY

The optimistic view of the future is that greater freedom and individuality are encouraged by the use of computers. Optimists note the individual benefits, such

Reprinted from Donald H. Sanders, *Computers in Society,* McGraw-Hill Book Company, 1977, pp. 225–227. (The outlook of pessimists is also considered on pp. 269–270 of this source.)

as those mentioned in preceding sections, and they expand and project those benefits into the future. They foresee no insurmountable problems in society's adapting to the changes brought about by increased computer utilization. The greater productivity that results from computer usage, they contend, will lead to an increased standard of living, a shorter work week, and increased leisure time. Although it will be a challenge for human beings to put aside age-old attitudes toward work and learn to use creatively the free time that they will have in the future, the optimists believe that people can learn to use their leisure in ways that are contemplative and self-fulfilling.

Also, it is argued, people will be freed from the basic struggle to maintain their existence and will have the time and resources to pursue the activities of their choice. (Since individuality has been defined as the freedom to exercise choice according to one's own scale of preference, it will thus be enhanced.) Aristotle's prophecy that "When looms weave by themselves, man's slavery will end" is cited by the optimists. Nonhuman slaves (computers and automated tools controlled by computers) will liberate many people from the unpleasant working conditions that have evolved from Charles Dickens's England of the 1800s and Upton Sinclair's United States of the early 1900s. No longer will people have to spend long hours at an assembly line, for example, tightening a few bolts on the monotonous widgets passing by, when a computer-directed and uncomplaining robot can do the work accurately and inexpensively.

MORE HUMAN AND PERSONALIZED SOCIETY

Optimists also believe that the sophisticated computer systems of the future will permit a more human and personalized society that will further reduce the need for individual conformity. They argue that the complexity of our present society, the millions of people crowded into it, and the inadequacy of our present information systems act to encourage conformity and thus to restrict personalization and human freedom of choice. However, when sophisticated information systems are developed and widely used to handle routine transactions, it will then be possible to focus greater personal attention on exceptional transactions. Therefore, more humanistic attitudes will emerge.

In short, optimists note that the following examples are merely the early tip of a future iceberg:

1 Automated health testing provides more information on each patient and greater personalization in patient care. Instead of using broad general standards or norms to evaluate a patient, a physician can obtain from the computer more specific norms for each patient, depending on the patient's age, sex, height, weight, etc.

2 After waiting hours to see a young and inexperienced intern or a harried and resentful senior-staff physician, a welfare patient at a clinic is often subjected to rushed, impolite, and haphazard medical care. When compared with this type of care, a polite and thorough computer program to determine a patient's medical history and current symptoms may be the more humane and personalized alternative.

3 Computer-assisted instruction techniques can give terminal-using students personalized lessons selected on the basis of the student's level of knowledge and past performance.

4 Reservation systems at airlines and hotels permit clerks to store more personalized information about customers than would otherwise be possible. If a customer needs unusual services, these can be entered into the system and provided at the proper time.

5 A computerized community "bulletin board" that stores offers by individuals to buy and sell items, indicates commonly needed services that are available in the community, and contains public service announcements can be established to draw a community closer together. In fact, Community Memory is just such a project of Resource One, a nonprofit group of San Francisco computer professionals.

CASE B DISCUSSION QUESTIONS

1 What will be the major benefits to individuals and organizations if the trends indicated in this "optimistic outlook" become a reality in future years?
2 Describe some of the arguments for a more pessimistic outlook concerning the future use of computer technology. What present evidences are there to point to a more pessimistic viewpoint?

SUMMARY OF CHAPTER 3

Computer-using organizations have experienced various changes that may be directly traceable to the computer. These changes have occurred in the administrative activities of planning, organizing, staffing, and controlling. Organizations making extensive use of computers are likely to be engaged in processing operations that have one or more of the following characteristics: (1) a large volume of input data, (2) repetitive processing tasks, (3) the need for speed in processing and retrieval, (4) the need for a high degree of accuracy, and (5) processing complexities that require or encourage computer usage.

The decision to introduce and use a computer in an organization has *implications that go far beyond* the mere acquisition of a piece of technical equipment. Information vital to the support of planning and control decisions is affected by the computer system that develops; the entire organizational structure may undergo stress and alteration; the nature and number of jobs are affected; the economic consequences are often hard to predict; and the decision-making techniques that have been used by managers in the past may have to be changed.

Chapter 4

Planning for Computerization

From an economic standpoint, the acquisition and use of a computer cannot be taken lightly. An investment decision involving many thousands of dollars (or a few million) must be made. This has never been an easy task. We know from Chapter 1 that a computer *can* improve the economic position of an organization. But there is no guarantee that economic benefits *will* be obtained merely because a computer is installed. On the contrary, many organizations have invested large sums in computers and have received benefits of *less* than a dollar for each dollar spent. One large bank, for example, decided to implement a total information-processing concept consisting of six large information systems. Unfortunately for the bank, however, only one system was eventually completed, and the loss sustained in the futile attempt to develop the other five is estimated at $12 million. And a recent report of the federal government General Accounting Office noted that after nine years and $7.7 million, the Federal Aviation Administration was still trying to develop several information systems (poor systems studies accounted for this lack of success).

The computer feasibility studies conducted in the early and middle 1960s were usually made to determine if money could be saved (i.e., the decision to acquire a computer was often based on estimates of cost displacement). But the economic picture of an organization may also be enhanced if information is provided that will enable administrators to make better decisions and give better service to patients, clients, customers, etc. Unfortunately, it is difficult (perhaps even impossible) to assign a precise dollar value to such benefits.

Yet is is the opinion of several authorities that the information systems that designers are now working on are often more than merely data processing systems and thus should not be justified solely on the basis of earlier tangible cost-displacement criteria. Rather, it is argued, the value of information should be determined by what administrators can do with it instead of what it costs to produce. In short, many of the important benefits of these new systems will be intangible, and although by definition intangible benefits are not subject to precise quantitative measurement, designers and managers are still faced with the problem of assigning approximate values to them. But in quantifying intangibles, there is always the danger that errors in assumptions and judgment will lead to economically unsound systems decisions.

In planning for computerization, decisions must be made concerning (1) the information systems analysis and design activities and (2) the acquisition and/or upgrading of computer resources to make such systems operational. As Figure 4-1 shows, there are many considerations which have a bearing on these decisions. For example, such variables as the personnel, material and financial resources of the organization, the differing informational needs of users, the different design tools, techniques, and guidelines employed as standards by different organizations, the different methods of data processing (manual, electromechanical, electronic) that may currently be used, the wide range of

Figure 4-1 Some considerations bearing on the design process.

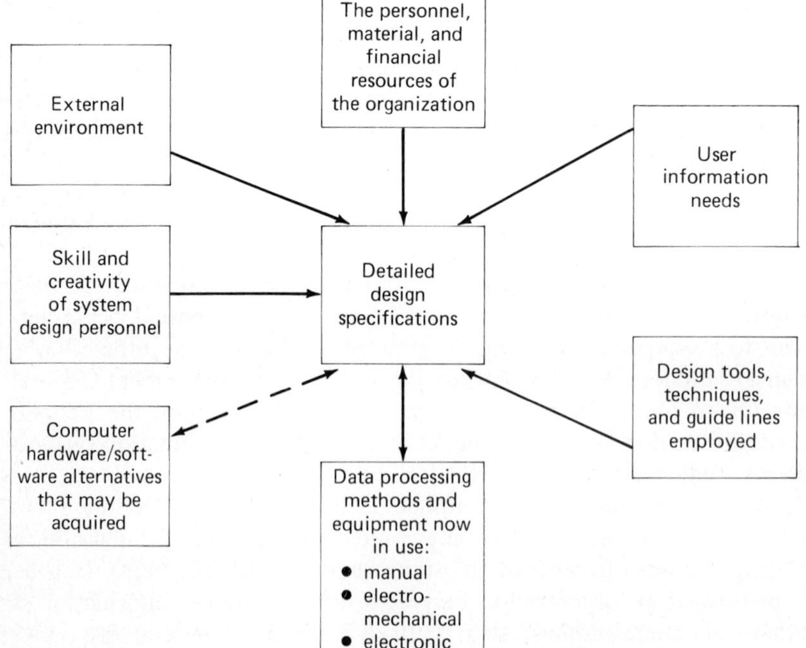

computer hardware/software that may now be installed in, or may be acquired by, an organization, the speed with which new hardware/software alternatives are introduced, the skill and creativity of the designers, the lack of static testing conditions caused by a rapidly changing environment—all of these ingredients have a bearing on the design process, add to the difficulty of the design task, and present practical limits to the number of system alternatives that can actually be evaluated. A system study is often conducted to provide answers to such questions as: (1) What data processing improvements are needed? (2) Should new information systems be designed? and (3) Should a computer be used to achieve data processing objectives? In answering these and other questions, the team making the study should follow a step-by-step system development approach to (1) *accomplish planning prerequisites and identify the objectives,* (2) *gather data on current operations,* (3) *analyze current operations,* (4) *determine feasible solutions,* and (5) *decide on the most appropriate solution.*

Although many considerations prevent the formulation of *exact* rules to follow in creating a system solution, it is possible to develop a better understanding of several of these design factors, and it is possible to discuss some of the general concepts and guidelines that may be a part of the design process. Thus, in the following pages of this chapter we will study (1) some basic *issues* in systems analysis and *the determination of design alternatives,* (2) some *tools and techniques used in system design,* (3) the format of the *detailed design specifications* that should be prepared, and (4) some *guidelines for hardware/ software evaluation, selection, and acquisition.* We shall also briefly outline the contents of the *system design report* that the team should prepare at the end of the system design phase.

THE SYSTEM ANALYSIS STAGE

The *system analysis* stage includes the early steps in the system development effort, and we shall now take a closer look at these steps.

Planning Prerequisites and Identification of Objectives

It is usually necessary for the study team members to hold preliminary sessions with the managers of all departments that the study will affect. Such *requirements sessions* allow these managers to participate in setting or revising specific system goals and should give each manager the opportunity to (1) identify those factors that are critical to the success of his or her contribution to the system's goals, (2) determine how these critical factors can be measured, (3) determine, for each critical factor, what *quantifiable* measurement constitutes success, and (4) acquire information that will be needed to ensure achievement of "success measurements."

This participation of end users is both necessary and logical; it enables those most familiar with existing methods and procedures to make suggestions for improvement and to benefit personally from the change. Furthermore, these managers are the ones whose performance is affected by changes, and they are the ones whose cooperation is needed if the study is to yield satisfactory results.

Data-Gathering Operations

The study-team members must first gather data on current operations before they can design suitable alternatives to achieve specified goals. In short, they must find out where they are before they can determine *where they want to go.* In identifying objectives, it is likely that preliminary data were gathered. But more details are now needed to determine the strengths and weaknesses of current procedures. As a result of information brought to light during this study step, it may be desirable to revise the scope and goals of the investigation. The iterative process may be continued.

The data gathered must be accurate, up to date, and sufficiently complete, for they will become the input to the design stage. On the other hand, however, if the analysts are not careful, they may become so mired down in relatively unimportant details at this stage that time schedules cannot be met.

Analyzing the Current System

During the data-gathering operations, emphasis is placed on *what* was being done. Next it is necessary for the team members to analyze their findings. The purpose of analysis is to learn *why* the system operates as it does and to prepare suggestions on *how* the study goals may best be achieved. More specifically, the team members are interested in analyzing and documenting their findings in order to (1) identify the decisions that the system must support and the data and procedures in the system that are essential to the decision makers in the organization, (2) identify the weaknesses and problems in the present system so that they will not be carried over to a new system, (3) clean up any contradictions or inaccuracies that have developed to this point in the investigation, (4) reconsider the appropriateness of the original study objectives, and (5) prepare a progress report for user and executive approval.

After evaluating the study team's progress and recommendations report, responsible managers may decide to revise the study goals or cancel the project, postpone system development until a later date, allow the team to proceed to the system design phase with the understanding that economic and operational feasibility tests must be met before a new system design will be given final approval, or give the team full authorization to design and implement the new system.

DETERMINATION OF ALTERNATIVES: SOME ISSUES INFLUENCING DESIGN

A *preliminary step* that must be taken by the system designers is to make sure that they have a clear understanding of what is expected of the new system. Once this initial step is accomplished, the designers are then ready for the *next step, which is to determine feasible alternatives* that could supply the necessary results. There are usually a number of issues involving methodology and the use of resources that must be resolved before this step can be concluded. *Included in these issues are questions about* (1) the type of conceptual design model that should be employed, (2) the flexibility that should be designed into the system, (3) the nature and number of the control provisions that should be included, (4) the advisability of "making" the system in-house or of "buying" it from an outside supplier, (5) the attention that should be given to human factors and organizational considerations (the operational feasibility issue), and (6) the economic tradeoffs that should be made (the economic feasibility issue).

Let us now look at each of these areas of inquiry.

Conceptual Design Issues

You may remember from Chapter 2 that obtaining well-designed information systems is a challenge that organizations are now facing as they attempt to adapt to the information revolution. This does *not* mean, of course, that designers have not been successful in producing information systems that are much more responsive and comprehensive than those that existed just a few years ago, for we know that they have. But progress has not yet measured up to the predictions made several years ago by a few zealots who envisioned a completely integrated "total system" built around a single online data base that would instantly give managers and other users in the organization all the information they needed to make their decisions. Perhaps one reason for this "lack of progress" was that the total system model was a fallacious design concept that failed to recognize the complexities of operating a modern business.

Although some authorities equated the total system model with a management information system (MIS) and then concluded that MIS was a *mirage,*[1] most MIS designers have always followed less ambitious conceptual models or long-range plans that take an evolutionary approach. Generally, these models or plans allow for a gradual integration of information-producing systems and provide overall guidance to designers as they implement a series of shorter projects.[2] Obviously, then, the selection of a conceptual design model is important, since it affects the approach that designers will use in the shorter projects. However, there are usually a number of uncertainties associated with the selection of a conceptual design model to build on. Why is this selection a challenge? Let us first develop a few background ideas before we attempt to answer this question that you have so thoughtfully raised.

[1]As defined in Chapter 2, MIS refers to a number of systems (or subsystems, if the entire organization is viewed as a single system) that are integrated as necessary to provide timely and effective managerial information. Such a concept of MIS views integration as possibly desirable but not as absolutely essential, and such a concept is not a mirage.

[2]This approach is generally somewhat conservative because (1) broad studies take a long time, are quite complex, require the efforts of highly paid employees who may be in short supply, are likely to be risky, and often do not show any prospect of immediate tangible benefits; (2) substantial gains may be possible sooner if short-project applications are placed on the computer; (3) resistance is often encountered from employees who do not want to experiment with the familiar system on a very broad scale: and (4) the planning and coordination of broad studies is complicated, since in many cases no single individual can really understand such studies.

As noted in Chapter 2, the management of medium-sized and larger organizations is a complicated process which takes place on at least three levels.

Top executives perform vital *strategic* planning and decision-making activities. They are charged with weighing risks and making major policy decisions on such matters as new product development, new plant authorizations and locations, corporate mergers and acquisitions, etc. They must also consider future technological developments in planning long-range strategy. Thus, as we saw in Chapter 1, the key factors that must be considered by top executives as they study a problem often are of an external nature.

The *tactical* management decisions made by middle managers deal with the implementation of strategic decisions. Resources are allocated, authority is delegated, and control is maintained so that the strategic plans will be carried out. Lower-level *operating* managers make the day-to-day scheduling and control decisions that are needed if specific tasks are to be accomplished. Actual results of an operation are carefully checked against planned expectations, and corrective actions are taken as needed. Certain types of internal information resulting from operating decisions are summarized and fed back to upper managerial levels by existing information systems.

Figure 4-2*a* depicts the three management levels, each with its own information needs. In addition to what might be termed the *horizontal* structure shown in Figure 4-2*a*, an organization is also divided *vertically* into different business specialties or functions, which generate separate information flows (see Figure 4-2*b*. Combining the horizontal managerial levels with the vertical business specialties produces the complex organizational structure shown in Figure 4-2*c*. Underlying this structure in Figure 4-2*c*, we have a data base consisting, ideally, of internally and externally produced data relating to past, present, and predicted future events.

With the above concepts in mind, we are now in a position to better appreciate the problems and challenges that designers face. More specifically, system designers *must* grapple with the following questions:

1 *Should a "top-down" or "bottom-up" approach to the system development be followed?* The *top-down approach* begins with studies of (*a*) broad organizational goals and (*b*) the types of decisions made by organizational executives. From these studies comes a model of the information flow in the organization and design requirements for the system. The *advantages* of this approach are that it is a logical and sensible way to attack a problem (buildings, airplanes, and computers are essentially designed in this way), and it can make it easier to integrate system elements. The *disadvantages*, however, are that it is very difficult to define the organizational goals and the decision-making activities of executives in the precise terms required for system design, and there is thus the risk of building a large and expensive system that is not effective. The *bottom-up approach*, on the other hand, begins at the operating level with the existing procedures for processing transactions and updating files and then builds the add-on modules to support planning, controlling, and decision-making activities as they are needed. The *advantages* of this approach are that smaller

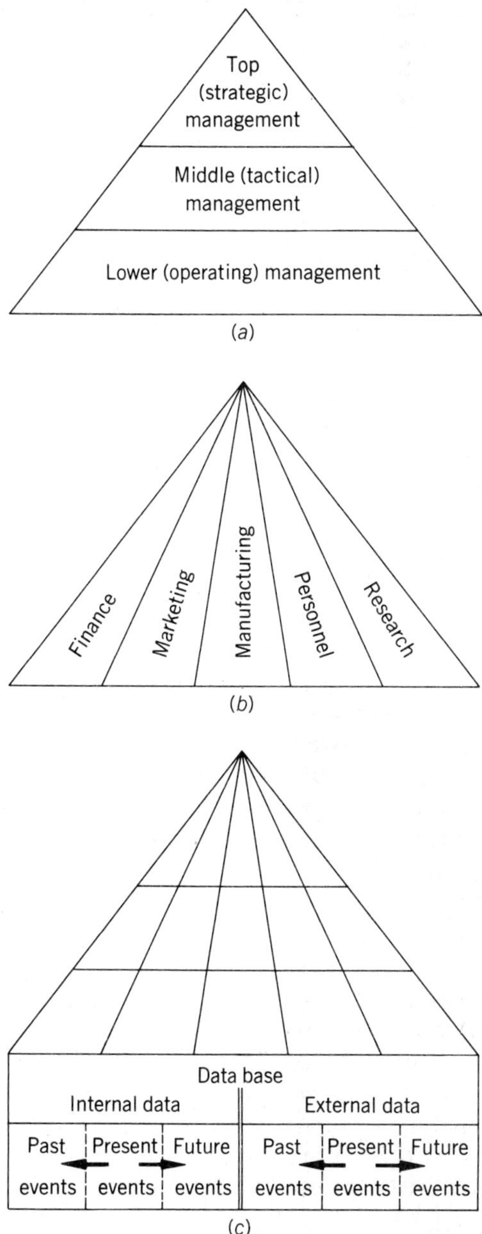

Figure 4-2

"bites" of work are tackled and the danger of building a large, complex, and ineffective system is minimized. The *disadvantages* are that this approach may not lead to the development of high-potential systems above the operating level, but if such higher-level systems *are* attempted it will then be necessary to redesign (at considerable expense) the existing programs and procedures to provide the integration of information that higher-level managers require. Given these considerations, it is not surprising that system designers often accept the challenge to develop a hybrid design philosophy that attempts to use the best attributes of each of these approaches.[3]

2 *Can a single data base be created to satisfy the differing information needs of the three managerial levels?* Most information systems today serve the needs of operating managers and, to a lesser extent, middle managers. They provide internally produced data dealing with past and current activities. Although some firms are using internal data and carefully developed planning models incorporating assumptions about external conditions to *simulate* responses to the "what if?" questions of top executives, the fact remains that most current systems focus on internal and historic events and produce output of only limited use in strategic planning. Whether to attempt to organize and structure a *single* data base to meet varying needs or to create *different* bases for different horizontal levels is a problem facing designers.

3 *Can different business specialties share the same data base?* Can the system supply from a single data base the information needed by marketing, production, finance, and personnel managers at different levels, or must separate vertically oriented data bases be designed for each specialty? Different business functions have generally had their own information systems. Attempting to integrate these separate systems into one or more corporate data bases that will serve the broader needs of many managers is a formidable challenge, but the effort is being made.

4 *Can externally produced data be incorporated into a data base?* To be of value to managers at the higher echelons, a system must supply information about the external world, and this information must be complete, timely, and accurate. But the quality of externally produced data is more difficult to control than internal data quality, and external data has been expensive to obtain. The growing availability of external data in machine-sensible form and/or the use of external data banks will make more data available to the firm's data bank. It is the designer's responsibility to see that these new facts are incorporated into an MIS in meaningful ways.

5 To what extent should an attempt be made to "solve the triangle"? That is, to what extent should the designers attempt to create an overall system that would simultaneously satisfy the information needs of most or all of the segments shown in Figure 4-2*c*? Although the tendency of some unwary organizations may be to attempt the triangle solution, the complexity of the problems involved usually dictates that designers take a more gradual and conservative approach.

From the discussion in this section, it should now be obvious why the choice of a conceptual plan or model for system design is so important—and so challenging. Certainly, the issues raised here will have a direct bearing on the

[3]For more information on conceptual design approaches, see Robert L. Paretta, "Designing Management Information Systems: An Overview," *The Journal of Accountancy,* April 1975, pp. 42–47, and John A. Zachman, "Control and Planning for Information Systems," *Journal of Systems Management,* July 1977, pp. 34–41.

alternatives considered during the design phase of the system development effort.

The Issue of System Flexibility

Another important issue that has a direct bearing on the design alternatives to be considered involves the degree of *flexibility*—i.e., the degree to which a system is able to adapt to a wide variety of circumstances—that needs to be built into the system. Such factors as the type of industry, the stability of the products made or sold, and the nature of the competition all help to determine the amount of flexibility that is needed. For example, those managers who work in a stable industry, have only a few staple products or services to sell, and are consistently able to capture a predictable share of their markets would probably not be as interested in information system flexibility as those who must function in a rapidly changing industry and who must attempt to produce, price, and keep track of a large number of complex products that are subject to the pressures of changing demand and competitive reactions.

The likelihood of future system changes obviously affects the need for flexibility. A fact that is sometimes overlooked in the design phase is that most systems are likely to be changed several times during their useful life. And these changes are often unpredictable. Furthermore, the cost of revising and maintaining systems to meet changing conditions is one of the largest cost elements in the use of computer-based information systems. Designers may thus face a dilemma: they can ignore the flexibility issue, produce a system that has (perhaps) lower design and implementation costs, and then incur the high costs required to periodically restructure the system, or they can initially spend the additional time (and money) to create a flexible design that may require fewer future changes. The *total cost* over the life of the system may well turn out to be less when flexibility is a design goal (see Figure 4-3). In short, given the unpredictability and cussedness of events, designers should perhaps adopt the motto that "if we can't make it right, we had better make it adaptable."

Another factor that affects the need for flexibility is the management style and philosophy of different managers. Two managers—A and B—who occupy the same position over a period of time will probably have different information

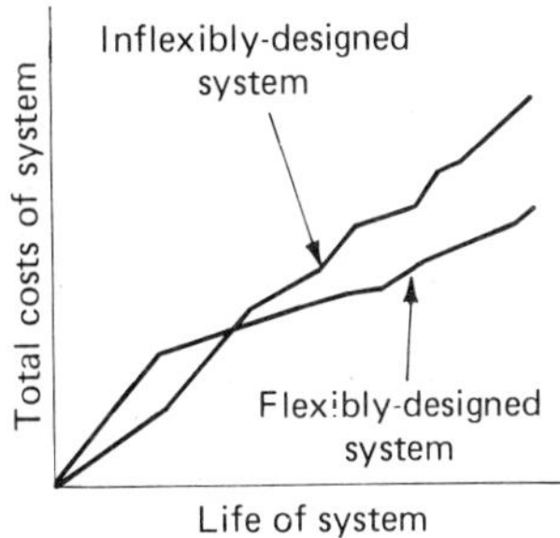

Figure 4-3 System costs.

needs. Manager A, for example, may want highly condensed reports with little detail, but manager B may wish to delve into detailed reports and seek many facts before making a decision. Political analysts tell us that former President Eisenhower was the type of executive who wanted fewer details, while former Secretary of Defense Robert McNamara was an executive B type who sought numerous facts. An issue facing the system designer, then, is how to make it possible for executive B to succeed executive A without requiring that the software be restructured. If staffing changes are possible during the life of a system, then a flexible design approach may be needed.

The issues and considerations that have now been outlined in this section should be evaluated by designers as they seek to establish efficient and effective alternatives during the design phase. A summary of questions bearing on flexibility that should be studied includes: (1) what data will be allowed to enter the system and what facts will be excluded, (2) how much detail will be permitted in the accepted data, (3) what approaches will be used to organize data elements and files, (4) to what extent, if any, will there be linkages or integration between data elements and files, (5) what approaches will be used to access data, and (6) what I/O and storage media and/or devices will be most suitable.

The Issue of System Control

An essential requirement of any system alternative considered during the design phase must be that vital and relevant data are not lost or stolen, errors are not introduced into the data before, during, or after processing, and data are not stored, retrieved, modified, or communicated without proper authorization. In other words, designers must make sure that procedures and controls are built into any alternative to ensure that the *integrity* of the data and the *security* of the system are not impaired.

Input and output error detection procedures, redundant checks on processing accuracy, provisions for system recovery in the event of failure, provisions for testing the logic of the system prior to its implementation—these and other control elements should be built into the system early rather than being added on later when the task would be much more difficult and expensive.[4] Since the implemented system will be subject to periodic audit reviews that test the adequacy of these control provisions, one or more auditors should play an active role in this phase of the design process. As a check on control procedures, auditors will trace transactions through a system from input to output. Thus, this *audit trail* must also be designed into the system.

A basic issue facing designers in the control area is how to balance the goal of a high degree of data integrity and system security against the possibility of creating a complex and "overcontrolled" system that is expensive to operate and that produces delays in getting the information into the hands of end-users.

[4]Control implications and procedures will be discussed in detail in Chapter 7.

The "Make" or "Buy" Issue

Should a new design be created in-house, or should an existing applications package or custom-built system be bought from one of the more than 800 outside suppliers?[5] Some of the pros and cons of using applications packages were briefly outlined in Chapter 2. Generally speaking, the make-or-buy decision often revolves around the lower cost, faster implementation, and reduced risk (the package is available for testing) advantages that may accrue to packages as balanced against the possible in-house or custom-built design advantages of greater operating efficiency and the ability to satisfy unique needs more effectively. (In trying to appeal to many potential users, the package product may sacrifice processing efficiency and effectiveness in areas important to a particular organization.) Whenever possible, however, the use of an appropriate application package should always be considered as an alternative in the design phase.

Some of the factors that should be considered in evaluating possible packages include:

1 *Package quality.* A check of current users should be made to evaluate the suitability, ease of use, performance, and reliability of the package.[6]

2 *Vendor reputation.* Is the vendor financially strong? Will adequate technical support be provided to install, maintain, and update the package?

3 *Documentation furnished.* Is documentation adequate to enable company personnel to maintain and modify the system?

Human Factors and Operational Issues

Will the proposed alternatives be easy for people to understand and use? Will decision makers be allowed enough time to learn to work with, and effectively use, the alternatives selected? (As Figure 4-4 shows, it would be unwise to install a new system without allowing time for managers to move up the learning curve.) Will the selected alternatives give prompt response, relieve people of unnecessary chores, and be pleasant to use? Will they handle exceptions gracefully and give individuals choices on how to deal with them? Will error-correcting procedures be effective and efficient? If the system contains personal data, will the alternatives safeguard *personal privacy?* These and many other questions bearing on the operational feasibility of a system must be considered when alternatives are determined. If a system is nonresponsive, and if it harasses and wastes the time of users and those it is supposed to serve, then

[5]It is estimated that there are more than 3,000 separate and distinct package products now on the market. Frost and Sullivan, a market research firm, further estimates that package sales will amount to nearly $900 million annually by 1984. Also, some vendors contract to supply a "turnkey system" to businesses. These custom-built system houses may sell the customer a computer (typically, it is a minicomputer) and then provide the custom programming, training, and maintenance support needed.

[6]For an evaluation of 199 popular packages, see Herbert L. Gepner, "User Ratings of Software Packages," *Datamation,* December 1977, pp. 117–121 ff. *Datamation* has published user ratings in each December issue for several years.

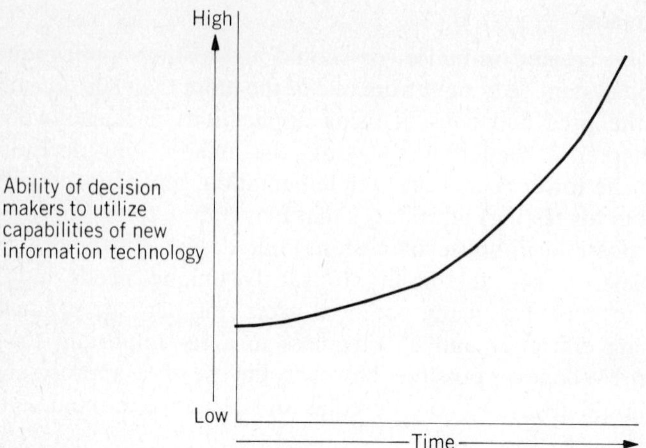

Figure 4-4 Management learning curve in using new information technology.

it will be resisted and it will not be trusted. Such a system will probably achieve few of its goals; at best, the results will only be marginal. A good design, on the other hand, will be easily recognized: People will not complain about it; they will just take it for granted! We will consider human factors and operational issues again in Chapters 5 and 6.

The Issue of Economic Tradeoffs

The economic issue has *not* been left for last in this section because it is less important than the others. Rather, it has been placed here because the question of economic feasibility underlies the whole system design and development effort. The decisions made by designers and other study team members in considering *all* the above issues (e.g., the conceptual design model to use, the degree of flexibility to design into the system, the decision to make or buy system components) can be reached *only* after careful thought has been given to the economic resources of the organization and to the economic criteria that have been established by those responsible for approving system projects.

A number of economic tradeoffs must typically be made before the final design alternatives can be selected. A very flexible data-base system that can immediately update and retrieve all records in the system might be nice to have, but the team elects to settle for a less expensive online processing approach that gives immediate access to records that are only periodically updated using batch techniques; designers on the study team would like the challenge of creating all components in the new system, but the team decides to give serious attention to a less expensive package from a vendor; auditors on the team would like to see a maze of control procedures built into the system, but others convince them that the additional development and operating costs involved would exceed the somewhat greater risks assumed.

EVALUATING ALTERNATIVES

Computer usage is justified when the tangible and intangible economic benefits to be gained are greater than comparable benefits received from other alternatives. The type and number of alternatives to be considered vary, of course, from one system study to another. In some situations, noncomputer options may be preferable; for some organizations the results of a study may indicate that the use of a remote computing service (RCS) or a timesharing service would be a desirable solution; in many cases, the system can be implemented using existing hardware and software; and in some development projects implementation may call for the acquisition of new hardware/software resources.

In selecting an RCS, the study team would consider such factors as: (l) the proximity, reputation, and financial stability of the center, (2) the quality of center personnel and their experience in dealing with similar systems, (3) the care exercised in safeguarding documents and providing backup facilities, and (4) the costs of using the center.

In choosing a timesharing service, the study team would be interested in such factors as: (l) the reputation and financial stability of the service; (2) the quality of service personnel and their ability to assist in system implementation; (3) the reliability of the service, e.g., its loading and therefore its response time, and its backup facilities; (4) the controls available to protect the security and integrity of user data and programs maintained in online storage; (5) the availability of programming languages and accurate library programs; and (6) the costs associated with using the service.

Regardless of whether an RCS or a timesharing service is chosen, the team should be required to present its findings and the economic basis for its recommendations to a top executive or steering committee for the final decision. For the remainder of this chapter we shall assume that the team believes that new computing hardware is justified. However, portions of the material that follows is appropriate in a study that does not result in the acquisition of new equipment.

Once the decision to obtain new equipment has been made (with the approval of top executives), there are a number of other questions that should be studied. These questions include:

1 *What equipment should be considered?* What hardware/software package would best meet company needs? Can consultants help in equipment evaluation and selection?

2 Which hardware/software package offers the greatest *return on investment?* Can the company afford the investment at this time?

3 Have all possible *acquisition methods* (rent, lease, or buy) been evaluated?

4 Have *organizational and personnel aspects* received proper consideration?

Equipment Evaluation and Selection

To select is to choose from a number of more or less suitable alternatives. Evaluation should be based on the ability of several computers and/or peripheral devices to process the detailed set of written system specifications that have been prepared.

If the new equipment is to replace or upgrade existing hardware, there will be a need to give consideration to the concepts of compatibility and modularity. "*Compatibility*" is a term that may be associated with the software of a computer. If the programming aids, data, and instructions prepared for one machine can be used by another without conversion or program modification, the machines are said to be *compatible.* Many manufacturers of third- and fourth-generation computers have designed "families" of machines to provide compatibility for the user. The IBM System/360 family of machines, for example, consists of several models differing in size and power. Yet some of these models are both hardware compatible, i.e., the basic machine language instructions of one model will run on others, and software compatible, i.e., the higher-level language programs are interchangeable, with little or no modification needed. Furthermore, System/370 models are compatible with each other and will run many existing 360 programs without change. Obviously, the team would place a high priority on selecting equipment that is compatible with, and does not require a costly rewriting of, the programs developed for the existing hardware.

An alternative to replacing existing hardware is to expand its capabilities. The concept of *modularity* (also called *open-ended design* and *upgrading*) allows a computer installation to change and *grow.* To the original CPU can be attached additional units as the need arises, just as additional freight cars can be hooked onto a freight train. Users can begin with small systems and build up the installation gradually; it is not necessary that final capacity be provided at the outset. In addition to *adding on,* true modularity also makes it possible to replace smaller components with larger versions while other hardware remains unchanged.

How does the modularity concept differ, then, from compatibility? *Two or more different* machine systems are compatible if they can accept the same input data and programs and produce the same output. A *single* system has modular capability if it can grow.

The evaluation and selection of equipment is a complicated task. *The selection approaches that have been widely used are summarized in Figure 4-5.* Regardless of the approach used, however, the study team should also compare the *quantitative and qualitative factors listed in Figure 4-6* to further limit the choices.

One final warning may be in order before we conclude this discussion of equipment selection. Figure 4-7 shows the findings of several organizations that have studied the relationship between software cost per instruction and hardware capacity. As Figure 4-7 shows, relative software costs may be expected

Figure 4-5 Equipment Selection Approaches

1 *Single-source approach.* This noncompetitive approach merely consists of choosing the hardware/software package from among those available from a selected vendor. There is a lack of objectivity in this approach; unfortunate results have been produced, but it has often been used in the "selection" of smaller in-house packages.

2 *Competitive-bidding approach.* System specifications are submitted to vendors with a request that they prepare bids. Included in the bid request may be a requirement that cost and performance figures be prepared for a specified *benchmark* processing run. The vendors select what they believe to be the most appropriate hardware/software packages from their lines and submit proposals. Sometimes this bidding approach yields excellent results. But frequently, vendors do not prepare the proposals they are capable of making. Other possible shortcomings in bidding include the facts that: (*a*) system specifications may be altered to improve procedures or, perhaps, place the vendor's package in the best possible light (the study team must then compare bids based on different specifications—a most difficult comparison indeed, as the vendors well know); and (*b*) program running (or throughput) times may be underestimated in the bids because inadequate allowance is made for housekeeping and set-up times.

3 *Consultant-evaluation approach.* Qualified data processing consultants can assist businesses in selecting the hardware/software package. Consultants can bring specialized knowledge and experience and an objective point of view to bear on the evaluation and selection problem.

4 *Simulation approach.* As we have already seen, specialized computer programs are available from a number of organizations to simulate the performance of selected hardware/software alternatives. Simulation programs are capable of comparing the input, output, and computing times required to process specific applications on all available commercial computers made in this country. Simulation provides fast, accurate, objective (and relatively expensive) evaluation.

Figure 4-6 Equipment Selection Factors

Economic factors

1 Cost comparisons
2 Return on investment
3 Acquisition methods

Hardware factors

1 Hardware performance, reliability, capacity, and price
2 Presence or absence of modularity
3 Number and accessibility of backup facilities
4 Firmness of delivery date
5 Effective remaining life of proposed hardware
6 Compatibility with existing systems

Software factors

1 Software performance and price
2 Efficiency and reliability of available software
3 Programming languages available (not promised)
4 Availability of useful and well-documented packaged programs, program libraries, and user groups
5 Firmness of delivery date on promised software
6 Ease of use and modification

Service factors

1 Facilities provided by manufacturer for checking new programs
2 Training facilities offered and the quality of training provided
3 Programming assistance and conversion assistance offered
4 Maintenance terms and quality

Reputation of manufacturer

1 Financial stability
2 Record of keeping promises

Figure 4-7

to increase rapidly as the hardware approaches 100 percent utilization. Yet many hardware procurement decisions have been made on the assumption that average software production costs will remain essentially unchanged, regardless of hardware limitations—i.e., that they will follow the dashed "selection myth" line. Such an assumption may, of course, lead to unwise equipment decisions. The study team should be aware that as hardware investment continues to decline as a percentage of total information systems cost, and as software costs continue to grow, the decision which will minimize the *total cost* of a new system may be to acquire enough hardware capacity to avoid the steep rise in the software production cost curve. (Of course, this does not mean that a giant computer should be initially acquired to handle all foreseeable applications, but it does mean that consideration should be given to selecting equipment with modularity and compatibility in mind.)

At this point (or perhaps at an earlier point) an estimate of the expected return on investment of the surviving choices should be made for economic justification and analysis purposes.

Estimated Return on Investment

The costs associated with the options remaining might be compared with the cost of improved current methods of performing the work. Let us assume that as a result of one cost comparison, it is expected that there will be negative effects on after-tax earnings for the first two years but that after this initial period substantial positive returns are anticipated. It is known that top executives believe that the equipment should yield a satisfactory return over a five-year period or it should not, at least for the time being, be acquired. Since the organization can earn a 20 percent return on investments made in plant and equipment, it is also the feeling of top managers that the equipment investment should be postponed if it cannot produce a similar return.

Equipment Acquisition Methods

It is the job of the study team to evaluate acquisition methods and recommend the one best suited to the company. *Equipment may be acquired in the following ways:*

1 *Renting.* In a majority of computer installations, hardware is rented from the computer manufacturer.[7] This is a flexible method that does not require a large initial investment. It is also the most expensive method if the equipment meets company needs for 4 or 5 years or longer.

2 *Purchasing.* Although the rental method is the most popular, there is evidence of a trend toward greater equipment purchasing. Greater interest in purchasing is due to (*a*) the fact that it is the least expensive method when hardware is kept for several years, (*b*) the greater reliability, longer physical life, and greater expected residual value of the latest hardware, and (*c*) the belief of some managers that the risk of becoming "locked-in" to a particular configuration is reduced by their ability to do a better job of long-range systems planning.

3 *Leasing.* Under one typical leasing arrangement, the user tells the leasing company what equipment is desired. The leasing organization arranges for the purchase of the equipment and then leases it to the user for a long-term period (usually, 3 to 5 years). This method combines some of the advantages of both renting and purchasing. Other leasing arrangements are possible. For example, IBM has a 1- or 2-year lease that is less expensive than its rental plan.

Figure 4-8 summarizes the advantages and disadvantages of each acquisition method. The study team should weigh these merits and faults carefully before making its choice.

MAKING DECISIONS

The complete analysis of the new proposed computerized activity usually will be performed by a study team which is assigned the task of investigating the feasibility of the proposal. Their report frequently will include the following points:

1 A restatement of study scope and objectives

2 The procedures and operations that will be changed

3 The anticipated effects of such changes on organizational structure, physical facilities, and company information

4 The anticipated effects on personnel and the personnel resources available to implement the change

5 The hardware/software package chosen, the reasons for the choice, and the alternatives considered

6 The economic effects of the change, including cost comparisons, adequacy of return on investment, and analysis of acquisition methods

7 A summary of the problems anticipated in the changeover

8 A summary of the benefits to be obtained from the change

Top executives must evaluate the recommendations made by the team to detect

[7]According to International Data Corporation, a research firm, 60 percent of all installed computers are rented or short-term–leased from the manufacturer, 28 percent are purchased, and 12 percent are leased from companies that specialize in computer equipment leases. For more information on acquisition methods, see "Should It Be Lease or Buy?" *Dun's Review,* July 1977, pp. 82–83 ff, and Ted Szatrowski, "Rent, Lease, or Buy?" *Datamation,* February 1976, pp. 59–62 ff.

Figure 4-8 Factors to Consider in Equipment Acquisition

Rental

Advantages

1 No large purchase price required
2 Risk of technological obsolescence reduced
3 Maintenance included in rental charges
4 Agreement may be cancelled without penalty after brief period
5 Greater flexibility in changing equipment configurations
6 Possibility of applying some part of rental charges to later purchase

Disadvantages

1 Most expensive if equipment is used for long period of time
2 Rental charges remain same throughout life of agreement
3 Rental charges may increase when monthly usage exceeds a specified number of hours

Lease

Advantages

1 Less expensive than rental over life of the lease
2 No large purchase price required
3 Maintenance is included in the lease charges
4 No additional charges when equipment is used beyond a specified number of hours monthly
5 Lease charges decline after specified period
6 Possibility of applying part of lease charges toward later purchase

Disadvantages

1 User contracts for equipment over long time period
2 Reduced flexibility—user is obligated to pay a contracted charge if lease is terminated prior to end of lease period

Purchase

Advantages

1 Generally, least expensive if machine is kept over long time period
2 No additional charges when equipment is used beyond specified number of hours monthly
3 Certain tax advantages accrue to the purchaser

Disadvantages

1 Equipment maintenance not included in the purchase price
2 Risk of technological obsolescence—of being "locked-in" to a system which does not continue to meet changing company needs
3 A large initial capital outlay is required

any evidence of bias[8] and decide whether the benefits outweigh the disadvantages. Suspicion of bias or of an inadequate effort may be justified if the points outlined above are not included in the recommendation. For example, suspicion is probably warranted if little or no mention is made of the personnel or organizational aspects of the change, if the alternatives considered are really just "straw men" which are obviously inadequate, or if feasibility depends solely on vaguely defined and suspicious intangible benefits.

REVIEW AND DISCUSSION QUESTIONS

1 (*a*) What is the purpose of the design stage of a system development project? (*b*) Why is system design a difficult task?

[8]After all, if the change is made, some members of the study team may expect to move into positions of greater influence.

2 Identify and discuss the basic issues that influence system design.

3 (*a*) Discuss the "total system" design concept. (*b*) Why is the selection of a conceptual design model important?

4 (*a*) Define and discuss the "top-down" approach to system development. (*b*) Define and discuss the "bottom-up" approach to system development.

5 Identify and discuss the factors that help determine the amount of flexibility that is needed in an information system design.

6 (*a*) Describe a system design that would offer a great deal of flexibility. (*b*) Describe one that would be relatively inflexible in a changing environment. (*c*) What are the advantages and disadvantages of each of the systems you have described?

7 What questions bearing on design flexibility should be considered?

8 "Designers must make sure that procedures and controls are built into any alternative to ensure that the integrity of the data and the security of the system are not impaired." Discuss this statement.

9 (*a*) What are the advantages and limitations of purchased software packages? (*b*) What factors should be considered in evaluating such packages?

10 What operational feasibility factors should be considered during system design?

11 "A number of economic tradeoffs must typically be made before a final system design can be selected." Discuss this statement.

12 (*a*) Discuss the possible computer acquisition methods. (*b*) What are the advantages and disadvantages of each method?

13 Computer hardware may be rented, leased, or purchased, but what about computer software? Contact representatives of several organizations offering programs to learn their acquisition policies.

Chapter 4 Readings

INTRODUCTION TO READINGS 11 THROUGH 14

11 In this article, Benjamin Knowles, Jr., emphasizes that a successful long-range data processing plan depends heavily on mature managers being willing to evaluate opportunities and problems and work for change. He analyzes some of the planning pitfalls that are often encountered and proposes a planning scheme that should lead to greater long-range success.

12 Most executives associated with computer operations have experienced various degrees of frustration in the development and implementation of systems to meet the information needs of their businesses. In this article, Charles F. Axelson tackles some of the pitfalls and offers some solutions to clear up the *MIS*understandings.

13 Success in the development of an information system must be defined in terms of both the *user* and the *data processing personnel.* In the second of a two-part article (see Reading 4), William Ainsworth indicates that it is often found that the criteria of each are quite different. The result has been an abundance of systems that have been successful from a technical standpoint but complete failures from the user's viewpoint.

14 It has long been acknowledged that *systems analysts* play a major role in the development of effective information systems. In this article William Feeney and Frea Sladek explore how effective system analysts must operate essentially as *change* agents in order to perform their jobs successfully.

Reading 11

Get Ready for Long Range DP Planning

Benjamin Knowles, Jr.

Managers of data processing departments have been characterized by reacting to one emergency after another. Long range planning for data processing is a method of identifying all the problems and opportunities of a department before attempting to solve any problems.

Successful long range planning depends first on a mature dp management team that is willing to evaluate opportunities and problems realistically and to join together in a commitment to make changes. Second, it depends on a flow of data, from planning studies through measurement of trends and achievements,

Reprinted from *Computer Decisions,* January 1977, pp. 38–42. Copyright © 1977, Hayden Publishing Company. Mr. Knowles is vice-president of Brandon Systems Institute.

to determine what management reactions are necessary to achieve or change the selected objectives.

DEAL WITH ISSUES

The long range planning approach is designed to deal with issues which are too time consuming to be completed in one year, and to deal with situations with more issues than can be addressed in the time allotted with resources which are available. With this approach, many potential issues are studied. Before the planning objectives are determined, all of the issues are viewed as a mosaic, rather than in sequence. No action is taken on any issue *per se*. Rather, the objective in planning is to separate constraints and minor problems from items or issues that require action, and to lay out a specific program to deal with the key issues.

Once the commitment to develop a long range dp plan has been made, the next step is to determine how to develop the plan. Since any effort is going to require scarce resources, the planning effort itself must be organized to be as efficient as possible. The first step in the "plan for planning" is to identify the major tasks, define the products and specify the interfaces which exist between each task.

While there are many variations in the long range planning process, one general approach is universally workable. It is composed of seven elements: premises and issue selection—the study and screening element; objective setting—the "what by when" element; strategy development and selection—the "how" element; consolidation into a strategic plan—the total impact element; feasibility tests—the iterative element; implementation and control—the tie to annual planning; and measurement—the feedback element.

WHICH SUBJECTS NEED INVESTIGATION?

In the premises and issues selecting element, it is necessary to study a variety of subjects affecting dp activities to determine which of them are appropriate planning issues. Most departments have study activities under way throughout the year. It should be obvious that these studies represent potential long range planning issues. In fact, any studies conducted during the previous two years (whether the results of the studies were implemented or not) should be included among the issues considered for long range planning.

The purpose of the premises study is to identify the major future events which are likely to require dp management attention and to determine what resources will be available to deal with these events. At this stage in planning, a critical issue may be overlooked or underestimated. The result is that the long range plan must be revised or abandoned. And while revision is an accepted part of the planning activity, it always has a negative impact on morale.

There is no mandatory set of premise areas to be studied, but there are four categories which almost always reveal high priority issues: basic workload analysis, parent organization goals, dp department capabilities, and impact of technology.

ASSESS THE RESOURCES

Basic workload analysis involves investigating working application systems to assess the resources required for software maintenance and to determine which system will require redesign. Second, it involves examining changes in user requirements which may lead to new systems. Third, it involves the investigation of the impact of volume changes on computer capacity.

The category of parent organization goals includes the dp department mission. The dp department may say that its mission is to provide service to users, but for many years there has been a growth in the use of dp systems to meet parent organization priorities. Corporate application systems may be treated as the needs of a user, albeit a very high priority user. But the questions of organization-wide control of dp expenditures, of dp managed consolidation of technology across multiple user functions, or of the support of different users based on different parent organizational priorities are clearly more important than a single applications system category.

These mission-oriented questions are of such importance that they should be clearly identified and approved by top management. Any action taken should be recognized by the user community as different from the traditional service mission of the dp department.

Even if these politically sensitive questions are ignored, one issue must be considered: What budget will be available to support dp activities? Obviously, the size of the budget will either motivate or constrain all major dp activities. The more limited the budget, the harder the dp department will have to work to set priorities and to achieve high productivity.

The third category is dp capabilities. This category examines the dp department from the inside. Issues center on resource constraints (budget, head count), cost of resources including the impact of inflation, changes in the quality of resources (experience or training of staff, reliability of services for vendor software and hardware), availability of resources (skilled people, necessary software), and dp management practices and their effectiveness.

THE EFFECT OF TECHNOLOGY

Impact of technology issues makes up the last category to be studied. This area is the sole responsibility of those who claim to be dp professionals. Even in technologically stable organizations, the dp planner must evaluate trends in the costs of existing products and services, examine new products and services, and establish standards for vendor performance.

The result of studies in these categories will be recommended actions for the dp department over a long planning period. It is not unusual for planners to

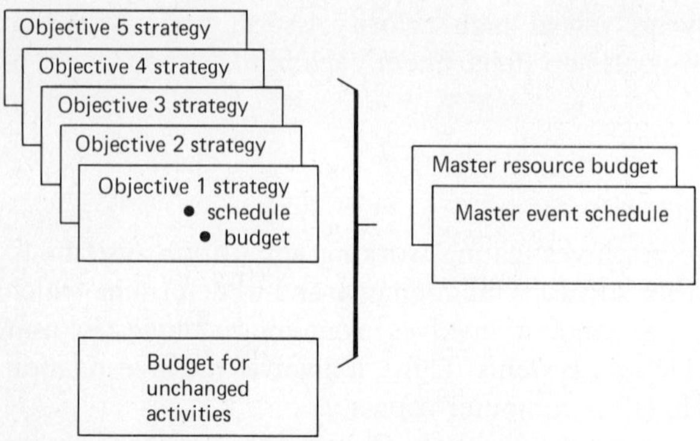

Figure 1 Strategies and budgets: The desired changes in dp operations can occur only with the proper combination of strategic and financial resources.

make 40 recommendations with varying long range impacts. Obviously, this is a greater number of strategic activities than even a very effectively managed dp department could handle over a three-to-seven-year planning horizon and still administer the dp department on a week-to-week basis. Choices must be made, and these choices lead us to the second phase of the premise development activity, the screening part of long range planning: issue selection.

The first step in issue selection is assigning priorities to the study recommendations. There are four key criteria:

- Timing—When is the latest a resource must be assigned in order to respond adequately to the issue?
- Cost of recovery—What is the cost of recovery from an error in judgment?
- Mandatory—Is a law, regulation or parent organization directive involved?
- Size of the opportunity—Does the issue offer a major, tangible benefit to the parent organization or a key user?

In the selection process, some recommended issues will be allocated to the operating year, some will modify the mission of a sub-organizational unit of the dp department, and some will be rephrased as planning guidelines or constraints. These minor issues will influence the plan but will not become objectives. As a general rule, any recommended issue based on such vague assumptions that no effective action can be planned (assumptions about the specifics of anticipated legislation or features of an unannounced vendor product) should be postponed until specifics are available.

Unless specific resources must be allocated during the first year in the planning horizon, a recommended issue should be made a guideline rather than an objective.

REDUCE THE STEPS

These steps will be used to reduce the total number of potential issues to from three to 10. In early plans the number of issues must be small, perhaps three. In more dp departments with more planning experience, a larger number of issues, perhaps 10, may be selected. Choosing more than 10 issues indicates that the dp management team has either failed to define issues at a high enough level of abstraction or failed to resolve the problems of priority. Planning with too many issues leads to overcommitment of dp resources; experience has demonstrated this point over and over again. The planner must try to achieve a few important goals rather than risk failure because of fragmented management attention.

The objective development step is basically to convert the recommended issue into a meaningful statement which describes the result desired by the planner in terms of a change in a measurable variable and limits the time of accomplishing the change. Simply stated, the objective says what will change by when.

At this point, issues have been assigned priorities or they have been eliminated, but no clear statement has been made about what the dp management team intends to accomplish, how performance is to be measured, nor when the intended result will be measurable.

Forecasts of limited budget growth, inadequate hardware capacity and major new user requirements indicate a major management challenge. But the identification of a problem does not, within itself, indicate what the planner will accept as an adequate solution. One manager would view survival in his job as a satisfactory solution; another would view an increase in budget as the desired result.

Other objectives might be increased productivity or more careful assignment of priorities to user needs. A specific objective in one of these areas will lead to significantly different dp activities. In addition, the determination of when the result is to be achieved will also lead to significantly different activities. An objective of action in one year rather than over three years would make a major difference to the planner in his attempt to describe how he will achieve the result.

The statement of the intended result, how it will be measured and when it is to be achieved is therefore the key to successful long range dp planning. If the objectives are too broad and vague, the plan will fail. Discriminating criteria are aids in choosing among available resources and competing methods to achieve the objectives.

DEVELOP ALTERNATIVE STRATEGIES

The next element in the structure is the development of alternative strategies for each objective and the selection of the most desirable strategy for each one. At the end of this activity, each objective will be paired with its selected strategy.

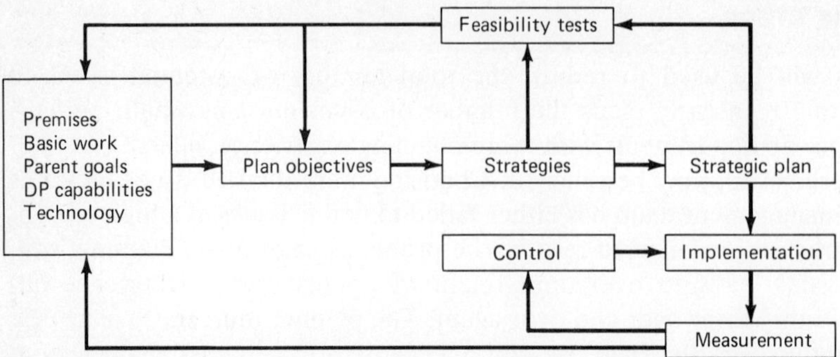

Figure 2 The total plan is composed of seven elements: premises and issue selection, objective setting, strategy development, consolidation, feasibility testing, implementation, and, finally, measurement.

This pairing concept is not new to long range planning, but is a key to making the planning process efficient.

A strategy answers the question of how dp resources will be used to accomplish the chosen objective. The chief distinction between the objective and the strategy is that the former deals with changes over time while the latter deals with men, machines and money (strategic resources) and schedules of events which will cause the desired change.

In the strategy development subelement, three to five alternative strategies are defined for each objective. Each alternative is described in adequate detail so that a comparison and a selection can be made. The effectiveness of developing alternative strategies is an important element in successful plans. An organization that has a well-developed philosophy of long range planning also has the kind of thinking climate where new ideas can be voiced and evaluated along with traditional solutions.

A long range dp plan that proposes the "one best solution" to planning issues and ignores other alternatives is frequently doomed to failure.

The strategy selection process may vary from organization to organization. It may be entirely internal to the dp department, or it may require approval of more senior management or a steering committee. The rigor of the selection process will vary also. Some dp organizations will do little more than a feature comparison between strategy alternatives, while others will perform investment analysis, risk analysis or other more quantitative types of analysis to support the selection of the most desirable strategy alternative.

At the end of this element of activity there will be three to ten objectives, each paired with the selected strategy. There is still one question to consider: What impact will these strategies have on the dp department and budget when they are combined?

This process is almost mechanical. For each planning year, the events described in the strategies must be combined into a Master Event Schedule and the resource requirements defined in the strategies must be combined with the unaffected resources to create a Master Resource Budget. The unaffected resources are those people, budget factors and hardware which were forecast as necessary for normal activities, but which are not involved in the changes required to meet plan objectives. Thus the merging of resources for change and resources for ongoing activities creates a pro-forma budget extending from the current budget year through the duration of the plan.

ADDITIONAL ANALYSIS

Starting with these two documents, the Master Event Schedule and the Master Resource Budget, additional analysis can be done. Problems with the schedule of events, problems with the resources required on a year-by-year basis can now be evaluated. Some changes will result. In some cases, strategies or strategy elements will be combined.

In some situations, problems will be so serious that premises or objectives will have to be reviewed. Thus, it is necessary for some provision to be made in the planning structure for iteration. This element is called feasibility testing.

The feasibility test element in the planning structure doesn't really represent a separate step in the process; rather, it points out the kind of checks which must be made during the strategy and strategic plan elements to assure that the plan is developing in a practical (i.e., feasible) manner. The feasibility tests ask very fundamental questions:

- Will the proposed plan achieve the dp department's objectives in a cost-effective way (economic feasibility)?
- Can the dp department actually accomplish the events scheduled in the long range plan and will the benefits projected actually be realized (organizational feasibility)?
- Can the dp department effectively install and apply the technology proposed by the long range plan (technological feasibility)?

When these feasibility questions are applied to each strategy alternative, a negative conclusion could lead to a change in objective criteria, or more study (a premises activity). When applied to the consolidated plan, a negative conclusion could lead to rejection of an individual strategy alternative because it doesn't fit with other choices. It could lead to consolidation of events from several strategies to form a more manageable plan.

BIG ENOUGH BUDGET?

Once the plan has been finalized, the first real test of its workability is whether the first year is budgeted. The best-laid plans are worthless if resources are not available to implement the events on schedule.

Some long range planners do not feel that a direct link between long term objectives and the annual budget is necessary. But how can all the work put into

Pitfalls of DP Planning

The first pitfall in long range planning is the dp manager's assumption that he can delegate the planning function to his staff. The problem is that planning is a management function: it must complement the leadership and control functions of management. There are many tasks which a staff may perform, but the basic issues, objectives and strategies are the manager's responsibilities.

Second, a long range plan may fail because the top dp executive becomes so engrossed in current problems that he spends insufficient time on long range planning, and the process loses credibility in the eyes of other managers and staff. This problem is the natural outgrowth of the successful manager's experience in dealing with current problems. Mature managers recognize that long range planning is a major means of avoiding the day-to-day problems which plague the "unorganized" manager. A long range plan frees the manager to solve major new issues while subordinates handle the majority of the current problems within the framework provided by the current plan.

Third among major pitfalls is the failure to develop department goals that are suitable as a basis for a plan. Typically, the plan is aimed at implementing the newest computer technology rather than at the more fundamental need of providing cost-effective service to the parent organization. There are several aspects to this problem.

Usually, the attempt to develop a plan starts with a goal or objective-setting exercise. Actually there is a significant amount of preplanning which should be completed first. The planner should review the needs of the parent organization and major users to develop an understanding of potential opportunities and threats involved in using dp systems. If possible, the long range plan of the parent organization should be examined for indications of required or desirable changes in dp service. In addition to reviewing the user environment, the planner must review present dp operations to isolate its strengths and weaknesses. This inner look is vital to assure that no weakness is fatal and that the long range plan is built on the department's strengths.

This preplanning effort is referred to as developing planning premises. Planning premises are not complete without a technological forecast, but the purpose of the plan should be to improve the dp department's service to the parent organization, not pioneer the use of new technology.

Once the planning premises are agreed upon, the task of setting objectives can begin. Problems result because the objectives are stated in very broad, vague ways and are excessively optimistic. These two faults cause the plan to be imprecise and usually unachievable. With such a start, it is no wonder that many plans fail.

The fourth pitfall is the failure to get major line personnel involved in the planning process. While planning is a management function, involvement of subordinate managers is necessary to develop alternative strategies, to develop a congenial climate in the department and to gain commitment to the resulting plan. This does not mean that planning is a committee activity, nor does it mean that all line managers should be involved in each phase of the process. A well-defined procedure must be developed and a method must be found to make each manager understand his role.

The final pitfall is the failure to use long range plans as standards for measuring managerial performance. Since there is a tendency for managers to rely on reactive tactics, there must be real incentive to assure that adequate emphasis is placed on developing and following meaningful strategic plans.

While these pitfalls are very common, even in dp organizations which have previously developed long range plans, there are straightforward steps which can be taken to improve the effectiveness of the process in almost any organization. First, recognize the maturity of the dp organization and its management. Planning, like other functions, should evolve in natural stages, and overly ambitious steps will only cause failure and frustration.

Second, select as a planning objective the creation of a climate which is encouraging to the planning process. Each manager needs to understand the process and his role in it. This requires an active management development program. It also requires that the benefits from planning be publicized.

Finally, develop formal planning procedures and a reliable planning database to support the process.

planning be justified if no tangible results can be observed? And how can tangible results be achieved without a statement of commitment to spend resources to achieve the intermediate steps?

It is critical that variations in the plan schedule or changes in the resource level be recognized by dp management. Aggressive corrective action must be taken to remedy any variation. The essence of planning is to provide a standard against which control can be exercised. Without control, planning is an exercise in futility!

As soon as a budget is approved, the first tasks can be assigned and the plan can get under way. However, if there is no follow-up, it is likely that little of the plan will ever be completed. A measurement step is needed.

First, task performance measurements must determine whether the assigned tasks are being completed satisfactorily. If not, redirection of short term resources is necessary. This is the control function previously emphasized.

There is a second reason for measurement. All of the work in long term planning was based on the planner's judgment about trends and his estimates of dp department capability. If these premises are inaccurate, there is little likelihood that short term control activities can fill the gap. In some cases, the plan must be revised. In all cases, the knowledge gained from the attempt to achieve the plan must feed back into the next cycle of planning. Careful evaluation of achievement is crucial to long range planning. Most systematic activities are dependent on this type of feedback in order to adapt to changing conditions; long range planning is no exception. A major method for assuring objective feedback is an audit of dp performance in relation to long range and annual plans.

The major benefits which the dp manager gains from long range planning are a better relationship with top management of his organization; better communication with his users; more efficient allocation of the resources available to him over a multiyear time period; and the ability to avoid involvement in activities which waste limited resources but don't contribute to his goal.

READING 11 DISCUSSION QUESTIONS

1 Critique the practicality of the *eight-element* long-range planning process described in the article. How universally workable would such a plan be?
2 Given the constant development and changes in computer technology, how realistic is it to commit the organization to long-range plans for data processing? Is a short-run process likely to be more effective?

Reading 12

How to Avoid Pitfalls of Information Systems Development

Charles F. Axelson

Compared with other functional areas of the business—such as sales, production, finance, etc.—the computer area is a relatively new development. However, it has come into its own, complete with unique characteristics and disciplines. Yet, in many cases, the computer area has not been recognized or managed by top management as a major business function. Too often, the computer area has been thought of as a special, technically oriented area beyond the practical orbit of the chief executive's attention. This should not be the case. While development problems are to be expected in any new endeavor, the companies that have had the least problems and frustrations in setting up computer-based information systems appear to be those that have plunged right into recognizing the computer area as a major function. And this recognition comes about by having some degree of personal attention and involvement on the part of the chief executive officer, active and continuing user involvement, adequate training programs, disciplined procedures in originating and managing information, and in general, the application of modern management methods and controls to the computer area with the same concern that is commonly given to a manufacturing plant or a production operation.

To follow through on this ideal, it is usually necessary that there be a knowledgeable high-level executive between the information systems manager and the chief executive officer. Whether this person should be a financial executive, or someone else, can only be answered on a case-by-case basis in each situation. As a rule, financial executives possess the extreme disciplines required for effective information systems management. Moreover, notwithstanding the amount of time given to the systems area, they may have the best qualifications to be the most effective liaison between top management and the information systems-computer people.

Liaison and discipline are not the end of the story, though. In these days of ever-increasing security considerations, financial executives must also be intimately aware of the need for sound and tight internal controls, including, of course, those applicable to the computer area.

The special world of information systems and its emergence as a major function, then require that all levels of management, from the chief executive officer down, recognize the importance of this function and their role in making it work.

We're all familiar with the horror stories of the computer world—the

Reprinted from *Financial Executive,* April 1976, pp. 25–31. Reprinted by permission of the Financial Executives Institute, New York, N.Y. 10013. Mr. Axelson is vice-president and controller of Libby, McNeill & Libby.

computer application that wasn't ready when it was supposed to be, the one that didn't come up with the right information that had been expected, another that released wrong information outside of the company and infuriated customers, and so on. Oftentimes, these situations involve substantial costs, loss of company goodwill and loss of confidence on the part of management in the ability of the systems-computer people to do the job that is expected of them. Invariably, a review of these situations reveals that the users were not sufficiently involved—on an hour-by-hour and day-by-day basis—in the planning and development of the computer application. The result was that they had insufficient knowledge and appreciation of precisely what it takes to tell a computer exactly what to do—in a manner that leaves no doubt and provides for every conceivable exception or contingency that could possibly arise. In a manual (noncomputer) information system, the unusual occurrence can be recognized by the human mind and handled as the individual sees fit; in the computer-based information system the computer can't even recognize the unusual occurrence unless a human has thought of it ahead of time and told the computer accordingly. Then the computer, after having been told (programmed) to recognize the unusual situation, doesn't know what to do with it unless it again has been told. The endless array of possible exceptions to any procedure, recognizing the possibility of their arising and making provisions, therefore, in computer programs, has much to do with the difficulties experienced in bringing computer applications into problem-free operation. All levels of management must really understand what nontechnical disciplines, such as consideration of every conceivable exception or contingency and constant involvement of users, are required to make an information system work. Only then can it function on an optimum basis. To accomplish this, there is ordinarily no need for general management to be involved in the technical aspects. This can be left to the experts. However, an appreciation of the nontechnical disciplines and a recognition of information systems as a major unique function which must be handled as such is vital to the success of any computer-based information system.

THE PITFALLS

Now what are the major individual, or separate, pitfalls in the development of information systems? More importantly, what can be done about them? The Management Information Systems Committee of the Financial Executives Institute recognized them as follows:

1 Late Completion Dates These may be due to a variety of causes, including incomplete specifications, unplanned interferences from other projects, lack of sufficient user involvement, employee turnover, level of employee competence, etc. It is unrealistic to set a firm completing date far in advance, for in most companies there are too many unforeseen interferences beyond the control of the systems-computer people. Rather, target dates should be set and then changed as necessary with the full consent and appreciation by top management of the factors that have necessitated the change.

2 Temptation to Proceed Too Fast This is a trait of American business people which is probably rooted in the competitive environment in which we live. This must be contained and obviously requires patience. Proceeding at a pace compatible with available resources and reasonable objectives calls for the sound exercise of human judgment. Proceeding too fast is fraught with hidden costs and further delays. On the other hand, proceeding too slowly may cause further loss of credibility. There is an optimum pace for the development of computer applications which is approximately right for each situation, and there's a right time to place a new computer application into operational status. Accelerating what is right can involve exposure to sloppy programs, incomplete documentation, incomplete procedures and other risks that will only make matters worse and more costly.

3 Temptation to Be First There's always an urge to be first with a new gadget or, in the computer world, a new piece of hardware, a new way of doing things, a new application. Here again the word is patience. If you're not a thorough professional running a clean shop, it's usually better to wait and see what others do before taking the plunge.

4 Higher Development Costs Than Anticipated Before being surprised by these, the company must ask itself whether it did a thorough professional job of realistically determining exactly what it would take to bring a particular application into operation and whether the company is measuring the particular cost correctly. All too often, costs exceed a plan because the plan itself wasn't realistic and costs applicable to other projects which have interfered have not been properly allocated to those projects. Escalation of original requirements, which increases costs, may result because the user and the systems people didn't plan properly and thoroughly enough at the study and preliminary design phase. Furthermore, poor planning may result in overlapping and redundant systems which unnecessarily increase both development and operating costs and eventually require that the overlaps be removed—all at a significant cost.

5 Higher Operating Costs Than Anticipated Always remember that once a computer application has been brought into being, it takes a certain amount of attention and hardware capacity to keep the application going. Program changes will undoubtedly arise, due to the changing needs of the business, the more sophisticated desires of the user or the operating requirements and opportunities for improvement within the systems-computer group. All of this costs money and should be planned accordingly.

6 Need for Expensive Machinery Computer manufacturers or internal staff may get carried away with what they think is needed. Management must insist that all alternatives be thoroughly explored and that the right equipment be secured at the right cost. Some excess capacity may be desirable to provide for expanding needs of the business and new applications. These decisions are not easy and may take a lot of time but they cannot be avoided.

7 Interference from Unplanned Projects It is unrealistic to expect that any active business will not have new situations or changed conditions which will interfere with previously planned prospects. This is a fact of business life, and thus management must either staff in excess of minimum requirements in order to respond to unplanned projects or accept the fact that existing projects are going to be delayed when higher-priority ones come along. Care must be taken, however, that personality-dominated projects do not attain importance and priority beyond their value.

8 Problems Arising from Operating Systems Provided by Computer Manufacturers These are sometimes tough to anticipate in advance, particularly if one is involved in a new or unique application. Caution again is called for: Don't be first if it isn't necessary. Manufacturers tend to work the bugs out of their basic operating systems before they are released. The problems are more apt to come from the vendor-supplied unproven software for specialized applications, and in particular the attempts of company computer people to modify software to accomplish things that were never intended by the manufacturer. There's a considerable difference between various manufacturers, however, in the ability to furnish and sustain as error-free systems as possible.

9 Unproductive Systems-Computer Staff This can be the result of poor internal organization, lack of training, high turnover, unrealistically low salaries, incompetent employees, poor management attitudes or any of one or more of various other reasons that apply to an unproductive segment of any business. And like any segment of the business that is experiencing personnel problems, the root causes must be examined carefully and appropriate corrective measures taken. Personnel with experience in the information systems areas should be transferred or promoted to user departments, and vice versa, whenever possible. The cross fertilization of ideas and the ability to better monitor developments is invariably beneficial to both parties. Judicious reduction of staff can often improve productivity and actually produce more on a lesser budget, but this calls for extreme disciplines in reducing the temptation to add staff just to accelerate the completion of computer applications. There is an optimum size staff for any organization that can get the job done with optimum productivity provided that top management will be reasonably patient and recognize that accelerated activities to get projects done earlier are not always wise expenditures of funds. It must be remembered, however, that the information systems area is a unique microcosm of most corporate functions and oftentimes such necessary disciplines as engineering, production and quality control considerations tend to get overlooked as they apply to the information systems function.

THE TEN COMMANDMENTS

While there are various means, as indicated, of avoiding or ameliorating the individual-case pitfalls, the real solutions of avoiding them in the aggregate lie in recognizing information systems as a major function and acting accordingly. These steps might be regarded as the ten commandments:

1 Heavy User Involvement User involvement means the assignment of one or more competent and knowledgeable people from the user department to work with the information systems group throughout the planning, development and implementation of the computer application. There is no getting away from the fact that this is a necessary ingredient for the success of any computer-based application. The heavier the user involvement, the more likelihood of early success with a computer application. It means pinpointed responsibility every step of the way with written requests and approvals at various stages, signed personally by the company officer responsible for the user function. It means endless meetings with systems personnel, a thorough recognition of exactly what is wanted as early in the game as possible and a constant awareness of all the contingencies and exceptions that, if not properly anticipated and programmed, may cause costly delays in bringing the application into full operational status.

2 Executive Steering Committee The chief executive officer, the officer in charge of the principal user functions involved with information systems, the head of the information systems-computer department and executives between that person and the CEO is the ideal—and vital—executive steering committee. This committee determines priorities, monitors progress on a periodic basis and considers the relative merits of various proposed applications. The frequency of their meetings would depend upon all considerations pertinent to a particular company, but they should meet at least quarterly.

3 Involvement of Chief Executive Officer Like any other major function of the business, the chief executive officer must devote a certain amount of time to the information systems area. If the area is completely foreign to the CEO a disproportionate amount of time may have to be devoted to it for a while. It is unrealistic to expect that the chief executive officer will be concerned with day-to-day activities. However, involvement in the periodic meetings of the executive steering committee (perhaps as chairman), in the budget for the activity (which would include major decisions to expand, contract and rearrange the activity) and in such major decisions as buying versus leasing, converting from one computer manufacturer to another, etc., should be a part of the CEO's activities.

4 Education and Training The need for constant training at all levels in the fast-changing environment of information systems must be recognized and handled. At upper management levels, this may mean an occasional presentation from the outside, a meeting of the executive steering committee largely devoted to this purpose, some reading, perhaps a short course within or without the company—but nothing too technical. Some companies see that their executives are familiar with detailed programming techniques. There is nothing wrong with this if the purpose is for the executive to gain an appreciation of exactly how involved it all is. But ordinarily it should stop there. It is not the role of the executive to necessarily learn the tools of the trade, which the technicians must possess. Below the executive level, there should be frequent training programs for systems analysts, programmers, machine operators and all others associated with the information system to keep abreast of developments and recognize new opportunities as they come along. Computer manufacturers provide courses that can be quite useful, and some colleges and universities offer such courses. In general, however, universities do not do enough in teaching the things that can be done with computers to aid in operation or management—they are more apt to be concerned with what the hardware and systems are all about rather than the concept of applying sound management principles to the information systems area.

5 Internal Organizational Arrangements within the Information Systems Department To successfully carry out an information systems program, constant attention must be paid to the best form of internal organization. Systems and programming teams are probably best organized along functional lines so that individuals gain expertise in the given functional area. The actual operation of the hardware is normally kept separate from the systems group, and sufficient provision for the administrative function (depending on the size of the installation) should be made to plan and coordinate the entire information systems function. The need for data control, a data librarian, physical security, internal control, backup facilities and disaster plan (including off-site storage of vital records and information) must be provided.

6 Administration of the Information Systems Function Planning for proper information management, apart from organizational considerations, includes adequate records and documentation in all areas. There must be properly designed forms for users to request preliminary proposals, feasibility studies, final application proposals and the acceptance of the final completed job. The users must give written approval that the feasibility study has been completed to their satisfaction, that the system specifications and design are adequate, that the testing has been sufficiently complete and that the final application has reached operational status. A post-completion audit review to see whether or not the objectives have been achieved should be made. The systems manager must approve every user request and sign-off approval, in

Steps in Systems Planning and Implementation

		Approvals required
1	Problem definition phase	User, systems manager
2	Preliminary survey phase	User officer, systems manager
3	Study and preliminary design phase	User, systems manager, executive steering committee
4	Design phase	User officer, systems manager
5	Detail business system design phase	User, systems manager
6	Detail computer system design phase	Systems manager
7	Programming specification phase	Systems manager or delegate
8	Programming phase	Systems manager or delegate
9	Programming test phase	Systems manager or delegate
10	System test phase	User, systems manager
11	Installation phase	User, systems manager
12	Post-completion audit phase	Executive steering committee

addition to approving the completion of the detail design, programming specification, programming completion and programming test phases. (See the table on the principal stages and user-systems involvement in the development of a computer application.) Daily reports of computer operations are a must, as is adequate documentation of all computer programs. While in smaller installations the more formal records may not be required, it must be recognized that when they do not exist, the information systems manager still cannot escape the responsibility to watch every facet of operations. Formal written requests and sign-offs from users should always be insisted upon.

7 Flexible Schedules The attitude towards schedules for the development of computer applications should be as flexible as possible. Estimated completion dates should be recognized as target dates and not as absolute commitment dates come what may. Software programs are available that can be of great assistance in forward planning of projects under development, after the estimated man-hours required have been associated with planned work-weeks, normal delays and interferences, vacations, level of competences, etc.

8 Cost-Benefit Considerations This is a debatable subject, but one that cannot be overlooked. Certainly, projects that represent mechanization of clerical activities should pay their own way. On the other hand, projects which furnish necessary information on which to run the business may be necessary regardless of cost—within reasonable bounds, of course. To try and determine a theoretical economic benefit may be more trouble than it's worth, and perhaps not too accurate anyway. There have been many projects that have never gotten off the ground because they appeared to be too costly, and yet the business will never know what it lost by not having the information available. Deciding whether or not to proceed with gathering new information, recognizing the probable estimated cost involved but not attempting to numerically measure the benefits should be a decision of the executive steering committee.

9 Cost Accounting in the Information Systems Area Considering the funds expended in a computer application, most companies should probably do more in developing cost accounting systems associated with information system activities. A company may have a fairly sophisticated cost for a relatively small production operation and have no system at all for a computer operation that is much larger. Oftentimes the basic data (man-hours of employees, overhead costs and equipment costs) are available and project costs can be accumulated fairly easily without a formal, sophisticated cost accounting system. For example, man-hours by projects can be extended by appropriate average rates which will indicate salary costs and employee benefits for each project. Whether the cost of an information system department should be allocated to users is a debatable subject. Many systems projects are interrelated with others in such a way that a number of users benefit and any single user accountability is impractical. Furthermore, some users balk at being accountable for heavy systems expense, and consequently deny themselves information which is vital to the operation of the business. Admittedly, this can be shortsighted, but an executive steering committee with a chief executive officer involved can often do a better job than an individual user in determining whether a particular project is worthwhile. It is usually desirable to inform the applicable users of the development and operating costs of a particular project with which they are involved, even though it is not formally charged to their budget.

10 The Tenth Commandment: Put the First Nine into Practice The last general step to avoiding pitfalls may be regarded as the Tenth Commandment, for if any one or more of the first nine are not put into practice the company is headed for trouble. Information systems are never problem-free, but the problems can be materially reduced if the nine previously indicated commandments are observed. A company may be cognizant of all nine but if it fails on any one, it only has itself to blame when things go wrong.

The pitfalls and suggestions enumerated here are nothing new to those with management experience in the information systems function. They apply equally to the large and the small company, although in the smaller company many of them will be combined. In each company, they will be approached differently. The M–I–S Committee of the Financial Executives Institute does believe, however, that following the principles outlined here will do much to reduce the mystique and problems associated with this developing major function of the business.

READING 12 DISCUSSION QUESTIONS

1 "Most executives associated with computer operations have experienced varying degrees of frustration in the development and implementation of the information

needs of their businesses. Indeed, it has been the computer area which has produced the largest problems for the executive." Discuss this statement.

2 Given the substantial budgets that are frequently allocated to data processing departments, why do there appear to be so many problems with computer usage? Is this the case, or are the problems exaggerated?

Reading 13

The Primacy of the User (Part 2)

William Ainsworth

Traditionally, data processing personnel have looked upon the implementation of a data processing system as being their responsibility. This has proven to be a shortsighted view of the situation, as it has tended to look only at technical and schedule responsibility. As the cost of installing a system has skyrocketed and its implications to the company have expanded, the DP operation has come to be involved with the overall profit responsibility of the company. Data processing personnel have to become aware of the profit responsibility of the user groups and what related performance goals this profit requires of these groups. In the past we have felt that cost justification of a system based upon personnel reduction or increased inventory turnover was sufficient for getting a go-ahead for the installation of a system. Lately, however, the broader implications of "bottom line management" has become predominant. This theory is based upon profit and results and considers the short-term effects on profit, even though the long-term effect is lowered cost. The DP personnel must now know and understand the profit motivation which is the user's responsibility. They must be able to put the systems project into this perspective and be prepared to discuss the impact of the project upon the profit picture of the company. It is not sufficient any longer to say that what is cost-justified on a long-range basis is profit-justified at this time. A user who is becoming increasingly aware of his department's profit responsibility to the company is becoming increasingly reluctant to invest in a system development effort.

If we accept that the prime responsibility today has become the maintenance of the bottom line of the profit and loss statement and that this responsibility rests with the user group, then we can perhaps accept the following areas of systems and decision responsibility prior to the decision to implement a system.

1 The goals which the system is to achieve must be those of the user, must be firmly stated and must be acknowledged in the system concept being proposed.

Reprinted from *Infosystems,* May 1977, pp. 50–54. Reprinted by permission from Hitchcock Publishing Company, Wheaton, Ill. 60187. Copyright © 1977, Hitchcock Publishing Company. Mr. Ainsworth is a principal at Peat, Marwick, Mitchell & Co. Part 1 of this article was presented in Reading 4 of this text.

2 The final approval decision must remain with the user and must be based upon his assessment of the cost and justification of the system and its impact on the company.

3 The user and the DP department should jointly develop and present all costs and schedule estimates upon which the project is based.

4 The approval of schedules should be the prerogative of the user. As we shall discuss later, this area may very well be the key to a successful implementation.

5 The DP department is responsible for providing the user with a technical analysis which he can understand thoroughly and with which he concurs.

6 The DP department is responsible for the choice of adequate personnel to meet the jointly agreed-upon schedule and for the design of a system which most effectively utilizes available hardware and software.

If the above rules are followed, system development should at least start out with a firm purpose, set goals, a believable schedule and a reasonable amount of harmony. Far too often, though, this harmony is superficial because of a lack of complete understanding. This lack of understanding may develop into an ever-widening gap as development proceeds unless each group's role and level of involvement is developed and maintained throughout the project.

In looking at the roles which have been established for computer system development in the past, we find that the DP personnel have assumed the dominant position in development. DP has pushed the system, forced decision and made installation go according to its schedule. The stated rationale for this has been, "If we didn't do it, nothing would ever get done." I cannot quibble with this, because, by and large, it was true then and is true today. What I suggest is that the thinking on this point be reversed and that DP personnal say, "If they don't do it, we won't." This is not an easy point to accept, but DP personnel must not only recognize the primacy of the user; they must encourage it and demand that he assert it. In order to do this, they will have to insist that the projects be so structured that the director always comes from a user group. The concept of user primacy says that, on any given project, the data processing personnel ultimately report directly to the user and are responsible to him for the conduct of the project. I will admit that this is contrary to all established practice and would appear to downgrade the data processing area. Such a drastic step is necessary in order to place responsibility where it belongs and to rescue data processing from the lowered prestige which technically sound but functionally ineffective systems have given to it.

Let's assume for a moment that you accept the concept of user primacy and that we have a project organized with a user director. The next step, before any final estimates and schedules are presented, is to work with the director to see that there will be a proper assessment of the need for involement on all levels

No matter what the system, there is a need for involvement on the corporate officer level, so we must always assume and insist on the involvement of officers. The exact type of middle management involvement and, where possible, the individuals concerned, should be discussed between the project director and the DP personnel. One of the most effective ways to determine just what middle management improvement is needed is for the DP personnel to attend departmental operating meetings. By attending these meetings, the DP personnel may be able to define operating problems caused by a lack of proper information. After discussion with the project director, they can then approach the man concerned with a suggestion of where he lacks information and how a new system might help. In this way one can gain the assistance of a man who might otherwise not realize he should be involved. He might not even have known he has a problem amenable to system solution, and in pointing it out to him, one may gain support as well as involvement. The involvement of this middle management group is the most difficult to cope with, the most ignored and also the most important of all areas. If DP personnel can get middle management interested and involved and, most importantly sustain that involvement during the duration of the project, the chances of success are increased many times.

Perhaps the most important area in the generating and sustaining of user interest lies in the scheduling of the project. This schedule of development is usually presented to the user by the DP group and is based upon their ability to develop the new system. This basing of schedules and commitments on the resources of the DP group is perhaps the single greatest mistake made today. The DP department can develop and implement a system in far less time than the user can adjust to the system. Thus a DP project schedule typically neglects three major aspects of the system development process:

1 The rate at which the user can participate in the development
2 The rate at which the user can absorb and utilize new systems
3 The balance of manpower availability between user and data processing

We should examine each of these areas in some detail and see how they affect system projects. We can also use this discussion to find out how we can incorporate these considerations into improved project schedules.

The rate at which the user can participate in the development is a function of that amount of time necessary for the user to completely control the project and contribute actively to what the system does, spread out according to his time available to work on the project. It is not the time necessary to sit down with DP and "rubber stamp" DP-proposed documents and procedures. User review presentations are insufficient vehicles for the user to control system design. One of the first things suggested to be done in starting a project is to determine level by level just who should participate in the project. When constructing the development schedule, the user analyzes how much each person should spend on the project. He then determines how much and what type of training is necessary to enable that person to have an effective voice in the project. He then schedules that person's input according to his available time. After doing this for each person, a master schedule of user commitment is drawn up. The DP schedules are then either drawn up or adjusted according to user availability.

This then becomes the design schedule for the project. It is obvious that, since the user can devote only part of his time to the project, the result is typically an extension of DP schedules. The way in which DP can cope with this is either to use less people or have several projects going at once. With this approach, we gain the user commitment to supply personnel and accept his responsibility, plus a realistic achievable schedule. It is the responsibility of the project director and the DP department to see that the required level of input is met. Under no condition should DP proceed with development in an area where the required user participation is not available.

If the user is kept constantly involved, the system should be well defined by the end of the development phase and should change little from that point. There may now be a long period of programming and debugging in which DP can operate without extensive user participation. Prior to starting programming, however, consideration must be given to the rate at which the user can utilize the new system. It is no good to write and test a system and then have it sit on the shelf because the user does not have the ability to install it. Remember, to the user the development of a new system is incidental to his main job of running the plant. Therefore, we must go back to him to develop an implementation schedule. Consideration should be given to early implementation of smaller pieces of the system to provide quick payback and less disruption. The schedule must include time for him to develop procedures for handling data, organizational changes, new job descriptions and many other things peripheral to the computer system itself. These must be done by the user and they must be done before implementation. If these are not done, no matter how good the programming is, that system will fail. Therefore, we must follow the same procedure with the implementation phase as we did with the development phase. The project director must identify what needs to be done, who should do it, and schedule the effort according to the availability of personnel. The DP schedule must then be adjusted to conform to the user availability schedule. The result will once again be a lengthening of the time to install the system. It is nonetheless better to have a good system in later than a poor system in early. The user primacy fact is proven by the number of inadequate systems installed today in which development proceeded rapidly but without complete user control.

Another point which is overlooked in the setting of schedules and which has a strong psychological effect is the fact that no one has an unlimited attention span. We all tend to get bored. In the development of complex systems, we invariably have a long-range plan (usually years) and a still longer time before payoff. Thus, there is very little psychological satisfaction or the feeling of a job well done associated with this type of system.

One of the most important and effective methods of assuming the maintenance of user involvement is the manner in which interface is conducted. Interface is a rather bad word used to describe how information is transmitted between groups. Its unfortunate connotation is that of a hard and formal method of meetings and presentations. Usually, large numbers of people are involved, and regular "progress meetings" are held. Little or no information is transmitted at a progress meeting. The progress meeting is an artificial situation at which political problems are discussed, but at which significant development considerations are not really handled.

The best way to handle development interface is on a man-to-man basis and by attendance at operational meetings. Of these, the man-to-man interface usually produces the most results. I have deliberately avoided touching on the formal education in DP of the users. My own belief is that if we establish a sufficient level of man-to-man communication. formal training is unnecessary. The idea of educating the user is also very condescending to him, as the DP man has just as much or more to learn.

If a relationship can be established with every user such that he knows that the system is going to help him and, above all, that he will influence the system design, formal education in DP is unnecessary. The mere fact of communication will educate both parties. Some ways this can be done are:

1 Let him discuss in detail what his job is.
2 Avoid the use of system terms and "computerese."
3 Do not try to rush him.
4 Encourage him to discuss where he has problems with his own management, not with his job.
5 Do not lead him to believe that the system will solve all his problems.
6 Try to let the ideas come from him. Let him have the credit.
7 Try to suggest some simple thing he can do which will improve his job. Let him gain some confidence in you.

DP has a long way to go to overcome the aggressive and overbearing attitudes of the past. They may have to be a little more humble in the future in their interactions with user groups.

A major forum for interaction which is almost totally overlooked is the regular attendance of concerned DP people at user department meetings and vice versa. It is not necessary that the visiting people contribute to these meetings, but that they observe and note what is taking place. A tremendous amount of actual (vs. theoretical) knowledge of the operations can be gained in this way. One of the major problems in a DP designed system is that it too often copes with how the business should work and not how it does work. The only way to find out how it does work is through regular attendance at user meetings. The information gained can then be discussed and observations enlarged through normal interaction with individuals of the user group.

Another interaction worthy of mention is the assignment of liaison personnel. DP often asks for a man to be assigned from a user group to work with them and to act as a go-between. This is the wrong way to go about liaison. DP is a single group trying to do several functions, while users are many groups, each with one function (i.e., production scheduling, material control, etc.) The correct way to get liaison is to have the DP department assign one person to the user departments. This eliminates the major problem of having someone from one user group trying to interpret and convey the requirements of other groups. The liaison man can be used to coordinate the information between the groups but cannot be used as a source of information. In this way the coordination function is accomplished, and the passing of erroneous interpretation of requirements is minimized.

Another aspect of the installation of a successful computerized system and the sustaining of user involvement is the recognition of key concepts—the numbers or needs which control the organization. This recognition and defining of key concepts should be the first step in designing a system. The investigation starts at the top of the information pyramid and works down, not vice versa. This has several advantages:

1 The investigation is uncluttered by a great deal of detail information.

2 The first contact is with management, and they are made a part of and given responsibility for what the system accomplishes.

3 By obtaining the ideas and key concepts of each level of management, you also obtain their support. The working relationship with the next level down is then much easier.

There is one pitfall to this approach which requires that DP be very careful about how they approach each user regarding control concepts. We all like to control our subordinates and measure their performance, but we do not want to be controlled ourselves. Therefore, while the concept of control numbers is originally greeted with enthusiasm, if it is pursued too hotly, a fear reaction sets in and we can be in trouble. A good balance is needed between emphasis and the arousal of fear.

In order to truly measure the success of a system, we must take into account many factors, of which the following four are perhaps the most important. Their importance may vary from installation to installation, so they should not be considered as listed in order of importance.

1 What direct costs, if any, are eliminated by the system?

2 Does the system provide accurate, timely information?

3 Does the management have better information which permits increased control?

4 Has capacity been increased so that the company can handle more business without increasing its staff?

Generally, the measurement of the success of a DP system fails to give consideration to these points, except for number 1, which is usually discussed under the initial justification. Even this is largely lost once the system is processing because by that time the system is running and, therefore, the system is successful. Once in this line of thought, DP people are placed in the position of constantly defending that system against charges that it does not satisfy the above four points. Take a look at each of the four areas and see how they contribute to success.

The idea of cost displacement and cost avoidance is the major source of defense of a system. It is often the least defensible of all the points because it is so quantifiable that it is usually accepted by opponents. However, unless it is completely overwhelming in its magnitude, it provides little shelter against other areas of system failure. It would be hard to find any manufacturing system which has achieved a significant direct cost reduction in salaries. The savings are usually to be found in increased turns and lowered inventory. The problem involved here is obtaining agreement on the benchmark level against which improvement is to be measured. If possible, these should be established and agreed to before conceptual system design gets underway. While lowered direct costs are great justification for implementing a system, they are not good for defending it after it is running. For this we need less tangible but more defensible success parameters.

Perhaps the one that can most be considered a measure of success is that the system is providing accurate and timely information in a usable fashion. If a manager can call or attend a meeting confident that he has good information for the making or defending of a decision, the system is not only justified in his mind, but he will also be a strong supporter of it. In this case, his success is a measure of the system's success. In order to achieve this, we must go back to the beginning of our design effort and must have developed this success parameter in every step of the installation.

Another factor which we tend to overlook is that cost displacement or cost avoidance affects the profit position of the company by lowering costs, but good information and resultant good decisions affect it by increased income. A company survives by income, not costs, so in all of our systems we should look to a system with a potential for increased income and not just cost efficiency.

The third area, that of increased capacity, is also income-oriented and too often neglected in measurement of success. We tend to think of this in terms of increasing capacity without increasing costs. There is nothing wrong with this, but we tend to ignore the benefits of increasing capacity even though increased costs may result. More business means more income and, I repeat, a company survives by income.

READING 13 DISCUSSION QUESTIONS

1 The author suggests that data processing departments frequently do not appear to appreciate *profit motives* in their operations. Given the *service nature* of data processing in many companies, is the profit motive a realistic objective? What would be the impact on other departments if data processing departments stressed the profit motive more?

2 "Under no condition should data processing proceed with development in an area where user participation is not available." Discuss the practicality of this statement. Can you identify areas in organizations where there may be exceptions?

Reading 14

The Systems Analyst as a Change Agent

William Feeney
Frea Sladek

Change occurs all the time in our world. People, technology, and companies change. At this moment people are being born at a rate faster than one per second. Men and women are changing their lives by getting married or divorced. Engineers and scientists are designing bombs to kill easier, vehicles to move people faster, and medical instruments to save lives more efficiently. From one day to the next, our lives and world change.

If the change happens too rapidly people can go into a state of shock. On the societal level, this is "Future Shock"; on a company level, decreased productivity results. In contrast , change which is too slow causes stagnation and boredom. Look at the great civilizations in Europe and Asia which disappeared because they became static and could no longer change or adapt. Or consider the companies forced out of business because their products were no longer in demand.

Whether change comes rapidly or slowly, people are responsible for introducing it. They are known as *change agents.* Revolutionaries, educators, consumer groups, and women's libbers act as change agents. Some have mastered contemporary change theory. Others have not. Their success depends upon their ability to understand change and customize their roles as change agents to achieve their goals.

And how about the systems analyst? His task is to plan and gain acceptance for organizational change. Yet while great care is taken to provide the analyst with technical skills for analyzing, designing, and developing new systems, rarely is much attention paid to training him to gain acceptance for organizational change.

Organizations are complex systems which have interacting parts. Each part influences all the other parts. For example, a new system in the accounting department may impact marketing and—ultimately—the company's suppliers and/or buyers. Further, organizations are made up of people, and it is with people that the change agent deals directly.

People find change difficult. Some theorists believe that extensive change is altogether impossible. Hoffer, in *The Temper of Our Time* (New York: Harper & Row, 1967), pointed out that the Jews spent 40 years in the desert primarily because the older generation could not change from being slaves to being free men. On the other hand, Toeffler, the author of *Future Shock* (New York: Random House, 1970), believes that some change is possible. When people

Reprinted with permission of *Datamation* ® magazine, © copyright by Technical Publishing Company, a division of Dun-Donnelly Publishing Corporation, a Dun & Bradstreet company, 1978—all rights reserved. The authors are associated with San Diego State University.

experience deep change, a kind of trauma sets in, but often they finally do adapt.

Then, too, people accept change at different rates. The young, for example, are more likely to accept and even introduce change. Mozart completed his first symphony at age eight, causing far-reaching changes in the world of music. Alexander the Great had conquered the civilized world by the time he was 27, forever altering national boundaries.

Too much change can cause people to become ill, or even die. For widows or widowers going through the first year without their spouse, the death rate is 10 times higher than it is for others their age. Holmes, a psychiatrist at the Univ. of Washington, has quantified personal change, ranking a list of commonly stressful events which may lead to illness. Almost 20% of these events are work-related. Sample events (and point scores assigned them) are: fired at work (47 points); retirement (45); business readjustment (39); change to different line of work (36); change in responsibilities at work (29); trouble with boss (23); and change in working hours or conditions (20). According to Holmes, if a person's total points during a year approaches 200, the person may become ill.

The successful change agent knows that people: (1) find change difficult, (2) accept it at varying rates, and (3) can become ill and ineffective because of too much change.

Because the systems analyst most often brings about change during a project, the sequence of activities followed during a systems effort is mentioned here. Fig. 1 shows in flowchart form typical tasks to be performed when putting a new software and/or hardware system into operation. (The tasks are listed as reminders of what should be done, not what absolutely has to be done, during a systems effort.)

While the systems effort is going on, the systems analyst uses his technical expertise in three major ways. These are shown by the hexagons in Fig. 1. Early in the effort he provides problem structure at a time when projects lack definition and scope. Later in the systems effort the analyst leads the project team in building the new system by choosing alternatives, designing software and procedures to perform the system tasks. Last, the analyst gets the new system running by guiding customer personnel in the use of the system.

Although the system effort is represented in Fig. 1 by neat, clearly distinct boxes, in practice there is no clear distinction between the stages. Further, in most systems efforts the activities are performed sequentially, but in some efforts they are worked on simultaneously.

How *should* a systems analyst act when he wants to change people in an organization? Should he use candy? Or a stick?

By being sensitive to his organizational setting, the systems analyst will have a better idea of the extent and force of change which will be acceptable and which will accomplish his project goals. In addition, the systems analyst has a variety of change agent roles to select from. Specifically, he may assume the role of persuader, catalyst, confronter, or imposer:

Persuader. The systems analyst attempts to persuade employees to accept

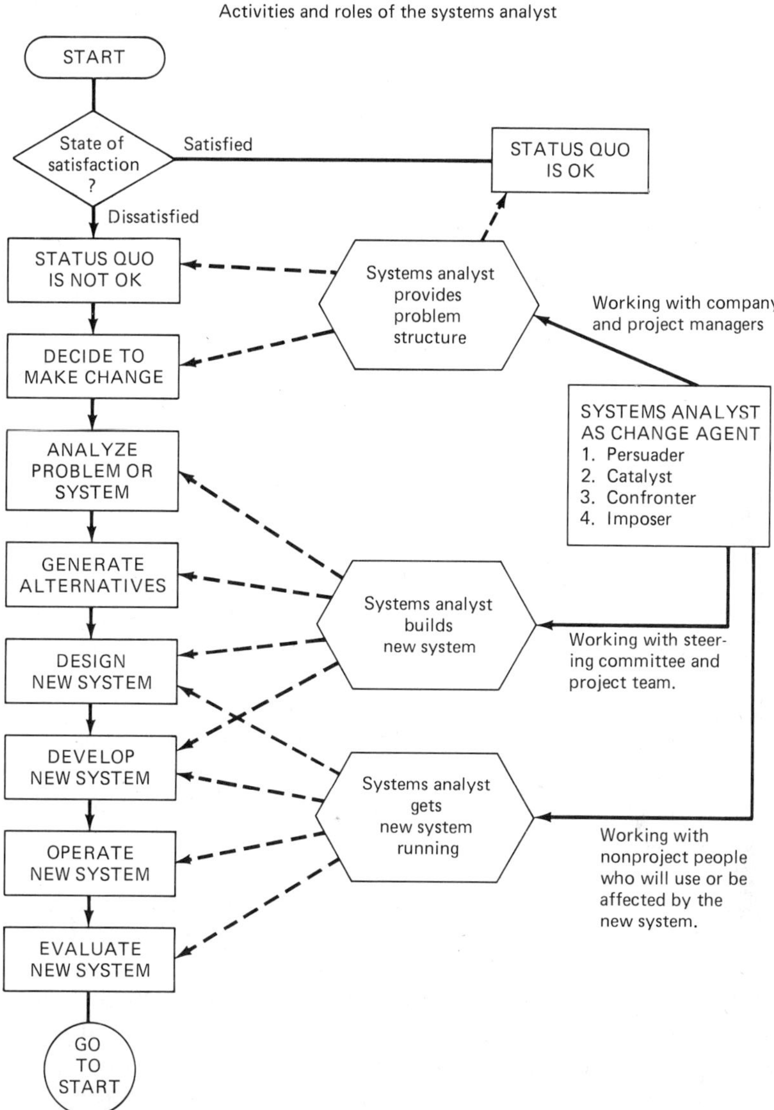

Figure 1 The systems analyst may work with many people at various stages in the development of a system, including managers, programmers, operators, and users. He may have to play a different kind of role—persuader, catalyst, confronter, or imposer—at each stage.

change dictated by the company and management. This is the mildest form of intervention for a systems analyst, merely helping people to change their attitudes and to adjust.

Catalyst. The systems analyst introduces new ideas to the change process, but lets the customer determine changes for himself. The amount of intervention is greater here than in the persuader role, but still the analyst is acting as a helper.

Confronter. The systems analyst sets himself in opposition to the customer because in the analyst's best judgment the customer will not achieve satisfactory change unless he is jolted into a completely different approach. This role frequently generates conflict and should be used with care.

Imposer. The systems analyst, with authority given by company management, imposes his plan for change on the customer. Severe ill feeling and even job reassignments are common when this role is assumed.

The nature of roles the analyst can assume as a change agent is best shown by examples. The following case histories illustrate the reasons for the choice of roles:

PERSUADER

An analyst was hired by a wholesale electrical distributor to design a computerized ordering system. The company management had received a sales briefing from a crt terminal sales team and was impressed with the capabilities of that kind of device. They wanted a time-sharing computer system using terminals.

The analyst, in conducting his own analysis, had determined that an online ordering system would indeed be best for the company. But when talking with the order clerks, the employees who would use the terminals, the analyst discovered they were uneasy about the new devices. They were concerned about typing on a keyboard connected to a computer. What if they made a mistake? Certainly the computer would catch it! Further, if the computer made the ordering task considerably more efficient, some of them would lose their jobs!

In choosing a role as a change agent the analyst could have imposed the use of the terminals on the clerks as a dictate of management. Take it or leave it! Some clerks might have done just that, leaving with a bad feeling and leaving behind them a group with a coerced feeling.

The analyst could have confronted them with their fears, pointing out how groundless these were. He could have explained that the clerks' not wanting the new system stood in the way of company growth, etc. Although the potential users might have bowed to this frontal attack, it is unlikely that they would have been won over.

The analyst could have acted as a catalyst, helping the employees to make their own decision about what they wanted. But if they hadn't come to the same conclusion as management and the analyst, the problem would have been still further from solution.

Last, the analyst could have, by patient and understanding listening, persuaded the clerks that the new system was best for all. And, in this case, he did. He arranged for the clerks to spend several hours each playing computer games on terminals similar to those they would be using. He pointed out the advantages of the new system to them, reminding them that they would be relieved from typing orders after having handwritten them, that they would not have to manually check each item ordered against a master catalog, and that instant credit information on all customers would be available.

By persuading the clerks that the new system would not embarrass them or cause them to lose their jobs, but would in fact make their jobs easier, the analyst won new allies. Even though persuading may have taken more time and effort than some of the other methods, it certainly worked to the advantage of the project in this case.

CATALYST

The chief analyst for a large savings and loan association on the West Coast heard during a lunch conversation that his firm was thinking about buying an automated portfolio selection system, instead of continuing with the manual method they had been using. The analyst made further inquiries in the trust department, and was asked in turn to help in the decision process. The new system was quite expensive. The analyst did a quick investigation of the success of the new system in firms which were using it, and compared these findings with the traditional manual portfolio selection success rates. There appeared to be no clear-cut advantage to the automated system, but several developments in selection simulation being made in three schools of business were promising better automated systems in the near future.

Because of his other commitments and because portfolio selection was new to him, the analyst did not exhaustively investigate the question. In meetings with the trust department, he chose a catalyst role, raising points which he felt were pertinent and providing structure to the conversations. In his catalyst role he did not come to the discussions with his own decision already made. Instead he came as a facilitator, to help others make a decision.

Another role the analyst could have assumed was that of confronter. He could have made a preliminary judgment about the new system, either for or against. If the trust department judgment had polarized on the opposite choice and the analyst had stuck with his choice, a confrontation would have been impossible to avoid. It is unlikely that the best interests of the company would have been served by the confronter approach. The portfolio selection process is based on subtle factors, not at all evident at a casual look. It is certainly best to let those most familiar with portfolio selection make the choice.

The analyst could have become an imposer if he had sold his decision to the trust department decision makers, and they had made the others in the trust department follow. But, given the analyst's involvement with this project, this role would have been even less appropriate.

The softer role of persuader would not have worked well either. The trust group was uncertain about what they wanted to do. They might have been persuaded to do something, but they really were the ones who should have made the decision, not the analyst, with his built-in limitations.

CONFRONTER

A company which manufactured custom engine heads and other parts for vans and four-wheel vehicles wanted to install a system to keep track of items it had sold to distributors and auto stores. Frequently the company received requests for products which it no longer had in stock. The person wanting such an item could purchase it from a retail store, if he knew where it was. One of the founders of the company, who had a large personal collection of microcomputers and various terminals, had determined that the company should acquire a minicomputer for a parts location system. He had pointed out to his two cofounders the advantages of such a system and the prestige of being able to provide a locating service to their customers. The two cofounders, not realizing the programming costs for such a system, gave their okay.

An analyst was hired to design the system. He immediately determined that such a system would not be in the best interest of the company. Further, he knew of an informal, mostly manual, system used by auto dealers for decades; it could be implemented instead of the proposed minicomputer system. Reaction time on this older system was one day for parts in the same city and two days for parts 500 miles away or less.

The analyst called a meeting to discuss the proposed system and only the one founder who wanted the minicomputer showed up. The analyst presented his views, even though he knew they would conflict with the founder's ideas. The two men talked until both realized that neither was going to change his views.

The founder asked the analyst if he would design such a system, even though the analyst had recommended against it. The analyst was convinced that the company would suffer a financial loss for at least a year if it bought the kind of system advocated and contracted the required programming. The analyst said no, he would not design a system that was not in the best interest of the company. The system was never built.

Although the company management never fully appreciated the financial burden it was spared, the founders did become more aware of realistic applications for computers. The analyst was never used again by that company. The role of confronter chosen by him had cost him future contracts with that company; but given the circumstances, he must have felt that was the only way he possibly could have changed their minds about the system.

IMPOSER

A service bureau which had enjoyed considerable success in processing savings and checking accounts for small midwestern banks was in serious decline because the banks were acquiring their own equipment. The future of the service bureau looked dim. The manager/owner of the business asked an analyst who worked for him part-time for suggestions.

The analyst made his report the following month, suggesting the bureau contact physicians, dentists, architects, and lawyers, offering to provide bookkeeping and customer billing services. The service bureau was already servicing several such professional people with custom programs, and the analyst felt that these could be revised to provide general programs for a wider population of users.

The bureau's programming staff was asked to a meeting with the manager and the analyst. It became evident that the three old-line programmer/analysts were not impressed with the suggestions for a new market, having built up the banking accounts from a few to over twenty in the heyday of the bureau. The old staff presented some general, off-the-cuff ideas about regaining the banking accounts, even though they had been requested by the manager to present some formal proposals. The manager felt a large measure of loyalty to his staff, but felt his business would go under in six months if new accounts were not brought in.

A week after the meeting, the manager assigned the analyst to work full-time to develop the professional service area. The analyst actively sought the aid of the old staff, but since they regarded him as a threat, they not only did not aid in developing the new programs, but on several occasions also caused slowdowns. The analyst took their ill-will personally and reported their obstructions to the manager. The manager in turn called in the staff and asked for an explanation.

About this time the manager's health failed and he had to place someone else in charge of the business. A computer consultant, a friend of the manager, was asked to step in. Faced with near anarchy, the consultant imposed a solution to the problem. The analyst was told to work on two of the four new areas, programs for physician and dentist billing and bookkeeping. The old staff was told to develop the programs for architects and lawyers.

Displeased with the apparent demotion, the analyst quit. A recent graduate in information systems was hired to replace him. One of the old staff resigned also and was not replaced. The two remaining programmer/analysts covered the two other applications.

The consultant could have tried other roles, but it is doubtful that a less forceful approach would have saved the company. As painful as the results of the imposer role are, it is used quite often in businesses which are in a state of flux. Employees who are to be relocated, laid off, or fired are rarely asked to participate in such decisions about their future. The boss, acting in the imposer role, performs these tasks.

SELECTING THE RIGHT ROLE

When does the systems analyst assume which role? Consider the kinds of situations he encounters. We've already talked about specific case histories. In Fig. 2 a theoretical framework of role selection strategies is presented. In general, the roles of persuader, catalyst, confronter, and imposer range from the mildest to most severe intervention. So when organizational conditions are not severe and people appear to have some tolerance for change, the persuader and catalyst roles are appropriate. On the other hand, when drastic change is required, it may be necessary to assume confronter or even imposer roles.

Over the life of a project, the analyst may take on any of the roles. No matter which role he selects, the goal is identical: to gain short- and long-term acceptance for the systems effort with a minimum of organizational agony. He can best achieve this goal by developing his awareness of change concepts, and

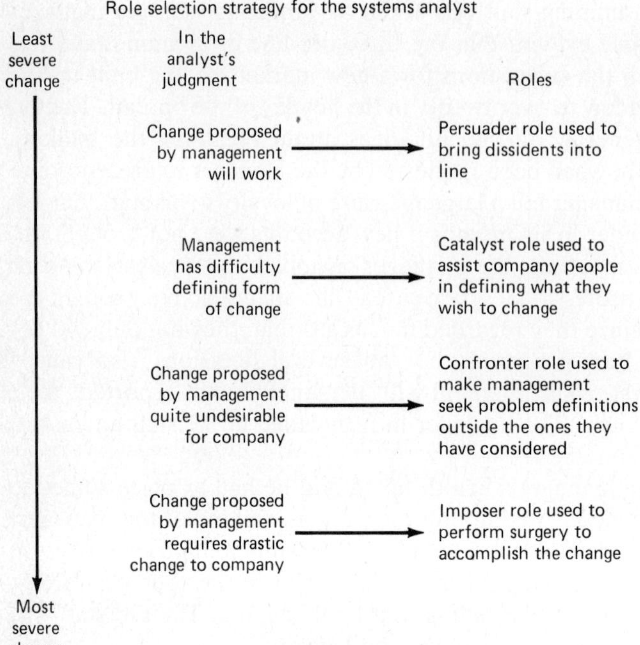

Figure 2 The severity of the change is a major factor in determining the analyst's role. Making the wrong choice may be fatal both to the project and to his career.

insightfully becoming a persuader, catalyst, confronter, or imposer as the situation demands.

READING 14 DISCUSSION QUESTIONS

1 "Revolutionaries, educators, consumer groups, and women's libbers act as change agents. So do *systems analysts.*" Is this so? Discuss whether the authors may (or may not) have overemphasized the role of the systems analyst.

2 If, as the author suggests, the systems analyst does perform a vital role as a *change agent*, what types of training should be required for this role? Are current requirements and job descriptions for *systems analysts* adequate?

Case C

The Disintegration of an Information System

Neil Milroy

Although accounting is usually regarded as having a restraining influence on wasteful practices, it is sometimes disturbing to find that a limited concept of its function in corporate life is often directly responsible for one of the most insidious causes of waste in many companies: inadequate business information.

Today's profit squeeze has prompted many business executives to seek various means to increase revenue and to cut production and administrative costs. These attempts arc normally carried on along organizational lines as each major activity is scrutinized for improvement. This "functional" approach usually fails to fully recognize the inadequacy of the information process, however, as it is seen only in segmented form.

It is surprising that many companies, while taking great pains to improve manufacturing technology and marketing effort, disregard the information process almost entirely. This is particularly serious when one considers the many corporate problems that are greatly compounded, though perhaps not uniquely caused, by the lack, inaccuracy, or excessive handling and interpretation of information. Consider for example: overinvestment in inventories; excessive overhead costs; "panic" material buying or financing; unproductive selling expenses; low labor productivity; rising clerical costs; poor communications; and prematurely obsolete equipment. The need for information to minimize the effect of these and other problems has stimulated many attempts to improve the process. Mechanized and electronic data processing techniques have been developed at a remarkable rate. Systems and methods improvements have been introduced. In many situations, however, such measures provide merely patchwork improvements on a fundamentally unsound process and the problem of information inadequacy persists.

Since the extent of the waste can mean the difference between success or failure for many companies, it would be advantageous for many to reappraise their information systems objectively to determine whether or not they are wasting hard-earned profits by neglecting the application of the accounting function in its widest sense.

To illustrate the problems of information inadequacy, their development and possible means of solution, let us consider the following case—a hypothetical one, perhaps, but only so in the aggregate and in the sequence of events. The detail occurs too often in industry to be imaginary. A company's development will be traced briefly through various stages of growth and each stage will be

Reprinted from *The Canadian Chartered Accountant,* vol. 82, no. 5, and *Management Controls,* June 1972, pp. 122–128. Reprinted by permission of *The Canadian Chartered Accountant* and Peat, Marwick, Mitchell & Co., New York. Neil Milroy is a manager in the Montreal office of Kates, Peat, Marwick & Co.

related to the information system employed to satisfy its evolving needs. Although these stages might span a period of several years, their characteristics can be seen in varying degrees and in different combinations in industries today.

ACCOUNTING MEETS ALL INTERNAL INFORMATION NEEDS (STAGE 1)

A small business enterprise made and sold its products in a comparatively captive market. The owner-manager supervised the production force directly, and sold through local merchants.

Its information system, adapted to support the company's expansion borrowing, was maintained by one bookkeeper and consisted only of basic books of account, monthly and annual financial statements (for treasury and tax purposes), and an informal system based on the owner's direct supervision and intimate knowledge of the current production marketing cycles. It was basic. Minimum manufacturing and sales information was supplied by the formal accounting system, and the need for further detail was obviated by the owner's informal information feedback.

ACCOUNTING IS EXPANDED TO MEET EXTERNAL DEMANDS (STAGE 2)

Faced with increased product demand, the company required further expansion capital. The owner-manager floated a stock issue, although continuing to run a "one man show." Since information was required by the company's new shareholders, the investing public, legislation, and external auditors, and since (at this stage) the internal requirements were few, the satisfaction of external demands received greater emphasis in the accounting system, as illustrated in Figure 1. These demands, though basic, were not easily satisfied. The company hired a qualified accountant to discharge the responsibilities created by the increased external demands.

At this stage in the company's development, financial accounting constitut-

Figure 1 Accounting meets all formal needs.

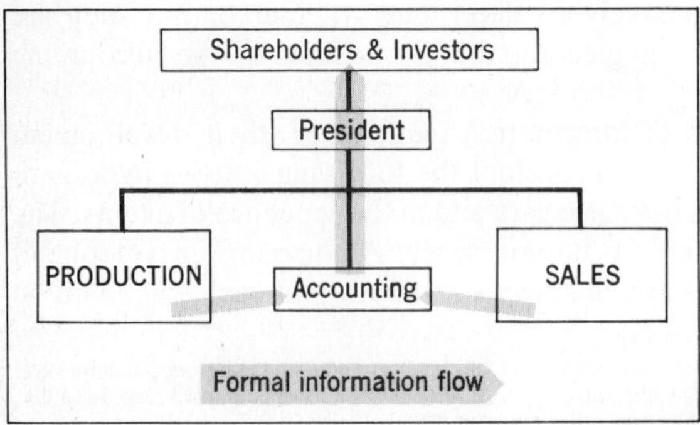

ed a corporate information system to the extent that formal data and reports were required. No matter how complex the operations, under the existing organizational and personnel circumstances, the financial accounting system was considered quite adequate by all concerned. The owner-manager-president, however, began to feel the strain of pressures imposed by his booming enterprise. He therefore delegated the responsibility for the two main functions of production and sales to two senior executives, and he himself retained control of product research and public relations.

His directives were quite specific. He charged the production vice-president with the achievement of two basic objectives: increased production efficiency and effective use of production facilities. The sales vice-president was charged with improving sales volume and improving the percentage return on sales. These overall responsibilities dictated the provision of specific information for each vice-president, without which neither the scope of their undertakings nor the channelling of effort could be defined. This information was basic, not specialized or requiring outside sources. It did require, however, detailed analysis of sales performance and costs, modification of the data-accumulating procedures and considerable clerical effort. Their information needs also included the establishment of valid standards and the subsequent comparison of actual performance against these.

The accountant's training might have suggested the adoption of a standard cost accounting system and use of high-speed data processing equipment, as well as a radical revision of the existing accounting system. However, circumstances conspired against him. A reluctance to accept standards in the valuation of inventories, the apparent high cost of data processing equipment, and the inertia of an accounting system that had proved satisfactory for years, all prevented—or at least seriously delayed—the necessary action.

The needs for information relentlessly continued. They were even desperate. The accountant was faced with mounting daily routine demands and countless technicalities raised by accounting theorists. The achievements of the system became further inadequate despite his increased efforts. Whatever the reasons, the transformation into stage 3 had now begun.

SEPARATE INFORMATION SYSTEMS CREATED TO FILL THE VACUUM (STAGE 3)

Attempts by the vice-presidents to obtain the statistics vital to the fulfillment of their duties were politely but firmly given second priority to financial requirements.

The production vice-president could not fathom why the system was unable to use his valid standards for both assessment of operating efficiencies and valuation of inventories. Finally he developed his own system to improve performance. It assigned attainable efficiency standards and measured performance against them.

The sales vice-president was forced to take a similar expedient course, creating his own sales statistics and analysis department. Even if the statistics had been produced originally, they would have contained marketing inaccuracies such as those caused by lack of indication of sales territories.

The creation of separate information systems, though not serious at this point, was rationalized by all concerned as providing essential specialized information service. It was argued that there was no duplication and that each one was designed according to particular functional needs. This information system might be illustrated as in Figure 2. Again only total production and sales information is incorporated into the official accounting system.

Despite arguments in favor of information specialization, however, it should be noted that all departments were deriving their basic historical data from the same sources and, further, that all this data was finding ultimate expression in financial statement terms.

The president began asking searching questions arising, ironically, out of the information supplied by the separate systems: Which products are yielding highest returns? Why are we still in that unprofitable market? Why is our gross profit down despite increased sales? Why are our profits down in spite of supposedly lower unit production costs? The answers could not be readily supplied. No single information system was equipped to do so. The systems were incomplete and contained arbitrary allocations of overhead costs that clouded the pertinent information required to provide answers to specific questions.

While modern accounting techniques using a marginal or direct costing approach could have readily provided greater insight into the nature and behavior of costs, such improvements had not been made due to many technicalities of an accounting nature. The accounting system, though accurately reporting results for financial purposes, fell more and more into operating disuse. More detailed and time consuming analyses were developed by all

Figure 2 Separate systems fill information vacuum.

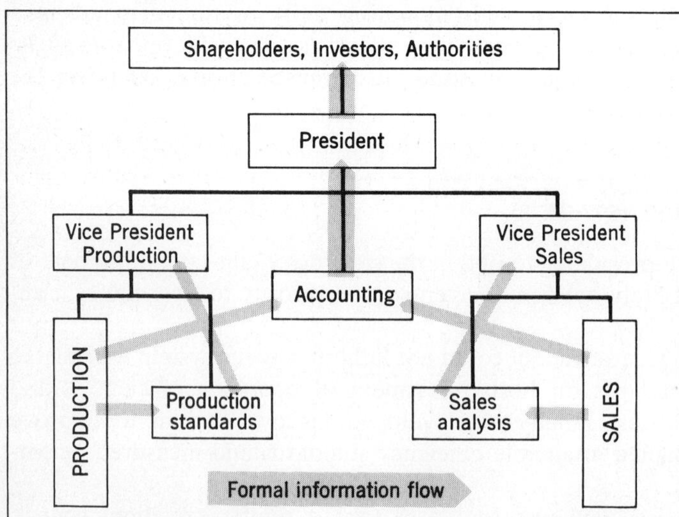

information systems to provide answers to the president's questions. As this process continued, the metamorphosis into stage 4 was accelerated.

DUPLICATION AND CONFUSION RESULT IN DISINTEGRATION (STAGE 4)

In this atmosphere of narrow information systems (which were, in effect, designed to satisfy specific requirements to the exclusion of others), the disintegration process became serious because the company experienced the following wastes, over and above the increase in clerical costs:

- Duplication in information coverage as each system used and interpreted the same data to suit its own needs.
- Breakdown in corporate communications as fundamentally identical information was distorted by different interpretations.
- Executive and management confusion as the decision-making process was complicated by the need to evaluate conflicting information supplied by different sources.
- Waste of specialized talents as some (whose aim in corporate life is the development, manufacture, or sale of products) were dissipating these skills by the need to administer what amounted to accounting routines.
- Inefficient data processing as no one system was large enough to justify the best equipment.

These costly results of the inefficient information system were overlooked while the various functions expanded to provide for their evolving information needs. The production division, requiring more accurate estimates of sales demands, organized a planning department over and above its standards and scheduling or "control" departments. The sales division, charged with the responsibility of moving the inventories, organized an inventory control section. And since the division was also responsible for improving the return on sales, a product control department was organized to support selective selling decisions with detailed product-cost studies.

Disintegration of the information system (illustrated in Figure 3) had, of course, been developing for some time, but it became a confirmed reality when the president never accepted information without a nagging doubt.

The president then made, in effect, a belated attempt to salvage what was left of the information system. He authorized the appointment of an analyst in the accounting department whose primary function was to restore some order to the information chaos. Our analyst, however, became another member of the accounting department which, under the circumstances, was of little help to either production or sales vice-presidents. The financial accounting system merely became more refined and the degree of "accuracy" increased but still within the same framework.

The production vice-president still maintained his own standards. Admittedly they were not accurate, as variances always existed, but how much more

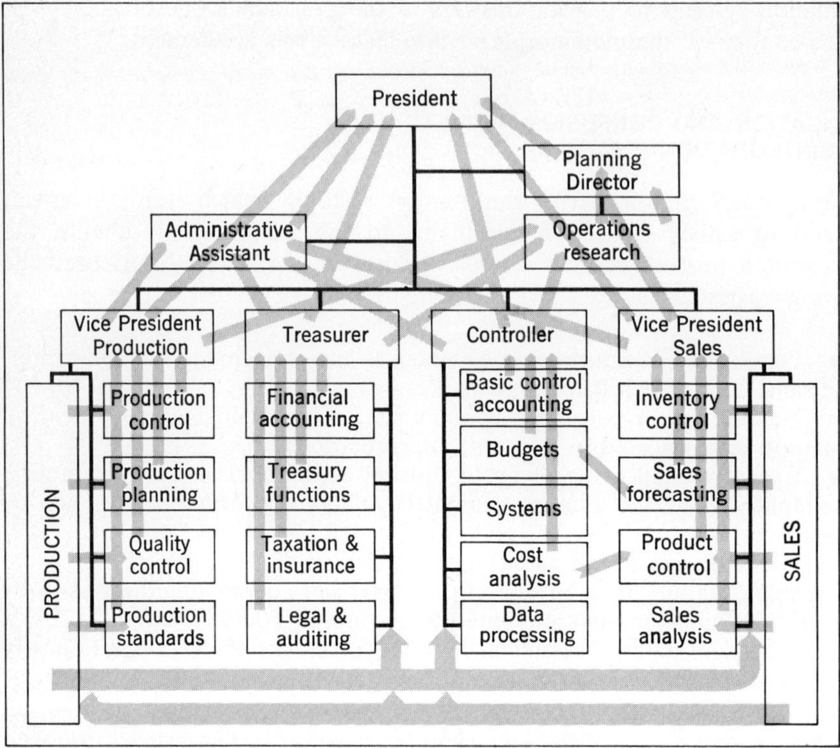

Figure 3 Duplication and confusion of conflicting information.

accurate were the "actual" costs which contained prorations, allocations, deferments, accruals and other adjustments? The sales vice-president continued to rearrange figures (instead of developing new business) because he had to prove to the president that market "X" was providing some return in spite of indications to the contrary by the company's absorption costing system.

Again the president tried. A controller was hired and the accountant was made treasurer to handle the task of providing shareholders and income tax authorities with "consistent" accounts. The controller assessed the situation as chaotic and hired a systems man and a data processing expert with all the necessary tools. These were all justified to the president on the basis of accounting needs and were intended to improve the accounting function even further.

The systems man devoted much time to streamlining accounting routines, forms and reports. Improved reports appeared containing an even greater degree of accuracy than before. Available time on the data processing equipment was used "productively" to analyze items of cost of relatively little consequence (such as postage and telephone costs) and even to calculate the cost of each mechanized application. Some attempts were made to provide for the company's need to plan its activities and to subsequently assess its actual performance against those plans. Corporate budgeting and basic control accounting were developed, but these potentially valuable control tools were weakened by their adherence to *financial* accounting principles.

The ultimate in specialized information refinement was being reached, but the fundamental problem had remained unchanged in nature and had greatly expanded in degree and cost. The situation was now ready for the development of stage 5.

ELABORATE STRUCTURE BUILT ON SHATTERED FOUNDATION (STAGE 5)

Our president, aging rapidly, then employed an administrative assistant whose primary function was to assist him in analyzing past trends for purposes of short- and long-range planning. The historical analysis was so time-consuming that formal planning became a hopeless task. A planning director was therefore employed who was later to be assisted by an operations research specialist. Both spent many long hours developing ways and means of using available information to discharge their responsibilities.

By then there was a wealth of information. There were five or six information systems operating at full capacity. Deciding on the relative accuracy of each and separating the wheat from the chaff took most of the time. Obtaining valuable information for decision-making and planning could receive very little attention. Our information system can perhaps be illustrated, again schematically, as in Figure 4.

The interaction of all these new information requirements resulted in the progressive refinement of each system. The whole process could have been written off to the pains of evolution, and the strong features of each system could have been salvaged. The situation could have been salvaged, in fact, at any of the previous stages, although at successively increased cost. Unfortunately, our company selected another approach.

THE FINAL IRONY (STAGE 6)

Having allowed the information "system" to develop haphazardly into such a time-consuming, confusing and costly monster, the president was advised that confusion would be minimized by the use of written instructions. Accordingly, a paralyzing blow was struck. The chaos was reduced to standard procedures, which had to be observed and could not be changed except after careful consideration and approval by a procedures committee. The laudable purpose was to ensure that current procedures were not amended unless all those affected approved of, or made due allowances for, the change. The effect, however, was to introduce an inflexibility that defied any attempts to centralize the information system. The creeping paralysis continued as more current procedures were reduced to writing and as more proposed changes were added

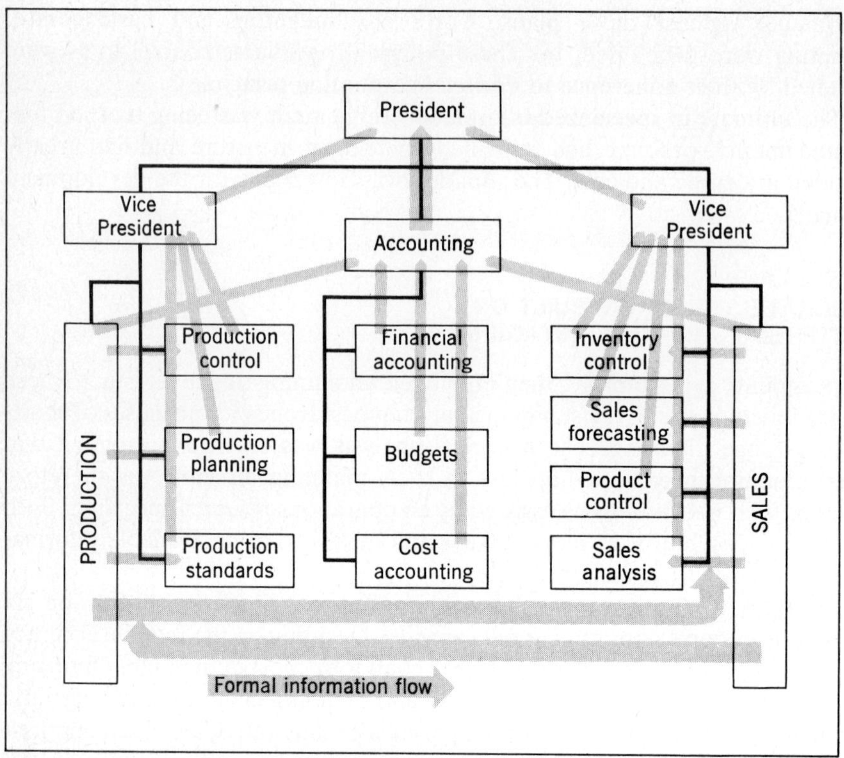

Figure 4 Fundamental error compounded in chaos.

to the agenda for the procedures committee. Nevertheless, the company earned some profits, not because of the system but in spite of it.

The company took many actions that were, in themselves, worthwhile. They were well intentioned and, in theory (as often in practice), desirable. To draw a contrary conclusion is not the intention. Neither should it be concluded that the personnel employed were unnecessary, that their potential value was not significant, nor that they acted irrationally. All the positions created and the departments organized could have provided the company with extremely valuable service had they been supported by an adequate information system. In this situation, however, their efforts were, to a greater or lesser extent, wasted and unproductive. Fortunately, in this case the president's final recognition of the intolerable situation, and its complexity, led to positive action.

RESTORATION OF ORDER (STAGE 7)

The difficulties of restoring order were, at this stage, very great and the cost of remedial action significant. Many personnel relationships had been formed and many practices and procedures developed. Highly refined and specialized techniques imposed further difficulties in coordinating and integrating the information requirements.

However, the president was sufficiently aware of the costs, both hidden and measurable, of dissipated skills, inefficient information processing and the many losses attributable to inadequate information, that he resolved to take drastic action. He further reasoned that since the restoration program required was complex, the opportunities for savings must be substantial. Fortunately, there was no question of redundant staff, as all specialists hired could be effectively used, so that support for the program was enlisted with relative ease once the information chaos was understood. The objectives of the improvement program seemed clear:

- To reduce the wastes and inefficiencies inherent in the system, and
- To provide for future information needs *so as to avoid the recurrence of the situation in which the information needs exceeded the capacity (both quantitative and qualitative) of the information system.*

To achieve these objectives a thorough review of the organization's information needs was carried out, giving thought to the organization structure and the company's objectives. Although it became apparent that some reassignment of major delegated responsibilities was necessary, the restoration program included the following major phases:

- Centralization of information processing under one senior executive responsible for the coordination of all planning activities, actual performance measurement and evaluation (including external reporting) and the development of control practices and systems. He was also responsible for the constant appraisal of new data processing techniques vis à vis the anticipated further evolution of information needs. This centralization (along the lines suggested schematically in Figure 5) was based on the premise that the processing of data is in itself a specialized function that should not be shared by the users of such information. Centralization was further justified by the economics of data processing equipment.
- An accelerated mechanization program to handle, intially, all basic information and paperwork routines, thus freeing accounting personnel to develop new systems and methods. In evaluating the feasibility of data processing equipment, however, allowance was made for all justifiable corporate information requirements and for their anticipated expansion.
- The design and implementation of modern management accounting techniques as most of the company's information requirements could be satisfied by such methods. These included flexible budgetary control, refined sales forecasting, improved capital expenditure evaluation, inventory planning, marginal or direct costing and integrated profit planning, to mention only a few aspects of modern management accounting.
- An advanced training program for all senior accounting personnel to enable them to appreciate the information needs of operating executives and anticipate improved control requirements. This phase included the hiring of competent accountants, as the company had learned that limiting the accounting staff had been shortsighted, as evidenced by the duplicate information systems.

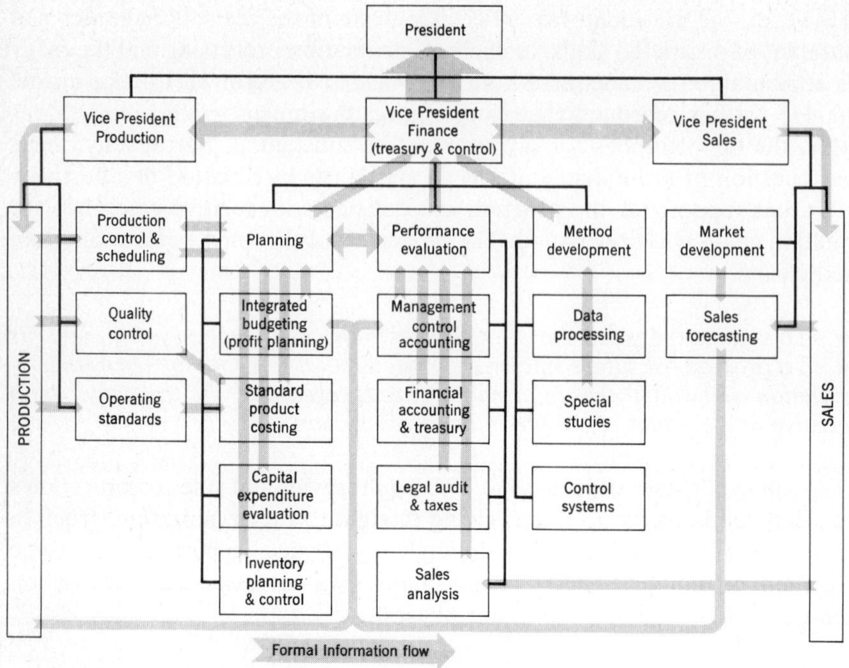

Figure 5 Integrated information system restores order.

In addition to these specific phases of the program, management was faced with the monumental task of objectively assessing the relative urgency of information needs and enlisting the cooperation of all staff levels. This reappraisal called for tact, patience, and an objectivity not often prevailing when day-to-day administrative responsibilities must be discharged.

The rewards, however, have been great and have not been affected by unpleasant staff reductions. The revision program was, by virtue of its complexity, sufficiently gradual that staff reductions were achieved by normal attrition. In any event, the rewards in terms of overall efficiency far exceeded considerations of savings in staff costs.

SOME CONCLUSIONS

Whatever the series of circumstances was that led to the disintegration of the information system, one conclusion emerges clearly: its disintegration resulted from the *inability of the accounting system to provide vital information.* Furthermore, since all requirements specified or implied in this case could have been satisfied by modern management accounting techniques, the accounting system's inability was in turn due to a fundamental flaw that is sufficiently prevalent in today's industry to warrant some concern: *the limited concept of the function of accounting in corporate life.*

The wider concept of accounting as a corporate information and control system receives little emphasis, considering its implications. Unfortunately, many accounting systems today are limited to a treasury or "custodial" capacity and, as such, often contribute directly to the development of separate information systems with all their attendant wastes.

Greatly improved modern management accounting, coupled with the speed of data processing equipment, permits the application of the wider concept. The existence of inadequate business information, therefore, is increasingly unjustifiable. The modern accountant appreciates this and is aware, perhaps painfully, of the need for accounting systems to be constantly adapted to suit evolving information needs. In other words, in spite of all the improvements made, *the accounting systems of today may be grossly inadequate tomorrow.*

Few companies can afford to be complacent about their information systems. The symptoms of disintegration can be seen all too frequently and the consequences of the disease can be too serious to be stoically and erroneously accepted as inevitable. The necessary reviews of information requirements and the methods used to satisfy them deserve top-management action to avoid the natural function biases that might prejudice subsequent revision programs. Company concepts of the function of accounting in corporate life should also be reviewed to ensure that its major purpose is to provide information in its broadest sense.

To do anything less can be extremely shortsighted. The cost of information inadequacy or of separate information systems can greatly exceed that of modernizing the information systems and the supporting organizations. Furthermore, the benefits are likely to continue long after the pains of critical reappraisal and revision are forgotten.

CASE C DISCUSSION QUESTION

What changes, if any, would you have made in the firm's restoration program?

SUMMARY OF CHAPTER 4

A systems study is made by an organization to determine the desirability of using a computer to achieve specified goals. Technical, economic, and operational aspects must be evaluated during such a study. Failure to plan properly for computers subjects the firm to probable financial loss; careful study, on the other hand, may yield positive benefits and may help the firm avoid common mistakes.

The steps in the systems-study approach are to (1) identify the scope of the problem and the objectives to be gained, (2) gather the facts on current operations, (3) analyze these facts and determine suitable alternative procedures, (4) choose the most appropriate alternative, and (5) follow up on the decision.

In a broad sense, the end result of a computer systems study is a single decision—to use or not to use a computer. But, as we have seen in this chapter, there are an uncountable number of decisions which must be made by the study team during the course of its work. The success of the information processing system produced depends on the quality of these decisions.

If a decision is made to acquire a computer, a bewildering number of technical preparation tasks must be accomplished before the conversion to the computer can be completed. Personnel must be selected and trained; data processing standards must be established; programs must be written, documented, tested, and debugged; file conversion must take place; the physical site for the equipment must be readied; and the actual changeover must be accomplished. Many months are required to perform these tasks. Computer vendors and consultants may be of assistance in the performance of some of these jobs.

Chapter 5

The Computer's Impact on Planning and Organizational Structure

An *organization* is a changing and ongoing system in which people and resources interact in a rational and orderly manner to accomplish common goals. Government agencies, hospitals, schools, churches, businesses, military units, Boy and Girl Scout groups, Rotary clubs—all these entities are organizations. Computer systems, by manipulating data and solving problems, may produce qualitative changes in an organization's information system. And since information is the cement that holds any organization together, the computer has had the effect of changing the structure and policies of many organizations.

The purpose of this chapter is to look at (1) the *administrative activities* which must be performed in an organization, (2) the computer-related tasks concerning the managerial tasks of planning and decision making, and (3) the impact that computers have on the organizational structure.

ADMINISTRATIVE ACTIVITIES

Computer-using organizations have experienced various changes that may be directly traceable to the computer. These changes have occurred in the administrative activities of *planning, organizing, staffing,* and *controlling.* As we saw in Chapter 1, these are important activities in any organization, because the successful achievement of organizational goals depends on how well they are performed. In a later section of this chapter we shall examine some of the computer's implications for the first two of these activities. Now, however, let us briefly summarize these administrative functions.

Planning

The planning function looks to the future; to plan is to decide in advance a future course of action. Thus, *planning* involves making decisions with regard to (1) the selection of both short- and long-run strategies and goals, (2) the development of policies and procedures that will help accomplish objectives or counter threats, (3) the establishment of operating standards that serve as the basis for control, and (4) the revision of earlier plans in the light of changing conditions. The steps followed in *planning and in arriving at rational decisions* are the same as those followed in conducting a systems study—i.e., the steps are: (1) *identifying the problem or opportunity,* (2) *gathering and analyzing relevant facts,* (3) *determining suitable alternatives,* (4) *evaluating and selecting the most appropriate alternative,* and (5) *following up on the decision(s).* Of course, administrative skill and quality information are needed during each of these planning activities.

Organizing

The organizing activity involves the grouping of work teams into logical and efficient units in order to carry out plans and achieve goals. Organizational units, for example, may be formally grouped according to (1) *type of work* performed, (2) *geographic area,* and/or (3) *type of physical good produced, handled, or distributed.* Administrators at each organizational level receive formal authority to assign goal-directed tasks; they then must motivate and coordinate team efforts if goals are to be achieved. The formal organizational (or authority) structure clarifies for employees the place in the organization of each job, the formal lines of authority and reporting relationships among positions, and the assigned role of a work unit in the total structure. Of course, an organizational structure must be flexible, because of constantly changing technological, social, and economic factors. When there is no longer a valid reason for some units to continue to exist, changes should be made in the organization to avoid duplication and waste.

Staffing

One aspect of the *staffing* function consists of selecting people to fill the positions that exist in the organizational structure. The staffing activity also includes (1) the training of employees to meet their job requirements, (2) the preparation of employees for promotion to positions of greater responsibility, and (3) the reassignment or removal of employees when such action is required. These topics are discussed in Chapter 6.

Controlling

Unlike planning, which looks to the future, the *control* function looks at the past and the present. It is a follow-up to planning; it is the check on past and current performance to see if planned goals are being achieved. The *steps in the control activity* which are covered in Chapter 7 are:

1 *Setting standards.* Proper control requires that predetermined goals be established by planners. These standards may be expressed in *physical terms* (e.g., units produced, quantities tested, or machined tolerances permitted) or in *monetary terms* (e.g., operating-cost budgets). The setting of realistic standards requires quality information.

2 *Measuring actual performance.* Timely and accurate performance information is essential to control.

3 *Comparing actual performance with standards.* Comparison information is action-oriented. Computers can provide this information to managers on an *exception basis only* when performance variations are outside certain specified limits.

4 *Taking appropriate control action.* If performance is *under control,* the administrator's decision may be to do nothing. However, if actual performance is not up to the standard, it may be because the standard is unrealistic. Therefore, replanning may be necessary to revise the standard. Unfavorable performance may have to be corrected by reorganizing work groups or adding more personnel. Thus, the control actions taken may require further planning, organizing, and staffing activities. If outstanding performance is noted, the appropriate action may be to reward the individuals or groups responsible.

The *order* of the administrative activities presented here is a logical one, and we shall use this order to present material in a following section. In practice, however, administrators carry out these activities simultaneously, and it is not practical to insist on a particular sequence in all situations.

PLANNING, DECISION MAKING, AND COMPUTER USAGE

We can look at this broad topic from at least two viewpoints. First we can examine the implications of *planning with computers,* and second, we can consider some computer-oriented *decision-making techniques* that are now being used.

Planning with Computers

As businesses have expanded in recent years within this country and across national borders, as separate firms have merged in order to expand markets and product lines, as the complexity of operations of such firms has increased, and as governments have increased the reporting requirements of organizations to include such things as occupational safety and health programs, affirmative action programs, and pension plans, the need for better planning tools and techniques has become critical. Generally speaking, *the use of computers can have an impact on planning activities by:*

1 *Causing faster awareness of problems and opportunities.* Computers can quickly signal out-of-control conditions requiring corrective action when actual performance deviates from what was planned. Masses of current and historical internal and external data can be analyzed by the use of statistical methods, including trend analyses and correlation techniques, in order to detect opportunities and challenges. Planning data stored online may permit managers to probe and query files and receive quick replies to their questions.

2 *Enabling managers to devote more time to planning.* Use of the computer can free the manager of clerical data-gathering tasks so that more attention may be given to analytical and intellectual matters.

3 *Permitting managers to give timely consideration to more complex relationships.* The computer gives the manager the ability to evaluate *more* possible alternatives (and to consider *more of the internal and external variables* that may have a bearing on the outcome of these alternatives). It makes it possible for managers to do a better job of identifying and assessing the probable economic and social effects of different courses of action. The awareness of such effects, of course, influences the ultimate decision. In the past, oversimplified assumptions would have to have been made if resulting decisions were to be timely. More complex relationships can now be considered and scheduled. In short, computers can furnish managers with planning information that could not have been produced at all a few years ago or that could not have been produced in time to be of any value.

4 *Assisting in decision implementation.* When decisions have been made, the computer can assist in the development of subordinate plans that will be needed to implement these decisions. Computer-based techniques to schedule project activities have been developed and are now widely used. Through the use of such techniques, business resources can be utilized and controlled effectively.

Computer information systems now regularly support the planning and decision-making activities of managers in a number of business areas.[1] In *marketing*, for example, data may be gathered that show consumer preferences from consumer surveys, results of market testing in limited geographic areas, and past sales data on similar products in an industry (obtained from the company's own past sales records and from subscriptions to data-gathering services). These facts may subsequently be processed by a computer to produce summary statistical measures (market percentages, arithmetic means, product rankings, etc.). These summary measures may then be analyzed by managers or by computer programs. These analyses, in turn, can be used as input to computerized statistical forecasting procedures that may be used to project sales volume into the future, given assumptions about pricing, economic trends, promotional effort, competitive reactions, and so on. Armed with this information, managers may be able to do a better job of planning marketing strategies. And in many companies, market plans become the basis for *inventory acquisition plans* and *production plans.*

Of course, provisions must also be made in a business to have adequate *financial* resources available to carry out marketing and production plans. The

[1]For more information on computer-based planning and decision-support systems, see Reading 1, Steven L. Alter, "How Effective Managers Use Information Systems," *Harvard Business Review,* November–December 1976, pp. 97–104; Reading 15, Eric D. Carlson, "Decision Support Systems: Personal Computing Services for Managers," *Management Review,* January 1977, pp. 4–11; "Management Gets the Picture," *Infosystems,* April 1977, pp. 37–38ff.

costs and revenues associated with alternative estimates of promotion plans and prices and sales and production volumes must be analyzed to determine the financial implications. To evaluate these implications (and to determine the expected profitability of various alternatives), financial managers frequently use computer programs to make cash flow analyses, time-series financial forecasts, and loan and interest rate projections. Decisions about the advisability of making investments in new plants and equipment are often made with the help of a computer.

Decision-Making Techniques[2]

A number of quantitative managerial aids have been introduced which utilize computers to provide the framework for decision-producing analyses. These techniques (which are often classified under the heading of *operations research or management science*) can be used to (1) speed up problem or opportunity awareness, (2) permit more timely consideration of increasingly complex relationships, and (3) assist in decision implementation. In particular, the computer-based techniques of *network analysis, linear programming* and *simulation* have decision-making implications.

Network Analysis Both PERT (*P*rogram *E*valuation and *R*eview *T*echnique) and CPM (*C*ritical *P*ath *M*ethod) are network models which are used to plan, schedule, and control complex projects. The basic concepts of PERT and CPM are similar. The following procedure is used to set up a network model:

1 All the individual *activities* to be performed in the project must be identified.

2 The sequence of each activity must be determined; i.e., it must be known what elements have to be completed prior to the start of a particular activity and what tasks cannot commence until after its completion.

3 The *time interval* required to complete each activity must be estimated.

4 The *longest sequence* of events in the project must be identified. The sum of the individual activity times in this sequence becomes the total project time, and this sequence of activities is known as the *critical path.*

The use of such a model in a construction project, for example, improves the *planning* function because it forces managers to identify *all the project activities that must be performed. Control* is also improved because attention can be focused on the sequence of activities in the critical path. Managers quickly become aware of potential problems. If a critical activity begins to slip behind

[2]For more details on the decision-making techniques that follow, see Gerald Adkins and Udo W. Pooch, "Computer Simulation: A Tutorial," *Computer,* April 1977, pp. 12–16; George A. W. Boehm, "Shaping Decisions With Systems Analysis," *Harvard Business Review,* September–October 1976, pp. 91–99; William G. Browne, "Techniques of Operations Research," *Journal of Systems Management,* September 1972, pp. 8–13; P. L. Kingston, "Concepts of Financial Models," *IBM Systems Journal,* vol. 12, no. 2, 1973, pp. 113–123; Thomas H. Naylor and Daniel R. Gattis, "Corporate Planning Models," *California Management Review,* Summer 1976, pp. 69–78.

schedule, steps can be quickly taken to correct the situation. By trading project cost against project time, several alternative paths can initially be computed to help in planning. By a greater commitment of resources, managers can often reduce the time required to complete certain activities in the critical path (and thus reduce total project time). The effect of a greater resource commitment, however, is often higher project cost (see Figure 5-l). Network models can simulate the effects on time and cost of a varying resource mix. Computations for small networks can be produced manually, but a computer is needed with networks of any significant size. Most computer manufacturers have PERT and CPM packaged programs available, and they are also available in the online program libraries of many timesharing services.

Linear Programming Linear programming models are used to find the *best combination* of limited resources to achieve a specified objective (which is, typically, to maximize profit or minimize cost). One important class of linear programming applications is in blending operations, where the objective is often to minimize the cost involved in the production of a given amount of blended product. For example, cattle feed may be a mixture of minerals, grains, and fish and meat products. The prices of these ingredients are subject to change, so the least expensive blend required to achieve specified nutritional requirements is subject to variation. Linear programming can help managers quickly determine the correct blend to use to minimize cost while meeting product specifications.

In addition to blending, linear programming is being used for such diverse purposes as preparing work schedules, selecting media for advertising purposes, determining minimum transportation costs from given supply points to specified points of delivery, and determining the most profitable product mix that may be manufactured in a given plant with given equipment. Practically all linear programming applications require the use of a computer (Figure 5-2). As a powerful *planning* tool, linear programming enables a manager to select the most appropriate alternative from a large number of options. It is also a technique that may aid the manager in carrying out his other functions. Its use in preparing work schedules, for example, has definite staffing implications.

Simulation In the physical sciences, experiments may be performed in a laboratory using small models of a process or an operation. Many complex

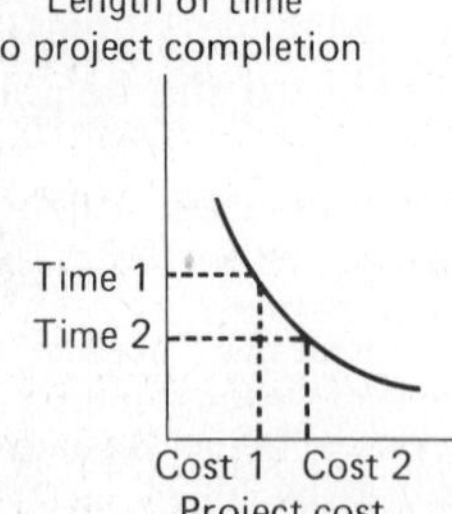

Figure 5-1 Reducing of project time may be possible if greater costs are acceptable.

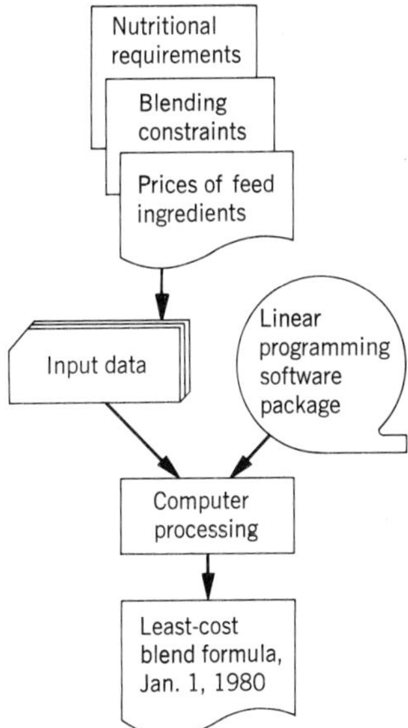

Figure 5-2

variations may be possible in these tests, and the results show the scientist what happens under certain controlled conditions. Simulation is similar to scientific experimentation. Perhaps Figure 5-3 will clarify the meaning of simulation. At its base, Figure 5-3 rests on reality or fact. In complex situations, few people (if any) fully understand all aspects of the situation; therefore, theories are developed which may focus attention on only part of the complex whole. In some situations models may be built or conceived in order to test or represent a theory. Finally, *simulation* is the use of a model in the attempt to identify and/or reflect the behavior of a real person, process, or system.[3]

In organizations, administrators may evaluate proposed projects or strategies by constructing theoretical models. They can then determine what happens to these models when certain conditions are given or when certain assumptions are tested. Simulation is thus a trial-and-error problem-solving *approach;* it is also a *planning aid* that may be of considerable value to organizations.

[3]Several programming languages have been developed for the special purpose of preparing simulation programs. Some of these languages are SIMSCRIPT, GPSS, GASP, and DYNAMO.

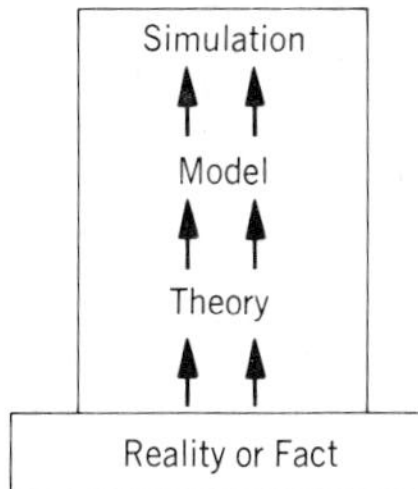

Figure 5-3

Simulation models have helped *top executives* to decide, for example, whether or not to expand operations by acquiring a new plant. Among the dozens of complicating variables that would have to be incorporated into such models are facts and assumptions about (1) present and potential size of the total market, (2) present and potential company share of this total market, (3) product selling prices, and (4) investment required to achieve various production levels. Thus simulation has helped top executives in their strategic planning and decision-making activities.

Simulation may also be helpful to *middle-level managers* in tactical planning and decision making. For example, simulation models are used to improve inventory management. The problem of managing inventories is complicated, because there are conflicting desires among organizational units, and what is best for one department may not be best for the entire firm. To illustrate, the purchasing department may prefer to buy large quantities of supplies and raw materials in order to get lower prices; the production department also likes to have large inventories on hand to eliminate shortages and make possible long—and efficient—production runs; and the sales department prefers large finished-goods inventories so that sales will not be lost because of out-of-stock conditions. The finance department, on the other hand, views with concern large inventory levels, since storage expense is increased, risk of spoilage and deterioration is increased, and funds are tied up for longer periods of time. Through the use of simulated inventory amounts and simulated assumptions about such factors as reorder lead times and cost of being out of stock, middle-level managers can experiment with various approaches in order to arrive at more profitable inventory levels.

Finally, simulation models serving managers at different levels may be integrated into an *overall corporate modeling approach* to planning and decision making. For example, Potlatch Forests, Inc., a producer of lumber and wood pulp products, has a corporate planning staff that has developed an overall corporate financial model. Given assumptions from top executives about economic conditions, capital expenditures, etc., for a 5-year future period, simulation runs produce estimated financial statements for each of the 5 years. Executives then analyze the simulated financial statements. If results are judged to be disappointing, executives may change variables in the model that are under their control—e.g., future capital expenditures—and the simulations are repeated. When acceptable financial results are obtained, they become the targets for planning at lower levels in the company. When feasible, lower-level plans are formulated (again, simulation models are used), and they are assembled into an overall corporate plan.

Of course, the output of simulation models is only as good as the facts and assumptions that go into the computer.[4] National economic data and assump-

[4]The U.S. Geological Survey uses a complex computer-based model to come up with estimates of the oil and gas reserves that might be found in the government's offshore tracts that oil companies bid on. In one area, 50 miles off New Jersey's shore, the model "estimates that reserves in the area range from 400 million to 1.4 billion barrels of crude oil and from 2.6 trillion to 9.4 trillion cubic feet of natural gas. But oilmen in Houston irreverently call this computerized approach SWAG—for Scientific Wild-Ass Guess." See *Business Week,* Sept. 20, 1976, p. 116.

tions about the national economy are usually an integral part of a corporate simulation model. Several organizations such as Lionel D. Edie, Data Resources, Inc., and the National Bureau of Economic Research provide extensive national economic data bases that are available to subscribers to their services. General Electric's MAP system is one that was originally developed for internal use by the organization but is now available to timesharing customers. When combined with a firm's internal information, the national economic data provided by these services may enable managers to more accurately model a firm's future.

To summarize several of the points that have now been made, the planning and decision process followed by many business executives may resemble the one shown in Figure 5-4. The strategies, goals, economic assumptions, etc., of these executives serve as the basis for market forecasts. This expectation of *how many* items can be sold then becomes the basis for determining (1) how and when to acquire materials and make the items (the production plans), (2) how and when to have the money on hand to pay for the acquired materials and produced items (the financial plans), and (3) how and when to promote and distribute the items (the marketing plans). And these plans are then used in simulations to estimate such variables as profit and return on investment. Of course, the results of these simulations may bring about changes in established plans and/or the results may cause changes in strategies and assumptions. Once initial simulations have been concluded and high-level plans have been made, operational plans at lower levels are often needed to implement the decisions.

From this brief overview, we can see that *computer simulation* offers such advantages as (1) controlled experimentation involving alternative policies and the consideration of many variables, (2) the ability to enhance operational understanding, and (3) the means of providing effective managerial training in

Figure 5-4

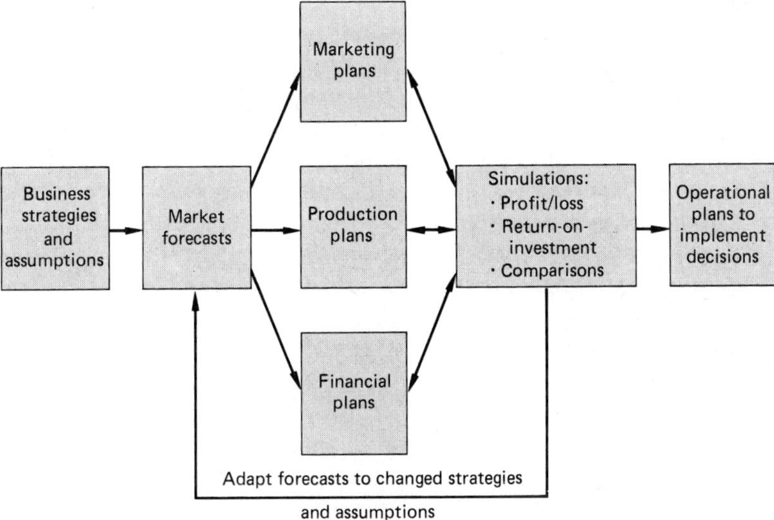

decision making. However, *simulation disadvantages may include* (l) the time and cost required to develop the model, (2) the use of oversimplified or incorrect assumptions hidden in the model, and (3) the possible lack of enthusiastic support for the model from managers who may be expected to use it.

ORGANIZATIONAL STRUCTURE AND COMPUTER USAGE

It was pointed out in Chapter 2 that when it is possible to introduce a new technological development into a business to improve on the process or to do something that was previously not feasible, then there will usually be those who will seek to take advantage of the new opportunity, even though changes in the ways individuals and groups are organized may then be necessary. Certainly, the introduction of computer technology into businesses has often resulted in such organizational changes.

When a computer is installed, for example, it may take over a large part of the work of several departments. If there is then no longer any valid reason for some units to continue to exist, changes are likely to be made in the organizational structure to avoid duplication and waste.[5] In other words, as computer-based management information systems are designed and implemented, there is often a need to reconsider the answers to several important and interrelated organizing questions. Included in these questions: (1) *Where will decision making occur?* (2) *Where will data be processed?* (3) *Where will data be stored?* and (4) *Where will computing resources be located?* As is so often the case, the "right" answers to these questions in one situation may be very wrong in another. Thus, what we will do in the following sections is look at some of the general implications of these issues.

Where Will Decision Making Occur?

The concept of centralization of authority[6] refers to a concentration of the important decision-making powers in the hands of relatively few top executives. *Decentralization of authority,* on the other hand, refers to the extent to which significant decisions are made at lower levels. In very small organizations, *all* decision-making power is likely to be centralized in the hands of the owner-manager; in larger firms, the question of centralization or decentralization *is a matter of degree*—i.e., it is a question of how much authority is held at different levels. The extent to which authority is delegated to lower levels depends, in part, on such factors as (1) the managerial philosophy of top executives, (2) the availability of qualified subordinates, and (3) the availability of good operating controls. Since all these factors may change, it is apparent that the degree of authority centralization is subject to revision.

Before computers came along, the general trend was toward *greater*

[5]Unless careful planning precedes such changes, however, they are likely to produce efficiency-robbing employee resistance in the affected departments.

[6]"*Authority*" is defined here as the right to give orders and the power to see that they are carried out.

decentralization of authority. To some top managers decentralization was more a matter of necessity than of choice. They often found themselves in a position where they could (1) wait for the necessary supporting information to arrive from lower levels before making a decision (in which case company reaction time suffered and opportunities were lost), (2) place their trust in experience, intuition, and their horoscope and make the decision without proper supporting information, or (3) delegate the authority to make the decision to a lower-level manager who was closer to the situation calling for the decision and who could thus be expected to react in a prompt and more informed manner. Given these alternatives, it is understandable that as businesses grew in complexity, the third path was frequently chosen.

With the introduction of quick-response computer systems, however, information may be processed and communicated to top executives at electronic speeds; reaction time may be sharply reduced; and thus the need for decentralization of authority may be lessened. But although new systems may make it possible to reconcentrate at the upper echelons authority and control previously held at lower levels, there is *no reason* why the information output cannot be disseminated via online terminals to lower-level managers to provide them with better support for decision-making purposes. In fact, if an organization implements the distributed processing concepts that were discussed in Chapter 2, the lower-level managers may have access to an entire hierarchy of processors that can supply them with decision-making information. Thus, the degree to which authority and decision-making powers are centralized or decentralized in an organization is now often determined more by managerial philosophy and judgment than by necessity. But the implications of the path selected for the organizational structure and for middle-level managers may be great.

Where Will Data Be Processed?

Prior to the introduction of computers, data processing activities were generally handled by manufacturing, marketing, and finance departments on a separate and thus decentralized basis. When computers first appeared, however, the tendency was to maximize the use of the expensive hardware by establishing one or more central processing centers to serve the company's needs. But in recent years, such developments as (1) the rapid reduction in hardware costs and (2) the arrangement of intelligent terminals, minicomputers, and larger processors into distributed processing systems have made it feasible for businesses to use either a centralized or a decentralized approach to data *processing*. Thus, many firms must now decide to what extent (if any) they will centralize their data processing operations. Should small computers be used by individual organization units, or should these units furnish input to (and receive output from) one or more central computer centers which can process data originating at many points? (See Figure 5-5.)

The possible considerations in favor of the centralized approach are:

1 *It may permit economies of scale.* With adequate processing volume, the use of larger and more powerful computing equipment may result in reduced

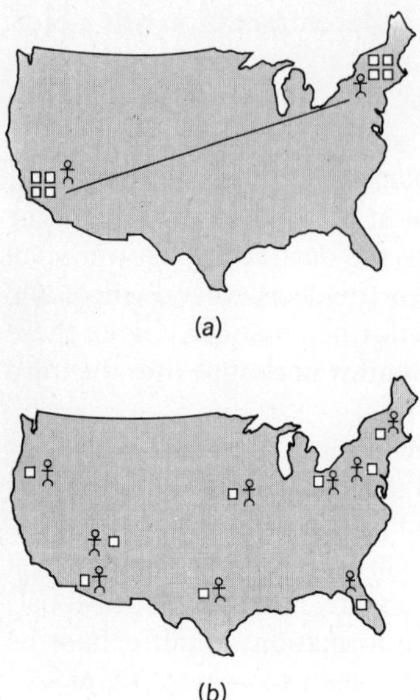
(a)

(b)

Figure 5-5 *(a)* Centralization or *(b)* decentralization of data processing activities.

operating costs. Also, duplication in record storage and program preparation may be eliminated; less expensive standardized forms can be used; and site preparation costs may be reduced since fewer sites are involved.

2 *It may facilitate necessary systems integration.* For example, achieving companywide standards on customer code numbers is a necessary step in integrating the procedures required to process customer orders. Such agreement is more likely to occur for efficiency reasons when order processing is handled at a central point. It may also be easier to establish and enforce the use of consistent corporate standards and controls at a central site.

3 *It has certain personnel advantages.* It may be possible to concentrate fewer skilled programmers at a centralized site and thus make more effective use of their talents. A sizable operation may offer more appeal to highly qualified computer specialists. Thus, recruiting may be simplified and a professional group will be available to help train new personnel.

4 *It may permit better utilization of processing capability.* With a centralized operation, companywide priorities can be assigned to processing tasks. Those jobs that are of greatest importance are, of course, completed first. With a decentralized approach, however, low-priority work may be processed in one division with excess capacity, while in another division a higher-priority application may be left unfinished because of inadequate processing capability.

In view of these benefits, it might seem that a decision to follow a centralized approach would be automatic. Yet there are limiting factors in centralization, which may cause a company to follow a more decentralized path. These limitations are implicit in the following discussion of the advantages of decentralization.

Included among the possible advantages of decentralization are the following:

1 *Greater interest and motivation at division levels.* Division managers in control of their own computers may be more likely to (*a*) maintain the accuracy of input data and (*b*) use the equipment in ways that best meet their particular operating needs. Greater interest and motivation, combined with greater knowledge of division conditions, may produce information of higher quality and value.

2 *Better response to user needs.* The systems standardization typically required for centralized processing may not be equally suitable for all divisions. With decentralization, special programs can be prepared to meet exact divisional needs. In addition, although a smaller machine will probably be slower than the centralized equipment, it should be remembered that central machine time must be allocated to several users. Information considered important by one division may be delayed because higher priority is given to other processing tasks. Thus, the fact that a smaller machine allows for prompt attention to a given job may lead to faster processing at the division level.

3 *Reduced downtime risks.* A breakdown in the centralized equipment or the communications links may leave the entire system inoperative. A similar breakdown in one division, however, does not affect other decentralized operations.

There is no general answer to the question of where data *should* be processed. Small organizations have usually opted for central computers because their departments often do not have sufficient volume to justify separate machines. Large organizations following the centralization approach have generally not created single huge installations. Rather, they have often achieved a greater degree of centralization by establishing several regional data centers. Some executives who have chosen to follow the *centralized processing* route have retained a *decentralized decision-making structure* by giving operating managers online terminals with which to obtain the necessary support information.

Firms with centralized hardware may also achieve greater interest and motivation at operating levels by maintaining some systems-analysis operations on a more decentralized basis. This can be a logical arrangement because (1) divisional systems analysts may have a better understanding of the information needs of the division, and (2) this approach can effectively counter the argument from division managers that since systems design is beyond their control, they cannot be held accountable for design results.

Finally, other organizations are following a *distributed processing compromise approach* to the centralization-decentralization issue by combining larger central computers (and centralized data files) with small processors, minicomputers, and intelligent terminals at operating levels. The central processor(s) serves the local processors by managing large data bases and by executing those jobs that require extensive computations (see Figure 5-6).

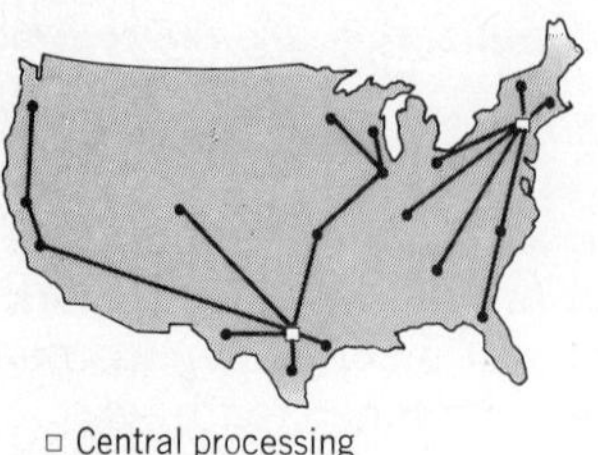

Figure 5-6 Distributed processing compromise approach.

Where Will Data Be Stored?

Before computers came along, data were typically stored at the using departments, although some summary facts needed to prepare companywide reports were maintained at centralized sites in large organizations. We have seen that when computers first appeared, however, the tendency was to maximize the use of expensive hardware by setting up centralized computer centers. Not surprisingly, the tendency was also to establish and store large centralized data bases at these central sites on such media as magnetic tape and disks.

In most cases, data with corporatewide significance will continue to be stored at a central site. But with the reduction in hardware costs, with the increase in data communications facilities, and with the development of distributed computing networks using intelligent terminals, minicomputers, and larger processors, there is no technical reason why applications-oriented files with local significance cannot be returned to the outlying user departments for storage and maintenance. Thus, many firms are now in the process of deciding to what extent (if any) they will relocate the storage of previously centralized computer-based data to using departments.

A decision to distribute some data base files from a central site to local levels might be made in the following circumstances:

1 When large volumes of data are produced at many local sites and quick access to the data is needed by local users. In a chain of retail stores, for example, local accounts receivable and customer credit records could be maintained at each store. Such records, of course, would be of little value to other stores in the chain.

2 When data are produced both centrally and at remote sites, when quick access to the data is needed by a number of remote locations, and when records can be updated from any site. For example, an organization may maintain regional warehouses to distribute a number of common inventory items. One or more inventory files containing records of these items may be updated centrally to reflect additions to inventory, while shipment transactions from each warehouse may be used to reduce inventory levels. To answer inquiries from salespersons about available items, warehouse personnel may need access to records showing local inventory levels as well as access to information about the inventory available at other warehouse locations.

In the *first* circumstance just described, a decision might be made to *partition* a centralized accounts-receivable file and distribute the data to the local stores. However, summary data from all store files could be transmitted to a central site in a timely manner for use in the preparation of periodic reports. In the *second* circumstance, a decision might be made to have *duplicate* or *replicated* copies of the inventory file(s) stored centrally *and* at each warehouse location. Updating of inventory records might be controlled by a central or host computer facility in a hierarchical computing network, or distributed processors at each warehouse location might communicate directly in a ring network structure.

There are *possible advantages to the centralized storage approach* in those situations where (1) unified control and strict adherence to standards is desired, (2) the partitioning or replication of files adds system security problems, (3) file sizes are large and many transactions do not originate at local levels, and (4) the application is too critical to run the risk of having data updated at one location and not at another.

On the other hand, however, there are also *possible advantages to a distributed data storage approach* in those situations where (1) data communication costs between central and local sites can be substantially reduced by moving frequently accessed records to the user's location, (2) the performance of data communications facilities and/or the central computing center presents system reliability problems for users, (3) user interest and motivation is improved through faster access to, and better control over, records that are locally stored, and (4) the redundancy found in replicated files can add storage backup and a degree of added data security to the system.

In summary, there is no general answer to the question of where data *should* be stored, just as there is no general answer to the question of where data should be processed. Some organizations may find it best to store and maintain data at a central site; some may prefer to use a partitioned approach to data storage; some may choose to use a replicated approach in order to distribute data base files; and many organizations may elect to use a combination of these basic data storage approaches.

Where Will Computing Resources Be Located?

Each business must determine the proper location for its main computer department. What is "proper" depends, in part, on the size of the company, the jobs to be processed, the degree of systems integration achieved and sought, and the importance attached to information systems by top executives. Three possible locations for the main computer department are designated in Figure 5-7. Let us look at each of these arrangements.

Location Number One Historically, the accounting department was often the first to see that a computer could be used to process large-volume applications such as customer billing. Since most of the early applications were of a financial nature, the computer was most often placed under the control of

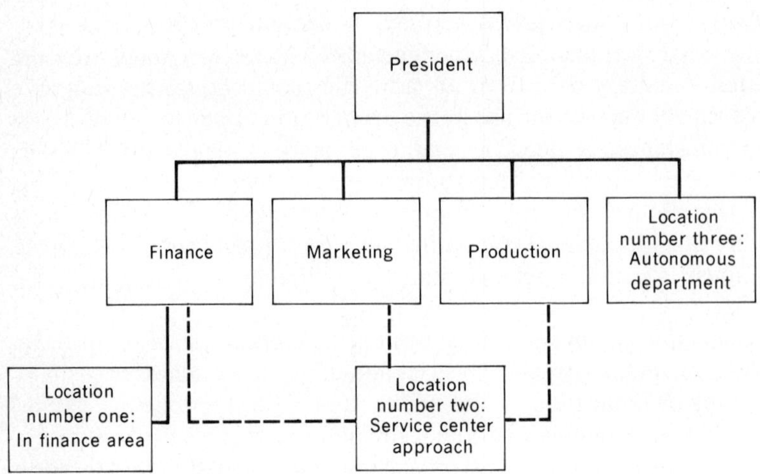

Figure 5-7 Alternative computer department locations.

financial managers. It still remains in this location in many businesses. But there may be several possible drawbacks associated with this finance-area location:

1 *Possible lack of objectivity in setting job priorities.* Computer-department personnel may tend to concentrate on accounting applications at the expense of important nonfinancial jobs.

2 *Possible limited viewpoint.* The computer department may continue to be staffed and managed by people whose viewpoint is limited primarily to accounting.

3 *Possible lack of organizational status.* Organizational status and authority are lacking when the top computer executive is interred several echelons down in one functional area of the business.

Location Number Two One approach which can avoid the lack of objectivity in setting job priorities is to establish a company "service center" to handle the various tasks. Each department may be charged its proportionate share of center costs. While the center manager may report to a neutral top-level executive or an executive committee, the service center basically occupies a position that is on the periphery of or outside the main organizational structure.

The main limitation of this type of organizational arrangement for business data processing is that the center manager generally has little status or authority outside his or her own department. Thus, little attempt is made to initiate systems improvements or develop integrated systems; a fragmented, every-department-for-itself approach may be expected.

Location Number Three In order to realize the full potential of the computer, a large number of managers have established an independent computer department as shown in location three of Figure 5-7. Their reasoning is that this location:

1 *Reflects the broad scope of information.* Independent status is needed to give impartial service to all organizational units that receive processed information. An interdepartmental viewpoint is required of data processing personnel.

2 *Confers organizational status.* The top computer executive should have a strong voice in determining the suitability of new and existing applications, should probably set processing priorities, and should study and make necessary changes in corporatewide systems and procedures in order to achieve better integration. To perform these duties, the information manager must have the cooperation of executives at the highest operating levels. In the event of significant change, such cooperation may not be received unless the information manager occupies a position that is no lower in the organization than the highest information-using department. Furthermore, in the event of a dispute, the information manager should report to an executive who is at a higher level than any of the disputing parties.

3 *Encourages innovation.* Personnel of an independent department can be encouraged to recommend improvement and change whenever and wherever the opportunity arises. They may also be encouraged to introduce, for the greatest total benefit, fresh ideas that may upset certain conventional approaches.

REVIEW AND DISCUSSION QUESTIONS

1 (*a*)What is involved in the planning function? (*b*) What steps must be followed in planning?

2 Explain what is involved in (*a*) the organizing function and (*b*) the staffing function.

3 Identify and discuss the steps in the control function.

4 (*a*) How may computer usage have an impact on the planning activities of managers? (*b*) Give examples of the use of computers for planning and decision making.

5 (*a*) Identify and explain the purpose of three computer-based decision-making techniques. (*b*) What are the managerial implications of these techniques?

6 (*a*) What is meant by centralization of authority? (*b*) What factors determine the extent to which authority is delegated to lower management levels?

7 "An organization may be centralized in one sense of the term and not in others." Discuss this statement.

8 (*a*) What developments have made it possible to centralize data processing activities? (*b*) What are the possible advantages of centralized data processing? (*c*) What are the possible advantages of decentralized data processing?

9 (*a*)What developments have made it possible to decentralize or distribute the storage of computer-based data files from central sites to outlying user departments? (*b*) What approaches might be used to distribute or relocate these files? (*c*) What are the possible advantages of a centralized storage approach? (*d*) What are the possible advantages of a distributed data storage approach?

10 (*a*) Identify and discuss three possible organizational locations for the computer department. (*b*) What reasons can be given to justify the establishment of an independent computer department?

Chapter 5 Readings

INTRODUCTION TO READINGS 15 THROUGH 17

15 As industry develops new ways to utilize computer technology more effectively, companies are assigning computer terminals to individual managers for direct, personal support of the job of decision making. In this reading, Eric D. Carlson analyzes the state of the art of such systems.

16. In this article, Carl H. Rodgers takes a look at the tangible and intangible factors that affect the centralization of the computer equipment within a company. He argues that the question of economy of scale, as it relates to the computer equipment itself, has for the most part disappeared.

17 It's important to understand the role of the dp department in a company's objectives before the organization begins to decentralize its data processing activities. Otherwise, James Hannan and Louis Fried argue, decentralizing may *not* be the thing to do.

Reading 15

Decision Support Systems: Personal Computing Services for Managers

Eric D. Carlson

Exception reports, models that produce optimal plans or answer what-if questions, and terminals that provide immediate access to current data on operations are among the services that computers provide for management in many organizations. However valuable these services may be, they really do not help a manager solve the unstructured problems typical of the real world of decision making.

Managers seldom rely on computers in making decisions such as choosing among alternative manpower allocation schemes with qualitative rather than quantitative differences or selecting products that best meet corporate objectives and comply with governmental regulations. In fact many managers complain that their computer services provide too much information or deliver information in the wrong form (not summarized or buried in the middle of a printout); therefore, they say, the computer really does not help much in decision making.

Even when the information is potentially valuable, the procedures for using today's computers often are so demeaning, complex, or time-consuming that

Reprinted by permission of the publisher from *Management Review,* January 1977, pp. 5–11. © 1977 by AMACOM, a division of American Management Associations. All rights reserved. Mr. Carlson specializes in decision support systems at the IBM Corporation, Research Division, San José, Calif.

most managers need staff support to make use of the information. Staff support in turn introduces additional costs, time delays, and communication problems that limit the utility of computer systems in supporting managers. In addition, managers normally expect to understand and direct their decision-making support, and understanding and directing today's computer services require too much time and effort for most of them.

A NEW TOOL FOR MANAGERS

Recently a number of companies have begun to use computers in new ways to provide direct, personal support for managers. Known as decision support systems (DSS), these new approaches to providing computer services to managers help them retrieve, manipulate, and display information needed for making decisions.

Gould Inc., for example, has combined a large visual display and video terminals with a computer information system. Designed to help managers make comparisons and analyze problems, it instantly prepares tables and charts in response to simple commands. IBM, working with the First National Bank of Chicago, has developed a similar system, which produces graphs and charts in color on a television screen.

Because professional judgments and insights are critical in decision making, a DSS must be designed to support a manager's skills at all stages of decision making—from problem identification to choosing the relevant data to work with, picking the approach to be used in making the decision, and evaluating the alternative courses of action. A DSS must produce information in a form managers understand, when such information is needed, and under their direct control.

Four main components can be incorporated into a DSS to achieve this base of support.

- The first is the ability to present information in ways that are familiar to managers and permit quick analysis of the data being presented. The graphs and charts used in both the Gould system and the Trend Analysis 370 system at First National of Chicago are examples of this feature. Good representations not only stimulate managerial insights and facilitate analysis but also can be used to generate new requests to the computer.

For example, by selecting points on a graph or locations on a map, a manager can request more detailed information. By subdividing a list or reconnecting groups on an organization chart, a manager can indicate a change to be made in the computer's data base.

- Once such representations have been chosen, the second main component comes into play—a set of easy-to-use operations that can be invoked to prepare and transform the representations. Simple commands to select data to be graphed, call up sales figures in a tabular format, or run a model to generate and display possible production schedules are examples of operations. Existing decision support systems use single, meaningful key words or phrases, such as SALES or RUN SCHEDULER, or selections from "menus" of operations as techniques for simplifying the selection of operations. The idea is to use representations and operations that will generate results useful to the manager.

- To save these results and to retain how the results were obtained, a DSS should provide a third component—memory. The memory should act like scratchpaper in developing intermediate results and like a file drawer in retaining results that are useful.
- And to make the representations, operations, and memories useful, the manager must be able to control them. This means letting the manager select or change the colors of a graph, the format of a table, or the place where subtotals appear in a report. Control of operations means letting the manager pick the order in which operations are performed and making it easy to select these operations. Control of memories means letting him decide what is to be saved, when it will be saved, and what names will be used to label the information that is saved. Because most managers are not accustomed to sitting down at a computer terminal, support for control may at first require an intermediary, or "chauffeur," to operate the DSS under the manager's direction.

Another important criterion of the usefulness of decision support systems is ability to be interactive, that is, quick response to commands and easy availability where decisions are made, such as in boardrooms and individual offices. (Gould, for example, uses a large video display in its boardroom and several smaller video terminals in the offices of senior managers.) Responsiveness and availability, combined with representations, operations, memories, and control, give a DSS the scratchpad and information-source capabilities that support the human skills used in decision making.

TECHNICAL REQUIREMENTS FOR A DSS

The development of decision support systems in organizations has been stimulated more by an increasing sophistication in data processing capabilities and improved computer technology than by a better understanding of decision making. Organizations that are developing systems have experience using computers for record keeping and transaction processing and have staff capable of utilizing recent developments in computer technology. A firm just beginning to rely on computers for record keeping and transaction processing is not likely to have the technology required for a DSS.

Decision support systems require three basic technologies: a computerized data base and data base management system, computer time-sharing support of interactive systems, and video terminals.

- A computerized data base provides the primary source of quantitative information. If a data base is not available, the DSS development will include a substantial data entry cost. The experience of the IBM Research Division in DSS development indicates that data entry costs can exceed the combined costs of DSS development and use.

The data base management system provides the technology for linking the DSS to the data base and for incorporating any other data a manager needs.

Again, without an existing data base management system, another substantial cost will be added to DSS development to provide data base management capabilities. (For the DSS developed by IBM Research, about one-third of the implementation cost went to provide data base management.)

• Several facts point to interactive, time-sharing computers as a requirement for DSS development. Decision making is not necessarily a routine or scheduled activity, and computing done by a DSS may not require a large computer. Nonetheless, the DSS will need access to the data base and data base management system—which probably will require a large computer. Also, the DSS should be available when the managers need it and be able to respond in time to help make decisions.

Several decision support systems—American Airline's AAIMS, for example—use an interactive, time-sharing computer with the programming language APL. Interactive, time-sharing services such as those provided by APL systems are report to reduce DSS development costs by over 50 percent while increasing the flexibility and convenience of using a DSS.

• Video displays—such as those used by Gould, the Trend Analysis 370 system, and several banks using a DSS marketed by Index Systems, Inc. and used in portfolio management—provide a mechanism for presenting information in a variety of forms (charts, graphs) and are easier to use than other technologies (typewriters, keypunches) that are available for communicating with computers. Decision support systems that have been developed without video displays incur costs (often hidden) for transforming the information produced into a graphic form and for the staff that transforms the manager's requests into a form that can be communicated through the typewriter or keypunch device. In DSS with video displays, these costs are eliminated or substantially reduced. And convenience benefits increase because color video equipment makes it easier for a manager to analyze data and permits display of information in ways that are familiar to managers.

Like the familiar cathode ray tube, video displays, moreover, are decreasing in price. A 10-in. (diagonal) video display that can produce black and white charts and tables costs about $5,000. A 19-in. (diagonal) color video display that can produce almost any form of graphic output costs about $100,000. A sophisticated video display system, including a large (7 ft. x 7 ft.) screen may cost over $300,000.

Each of these vital technologies—data base systems, interactive time-sharing systems, and video displays—is widely available. An organization already using them can expect the cost of developing a DSS to run about $250,000, an estimate based on five man-years (at $50,000 per year) for DSS design and implementation. But if developing a DSS includes installing one or more of these technologies, the costs will climb quickly to a million dollars or more.

HOW MANAGERS USE DECISION SUPPORT SYSTEMS

The expense of a DSS is justified only if it can be well used as a management tool. Systems in use today support a variety of decision-making activities. Some

DSS vs. Other Computing Services

Decision support systems incorporate features found in management information systems and in computer simulation and optimization models. Nonetheless, a DSS has a number of distinguishing characteristics that make it different from other computing services for managers. For example:

1 Decision support systems emphasize direct support for managers to enhance the professional judgments required in making decisions. The use of interactive systems and video displays in successful decision support systems are examples of this point. In DSS design, the emphasis is on helping the manager make decisions rather than on actually making decisions for the manager. DSS design also stresses presentation of information in a form that is useful rather than on presenting all the information that might be useful.

2 A DSS should be flexible enough to respond to the changing information needs and decision-making processes that are typical of a manager's job. A DSS should not require that a manager specify exactly what data will be required or what sequences of operations will be useful before the DSS is developed. It should allow the manager to select the relevant information and operations while using the system.

3 Decision support systems are intended to support all phases of decision making, including identifying that a problem exists, generating useful information, selecting a course of action, and explaining that course of action to others. Management information systems typically are used to generate useful information, and a computer-based model may help select a course of action. But such support is of limited value if it cannot be incorporated into the other activities involved in making decisions. In a DSS the representations, memories, and control are intended to help the manager use the information provided by the system's operations; in other systems the operations are available, but there is not much support for using the information they provide.

---

perform jobs such as data gathering and formating, tasks that ordinarily consume many hours of staff time, and their value in terms of cost displacement is directly measurable. Some, as indicated previously, are used as a workbench or scratchpad for developing decisions and thus are useful to managers in creating and comparing alternatives, and their value can be expressed in terms of increased management activity. A DSS also may lead to improved decisions through better analysis or investigation of more alternatives, but the contribution of the system to such improvements can be difficult to measure. Thus, the best measure may be the amount that a manager is willing to pay to use a DSS.

Another managerial activity where a DSS is supportive is the explanation or "selling" of a decision. The DSS can show why or how an alternative was chosen, provide a visual representation (such as a portfolio list) of the decision, and help other managers test or modify a decision. The value of the DSS in such activities will be increases in management productivity, plus intangible improvements that are best measured by the willingness to pay.

Two examples illustrate different uses of DSS as a management tool. As part of a four-year joint effort, IBM and First National Bank of Chicago analyzed some of the bank's managerial activities. They found that as much as 90 percent of the time spent in making decisions involved gathering and setting up information for the manager. The bank executives felt that information for analysis was hard to obtain, that information from different sources often was conflicting, and that not enough time was available for analysis.

The joint effort produced an information system that helps the bank's managers analyze asset and liability positions, decide on loan portfolios and interest rates, and check indicators of bank performance with respect to competitors. A variety of other uses also are anticipated. Through a video display, information can be called up in seconds in tabular form or on colored graphs or charts; a variety of other uses is anticipated. Although the bank and IBM have not released the cost/benefit data on this DSS, both companies are convinced of its value. Bank personnel give examples of cases where use of the DSS reduced the cost of providing information to decision makers by over $100,000.

Another DSS developed by IBM and used for the past five years by a number of organizations helps managers analyze and display data that can be related to a geographic location. Customer data, market surveys, and land characteristics are examples of the type of geographically related data that can be reached via this system. Called the Geo-Data Analysis and Display System (GADS), it has been used to make decisions such as allocating police manpower, setting school attendance boundaries, making territory assignments for repairmen, evaluating urban zoning, and planning equipment for fire stations.

Managers use a video display to select relevant data from the computer's data base, draw maps and graphs, compile lists, and manipulate the maps, graphs, and lists to help arrive at a decision. For example, a customer-service manager can use the DSS to display a map showing the location and equipment inventory of customers, to subdivide the map into territories for each service engineer, to draw a graph of the distribution of workload by territory, and to project the future workload by territory.

The system often is used by groups of managers to develop decisions together. It also is used by staff personnel to prepare information for managers. In six recent applications, users paid between $3,000 and $10,000 to cover the operating costs of GADS, and managers estimated that, for these applications, the cost of obtaining the same services from a consultant or from staff support would total $20,000 or more.

A key factor that makes both these systems useful tools is that they can be used directly by managers. Whether or not the manager directly operates the terminal or uses a staff chauffeur depends on the individual's style. What is important is that the DSS can provide information when it is needed in a form that the manager can understand and at an acceptable cost.

THE FUTURE OF DSS

Until recently decision support systems have been of interest primarily to academic and industrial research and development groups. Organizations using DSS tend to be large, with substantial experience and investment in computers. But as computer technology for DSS becomes cheaper and more available, a broader-based interest in DSS can be expected.

The rapidly decreasing costs of computer storage and improvements in data entry and data management systems make it increasingly likely that much or all of the information a manager needs to reach a decision will be stored in a computer, making decision support systems a necessary aid for managers. Without a DSS a manager will need other support to access information stored in the computer and to manipulate and transform it into understandable form.

Personnel costs already exceed 50 percent of most data processing budgets. Also, hidden personnel costs—such as programmers employed as management staff analysts, a manager's time spent trying to communicate his information needs to the data processing department, or personnel used for making slides or charts from data on a computer printout—may exceed the direct labor costs of data processing.

Indications are that a DSS can reduce personnel costs of providing information for managers; in the future this reduction alone should be enough to justify DSS, along with improved management productivity and perhaps even improved decisions that may result from increased use of decision support systems. More experience and better methods for measuring the impact of support systems on decision making are needed, however, before claims of such improvements can be fully justified.

Further developments in computer technology will not be enough to ensure the success of DSS. Technology still must be assembled into systems that are compatible with managerial styles and provide support that managers feel is valuable; decision support systems will have to fit into an environment where the relevant data and decision-making processes cannot be specified in advance; and they must be available even when not used on a routine basis. A DSS also should be able to support decisions where compromise or time constraints may be more important factors in reaching a decision than optimal solutions or standard operating procedures.

Achieving these goals will require new ways of using computer technology, uses that are different from how technology has been used previously in management information systems or computer-based models. But because only managers know what representations, operations, memories, and methods of control fit their styles of decision making, management involvement will be more important than computer technology in developing useful decision support systems.

READING 15 DISCUSSION QUESTIONS

1 What are some of the behavioral reactions that managers may expect as decision support systems such as those described in the text are introduced into a company?
2 Which areas of management would be most affected by decision support systems? Are there areas where such systems would be ineffective?
3 What type of *orientation* or *training* would be needed in an organization before these DSS systems are introduced?

Reading 16

Issues in Centralization

Carl H. Reynolds

The question of centralization-decentralization of computing resources has been under intensive study for five or ten years. Three economic considerations must be evaluated:

1. Personnel required to operate the hardware
2. Data processing applications programming efforts
3. The computing hardware

With respect to operations personnel, there usually is an advantage in centralizing the work done in support of the machine. Staging jobs, handling tapes, processing output, are all tasks which have built-in overhead. For example, we have to have at least one person there for a whole shift, even if he is needed only sporadically. I contend, however, that this is more a function of the means of processing than an advantage of centralizing the facility. As on-line processing comes into greater use, the operator expense will be less and less a factor in the centralization-decentralization decision.

Another factor works against centralization. In the small installation, it is relatively easy to have individual persons perform multiple tasks. For example, the supervisor can run the tape library and, as needed, assist in mounting and de-mounting tapes and/or loading or unloading printers. In large shops, these activities become more and more specialized. Personnel become rigidly assigned to tasks. Work rules develop, whether or not one is unionized, which prevent one class of worker from carrying out another class's tasks. Benefits from saving operations personnel do not seem to me to be a major issue in deciding the centralization issue.

When we centralized operations at Hughes Aircraft Company, we assumed there would be a major savings in applications programming. Hughes is comprised of a group of engineering and manufacturing elements, all of which have, theoretically, the same data processing problems to solve. Products must be designed, documentation must be released to the factory, materials and parts must be purchased, products must be fabricated and assembled, and goods must be shipped. If one could have just one production control system, one purchasing system, and one order status system for all factories, the costs of development and maintenance could be cut two or three times. In fact, we estimated that the costs could be cut by a factor of two, and that more than $1.5 million per year would be saved by the development and installation of such "common" systems.

Reprinted with permission of *Datamation* ® magazine, © copyright by Technical Publishing Company, a division of Dun-Donnelly Publishing Corporation, a Dun & Bradstreet Company, 1978—all rights reserved. Mr. Reynolds is corporate staff director of computing and data processing for Hughes Aircraft Company.

NOT ALWAYS FEASIBLE

This common system approach is reasonable for financial systems. The accounting department at Hughes, while reporting to individual line management, nevertheless has many common objectives and practices. They all use the same chart of accounts, for example. Accounting also is constrained by legal regulations, reviewed by outside auditors, and has a long, well documented tradition. This has led to most accounting operations using the same basic dp systems. Individual differences are accommodated by special data entry and output reporting programs. The dp requirements of engineering and manufacturing, however, are quite different. There are two reasons for this. In the first place, what is to be done by the computer, or even by the underlying production control or engineering support systems, is only beginning to be codified and taught.

Furthermore, production and engineering dp systems are part and parcel of the very fabric of everyday work. There is really no such thing as a weekly or monthly or overnight kind of cycle. All of those production and engineering people and all the systems that support them work in the here and now. In a very real sense, batch processing—historically developed in support of accounting—is totally inadequate to be a real help in manufacturing and engineering. It is in these very areas that time-sharing, hand calculators, and on-line systems have had the biggest impact.

The task of controlling a job shop that produces one or two items to individual order is a lot different from controlling a production line which produces thousands of a single item. Finally, a production control system is the embodiment of the management control system imposed by the factory manager. This product development and manufacturing system, which includes the discipline of engineering data control, varies with the managerial style, sophistication, experience, and desire of the management of the operation. Therefore, the data processing system will vary from factory to factory, and we have been unable to make any great progress in developing "common" systems in the manufacturing and engineering areas.

DO WHAT THEY WANT

We've come to believe that it is more important to do the job the people want than to save the money that would accrue in programming only one system. Data processing is a small part of the cost of the information system it supports.

The charge for keypunching the data, printing the checks, maintaining the employee records, and tax reporting is approximately 18 to 20 cents. If we add to that the cost of the department which administers the payroll system, the price goes up to something like 33 cents. And if we include in these costs the secretaries, timekeepers, and supervisors who keep track of things at the local level, I suspect we would have to add another 10 to 15 cents to each check. (This local work is required in part because the big, batch corporate system doesn't give back its answers for several days or even weeks after the data is sent in.) Here are some examples.

In one instance data processing is only four or five percent of the total cost of purchase orders. In another, one of our material control operations purchases, stores, and disperses items necessary for engineers to do their development task. This involves building bread boards, prototypes, and the like. Of the $2.3 million spent each year, about $400,000 is spent on data processing.

The point is that we are not out to minimize data processing costs, or at least that it is not the most important thing to worry about. The most important thing is to work on 33 cents for payroll checks. I have found that it is indeed true that making systems fit the special requirements of the individual organization is considerably more cost effective than trying to change the organization to fit some data processing operation. This is true even in cases where programming itself is quite expensive.

In summary, applications programming is an issue in centralization only to the extent that the management of the supported organizations is really centralized. The rising cost of programmers and the growth of packaged programs is quite another issue, which cannot be addressed here.

From a perspective of 1969 or 1970, you could do yourself a big favor by getting a 370/165 if you had sufficient work for more than one 360/65. Fig. 1 is a picture of the performance per unit price as the function of absolute performance of IBM 360, 370, and "375" lines.

Taking a 1969 perspective on this data, we can see that the 165 was better than twice the absolute performance of the 65 and twice as cost effective. The 155, while about 25% more cost effective than the 65, was about the same in absolute capacity. It is pretty clear then, that in 1969 or 1970, if you had sufficient work for more than one 65, you could do yourself a big favor by getting a 165.

Let's take a look at the present, however.

If again you needed to increase your capacity, it's apparent that the 168 is

Figure 1 Performance and cost relationships of IBM computer generations.

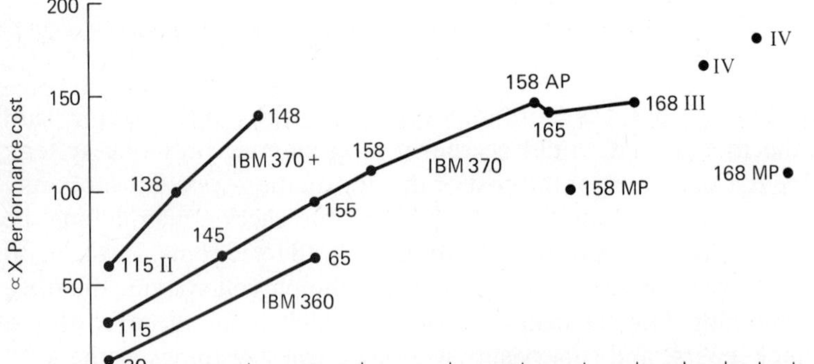

not a whole lot more powerful than the 165 and is no better at all in price performance. The chart information actually favors the large machine because the data is heavily dominated by cpu performance, not I/O performance. The larger the machine, the less effective or efficient becomes the I/O. This is especially true above the 145, since all of the I/O devices are the same.

It is interesting to note several things from the accompany chart:

1 The IBM 165 is as good a price performer as IBM makes, with the exception of its 168 attached processor, a very large, specially priced machine.

2 Two different evaluations of the Amdahl are both considerably better than the 165. The higher Amdahl estimate (IV at the 90 performance level in Fig. 1) is ours, and the lower estimate (IV) is IBM's. Note that the performance/cost improvement of the Amdahl over the IBM 370/165 is less than the improvement of the 165 over the 360/65. It is concluded that no current technology can achieve a jump equivalent to that of the 370 over the 360 line.

BIG VS. SMALL

Table 1 is an indication of the role of performance of some of the different machines which we've looked at. The Whetstone is an instruction sequence that's derived from the analysis of some typical scientific programs. It is really a measure of cpu performance. The Data-General C300, the IBM 155, and the DEC-10 are all the same power on this particular application. They range in price from \$100,000 to \$1,000,000. While one can't draw complete conclusions from this, it is clear that price and performance are no longer directly connected in this business. It is erroneous to assume that the 155 is a better machine for all applications just because it costs a million dollars.

The figures for the HP 3000 are for the Model I. The Model II HP 3000 is two to four times the Model I, and thus in the same ballpark as the Eclipse (C300). The fact that you must be careful and thorough is shown by the HP 2100, which only costs \$11,000 but performs at a performance divided by price of seven, the best on the page. There are a lot of other things to consider, too, like elapsed time, and total I/O load.

Table 2 gives you some indication of the reasons for this equivalency of

Table 1 Some Rough Comparisons—Big vs. Little

Machine	Approximate whetstones/sec	Approximate CPU price	Approximate perf/ approximate price
IBM 165	1440	\$1,800,000	0.8
IBM 155	400-500	\$1,000,000	0.4-0.5
Data Gen C-300	500	100,000	5.0
HP-3000 II	250	100,000	2.50
HP-2100	76	11,000	7.00
DEC-10	500	200,000	2.50

Table 2 Component Cost

Machine	Disc $'s/MB	Main memory $'s/B
IBM 360-65	1081	155+
IBM 360-165	446-274	0.52
IBM 360-168	224-126	0.27
HP-3000	404	0.09
DG-0300	242	0.12
MICRO S	4000	.05

capability regardless of the size of the machine. The top part shows memory costs for a variety of equipment. Memory costs used to be around $1.55 per byte (1969–70), and they today range from 9 to 27 cents per byte. Today all these memories are made the same way, by use of semiconductors and large-scale integration techniques. In fact, the memories seem to be the same in all machines, whether large or small. It's just a matter of how many chips you put together.

There is one thing which does change with memory size, however, and that is disc storage. As we can see, in quantities of 100M bytes or less, the memory seems to cost $400 to $500 per million bytes. When one gets up to the several hundred million bytes, the price drops to around $100. Note, however, that this is just a factor of four at the very outside, not factors of 10 as we were looking at in the other chart for cpu's. It is interesting that the cost of a floppy for the minis—a mini floppy from Shugart Associates—is about $395 for approximately 100 kilobytes. In this case, the cost is $4,000 per megabyte or an order of magnitude more expensive than on the large machines. On the other hand, you're talking about absolute cost of only $400.

IMPORTANCE OF HARDWARE

Finally, and perhaps most important, is the nature of the hardware. Raw computing and high speed on-line storage show, at present, no economy of scale. Off-line storage, disc, and probably tape still show better price performance in the large economy size. However, systems come in all sizes—$1,000 to $10 million at very nearly the same price performance. In the past two major factors influenced centralization of hardware and people in the computing business: the hardware, which historically was cheaper the bigger it was; and hope that one set of programs could solve all requirements for particular functions. While the latter is still a hope, its validity is quite independent of whether or not the hardware and the personnel are centralized. That is, the package program approach is in fact growing and will continue to grow. It is just as applicable to decentralized hardware and operations as it is to centralized. Grosch's Law, however, no longer seems to hold. There is, today, no economic justification for lumping a lot of problems together to get a big machine. There is, rather, considerable evidence that if you misapply large machines, you're going to spend more money and do a poorer job than if you did them separately on small machines.

COMPLEXITY

The next major issue in centralization is the complexity of the large, modern data base/data communications system. With respect to complexity, there are really two forces at work. First is that in the IBM world, software has evolved over 10 or 15 years from original design premises, which are no longer valid. Too many new things were attempted prior to actual field experience, and too many people got committed to those early errors. A great many of today's complexities are due to the necessity of handling large volumes of batch work as it seemed to be back in 1960–1962. An indication of this complexity is shown (Table 3)—the allocation of memory to the various software functions. You can see that three million bytes out of six million are devoted to various kinds of operating and control programs. This is only resident space. Each of these areas has many times that much space reserved to it on disc or drum. The second element of complexity is the sheer size of the hardware and software. An idea of this is shown in Table 3, which does not include the teleprocessing network and equipment.

MANAGING MAINTENANCE

Another major issue which must be addressed in large centralized installations is the management of maintenance. Size brings functional specialization. Size also means isolation and the inability to see the total situation from any one place. The result is that very specific management effort has to be directed to integrating these specialities to yield effective maintenance of the system. In our paper in *Datamation* (November 1975, p. 106), Jack van Kinsbergen and I discussed how we go about this. We have trouble logs; every failure is recorded; a group of two or three specialists spends full time tracking down the cause of

Table 3 Core Map—Dual IBM 165's

Component system	S_1	S_2
OS	708	694
ASP	750	
IMS control	530	
ATS		166
TCAM		104
TSO control		128
User	1084	1980
(Total = 3064)	——	——
Total Kilo Bytes	3072	3072

each system failure. This is not to say that in the small shops one need not worry about such detailed tracking. It is to say that it is easier in a small shop to assess whether or not the level of reliability is adequate to the task. The man in charge of a small shop knows those things. Software and hardware are less extensive, so he spends less time chasing down the bugs. The impact, the remedy, and the effectiveness of operation are more easily visible in the small shop than a large one.

We have found in many cases that certain bugs are not completely defined for weeks after their occurrence. There are other bugs which occur once and never occur again. One cannot afford not to keep track of these in a large shop because of the large impact should the bug recur or turn out to be a permanent problem.

IMPACT OF FAILURE

The whole issue of overall effectiveness of the operation becomes clouded and complicated. A large, general purpose industrial installation serves a multitude of users with a wide variety of services requiring a whole set of disciplines. We have almost no personal, direct knowledge of what the users do with our services, or what the impact of partial and total failures of one or several of the services has on the company. As a result, we must have elaborate procedures for measuring performance. For example, we record the timeliness of every single report and group of reports out of our company. This is a good idea in any shop, but it takes on an added complexity in a place of our size. It even becomes difficult to know whether these facts are correct. Events occur on second shift in a variety of locations for a variety of users. Many hands are used to gather performance data. Therefore, we must check even the reliability of our performance recorders. In a smaller operation, dp is closely coupled to the needs of the group it serves, and the effectiveness of dp is much more easily judged.

MOTIVATION

A major issue in centralization is motivation of the organization: the data processing people, the personnel using the data processing, the company management. In 1970, when Hughes decided to centralize, I discounted the warnings of several users that our dp organization would not be responsive to their needs. I had set up a pseudoprofit center. We would have to "market" our services to the users. If we did not satisfy their needs our organization would be eroded. Now, however, I recognize several flaws in my plan. First, the central dp organization is not really a profit center. Most of our business is captive: we know it and they know it. That knowledge lets us use daytime resources to return production systems that failed last night—even though that disturbs the open shop daytime users. Another example is that the production users are stuck with the costs of reruns. Thus we are not a separate business, and our people are motivated by things other than user happiness.

Some examples:

- Systems programmers rarely see a real user, and most never see the results of computing on a user organization. This isolation, plus the difficulty of their task, leads them to be motivated mostly to build their specialty. Vendors subtly encourage this. "Keep your resume updated by getting all the latest versions of the software," says the salesman, in effect. "I know it's not debugged, but think of the knowledge you'll gain debugging it for us. Your skills will be in even greater demand."
- All dp shops have procedures. All dp shops break the rules when the "situation warrants." We understand dp reasons for breaking procedure, but seldom are sympathetic to letting problems in other areas of the business influence our rules. "I cannot put that change in without a department manager's approval. It's not our fault he didn't do it yesterday before he got sick." You all know the problem.
- Priorities can be looked on as motivation-dependent, too. Suppose you've had a serious overnight problem and the finance systems must be rerun to get the billing out. Suppose a series of open shop computer runs is needed to complete a proposal for a new contract. Which should get priority? Actually, only the general manager could make that decision.

An example of the problems with user motivation, or perhaps a parable, illustrates the impact that the inability to make choices has upon users. Some time ago, my wife had some difficulty with the phone company, and had been given the treatment that, "Well, that's the way it is because that's the way it is and we're not going to do anything differently." When I got home from work she was quite upset by this and carried on for 15 or so minutes blaming the telephone company and saying she'd do anything if she could just find a way to get along without using their blanketyblank services at all. I said, "Gee, you sound just like one of my users when the service goes sour."

As long as someone has no choice in the matter you can always expect that he will be dissatisfied with that service. If a user selects an alternate vendor, then he will tolerate a lot more failures on his part than if he is forced to pick the in-house supplier. It may be wrong, but unfortunately, it's true. The more certain the user can be that the dp personnel are measured by the performance of his business unit, the more satisfied he will be with the level of service.

The interesting thing to watch, which is not often considered, is the line management of the user organizations. Management, in general, is not terribly enthusiastic and interested in data processing. They have many other interesting things to do—development, sales—anything but data processing. When the corporate management says the central data processing organization is "in charge of data processing," that is almost always interpreted by line management as "totally responsible." Nothing can go wrong with the information system—manual, automated, or even peripheral to the real system—that management doesn't look upon as a data processing problem. In fact, many system problems are outside of dp's control and even knowledge.

And there is the problem of resource allocation. Since none of the line management knows how much he's getting out of this corporate thing or how much he needs to do a good job, he is reluctant to spend resources on it. After all, corporate resources are limited. All line managers have more ways to spend money usefully than they have money to spend. All good managers believe they can spend dollars better than their peers. Thus the problem of resource allocation becomes one of "wait till disaster hits"—then reorganize dp.

Managing a big dp organization is a big task. It involves major resources, specialized skills, and management of complexity. The major motivation for taking on this task used to be computer economy of scale. That part of the scale economy which relates to the computer equipment itself has disappeared. Organizations will, therefore, be wise to reexamine their dp organizational direction in the light of current technical realities.

READING 16 DISCUSSION QUESTIONS

1 What are some of the major arguments in favor of centralizing the data processing facility within a corporation?
2 What impact would a centralized data processing system have on the managers in various departments? How would they be affected by a decentralized system?

Reading 17

Should You Decentralize?

James Hannan
Louis Fried

Many articles are being written about distributed processing, decentralization, networks and other methods of computer organization and processing. Before jumping on any bandwagon, however, managers should carefully assess the role of the data processing department to determine whether decentralization would meet corporate objectives.

If recent events are any indicator, there is no clear-cut trend towards either centralization or decentralization. First National City Bank, for example, has decided to decentralize its dp operations. The rationale: reduced costs. North American Rockwell, in contrast, has centralized its operations within the past two years to reduce costs.

Resolving this apparent contradiction is a difficult task. Outlining the arguments on both sides will help to clarify the issues involved in making a decision either for or against centralization.

Reprinted from *Computer Decisions,* February 1977, pp. 40–42. Copyright © 1977 by the Hayden Publishing Company. Reprinted by permission of the publisher. Mr. Hannan is associate editor of the Auerbach Information Management Series. Louis Fried is an independent dp consultant.

REASONS FOR CENTRALIZATION

Both centralization and decentralization result in economies of scale, allow greater sophistication of applications, improve the systems development process and provide better control of dp expense.

The most frequent argument advanced in support of centralization is that it results in economy of scale. The reduced costs are the result of several factors:

- Decentralized small computers may have unused capacity.
- Individual small computers may be overloaded, generating pressure for upgrading equipment or purchasing expensive service bureau time.
- In a single large installation, the costs for items such as floor space, electricity, air conditioning and other facilities are less than in multiple small installations.
- Large installations need fewer support personnel than small installations.
- Large installations require fewer management and staff personnel.
- A large computer is more cost effective. H. R. Grosch advanced that hypothesis over 20 years ago, and the more recent studies of Kenneth Knight confirm it.

Large computers, with their higher internal speeds, greater primary storage and higher channel capacity, may make certain applications practical that are not feasible on smaller equipment. Examples of this include scientific computation, database management systems and the maintenance of an access to hierarchically structured files for manufacturing systems.

Quality of Systems Developed

There are several reasons for centralizing the systems development and programming functions. Centralization permits the design and use of common databases as well as common standards for data entry and input validation. It can also facilitate the use of development and project techniques that result in specific benefits to the organization.

In addition, larger installations seem to attract and retain highly qualified technical people. These individuals can provide management with a wide range of alternative solutions to problems. This fact reduces the cost of development, operation and future maintenance of the systems. Furthermore, a lower personnel turnover rate can help to reduce both maintenance costs and risk exposure on systems.

There are also a number of reasons for centralization that can be grouped under the general topic "Controlling the cost of dp on an organization-wide basis":

- Decentralized installations are difficult to audit for operation or project development efficiency, effectiveness and conformity to overall organizational standards.

- Smaller installations generally do not have personnel with the skills and experience to do a good job of equipment selection.
- Smaller installations generally do not have the necessary negotiating power or experience to develop favorable contracts with hardware and software vendors.
- Centralization reduces the cost and improves the quality of personnel training.
- Smaller installations generally lack sufficient information to perform adequate advance planning.
- Decentralization tends to obscure management perspective of the total cost of dp for the entire organization.

REASONS FOR DECENTRALIZATION

The arguments advanced for centralization are generally based on efficiency. In contrast, the arguments for decentralization deal with effectiveness.

Until recently, no one could argue that decentralization offered anything but added cost. In the last few years, however, the minicomputer has held out the promise of substantial savings.

A single-purpose mini, programmed for a specific application, is relatively inexpensive. If it is used as an office machine, it does not require a trained operator or the programming and technical support that a general-purpose computer does. Some minis can provide online inquiry, saving the cost of telecommunications. The high cost of telecommunications, the overhead associated with large general-purpose computers, and the possibility that a large installation's capacity will not be fully utilized combine to weaken the case against decentralization.

In the area of applications, there are two disadvantages when a company attempts to meet divisional needs from a central site. Often, applications developed for a centralized operation are far more complex and costly than those developed for divisional needs. Also, maintaining the system for one division could potentially affect all divisions. If the central computer is disabled, all divisions are adversely affected. Not only are the risks increased, but centralization forces divisions into a common mold that may be inappropriate for their needs. These different needs could be satisfied by smaller installations at reduced cost and complexity.

Attuned to Local Needs

Proponents of decentralization argue that local analysts are more attuned to local needs and have a deeper understanding of divisional operations, managerial preferences and organizational strengths and weaknesses. This enables them to establish requirement specifications and to design systems that are best suited for the local user.

The local analyst can also respond more quickly to emergencies and changes in priorities of local management. In contrast, a division manager in a centralized environment has to battle with other users for the central systems development resources.

The close association between the analyst and the user also means that the user will be better informed about the benefits and limitations of dp. The user can assume tighter control over dp personnel and the quality of their work.

Even though most centralized installations allocate their costs to users according to the resources used, the division manager feels little responsibility for the total dp cost. Salaries paid to central personnel, overhead rates, choice of equipment, time spent on projects and share of resources used all seem to be beyond the division manager's control. As a consequence, the allocations are viewed as "paper dollars." The manager's only objective is to obtain as much service as he can from the centralized installation. In the long run, this drives up costs. If the dp resource is local, the division manager has direct knowledge of all the elements of cost and an incentive to control those costs.

ORGANIZATIONAL OPTIONS

Fortunately, the dp manager does not have to choose between these apparently mutually exclusive alternatives. There is a wide range of choices for organizing dp functions. In fact, the systems development and operation functions do not have to be organized in the same manner. The most common methods of organizing dp operations are distributed input and control, distributed processing, and remote job entry.

The techniques of distributed input and control are as old as commercial data processing. In its simplest form, the user has the responsibility for controlling input and converting input to machine-readable form. Users may have their own data entry equipment (keypunches or key-to-magnetic media) or may contract the work to outside vendors.

Developments during the past few years have made distributed input and control increasingly attractive. Data communications techniques have reduced the time of transmitting the data before and after processing. Online and key-to-disk data entry permit extensive editing and validation of data prior to processing. Where central computer capacity is available, online data entry also makes the resultant files ready for processing or can provide for online updating of databases.

The term distributed processing describes a configuration in which data are processed at separate computer installations that transmit data to each other. The variations of this technique may include partially or completely distributed databases.

One company maintains its inventory records through the use of minicomputer-based online systems in all locations. Summarized inventory status is periodically transmitted to corporate headquarters for updating central files. All invoicing, order entry, and inventory-related accounting is done locally on the mini.

Decentralized Analysis

Advantages
Local direction, flexibility and assignment of priorities through user control of the staff
Analysts more responsive to the user
Analysts more responsive to user problems, personnel and requirements
Analysts more protective of the user
More rigorous acceptance testing prior to implementation
Dp costs more visible and easier to control because of user project managers
Disadvantages
Vulnerability of small staffs to turnover
Difficulty in maintaining corporate documentation and design standards
Deviation of selection of projects from corporate return-on-investment guidelines
Friction between the divisional analysts and central programmers/analysts may result from conflict over design criteria
Difficulty in maintaining control of applications design as it affects the economic utilization of hardware
Tendency of divisions to invent solutions to their problems rather than use corporate-wide systems

Remote job entry is a well-established processing method that permits use of a central computer (or time on a service bureau computer) by a local station that has tape or card I/O devices and a printer.

SYSTEMS DEVELOPMENT OPTIONS

There are several systems development options in use that fall somewhere between centralization and decentralization. The most popular options are user group liaison, decentralized analysis, and decentralized analysis and programming.

In many dp organizations, user group liaison is a continuing problem that seems to have no economical solution. There are, however, two solutions that work reasonably well.

A person with dp experience can be assigned to a division staff. Unless the dp organization is lucky enough to have an analyst familiar with the user division and its problems (and can spare the analyst), it is difficult to find someone with knowledge of both worlds. This gives the company two options: transferring someone from dp and training him in the needs of the organization, or moving a person who knows the user departments into the dp department, training him as an intern, and then sending him back to the user staff. Both techniques have been used successfully throughout the industry.

Another way to handle the user group liaison problem is to assign a dp analyst as an account manager to specialize in the needs of particular division or

Operations Options

Distributed input and control	Distributed processing	Remote job entry
User feeling of responsibility for the system	Down-time affects only the immediate local operation	Speed of transmitting input and output
Data entry costs removed from dp budget	User feeling of system responsiveness	Extending use of existing central computer capability at low cost
	Advantages	
Lower dp costs through user control of input and validation of output	Costs comparable to RJE because of ability to operate with a less powerful computer	User feeling of increased system responsiveness
Data entry problems corrected by direct user involvement		
Reduced costs through the use of data entry personnel for clerical and control tasks at user site		
Higher equipment costs and under-utilized capacity	Less corporate visibility in local operations	Reduction of control over program library because user's ability to create or modify central programs from RJE terminals
	Disadvantages	
Need for additional supervisory personnel (depending on the size of the installation)	Development of dp autonomy by local divisions	Difficult to control users Tendency for users to develop their own dp department

user function. While this method provides greater control by the dp group, experience seems to indicate that it does not satisfy the user emotionally.

Decentralized analysis has been recommended as a way of improving user satisfaction while retaining the benefits associated with centralized design and programming. With this technique, the user maintains a staff of analysts who define system requirements, establish user priorities, participate in acceptance testing and direct users in implementation.

An American Management Association research study performed in 1968 pointed out that large corporations tend to encourage divisions to maintain their own systems staff; the programming staff is with the hardware. Several authorities in the industry indicate that this seems to be a frequently selected organization pattern.

Decentralized analysis and programming emphasizes many of the advantages and disadvantages of decentralized analysis. The advantages that relate to user responsiveness are enhanced. On the other hand, acceptance testing and cost control of the project may suffer. The disadvantages associated with maintaining standards and system redundancy tend to become more intense.

COMBINED METHOD

Once a company realizes that the hardware and the systems development function are not necessarily coupled, it has another alternative: combining some of the features of both centralization and decentralization.

It can use centralized hardware with decentralized analysis, or analysis and programming. It can combine centralized analysis and programming of distributed small (or mini) computers. Or it can organize by application, with corporate-wide systems centralized and exclusive division systems decentralized with hardware alone, or with hardware and development.

The average organization is well advised to avoid change unless it is justified. A key question should be raised before any detailed analysis is performed: Why is the centralization-decentralization issue being raised at all?

If the answer is that the issue is politically motivated (and it frequently is), the manager should attempt to resolve those political factors that prompted the call for change. This will save the time and cost of performing the studies and eliminate the need for any changes.

If the problems are in the realm of service, effectiveness and cost, they are real problems. It will then become necessary to balance the requirements of the division against those of the organization as a whole.

In this evaluation, the manager should pay close attention to developing alternative organizational designs and comparative costs. Cost information may be all that top management needs to resolve the problem. However, if top management is primarily concerned with service rather than cost, a different approach will have to be taken. Each dp manager must determine the organizational and management climate of his or her corporation.

READING 17 DISCUSSION QUESTIONS

1 Discuss the major advantages and disadvantages of decentralizing the data processing activities within an organization.
2 What technological developments in the last ten years have influenced the organization of data processing activities?

CASE D

New Trends in Data Processing

The announcement of a new family of computers is obviously an extremely important event for users, and industry observers are betting that International Business Machines will unveil more advanced equipment in a year or so. Asode from that, several trends currently underway in the computer industry will have a significant effect on the way computer users operate in the future. Among the most important are distributed data processing, data base systems and remote computing.

Basically, these developments have one thing in common: They make it easier for the user of data to get the information needed in a timely and efficient manner. They will not account for all computer applications and uses in the future. Basically, they offer the user new alternatives for handling data flow.

THE QUESTION OF NEW SYSTEMS

But many companies will want to—and should—stay with batch processing systems that allow all the work to be handled in an essentially serial manner, with each job run in the order it is received by the computer center. Just because there is something new in the field does not mean that it is necessarily better. In fact, many of the newer systems may be less effective for a firm than the present way of doing business. For example, distributed processing may be made to order for a decentralized firm with widespread operations, but it may have no place in a highly centralized operation.

Distributed processing is in a state of flux. But essentially it involves providing computing power out in the field, where it is used, instead of concentrating the function in a central location; in addition, it provides a means for communicating among the various centers.

"Distributed processing is really, in fact, convenience computing," says Carl Masi, director of product marketing for Wang Laboratories. "It provides the ability to deliver results easily and reliably so that a user—whoever he might be—can get done what he needs, when he needs it, where he needs it, in the form he needs it."

In many ways the "new" concept of distributed processing is really a throwback to the past, notes John J. Hunter, a project editor for Auerbach Software Reports. In the early days of computing, the machines were used directly by the people who needed the data or the power of the computer. With the advent of more sophisticated systems, computers were centralized; professionals ran the centers, coming between the end user of the data and the machine. At the time, this was the most efficient way to ensure that the equipment was used effectively. It eliminated costly duplication of hardware, software and people.

Reprinted with special permission of *Dun's Review,* July 1977, Copyright 1977, Dun & Bradstreet Publications Corporation.

But many of these systems became overloaded, says Hunter, resulting in an "alarmingly high incidence of missed schedules." Thus, there was a move to redistribute the processing power to the ultimate users of the system, and industry came back full circle to the "new" concept of distributed processing. This "new" trend was possible because the price of computer hardware was dropping rapidly and the minicomputer came into prominence, with its ability to perform a wide range of functions.

"For the first time in the history of electronic data processing, many users can afford to tailor data-processing functions to fit their corporate operating structures," says Stephen J. Callahan, managing editor of the Auerbach Computer Technology Reports. "Distributed computing returns the control over information back to where it was before computers: with the data users."

CUTTING ERRORS

Allen Lay, senior vice president and group officer for Pertec Computer Corp., cites one example: distributed processing allows the inventory control clerks and order entry clerks most familiar with data to enter it into a system, which should significantly cut errors.

A prime mover in distributed processing is New York's Citibank. It did not invent the technique, but its name has become synonomous with the concept because it was truly a pioneer in the area. The bank did not start with the idea of developing a distributed network. Rather, it was seeking ways to shift labor costs into capital costs when it embarked on the distributed route, Vice President Jon Gould reports in a *Computerworld* interview. This move toward automating manual operations led the bank into minicomputer-based systems.

Today, Citibank has hundreds of small processors performing tasks in almost every area that previously required interaction with a central data-processing site or were done manually. In many cases, similar procedures are now being developed by different groups using different machines. In some businesses, this would be regarded as an unnecessary duplication of effort, but not at Citibank. "We're riding a technology curve," Gould says. As long as the cost of the automated transactions is less than the cost of having the same work done manually, the duplication is not critical.

CITIBANK'S APPROACH

Citibank has a central group that advises individual managers who are developing procedures on their own machines and encourages departments working on similar problems to share experiences. But the interaction is not mandatory, and it often is neglected. The key to the Citibank data-processing approach is that each manager decides how he will achieve his assigned work load within his budget. "He decides how best to set up his shop," Gould says. Many departments use outside software consultants to speed development programs.

Although each manager develops applications as a self-contained data processing operation, he is still subject to management controls. The result is a classic example of distributed processing, although the original goal was simply to cut costs and increase efficiency.

Citibank's cost savings have been impressive—an estimated $80 million since 1970. If operating expenses had continued to grow at the rate they had during the 1960s, 1975 costs for the functions that were computerized would have been $400 million instead of the actual $240 million. The difference of $160 million would have meant a net savings after taxes of about $80 million, Gould explains. In effect, an increasing labor cost of 14%-to-18% per year has been replaced with automated procedures that are benefiting from the decreasing costs of technology, he adds. In the process, the bank's staff for the activities involved has been cut from 10,500 in 1970 to about 5,000 now. In almost all cases, the work force was cut through normal attrition.

Another firm using a distributed network is Converse Rubber Corp. of Wilmington, Massachusetts, which makes rubber footwear. It has been able to pare its service bureau costs $8,000 a month by moving to an in-house network of minicomputers.

In addition to saving money, Converse has gained other advantages. For example, the elapsed time from the receipt of an order to shipment and billing has been reduced from two weeks to 36 hours, and the personnel in the key-punch department and the clerical staff have been trimmed by the move.

Here's how the system works: A five-station network extends across the U.S. to support several essential company functions: order entry, shipping and accounts receivable. Terminals are set up in warehouses in Contoocook, New Hampshire; Charlotte, North Carolina; Elk Grove, Illinois; and Reno, Nevada, as well as in Wilmington, Delaware. In a departure from common practice, the distributed network is isolated from the company's IBM 370/138 mainframe, located in Wilmington. Data is transported "across the hall" between the two systems on magnetic tape, according to senior software technician Frank Sinclair.

During the week, clerks at each installation enter orders through cathode-ray tube terminals controlled by the minicomputers. As the order is entered, it is validated for product code, size and unit price. Requested terms (for example, payment in 129 days) are checked against the terms granted to the specific customer (for example, cash in advance). If there are any errors, appropriate error messages are displayed and corrections are keyed in.

RECORDED ON DISK

If everything is satisfactory, the order is accepted and recorded on disk at the installation. At the end of the day, the accepted orders are copied to tape at the remote sites to await transmission to Wilmington after working hours.

In Wilmington, transmitted data is moved to the 370/135, where the central open order file is updated. This routine also produces five shipping order print image tapes—one per site—for transmission back to the originating stations.

Back in the warehouses, the data is loaded into the open order file, the shipping orders are printed and the stock is pulled immediately for shipment. The completed orders are then transmitted back to Wilmington, using the same tape-to-tape technique, where the invoices are prepared on the 370/135.

The move toward data base systems is also affecting the way many businessmen run their computer operations. This technique allows a firm to collect all, or almost all, of its data in one form so that it can be used in a wide variety of applications.

Previously, each program had particular data associated with it and that data could not be easily used in other programs run by the same firm. If the data was needed by another program, it had to be created especially for that program, leading to redundancy in the system.

One of the best examples of this redundancy is visible in banking. Many banks may have several different files on a single customer—one each for his checking account, savings, car loan, home improvement loan and mortgage, among others. Under the older methods of doing business, these files are separate; and all are essentially redundant in that they all contained the same personal information—residence, place of birth, age, credit rating, and so forth. In addition, they could not be easily matched. For example, on the checking account the file might be in a joint name; for the car loan, it might be John L. Doe, and for the mortgage, J. L. Doe.

But banks are now moving more and more into what are called Central Information Files, which are essentially data base systems. Under this arrangement, each transaction a customer has with a bank is recorded in one file, and the customer gets one statement listing all of the separate transactions—a savings to the bank in computer storage and processing and an aid to the consumer in consolidating all information on his banking business.

The advantages of such systems are apparent, according to Bill Casey of Cullinane Corp., a producer of data base management systems: redundancy of data is eliminated, more data is available to individual programs, the data base can be changed without changing the applications programs, and the same data can be used in different ways.

Of course, all data can be collected in one place, but getting to this data is the key to the success of these systems. It is like a farmer putting all of his grain in a silo instead of having it in different locations—how does he get to the specific grain he wants when he wants it?

FUNCTION OF DBMS

This is the function of a data base management system—DBMS in computerese. These software systems—available from a wide range of vendors, both independent and computer manufacturers alike—set up certain guidelines for how data should be kept in the files and they provide a mechanism for assessing that data. Each program just has to request a certain type of data and the DBMS finds it within the data base itself.

To date, most of the data base systems run on large centralized computer systems. But systems have also been developed to operate on distributed networks, which each local minicomputer has a data base pertinent to its operations; a central index or data base is also maintained at headquarters.

In this application, each local plant has all the information it needs on its production, inventory, payroll, accounts receivable and payable and so forth in its data base. But weekly or even daily, it transmits the gross figures to a central location for the use of top management.

Remote computing, as a concept, has been around the computer industry almost since its inception, but several trends are coming together to make it more practical today.

DISTRIBUTED PROCESSING

Basically, in a remote computing network, terminals are spread around the country—or world—all communicating with a central computer. It is allied to distributed processing, but in the latter the actual processing power is distributed among several locations, while in a pure remote computing network the processing power is all in one location, with input and output handled remotely. In a distributed system, the user can actually process some jobs without communicating with the large computer in the system—if there is in fact such a large computer. But in a remote system, all work is done at the central location.

A major reason such a system is possible is the rapid decline in the cost of communications with the advent of independent, specialized non-Bell common carriers, satellite systems, packet switching, and new, reduced rates from American Telephone & Telegraph itself. With this lowering of communications costs, nationwide and even worldwide terminal networks are possible and can be cost-effective. Proponents of such systems claim that a well-run central computer center with one or more large mainframe computers is more efficient than distributed smaller centers. By having all the processing done at one point, they note, a company can afford several super-large machines as opposed to several smaller systems. The economies of scale apply here, the proponents say.

At the same time, the central operation can be controlled better than several smaller sites; its performance and operation are easier to monitor. Furthermore, with a central site, only one group of programmers and operators needs to be hired and trained, making it more cost-effective because of reduced redundancy.

But there are numerous disadvantages to a centralized system (for example, less flexibility, more likelihood of congestion, the high cost of back-up equipment), just as there are advantages to a decentralized set-up (for example, easier access to local files, greater availability, easier tailoring to local needs). The important point is that there are now more options so that the computer user can employ the one best suited to his own operation.

CASE D DISCUSSION QUESTIONS

1 Identify the major trends that are taking place in data processing.
2 What do you project will be the impact of these trends on managers and their jobs?

SUMMARY OF CHAPTER 5

To achieve organizational goals, managers must perform the activities of planning, organizing, staffing, and controlling. The information produced by a computer-based system can have an impact on *planning* by (1) quickly identifying problems and opportunities, (2) supporting problem analysis and selection of alternatives, (3) influencing the choice of the most appropriate option, and (4) supporting decision implementation. Computers can also be used to apply decision-making techniques such as PERT/CPM, linear programming, and simulation to problems.

In addition to these planning implications, computer usage also raises a number of questions which have organizing implications. Although there are no general right or wrong answers that apply in every situation, executives must consider such questions as: (1) Where will decision making occur—i.e., will decision making be centralized or decentralized? (2) Will the data processing be centralized or decentralized? (3) Will the storage of data be centralized or distributed? and (4) Where will the computing resource(s) be located within the organization?

Chapter 6

Staffing Implications of Computer Usage

In this chapter we shall examine some of the internal effects of computer usage on business organizations by studying some of the personnel and staffing implications of computer-based information systems. In addition, we shall explore (1) *the types of personnel that are needed to staff a data processing center,* (2) *some of the problems of employee selection, training, and motivation,* and (3) *the alternative administrative structures that are possible for organizing these personnel.*

INTERNAL EFFECTS OF COMPUTERIZATION

We saw in the last chapter how computers may affect the organization structure of a business. And as computers change an organization, they are bound to influence the lives of its employees. The nature of these effects will depend on decisions consciously made and on the indirect and perhaps unintentional impact of the application of computerization techniques.

Changes in Job Duties

Both *managers* and *employees* may *benefit* from changes in job duties brought about by their organizations' use of computers. *High-level executives* have, in some cases, been able to use better and more timely information in order to reassume some of the decision-making powers previously delegated to subordinates. In other cases, executives have, with a greater feeling of confidence in their ability to monitor performance through computer-produced reports, delegated additional authority to subordinates. However, the primary role of top executives lies in formulating objectives and policies and planning and guiding overall organizational strategy. Computer-based systems should, through the use of improved simulation techniques, help remove some of the uncertainties from the usually unique and ill-structured problems that top administrators face. But substantial changes in the top executive role have not occurred, nor are they expected in the near future.

A most important role of *lower-level supervisors* is to provide face-to-face communication, direction, and leadership to operating employees. But these administrators have, in the past, been caught in a squeeze between rising personnel and materials costs, on the one hand, and the need to maintain cost controls and remain within budget limits, on the other. Computer usage has benefited supervisors by permitting them to (1) schedule operations more efficiently, (2) maintain better control over economic resources, and (3) cope with a generally increasing level of paperwork. By relieving supervisors of many of their clerical duties, computers have thus made it possible for them to give more attention to the important personnel administration aspects of their work.

Administrators occupying *middle-level positions* in an organization,[1] like all managers, must perform the activities of planning, organizing, staffing, and controlling. As a result of computer information systems, some middle managers no longer need to spend as much time in controlling, because the computer can take over many of the clerical control activities—e.g., it can signal with a "triggered" report whenever actual performance varies from what was planned. Time saved in controlling has enabled some middle-level administrators to devote more attention to planning and directing the work of subordinates. More accurate and timely organizationwide information supplied by the computer has given some administrators the opportunity to spend more time identifying problems, recognizing opportunities, and planning alternate courses of action. In this respect, then, their jobs have become more challenging and more nearly resemble those of chief executives. With more time to devote to departmental employee matters, improved morale may be expected; furthermore, the more timely information that is now available to some middle managers puts them in a position to be able to react more rapidly to external changes.

Operations research employees using the techniques of linear programming, simulation, etc.; *scientists* conducting research into complex problem areas that could not be considered without computers; *design engineers* and *architects* using

[1] "Middle managers" may be defined as those who are above the lowest level of supervision and below the highest level of a self-contained operating organization; i.e., they occupy positions between foremen and first-rung supervisors, on the one hand, and company presidents, executive vice-presidents, and division managers of larger corporations, on the other. Thus, the term "middle manager" is rather nebulous and is applied to a number of levels. The difficulties of generalizing about such a wide range of positions should be recognized.

computers to simplify design work and increase the alternatives that can be considered; *structural engineers* using computer models to predict the effect of stresses on different structural configurations; *sales personnel* who receive more timely information about customers and product inventories and who are able to promise more efficient handling of sales orders in order to serve their customers better and thus improve their own sales performance; *clerical employees* whose job duties have changed from routine, repetitive operations to more varied and appealing tasks—all these individuals are also among the beneficiaries of the use of computers in organizations.

In short, computer usage has often made it possible for many people to eliminate routine procedures and to use their creative abilities in more challenging and rewarding ways.

Unfortunately, however, some company personnel have been the *victims* of computer usage. *Top-level executives* are the ones who approve the installation of computer systems. In giving their approval, they obviously do not expect to be victimized. And yet, in a sense, a number of top administrators have been computer victims. Many have been disappointed in the economic effects of their installations; some have discovered too late that poor security provisions in the computer center have left their organizations *more* vulnerable to theft, espionage, and sabotage; and more than a few have been disappointed because their new information systems have not given them the service and support for decision making they were led to believe would be provided. Some top administrators also feel more constrained because they are now more dependent on their systems staff for information.

Some *administrators below the top levels* whose decisions were highly structured and repetitive have found that those decisions were progammable on a computer. The information systems have therefore taken over those duties, and the need for as many people to perform the remainder of the job duties has been reduced. In some organizations, those who were not displaced found their jobs less challenging because, although they retained the duties that required less judgment and skill, their other tasks that required the skilled interpretation of systems information were moved upward in the organization or were taken over by the information systems staff. And in some cases, managers are finding that they have little voice in determining the information they will receive or in the design of the new systems which will be used to monitor their performance. (In one retail chain, store managers dread Monday mornings because they may receive a critical telephone call from their boss if the previous week's sales are down. This is because the boss has a report prepared by the computer over the weekend, while the store managers do not receive the figures until later in the week.) Managers caught in this type of situation have experienced the same frustrations as many employees whose duties and performance have been put under the microscope of a time-and-motion study engineer. Many administrators, of course, have not meekly accepted new systems changes which they perceive to be a threat, as we shall see in a later section on resistance to change.

Many *lower-level clerical supervisors* and their employees have suffered because their departments have been eliminated, merged with others, or reduced in scope and status as the result of the installation of computer information systems. When such changes occur, they can lead to changes in the employment status of individuals.

Changes in Employment Status

The use of computers has created hundreds of thousands of new jobs, and many of these employees are currently working in challenging and satisfying positions. But computer usage has also been responsible for the elimination of jobs and the displacement of employees.[2] On balance, then, what is likely to be the net effect of computer usage on employment? Will the net result be greater unemployment or increased job opportunities? Printed sources can be found to support each position.

Nature of the Controversy To some extent the employment controversy is fed by a failure on the part of some writers to make a distinction between unemployment and displacement. Those who are optimistic about the effects of computers on employment are generally looking at the effect of technological change on the *total employment* picture; i.e., they are looking at the effect on the *total number of jobs* in the labor market. Those who view the picture pessimistically are frequently looking at the short-run effects of *displacement* on *specific occupational categories;* i.e., they are looking at the reduction in the number of jobs in a specific segment of the labor force.

Unemployment and displacement are not the same. Unemployment refers to the total number of people involuntarily out of work. *Displacement* occurs when the jobs of individual workers are eliminated as a result of technological change. *If* these displaced workers cannot find similar jobs elsewhere, and *if* they cannot find work in other occupations, then there is, indeed, an increase in the unemployment figures. But has the use of computers caused a larger number of people to be unemployed than would otherwise have been the case? In other words, have computers reduced the total number of jobs available in the total labor market? Many economists are of the opinion that although computers do cause displacement and some displaced workers become unemployed, unemployment may not be created in the sense that more people are out of jobs than would have been if computers had not been used. Why? Because there are those who owe their jobs to computer usage, and there are probably many more who might have joined the jobless if new technology had not been used to maintain a competitive level of productivity with other countries of the world.

Regardless of the ultimate effects of computers on total employment, to the employee being displaced today, the future consequences are of secondary importance. The displaced victim is likely to be in sympathy with the famous economist who noted wryly that "in the long run we are all dead."

[2]New York's Citibank has established a distributed processing network of hundreds of small computers in recent years. "In the process, the bank's staff for the activities involved has been cut from 10,500 in 1970 to about 5,000 now. In almost all cases, the work force was cut through normal attrition." See "New Trends in Data Processing," *Dun's Review,* July 1977, p. 96.

Business Displacement Experience The extent to which displacement has actually occurred in business, and the significance of the problem in particular cases, has depended in large measure on the following factors:

1 *The rate of growth of the firm and the economy.* If the company is growing rapidly, so that more work must be done to handle the expanding business, then there may be little or no effect on the number of clerical workers employed. The use of a computer enables workers to be more productive, but increases in the demand for a company's output can prevent a layoff problem. Reassignment of surplus workers to different departments may, of course, be required. If workers must be laid off, they will have greater opportunity to find employment elsewhere if the economy is in a period of prosperity. It is fortunate that most computer installations have occurred during relatively prosperous periods.

2 *The objectives sought.* Is the company introducing a computer system for processing purposes that could not otherwise be considered? Is the goal to do more work with present employees? Or is it to save money by eliminating existing jobs? Objectives obviously play a part in determining the degree of displacement.

3 *The care in planning and preparation.* Business executives should give careful thought to the displacement problems that they are likely to encounter. It should be noted that fear of displacement is a cause of resistance to change. If displacement is not expected, employees should be so informed; if jobs are to be eliminated, plans should be made to protect present employees as much as possible. Employees in departments where reductions are expected can be given the first chance to fill vacancies occurring elsewhere in the company.

4 *The type of occupations threatened.* Up to the present time most of the jobs that have been eliminated have been of a clerical nature and have usually been held by people who can be transferred to other departments without too much difficulty. In the past, few clerical workers were laid off in larger businesses when job reductions occurred.[3] This was possible because those workers in affected departments who quit during the many months between the time the computer order was placed and the time the conversion was completed were simply not replaced. Thus, a potentially serious layoff problem often has not developed. When the affected jobs are *not* of the clerical type, the displacement problem is likely to be much more severe. Attrition and turnover in these situations may not be of much help. The affected workers may be older employees or lower-level managers whose skills are no longer needed. They are not likely to quit, but they may find it difficult to retrain for jobs at an appropriate level. In some *production-oriented occupations,* for example, displacement is occurring as a result of the installation of computer-controlled machines (e.g., certain machine tools and typesetting machines). Employees in these occupations are protected to some extent by union contract agreements, but the demand for their skills is declining.

Personnel Resistance to Systems Change

It was observed that if people in the operational areas that prepare the data input and use the information output are not sold on the new system and do not

[3]Small firms have not been as successful in preventing layoffs, possibly because there may not have been other departments to which surplus workers could be reassigned.

want to make it work, it is likely to fail to achieve its goals. In too many cases, however, company personnel *have not been convinced* of the merits of the changes taking place and no attempt has been made to counter this attitude. Why not? One reason is that executives and data processing specialists have too frequently become so preoccupied with system problems of a technical nature that they have ignored the human factors involved in the transition. In short, the emphasis has too often been placed on work rather than on workers.

Personnel preparations should receive considerable attention during the system-study period, and at the same time that technical preparations are being made, so that employees will accept changes with a minimum of resistance.

Forms of Resistance Resistance to change is the rule rather than the exception, and it may appear in many forms. At one extreme employees may temporarily feel threatened by a change, but after a brief adjustment period they resume their previous behavior. At the other extreme reaction may be evidenced by open opposition and even destruction. Between these extremes may be found a number of other symptoms, including the following:

1 *Withholding data and information.* It is not uncommon during the system study for employees to withhold information about current operations.

2 *Providing inaccurate information.* Input data containing known inaccuracies are submitted to sabotage processing results.

3 *Distrusting computer output.* Some employees continue to maintain old methods after the conversion is made.

4 *Showing lowered morale.* A general lowering of employee morale may result in lack of cooperation, sullen hostility, sloppy effort, an attitude of indifference, jealousy among workers, etc.

Although employee reaction to change depends, of course, on the individual, it also depends on answers to such questions as: (1) What are the nature and magnitude of the changes? (2) Why are they being made? (3) Who is backing them? (4) Who will administer them? (5) When will they take place? (6) In what departments will they be felt? (7) What has been the extent of personnel preparation? (8) Does the firm have a history of good personnel relations? (9) Does the firm have a reputation for innovation and change?

Reasons for Resistance We often see that there are those in an organization who are motivated to seek change because of their dissatisfaction with the status quo and because of their desire to create and be leaders in the use of new techniques. But the changes sought by some may appear to others to be a threat—a threat that may take one or more of the following paths:

1 *The threat to security.* Computers have a reputation for replacing people; therefore, there is the understandable fear of loss of employment and/or of reduction in salary.

2 *The reduction in social satisfaction.* The introduction of a computer system often calls for a reorganization of departments and work groups. When change causes a breaking up of compatible human relationships and a realigning of personnel, it also causes a reduction in social-need satisfaction. Resistance to such a proposed change may be anticipated.

3 *The reduction in self-esteem and reputation.* Individuals need to feel self-confident, but self-confidence may be shaken by the lack of knowledge about and experience with a computer system. The equipment is strange to them, and they may fear that they will be unable to acquire the skills necessary to work with it. In short, their self-esteem may suffer as a result of the change; therefore, the change may be resisted. Egoistic needs relating to the reputation of the individual are also threatened by change. Fear of loss of status and/or prestige is an important reason for resistance by both managers and employees. Department managers, for example, may oppose a change because to admit that the change is needed may imply that they have tolerated inefficiency—an admission that can hardly enhance their reputations. And employees knowledgeable in the ways of the old system may also suffer a loss of prestige because when new procedures are installed, they may no longer be looked to for information.

Employees Who Resist In summary, then, *nonsupervisory employees* may resist change because they fear they will (1) lose their jobs or be downgraded, (2) be transferred away from their friends, (3) be unable to acquire the needed new skills, and/or (4) lose status and prestige. A greater obstacle to successful computer operations, however, may be *managerial* resistance to change. Although managers may suffer economic loss because of the change to computer processing, the more usual motivating force behind their resistance is the threat of a reduction in ego-need satisfaction. Many managers feel that their positions are being threatened (and indeed this is sometimes the case). In a very real sense, those who may be most affected by the change are being asked to help plan and implement it. But it is unrealistic to expect a manager to be enthusiastic about changes that threaten his or her position. Proper personnel preparation must include managers as well as nonsupervisory employees.

Suggestions for Reducing Resistance Although there is no simple formula that prevents resistance and ensures successful computer usage, *there are some guidelines*—developed as a result of practical experience and social research—*which may, when used with care, help to reduce the level of organizational resistance.* Included in these guidelines are suggestions to:

1 *Keep employees informed.* Information relating to the effects of the change on their jobs should be periodically presented to personnel at all levels. Topics discussed should include loss of jobs, transfers, the extent of necessary retraining, the reasons for (and the benefits of) the change, the effect on various departments, and what is being done to alleviate employee hardships. Basic company objectives should be reviewed; the motives behind these objectives should be identified; and the contribution that the change makes to goal achievement should be explained. When possible, employees should be assured that the change will not interfere with the satisfaction of their personal needs.

2 *Seek employee participation.* Employees are more likely to support and accept changes that they have a hand in creating. In addition to yielding valuable information during the system study, requirements and review sessions also help reduce later resistance by allowing managers to have a say in the planning of the project. Psychologists tell us that *participation has three beneficial effects. First,* it helps the employee satisfy ego and self-fulfillment needs. *Second,* it gives the employee some degree of control over the change and thus contributes to a greater feeling of security. And *third,* the fear of the unknown is removed. The *participation of supervisors and informal group leaders* may greatly reduce the level of resistance. But participation is not a gimmick to manipulate people. Employees asked to participate must be respected and treated with dignity, and their suggestions must be carefully considered.

3 *Use managerial evaluation.* Make their ability to handle change one of the criteria for evaluating supervisors' managerial capability. Let them know that this criterion has been established.

4 *Consider the timing of the change.* Do not set unreasonable conversion deadlines. Give personnel time to get used to one major change before another is initiated.

STAFFING THE COMPUTER FACILITY

Since people are the most important resource in any computer facility (Figure 6-1), the procedures that are followed in a facility to *select* and *train* employees and the approaches that are used to *motivate* computer personnel are of particular significance.

The Selection Process

The selection process consists of (1) *determining the nature and number of positions to be filled,* (2) *recruiting potential candidates for jobs,* and (3) *selecting from among the job applicants.*

Personnel Needed A prerequisite to the selection process is the preparation of job descriptions and job specifications for any new positions to be filled. A *job description* defines the *duties that must be performed* and the equipment that is used, indicates the degree of supervision that is given and received, and

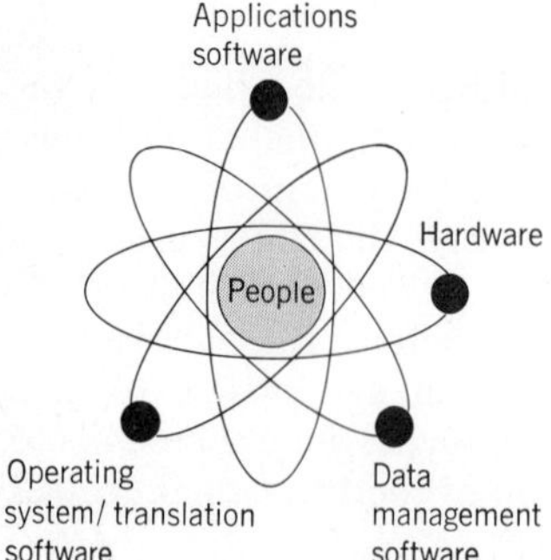

Figure 6-1 All elements of a computer-based information system revolve around the system's personnel.

describes the working conditions associated with the position. A *job specification* identifies the *qualifications that candidates for each job should possess.* Job specifications include the levels of education, experience, and training considered necessary to perform each job adequately. Also included is a statement outlining the physical and communication skills needed, as well as the personality traits desired. These facts are useful for (1) staffing purposes (since both the recruiter and the candidate must know what is needed and expected) and (2) wage purposes (to determine the relative worth of the new job).

Most of the positions to be filled in a computer facility can be classified into the following occupational categories: (1) *information systems management,* (2) *systems analysis and design,* (3) *program preparation,* (4) *data base administration,* and (5) *computer operation.* Very brief descriptions and specifications for such positions might include the following points:

1 Information systems management. *Information systems managers,* like all managers, must perform the functions of planning, organizing, staffing, and controlling (i.e., the functions discussed in Chapter 5). To be able to plan effectively and then control department activities, such managers should possess technical competence in addition to managerial ability. But too much emphasis on technical competence at the expense of managerial ability should be avoided. Too often in the past, the most skilled technician became the manager, only to demonstrate, very soon, incompetence in the techniques of management. It is likely, in fact, that the larger the data processing department, the more important managerial skills become in the total mix of skills required by the manager (Figure 6-2). The manager selected should understand the company's business, its purpose and goals, and its data processing procedures; he or she should be able to communicate with and motivate people; and he or she should possess the poise, stature, and maturity to command the respect of other company executives as well as data processing employees.

Increasingly, people planning to seek a career in information systems management must first acquire a college degree. Courses in business administration, economics, data processing, and statistics are desirable.

Figure 6-2 Total mix of skills required by the information systems manager. (Adapted from R. L. Nolan, "Plight of the EDP Manager," *Harvard Business Review*, May–June 1973, p. 145)

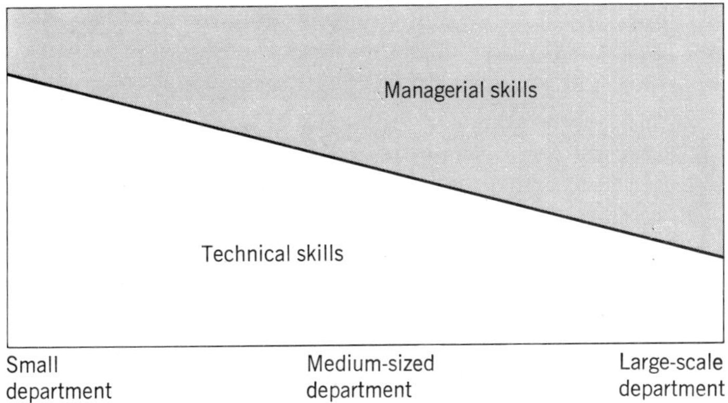

*2 **Systems Analysis and Design*** Although there are several grades of *systems analyst* (lead, senior, junior), the job basically consists of (1) gathering facts about and analyzing the basic methods and procedures of current information systems, (2) determining information needs, and (3) modifying, redesigning, and integrating these existing procedures into new system specifications as required to provide the needed information. In addition to making the most effective use of existing data processing equipment, the analyst may also (as in the case of the system study) recommend justifiable equipment changes. Analysts must usually be very familiar with the objectives, personnel, products and services, industry, and special problems of the specific firms that employ them. They must also know the uses and limitations of computers as well as other types of data processing equipment, for they are the interpreters between managers and data processing specialists. They must understand programming basics; they must be able to determine which jobs are candidates for computer processing; they must have logical, reasoning ability; they must have initiative and the ability to plan and organize their work, since they will frequently be working on their own without much direct supervision; and they must be able to communicate with and secure the cooperation of operating employees and supervisors. Educational backgrounds vary, but a college degree or the equivalent is generally desired. Courses that have proven valuable to the types of systems analysts described above are the same ones mentioned for data processing managers.

*3 **Program Preparation*** The job of the typical business *programmer* (as defined in this book) is to take the broad systems designs of the analysts and transform these specifications into workable, coded machine instructions.[4] However, there are different programmer categories, and their duties vary in different organizations. In some companies, for example, a person with the title of "programmer" may perform *both* the systems-analysis and programming functions.[5] And since job descriptions vary, there are also varying opinions about the educational background required of business programmers. Such factors as the duties of the programmer, the degree of separation between the systems-analysis and programming functions, the complexity of the data processing systems, and the industry in which the business operates should probably be considered by the company in establishing educational standards. As the programmer's job is defined here, a college degree is not an absolute condition for employment in many organizations. What *is required,* however, is that the programmer have (1) analytical reasoning ability, (2) the ability to

[4]We are referring here to *business applications* for the most part. In scientific programming a strong mathematics background is required. Systems programmers—i.e., those who write the complex operating system software and translating programs discussed in Chapter 2—are also likely to have a more scientific background than business applications programmers.

[5]The degree of separation of systems analysis and programming has depended upon the size and complexity of the company and its data processing systems, the ability of data processing personnel, and the desire of high-level executives to reduce communication problems and fix responsibility for each application on a single person. The lack of general agreement on the definition and description of systems-analyst and programmer positions presents some personnel management problems for the data processing manager, who is expected to recruit, select, train, evaluate, and compensate the employees who occupy these positions.

remember and concentrate on small details, (3) the drive and motivation to complete programs without direct supervision, (4) the patience and perserverance to search for small errors in programs, (5) the accuracy to minimize the number of such errors, and (6) the creativeness to develop new problem-solving techniques.

4 Data Base Administration The *data base administrator (DBA) function* does not yet exist in many installations. The activities of this administrator are to (1) establish and control data definitions and standards, (2) act as a file-design and data-base consultant to others in the organization, and (3) design the data-base security system to guard against unauthorized use. Although the DBA function may be located at a lower level in the organization, a good case can be made for locating it, as shown in Figure 6-3, because of the departmental cooperation and compromise that is needed if the job activities described above are to be accomplished.

In addition, the DBA is responsible for (*a*) monitoring and auditing data-base operations in order to improve effectiveness and efficiency, and (*b*) investigating new data management software packages that might also be used to increase effectiveness and efficiency. To perform these duties, a DBA must have a high degree of technical ability; furthermore, the DBA must also have the ability to communicate effectively with a large number of users with dissimilar backgrounds. It is not surprising then that the DBA has sometimes been referred to as the "superman" (superperson?) of the data processing community.[6] Educational backgrounds again vary, but a college degree or the equivalent is generally needed.

5 Computer Operations The duties of the *computer operator* include setting up the processor and related equipment, starting the program run, checking to ensure proper operation, and unloading equipment at the end of a run. Some knowledge of programming is needed. *Keypunch* and/or *key-to-tape*

[6]For more details on this emerging occupation, see Edward K. Yasaki, "The Many Faces of the DBA," *Datamation,* May 1977, pp. 75–79.

Figure 6-3 Possible staffing arrangement along functional lines.

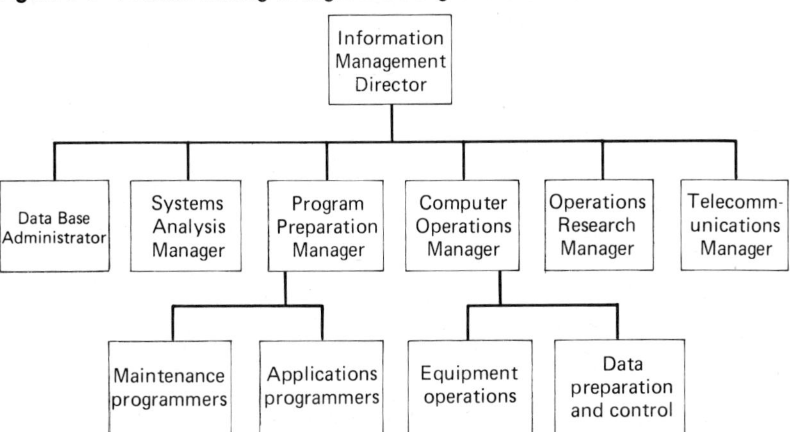

operators, a media *librarian* who maintains control over master tape and card files, a *scheduler* who plans the daily flow of work to be accomplished and assigns the necessary personnel, and various other clerks and operators of peripheral equipment may be needed in the operations area.

Recruiting Potential Candidates

To fill the jobs described above, it is necessary to *recruit* potential candidates and then to *select* from among those candidates the right people for the jobs. Figure 6-4 summarizes the recruitment and selection steps in the selection process that are discussed in this section and in the section that follows.

Two general procedures are often used to *recruit* candidates for new jobs. *One procedure* is to review personnel records and supervisory recommendations (or application forms and references, in the case of nonemployee candidates) to compile a selective list of people qualified. People on this screened list are then contacted to see if they might be interested. The main weakness of this approach is that qualified candidates may be overlooked. A *second "reserve pool" procedure* is to announce the openings to all employees and invite them to make application if interested. Those applicants who appear to possess the necessary qualifications join the pool from which initial and subsequent openings are filled. Printed advertisements, college placement offices, outside employment agencies, contacts made at professional meetings, the knowledge of vendor representatives—all these resources can be used to secure nonemployee applications.

The information systems manager may sometimes be hired from an outside source to supervise an initial computer installation. The big disadvantage of this approach is that the person hired has little knowledge of the firm or of the people with whom he or she must work. Perhaps a preferable choice would be to appoint someone in the company who has the managerial qualifications and give him or her the required technical training. In staffing other vacancies, too, most firms prefer to select suitable candidates from within and to train them in the necessary skills. This approach is particularly valid in the case of systems analysts who must be familiar with company operations.

Programmers are more likely to be recruited from outside than analysts and other data processing employees. This may especially be true when the programming job is considered to be basically coding and includes little in the way of systems work. In staffing programming jobs requiring some degree of systems analysis, a firm may give technical training to people possessing a knowledge of the business, or it may hire experienced programmers (or programmer trainees) and school them in company policies, problems, and operations. Businesses have usually found that *when suitable candidates are available,* the first approach is preferable.[7] In spite of these considerations,

[7]There are several *advantages associated with internal selection:* (1) employees have a better understanding of the business; (2) their work habits and personality traits are easier to appraise; (3) having demonstrated some degree of company loyalty, they may be less inclined to leave the firm after they are trained; and (4) internal selection can improve employee morale. In some situations, too, union contract agreements may specify that selections be made internally.

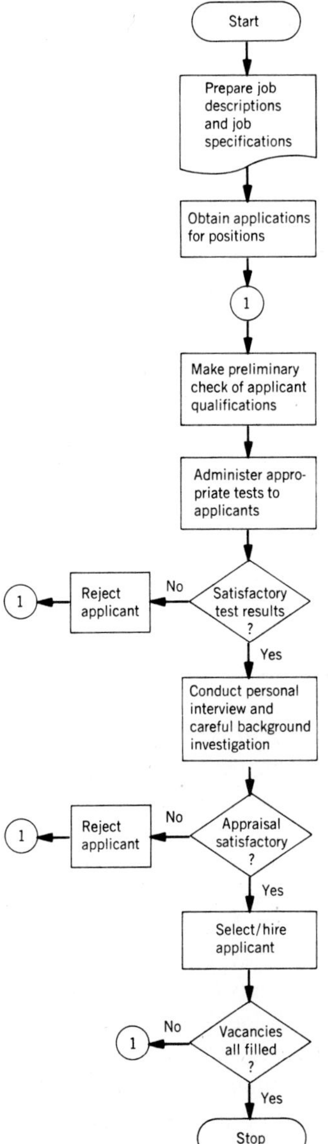

Figure 6-4 The selection process.

however, hiring experienced programmers may help speed up a conversion to new hardware. Many organizations have found that programmers skilled in the use of the hardware ordered for a new system are a valuable complement to company trainees.[8]

Selection Procedures When possible candidates have been identified, it is then necessary to balance and compare their qualifications with those listed in

[8]Of course, there is always the danger that they may select an "experienced" programmer who is interested in keeping one jump ahead of past mistakes.

the job specifications. Sorting out the "best" applicants is a difficult job. The screening process generally involves the use of such selection devices as *aptitude or skill tests, personal interviews,* and careful *examination of records* indicating the candidate's educational background, experience, and work habits. A frequently used approach in the selection of analyst and programmer *trainees* is to give candidates an aptitude test[9] and then to follow up with interviews and careful record examinations on all who receive satisfactory test scores. In the selection of *experienced* programmers, personal interviews and personal or telephone contacts with parties familiar with the work of the candidate are of particular importance. Proficiency tests are sometimes used to check on the ability of a candidate to program a test problem. Tests may also be used in the selection of computer-operations personnel. These tests measure manual dexterity, mechanical aptitude, clerical aptitude, etc., and they generally yield satisfactory results.

Selection decisions follow the testing, interviewing, and background-investigation phases. The chosen candidates must then be trained to prepare them for their new duties.

Training Selected Employees

Extensive preliminary training is likely to be needed by those selected to be systems analysts and programmers. Trainees selected from within the organization will need to master the necessary technical details, and experienced analysts and programmers hired from outside will have to learn a great deal about the business. Of course, in addition to having a *knowledge of the business and the industry,* the systems analyst must also understand the *techniques of systems analysis and design.* There is lack of uniformity at the present time in the methods used to train (*educate* is probably a better word) analysts to meet the latter requirement. A good grounding in the "core" courses found in collegiate schools of business combined with further emphasis on accounting systems, communication skills, mathematics, and statistics are felt by many to be prerequisites to more specialized systems training. Graduate and undergraduate programs for additional specialized work in systems analysis and design have been proposed by the Association for Computing Machinery (ACM).[10]

Consulting firms, private institutes, and organizations such as the American Management Association conduct systems-analysis seminars on a limited basis.

[9]*Programmer aptitude tests* are math-oriented exams that *attempt* to measure the ability of trainees to acquire whatever skills are needed to become successful programmers. Although there is lack of agreement about the ability of these tests actually to measure what they claim to measure, when carefully used they may give an indication of a trainee's ability to reason in arithmetic and abstract terms. Since this ability is considered to be an important prerequisite for many data processing jobs, the test may serve as a screening aid. But good test performance alone does not necessarily mean that the candidate will be a successful programmer. The tests do not measure motivation, and they may not begin to measure all the other qualities that may be required.

[10]Details about the graduate programs are found in R.L. Ashenhurst (ed.), "Curriculum Recommendations for Graduate Professional Programs in Information Systems," *Communications of the ACM,* May 1972, pp. 363–398. The details on undergraduate programs are found in J. Daniel Couger (ed.), "Curriculum Recommendations for Undergraduate Programs in Information Systems," *Communications of the ACM,* December 1973, pp. 727–749.

Correspondence courses in systems work are offered by the Association of Systems Management and others. Also, an in-house systems training program utilizing senior analysts as instructors has proved to be effective. For years, computer manufacturers have contracted to teach machine-dependent skills to their customer trainees. Their programs in formal systems training are newer, since systems analysis is independent of machines; however, their systems representatives have provided some on-the-job-training in analysis and design techniques to customer personnel over the years.

Programmers must obviously possess *an understanding of computer hardware and software.* (The formal training given to analysts in this area may parallel or be identical with the formal training received by programmers.) One method employed to introduce those programmer students who have been selected from within the firm to hardware and software concepts is to enroll them in the vendor's programming classes. These classes introduce the students to the vendor's hardware and software that can be used. Such courses vary in length from one to six weeks, they are usually offered at the vendor's educational center, and they generally emphasize coding. Following satisfactory completion of the vendor's course, the students may receive additional on-the-job instruction from other experienced programmers who may be available. Alternatively, the students may receive all their training from in-house educational operations and/or from courses offered by independent training organizations.

Programmer training is a continuous, lengthy, and expensive process. To the surprise (and dismay) of many executives, it has been found that *at least six months* is generally required before programmers attain a *minimum* level of proficiency. Training costs per programmer may run into the thousands of dollars. Of course, in addition to the training available from vendors and through in-house activities, programming skills are also taught by consultants, professional organizations, colleges and universities, and vocational schools.[11]

Equipment manufacturers and vocational schools also offer brief courses to train operators of peripheral equipment. On-the-job training is often the only preparation required. Because of their need to know some programming, computer operators are often sent to the vendor's programming course or they receive the necessary in-house training.

Selecting and training employees for vacancies in the computer department are important aspects of staffing. But managers must also motivate computer personnel if they hope to achieve organizational goals.

Motivating Computer Personnel

Although the problem of turnover among skilled employees in the computer department has been reduced somewhat in recent years, it has not disappeared. Locating and training replacements remains a time-consuming and expensive

[11]More information on these training organizations (and on training approaches) may be found in Gerald M. Weinberg and Daniel P. Freedman, "Training and Motivation of ADP Personnel," a chapter in *Automatic Data Processing Handbook,* McGraw-Hill Book Company, New York, 1977, pp. 5-23–5-31.

activity in many organizations. Furthermore, department productivity may suffer seriously because of the departure of key personnel. It is therefore important for computer managers to keep turnover to a minimum. Psychologists have outlined the needs and factors that *influence* and *motivate* human behavior. Since motivated employees are less likely to leave an organization and are more likely to be highly productive members of a department, the manager should be aware of these important behavioral concepts.

What are the needs and factors that *influence* and *motivate* behavior? What is likely to cause job satisfaction and dissatisfaction among computer staff members? Behavioral scientists tell us that human needs may be classified into a series of ranks or levels, as summarized in Figure 6-5.

Professor Frederick Herzberg of the University of Utah has made a distinction between those factors that motivate and those that only influence behavior. The *motivating* factors are such high-level needs as (1) the need to *achieve* something useful, (2) the need to be *recognized* for such achievement, (3) the need to have the *work itself be meaningful,* (4) the need to be *responsible* for making decisions, and (5) the need to *grow and advance.* In short, job satisfaction, high production, and low employee turnover are related to the self-fulfillment of people on the job.

The lower-level *physical, security, social,* and *status* needs are sometimes called *maintenance* factors. According to Herzberg, the presence of these factors, along with economic and employee-orientation factors, does *not* necessarily motivate workers, because such factors tend to be taken for granted. The absence of one or more of these factors, however, may have an *adverse influence* on employee behavior and may result in job dissatisfaction, low production, and high turnover.

The information systems manager must therefore look beyond the lower-

Figure 6-5 Employee Need Classifications

Need classification and explanation
1 *Physiological needs.* Included in this lowest-level category are the needs for food, clothing, shelter, and sleep. They are necessary for survival and thus receive first priority. When thwarted, these needs override in importance all others in influencing behavior; when regularly satisfied, they cease to direct human behavior.
2 *Safety needs.* The needs for protection against danger, threat, or deprivation begin to dominate human behavior when the physiological needs are satisfied.
3 *Social needs.* When the above needs are satisfied, social needs, i.e., the need to belong to a group and to associate with and be accepted by others, become important influencing factors.
4 *Ego needs.* When the first three need levels are reasonably satisfied, ego needs become important in behavior motivation. There are two kinds of egoistic needs: (1) those that relate to the *self-esteem* of an individual, e.g., the needs for self-confidence, achievement, and independence, and (2) those that relate to the *reputation* of an individual, e.g., the needs for status, recognition, and respect. Unlike the lower needs, these are rarely satisfied; people strive for more satisfaction of these needs once they have become important to them.
5 *Self-fulfillment needs.* The final level in the need hierarchy reflects the desire of individuals to realize their own potential, continue to develop, and be creative.

level needs in motivating his or her staff. These needs *must* be satisfied, of course, but frequent raises and private offices may not be enough to reduce turnover and produce motivated employees. What are likely to be more important in achieving these desirable ends are (1) the promise of challenging work, (2) the assignment of greater responsibility to staff members, (3) the setting of realistic and carefully thought-out objectives, and (4) the opportunity to grow and develop through such means as carefully planned training programs.

ORGANIZING THE COMPUTER FACILITY

In Chapter 5, we considered such important organizational questions as where the data will be processed, where the data will be stored, and where computing resources will be located within the business. In this section, we will now look at the organizational composition of the computer department itself. Of course, the decisions made in response to those earlier questions will have a direct bearing on the composition of a particular computer facility. For example, a facility located at the headquarters of a company that has elected to use a centralized data processing and storage approach would probably not be organized like the headquarters facility of a firm that has distributed most of the data processing and storage functions to outlying branches.

The composition of a computer facility thus depends on the scope and magnitude of the data processing work that must be performed and the extent to which this work is carried out by the particular department. It is usual, however, to include the activities of system analysis and design, program preparation, and computer operation in the department. Although other logical arrangements are possible, Figure 6-3 provides us with an organizational framework from which combinations or further subdivisions of activities may be made as needed.[12]

Because of the close cooperation that must also exist between programmers and systems analysts, it is generally desirable that both groups report to the same executive to minimize friction. The *systems-analysis section* acts as the vital interface between outside operating departments and the other sections in the computer organization. As noted earlier, it may be desirable to maintain systems analysts in the operating divisions of large firms with centralized computer centers.

There is no reason why a single supervisor could not be in charge of both systems analysis and program preparation. In medium-sized and large organizations, however, a separate supervisor is frequently found. The *programming function* is sometimes subdivided into (1) the preparation of new applications and (2) the maintenance of existing programs. Authority may also be given to one or more individuals to make sure that proper standards and documentation levels are maintained. In order to fix total responsibility for the design, implementation, and maintenance of a new system, it is often desirable to establish a *project group* of analysts and programmers. (Such a group might

[12]For the pros and cons of this and other organizational possibilities, see Thomas R. Gildersleeve, "Organizing the Data Processing Function," *Datamation,* November 1974, pp. 46–50.

employ the chief programming team or egoless programming team concepts.) Under this type of *project organization* (Figure 6-6), a project leader might report to a manager of new system development. There may be training and motivational benefits from this type of approach.

The function of the *computer-operations section* is to prepare the input data and produce the output information on a continuing production basis. Multiple shifts may be required. The control of equipment time and the scheduling of processing activities are an important part of the duties of the operations supervisor. Controls must also be established to make sure that input data are accurate. Computer operators, operators of peripheral equipment, keypunch operators, and media librarians are found in this section. The total number of employees may be large, and turnover is likely to be high; thus, personnel-management considerations may occupy a significant part of the operations supervisor's time.

The *operations-research section* may logically be assigned to some other corporate planning element concerned with the overall study of company operations. But since the use of computers and data files is required to support many of the mathematical models which operations-research (OR) personnel create, there may be good reasons for assigning them to the computer department for coordination purposes. Certainly, the work of the OR and systems-analysis groups should be closely coordinated. It makes little sense to develop a mathematical model if the system will not provide the necessary input data.

The *telecommunications function* may also logically be assigned to some other organizational unit. However, there is a growing tendency to place the responsibility for both computing and telecommunications services under a single information management executive. In some smaller firms, an analyst or programmer might be able to make the necessary telecommunications decisions.

Figure 6-6 Possible project organization of computer facility.

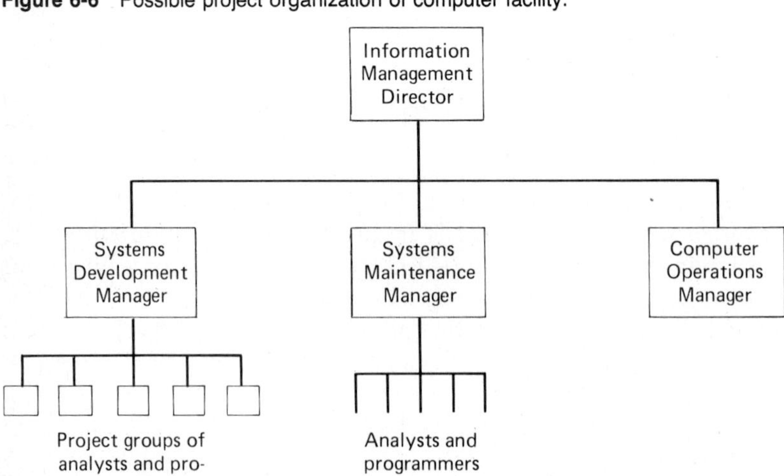

But as the distinctions between data processing and data communications become more blurred, as the knowledge needed to efficiently manage the complex communications networks that many organizations are now planning becomes more specialized, and as new techniques and services to carry voice, data, and facsimile messages between remote points are implemented, the need for a separate telecommunications function located as shown in Figure 6-3 may become more acute.

REVIEW AND DISCUSSION QUESTIONS

1 (*a*) How may individuals benefit from changes in job duties resulting from computer usage? (*b*) How may their job duties be adversely affected?

2 What changes in employment status may result from computer usage?

3 (*a*) What activities may be performed by a data base administrator? (*b*) Can you think of any reasons why the DBA function might be located outside the computer department?

4 What advantages might there be to organizing analysts and programmers into project groups?

5 *a*) What steps are included in the process to select computer personnel? (*b*) What is a job description? (*c*) What is a job specification?

6 Give brief job descriptions and job specifications for the following positions: (*a*) information systems manager, (*b*) systems analyst, (*c*) programmer, (*d*) data base administrator, (*e*) computer operator.

7 Discuss the possible procedures that may be used to recruit candidates for new jobs. (*b*) What selection procedures may be used to fill data processing positions?

8 What are the needs which influence and motivate human behavior?

9 (*a*) What is likely to cause job dissatisfaction among computer staff members? (*b*) What is likely to motivate employees?

Chapter 6 Readings

INTRODUCTION TO READINGS 18 THROUGH 20

18 Organizations constantly face the difficult job of motivating professionals, and in this reading Professors Cougar and Zawacki analyze some of the problems involved with the development of an efficient dp organization.

19 Organization change can produce employee resistance in the forms of hostility and aggression. In this reading, Louis Fried points out how these symptoms appear, why they are caused, and what managers can do to avoid them or to combat their effects.

20 Information security is changing the way that systems are designed and made operational. In this article, Belden Menkus emphasizes *management's responsibility for safeguarding the information* in an organization.

Reading 18

What Motivates DP Professionals

J. Daniel Cougar
Robert A. Zawacki

On a recent trip to Des Moines, we were forced to make a change of planes in Lincoln, Nebraska. While we were waiting in the terminal, another passenger made a surprising seat request. He wanted to sit in the middle seat in the three-abreast arrangement of the Boeing 727. One of us asked the Frontier clerk if this request was as unusual as we suspected. "First time it ever happened in my five years with the airline," he responded.

Odds are that this passenger wasn't a programmer or an analyst. We have just concluded the first part of a survey on what motivates dp employees. The survey revealed that systems professionals have a startlingly low proclivity for social interaction. In fact, the results showed that these jobholders have *negligible* need to work with other individuals.

It follows that programmers and analysts are not necessarily seeking the kind of interaction that programming team concepts are imposing. (Other results suggest that systems professionals won't readily take to the increased specialization that team concepts call for either.) These approaches might be well accepted in other fields, but their implementation requires special considerations for dp personnel.

Dp professionals are different from others in a variety of ways, the research shows, including having a higher need for personal growth than other profes-

Reprinted with permission of *Datamation* ® magazine, © copyright by Technical Publishing Company, a division of Dun-Donnelly Publishing Corporation, a Dun & Bradstreet Company, 1978—all rights reserved.

sionals do. The results show much more, too, verifying some of the suspicions we have always had about dp professionals, and providing some surprises in other areas.

We're learning that the computer profession, now more than 25 years old, may be assuming some of the behavioral problems characteristic of older disciplines, such as engineering and accounting. Worker alienation is a major problem in many fields today. Jobs have not kept pace with changes in our society such as in worker attitudes, aspirations, and values. Managers have attempted to reduce alienation and improve the quality of work life by trying a plethora of ideas for humanizing work, including sensitivity training, management by objectives, shortening the work week, expanding worker involvement in the decision making process, etc.

Those old signs of job dissatisfaction are emerging in the computer field too. Although the aura of excitement of a dynamic field continues to attract persons into the profession, it no longer retains them. Individuals are seeking a more meaningful experience than just being part of a fast-growing profession. The job itself must produce the essential elements of satisfaction.

The behaviorists have identified factors key to motivation and satisfaction in other disciplines. But are they the same for our profession? Even if they are identical, does each factor have the same degree of importance in our field as in others? What does motivate the dp employee?

A straightforward way of answering those questions is to compare the data processing professionals' perceptions of their jobs with job perceptions of other professionals. This can be done using the model in Fig. 1.

Figure 1 According to the behaviorists' model, developed by Hackman and Oldham, the presence of five key job characteristics leads to the employee feeling that he experiences meaningfulness from his work, responsibility for outcomes of the work and knowledge of the results of the work. These "critical" psychological states, in turn, lead to high productivity and low job turnover.

Numerous studies have been done, using a Job Diagnostic Survey, to determine whether those core job dimensions are available in various jobs. The authors have tailored the survey mechanism to fit dp employees, making it possible to learn how dp employees see their jobs and whether their perceptions of their work differ from those of other employees.

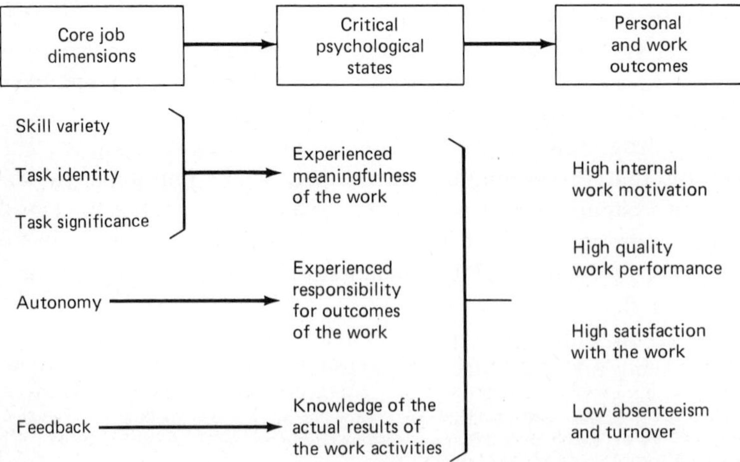

KEY JOB FACTORS

The model identifies five important characteristics of a job (called "core job dimensions" by the originators of the model). Skill variety (tasks that challenge the individual's skills and abilities), task identity (completing a "whole" and identifiable piece of work), and task significance lead to experienced meaningfulness of the job. Task autonomy leads to experienced responsibility for outcomes of the job. Finally, feedback concerning effectiveness of the employee's efforts provides knowledge of results of the job.

Since the model has been used to collect information on other professionals, it allows us to compare dp professionals to some kind of a norm. It turns out that systems analysts and programmer analysts rate their jobs higher, in terms of the existence of these key job dimensions, than other professionals do. However, programmers rate their jobs slightly lower than other professionals do. (See Table 1.)

The model identifies three "critical psychological states" associated with high levels of internal motivation, satisfaction, and quality of performance—and with correspondingly low levels of absenteeism and job turnover.

The two behaviorists who developed the model, Greg R. Oldham from the Univ. of Illinois and J. Richard Hackman from Yale Univ., use the three "psychological states" experienced by a golfer to illustrate the effect of core dimensions: "Consider, for example, a golfer at a driving range, practicing to get rid of a hook. His activity is *meaningful* to him; he has chosen to do it because he gets a 'kick' from testing his skills by playing the game. He knows that he alone is *responsible* for what happens when he hits the ball. And he has *knowledge of the results* within a few seconds." (J. R. Hackman, G. R. Oldham, Robert Janson, Kenneth Purdy, "A New Strategy for Job Enrichment," *California Management Review,* 1975, vol. 17, no. 4, pp. 57–71.)

1 *Experienced meaningfulness.* The individual must perceive his work as worthwhile or important by some system of values he accepts.

2 *Experienced responsibility.* He must believe that he personally is accountable for the outcomes of his efforts.

Table 1

	Data processing professionals			
Core job dimension factors	**Analysts**	**Prog./analysts**	**Programmers**	**Other professionals**
Skill variety	5.55	5.45	5.23	5.36
Task identity	5.37	5.29	5.00	5.06
Task significance	5.75	5.72	5.46	5.62
Autonomy	5.31	5.48	5.13	5.35
Feedback from job	5.20	5.05	5.10	5.08

Data processing analysts and programmer/analysts rate their jobs higher in terms of key job characteristics than do "other" professionals. Programmers, on the other hand, rate their jobs lower.

The "other professionals" data comes from studies by Hackman and Oldham of over 6,000 persons in the sciences, law, religion, education, writing, art, and entertainment and recreation fields. (Scale: 1 to 7.)

About the Survey Project

To what extent does doing the job itself provide you with information about your work performance? That is, does the actual work itself provide clues about how well you are doing—aside from any "feedback" co-workers or supervisors may provide?

1 - - - - - 2 - - - - - 3 - - - - - 4 - - - - - 5 - - - - - 6 - - - - - 7

1	4	7
Very little; the job itself is set up so I could work forever without finding out how well I am doing.	Moderately; sometimes doing the job provides "feedback" to me; sometimes it does not.	Very much; the job is set up so that I get almost constant "feedback" as I work about how well I am doing.

We began our research project with the hypothesis that data processing professionals *are* different. We sought to identify key variables in job satisfaction and motivation. The ultimate objective is to identify ways in which jobs can be redesigned to improve satisfaction and productivity.

Our research team (a computer scientist and a behavioral scientist) organized the project into three phases, only the first of which has been finished. *Phase I* involved identifying norms for the field. We surveyed data processing personnel in 25 organizations, both in industry and government. The industries represented include: food processing, airlines, electronics, retailing, banking, insurance, and mail order sales. Their data processing organizations ranged in size from 25 to 150 employees and were located in all geographic regions of the United States.

The government organizations included operations at the city, state, and federal level. Their dp groups varied in size from 30 to 200 employees, and were located in 15 states.

Together, more than 600 dp professionals (analysts, programmer/analysts, and programmers) were surveyed, as were more than 1,000 persons in other dp jobs. Tentative findings are presented here on the motivating potential of the three types of "professional" jobs within our career field, and on the motivation patterns of the people in our profession.

Phase II of the project will continue through next year. In it, five to eight firms in five different industries (including, incidentally, the software development industry) will be surveyed to determine the interindustry differences. Government versus private industry comparisons also will be made.

In *Phase III*, which will go on through 1980, we will use techniques proven in other fields to analyze dp jobs for ways to improve job satisfaction, employee motivation, and productivity. This research will include all jobs within a dp unit: key entry, data control, computer operation, programming, systems analysis, programming analysis, supervision, and management. (These job redesign projects begin this year under a government grant. Similar projects will be undertaken in private industry as funds become available.)

We originally sought to define a survey instrument tailored to the dp field. After two months of evaluating various instruments we decided to use, instead, the Job Diagnostic Survey (JDS) developed by Oldham and Hackman, for two principal reasons:

1. The Hackman/Oldham instrument is conceptually sound. Its validity and reliability have been substantiated in studies of more than 6,000 subjects on more than 500 different jobs in more than 50 different organizations.

2. A major objective is to compare our results with prior studies of personnel in other professions. Our hypothesis on the difference between dp professionals and other personnel could be tested if we used the JDS.

We expanded the survey questionnaire to include other elements: employee perceptions on relative importance of problems relating to maintenance, realistic work schedules, access to the computer, access to supervisors and access to others (such as users or personnel in other departments whose work affected ours). Also added to the survey instrument was a section on the relative importance of eight categories of compensation.

The resulting Job Diagnostic Survey contains 94 questions and produces information on 45 variables. The survey is administered individually, in approximately 30 minutes.

Most survey questions ask participants to record their response on a scale of one through seven, as in the example above.

All survey results were analyzed with the computer packages for Analysis of Variance (ANOVA) and SPSS (Statistical Processing for the Social Sciences).

3 *Knowledge of results.* He must be able to determine, on some fairly regular basis, whether the outcomes of his work are satisfactory.

If these conditions exist, a person "tends to feel very good about himself when he performs well." Those good feelings motivate him to try to continue to do well. This is what the behavioral scientists mean by "internal motivation," as opposed to external motivation factors, such as incentive pay or compliments from the boss.

The relationships between the three psychological states listed above and the on-the-job outcomes are illustrated in Fig. 1. When all three are high, then internal work motivation, job satisfaction and work quality are high, and absenteeism and turnover are low.

Data processing employees, according to our results, feel they experience about the same level of meaningfulness from their jobs as do other professionals, but have lower perceptions of the degree of responsibility and knowledge of results. (See Table 2.) The poor ratings on "knowledge of results" stems directly from another category we tested, "feedback from supervision," since feedback from the job itself is about the same for our industry as for others. It appears that our supervisors are not doing anywhere near as good a job as their peers in other professions in providing feedback to employees. (See Fig. 2.) This is an area where immediate improvement is possible.

Also, using the model, a single index can be computed which characterizes a job's motivating potential. That index is called the "motivating potential score," and can be used to compare dp jobs with others. The meaningfulness of this index can be illustrated by showing its relationship to things like absenteeism and job performance, as in Fig. 3.

The right hand side of the model (Fig. 1, again) pictures the "personal outcome" from an individual's job. However, the Job Diagnostic Survey (JDS) used with the model does not measure actual work outcomes: productivity, employee perceptions of their productivity, turnover, or absenteeism. Instead,

Table 2

	Data processing professionals			
Psychological state	**Analysts**	**Prog./analysts**	**Programmers**	**Other professionals**
Experienced meaningfulness	5.56	5.49	5.23	5.40
Experienced responsibility	5.31	5.48	5.13	5.75
Knowledge of results	4.59	4.42	4.55	5.00

In measures expressing how meaningful they feel their jobs are, or how responsible they feel for the outcome of these jobs, dp professionals—especially analysts and programmer/analysts—are not far different from other professionals. In terms of feedback on the results of their work, however, dp employees rate their jobs lower than other professionals do; their supervisors may be at fault for that. (Note that the ratings are derived from those in Table 1. Scale: 1 to 7.)

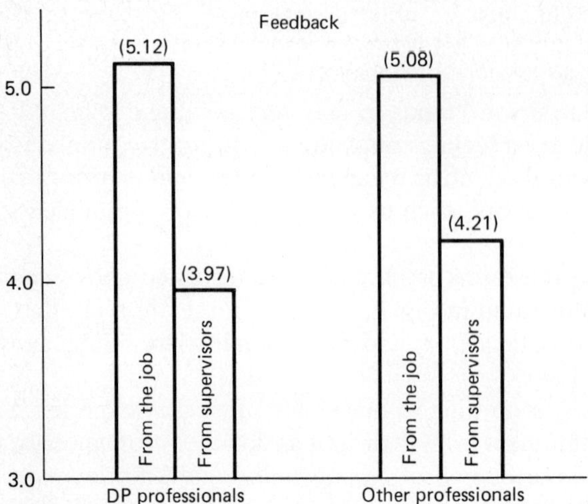

Figure 2 Data processing professionals say they receive most of their feedback on their performance from the job itself, as do other professionals. But the amount of feedback dp employees feel they get from their supervisors is substantially lower than that seen by other professionals—an obvious place for improvement. (Survey responses are given on a scale of 1 to 7.)

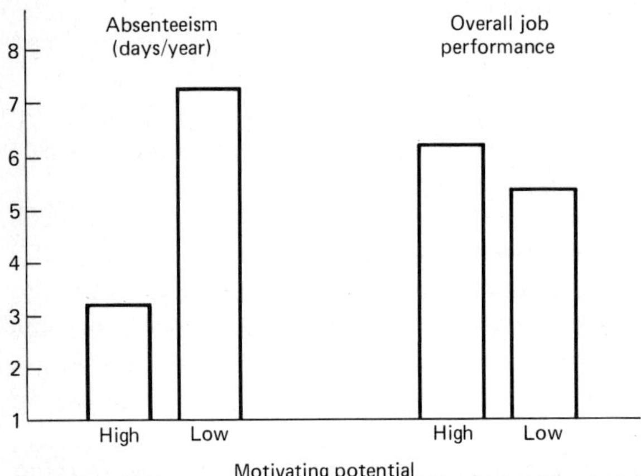

Figure 3 The motivating potential of various jobs can be calculated from the results of the Job Diagnostic Survey, and the index proves to be very well related to things like absenteeism. The results above are from the Hackman/Oldham study of more than 1,000 employees working on about 100 jobs. (The job performance is as rated by supervisors on a 1-to-7 scale.)

employees report directly how satisfied (or dissatisfied) they are with various aspects of their job. Table 3 provides those results. It indicates that dp professionals generally are satisfied. However, although their general satisfaction is higher than that of other professionals, they are less satisfied with supervision.

The JDS proved to be an especially good discriminator. One organization surveyed was not "healthy," in behavioral terms. All others were. In fact we

Table 3

	Data processing professionals			
Measures of satisfaction	**Analysts**	**Prog./analysts**	**Programmers**	**Other professionals**
General satisfaction	5.10	5.37	5.30	4.88
Satisfaction with co-workers	5.01	5.22	4.96	5.48
Satisfaction with supervision	4.64	4.60	4.60	4.89

The results show that dp professionals are fairly satisfied with their jobs in general, somewhat less satisfied with co-workers, and even less satisfied with their supervisors. (Scale: 1 to 7.)

attempted to survey only organizations whose working environment was healthy, because we wanted to build "norms"; in the past our profession has been without benchmarks in the behavioral areas. The unhealthy organization was significantly below the norms on most of the core job dimensions. With the information from the model we have a substantive basis for beginning the job redesign process in that organization.

GROWTH NEED VERSUS SOCIAL NEED

We expect that people who have a high need for personal growth and development will respond more positively to a job high in motivating potential than people with low growth need strength will.

Obviously, not everyone is able to become internally motivated—even when the motivating potential of the job is quite high. Behavioral research has shown that the psychological needs of people determine who can (and who cannot) become internally motivated at work. Some people have strong need for personal accomplishment—for learning and developing beyond where they are now, for being stimulated and challenged, and so on. These people are high in "growth need."

The need for growth is quite high for dp professionals, compared to other professionals and to other job categories. Table 4 shows this effect. This outcome has little surprise for managers accustomed to insistence by their staff that they be provided training, be allowed to attend conferences and seminars, etc. (A frequent result of behavioral research is that intuitive beliefs are substantiated. Survey data on growth need is a good example.)

However, the key reason for computing growth need is to compare it with the job's potential to fulfill that need. A job low in motivating potential will frustrate a person with high need for growth. It is a perfect example of the old cliche of a round peg in a square hole.

The motivating potential score shown in the right column of Table 4 enables a comparison of the job potential to the employee growth need. Hackman's and

Table 4

Job category	Growth need	Motivating potential
Dp professions	6.02	157.5
Other professions	5.59	153.7
Sales	5.70	146.0
Service	5.38	151.7
Managerial	5.30	155.9
Clerical	4.95	105.9
Machine trades	4.82	135.8
Bench work	4.88	109.8
Processing	4.57	105.1
Structural work	4.54	140.6

Putting an employee with high growth need into a job with high motivating potential leads to a high quality performance and to low absenteeism and turnover. Trying to put an employee with low growth need in such a job such as the structural worker in this table, risks overstretching the individual.

Fortunately, there is a good match in what dp jobs have to offer and what dp employees need. (The scale for growth need is again 1 to 7, the "motivating potential" scores are derived numbers and are not relative to any scale.)

Oldham's survey results shown include an example of the imbalance of growth need and motivating potential. Notice that the lowest growth need is for structural work. On the other hand, the motivating potential for that field is near the midpoint for all jobs reported in the table. Thus, jobs in that industry have a motivating potential above the growth needs of the workers.

The dp field provides some better matches. Both the dp individual's growth need and the dp job's motivating potential score are high—the highest in the table. (Unfortunately, our research indicates that such a balance is not so prevalent among the other jobs in the data processing organization.)

Although the average for all organizations in our study showed a high positive correlation between growth need and motivating potential, this was not always the case for individual organizations. For example, the organization with the next to the highest growth need in our survey was the lowest in motivation. In contrast, another organization with the lowest growth need was highest in motivation. Now that they are aware of this disparity, these organizations can analyze their jobs to reduce the inequity.

The most surprising result of the survey was the measurement of the variable labeled "social need." Survey questions related to this variable determine an individual's need to interact with others. The average score on this variable for all other professionals was 5.48. For all data processing professionals in our survey, the score is 4.19. (See Fig. 4.) However, for five organizations the average was only 2.23! So, while some professions attract people who have a high propensity for—and reinforcement from—interaction with others, our profession does not appear to exhibit this characteristic.

The implications are significant. Programmers and analysts have increasingly been grouped into teams in anticipation that productivity will be increased. The chief programmer team concept has been widely publicized and advocated.

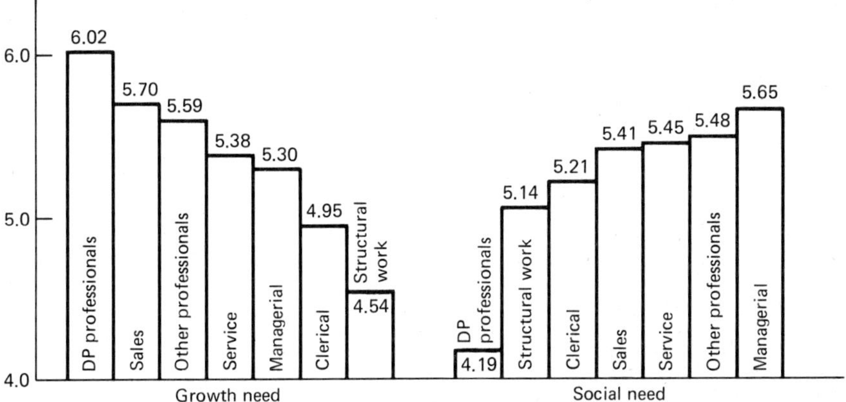

Figure 4 Are programmers, analysts, and programmer/analysts "loners"? The results seem to confirm that. They are also unusual in their need for individual growth. (As before, responses are on a scale of 1 to 7.)

Some have suggested that it is the social interaction of the team that has produced whatever productivity benefits resulted from the programmer team approach. If our study is representative, it mandates caution in accepting such views.

What does this survey statistic mean to a manager of dp professionals? The lack of need for social interaction does not mean that teams should not be utilized. It simply indicates that dp professionals are not actively seeking a team experience. (Managers of other parts of the company will find their employees eager to interact, and a team approach is a natural organization to facilitate such interaction.) This conclusion is supported by data from Table 3. Dp professionals in the survey organizations were satisfied with their co-workers. In other words, they were getting the interaction they needed—as long as it was not overdone.

Our industry, like others, has a number of experientially derived theorems that have not previously been validated by statistical studies. For example, how often have you heard the comment that programmers are "loners"?

The growth need section of our study lent authenticity to one of those theorems. Here is another case. Perhaps the theorem is best expressed by Gerald Weinberg in his widely quoted *Psychology of Computer Programming* (Van Nostrand Reinhold Co., N.Y., 1971). "If asked, most programmers probably say they preferred to work alone in a place where they wouldn't be disturbed by other people."

However, we interpret the survey results on social need as follows: management does not need to reduce emphasis on the project team, it just needs to control the frequency and duration of team meetings. Consider the oft-cited guideline that structured walkthroughs should be limited to two hours. You don't find similar guidelines in the literature on management meetings! (The social need strength for managers in the Hackman/Oldham surveys was 5.65. Managers could be in meetings all day—and love it.) The structured walk-through guideline was empirically derived, probably by judging the increasing level of impatience by analysts and programmers when a meeting dragged on.

Also, a low social need may indicate the need for additional training on supervisory techniques when dp professionals are promoted to management positions.

WHAT IT MEANS

Although we have barely begun the in-depth analysis of our data base, some tentative propositions are:

1 *Dp professionals have some unique differences from the general population.* They have substantially higher growth need strength than *any* of the job categories surveyed by Hackman and Oldham. This is true of analysts, programmer/analysts, and programmers. Also, they have the *lowest* social need strength among professionals—significantly lower than others.

2 *A good job match is possible.* For the survey firms—intentionally selected because they are healthy—the motivating potential of the jobs match the growth needs of dp professionals.

3 *Supervisory feedback to employees can be improved.* Employees in the survey firms are generally satisfied with co-workers and with supervisors. Nevertheless, they believe that feedback from supervision should be improved. They rate this category lower than do their counterparts in the other professions.

4 *An appropriate conceptual model exists.* The Hackman/Oldham model is applicable to the computer field. Our analysis substantiated that of the original researchers, with comparable statistical reliability and validity. The conceptual model (in Fig. 1) is useful for management in our field to analyze individual motivation patterns, and the Job Diagnostic Survey is useful to gather data to determine satisfaction levels and work outcomes.

5 *Job redesign has potential.* Studies of other industries show that job redesign can increase satisfaction and productivity. With the norms resulting from our study, managers in the computer field have the basis for determining which jobs have potential for improvement.

Productivity consists of two parts—improved techniques and increased motivation to utilize those techniques. An enormous amount of time and energy has gone into the first part, technique improvement. Why has the second part, motivation, been given so little attention?

Is it the qualitative nature of that part? Are we so oriented to the analysis of the quantitative part of the job that we willfully ignore the harder-to-measure aspects of employee motivation?

Or is it the fact that we are "systematic" people who deal in practicalities? We want something we can touch or see. "Lines of code per hour" is a measurement that can be substantiated. Degree of motivation cannot be seen, felt, tasted or smelled—but it exists.

We are emulating the industrial engineers of the 1940s, who kept chipping away at each job on the auto assembly line until it was splintered into the ultimate level of specialization. We seem to be concentrating just as fervently on fragmenting the jobs of analysis and programming. The chief programmer team concept is the latest in the long list of moves for enhancing specialization. The analysis/programming task now is fragmented into the elements performed by the chief programmer, the moderator, the librarian, the recorder, etc. Perhaps jobs should be *enlarged* in scope, rather than reduced.

If we devote equal time to the analysis of motivation and the ingredients of job satisfaction, this alone may increase productivity. However, productivity increase is the wrong reason for initiating such a study. Shouldn't a supervisor gain as much satisfaction from helping employees achieve fulfillment as from meeting cost/schedule objectives?

Fortunately, researchers like Hackman and Oldham have proved in other industries that productivity can be increased by a better matching of jobs with individuals.

We already have a data base rich with information for further analysis. For example, our data on problem areas and on compensation preferences presently is being analyzed for another *Datamation* article.

During the next year we will be increasing our data base to include more than 2,000 professionals, to ensure a representative set of "norms." At the same time, we will be conducting job redesign studies, to better understand the factors which produce job satisfaction.

Our profession has been very progressive in developing new product-related techniques. Let's hope that progressive attitude will now extend to better utilization of the behavioral sciences.

READING 18 DISCUSSION QUESTIONS

1 What type of motivational approaches can be used to improve the performance of *professional* employees such as those in data processing departments?
2 Are there special differences that require alternative motivational approaches for data processing department employees?

Reading 19

Hostility in Organization Change

Louis Fried

The Chairman of the Board of a large international manufacturing company managed to coax away one of his chief competitor's top men. This man, a successful and independent thinking executive, was appointed President of the company. He brought with him a few key men with whose aid he proceeded to change some of the company's operations and make specific changes to product

Reprinted from the *Journal of Systems Management,* June 1972, pp. I4–21. Reprinted by permission from the Association for Systems Management, 24587 Bagley Road, Cleveland, Ohio. Louis Fried is vice president and management services manager for the Title Insurance and Trust Company, Los Angeles.

design. He also introduced a different style of management with little respect for conventional organization structures.

Although the company had three strong Vice Presidents, the Chairman of the Board felt that none had a broad enough background to manage the entire company. Furthermore, the appointment of one might make the other two unhappy. Bringing in an outsider who had a top reputation in the field seemed like an ideal solution.

Nineteen months later, at substantial cost to the company, the Chairman of the Board fired the President rather than lose a number of top level and talented executives, including at least one of the Vice Presidents.

During the nineteen months the President and Vice Presidents frequently countermanded each other's orders. Previously hidden personality conflicts at top levels came to the surface. Discontent within the top echelons of the organization became apparent as complaints were forwarded around the President to the Chairman of the Board. Morale throughout the organization plunged.

This well-known story of the Ford Motor Company in 1969 provides a prime example of hostility and aggression resulting from organization change.[1]

Whenever there is a significant change in management personnel in almost any organization, there is also generally a change in the style of management.[2] This change in style alone could account for such a depth of hostile reaction, but any organization change will arouse some reaction.

Some changes are more likely to arouse aggressive response than others. These types of change would include:

1 The merger of two organizations into one

2 The firing or demotion and subsequent replacement of an organization head

3 Improperly introduced major changes in work rules, equipment, or methods (this excludes the types of changes characterized by the Hawthorne experiments)

Recently, it has become popular to maintain that man is instinctively aggressive and that this is his natural state. Several best-selling books contend that humans work together only when their needs overpower their basic aggressive instincts. Robert Ardrey, in *The Territorial Imperative,* imputes to man a drive toward territoriality and its aggressive defense. Anthony Storr, in *Human Aggression,* combines the Freudian concept of the death-wish with an instinctive aggression. In *On Aggression,* Konrad Lorenz develops an evolutionary theme to illustrate the basic nature of human hostility.

It does not seem necessary, however, to go so far afield to find the genesis of aggression and hostility arising in the context of organizational change, though determining the reasons for aggressive reaction in this context may be rather like

[1]L. G. O'Donnell and G. A. Nikolaieff, "Bunkies' Downfall," *The Wall Street Journal,* Sept. 17, 1969, pp. 1, 10.

[2]G. A. Bassett, *The New Face of Communication,* American Management Association, 1968, p. 164.

peeling an onion, and require exposing several layers before getting to the core of the problem.

In examining the layers of this onion (Figure 1) we must recognize that there is a mental and emotional inertia in both individuals and groups. Robert Tannenbaum says that the most characteristic individual and group reaction to change is resistance.[3] Even before the nature of the change can be determined it appears that change itself is charged with negative valences.

The obvious manifestation of hostility is overt aggressive action. This may take several forms, ranging from reduced job efficiency to leaving the organization. The type of action taken by the individual is a product of his life-long conditioning coupled with his understanding of the nature of the change. Each person interprets change differently, so that the change is not precisely recognized for what management intends it to be, but what the employee perceives it to be.[4]

The proximate cause of overt aggressive action is frustration. Frustration results when an external barrier stands between a motivated individual and his goal.[5] These goals may be rational, consciously recognized objectives or they may be human needs far down on Abraham Maslow's "need hierarchy" list.[6]

Frustration is born of the conflicts that arise between the requirement to

[3]R. Tannenbaum, I. R. Weschler, and F. Massarik, *Leadership and Organization,* McGraw-Hill Book Company, New York, 1961, p. 80.

[4]J. B. Miner, *Personnel Psychology,* The Macmillan Co. of Canada, Limited, Toronto, 1969, p. 72.

[5]B. Berelson and G. A. Steiner, *Human Behavior,* Harcourt, Brace & World, Inc., New York, 1964, p. 267.

[6]A. Maslow, "The Need-Hierarchy," *Management and the Behavioral Sciences,* Allyn and Bacon, Inc., Boston, 1968.

Figure 1

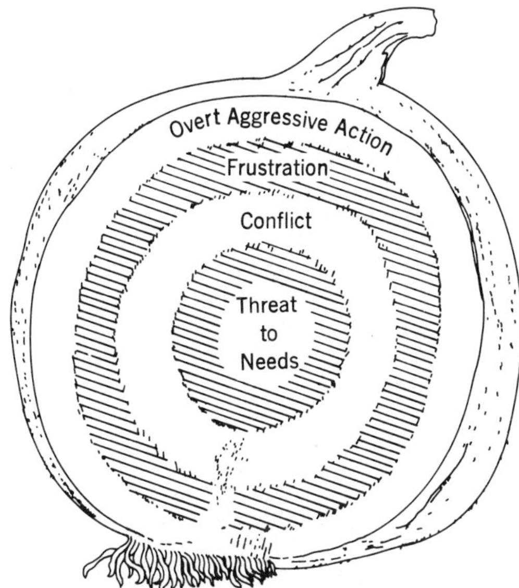

accept the externally imposed change and the forces driving the individual to reject change. The intensity of the conflict depends on what the individual perceives the impact of the change to be on his goals or needs. The core of the onion then, the central reason for aggressive resistance to change, is the threat to the satisfaction of human needs. The threat of change seems first to attack the highest level needs and gradually work its way down the pyramid. Prior to examining specific types of activity, there is a second model to keep in mind. (Figure 2.)

FEAR

Change is strange, threatening, and full of uncertainties. In fact, uncertainty itself is always threatening. This generates fear.[7] The fear syndrome generates a "fight or flight" conflict which leads directly to overt aggressive activity or departure from the organization.

Both models exhibit the common characteristic of conflict. This conflict is normally resolved before any action is taken by the individual. All goal directed activity involves some degree of conflict, but usually there is no frustration as long as satisfactory progress is made toward the goal. The employee who remains with the organization may adapt to frustration by regressing, by becoming aggressive and hostile, by developing a tendency to blame others, or remain frustrated by doing nothing (which leads to more tension).[8]

[7] L. R. Sayles and G. Strauss, *Human Behavior in Organizations,* Prentice-Hall, Inc., Englewood Cliffs, N.J., 1966, p. 304; and R. Tannenbaum and others, op.cit., p. 82.

[8] C. Argyris, *Personality and Organization,* Harper & Row, Publishers, Incorporated, New York, 1957, p. 78.

Figure 2

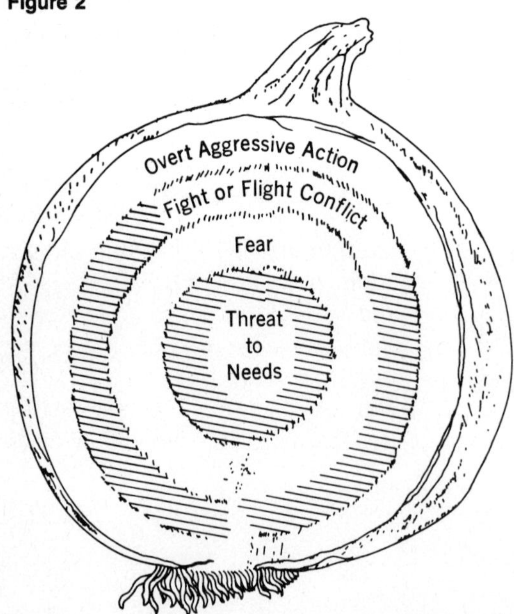

Individual resistance to change may be indicated by reduced job efficiency. On an individual basis this inefficiency may be involuntary. However, group resistance may be evidenced by a conscious restriction of output.[9]

Every group is a social system, and any change in one of its component parts is likely to require or result in alteration of other parts. A change in the number of orders given to subordinates. This results in a change in interpersonal relations, which can lead to additional resistance.

Each person is influenced by his attitude toward the objectives of the organization, by his group loyalties, and by his personal relationships. According to the way they perceive the impact of change on themselves, the individual's positive or negative feeling about the change may dominate his attitude.

This could result in previously buried factional differences arising with renewed strength, as in the example of the Ford Motor Company. At this point the regressed individual is sunk in a morass of ineffectuality. He has now reached a point of protracted regression at which it is frequently converted to active aggression and hostility.[10] His aggression may be expressed verbally, through griping or rumor-mongering, or it may take physical form.

Where the change is one of work method and the organization consists of old, trusted management, aggression may be displaced to the "efficiency experts" or to minority groups attempting to enter the work environment.

The organization must continually be viewed as the social group within which the individual functions. The group strongly influences the behavior of its members by major pressures toward conformity.[11] Very high-ranking influential members of a group do not conform as strictly, and are more central in the group's interaction. It is these individuals who prove to be the focal points for factionalism within the informal group when their perceived personal interests are best served. Conflict comes from a lack of firm formal direction, as in an unstructured group. Furthermore, when changes in work methods or objectives are introduced they tend to change the importance of different functions and activities, threatening the power and independence of old groups.[12]

DEFENDING STATUS

The individual's fifth level needs for self-realization and self-fulfillment are the first to be threatened by the process of regression. At this point he will fall back to defend his needs for status, recognition, and respect.

Consider the case of a group whose manager has been fired by the top management of the organization, and who has been replaced. Assume also that the prior manager had been in the organization for some time, was reasonably well-liked, and had had some opportunity to direct and develop individuals within his organization.

[9]Tannenbaum and others, op.cit., p. 81.
[10]Argyris, op.cit., p. 41.
[11]Berelson and Steiner, op. cit., p. 337.
[12]Tannenbaum and others, op. cit., p. 323.

Initially, the act of firing this manager implies to members of the group that the goals and directions of the manager and the group are questionable in the eyes of top management. Members of the group who felt that they were doing a good job must now re-examine their values. Those who had patterned themselves after the manager in an attempt to emulate his success now find that top management does not recognize or respect this image and has assigned it an extremely low status. At this point group members are defensively dropping back to third level needs for a sense of belonging and identification as a member of a known, respected group. Those members of the organization most likely to manifest concern are in the middle range of status, compensation, and capability. They are the ones aspiring to advancement and who view themselves as capable of advancement.

Those who feel that they cannot advance, either because they are relatively secure in their positions, or because their self-image is one of having reached their maximum of development, tend to accept organization change with relative equanimity.

If the new manager is then appointed from outside the original group, a final blow is dealt to the self-respect of members of the group and they are forced back to concern about second level needs of security or protection against deprivation. In this case the total impact on the individual is readily visible. The individual who stays with the organization and cannot accommodate the changes is subject to exhibiting responses such as regression, overt physical or verbal aggressiveness, and impaired efficiency.

Other symptoms also characterize the individual involved in resistance to change. The individual may escape the situation through apathy, or chronic absenteeism, or tardiness. Tardiness may also represent a physical method of indicating aggression.

In a quest for information to help him formulate his position, or as an expression of hostility, the group member may employ a full range of "testing" activities to determine the relative strengths and weaknesses of the new management resulting from a reorganization. Absenteeism or tardiness may be used to test the guidelines of permitted behavior and help the group member to determine normative behavior as defined by the new management.

New management is not only probed to determine the limitations of behavior that will be permitted, but they are also probed to determine the extent of their skills and knowledge of the area being supervised. The employee does this by observing the reaction of the new manager and the decisions of the new manager when faced with a situation that the employee allowed to arise, or when approached by an employee to make a decision. Most often, the employee has already determined what the answer should be, and is simply trying to find out if the new manager can arrive at the same decision.

In another type of hostile activity, the employee sets out to "punish" the organization for his imagined maltreatment. He may do this by withdrawing from contact with management and sometimes other employees, in an attempt to deny them the benefits of his association.

LEAVING THE ORGANIZATION

The final, and most complete, form of resistance to change is leaving the organization. The reasons for leaving an organization that are recorded in exit interviews rarely contain the truth. This may be because the employee does not want to jeopardize the value of the reference for future positions that can be given by the organization he is leaving. It may be because the employee cannot verbalize or does not realize the real reasons for his leaving. It may also be the fault of the interviewer, who might lead the interviewee into a preconceived direction of thought.

The recorded reasons for leaving do contain some elements of truth and therefore cannot be completely ignored. One study yielded some of the following reasons for members leaving the organization when changes in management and organizational objectives created a new power situation with new patterns of leadership.[13] The reasons given were that functions were being disregarded or that there were not the tools to do the job. Some left because they did not want to go through the extensive readjustments that they felt would be necessary. Others left because they claimed that new policy did not allow them to do the work in which they were interested. Some left because they did not want to engage in a factional struggle.

The more basic reasons may include the fact that turnover results not only from frustration produced by conflict, but also from a direct attempt to escape from the region of negative valences because the future also seems hopeless. The inability to resolve the conflicts underlying his frustration may lead the individual to a potentially self-destructive rage. He seeks the opportunity to strike out against the organization as the symbol of his frustration in a manner that will bring the most attention to his situation and do the most damage to the organization. In what amounts to a kamikaze attempt to damage the organization regardless of personal cost, the employee may quit. This, in effect, is a symbolic suicide of protest.

INTRODUCING CHANGE

The organization manager encounters two sets of pressures. One, from below, is a strong resistance to change. The other, from above, is the pressure to successfully implement the change or lose his position. He must somehow convince his subordinates that the change is right, proper, and for the best.

He must face the fact that there are generally accepted legitimate norms about the rights and responsibilities of both managers and subordinates. These norms are established by a procedure of implicit bargaining, which often includes the process of "testing" described earlier. Change, however, violates the implicit bargain unless carefully introduced.

In the problem of introducing changes to work methods and rules, we are faced with the question of timing. The established manager must consider that

[13] Tannenbaum and others, op. cit., p. 320.

fast changes may lead to violent resistance and disrupt the entire organization. On the other hand, slow changes may invoke some resistance, but it will be less intense at any given time. Even the slow change must be clearly communicated to all employees, or exaggerated fears will arise about where the change is leading.[14]

It is sometimes desirable for a new manager to make all his changes at once. This clearly defines the new "rules of the game" to all members of the organization. The abruptness of this method does incur the risk of losing some employees. However, this risk is a normal part of the management considerations involved in introducing any change.

Even so, a new manager often should wait before taking action until he knows more about the organization and the people. Reality dictates that this waiting period may often be short, since the manager cannot ignore top management pressure for rapid change to improve the performance of the organization.

One general characteristic of changes in methods and work rules, or in the mergers of two organizations into one, is that they can be introduced gradually to the members of the organization. Changes are invariably resisted if the staff is not previously advised or conditioned, and resistance springs from fear of the unknown. It can be reduced by providing appropriate information. Employees who are concerned about meeting their needs are the chief contributors to the "rumor mill." They are so hungry for information that the slightest nuance in an ordinary statement is subject to extensive interpretation. To prevent this the manager must meet the situation head-on.

The manager has one preliminary decision to make. He must decide if he will keep or replace all or part of the present staff. If complete replacement is intended, then his path is clear. He must move as rapidly as possible to accomplish that objective, and may for the most part, disregard the present staff. However, new staff members should be either carefully indoctrinated by the manager personally or segregated from the old staff members to prevent communicating the poor morale of the original organization members to the new organization.

If, however, he intends to retain all or part of the original organization members, then he must find some way to use (or give the illusion of using) participative decision-making techniques. He must make them feel involved in the decision to make the changes and the methodology for implementing the changes.

GROUP DECISION-MAKING

The members of an organization will feel less threatened if it appears that they have some degree of control over their own destiny. It is best for the individual or the group to have some self-direction or control over the impact of the

[14] Sayles and Strauss, op. cit., p. 319.

change. It is always desirable to at least provide the illusion that this is happening. Group discussion and decision-making involves subordinates actively in the process of introducing change and enhances their sense of control over the environment. It also helps to "unfreeze" attitudes so that they can be re-examined.[15]

Group decision-making is a dangerous tool in the hands of the inexperienced manager. The group may decide on a course of action completely opposite to that desired by the manager. He must, therefore, ultimately demonstrate his authority to the group. One way to prevent this ultimate exercise of authority from being too obvious is to return decisions to the group for further consideration of pertinent points until the decision that emerges from the group is either that which the manager desired or an equivalent or better substitute.

Sayles and Strauss feel that when individuals are permitted to participate in making the final decision on a change, it is sometimes useful to ask the group to accept the change on tentative, trial basis. This enables employees to test their reactions and provides them with more facts on which to base their decision. It may also help to unfreeze their attitudes and think objectively about the proposed change. A tentative change appears less threatening and generates less resistance than a permanent change. They also feel that where individuals do not participate in making the final decision, tentative changes may be unwise since they prolong the period of uncertainty and tension. There is also always the chance that employees may effect the final decision by resisting or sabotaging the tentative change.

If the group's participation in the decision-making is only illusory, then the technique of the tentative change is probably unwise. The manager risks being forced to show his hand if the group rejects the change after the trial period.

FRINGE BENEFITS

There are several fringe benefits associated with the use of the group decision-making technique. Participation of the individuals generally results in diminishing the time required to establish new group norms. Individuals who fail to live up to standards of proper conduct as redefined by the group are subjected to pressure to conform. Group decision-making commits each member of the group to carry out the decision that is agreed on. It also serves to improve the group member's image of the group manager.

The group decision-making technique can have some disadvantages. The decision of the involved group may be contrary to the good of the entire organization or differ from the intentions of higher management. Such decisions may frequently be inconsistent with the organization's long-range plans. This may be true if only because the organization members participating in the decision-making do not normally have access to all the facts available to top management.

[15]Sayles and Strauss, op.cit., p. 314.

Group decision-making in a contracting organization environment is probably inappropriate. Because needs for security are much more obviously threatened, one should expect greater resistance to change in a company which is contracting or stationary in size than one which is expanding and providing a greater number of opportunities, even though this involves change. In the contracting organization the group may be forced to decide on preserving or elminating the job of one of its members. This is not only a decision which it is ill-equipped to make, but also a decision that is unfair for management to ask.

Three difficult-to-manage and frequently interrelated conditions do not lend themselves to group decision-making. These are decisions relating to the contracting organization as described above, decisions on which management cannot provide group members with all of the appropriate information even though it is known, and those in which the head of the organization is to be terminated and replaced.

It is obviously as unwise to require a group to make a decision on which all necessary information is not available as it is for a manager to make a decision on the same basis. For this reason, unless the organization can derive some peripheral benefit and is able to absorb the expense of the group operating on a trial-and-error basis, group decision-making should be avoided in this circumstance.

Strategic security reasons may also prevent management from disclosing all information that it has available. Management may suspect a member of the group of relaying proprietary information. Information relating to marketing techniques, products, and manufacturing methods may often require strict secrecy until they are publicly announced in order to derive the maximum tactical advantage. Under these circumstances, group decision-making is again inappropriate.

Finally, it is in the extremely sensitive area of terminating and replacing a group head that group decision-making cannot be used. No successful business organization can be run as a democracy.

No manager can relinquish the decision or the responsibility for naming the subordinate to whom he will delegate authority and whom he expects to hold responsible for its appropriate exercise. Furthermore, no manager can be expected to operate efficiently if each decision must be conditioned by his need to maintain personal popularity with the group.

Each executive, due to the limitations of his span of control, is forced to delegate some of his authority. He shapes the entire character of the organization under him by the appointments he makes to those positions reporting to him. Each appointee subsequently constitutes his staff of members with whom he can comfortably communicate and in whom he has trust. An important corollary to this is that the follower must be able to identify with the leader. Control cannot be exercised if those who wish to control are too different from those who are to be controlled.[16]

[16]J. Klein, *The Study of Groups,* Routledge and Kegan Paul, Ltd., London, 1956, pp. 136 ff.

The appointment of a top-calibre manager to a group whose previous performance was unsatisfactory will generally result in the manager reconstituting the group with personnel closer to his ideals. It will furthermore cause members of the original group to be extremely restive, since they cannot adequately communicate with their new superior.

Given, then, that the group cannot participate in this decision, that no information will be provided by higher management to the group or its original manager prior to his termination, and that no information can be provided to the group relating to the actions of the new manager, this becomes the most difficult introduction of change imaginable. How, then, can it be handled?

INTRODUCING THE NEW MANAGER

Observation of many changes indicates that most managers intuitively feel that where no information can be provided to group members, as little material for conjecture as possible should be allowed to reach the "rumor mill." For this reason many will approach a termination so that once the news has been made public, the terminated group head will be removed from contact with the group as rapidly as possible. This condition assumes normal popularity of the group head with his subordinates and some reasonable question as to whether or not his performance had been inadequate. If the group head is terminated for obvious cause, or if he had been unpopular with his subordinates, no such minimizing of publicity is necessary.

Some brief announcement of the reasons for the manager's removal must be made to the group. This announcement should be as brief, objective, and unambiguous as possible. It should provide as little room for misinterpretation as possible. If the organization desires to retain the members of the affected group, the terminated manager's superior must clearly state to the group the effect of this change on their individual positions.

Several possible courses of action are open to management. They may break up the group and distribute its members through other groups in the organization, they may appoint an interim manager or they may appoint an immediate permanent replacement for the terminated manager. Breaking up the group could normally result in the loss of some of the group members to the organization. The symbolic death of the group with which they identified may so shatter the identification of the individual with the organization that he might be unable to adjust to other groups.

The appointment of an interim manager suffers from the same drawbacks as the introduction of interim change when the group will not be responsible for the decision. In addition, the interim manager cannot be expected to make any but extremely short-range decisions. His immediate superior would be required to make most of the decisions for the group. The personal relationships within the group have been disrupted, the goals of the group are ambivalent, and the temporary manager must face some loss of status when he returns to being an ordinary member of the group. Under these circumstances, very little productive work will get done. The best possible solution is the appointment of a new manager as soon as possible after termination of the original manager.

The ease with which the new manager can assume his role is directly proportional to the briefness of the time between these events. The group which has suffered the shock of losing its leader can absorb the appointment of his replacement as a part of the same event. The norms and patterns of personal relations within the group have only been disrupted one time. On the other hand, if an extended period of time has elapsed, the group has adapted to the circumstances and established a new set of norms and interpersonal relations. These are disrupted again when the permanent appointment is made after some time has elapsed.

It is also difficult, at that time, for the new appointee to say anything reassuring to members of the group regarding the security of their personal position. He does not have enough first hand knowledge to reliably evaluate group members, and they know it. Almost anything he says regarding group member security will be questioned. It is therefore incumbent upon his superior to make any such statements.

The newly appointed manager requires some time before he can be expected to deal appropriately and believably with the problems of group members. With the personal expectations of the new manager being an unknown quantity, the level of frustration within the group can be expected to rise. This frustration is generally undirected and will be manifested in many of the ways previously described.

Until he is prepared to make some believable definitive statements as to his own expectations for group member performance and as to meeting the needs of the group members individually, he should probably avoid meetings of the total group. Such meetings might only serve to provide the group with a focal point for hostility and aggression.

The new manager's first requirement is time . . . time to evaluate the members of his staff . . . time to absorb the situation and the organizational environment. The manager is generally required to maintain at least as good performance as the group had before, even though he may not be able to improve it immediately. It is necessary for him to resist higher management pressures for rapid results until he can make sound, well considered moves. Assuming that he has the necessary management support and has convinced them of the need (and his ability) to establish his own timetable, he must then find a way to buy the necessary amount of time from the members of the group.

If there existed any group cohesion in the past, it has probably been severely damaged by the management changes. However, a large part of the informal organization must still exist. This informal organization has its leaders and high status members. The key to maintaining group performance is the informal leader. By identifying and forming a working relationship with these leaders, he can generally prevent a drastic reduction in the group's performance level.

Re-establishing individual cooperation and group cohesion is extremely important. If these informal leaders do not react in a positive fashion to the manager's approach, they represent a major threat to the effective performance of the new manager. For this reason, if he cannot obtain their cooperation, his only recourse is to remove them from the organization. While their removal might temporarily create an added disturbance, it will allow group hostility to diminish in a shorter time, since some major elements fueling that hostility will be removed.

The new manager must make every effort to get acquainted with his key personnel as soon as possible. While the formal structure of a group meeting should be avoided, individual informal talks provide an excellent method for both evaluating employees and forming interpersonal relations. As soon as possible, those people who can form the cadre of a rebuilt organization should be identified. This cadre and all those whom the manager determines are of value to the organization should be apprised of the manager's opinion as soon as possible. This feedback will help to satisfy their needs for reassuring their security.

Such a selected cadre should be made to feel that they are the manager's "chosen" group. This cadre, whose needs have been met through the highest levels, as well as any new members of the organization hired by the new manager have a vested psychological interest in supporting him.

In the information of new group norms, and in creating the new implicit bargain between the group and the manager, these people form a "voting block" to support the manager. This must be done carefully in order to avoid formation of a clique. The objective is to have all members of the group join the cadre rather than to form separate opposing forces.

Original group members have suffered a blow to their self-image which was modelled on the previous group leadership. It is important that these people change the image with whom they identify. Those who are to remain with the organization must be "imprinted" with a new image in keeping with the objectives of new management. Imprinting must be done with someone not too remote from the group members themselves, someone with whom they can identify or choose as an ideal image.

Because of this need for identification, there may be too much difference between the group members and the manager for such imprinting to take place. Those selected for membership in the cadre must be carefully chosen for those qualities the manager would like to see spread throughout the group. Screening of new applicants is very important at this stage. Outsiders brought in must be technically competent enough to rapidly earn the respect of the original group members and to demonstrate the good judgment of the new manager.

Members of the restructured group need to enhance their prestige and demonstrate their ability to function successfully as a group. Discreetly managed participative goal setting should be introduced for the purpose of establishing short-term objectives. Long-term objectives and projects do not provide the immediate reward necessary. Short-term objectives that can be readily accomplished provide a rapid, rewarding experience to group members.

After the psychological damage to their self-image, group members badly need the victory that goal accomplishment provides, and some token of recognition from higher management for their contribution. Another method could be winning a long-standing argument with another group. These events can often be arranged without too much trouble.

MINIMIZING THE IMPACT OF CHANGE

Since the problems have been created by change, it is necessary to minimize or eliminate any forms of change that are not absolutely required. Unless it is the intention to replace the group, the manager should not change the offices or the physical location of the group. Even when such a change would appear to enhance the prestige of the group, the slightest disadvantage of the new location will create another focal point of controversy.

Under these circumstances any change appears to be an attack against the previous norm. While a given change may not really be an attack against the previous norm, the group accepts the change as a symbol of such an attack. For example, changing the time of a coffee break is not an attack on the entire previous system, but it may be taken as such. The manager must try to preserve some of the "institutions" of the previous system.

Until all possible imprinting is completed and the manager is secure in the support of his "voting block," it is unwise to directly criticize prior management. This criticism has been implied most severely by the management change itself. The new manager may not be directly associated as yet with the organization elements that caused the change. He can maintain a neutral position with members of the group by criticizing "circumstances" and "the environment" or he can blame changing needs on the part of the organization for the failure of the prior manager. This would be taken as less of a personal affront to group members and gives them a "way out."

The generally pessimistic attitude that exists immediately after the organization change is emphasized by critical interpretation of the new manager's most innocent comments. The group member who feels that he has been dealt with unfairly by higher management expects duplicity on the part of the new manager. The manager must be scrupulously fair and open to the greatest extent possible. He must be especially candid in reviewing the performance of staff members and in appraising their future opportunities within the group. Any action taken that is contrary to his expressed intent will be taken as further evidence of duplicity. For this reason, he should be precise and concise in his discussions with group members. Until he is fully accepted, he should not "philosophize" with members of the group so that he cannot be misinterpreted. Yet, he should gradually associate with group members through brief informal contact to reduce tension and reinforce the manager's "human" image.

Charges of duplicity can also arise from skipping the chain of command. Such action makes an already insecure subordinate become even more insecure. The supervisor who has been skipped over is pushed into regressive action which actually does decrease his efficiency. In this, the manager who suspects inefficiency on the part of the supervisor can actually create it. Furthermore, he demonstrates to group members that he has a low regard for the skipped-over supervisor. While this may not actually be true, it is the way group members are most likely to interpret the action.

Should it be necessary to review all current work or work methods, remaining members of the original group must be dealt with in a manner that will allow them to feel secure and save face. If a project must be temporarily stopped, it is important to find other tasks to keep those people formerly on the project busy. The manager must be careful to avoid insulting the creators of the project itself directly. He can permit face-saving by such devices as crediting poor past performance to improper direction, changing company needs, technical obsolescence, or new factors making the previous approach uneconomical.

CONCLUSION

Despite the manager's best efforts, he will probably lose some group members that for one reason or another he would prefer to keep. The manager who tries to keep an employee who is resigning is probably making a mistake. The employee has reached a point of frustration at which nothing will permanently satisfy him. While a promotion or a salary increase may temporarily dissuade him from leaving, it also denies him the satisfaction of "getting even," which further frustrates him.

The manager can expect to lose those employees who have suffered a loss of authority, status, or prestige as a result of the change. He must carefully reinforce the authority of those that he wants to retain in the organization.

Each person and each environment is different. While studies in group psychology and in individual reactions to frustration may point to some generalized causes and effects, and may permit the establishment of some guidelines for overcoming hostility and aggression that result from organization change, there is no "cook book" answer. There is no clear-cut list of "do's and don't's" But, one must be able to handle change because change will probably be the hallmark of the organization of the future.[17] This is emphasized by observation of one of the more effective methods of handling change. Today's aerospace, electronic, and fashion industries have handled the problem of change by making change a constant part of the organization environment. This may be the ultimate answer for the organization of the future.[18]

READING 19 DISCUSSION QUESTIONS

1 What changes are likely to arouse aggressive response?
2 What conditions do not lend themselves to group decision making?
3 What can be done to minimize the impact of change?

[17]"The Seventies: Institutions," *Business Week* Dec. 6, 1969, pp. 126-148.

[18]Sayles and Strauss, op. cit., p. 319.

Reading 20

Management's Responsibility for Safeguarding Information

Belden Menkus

Information is an organizational asset. It has form, function and a demonstrable value. Information must be protected and managed in the same way that other organizational assets are controlled and safeguarded. Management will be held accountable (as it is for the use of other assets) for what happens to the organization's information base. Management is being held ever more accountable by stockholders, government agencies and the public for the manner in which information is accumulated and employed by the organization.

Management of information assets is a new task for the organization. It changes many of the ways in which executives do their work. It alters goals and also the methods for achieving those goals. New problems and opportunities are created by these needs and obligation to manage information assets.

BUSINESS INTELLIGENCE

The business intelligence function creates a new basis for corporate growth and survival. *Business intelligence* may be defined as "the collection and systematic analysis of all of the available information about the economic, social, cultural and political environment in which the organization must function." (Unfortunately a legitimate but inadequately controlled business intelligence effort may lead an organization into its counterpart—industrial espionage, which is unauthorized access to the proprietary or privileged information of other organizations.)

An effective business intelligence activity necessitates learning in legitimate fashion as much as possible about the present and future resources, plans, policies and activities of customers, competitors, suppliers, government agencies and employees. (Figure 1.)

NEW OBLIGATIONS

The increased size, scope and complexity of organization information assets creates new obligations that it owes to stockholders, government agencies, employees, competitors and the general public. Among other things:

- Through various Federal Trade Commission orders and decrees corporations have been forced to inform competitors in advance of the release of

Reprinted from the *Journal of Systems Management*, December 1976, pp. 32–38. Reprinted by permission from the Association for Systems Management, Cleveland, Ohio. Mr. Menkus is a contributing editor of *Administrative Management* and editor of *Computer Security*.

Data elements in some categories may not be subject to data center access and handling. However, exposure to compromise is increased materially when data is transmitted by communications common carrier to and from remote operating locations or is processed by external data service organizations.

1 *Assets.* Plant and equipment location, size, type, and performance capabilities.

2 *Stock.* Purchases of raw materials, subassemblies, and operating supplies, and sales or transfers of surplus stocks to others.

3 *Production.* Units produced or warehoused, volume scrapped or reworked and the number and nature of defects and volume produced for private label.

4 *Sales.* Dollar volume by product, product line, industry's type, customer's size, and geographic location; discounts given.

5 *Sales planning.* Promotions, advertising, exhibits and relations with representatives and distributors.

6 *Financial.* Condition and status of accounts receivable and payable, as well as capitalization—both short and long term.

7 *Personnel.* Salary, bonus and benefit structure (including labor contact provisions); job assignment and duty locations; career development; records indicating probable future promotions and assignment.

8 *Research and development.* Product, process and material substance qualities and performance.

Figure 1 Basic business intelligence data categories.

certain new products and to share formerly proprietary technical knowledge with those competitors.

- The Federal Internal Revenue Service and the Securities and Exchange Commission as well as numerous Federal, State and local regulatory agencies have required that organizations reveal vastly increased information about their critical financial transactions and the manner in which they do business in the United States and foreign countries.
- The scope and type of data that organizations can legitimately gather about employees and customers have been severely restricted by a number of legislative acts and court decisions expanding individual rights.

Together these vastly increased information accumulations and restrictions on their use create a new set of legal problems and operating rules whose impact has not yet been clarified by the legislative/judicial process.

Among the already apparent problems are these:

- Data copied without authorization from one data processing magnetic tape to another cannot be said to have been *stolen*—in a legal sense—because the basic record remains in the possession of its legitimate custodian. And, existing legal precedents recognize the theft of business records only when the material is physically removed from the custodian's possession.
- Data processing equipment operators have been determined in many

cases to have *control over organization assets* comparable to that exercised by corporate officers.[1]

- Information systems designers ultimately will be held responsible through an extension of the *product liability* doctrines[2] for the way in which these creations function—in terms of accuracy, reliability and consistency.

INADEQUATE GUIDELINES

Key executives have been given significant information asset management responsibilities and then provided with conflicting guidelines—or no guidelines at all. The resulting organizational conflict is best exemplified in the Federal Government by the tension faced by agencies executives attempting simultaneously to comply with the information disclosure requirement of the Freedom of Information Acts (Public Laws 89-487 and 93-502) and the information protection requirements of the Privacy Act of 1974 (Public Law 93-579).

Because of this lack of consistent guidance, the means for resolving the social, moral and legal problems associated with effective information asset management must be developed by each organization in the context of its needs, goals, resources and operational environment. This is one of the rare instances in the practice of management when it may *not* be possible to look to the policies and practices of other organizations in the same industry for guidance. What they do—or plan to do—may not be wise, proper or legally responsible.

Any effort to determine how the organization's social, moral and legal responsibilities for managing its information assets are to be effectively discharged properly begins with a definition of what those assets are. They may be described under four general classifications: corporate secrets, employee job performance and personal data, information gathered through transactions with customers and suppliers, and Federal Government agency classified information.

Corporate Secrets

Corporate secrets are the categories of information generally classed as business intelligence and further defined by the restrictions and qualifications described in Figure 2. This type of information is subject to compromise through industrial espionage efforts. The act of corporate recording secrets on magnetic tape reels or disk packs does not lessen this exposure to compromise. The creation of a secure use environment will reduce—if not eliminate—that exposure. Figure 3 lists aspects of such an environment.

There is a continuing financial and competitive risk for the organization if corporate secrets are prematurely disclosed. There is possible legal and moral

[1]*Accounting Standard Statement 3,* American Institute of Certified Public Accountants, New York, December 1974, paragraph 23.

[2]E.J. Grenier, Jr., I. J. Martin, Jr., and R. L. Winkler, *Liability For Breaches of Computer Data Security—How Courts Consider Standards of Care and Technological Feasibility,* paper presented to International Computer Congress 74, Stockholm, August, 1974.

Broadly, a *corporate secret* can be defined as "information not otherwise readily available, but known (accessible) to a limited number of persons within the organization and used to produce, or facilitate or control the use of some product or service." It appears to be difficult to define the concept more exactly than that. However, the courts have tended to expect the holder of a claimed *corporate secret* to answer such questions as:

1 Is this information readily available in this form to other corporations? (Legitimate access to the information is assumed but may have to be demonstrated during a legal action.)

2 How expensive and time-consuming would it be for others to collect this data and create files of comparable scope and accuracy? This is the value of this information to the legitimate holder and to its competitors. This economic worth can be developed from the organization's financial investment and system development experience accumulating, organizing and preparing the information for use. However, where information is no longer accessible because of changing social, cultural or economic factors, or was accumulated as a result of unique relationships or events, this fact should be demonstrated and some attempt made to allow for it in the valuation process.

3 What efforts have been made to protect the secrecy of this information—in particular, to identify and record unauthorized access by employees, competitors, and the general public? The answer to this question is developed from a review of the data security program, concentrating on access controls and data transmission security.

Figure 2 What are corporate secrets?

liability if derogatory informal information is not promptly disclosed to government officials and even the public at large. The courts and various regulatory agencies have held that management is responsible for timely disclosure of such things as excessive flammability and similar product construction defects, possible carcinogenic exposure to employees working with—or

Figure 3 Ways to reduce corporate secret compromise.

1 Limit the number of those who know of the existence of particular corporate secrets.

2 Release this information only to reliable employees on a strict need-to-know basis.

3 Assure that all who have access to this information understand its value and are capable of protecting it.

4 Use code words wherever feasible rather than generic or descriptive terms to identify data about performance of products, processes, production activities, marketing plans and similar critical matters.

5 Restrict reproduction, transmission and distribution of this information. (**a**) Destroy promptly used typewriter and impact printer film ribbons, carbon paper, spoiled document copies. (**b**) Avoid sending this information through the mails or over common carrier telecommunications circuits.

6 Change locks periodically on rooms, desks and records; storage containers in which corporate secrets are housed.

7 Escort visitors to and from offices. Do not permit them to have unaccompanied access to sensitive work areas—including the data processing facility.

8 Encourage employees to report all efforts—including offers of gifts or other rewards—by outsiders to get them to disclose corporate secrets.

individuals using—a product, and likely negative environmental consequences of production techniques or manufacturing methods.

Employee Data

Employee data is accumulated as a result of the process of selecting an individual for a particular position and retaining that person as an active employee. Typically this classification will encompass some information about individuals whose applications for employment were rejected. It may also include information about terminated or retired former employees.

Included in this information collection will be such things as data on the nature of the tasks performed in various job assignments, the quality of work performed and the nature of training received. It may also include information about the individual's personal, financial and legal problems experienced both on and off the job. It can include data gathered from outside sources—credit agencies, educators, criminal justice agencies, and the like.

Enhanced problems with—and liabilities for—the conscientious control of employee data collections are created by the growing acceptance of the concept of an individual's right to *data privacy*. This theory provides that the individual has a basic interest in the nature and extent of the information that others collect about him or her, the way in which it is used, and the access that third parties will be given to it. Development of this data privacy concept has led to the elaboration of additional rights and obligations. Generally these provide that:

1 Personal data accumulations must be protected against unauthorized access or use.

2 Data accumulated must be limited to that information essential to the purpose stated for its collection.

3 The subject of the data should be able to verify the completeness, currency, and accuracy of the record and to correct or amend it when disagreements about fact or interpretation occur.

4 Data must be promptly purged from the information file when it is no longer current or pertinent.

Balanced against these new obligations to protect data against improper disclosure or use are continuing obligations to disclose selected information to other organizations. These may be job histories provided to another employer, or information on job-related problems or accomplishments supplied to educational, credit evaluation or criminal justice agencies.

Unauthorized disclosure of some employee data may expose the individual concerned to possible blackmail or other types of harassment, and may expose the organization to legal action for libel. Among other things, the courts are beginning to hold that certain types of negative "recommendations" for terminated employees may be libelous.[3] The act of disclosure itself may create new, or intensify existing, labor problems.

[3]See Laurence Steisen in *The New York Times,* December 7, 1975.

Customer and Supplier Information

Continuing contact through normal transactions with customers and suppliers—both actual and potential—leads to the routine accumulation of significant information about them. The data collected can include, but is by no means limited to, such things as summaries of purchase and sales histories; analyses and evaluations of financial and credit conditions; and reports on these companies' executives, products, production and marketing practices and relations with their employees, customers, competitors and suppliers. Some of this information is gathered formally. Some of it may reflect difficult to verify "trade gossip."

Typical of the valuable data in this category are lists of customers or suppliers valued by corporate size, financial condition or similar factors. These files are potential marketing tools and have been stolen in the past. Figure 4 suggests ways to prevent unauthorized use of such lists.

The already discussed data privacy protection liabilities and authorized obligations are incurred as well in the accumulation and handling of this type of information. So, too, are the already mentioned exposures to blackmail and other harassment and libel actions.

Competitors

It is reasonable and customary to accumulate and maintain information about the plans, prospects, activities and accomplishments of actual or prospective competitors. Most information collections of this type are created within traditional legal and ethical constraints. If the data gathered is that which the competitor has openly and intentionally disclosed, the subterfuge and ethical compromise implicit in *industrial espionage* is avoided.

Because of the intricate care that must be used in separating ephemeral from significant data the *information accumulating net* often must be drawn widely to encompass such things as "trade gossip," inadvertent or indirect revelations in the trade press and professional journals, annual reports, and disclosures in documents filed with the Federal Securities and Exchange Commission, as well as other international, Federal, state and local government agencies. A focal point of continuing opposition to some aspects of the Freedom of Information Acts has been the access that some can secure, through applying

Figure 4 Preventing unauthorized address list use.

1 Include a liberal number of *dummy* names in each list.
- Assure that management controls do not confuse them with legitimate entries.
- Select a significant number of these *dummy* entries in any list sampling.

2 Change a sampling of key dummy names monthly or every time the list is run.
- Record the identifiers used (an alteration of firm names, or a post office box number alphabetic suffix) to be able to verify probable data and file status if it is discovered to have been duplicated or used without authorization.
- Consider setting an identifying code field in each dummy name to identify use. Standard computer job initialization routines can assure that this is done routinely as an integral part of processing the file.

these provisions, to data claimed to be proprietary or confidential but required to be disclosed under other statutes.

Data collected about competitors plays a critical role in making production and marketing decisions. Its unauthorized or uncontrolled release to third parties can expose an organization and its management to possible charges of theft of corporate secrets of other organizations or negligent violation of trust.

Federal Government Classified Information

Organizations that are contractors to the Department of Defense, Energy Research and Development Administration and similar Federal Government agencies may from time-to-time possess classified information. This data may be provided by—or through—the agency using the contract. Or it may be generated by the organization itself in carrying the terms of the contract. Traditionally circulation and access to such information has been closely restricted.[4] However, as evidenced by periodic "leaks" and sale of such information, management may experience some difficulty at times in monitoring those restrictions.

THREATS TO CONTROL INFORMATION

The management of any organization that desires to maintain consistent and responsible administration of its information assets must be prepared to counter five basic procedural threats to that control. These are:

1 *Accidental disclosure.* Inadvertent release of sensitive data of all types occurs because either: (a)Those working with the information are unaware of its significance or value or the risks inherent in giving others unauthorized access to it, or (b) the system for accumulating, processing, storing and distributing the data has not been designed to identify, isolate and frustrate accidental disclosure possibilities.

In the first instance several things can occur. Employees may simply "gossip" to others about specific facets of the information that they work with: Corporate secrets may be included or customers or competitors may be identified in professional journal papers or press releases. Or, circulation of copies of memoranda, reports or computer-produced statistical summaries and analyses may not be fully controlled.

In the second instance too much stored data may be too readily accessible to unauthorized remote terminal inquiries, or the system may ignore the occurrence and the consequences of telecommunications system switching errors.

2 *Intentional infiltration.* This threat involves the conventional *industrial espionage* exposure generated by someone from the outside seeking to secure unauthorized access to proprietary or otherwise sensitive data. In its simplest form, someone may simply walk in, copy and remove the data sought. Or the threat may involve, in its more sophisticated manifestations, interrogation of

[4]Typical of these restrictions are those contained in the *Department of Defense Industrial Security Manual for Safeguarding Classified Information.*

the crucial data files from a remote site; the culprit may never physically enter the organization premises.[5]

3 *Data loss.* Critical data simply may become at times unavailable to the organization. Popular concepts to the contrary, this condition rarely results from someone's industrial espionage activities or from the vandalism of a malicious or vindictive employee. In most instances, both desire to leave as little evidence of their undertakings as feasible. It is more likely that the data has been misplaced or erased through an operational error. In both circumstances, loss of the data reflects a defect in management's control of some aspect of the data handling and distribution process.

4 *Defective data.* Information maintained about a particular subject or incident rarely is completely erroneous. But mistaken, distorted and noncurrent information may be included with that which is correct and may need removal and correction. It has been a concern for the routine identification and correction or elimination of errors in accumulated data that has generated the continuing broad public support for data privacy protection legislation. Most problems with data file accuracy can be eliminated by careful planning and control of the data collection process.

5 *Standards lack.* Management's failure to develop and apply consistent rules for the design and operation of information systems can contribute to the possible occurrence of each of these other threats. Examples of this include lack of standard:

a *access* controls, which can lead to accidental disclosure of data and make intentional infiltration possible.

b *operation* controls, which can lead to data loss and the retention of defective data.

c data *collection* practices, which can lead to the initial accumulation of defective data.

Personnel

The fact that people are involved in the creation, maintenance and use of data stores accounts for a separate set of threats to these organizations' information assets. These dangers are posed by information users, data producers, system operators and intruders.

Most of those in the first three categories will be employed by the organization. Arthur Miller of the George Washington Law School has defined the employee's obligation to protect information.

> An employee owes loyalty to his organization under the . . . law . . . The technical word is that he is in a fiduciary relationship. To breach it, he might be enjoined by a court or held liable in damages. Furthermore, if he discloses "trade secrets" he might, under the laws of some states, be punished criminally. Speaking generally, there is an obligation to keep a confidence if the person knows it is a confidential matter . . .[6]

[5]Edward Yasaki, "A Package is a Trade Secret—At Least in Santa Clara," *Datamation*, October 1972.

[6]From an address to a January 30, 1971, conference on Professional Responsibility.

To establish basic rules for secure and responsible handling by employees of information assets it will be useful to have all employees sign a nondisclosure agreement (Fig. 5) as part of the hiring process.

As a supplement to such agreement, and because of their greater–and potentially unrestricted–access to data file contents, some organizations require computer operators and other data processing activity staff to annually sign a statement acknowledging that they understand and affirming that they will adhere to a *code of ethics.*

One such code statement[7] recognizes that someone assigned to data processing is not an ordinary employee. He or she is deemed by organization management to occupy a sensitive position of trust. The employee agrees under the code, as an integral part of the conditions of employment and subject to disciplinary action for nonadherence, not to:

- Submit to or permit unauthorized use of any information in data center files.
- Seek—or permit others to seek—to benefit personally from any confidential information which has come to him or her by virtue of work assignments.
- Exhibit or divulge the contents of any record to any person, except in the conduct of his or her work assignment.
- Include, or cause to be included, in any record or report, a false, inaccurate or misleading entry.
- Remove, or cause to be removed, copies of official records or reports from any file, or from the office where it is kept, except in performance of assigned duties.

There are, unfortunately, realistic limits on what can be accomplished in safeguarding information through the use of written statements. Careful monitoring of information procedures (such as might be done by members of an internal audit staff) will help further improve controls on access to and use of critical data. The most valuable thing that management may be able to do in this regard is to initiate a continuing employee information protection education program. Such a program is designed ideally to make employees more aware of

[7]*Computer Security,* September/October 1975.

Figure 5 Employee nondisclosure agreement.

Without the prior consent of the company, either during or after my employment with it, I will not use or divulge to others any proprietary data including trade secrets and unpublished financial and business information which I produce or otherwise obtain during the course of that employment with respect to any business in which the company is—or has been—concerned, or which is entrusted to the company by others. At the time my employment with the company is terminated I will promptly surrender to it all documents in my possession or under my control which contain proprietary information which belongs to or has been entrusted to the company by others.

NOTE: it may be advisable to enumerate in the agreement the broad classes of information or records that it covers.

the value and relative sensitivity of the information that they handle. The program may be integrated with a general employee training effort or it may prove more effective if given a separate identity and emphasis. Particular targets for the program, apart from the data center staff and key information-using executives and supervisors, include keypunch operators and others involved in collecting and preparing raw data for subsequent processing; individuals who maintain and retrieve files; and those people responsible for answering inquiries from customers, suppliers and the general public. Elements in successful programs of this type include posters, paycheck envelope inserts, and written reports of procedure violations, as well as formal classroom experiences.

Outsiders

Outsiders, such as trade association representatives, auditors, and agents of the United States Internal Revenue Service and various Federal and State government regulatory bodies, present a separate set of information asset access protection problems. These people have a legal right to access to certain data, but they do not have a right to unlimited access to the organization's information. Unlike the organization's employees, the responsibility for what these people do with what they learn through this access is not as clearly defined legally or ethically. Increasingly the organizations for whom these "outsiders" work are becoming more aware of this problem and the need to resolve it. Typical of these is the Occupational Safety and Health Administration (OSHA) of the United States Labor Department. It offers to help employers protect corporate secrets while one of its inspectors is examining the premises. Among other things it suggests that the OSHA representative be told where sensitive areas and operations are located. The agency also offers to write violation citations in language that will not reveal confidential data about products, processes or equipment.

AN EXPANDING, CONTINUING OBLIGATION

Management's growing obligation to safeguard its information assets and the way in which they are used is changing the way in which data handling systems are designed and operated. As the scope of these legal, social and moral responsibilities continues to expand, management's obligation to be a prudent user of information can be expected to intensify. The impact of these events on the organization can be eased by careful and expeditious development and installation of protective policies and procedures.

READING 20 DISCUSSION QUESTIONS

1 Has computer usage created more problems concerning the *safeguarding of information?* Why?
2 What can be done to provide management with the ability to control the safeguarding of the information?

Case E

Behavioral Reactions to the Introduction of a Management Information System at the U.S. Post Office: Some Empirical Observations

Gary W. Dickson
John K. Simmons
John C. Anderson

INTRODUCTION

Usually the rationale underlying the introduction of management information systems into organizations is that the resulting cost savings and benefits from better information for use in management decision making outweigh the costs of developing the system. Too frequently, dysfunctional behavioral reactions to the system on the part of persons interacting with the system prevent the benefits from being achieved. As an example, consider what happened when the United States Post Office Department introduced a new information system. The system was tested in the Minneapolis Post Office and an expanded nationwide system development was subsequently undertaken.

In order to find out how people reacted to the introduction of the system in Minneapolis, researchers conducted a survey two years after its introduction in this location and while the national system was being developed and implemented. In addition to surveying reactions to the system, the research team also attempted to investigate why these reactions occurred. What follows comes from a paper written by the research team describing the situation they found and attempting to explain the conditions. The statements and conclusions are opinions of the research team.

PROLOGUE

During the first few months the management information system operated paper clips were inserted in source recorders, and workers were "ready to sabotage the whole system." The situation at the managerial level was not appreciably better. Foremen and supervisors found the "information" provided to be of limited usefulness and generally disliked the new system.

These were the conditions that existed following the introduction of a prototype management information system in the Minneapolis Post Office. This

This case is a working paper prepared in the School of Business Administration, University of Minnesota. Reprinted by permission of the authors. Gary W. Dickson is professor of management information systems, John K. Simmons is a professor of accounting, and John C. Anderson is professor of management science, all of the School of Business Administration, University of Minnesota.

paper reports the results of an exploratory research project designed to investigate the organizational reaction (at all levels) to the introduction of a management information system. Another objective of the study was to identify the variables causing dysfunctional behavioral reactions to the introduction of an information system.

THE SYSTEM

In an attempt to improve the Post Office management to enable it to cope with the increased size and complexity of operations, Post Office Headquarters proposed a trial postal management information system for installation in Minneapolis, Minnesota. The prototype system, called the Postal Source Data System (PSDS), was planned, designed, and implemented between 1961 and 1965.

The PSDS was designed to be a management information system which collects data relative to employee time and mail volume. The system consists of three broad categories of components: (1) input equipment (badge readers and scales), located at employee work stations; (2) "compiler" equipment for translation of inputs from these stations into computer-readable form; and (3) the computer which performs calculations and prints the outputs.

System Inputs

The inputs to the system are provided by the postal workers, clerks and mail handlers, and are basically of two types—time and mail volume. To record time, the employee places his prepunched, plastic identification card in a badge reader and by using a "send" button, records the appropriate type of transaction. Transaction types include: begin tour, end tour, out to lunch, back from lunch, and a change of work center. The latter type of transaction is especially important for use in the PSDS because it allows the calculation of total hours worked in any work center. The mail volume passing through each work center is measured by electronic scales on which the workers weigh all mail. Weight/volume standards make possible the conversion of weight to pieces of mail processed.

System Outputs

The system outputs consist of the following four types:

1 *Time and Attendance.* At the close of each pay period, the total hours for each individual are reported to each post office. Pay hours are transmitted to the postal data center where payroll checks are prepared.

2 *Labor Distribution.* The total number of hours worked in each work center during each tour is reported.

3 *Mail Volume.* The volume of each type of mail passing through each work center is reported.

4 *Work Measurement.* The combination of labor distribution and mail volume allows a productivity measure to be calculated for each work center.

System History

During 1961 and until June 1962, the system was planned and tested. The first equipment was installed in the Minneapolis Post Office in the fall of 1963. In August of 1963, training classes were held for employees concerning the use of the system. The time, attendance, and payroll applications were begun in June 1964, and were employed in a dual mode until May 1965. In March 1965, a mail volume system utilizing the new equipment was initiated. This was run in a dual mode with the old system (with reliance placed on the old system) until October 1965. The total switchover period lasted one year and four months.

The reaction of postal management to the "prototype PSDS" was favorable, as indicated by the following statement:

> The prototype proved conclusively the feasibility of using modern, high-speed data collection, data processing and communications techniques and equipment to reduce great masses of data to timely, accurate and meaningful end products, whether a salary check or a management report.[1]

Thus, based upon the prototype experience in Milwaukee and Minneapolis, the Post Office Department decided to implement a new and expanded PSDS to connect the nation's 75 largest post offices. The system, based upon the prototype but technically much superior, was to contain over 8,000 pieces of equipment and has been forecast to cost in excess of $25 million.

According to the same document, the goal of the nationwide PSDS is:

> . . . to provide all levels of management with timely, accurate information with which to better cope with the great masses of data being generated by their operations.

RESEARCH METHOD

Depth interviews were conducted at the Minneapolis Post Office during the Spring of 1967. The interviews were intended to find out how people reacted to the introduction of the system and to attempt to explain why certain types of reactions occurred. Two interview schedules were used, one for clerks and mail handlers, and another for operating managers and top management. Figure 1 presents the type of persons interviewed, their category, and the number of each type.

The interview schedule was slightly different, depending on whether or not the respondent had been at the Post Office at the time the system was introduced or whether he had been employed after the system had been totally implemented (October 1965). Twenty-five workers fell into the "old" category and fourteen were classified as "new." All management personnel were employed when the system was installed. Each interview lasted approximately 60 minutes.

[1]"Postal Source Data System," Post Office Department Publication 109, United States Post Office Department, June 1967, p. 3.

Figure 1 Interview Composition

Category	Position	Number
Worker	Clerk	23
	Mail handler	16
Operations Management	Foreman	13
	General foreman	5
	Tour superintendent	3
Top Management	Postmaster, Director of Operations, et al.	7
Total		67

REACTION TO THE SYSTEM

During the first few months of its operation, the system was plagued by input errors, i.e., errors in the transactions made by the employees. In one month, for example, out of 4,300 total transactions, 400 had some type of error. Another problem which plagued the system was physical sabotage. Source recorders were rendered inoperable by having paper clips inserted in them. In one interview, it was mentioned that honey had been poured down a source recorder.

Another indication of the workers' reaction to the system involved what the workers recalled of their peers' reactions to the system. Statements such as: "They didn't like it, but they figured it was necessary"; "There was much grumbling, confusion and fear"; "It was terrible, they wanted to go back to cards"; "The seven dial system confused the hell out of them"; are typical of the workers' recollections of how people reacted to the system.

Operating management related similar kinds of worker reaction to the prototype PSDS. Sabotage, threats, and union resistance were all mentioned. Similarly, top management stated that the workers objected to the system and, in one instance, suggested that volume data was being deliberately falsified in order to "beat the system."

The perceptions of the members of the various groups concerning their own reaction to the system, the reaction of others in their membership group, and the reaction of the members of other groups are summarized in Figure 2. For example, the figure shows that of 25 workers interviewed, 17 said they had been negative regarding the system, whereas 24 out of the 25 responded in a manner suggesting that other workers had been negative.

Each group overwhelmingly perceived that the workers reacted negatively to the system when it was installed. Although not as strongly, the groups perceived that the supervisors also reacted negatively. Over half of the workers were uncertain how their supervisors felt about the system. Even the top management group perceived that both the workers and supervisors were "against" the system. Two people in the top management group admitted reacting negatively to the system. A few more persons were positive regarding

Figure 2 Attitudes toward the Prototype PSDS at Installation

Respondents	Attitude of:	Feeling about system			
		Positive	Neutral	Negative	Uncertain
Workers N=25	Self	6	2	17	—
	Peers	—	—	24	1
	Supervisors	3	1	8	13
Operations Management N=21	Self	8	6	6	1
	Peers	5	5	8	3
	Workers	—	1	20	—
Top Management	Self	5	—	2	—
	Supervisors	3	—	4	—
	Workers	2	—	5	—

the system when they recalled their own perceptions contrasted with their perceptions about peer feelings.

The reaction of both workers and management to the prototype PSDS in Minneapolis can be summarized as being very negative. Evidence such as error rates, mention of sabotage, and perceptions of the interview subjects all indicate that the introduction of the system was met with hostility at virtually all levels of the organization. The question begged by these results is—What caused this sort of behavior on the part of the members of the organization?

UNDERLYING CAUSES

In the case of the prototype PSDS there were, we believe, several factors in addition to the manner in which the change was introduced which materially contributed to the outcome described above. We consider all of the following variables to have affected what happened: (1) environmental factors, (2) method of introduction, and (3) work relationships.

The Environment

Three environmental conditions existed at the Minneapolis Post Office prior to the introduction of the PSDS which we believe definitely influenced the manner in which the system was received. These conditions are somewhat related but are separated for purposes of discussion.

1 The Managerial Climate An article in *Fortune* concerning the Post Office Department states that postal employees "work in an atmosphere that is ruinous to morale."[2] Low pay, bad hours, and little opportunity for advancement are pointed out as the causes of many of the difficulties. Our interviewees mentioned all these factors when asked what they did not like about their jobs. The only strong factor mentioned in favor of the job was security. The lower levels of supervision also indicated a lack of enthusiasm for their jobs. Concerning the supervisors, the *Fortune* article says:

[2] "It's Now or Never for the Post Office," *Fortune,* March 1967, p. 136.

> The picture is hardly better at the supervision level. Until recently, promotions depended to a considerable degree on political influence. There was—and is—nothing automatic about the rise to the top of the best qualified candidate. When a man of superior abilities does not advance, he may well discover more frustration than satisfaction. Hemmed in by hundreds of petty regulations and caught between a politically appointed postmaster and frequently belligerent subordinates, he is asked to do his job without any real training in management techniques.

Both workers and supervisors in our interviews mentioned the political aspects of advancement. The gap between the worker and his management is indicated by the responses given to a question regarding the feelings of various groups of persons (workers, supervisors) toward the system at the time of the interview (as opposed to the feelings at the time of installation). Thirty-one out of thirty-nine clerks and mail handlers had no idea how their supervisors felt about the system, whereas thirty-two out of thirty-nine were able to respond concerning how their co-workers felt. The response shown in Figure 2 to a similar question further indicates the lack of informal communication between workers and their immediate management.

2 The Union Another factor, and one definitely associated with the managerial climate, is the role played by the union vis-à-vis the system. Some 92% of all postal workers are unionized, and as the *Fortune* article says:

> The union leaders declare publicly they have no fear of mechanization, but they find fault with almost every device the Post Office installs. Some claim that new mechanical letter sorters, which compel operators to keep pace with their sixty-a-minute pace, are too nerve-racking and fatiguing.

In the case of the prototype PSDS, the unions were in great opposition to the system at its earliest phases. In fact, the day before our interviews were to take place, all union members (clerks and mail handlers) received a letter from the union mentioning our interview and restating the union's opposition to the system. A check of the responses of the persons who had received the letter against those of the non-union members who had not received it indicated that the letter apparently had no effect on the way in which our questions were answered.

3 Automation History At the time our interviews were taking place, the Minneapolis Post Office was still having difficulty getting persons to man the automated letter sorters mentioned in the quotation above. Many of these machines were sitting idle while mail was sorted by hand. Several other attempts at levels of mechanization of operations had met with relatively little success.

Method of System Introduction

Another variable contributing to the behavior associated with the reactions which occurred when the prototype PSDS was introduced is the method by which the system was presented. Essentially, the method employed was to install the equipment and later have employees attend a class in which they were shown how to use the equipment (but told very little about what the system did). The equipment orientation is demonstrated by the fact that only 13% of all employees responding to a question concerning how they learned about the system mentioned anything about attending a class. Far more prevalent answers were: seeing the equipment (37%), and a letter announcing the system (17%). Figure 3 shows the relative lack of knowledge on the part of all levels of postal personnel concerning the uses of the system.

The responses shown in Figure 3 are arranged in order of increased understanding of system use beyond knowledge that the system was used for payroll purposes. Almost half (6/15) of the responses from persons employed since the system was introduced had no idea what the system did beyond payroll applications. The worker responses tended to cluster around three areas: (1) the system keeps track of where employees are (called "spying" in one case), (2) it keeps track of vacation-time, sick leave, etc., and (3) the weighted mail is somehow entered into the system.

The foremen, perhaps because of their concern with keeping track of their employees, frequently mentioned the employee location uses of the system. They also recognized that the system had something to do with weighing mail, but totally ignored the relationship between mail volume and work centers. Recognition of this use was, however, pointed out by the mention of use in work measurement by four respondents. To be coded under the work measurement category, a response had to indicate an understanding that the system calculated a productivity measure by comparing work center mail volume to hours worked in the center. Top management also failed in a number of instances to show a good understanding of how the system was supposed to be used.

It is possible to infer that the relative lack of understanding about the system on the part of management (foremen and above) may be associated with a lack of use of the system. Another factor contributing to managerial attitudes about the system may stem from the fact that the system was initiated, designed, and implemented from the Post Office Department in Washington, D.C. The interviews indicated that many of the top management personnel felt that

Figure 3 Knowledge about System Use

Level of Knowledge	Work Groups			
Response	Workers (old) N=25*	Workers (new) N=14*	Foremen N=13*	GF & TS N=8*
Don't know	4	6	1	1
Employee location	6	6	6	0
Sick leave, vacation	10	0	4	2
Hours/work center	5	2	3	3
Weighing mail, volume	10	1	7	4
Volume/work center	3	0	0	0
Work measurement	0	0	4	3

*Multiple responses to the question are recorded

matters would have gone much more smoothly had they been able to participate in the design and installation of the system.

Technical Factors

There were a number of technical considerations that were peculiar to the type of organizational change represented by introducing a management information system. In the case of the prototype PSDS, the workers were especially bothered by technical factors. Specifically, the lack of a visual record of their transactions (as would be the case with a time card) was mentioned time and again as a problem with the system. Further, the inability to check their sick leave status and accrued vacation time bothered the workers. The latter point represented a change from the former system that upset the informal organization at the Minneapolis Post Office. Under the previous system, accrued vacation and sick leave time was posted for all employees in a public place. It was frequent practice for employees to gather at this spot to compare time they could take off. With the new system, no public postings were available and the employees missed the opportunity to gather and discuss a subject of mutual interest.

The new system also eliminated a few jobs of timekeepers. Widespread negative reaction to the job elimination was present, but it is difficult to say what was the most important cause. Clearly, the elimination of the jobs themselves was a factor. Informal behavioral considerations associated with these jobs, however, may have been even more important. First, the job of timekeeper was very popular and senior employees could "bid" to take these positions as they became available. Thus, "high status" positions available were lessened. The timekeepers, furthermore, by making daily rounds among the employees, served as an informal communications system for the organization. Reduction in the opportunities for this type of informal communication may have been a very important contributor to negative feelings. The elimination of the posted vacation and sick leave time and the elimination of about ten timekeeping jobs were the only work relationships disturbed by the system.

Other technical factors which caused the workers difficulty included (1) system malfunctions, (2) extra work and standing in line, and (3) clock differences. The workers claimed that one could shorten or extend one's shift depending on which remote terminals they clocked in and out on because the clocks at the stations varied by as much as five minutes. We encountered a great deal of hostility on the part of workers because of these clock differences. Yet, the technical personnel assured us that all clocks on the terminals were synchronized with a master clock. We have no satisfactory explanation for this seeming discrepancy.

EPILOGUE

Three years after the survey was conducted at the Minneapolis Post Office concerning the prototype PSDS system, an article appeared in *Computerworld*[3]

[3]J. Hanlon, "Post Office Shows How Not to Develop Information System," *Computerworld,* Aug. 4, 1971, Copyright by Computerworld, Newton, Mass. 02160.

commenting on what happened to the national system's development and introduction. It should be noted that the Post Office Department was not interested in the research study reported above and had no knowledge of its findings.

Post Office Shows How Not to Develop Information System

Washington, D.C.—The Post Office Department's computerized management information system (MIS) costs more and is less useful than previous manual systems, according to the General Accounting Office (GAO).

The GAO report on the Post Office Department (POD) is virtually a textbook of how not to develop an MIS.

When POD started developing the system in 1966, POD said the system would reduce paperwork and at the same time produce more timely and accurate reports. Employees producing manual reports were to be reassigned to other tasks at a saving of $4.5 million per year.

But inadequate planning, insufficient testing, and excessive haste, the GAO said, resulted in a system that:

Was over two years late
Will cost $60 million, almost twice as much as expected
Requires more rather than fewer people
Has "substantially increased costs"
Has a high error rate
Produces useless reports

The Postal Source Data System (PSDS) automatically collects data at the 75 largest post offices concerning mail volume, employee attendance and hours.

Automatic employee badge readers, electronic mail scales, and keyboards at each post office send data in real-time to dual Control Data Corp. 1700s at one of five concentrator centers.

Data is then sent to dual CDC 3300s at one of two main DP centers. Reports are produced on high-speed printers at the post offices, sometimes within two hours of the original data inputs.

Despite the difficulties with the system, it is now being expanded to 35 additional post offices, an action that drew particular GAO criticism.

Poor Planning

The POD first tested an information system in Minneapolis and Milwaukee from 1962 to 1965. The test was unsatisfactory, according to GAO, and a POD study team recommended further testing be confined to those two offices until the system was made to work.

Instead, the POD decided to implement a significantly different system, PSDS, at all 75 large post offices.

In 1966, the POD negotiated a $22.7 million contract with CDC for purchase and installation of the entire system, despite the fact that there had been no testing and despite the recommendation of POD's own ADP Management Division that a lease-purchasing approach be used in case the system proved unfeasible.

In its haste to get the system, the POD did not prepare detailed specifications prior to purchase. During the first five months after purchase, the specifications were changed four times and then totally scrapped. CDC was forced to halt programming until the POD decided what it really wanted.

Other POD changes further delayed implementation of PSDS, but the equipment was delivered on schedule, which meant that one 3300 was little used for 20 months.

Prior to awarding the contract, POD officials visited only eight of the 75 post offices. When the other post offices were actually visited, officials found the system would require "substantially" more equipment than projected. The contract with CDC has increased from $22.7 million to $36 million.

"If precise equipment requirements had been known prior to the award of the contract, more competition might have been generated and lower prices for the large quantities might have been offered by the bidders," declares the GAO report.

Further, in estimating costs POD assumed that computer equipment could be installed at post offices without difficulty. When installation began, it found that of the first 47 offices, only 11 had adequate electrical power and air conditioning.

System Doesn't Work

The delays and cost overruns would not be too serious if the system actually worked as planned. But the GAO report notes that rather than saving the POD money, it now costs more to perform employee time and attendance functions than under the former manual system.

Not only have no employees been reassigned to other duties (which was to produce the bulk of the financial saving), but "some post offices have found it necessary to employ full-time and attendance clerks to prepare the necessary payroll forms, whereas before the installation of PSDS, such forms were filled out by production employees in their spare time," the report declares.

Reports Not Useful

During one two-week period, a single post office received a 12-ft high stack of reports. "We question whether such volume of data can be examined timely and adequately for effective use by management," charges the report.

In late 1969 (the time of the GAO field review), post offices were still maintaining manual records "because the reports produced by PSDS were inaccurate or incomplete, or were received too late to be of use."

For example, error reports, such as an employee checking in at 8 a.m. and 1 p.m. but not checking out for lunch are supposed to be produced within two hours while an employee is still at the office. But the reports were sometimes received as much as 14 hours late, the GAO says.

Up to 1 million uncorrected error messages remain in the system at the end of each pay period and are simply purged, the GAO notes.

Ironically, the large number of unneeded reports seems to be bogging down the system and causing the errors, while system users demand the extra reports as a way of compensating for errors.

"The reports being generated by PSDS at the time of our review were less timely, less meaningful, and less accurate than reports available prior to installation of PSDS," concludes the GAO report.

The POD declined to comment to CW, but a letter of reply is included in the GAO report. It admits many of the charges made by the GAO, but states that the problems are being corrected. In particular, it claims that reliability, effectiveness, and timeliness of reports have been improved since the GAO did its study.

CASE E DISCUSSION QUESTION

1 What might postal authorities have done differently to avoid the problems discussed in this case?

SUMMARY OF CHAPTER 6

Before the conversion to new computer systems can be made in a way that will satisfactorily achieve company goals, attention must be given to the staffing function.

Plans must be made to recruit and select personnel to fill positions that computer usage may create. A prerequisite to sound recruitment and selection is the preparation of job descriptions and job specifications. Positions may be filled from a pool of present employees or from candidates recruited from external sources. Most businesses have found that when suitable employee candidates are available, it is preferable to give them the necessary training to prepare them for the data processing jobs. However, when suitable candidates are not available internally, the company must resort to external sources. Workers are usually selected on the basis of aptitude-test scores, personal interviews, and background records.

The most extensive training, of course, must be given to analysts and programmers, but it is desirable that noncomputer personnel receive exposure to data processing concepts. Training given for equipment operators may consist of formal classes combined with on-the-job training or on-the-job training alone.

Chapter 7

Control and the Computer

There are numerous controlling implications associated with the use of computer-based information systems that are of concern to managers in business organizations. A primary concern, of course, is that managers have ready access to a good information system in order to control the business operations for which they are responsible. In addition to this *managerial control* consideration, however, executives and auditors are also vitally interested in—and responsible for—maintaining the necessary *internal control* over the *information system itself* so that the system is operating efficiently and the integrity and security of data, records, and other business assets are preserved. In this chapter, we shall (1) examine the implications of computer usage on the areas of managerial and internal control and (2) study the various aspects of controlling the actual facility itself in terms of performance and integrity.

MANAGERIAL CONTROL IMPLICATIONS

You will recall from Chapter 5 that the general control procedure consists of several steps: (1) the establishment of predetermined goals and standards, (2) the measurement of performance, (3) the comparison of actual performance with the standards, and (4) the making of appropriate control decisions.

The information output of the computer can help the manager carry out this procedure in many ways. First of all, better information can lead to better planning and the creation of *more realistic standards.* Computer simulation can assist managers in setting goals by showing them the effects of various alternative decisions when certain conditions are assumed; and computer-based network models such as PERT and CPM can improve planning (and therefore control) by forcing managers to identify all project activities that must be performed.

Computer processing systems can also help managers control by gathering, classifying, calculating, and summarizing *actual performance data* promptly and accurately. Once performance data are read into the computer, it is possible for the machine to *compare* the actual performance with the established standards. Periodic reports showing this comparison can be prepared. In some systems, triggered reports, based on the *principal of exception,*[1] may be furnished to the manager only when variations are outside certain specified limits.

It is also possible to program the computer so that it signals when *predetermined decisions* should be carried out. For example, a program may specify that when the inventory of a certain basic part falls below a given level, an output message signals the need to reorder and indicates the reorder quantity. By thus relieving people of many of the routine operational control tasks, the computer frees them to devote more time to (1) planning future moves and (2) leading the all-important human resources of the organization. Such a human/machine relationship, in other words, makes it possible for people to concentrate more of their attention on the heuristic area of intellectual work—an area in which they are far superior to the machine—while the machine is permitted to take over the well-structured control tasks. Figure 7-1 illustrates the place of a computer system in the overall managerial control process.

Internal Control Implications

Managers and auditors are responsible for *internal control;* that is, they are responsible for the controls needed to (1) safeguard assets against theft and destruction, (2) check on and maintain the accuracy and security of company data, (3) promote operating efficiency, and (4) encourage compliance with company policies and procedures.

Need for Internal Control Some managers have been surprised to learn that the introduction of a computer system often requires reexamination of internal control procedures. Why? How thoughtful of you to ask. A review is required because in noncomputer systems the data processing activities are typically separated into several departments, with a number of employees being responsible for some portion of the total activity. For example, in the processing of a customer order, credit approval may come from one location, control of the inventory of ordered items may reside in another department, customer billing

[1]In chapter 18 of Exodus, Jethro gives good advice when he tells Moses to delegate some of his routine leadership duties to subordinates and concentrate his attention on the more important exceptions, which the subordinates are unable to handle. This idea is called "the principle of exception" in management literature.

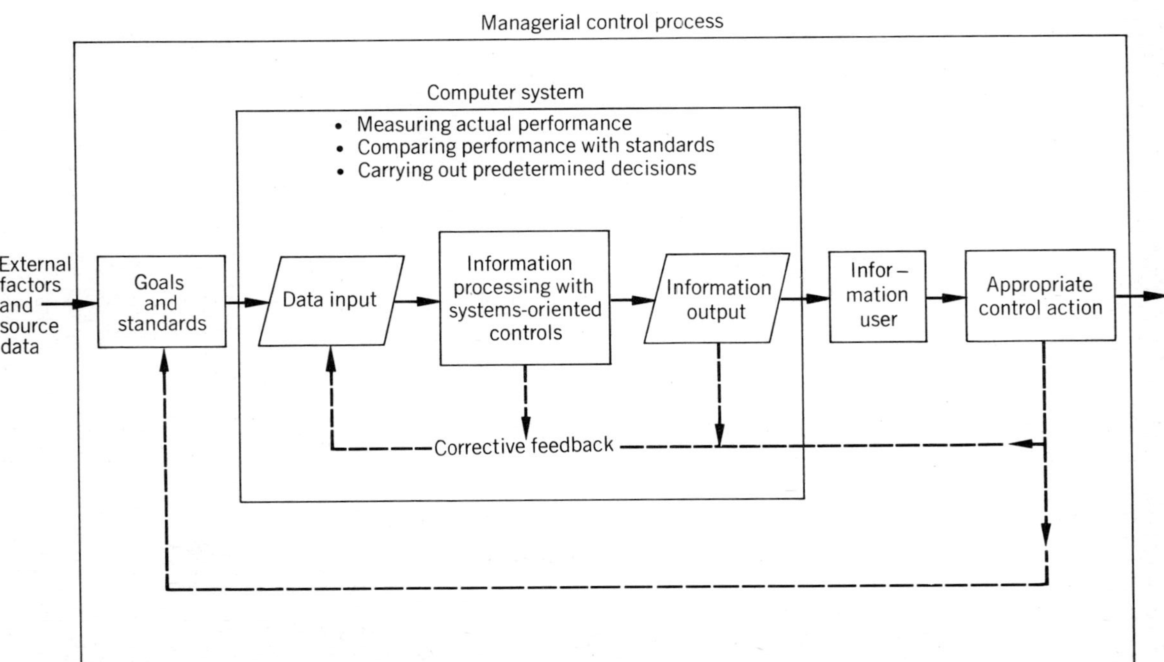

Figure 7-1 Managerial control and the computer.

may be handled by a third department, and receipt of payment for items shipped may be in a fourth location. Thus, the organizational structure separates those who authorize and initiate the order from those who record and carry out the transaction. And both of these groups are separated from those who receive payment for the order. Such a division of data processing activities makes it difficult for fraud to go undetected, since several people from different departments would have to be a party to any deception. Also, personnel in each organizational unit can check on the accuracy of others in the course of their routine operations. Thus, internal control has been achieved by the reviews and cross-checks made by people at separate points in the company. In other words, *internal control* was *employee-oriented.*

But computer usage may make it possible for processing steps to be consolidated and integrated so that these steps may all be performed by only one or two departments. With fewer departments involved, however, and with the likelihood that fewer people are cross-checking data, it may *appear* that even though source documents originate outside the computer department, the use of computer systems results in a reduction of internal control. Responsible managers have sometimes been distressed to learn that such a reduction *can occur* in an *inadequately controlled* computer department and can produce the following related and unhappy results:

1 Failure to Safeguard Assets Knowledgeable employees (or even a skilled outsider) can steal data and/or programs and sell them; they can acquire and use them intact to support an ongoing fraud or embezzlement; they can add, subtract, or substitute transactions in the data for fraud or embezzlement purposes; and they can do these things at the computer site or at a remote terminal hundreds of miles away. Thieves have become interested in computerized financial records because the job of accounting for the assets of many organizations has now been entrusted to computer systems, and the moves by the banking industry in the direction of EFTS will simply hasten this trend. In the past, paper money was introduced and thieves used presses; now, plastic money (credit cards) and magnetic money (money cards with magnetic strips, computer tapes, and disks) are used, and thieves are using embossers and computers. And they are making big "hauls." The average computer embezzlement loss suffered by organizations is reported to be between $500,000 and $1 million—5 to 10 times higher than the average manual system loss. A widely discussed example of a "computer crime" is the case involving the chief teller at a Union Dime Savings Bank branch in New York City who was charged with stealing about $1.5 million from the bank's accounts. Hundreds of legitimate accounts were manipulated; money was transferred to fraudulent accounts and then withdrawn; and false information was fed into the bank's computer so that when quarterly interest payments were due the legitimate accounts appeared intact. And all this was done by a person who did not have direct access to the computer. Other techniques used by computer-wise thieves include (*a*) deducting a few cents in excess service charges, interest, taxes, or dividends from thousands of accounts and writing themselves a check for the total amount of the excess deductions and (*b*) reporting inventory items as broken or lost and then transferring the items to accomplices.[2] In short, it has been estimated that losses suffered by organizations as a result of fraud and embezzlement now exceed those caused by robbery, loss, and shoplifting—and the computer is playing an active part in an increasing number of theft cases.

*2 **Failure to Maintain the Physical Security of the Computer Site*** The very existence of some organizations would be threatened by the physical destruction of the files and software that may now be concentrated at a *single* site. Among the possible hazards are *fire, flood,* and *sabotage.* Thousands of military records were destroyed by fire at the Army Records Center in St. Louis; numerous computer centers were flooded in the mid-Atlantic states by the rains that accompanied tropical storm Agnes; and cases of disgruntled employees changing programs to sabotage records and using magnets to ruin tapes containing programs and data have been reported. Several computer centers were also destroyed by bombs during the antiwar period of the late 1960s and early 1970s.

*3 **Failure to Maintain Data Integrity*** If input data are accurate and complete when they *enter* the computer system; if they are *classified, sorted,* and updated properly when necessary; if they do not become inaccurate through subsequent errors of omission or *calculation;* and if they are not distorted or lost through system malfunctions or operating mistakes, then a manager can be confident about the *integrity* of the data. Unfortunately, the internal control procedures in many businesses have sometimes failed to maintain a high degree of data integrity.

*4 **Failure to Maintain Data Security*** As Figure 7-2 indicates, a modern computer system is vulnerable to attack and penetration at many points and from many people, both inside and outside the organization. Programmers, operators, and maintenance personnel usually have the opportunity to penetrate systems security, and they may do so for personal grudges or for personal gain—e.g., for a bribe from an outsider. Operators, for example, can make duplicate copies of master tapes for outsiders in a few minutes, and programmers can insert code into an operating system in such a way that it provides a "trap door" for penetration at any convenient time in the future.[3] But even without help from within an organization, unscrupulous outsiders may gain access to the secrets and confidential records stored in an organization's computer system. Among the techniques employed against online systems are

[2]For additional techniques and examples, see Brandt Allen, "The Biggest Computer Frauds: Lessons for CPAs," *The Journal of Accountancy,* May 1977, pp. 52–62; Brandt Allen, "Embezzler's Guide to the Computer," *Harvard Business Review,* July–August 1975, pp. 79–89; Richard G. Canning, "The Importance of EDP Audit and Control," *EDP Analyzer,* June 1977, pp. 1–13; Hal Lancaster, "Rise of Minicomputers, Ease of Running Them Facilitate New Frauds," *Wall Street Journal,* October 15, 1977, pp. 1ff; Laton McCortney, "Is Paper Products Case Tip of the Iceberg?" *Datamation,* March 1977, pp. 148–149; Donn B. Parker, *Crime By Computer,* Charles Scribner's Sons, New York, 1976; Marshall Romney, "Detection and Deterrence: A Double Barreled Attack on Computer Fraud," *Financial Executive,* July 1977, pp. 36–41; K. S. Shankar, "The Total Computer Security Problem: An Overview," *Computer,* June 1977, pp. 50–61.

[3]For further information on this penetration technique, see Richard G. Canning, "Protecting Valuable Data—Part 2," *EDP Analyzer,* January 1974, pp. 1–3.

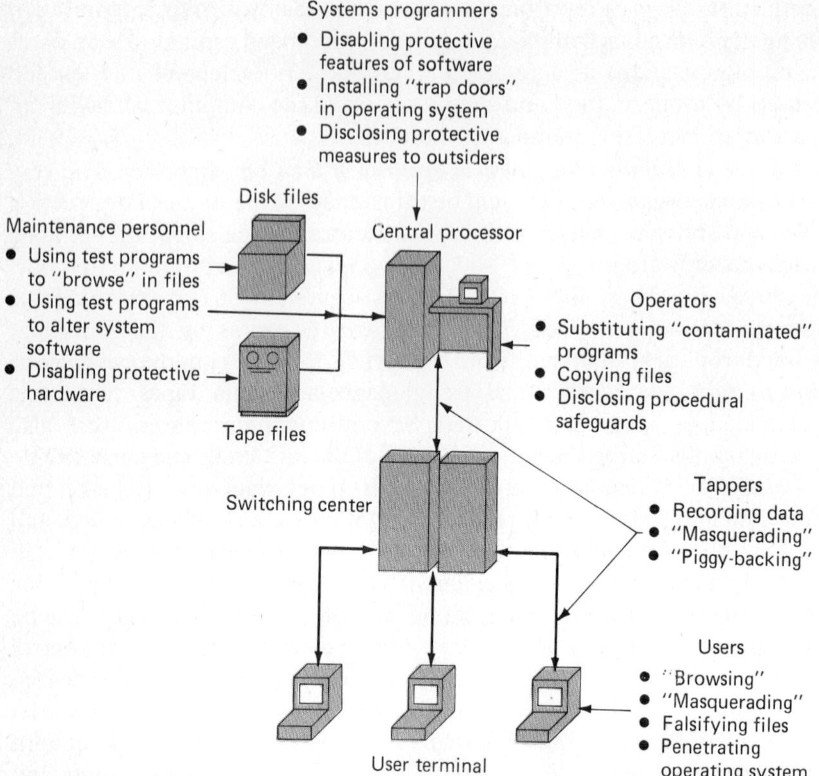

Figure 7-2 (*Source:* Tom Alexander, "Waiting for the Great Computer Rip-off," *Fortune,* July 1974, p. 144.)

"masquerading" and "piggybacking." Penetrators obtain the passwords of legitimate users by wiretapping or other means and then use these passwords to masquerade as authorized users in order to get access to the system and to other people's files. The piggybacking approach is similar in that a small computer or "bootleg" terminal is attached to a tapped communications line, where it may intercept and modify legitimate messages. In summary, then, those with motivation, financial resources, and access to computer skills may find that, as one authority has stated, penetrating today's computer system is about as difficult as solving the crossword puzzle in a Sunday paper.

5 ***Failure to Protect Privacy Rights of Individuals*** Unlike the information stored in older systems, files maintained in large, integrated computer data banks may be more complete, less subject to deterioration, and therefore more worthy targets for unscrupulous persons bent on ferreting out information of a private and confidential nature. Seemingly innocent data recorded and stored at one time may be retrieved and correlated quickly and inexpensively by the computer (perhaps through the use of Social Security numbers) with other data collected from different sources and at different times to reveal information about individuals that might be damaging to them. It has only been in recent

years that some managers have recognized the importance of safeguarding the privacy rights of those whose records are stored in their computer systems.

In spite of the possible dangers inherent in an inadequately controlled computer system, however, *there is no reason that a company should have less internal control because of computer usage.* On the contrary, there is no reason that *system-oriented controls,* in the form of computer programs, cannot be substituted for the employee-oriented controls of manual systems. Also, there is no reason that the separation of duties and responsibilities cannot be maintained *within* the computer department to safeguard the integrity of the system-oriented controls. In fact, there is no reason that a firm cannot achieve better control because of (1) the computer's ability to follow policies and execute processing procedures uniformly, (2) the difficulty of changing and manipulating, without detection, proper programmed systems controls, and (3) the computer's inherent accuracy advantage when given correct input data. Of course, top executives expect auditors to be sensitive to, and knowledgeable about, internal control arrangements that will avoid negative consequences.

Auditors, Auditing, and Internal Control[4] Auditors may either be employees of the organization *(internal auditors)* or be independent certified public accountants employed by the board of directors *(external auditors).* Periodic examinations or *audits* are performed by these auditors to evaluate the existing internal control arrangements. In studying these arrangements, auditors check to see if there is an *organizational separation of activities* within the computer department between those who design and prepare the new systems and those who prepare the input data and operate the equipment. In other words, analysts and programmers should design, maintain, and make necessary changes (according to specified procedures) to programs, but they *should not* be involved with day-to-day production runs; equipment operations, on the other hand, should not have unrestricted access to completed computer programs nor should they be involved with making changes in data or programs.

In addition to their concern about a proper separation of duties that can help safeguard assets, auditors are also concerned about whether adequate controls have been created to maintain data integrity and security. Thus, during the audit attention is turned to the *audit trail* to monitor systems activity and to determine if security and integrity controls are effective. The audit trail begins with the recording of all transactions, winds through the processing steps and through any intermediate records which may exist and be affected, and ends with

[4]For additional information on the effects of computer usage on auditors, auditing, and internal control, see Richard G. Canning, "The Importance of EDP Audit and Control," *EDP Analyzer,* June 1977, pp. 1–13; "Data Processing Audit Practices Report" and "Executive Report," *Systems Auditability and Control Study,* Institute of Internal Auditors, Inc., Altamonte Springs, Fla., 1977; Elise G. Jancura and Fred L. Lilly, "SAS No. 3 and the Evaluation of Internal Control," *The Journal of Accountancy,* March 1977, pp. 69–74; John B. Wardlaw, "Security, Control, and Auditing in a Dispersed Data Processing Environment," *The Internal Auditor,* June 1977, pp. 66–73; Bryan Wilkinson, "An Application Audit," *Datamation,* August 1977, pp. 51–55; and Edward K. Yasaki, "Who is the DP Auditor?" *Datamation,* August 1977, pp. 55–58.

the production of output reports and records. By selecting a representative sample of previously processed source documents and following the audit trail, the auditor can trace these documents through the data processing systems to their final report or record destinations as a means of testing the adequacy of systems procedures and controls.

In a manual system, a visible and readily traceable paper trail is created from the time source documents are prepared until output reports are produced. With the introduction of computer systems, however, the form of the trail has changed. Of course, *it cannot be eliminated* because of the desire for good internal control and because of tax and legal requirements. The Internal Revenue Service (IRS), in a report on the use of EDP equipment, has said that the audit trail, or the ability of a system to trace a transaction from summary totals back to its source document, must not be eliminated. Nevertheless, intermediate steps in the information systems that were previously visible have *seemed to vanish* into magnetizable and erasable media.

Nor will the audit trail become more visible in the future. The increased use of online direct-access storage devices to hold intermediate data and the substitution of online processing techniques for batch processing will result in an even greater decrease in the visible portion of the trail. For example, source documents may be replaced by machine language recordings made with transaction recording equipment; input data will originate from widely dispersed locations through the use of remote terminals (again, no paper documents need be involved); and a reorder message for a basic part may be transmitted by the computer to the supplier through the use of data communications facilities, with no paper documents being prepared. In examining such systems, the auditor must be satisfied that adequate controls are incorporated to prevent unintentional or deliberate damage to "invisible" files and records stored in an erasable medium. To comply with IRS requirements, for example, source data originating from online terminals may have to be "logged," or collected, in a separate operation by the system as they are processed. At prescribed intervals, the collected input data may then be sorted, listed, and stored in a suitable form so that the audit trail is preserved (see Figure 7-3).

Test data may be used in the examination by the auditor. Just as the programmer uses simulated input data to check programs during the debugging and testing stage, so, too, may an auditor use test decks to check on program integrity and security controls. Both valid and invalid transactions are included in the test data. Of course, the fact that a program passes the auditor's test does not mean that the tested program always receives accurate input data or is always the one that is used during processing. Reasonable but incorrect input data may be supplied, and a fraudulent patch may be inserted into the program during subsequent processing runs.

The *function* of the auditor will probably not change in the future, but his or her *techniques* will certainly be subject to revision as a result of computer usage. One of the greatest challenges facing the systems designer and the auditor will be to devise ways of preserving an audit trail that (although it may appear to

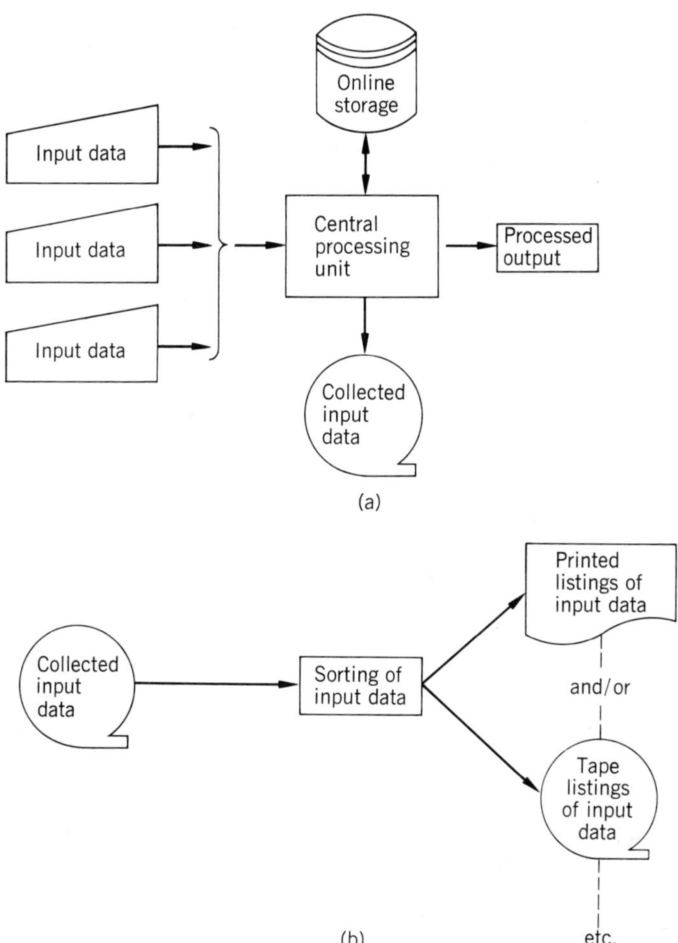

Figure 7-3 Preserving audit trail in online processing environment. *(a)* Collecting source data originating at online terminals. *(b)* Periodic sorting, listing, and storing of collected source data.

be nearly invisible) must be readily retraceable. Furthermore, this trail must be kept as simple as possible, and it must not require great masses of supporting printed detail.

A Final Note on Management Responsibility

We have now seen that the inadequate control of a computer system can lead to a lack of data integrity/data security, and to a failure to safeguard vital assets (including the computer system itself). Furthermore, a lack of control can compromise the legitimate privacy rights of those whose records are stored in an organization's computer files.

Since poorly controlled computer systems are, at best, likely to produce unreliable information for management decision-making purposes, and since, at worst, such systems can endanger the very existence of the organization, the *primary responsibility* for establishing overall internal control policies and procedures must reside with top-level executives. Furthermore, the *operational responsibility* for the accuracy and completeness of input data and output information should reside with the managers of using departments. With proper management support, auditors *should* be expected to design appropriate controls into new systems and to perform periodic audits to ensure that these controls are reliable and efficient. But auditors *cannot* be expected to function effectively in an environment where top managers and users have simply assumed that data processing specialists will provide whatever controls are needed.

CONTROLLING THE COMPUTER FACILITY

The workload for a computer facility should be determined by decisions made by top-level executives and users relating to the facility's mission and the projects it *should* be working on. In addition to having a keen interest in how effectively a facility is being used, however, executives, users, and data processing managers are also intensely interested in the controls that may be used (1) *to improve operating efficiency* (e.g., to reduce department costs or to permit more work to be done at the same cost) and (2) *to avoid the problems that may result from failure to safeguard data integrity, system security, and personal privacy.* Let us look at these control topics in the remaining pages of this chapter.

Control of Operating Efficiency

The basic procedure to be followed to control the efficiency of computer department operations consists of the same steps used to control any other activity. That is, acceptable standards of performance for the department must first be established; actual operating performance must then be measured; the actual performance must next be compared against the standards; and, finally, the appropriate control actions must then be taken.

Establishing Department Standards of Performance The importance of *methods standards* (i.e., the procedural rules and instructions that are to be followed in performing specific tasks) were pointed out earlier. *Performance standards* are then used to specify *how well* the particular tasks are to be performed by both people and equipment. A method standard, for example, might spell out the steps to be completed during the data-gathering phase of a system study; a corresponding performance standard might then specify, for a study of a given complexity, the length of time that should be needed to complete the data-gathering phase. Obviously, then, objective and realistic performance standards cannot exist in the absence of clearly defined methods standards.

A computer facility may establish standards of performance for both equipment and personnel. *Equipment performance standards* (which may be applied to each separately operated piece of hardware) may specify the time that should be spent on such activities as (1) set-up, (2) testing, (3) production, (4) reruns, (5) training, and (6) scheduled and unscheduled maintenance. Such standards can be used in assigning processing tasks to facility hardware and in evaluating the performance of equipment operators.

Although *personnel performance standards* for equipment operators may be based on general equipment standards, it is usually much more difficult to establish realistic performance criteria for those engaged in the creative activities of systems analysis/design and programming. To illustrate, the number of key strokes per hour at a data input device can be counted, and such counts can be used to establish keying performance standards. The number of lines of code (LOC) produced by programmers over a given period can also be counted, and LOC performance standards can then be established.[5] But it is quite possible for one programmer to prepare a flexible program with 200 lines of code that is tested and ready on schedule, is straightforward and relatively easy to maintain, and is efficient in the use of machine time. Another programmer assigned to the same project might use 250 lines of code to prepare a program that lacks many of the desirable qualities of the shorter program. Yet if a rigid LOC performance standard were applied, the second programmer would likely receive a higher performance rating.[6] In spite of the hazards involved, however, many data processing managers are currently attempting to create systems and programming performance standards by (1) dividing each project into clearly defined tasks and deliverable outputs, (2) evaluating the project in terms of its size and complexity, and (3) estimating completion times on the basis of the past performance experience of the facility.[7] (The actual project performance is then measured and compared against the estimates. Subsequent project plans and controls are then influenced by this additional experience.)

Although departmental standards of performance are needed if managers are to control the operating efficiency of their computing resources, such performance standards do not exist at all in many organizations. And when performance criteria have been established, the emphasis has generally been on equipment usage.

Measuring Department Performance Evaluating the performance of creative personnel is more an art than a science, and the approaches currently used vary from one facility to another. The success with which analysts and programmers perform their work, the satisfaction of users with the finished product, and the degree of success or failure detected in follow-up project performance reviews conducted by internal auditors are probably the best

[5]The case for using LOC as a measure of productivity is found in James R. Johnson, "A Working Measure of Productivity," *Datamation,* February 1977, pp. 106–107ff.

[6]In later periods, of course, the first programmer would likely produce code that was complex, voluminous, and redundant.

[7]For further discussion of this topic, see John Toellner, "Performance Measurement in Systems and Programming," *Infosystems,* Part 1, December 1977, pp. 34–36, and Part 2, January 1978, pp. 60–62.

current indicators available to measure the performance of creative personnel.

The performance and efficiency of the computer system itself can suffer from such causes as the wrong hardware configuration, poorly written programs, and/or poor scheduling of the jobs to be processed. Unfortunately, both the causes and cures of inefficiency are seldom obvious. Thus, performance-measuring tools have been developed to break down computer usage time into productive and idle components. *Included in these computer performance evaluation (CPE) tools are:*[8]

1 *Hardware monitors.* A hardware monitor is an electronic data-gathering device that is usually connected by probes to the circuitry of the CPU. These probes collect timing and resource usage data from the processor during normal operation by sampling the electric pulses or signals that represent data flowing through the CPU. The data gathered by the monitor are recorded on magnetic tape for further analyses to determine system component utilization. These analyses may identify overworked components, bottleneck situations, and resource conflicts. An analysis package supplied with the monitor may provide plots and graphic displays to aid the manager.

2 *Software monitors.* This CPE tool is a computer program that is patched into the computer's operating system program. The status of system resources is periodically sampled and recorded on tapes or disks for subsequent analysis. An analysis software package may be provided with the monitor to produce reports on resource usage (e.g., on disk space utilization and on paging activity in a virtual storage environment) and on software performance. Unlike a hardware monitor, which imposes no load on a system and does not interrupt normal operations, a software monitor does add a small additional burden on the system by taking up storage space and by periodically interrupting normal activities in order to gather data. The software monitor, however, is less expensive.

3 *Job accounting packages.* Many operating systems contain routines to gather job accounting statistics as a byproduct during processing runs. These job accounting packages are supplied by computer manufacturers and by a number of independent software vendors. Two purposes may be served by the use of these packages: *First,* data dealing with such things as CPU usage, channel usage, elapsed times to process applications, peripheral device allocations, and storage utilization may be gathered to evaluate system performance; and *second,* the usage statistics may be converted into dollar figures by the operating system for user billing purposes.

[8]A wealth of information is available on CPE tools. See, for example, Israel Borovits, and Phillip Ein-Dor, "Cost/Utilization: A Measure of System Performance," *Communications of the ACM,* March 1977, pp. 185–191; "Data Processing Audit Practices Report," *Systems Auditability and Control Study,* The Institute of Internal Auditors, Inc., Altamonte Springs, Fla., 1977, pp. 167–171; John R. Hansen, "Evaluating an Awesome Computer Facility," *Infosystems,* January 1978, pp. 66–67ff; Thomas M. Hoger, "Monitors: How the Computer System Behaves!" *Infosystems,* October 1977, pp. 80ff; "How to Squeeze More out of a Computer," *Business Week,* September 13, 1976, pp. 96ff; Phillip C. Howard, "Monitors and Merriment," *Computer Decisions,* September 1975, pp. 40–42ff; John J. Hunter, "Measure for Measure," *Computer Decisions,* September 1976, pp. 54ff; Neil D. Kelley, "Cutting DP Costs," *Infosystems,* June 1977, pp. 80–82; G. Jay Lipovich, "DP Manager and Performance Measurement," *Journal of Systems Management,* March 1977, pp. 22–27; and Barry Stevens, "Sharp Management Notes Performance," *Computer Decisions,* September, 1975, pp. 27ff.

Comparing Actual Performance with Standards and Taking Action These final control steps need little further discussion here. Significant variations of actual performance from established equipment usage standards, for example, would certainly call for an appropriate response. The response might be to institute an operator training program, consolidate underutilized resources, make hardware substitutions to alleviate bottlenecks, have equipment repaired, etc. Some examples of actions that have actually been taken to improve operating efficiency are:

1 American Airlines reduced its orders for CPUs and peripheral devices by 10 percent to 15 percent after monitors showed that program faults were misdirecting some of the 2.5 million reservation system messages processed each day.

2 INA Corporation sold one of its four large CPUs after performance measurement showed that the company's processing volume could easily be handled by the other three. The savings in annual maintenance costs alone amounted to about $40,000.

3 General Electric Company rescheduled the workflow of one computer—an action that resulted in the elimination of $140,000 worth of new equipment. Overall, G.E. has saved $1.5 million by measuring performance of existing systems and getting them to produce more work.

Charging for Computing Resources In addition to performing the steps listed above to control the efficiency of computer department operations, the department manager should probably also establish some mechanism whereby computer users are "charged" a fair price for the computing resources that they use.[9] Although a *no chargeout* approach that provides services to users on a no-charge basis and that treats all computer costs as a company overhead expense has the advantage of not requiring a user billing system, it also tends to encourage waste, since users have little incentive to utilize computing resources in the most efficient manner. In the interest of promoting greater efficiency, then, the department manager may consider using one of the following *alternatives to the no chargeout approach:*

1 *Full chargeout for resource usage.* In this approach, all operating expenses are absorbed by users and the computer facility is run as a cost center. Chargeout computations are calculated frequently (e.g., weekly or monthly), and the chargeout rates can vary for the same application from period to period due to usage fluctuations. (If a system is fully loaded, the charge for processing the application will be lower, because many users are sharing the total costs; if

[9]The following sources give further information on charging for computing resources: Richard G. Canning, "The Effects of Charge-Back Policies," *EDP Analyzer,* November 1973, pp. 1–13; John Dearden and Richard L. Nolan, "How to Control the Computer Resource," *Harvard Business Review,* November–December 1973, pp. 68–78; Richard L. Nolan, "Effects of Chargeout on User/Manager Attitudes," *Communications of the ACM,* March 1977, pp. 177–184; Carol Schaller, "Survey of Computer Cost Allocation Techniques," *The Journal of Accountancy,* June 1974, pp. 41–42ff; J. J. Sobczak, "Pricing Computer Usage," *Datamation,* February 1974, pp. 61–64.

the system is underutilized during a period, however, the user's application must absorb a higher percentage of the total costs.) Since individual users have little or no control over these usage fluctuations, they also have little or no control over their charges from period to period. This lack of internal price stability often causes users to buy computing services outside the organization—an action that can result in further decreases in in-house users! Of course, the advantages of a full chargeout system are that (*a*) users realize that the computer is not a "free good" and (*b*) the computer department must offer rates competitive to outside facilities or risk losing user business.

2 *Partial chargeout for resource usage.* To overcome the disadvantage of charging fluctuating prices for the same tasks while retaining the advantage of giving users an incentive to make efficient use of computing resources, many organizations have settled on some form of partial chargeout system. Typically, a constant rate based on some usage activity (e.g., seconds of CPU time used) is set at the beginning of a period and is then changed only infrequently. Some or all of the costs incurred to develop new applications may be charged to company overhead. Billing statistics are typically gathered by the job accounting packages discussed earlier. A computer chargeout program (which may charge less for jobs run during the evening hours and more for jobs that utilize those resources of the facility that are relatively scarce) then uses these statistics to prepare user bills.

Control of Data Integrity, System Security, and Personal Privacy

The unhappy managerial and social consequences of a lack of control over data integrity, system security, and personal privacy were discussed earlier in this chapter. The purpose of this section is to outline briefly some of the integrity, security, and privacy controls that have been devised in the attempt to control the negative effects of computer usage.

Integrity Controls[10] To be assured that a computer department will provide accurate, complete, and reliable information, managers and auditors should periodically check to see that (1) all *input* data are correctly recorded, (2) the *processing* of all authorized transactions is accomplished without additions or omissions, and (3) the *output* of the system is distributed on a timely basis and only to those who are authorized to receive it.

The purpose of *input controls* is to make sure that (1) *all* authorized input transactions are identified, (2) these transactions are *accurately recorded* in a machine-usable form at the *right time,* and (3) *all* these transactions are then sent to the processing station. *Among the input control techniques that may be adopted are:*

[10] A wealth of additional information on this topic may be found in Richard G. Canning, "The Importance of EDP Audit and Control," *EDP Analyzer,* June 1977, pp. 1–13; "Data Processing Control Practices Report," *Systems Auditability and Control Study,* The Institute of Internal Auditors, Inc., Altamonte Springs, Fla., 1977; William C. Mair, Donald R. Wood, and Keagle W. Davis, *Computer Control and Audit,* 2d ed., The Institute of Internal Auditors, Inc., Altamonte Springs, Fla., 1976; D. E. Morgan and D. J. Taylor, "A Survey of Methods of Achieving Reliable Software," *Computer,* February 1977, pp. 44–51; and Robert L. Patrick, "Sixty Ingredients for Better Systems," *Datamation,* December 1977, pp. 171ff.

1 *The use of prenumbered forms.* Whenever possible, a simple and effective control is to use serially numbered forms so that documents may be accounted for. A missing number in the sequence signals a missing document.

2 *The use of control totals.* When batch processing is used, certain totals can be computed for each batch of source documents. For example, the total dollar-sales figure may be computed on a batch of sales invoices prior to, perhaps, keypunching. The same calculation can be made after keypunching to see if the figures compare. Control totals do not have to be expressed in dollars. They can be the totals obtained from adding figures in a data field that is included in all source documents being considered. A simple count of documents, cards, and other records is an effective control total. For example, the number of cards processed in the computer-operating department can be compared with the count of the number of cards that are delivered for processing. Similar comparisons between records read on magnetic tape and the number of input source documents may be possible.

3 *The use of transcription methods.* One means of controlling data transcription is to have knowledgeable clerks conduct a preaudit of source documents prior to recording the transactions in a machine-usable form. If input is by means of punched cards, the card verifier can be used. Transaction recording devices are available that can reduce errors caused by recopying, keypunching, illegible records, and loss of documents.

4 *The use of programmed checks on input.* Program instructions can be written to check on the reasonableness and propriety of data as they enter the processing operation. For example, program checks can be written to determine if (*a*) certain specified limits are exceeded, (*b*) the input is complete, and (*c*) a transaction code or identification number is active and reasonable. When online processing is used, lockwords or passwords may be required from remote stations before certain files can be made accessible.

Processing controls are established to (1) determine when data are lost or not processed and (2) check on the accuracy of arithmetic calculations. These controls may be classified into hardware and software categories. Important *hardware processing controls include* parity checks (i.e., checks that test whether the number of digits in an array is odd or even) and the use of dual reading and writing heads in I/O equipment. *Software or programmed processing controls include:*

1 *The use of record count.* As a check against a predetermined total the computer can be instructed to count the number of records that it handles in a program run.

2 *The use of tape labels.* The *external* labeling of magnetic tapes should be carefully controlled. These outside labels may give those interested such information as the tape contents, program identification number, and length of time the contents should be retained. *Internal* header and trailer control labels may also be recorded on the tapes themselves. The first (or *header*) record written on the tape gives the program identification number and other information. Before actual processing begins, then, a programmed comparison check may be made to make sure that the correct tape reel is being used. The last (or *trailer*) record contains a count of the number of other records on the tape.

3 *The use of sequence check.* In batch processing, the records are in some kind of sequence, e.g., by employee number or stock number. Programmed checks to detect out-of-sequence and missing cards and records prevent a file from being processed in an incorrect order.

4 *The use of structural check.* A test of the transactions to be processed can be made to determine whether the debits and credits called for represent acceptable combinations. Transactions with unacceptable debit and credit combinations are rejected.

Output controls are established as final checks on the accuracy and propriety of the processed information. *Among the output control methods that may be employed are:*

1 *The use of control totals.* How do the control totals of processed information compare with the input control totals? For example, is there agreement between the number of records that were delivered for processing and the number of records that were actually processed? A basic output control technique is to obtain satisfactory answers to such questions.

2 *The review of interested parties.* Feedback on a regular basis from input-initiating and output-using departments points out errors that slip through in spite of all precautions. Follow-up action must be taken to correct any file inaccuracies that may be revealed.

3 *The use of systematic sampling.* Auditors can check on output by tracing randomly selected transactions from source documents through the processing system to the output destination. This should be done on a regular and systematic basis.

4 *The use of prenumbered forms.* Certain output forms should be prenumbered and accounted for in the same manner as input documents. Blank payroll-check forms, for example, should be closely guarded.

System Security Controls[11] Since easy access to the computer by people with the skills needed to manipulate the system is a primary reason for the difficulty in maintaining security, an important step in achieving a more secure system is to separate the activities of those working *within* the computer department as noted earlier in this chapter. In addition, *system-design, programming, computer-operation,* and *retention* controls should be enforced.

Systems should be designed (and documented) with audit and control considerations in mind. (It is expensive to ignore control aspects and then have to revise and rework a designed system. The participation of a knowledgeable auditor in the design phase so that proper controls may be built in is thus a wise

[11] A number of the sources cited in the preceding footnote also provide information on system security. Additional references on this subject are: Richard G. Canning, "Integrity and Security of Personal Data," *EDP Analyzer,* April 1976, pp. 1–14; "Comprehensive EDP Security Guidelines," *The Australian Computer Journal,* March 1976, pp. 25–37; Lance J. Hoffman, *Modern Methods for Computer Security and Privacy,* Prentice-Hall, Inc., Englewood Cliffs, N.J., 1977; Jerome Lobel, "Planning a Secure System," *Journal of Systems Management,* July 1976, pp. 14–19; K. S. Shankar, "The Total Computer Security Problem: An Overview," *Computer,* June 1977, pp. 50–61; and August W. Smith, "Data Processing Security: A Common Sense Approach," *Data Management,* May 1977, pp. 7–8ff.

precaution.) One of the most important controls that can be exercised over systems design is to assign authority to one or more individuals to make sure that systems and program flowcharts, decision tables, manuals, etc., are correctly prepared *and maintained.* Specifically written control procedures should be established for this purpose.

Programming controls should be formulated to handle *program changes.* Changes should be made only after written approval is given by someone in a position of authority—e.g., the manager of the affected department. It is sometimes a good policy to postpone making a number of minor changes until the end of an accounting cycle so that data handling remains consistent throughout the accounting period. Changes in programs should be made by authorized programmers and not by computer-operating personnel. All changes should be charted and explained in writing; when completed, they should be reviewed and cleared by someone other than a maintenance programmer. All documents related to the change should be made a part of the permanent program file.

Some of the *computer-operating controls that may be established are:*

1 *Control over console intervention.* It is possible for computer operators to bypass program controls. They have the ability to interrupt a program run and introduce data manually into the processor through the console keyboard. With organizational separation of program preparation and computer operation and with operators having access to object programs and not source programs, it is unlikely that an operator will have enough knowledge of the program details to manipulate them successfully for improper purposes. But the possibility of unauthorized intervention should be reduced in a number of ways. Since, for example, the console typewriter may be used to print out a manual intervention, the paper sheets in the typewriter can be prenumbered and periodically checked. Other approaches using locked recording devices may be employed. Additional control techniques include rotating the duties of computer operators (or others in sensitive positions).[12]

2 *Control over physical security.* Definite controls should be established to safeguard programs and data from fire and water damage or destruction. Duplicate program and master file tapes may have to be kept at a location away from the computer site. A waste-disposal procedure to destroy carbon papers and other media containing sensitive information should be followed.[13] Only authorized personnel should be allowed access to the computer site.

[12]Managers should be alert to the risk inherent in having employees who never take vacations, who refuse promotion or rotation, who have access to the premises when no one else is present, and who are always around when the books are closed at the end of an accounting period.

[13]Almost $1 million in telephone equipment was stolen from Pacific Telephone & Telegraph Company by a clever thief who, at the age of 16, found in the telephone company trash cans information on Bell System operating procedures, manuals on "system instructions," and a guide book on "Ordering Material and Supplies." Catalogs and authority code numbers were also acquired from trash cans! The thief obtained a special input device and then accessed the Bell System computer to input coded order and authority numbers. The ordered equipment was then picked up by the thief at a company warehouse (he had also bought a used telephone company van for the purpose). See Leo Anderson, "This Man Stole Almost $1 Million from a Telephone Company," *Telephony,* November 17, 1972, pp. 36–38. (After being caught and paying his debt to society, the thief started a consulting service called EDP Security, Inc.)

3 *Control over terminal usage.* Control procedures to identify authorized users of the system should obviously be given special attention. Such identification is typically based on something that users *know* (e.g., a password), on something they *have* (e.g., a card with a magnetically coded identification number or a key that is used to unlock the terminal keyboard), on some *personal characteristic* they possess, or on some combination of these elements. Passwords are most commonly used, but when used frequently (and carelessly), these words lose their security value. A better approach, perhaps, would be to have the computer provide the user, each day, with a different word or code that the user could then modify by following a secret procedure in order to gain access to the system. For example, "the computer might send a five-digit password. The user then adds today's date to it, and then sends back the second and fourth digits of the sum."[14] Once an authorized user has been identified and has gained access to the system, various techniques employing cryptography—that is, "hidden writing"—are available to thwart those who would intercept the messages traveling between the computer and the remote terminal.

The security of records *retained or stored* in machine-readable form for extended periods of time must also be maintained. Such retention is often necessary in order to satisfy an IRS ruling that *requires* the preservation of certain machine-readable records by computer-using organizations for tax audit purposes. A second reason for retention control (although, given the "persuasiveness" of the first reason, a second is not required) is that management decision making may be aided by having historical data readily available and easily incorporated into simulation models that might uncover possible trends and relationships.

Although punched paper media, microfilm, and magnetic disk packs may be used for long-term data storage, magnetic tape is by far the most popular retention medium. Thus, controls in most cases must be designed to protect archival magnetic tapes against dust, improper temperature and humidity fluctuations, and electromagnetic radiation.

Privacy Controls[15] An individual's "right" to privacy has been discussed at various times in this book, but privacy is not one of the rights specifically mentioned in the Bill of Rights of the Constitution. (In fact, the word "privacy" does not appear anywhere in the Constitution.) Furthermore, what one person may consider to be a privacy right may be in direct conflict with one of the rights

[14]Richard G. Canning, "Protecting Valuable Data—Part 2," *EDP Analyzer,* January 1974, p. 8. This is a good source for further information on securing online terminals.

[15]Additional privacy control information may be found in the following references: Paul B. Demitriades, "Administrative Secrecy and Data Privacy Legislation," *Journal of Systems Management,* October 1976, pp. 24–29; Jerome Lobel, "Computer Privacy States' Side: Seeking Cooperation Amid Confusion," *Data Management,* April 1977, pp. 12–15ff; *Personal Privacy in an Information Society* (Washington, D.C.: U.S. Government Printing Office, Superintendent of Documents, Stock No. 052-003-00395-3, July 1977); Willis H. Ware, "Handling Personal Data," *Datamation,* October 1977, pp. 83–85ff; and J. T. Westermeier, Jr., and Kenneth D. Polin, "Privacy Report to Alter Relation of Business to the Individual," *Data Management,* September 1977, pp. 30–33.

that *is* explicitly mentioned in the Constitution. For example, if a newspaper reporter unearths the fact that a member of Congress has put a number of relatives on the government payroll for no good purpose, and if the reporter then reveals this fact and prints the names and salaries of the relatives, he or she has undoubtedly infringed on their privacy. But the reporter has also used rights guaranteed in the Bill of Rights (the First Amendment's freedom of speech and freedom of the press) to perform a public service. Thus, there may be legitimate rights operating against privacy in some situations. In short, since privacy is not one of the specific constitutional rights, and since a balance has to be struck between the need for privacy on the one hand and society's need for legitimate information on the other, *the extent to which individuals are given privacy protection must depend on judicial and legislative decisions.* That is, the *continuous* task of balancing human rights against basic freedoms in order to establish privacy controls is the responsibility of the judicial and legislative branches of government.

Recognizing that rapid advances in computer technology have given users of that technology the ability to gather and store information that (1) goes beyond the legitimate information needs of society and (2) can lead to excessive and unnecessary intrusions into an individual's personal privacy, lawmakers have been busy in recent years in the effort to restore some balance in favor of privacy. The result has been that federal statutes and dozens of state bills have been passed over a brief time span to control the invasion of privacy.

Some *examples of existing privacy laws* are:

1 *Fair Credit Reporting Act of 1970.* This federal law gives individuals the right to know what information is kept on them by credit bureaus and other credit investigation agencies. Individuals also have the right to challenge information they consider to be inaccurate and to insert brief explanatory statements into the records in disputed cases.

2 *State "Fair Information Practice" laws.* The California Fair Information Practice Act of 1974 spells out the rights of individuals when dealing with state government data banks. Individuals have the right (*a*) to know what information is kept on them in the various state computer data banks; (*b*) to contest the "accuracy, completeness, pertinence, and timeliness" of the stored data; (*c*) to force a reinvestigation of the current status of personal data; and (*d*) to resolve disputes in ways spelled out by the law. The Minnesota Privacy Act (and acts passed by other states) contains similar provisions.

3 *Privacy Act of 1974.* This important privacy legislation was passed by Congress late in 1974 and signed into law by President Gerald Ford on January 1, 1975. It became effective late in September 1975. The act is aimed at some of the uses and abuses of *federal government* data banks. Some of the provisions of this law are: (*a*) With the exception of classified files, Civil Service records, and law enforcement agency investigative files, individuals have the right to see their records in federal data banks; (*b*) they may point out errors in their records, and if these errors are not removed, they may ask a federal judge to order the correction; (*c*) when federal agencies request personal information, they must tell individuals whether their cooperation in supplying the information is required by law; and (*d*) no federal, state, or local government agency can design a *new* information system based upon the use of the Social Security number. A Privacy Protection Study Commission was also established to monitor enforcement of the law and to study issues that will have to be resolved in the future. For example, the Commission was specifically given authority in the act to examine personal information activities in the medical, insurance, education, employment, credit and banking, credit reporting, cable television, telecommunications and other media, travel and hotel reservations, and EFTS areas. After a two-year study the Commission issued a final published report in July 1977. At this writing, it appears that additional laws will eventually be passed to incorporate the Commission's recommendations and to expand the scope of the Privacy Act to include data banks maintained by federal, state, and local law enforcement agencies, state and local governments, and businesses.

REVIEW AND DISCUSSION QUESTIONS

1 How can computer systems help managers control business operations?

2 (*a*) What is internal control? (*b*) Why is it needed? (*c*) Identify and discuss the types of information system failures that can result from poor internal control.

3 Of what significance is organizational structure in maintaining internal control?

4 (*a*) What is the audit trail? (*b*) Why is it needed?

5 "Data integrity, data security, and personal privacy are interrelated." Define these terms and discuss this statement.

6 Why must the primary responsibility for internal control reside with top-level executives?

7 "The basic procedure to be followed to control the efficiency of computer department operations consists of the same steps used to control any other activity." Identify and discuss the use of these steps to control computer efficiency.

8 (*a*) What is a performance standard? (*b*) Why is it difficult to establish realistic performance standards for system analysts and programmers?

9 (*a*) What is the purpose of using computer performance evaluation tools? (*b*) Identify and discuss three CPE tools.

10 (*a*) How may charging for computing resources lead to greater efficiency? (*b*) Compare the full chargeout and partial chargeout approaches to charging for computing resources.

11 (*a*) What is the purpose of data integrity controls? (*b*) Into what three categories may integrity controls be classified? (*c*) Give some examples of integrity controls.

12 (*a*) What is the purpose of system security controls? (*b*) Into what categories may security controls be classified? (*c*) Give some examples of security controls.

13 "The extent to which individuals are given privacy protection must depend on judicial and legislative decision." Discuss this statement.

Chapter 7 Readings

INTRODUCTION TO READINGS 21 THROUGH 23

21 Computer-related and computer-assisted frauds continue to present a serious problem. In this reading, Brandt Allen discusses potentially vulnerable areas in a computerized system and emphasizes that knowledge of the company's procedures can provide a would-be embezzler with the background necessary for success.

22 Preventive measures that can be taken to improve data security are also discussed in this reading by Marvin Wofsey. Many of the risks associated with the use of computers are pointed out in his wide-ranging article, and both preventive and ameliorative measures are suggested to reduce the possible dangers.

23 As many companies have centralized their data processing activities, they have found the need to formalize the procedures for providing service to the user departments. In this article, Richard L. Nolan discusses seven steps that companies can take to design an effective chargeout system whereby they can place more control in the hands of those who use data services and hold them accountable for the services they use.

Reading 21

Embezzler's Guide to the Computer

Brandt Allen

With the assistance of an on-line computer system, a young graduate student stole about a million dollars' worth of inventory from a large utility in California. The student acquired knowledge of the system by posing as a magazine interviewer, retrieving computer manuals from wastebaskets, and phoning employees. Eventually he was able to accumulate enough data, including system instructions and practices, ordering and operating instructions, catalogs, passwords, and the like, to gain access to the equipment order system.

With his knowledge of company procedures and his access to the on-line system used for part of the inventory control system, the student was able to place orders for equipment to the utility's central supply division. The equipment would then be shipped to various designated warehouses, where, at early hours in the morning, in a disguised truck, he would pick it up, along with the bill of lading. He spread his thefts over a number of field locations so that no single loss would arouse suspicion, and sold the equipment through a company he had formed.

Reprinted from *Harvard Business Review*, July–August 1975. Copyright © 1975 by the president and fellows of Harvard College; all rights reserved. Brandt Allen is on the faculty of the Colgate Darden School of Business Administration at the University of Virginia.

By entering fraudulent data into the bank's computer from a remote terminal in his branch office, a chief teller of a major New York savings bank stole a million and a half dollars from hundreds of accounts. When quarterly interest was due, he would simply either redeposit some of the money or indicate that it had been redeposited. The manual auditing and the computer controls failed to show any fraudulent manipulation. The teller was not detected until a police raid on a gambling operation revealed that he was betting up to $30,000 a day on professional sports. Even then the teller had to explain his manipulations to the bank executives for them to fully understand what he had done.

As you can see from these examples, embezzlement may be the best game in town; it certainly beats the market for yield and return, and it is probably less risky. In fact, it is estimated that embezzlers take two to three billion dollars a year in the United States. (Since many if not most embezzlers never go public, only a sixth of the winnings and related incidents ever get reported in the press.) If embezzlers are detected, their penalties are almost always small. They rarely go to jail. The young graduate student in California, for instance, spent less than a year in detention.

As businesses and other organizations have automated more and more of their accounting and record keeping, embezzlers have found themselves faced with the problems of mastering and profiting from the new technology. Fortunately, the prognosis is good. Virtually all of the traditional peculation opportunities of the past may be safely run through the computer, and a host of exciting new schemes is possible as well.

To sweeten the pot, computer technology tends to confound auditors and managers to the extent that they are rarely in a position to detect or prevent computer-based embezzlement. For example, of the more than 50 case examples I have studied, fewer than half were first detected by auditors or internal controls.[1] A great many of these cases involved very simple schemes that could have continued to be successful for much longer, or for indefinite periods of time, had the perpetrator been a little more clever.

This guide is written both for the accomplished embezzler who wishes to polish his skills with computer technology and for the novice who correctly sees this field as a ripe new opportunity. The schemes most likely to be successful will be discussed, along with explanations of just how the computer must be manipulated. Examples of once successful but recently detected cases will be presented. Finally, a list of common misconceptions and important truths about computer fraud will be outlined. This is important since you, a would-be embezzler, may often profit from others' misconceptions.

THE BEST-LAID PLANS

To steal from an organization, it does not really matter what industry you are in or whether you work for a profit-oriented, governmental, or not-for-profit

[1]See Lee Seidler, "What Will They Think of Next?" (Ideas for Action), *Harvard Business Review,* May–June 1974, p. 6.

group. It does help, however, if you are in a position of responsibility and are a "trusted" employee—the greater your responsibility, the better. Knowledge of basic accounting, record keeping, and financial statements is also necessary, though the same is not so of the computer. You are in the ideal position of not needing to know a lot about computer technology in order to beat it. The auditors and management must, however, know a great deal in order to catch you at it. The best embezzlement schemes have to be well executed to work, but the ideas are simple.

Disbursements Fraud: "A Voucher Is the Next Best Thing to Money"

Without a doubt, the best place to start is with the fraudulent disbursements game. This fraud has historically accounted for more embezzlement losses than all others. The approach is actually quite simple: your company, bank, or organization is fooled into paying for goods and services that it did not receive or did not receive in full measure. Payment is made to your bogus company. Arranging to cash checks issued to your company is certainly no problem; fooling your employer into issuing those checks is a bit tougher. Here are five things to remember when you start:

1 Carefully examine the accounting and record-keeping systems of your company. This can be done by personal inspection, unobtrusive questioning, and often simply by reading policies and procedures manuals or computer system documentation.

2 Study the purchasing function. Most organizations use a "purchase order" or similar document to order merchandise. Determine: who has access to blank forms; who is authorized to approve them; where copies are stored once the order is prepared and sent (in companies with advanced computer systems, the "image" of the purchase order is kept in the computer and may be read by authorized personnel in various departments; in this case there may be no written copies of the order); how form numbers are controlled (if at all); and what procedures are used for partial receipt of goods, cancelled orders, changes to unfilled-outstanding orders, and for all unusual transactions. This last item is particularly important; because the controls for nonstandard procedures are often the weakest, you should concentrate your efforts there.

3 Study the procedures for receiving merchandise. Often someone at the warehouse or receiving terminal verifies that the shipment corresponds to what was ordered by comparing the shipment to a file of open purchase orders. You must determine what verification is made and with respect to which documents, and what notification of receipt of merchandise is prepared, to whom it is sent, and where all the copies are maintained.

4 Watch out for vouchers. At this point in a purchase transaction, organizations often initiate a voucher record or document that uses vendor, purchase order number, account code, amount, receipt of merchandise document number, and related information. Learn as much as you can about this process and about the vouchers and the voucher file, because a voucher is the next best thing to money.

5 Find out how invoices are processed. The invoice is matched against the voucher to ensure that the invoice is correct and that the merchandise has been received; normally, a check is then prepared. Generating an invoice is the least of your problems, of course, since it comes from your bogus company through the mails.

The key point of the purchase transaction is this: whenever an approved purchase order is matched with a receipt of merchandise and with an invoice from the vendor, a check will be issued. You must be in a position to alter or fabricate both a purchase order and a merchandise receipt. After that, it is a simple matter for you to see that the invoice is rendered.

Exactly how you arrange to falsify the two key documents or records is, of course, the difficult part. If you work in purchasing, you can generally find some way of generating fraudulent purchase orders by forging names of legitimate buyers, altering otherwise proper orders, or canceling an outstanding order and using that purchase order number and authorization to issue a fraudulent order to your bogus company. Your problem will be to generate the merchandise receipt or record. The easiest method is, of course, to collude with someone in the receiving terminal, but many other devices, short of collusion, may be used. Sometimes this is as simple as printing either packing slips for your bogus company or merchandise receipts (employer's), forging them, and sending them through the company mail to data processing or accounting.

It is often much easier to establish both the purchase order record and the merchandise receipt if you work in accounting or data processing. Sometimes it is as simple as punching a few cards and entering them as if they were legitimate into a batch of transactions. The danger of doing this in second-generation computer systems is that the computer files of open purchase orders and merchandise receipts would not correspond to the various duplicate files maintained elsewhere—a constant threat. More modern computer systems often lack duplicate files because "purchase orders" and "merchandise receipts" are entered into a centralized set of computer files through computer terminals or data-collection devices. Here's an example to get you thinking:

> Over a six-year period, the chief accountant of a large fruit and vegetable shipping company embezzled more than a million dollars. While running the accounting work at a computer service bureau, he developed a model of the company on which he experimented with both real and fraudulent disbursement transactions. He determined which company accounts he could take large amounts of money from without being detected. He then charged these accounts with phony purchase orders and receipts from punched cards he had prepared. By increasing these expense and inventory accounts, the accountant made the difference between what was actually owed and the recorded amount payable to a dummy company he had established.

The embezzler must be aware that his scheme is not complete just because he has been able to close the purchase order/merchandise receipt/vendor/invoice circle, and his dummy company has received the check. He has left "footprints" that are a potential threat to him behind in the company records. One footprint is that some account was charged for merchandise or services not received. It may have been an inventory account, in which case the book inventory figure is higher than the actual physical inventory by the exact amount of the theft. When the count of the physical inventory is made, your peculation should be exposed. There are, of course, many steps you can take to minimize such occurrences; these four stand out:

1 Select inventory accounts with high activity and high value, accounts that are physically difficult to count, where security is a continuing problem, where responsibility is shared among many, and where a certain amount of loss is "expected."

2 Do not "hit" any account too hard. Try to find out how much shortage will be tolerated in each account before someone triggers a thorough investigation. Remember that there are likely to be other white collar thieves at work (as well as thieves without collars).

3 Select accounts supplied by many new and constantly changing vendors.

4 Be aware of managerial style. Some managers are detail oriented. They pore over the financial statements, analyze the operating variances, and scrutinize the purchases, prices, terms, and inventory levels. Other managers are just the opposite. When charging a fictitious purchase to an inventory account, pick on the latter.

Many of the same arguments also hold for charges to expense accounts. Pick accounts that are difficult to monitor—ones such as freight, taxes, employee benefits, indirect labor, supplies, services, and so on. Avoid charging to small departments, departments run by detail men, and basic accounts, such as fuel, that tend to be watched closely.

Remember that all your efforts must be conducted through an accounting system with a number of tests and controls, checks and balances, cash totals, and batch counts. Fortunately, most of these controls are documented in the computer system descriptions or are the major topic of conversation of the data control group. You can also test for them by occasionally rearranging proper transactions; when the "real" test occurs, "they" will just think it is an error.

Inventory: "It Is Easier to Convert Goods to Cash"

Do not ignore inventories as a possible sorce of revenue. In many cases, it is easier to convert goods to cash than it is fraudulent checks, especially since the former are harder to trace. Although smaller, homogeneous articles might be easier to steal, size should not be a primary consideration, as the following example at an East Coast railroad suggests:

> One or more employees in a railroad's computer center allegedly altered input data to aid in the theft of over 200 boxcars. It is thought that the rolling stock inventory file was altered to reflect that the cars were either scrapped or wrecked, when they were actually shipped to another company's yard and repainted. The U.S. attorney handling the case stated that the actual thefts could not have gone undetected without the collusion of someone who had access to and was able to manipulate the

railroad's computer records. If they can take 200 boxcars—just think what you can do!

Computerized inventory systems lend themselves to penetration for two basic reasons: they account for a large amount of material, and the controls on access systems are normally lax. Depending on the company and the location of its warehouses, inventory transfers or shipments are either recorded on supporting documents first and later keypunched and entered into the computer, or they are entered directly into a central system via computer terminals. Both systems are vulnerable to theft. (By this time you have probably noticed that I use the terms *fraud, theft,* and *embezzlement* interchangeably. See the ruled insert on page 371 for more complete descriptions of the terms and some idea of the penalties connected with the crimes.)

The computer can assist you because it lessens the visibility of your acts and may make it easier for you to gain access to the inventory files. Also, as in the example described at the beginning of this article, interwarehouse transfers are often subject to less control because no one outside the company is usually involved in the transaction.

One day soon you will read about the following now-hypothetical inventory fraud:

> A large manufacturing/wholesale company operating through a number of geographically separated warehouses linked by computer-communications to a centralized order-processing system found that several of its warehouses had been virtually "cleaned out." Apparently a computer other than that of the corporation was connected to the system and used to send shipping instructions to the warehouses. Because the company had relied on its central computer to keep records of all shipping instructions, there were no extra copies other than the bill of lading and the mailing labels, which were printed at the warehouse. As a result, there was no record of where the goods had been shipped.

Sales Manipulation: "Shipping Documents Are Vulnerable"

Another fruitful area for the embezzler is the manipulation of shipments, sales, and billing procedures. Your objective here is to confuse your company into:

- Shipping a product to a customer without sending the bill
- Shipping one thing and billing the customer for something else
- Billing a shipment at the wrong price
- Granting improper credits or adjustments on returned or damaged products
- Manipulating the sales commissions, allowances, and discounts on merchandise shipped

For homework, prepare a flow chart of sales-order processing. Determine how all sales orders are received, written up, logged, and checked; how logs or registers are prepared, verified, and checked; and how sales commissions are processed. Study the flow of sales orders to the warehouse or plant and observe how orders are picked, packed, and shipped, and how all logs and registers are maintained there as well.

From your research you should have little difficulty in determining how to place an order (through a dummy company or one controlled by an accomplice). Your key task will be to intercept the shipping document or processed sales-order statement after shipment but before it is processed by the accounting department. For example, in many warehouses one can simply destroy a processed sales order after the order has been shipped. A helpful hint: most of the checking, logging, and registering controls you will have to beat were set up to ensure that the customer receives his order, *not* to ensure that your company bills correctly. Shipping documents are vulnerable to manipulation all the way from the warehouse to the accounting records in the computer.

In many computerized order-entry systems, the sales-order record is maintained on a computer file and is not normally updated or maintained until the order is shipped. When word is received that the order has been shipped, the sales-order record becomes the primary source of data on the shipment to accounts receivable and billing. The weak point in these systems is that the sales-order record can be changed after the shipment has been made but *before* the billing processes are triggered. The time delay here may be hours or just seconds, but in all systems there is still a point of vulnerability. For example:

> A middle-level manager in one large manufacturing company had access to the company's on-line order-entry, billing, and shipping systems. He was able to place bogus orders, which initiated the shipping of merchandise to a cover address. Then he would initiate billing cancellations due to alleged loss, damage, or destruction of the shipment in transit.

As I have noted, some companies have such weak controls that you can simply destroy the sales-order record after shipment and it will not be detected. In most cases, however, a register of sales orders filled is maintained, and a missing record would be noted. In this case, you may have to destroy the document after it has been checked against the log, or you might alter the record so that the eventual bill is much lower than what it ought to be. For example:

> In a large Canadian department store, a systems analyst, using his knowledge of the sales-order processing system, was able to place orders for expensive appliances and have them coded as "special pricing orders." He was then able to intercept these orders in data processing and change the price to only a few dollars. When the appliances were delivered, he paid his account and closed the loop.

In most cases it is best to stick to only a few items per order and to order only items you know are in stock. In some cases, however, where a company's control over back orders and partial shipments is weak or nonexistent, just the reverse is true.

Payroll Fraud: "It Is Easiest in Companies with a Large, Varying Work Force"

If you apply yourself, the payroll processing function in most large organizations with computerized control systems is a ready source of funds. There are a number of ways to manipulate your organization's payroll, but probably the most popular are:

- Padding the payroll with nonexistent employees.
- Leaving former employees on the payroll after termination.

Once you understand the payroll process thoroughly, you are ready to start. Employees in data processing, payroll, and programming are in ideal positions for these schemes. Perhaps the simplest method is to pad the payroll with extra hours, for oneself or for others as well, by altering input data; this does not require forging time records, or any other details. For example:

> Over a five-month period a computer center employee who had both input and monitoring duties initiated checks payable to herself. Although she regularly deleted the check from the disk record, a surprise audit revealed that overpayments had been made, and she was discovered.

Such payroll schemes are, however, limited as to the amount it is possible to take and involve more and more risks as the number of people involved increases. These schemes are also the ones payroll managers fear the most, and thus the ones they know how to control the best. As a result, unless controls are extremely lax, these schemes should be avoided. There are better ways.

Data-processing employees are often in the best position to create fictitious personnel, which is usually easiest to do in companies with lax controls and a large, varying work force. Supervisors of large departments often have neither the time nor the desire to verify the existence of each individual listed on the periodic check register (which they may or may not receive). In addition, the personnel department's employee data files are usually maintained in the EDP department and are subject to similar manipulation so that both files can be made to reflect the same fictitious employees. For example:

> An employee in the data center at the welfare department of a large city entered fraudulent data into the payroll system and stole $2.75 million over a nine-month period. He and several of his friends created a fictitious work force identified by fake social security numbers that were processed weekly through the payroll routine. The computer would automatically print a check for each fake employee. The conspirators would intercept the checks, endorse them, and cash them. The conspirators were uncovered when a policeman discovered a batch of over a hundred of the fraudulent checks in an overdue rental car he found illegally parked.

In those companies that have numerous branches employing a varying

Know what you are doing, or let the punishment fit the crime!

If you are going to steal in style, it would be wise for you to understand the nature of your thefts, their legal classifications, and the statutes involved. Although the laws and statutes vary from state to state, the following are generally accepted descriptions of the illegal activities you will undertake.

1 Larceny is the theft of assets, with the intent to convert them into cash without the consent of their lawful owner.

2 Embezzlement involves the theft of property by someone to whom the property has been entrusted (i.e., "larceny after trust").

3 Collusion occurs when more than one person is involved in cooperation for a fraudulent purpose.

4 Fraud involves the intentional misrepresentation of the truth to deceive the owner. In computer crimes the fraud occurs (*a*) when a thief attempts to conceal his actions through incorrect entries or changes in the company's records or files, and (*b*) when he is not entrusted with the assets that he actually steals. Most computer crimes fall into the fraud category.

If you simply steal inventory, it is theft, and if detected you may be charged with larceny. If you are an employee who steals and you disguise the theft, as was allegedly done at the railroad, that is fraud. If, however, you are the individual charged with responsibility for the inventory, your fraud is an embezzlement. If there is more than one of you, your embezzlement is collusion. For some delightful reason having to do with blue collars and white collars, thieves go to jail when caught, but embezzlers generally do not.

In a large percentage of cases, embezzlers are not even prosecuted. Because embezzlement is a crime against an entity and not an individual, a concept dating back to English common law, the criminal is often absolved if he or she simply returns the money. Also, because embezzlers are in positions of trust, they are often high up in the organization and friends of the top management, if they are not top managers themselves. Organizations, naturally preferring to hang their dirty laundry inside, settle such matters between friends.

number of employees, like opportunities exist. A branch manager can easily submit to the central processing group fraudulent information on temporary employees he has "put on the payroll." When the periodic checks are delivered, all he has to do is pocket those for the fictitious members of his work force.

Programmers who have complete understanding of payroll system controls and auditing methods have many, and often much more subtle methods that they can employ. A payroll program may be written to take a few pennies from each person's check and add them to that of the programmer. A better approach is to use the same scheme with income tax withholdings. The programs should, however, be designed so that the fraud segments can be activated or deactivated at will.

Pension Benefits and Annuities: "Keep a Deceased Pensioner on the File"

You can often embezzle from funds destined for the payment of pensions, employment benefits, and annuities. While insurance companies and pension funds are the most fertile grounds for such frauds, a surprising number of other organizations also handle pensions, even if only on a small scale. Many businesses have small groups of special employees who, for one reason or another, have pension and benefit programs that are administered directly by the company rather than being taken care of through a pension fund.

The actual steps to be taken will vary, depending on the size of the company and the extent and type of the pension and benefit programs. Regardless, you will first need to become familiar with the details of the operation to be embezzled: the numbers and list of beneficiaries, how beneficiaries are validated and revalidated, how benefits are determined, the addresses changed, and so on.

One of the most elegant frauds in the pension area—one that can run undetected for a considerable period of time—involves changing the address of a legitimate beneficiary to that of the embezzler or an accomplice at the time of the beneficiary's death. It is best to select beneficiaries with no life insurance. Also, since particular attention should be paid to how death notifications are received and processed, employees of the computer center are often in the best position to operate this embezzlement. For example:

> In a West German company, an employee operating a pension fraud left the deceased recipients' records in the computer system files but changed their bank account numbers, to which the checks were paid, to his own. When the pensioners were required to verify their existence, auditors uncovered the scheme.

If you are to be successful here, you must keep a deceased pensioner on the file only for a limited time, and then "kill" him.

If an estate does not claim death benefits after a beneficiary dies, you can claim them yourself through an accomplice. Again, personnel in the data center are often in the best position to know the status of each account, the requirements for processing claims, and if there has been communication between the company and the estate.

Rather than claim death benefits, it may be possible for you to claim the annuity or retirement benefits of a former employee who, for whatever reason, has not applied for his legitimate benefits after a period of time. To protect yourself, you can make private inquiries as to why the person has not applied and, if the risk is low, proceed to claim them yourself.

Accounts Receivable: "The Computer Can Be Your Scapegoat"

Theft from accounts receivable "robs Peter to pay Paul" by making good on one account with payments diverted from another. Popular long before the advent of computer systems, this "lapping" method does not necessarily require access to cash, though it does require constant vigilance; the amounts involved can mount up. The computer improves on the old scheme in several ways: in most cases, access to computer records is easier than to old manual records; your actions have less exposure when committed through a computer system; and the computer accepts all input as truth. Should a customer become suspicious because of repeated billings of a previously paid bill, a computer foul-up can be your scapegoat.

To succeed in this fraud, your main concern will be to shuffle the accounts continually. In addition to the accounts receivable section, ideal positions from which to operate this scheme are in the keypunch, data control, or computer operations departments. For example:

> Two men diverted over $61,000 in bill payments sent by insurance companies to a university medical center and deposited them in dummy accounts they had established. To cover their scheme, which lasted for ten months, the men deleted accounts from the medical center's computer records by making them uncollectible, or by purging them from the files. This fraud, like so many others, was uncovered by accident. One account was mistakenly left in the system, causing a second bill to be sent to an insurance company. A complaint followed, which led to the discovery of the culprits.

If you install what is commonly called a program "patch" into a computer program, you can alter the program so that thefts can be more permanent. To accomplish this, you will need a good working knowledge of computer programming, to know how to alter a program, and access to the program library.

It may also be necessary to "pass inspection" by the internal audit group, but this is not as difficult as it might appear, since, as a practical matter, computer programs can only be tested by checking the results of test data. This method of inspection can ensure only that the program "does what it's supposed to do" not that it "doesn't do anything else" under unusual conditions, such as perform a different task when a particular switch is set "improperly" at the machine console, or when "unusual" transactions appear. In the trade, these are called "triggers."

An "unusual" transaction might be a debit and a credit of the same amount on the same day where the amounts are equal to the numeric data, e.g., a debit and a credit of $112.75 on January 12, 1975 (01-12-75) might trigger a secret patch. The best trigger is one that, like the "unusual transaction," can be controlled from outside the organization. In theory, a complete test procedure should detect such tricks, but there is no guarantee; the internal auditor is always playing catch-up ball against you. Here is a good example of a patch:

> A bank programmer patched a program in such a fashion that it added ten cents to every service charge less than ten dollars and one dollar to those greater than ten. The excess charges were credited to the last account, which he had opened himself, under the name of Zzwicke. He was able to withdraw several hundred dollars each month until the bank, under a new marketing campaign, tried to honor the first and last names on their customer list, and discovered that Mr. Zzwicke did not exist.

Since they have the potential to enable the thief to prove that two plus two equals five, program patches, in spite of their difficulty and complexity, may be the embezzlement technique of the future. Companies have developed extensive controls over the processing of input data, in both receivable and payable accounts, primarily to detect and correct errors, but secondarily to prevent fraud. The "books" are assumed to be in balance at the beginning of the day, and if the day's transactions are clean and balanced, the ending totals are assumed to be correct and in balance. Thus the focal point of the controls is on the processing of inputs.

Using a program patch to cover fraudulent increases or decreases in balance can be especially profitable in large banks. The computer can be made to perform the old "adding machine trick" of the manual bookkeeping days in which bookkeepers totaling a series of ledger accounts could cover up a theft by advancing the tape, adding the stolen amount, and then repositioning the tape before finally punching the total key to get a desired but erroneous "balance." The computer program can also be made to "add" to the "correct amount," although not correctly.

A LITTLE LEARNING IS A DANGEROUS THING

There has been a paucity of published material about computer-related fraud, and because of this there are perhaps too many misconceptions about just how difficult it is to carry off. For some time, embezzlement has been the social disease of corporations, and they go to great pains to avoid any publicity when incidents occur. As a result, there is only skimpy knowledge on how to do it successfully. Perhaps some of the following truths and fictions will help you.

Fiction: It's Best to Stick to Banks

A number of computer frauds and embezzlements have indeed been detected in banks, insurance companies, brokerage houses, and other financial institutions. In fact, perhaps the first detected case of computer fraud was in a Minneapolis bank in 1966.

Embezzlement in financial institutions has received more publicity, probably because these organizations are, in many cases, regulated and investigated by federal agencies. But computer fraud has not been limited to financial institutions. There have been a number of examples of detected, computer-related frauds in manufacturing companies, wholesalers, utilities, chemical processors, railroads, mail order houses, department stores, hospitals, and government agencies. Given the reluctance of corporations and other organizations to publicize their own problems with embezzlement, these case histories, at the least, are examples of detected fraud in organizations that were unable to prevent publicity. However, it is evident, even from this small sample, that computer embezzlement works in places other than financial institutions.

Truth: Any Organization Can Be a Target

Fortunately for you, many executives believe just the opposite; they think embezzlement is something that happens to the other guy. This is, of course, the classic rationalization, and is the reason that general security in many organizations is poor. The potential for embezzlement varies with the type of firm, size, extent of controls, degree of audit, capability of the management and auditing personnel, as well as a host of other factors that are often unique to the organization. But there is probably no business organization, government agency, foundation, or not-for-profit organization that cannot be a successful embezzlement target. (Furthermore, the executive who says it cannot happen to him always makes the best patsy.)

Fiction: You Need Access to Cash

Probably the most strongly held and most dangerous misconception executives hold is that the successful embezzler has access to cash or cash equivalent items, such as securities, in his day-to-day activities. Do not believe it. Many of the most exciting and lucrative embezzlements have been conducted by individuals who had absolutely no access to cash. Of all of the embezzlement schemes in this guide, only one involved people who had access to the "real thing." In fact, as most organizations have better control over cash and the people who handle it than any other part of their accounting system, there is a greater chance of embezzling funds if you do not have access to cash in your job assignment.

Truth: Collusion Is Beautiful

Corporations act as if there were some unwritten law of business that holds them responsible for embezzlement losses incurred by single individuals, but leaves them blameless if such losses are due to collusion. This is, of course, a ridiculous but nevertheless advantageous belief for the embezzler. Furthermore, if you are willing to take the added risk, collusion can mean a many-fold increase in the take.

A good place where collusion works well is in banks. Employees in positions to make noncash, uncleared deposits appear as if they had been cash can and do bilk banks of thousands of dollars a year. With help, those thousands can become millions. There is nothing that a wise controller fears more than collusion between key individuals, and with good reason. For example:

> Five men, including a vice president of one big New York bank and a branch manager of another, stole $900,000 by running a float fraud between the two banks for four years. Deposit records were altered in the banks' data-processing centers so as to appear as cash deposits; the men would then withdraw cash. The fraud was detected only after a bank messenger failed to deliver some checks for a fraudulent "cash" deposit, and they overdrew one of their accounts by $440,000. Otherwise the scheme could have continued indefinitely.

Fiction: Small and Poorly Managed Companies Are the Best

It is true that small companies are not able to maintain the same degree of internal control and separation of job responsibility and job assignments that a larger one can handle. It is also true that the internal controls and financial-system designs of poorly managed companies are more easily exploited than are those of well-managed ones. However, it is certainly a misconception that computer frauds have taken place only in small, poorly managed organizations. Some of the largest losses have occurred in the large companies. Furthermore, big companies are less apt to become suspicious of large losses than smaller companies are.

Truth: Look for Special Circumstances

One good rule of thumb is to always be on the watch for special circumstances that create opportunities for fraud, such as when a company converts from manual processing to a computer system or switches from one system to another. At these times unusual activities are less noticeable, and improper transactions and manipulations can be covered up. Exactly what you do is dependent upon what changes are being made and what position you occupy at the time.

Fiction: The Old Schemes Will Not Work Any More

Many age-old embezzlement schemes work just as well today as they did before computers were commonplace; many are even more successful because the computer makes transaction processing more predictable and reliable. Theft from dormant bank accounts is a good example. Long before computer systems were installed, bank embezzlers transferred money from accounts that showed very little activity to their own or to that of an accomplice. Today, the task is easier because more persons have access to the subsidiary ledger files, via the computer, and money can be transferred through a number of accounts at a faster rate. This makes the embezzler's actions harder to trace. For example:

> A computer systems vice president and a senior computer operator of a New Jersey bank, along with three nonemployees, stole $128,000 from little-used savings accounts by transferring the funds to newly opened accounts. The actions were uncovered when the bank switched to a new computer, disallowing the culprits a chance to erase their withdrawals as had been planned.

Truth: Some Schemes Are Never Detected

By definition, the only schemes known of are the detected ones. Considering the fact that a great many schemes are uncovered by chance, there must be a large pool of undetected embezzlement operations. For example:

> A large bank in New York recently suffered a severe setback in trading in foreign currencies. That loss, together with certain other conditions within the bank, led to the suspension of dividends, a large run on the deposits of the bank, and eventual collapse. In the course of a full and complete examination of the bank, investigators discovered a large embezzlement scheme, unrelated to the losses on securities trading, that had escaped detection by the bank auditors and examiners. In the absence of the securities trading losses, this embezzlement scheme could have run for a long period of time.

This and other accidental discoveries of embezzlement schemes lead one to believe that there is a great deal of embezzlement that goes undetected. In fact, *all* successful embezzlement is undetected.

A final word of encouragement: In just the few examples mentioned in this article, embezzlers stole over $15 million with the computer's help. They were caught—but you can be smarter!

READING 21 DISCUSSION QUESTIONS

1 As the controller of a company that is about to install its first computer, what steps would you take to prevent some of the problems discussed in Brandt Allen's article?
2 Many writers look to future solutions to the computer security problem as evolving from *people-oriented* controls, whereas others see *system-oriented* controls as the answer. Describe some of the arguments in favor of each of these directions.

Reading 22

Data Security

Marvin M. Wofsey

The computer is the Achilles heel of modern business. In many cases the firm has lost the ability to revert to manual or electric accounting machine operations. As time passes, more and more applications are put on the computer. People who knew how to do the work before it was taken over by the computer leave for other positions, retire or die.

Had the telephone dial not been invented, all of the women in the United States would be needed as telephone operators in order to handle today's volume of calls. If today's on-line airplane reservation systems or insurance companies' records were not on the computer, the number of people who would be needed would be very large. The move to computers cannot be reversed.

Each month brings reports of computers destroyed by bomb, fire or other means. There are ready headlines such as: COMPUTER FACILITY BOMBED—ONE KILLED, or STUDENTS BURN COMPUTERS—DESTROY TAPES. Such occurrences can force the company out of business. The aftermath usually fails to make news. Companies have failed due to damage to their computer programs and tape or disk files. Others have suffered losses so severe that it took years to recover. But these stories rarely make the headlines.

Management has paid little attention to this problem. Ignoring it, however, will not cause it to go away. There is a well-known saying that lightning only strikes once in the same place. After it strikes there is nothing left to strike again. A catastrophe in the computer room can be just as devastating. Without

Reprinted from *Data Management,* September 1972, pp. 80–86. Reprinted by permission from the Data Processing Management Association, 505 Busse Highway, Park Ridge, Ill. Professor Wofsey is on the faculty of George Washington University.

adequate countermeasures there may be no company left to suffer another catastrophe. Managers can no longer ignore the risk involved in using computers. It is too vital. The hazards in using computers should be analyzed and treated as any other business risk.

Various risks are associated with the use of computers. Both preventive and ameliorative measures are suggested with a rational method for deciding which measures to adopt.

CATASTROPHES

Fire Back in 1959 a fire in the Pentagon destroyed a large computer installation. The fire started in a light fixture, but spread quickly through the area. Flames, heat and smoke destroyed computers valued in the millions. This, however, was only the visible part of the iceberg. Losses in programs and data far exceeded the cost of replacing the computers. It took years for the Air Force to recover from this fire. Few businesses would have been able to resume operations after such damage. Shortly after the Pentagon fire another computer a half mile away caught fire. A guard ruined the computer by using a fire hose, instead of carbon dioxide. There have been so many fires in data processing installations since 1959 that they no longer are worthy of headlines. They appear as small items in the middle of the paper and/or in bankruptcy, dissolution or merger.

Explosion Although not as common as fire, explosions are another hazard to data processing. Gas, chemicals, or explosive materials have resulted in accidental damage to buildings. A computer in the building is at least as vulnerable as the building and its other contents.

Natural Disasters Floods, hurricanes, cyclones, tidal waves and earthquakes have caused much destruction in computer installations. Hurricane Celia in 1970, for example, tore power lines, flooded computer centers with salt water, and wrecked buildings housing computer installations. In 1971 an earthquake in California disrupted power and ravaged computer centers.

Sabotage Deliberate sabotage of computer installations may be categorized into two areas: protests based on social considerations and revenge. Examples of the former are: peace demonstrations and those for civil rights, the fighting of poverty, and those attempting to safeguard the ecology. These outbreaks may not be a passing idea of college boys or radicals. Instead they may represent a basic shift in values established by society. These carefully planned attacks on the focal points of operations of business, government, and educational institutions can be expected to increase, rather than decrease. Disgruntled employees and customers recognize that the greatest damage can be wrought in the computer system with the least effort and least danger of apprehension. A humanities course offered at Syracuse University was reported to be a workshop on the nonviolent sabotage of computer installations.

Social Protests The right to personal property—to use it in any way you desire—is no longer sacrosanct. Bombs in universities in Wisconsin, California and Kansas attest to this. Welfare recipients occupied the Welfare Department's computer center to protest the withholding of their checks. Students in Massachusetts took over the college data processing center. They did no overt damage, but held the installation as ransom to force the college administration to accept a number of demands. This installation was particularly vulnerable, since there were no backup files. Furthermore, no data could be processed until the students released the center.

Many companies bill customers on pre-punched cards, which are to be returned with the payment. Most of these systems anticipate only a small number of exceptions. It doesn't take very many customers spindling, folding, or stepping on the return card with spiked golf shoes to swamp those handling exceptions. A concerted effort by customers protesting a company policy could completely disrupt the system.

Environmental Problems Only in a minority of cases is the computer installation a part of the original plans of a building. More often the computer installation is built within an occupied building. Compromises with the existing structure are necessary. It is fairly common to see water pipes or steam pipes running through such installations. Leakage or bursting of these pipes could cause great damage. Quite often newspapers report damage to a seemingly impervious installation. In at least two occurrences completely fireproof computer installations were damaged severely by fires on contiguous floors. Once water to put out the fire on the floor above the installation deluged the computer. Another time a fire on the floor below resulted in the computer falling into the basement. Elsewhere a computer was installed above a bank vault. Yeggs dynamited the vault, seriously damaging the computer above it.

Power Difficulties Most managers recognize the possibility of power failure. Since such disruptions normally are of short duration and comparatively rare, they usually are treated as calculated risks. When such failure lasts for hours or even days, the ramifications can be great. Many computers in England were "off the air" for long periods of time in 1970 because of power stoppage.

More insidious than power failure is damage from power brownouts or temporary surges or drops in power. Many computers can tolerate power variances of plus or minus 10 per cent. The brownouts of 1970 were reported to be decreases of 5 per cent to 8 per cent. It does not take much of a temporary drop at these times to exceed the 10 per cent tolerance. Furthermore, it is possible that in coming years it may be necessary to reduce power more than 10 per cent in order to prevent a complete blackout. Surges or drops in urban electrical power are fairly common and expected at particular times of the day.

A sudden storm or change in temperature or cloud coverage can result in such surges or drops.

The damage to the computer from such variations in power can be recognized and corrected. Damage to programs, files, and reports may not be discovered until much later, if ever. Power variations have resulted in the updating of wrong records in a vendor master file. In another case data when read from disk were written erroneously in core. Errors also were found in writing on disk from core. Drops in power have caused disk drives to go out of operating status, aborting the run, and necessitating a rerun.

Loss of Programs and/or Data Earlier reference was made to loss of programs or data due to fire. Not as well publicized, but more often occurring, are such losses because of misoperation or environmental difficulties.

An installation experienced data damage on tapes, which at first could not be explained. It was noticed that this damage was only on tapes stored on the bottom shelves of the tape vault. Eventually the trouble was traced to a floor buffer, which set up a magnetic field and distorted the patterns of magnetically stored bits on the tape. Similarly, tapes containing data and programs were damaged by magnetic fields from a hand vacuum cleaner. Operator errors have resulted in writing data on tapes over the only copies of master files or programs. Also, data stored on disks have been lost. At best, if others are available, such loss results in the use of extra machine time. If backup copies of data dumps are not kept, reconstruction costs and time used can be considerable, if not impossible.

If you are using a time-sharing company for running programs, there is another possible loss of data or programs that is often not recognized. If the time-sharing company were to go bankrupt, as so often has occurred, how do you get your property back? You might have a difficult time convincing an officer of the court that, although the tape or disk belongs to the time-sharing company, the data belong to you.

External Radiation Even tapes stored normally within computer installations are not safe from external radiation unless special precautions are taken. A newspaper report indicated that several, perhaps hundred, of Internal Revenue Service tapes were erased by airport radar. In another case the computer was installed in the basement of a building. An electrical motor outside the computer installation created a magnetic field, wiping out tapes shelved on the adjacent wall inside the tape storage area. Many tapes have been wiped out while being shipped from one installation to another. En route the box may have been within a magnetic field. When the tapes arrived the data were hopelessly damaged.

Mechanical or Electronic Breakdown Outright failure or intermittent misfunction of computer equipment is another hazard. The former usually results in a small amount of time lost, necessitating reruns. If, however, a replacement part is not available locally, the installation may be down for days.

Intermittent failures, however, are more dangerous, because one may not realize they have occurred. Wrong accounts may have been updated. Files may contain erroneous data. If the malfunction is not located quickly and the tapes with errors corrected, the backup tapes may be released for other purposes. In this event recovery may be difficult and costly, if not impossible.

In a large computer installation an operator got a read error signal on a disk drive. The problem really was a faulty read head, which in fact was ruining the data on the disk. Thinking the problem was with the disk he removed it, and substituted the backup disk. By the time the real problem was discovered recovery was time-consuming and expensive. It involved punching cards from the last printing of the files and then doing all subsequent runs. This could have been catastrophic if the complete file had been printed.

Operator Error As long ago as the early forties, when Mark I and II were running at Harvard University, operators have been mounting wrong tapes. To this day they use tape rings improperly, forget to set switches, or damage cards. These are only a few of the many ways that operator errors occur. The results range from loss of time for reruns to loss of good will because of wrong billing of customers. In some cases recovery is made within the hour. Other times it takes weeks of costly effort.

Data Theft Newspapers are continually reporting individual thefts of data from computer installations. According to such reports an encyclopedia publisher allegedly found that former employees were selling their mailing list even to the company's competitors. An airline "lost" information worth $5,000,000. Policemen in New York were convicted of using computer output files maintained manually to sell information to detective agencies and airlines. In Sweden employees in a service bureau "borrowed" tapes with population registry information. Among buyers of the data were a private statistics office and a political party. When the tapes were missing prior to a special run this theft was discovered.

On-line, time-sharing installations are particularly vulnerable to data and/or program theft. FBI agents arrested an eighteen-year-old youth for using leased telephone lines to steal data. According to the agents the youth was close to bypassing completely the file security programs. About a month later another man was charged with grand theft—the stealing of proprietary programs from the computer of a time-sharing company. It was reputed to be the first theft by plucking the brains of a computer.

One of the top computer software experts in the world recently said that any enterprising person can get through the software security of any time-sharing system. Furthermore, it is comparatively easy to copy any data sent over wires. Computers have been wiretapped with portable recorders. An unshielded line may be tapped without others knowing that it has occurred. It is possible to record from outside the building input and output without those within the installation being aware it is being done.

Other Thefts Computer time and equipment are also prime targets for thieves. In Chicago five employees were accused of using their employer's equipment during slow hours to set up their own data processing firm. In the encyclopedia company mentioned previously the employees were said to have used the company's equipment to copy the tapes. A governmental employee used time on the night shift to run jobs for his own clients. He did this for some time before he was discovered and discharged. He then set up his own service bureau to continue servicing his clients from the spurious operation. Since he now had to pay for machine rental, he had to raise prices considerably. At costs ranging into the hundreds of dollars per hour, computer installations may be paying a great deal of extra rental and other costs for such illicit use. These are only a few examples where the culprits were caught. How many others have not been detected?

In many instances programmers have learned company secrets or the details of sophisticated programs. Competitors have enticed such programmers to transfer to their employ. The programmers have too frequently made the secrets and/or program details known to their new employers.

Computerized larceny has one great advantage over other forms of larceny. It is seldom discovered. When it is discovered, it is hard to prosecute. There has always been a good market for stolen cards, tapes, or disks. With the miniaturization of computers the theft of the computers themselves can be expected.

Fraud A bank was victimized by a systems analyst who was alleged to have funneled deposits of various customers into his account. A city employee was charged with selling raises in pay to other employees. These raises were effected by changes made during night computer runs. Stolen credit cards cost New York banks about $500,000. In this case, however, computer analyses uncovered the credit ring. In Los Angeles a swindle netted about $50,000 in false welfare payments. A stockbroker was reported to have been bankrupted by fraudulent manipulations of its computerized accounts.

An accounts clerk in Britain was convicted of using the computer to defraud a small grocery store owner of almost $120,000. He fed in a bogus account number of a store owned by a friend. Periodically he would actuate payments to that number, even though no goods were delivered. It was only by accident that another clerk noticed an unfamiliar code and started an inquiry.

Law Suits Newspapers are replete with reports of cars repossessed because of "computer error" or credit reputations damaged for the same reason. Increasingly the damaged party seeks recourse through suit. A retail store owner admitted he blamed errors on the computer, even though he didn't have a computer. With the bad press they are getting, computers and computer systems do not rank very high in the average man's opinion. Juries increasingly rule against the computer user in such suits. In these cases the verdict should depend upon whether or not all prudent precautions were taken to ensure against such errors. This loss of repute should recall to managers the saying about Caesar's wife having to be above reproach.

In New Orleans a company was in dispute with the computer manufacturer in renegotiating an expired contract. It withheld rent and maintenance payments. The manufacturer sued, and the judge granted a "Writ of Sequestration," ordering the Federal Marshal to seize the computer.

Suits by computer users against vendors of hardware and/or software are increasing. In addition, thousands of users have settled out of court or absorbed the loss without recourse. In 1971 at least three major suits had not yet been settled in court. A verdict in favor of the plaintiff could result in a large increase in such suits. Win or lose, such suits are expensive, especially where the lawyer is not thoroughly grounded in computer technology and its related jargon.

At first glance these suits may appear to be a potential benefit, not a hazard of data processing installations. The vendor ultimately must pass these costs down to the consumer in the form of increased prices. Furthermore, at best, the user can only hope to break even. Often the lawyer will be the only one with a profit. If the suit is lost the user will have to absorb the additional legal fees and possibly court costs.

Looking at this from the other standpoint, many computer installations sell or rent hardware time, software and/or operating services. In these cases they are vendors, just as much as the hardware and software vendors mentioned previously. As such, they easily could be defendants in similar suits.

Company officers can be sued by stockholders for poor management. The many examples of poor management of computer installations and recent surveys attest to this. Such derivative suits for mismanagement can readily exceed the total assets of the managers involved. The law is developing rapidly to reflect social changes. The citizen's right to call officials to account is being extended. It appears to be logical to extend this trend to computer managers, even in private companies.

PREVENTIVE MEASURES

Few, if any, data processing installations have the funds and need to take all of the following precautions. They are discussed to furnish reference points for deciding which measures to employ. These possibilities are segregated into five categories: location, site construction, operating procedures, data protection, and legal protection.

Location If location of building choice is possible, one should consider possible catastrophes. If the area is subject to hurricanes and/or floods, don't build on the waterfront. Select a higher and protected location instead. Don't build over a fault. There might not be an earthquake, but if there is one, damage normally is much greater over a fault. Select or erect a strong, fireproof building in a safe location. It would, for example, be rash to have such a building at the end of a busy airport runway or next to an explosives plant. Similarly, sharing a building with a firm housing volatile materials would increase the danger of a catastrophic fire. Location within the building should also be considered. The safest location is as close to the center of the building as possible, and on the lower floors. In a multibasement building it might be on the first floor below street level. This would provide the best protection from sabotage and radar. Of course, if it were necessary to put the computer in a building close to the waterfront subject to floods, a second or third floor location may be preferable. The lower in the building the computer is, the less will be the danger of earthquake damage. Aside from these precautions, one should select a location away from the regular stream of pedestrians, out of sight, and not contiguous to danger. For example, the computer center should not be next to Selective Service or munitions manufacturers' offices, since these often are the objects of protests. In such protests the innocent bystander often gets injured.

Site Construction Fireproof computer sites constructed in fireproof buildings provide the best protection against fire. To prevent damage from leaks no wet pipes should be in the computer installation. Carbon dioxide fire extinguishers are dangerous to people. Sprinkler systems can damage the computer severely. Halon 1301 is a less destructive fire extinguisher but costs more than carbon dioxide or water.

Most sprinkler systems have wet pipes, which have the ever-present danger of leak. There is, however, a dry pipe sprinkler system. If the temperature below the sprinkler rises to 140° a solenoid allows water to flow into the pipe. If the temperature below the sprinkler approaches 212° water is released. When the temperature drops below 140° the sprinkler turns off.

Faraday Cages or RF shielding provide the best protection against emanations from external sources. These precautions, however, are costly. Grounding will help dispel the energies of such emanations.

A voltage regulator with a flywheel should keep power fluctuations within the plus or minus 10 percent range. In case of power stoppage it will enable a "slow stop," thus preserving data. Temperature and humidity controls will prevent many computer malfunctions.

Carpeting on the floor normally should be avoided. Carpets cause static electricity to build up when the humidity is low. When the IBM 360-30's first came out a chemical manufacturer had a great deal of trouble with programs failing because of static electricity generated from plastic-covered chairs and from carts being pushed near the computer.

Locked, maximum-security doors provide the best protection against undesired intrusion. A plain lock, which can be opened easily from inside the installation, is preferable. Under normal conditions locks opened by specially treated cards work very well. If for any reason, such as fire, the electricity is cut off, these locks do not work. Unless optional means also are available people cannot get in or out of the installation. In an Air Force base with a tube computer a card identification lock was used. A power failure shut down the computer and the air conditioning system. Personnel could not get out for hours. Had the power been cut by fire a tragedy might have resulted.

In the 1970 California earthquake the door to the computer room could only be opened by the guard outside. He fled, leaving the computer operator imprisoned in the computer room.

To protect against both unwarranted intrusion and the carrying of metals to the computer room, a double door system with a scanning zone between might be used. The first door, opened by a key, must be closed and locked before the person entering is able to pass between the electronic metal scanner. He then can open the inside door if he passes inspection. If not, he must telephone for assistance.

For protection against theft, unauthorized use of the computer, and sabotage during off-hours, closed circuit TV provides comparatively inexpensive protection. A continuous picture of the computer installation can be relayed to the guard's station. If the danger is great enough an ultrasonic detector system, with alarm to both the guard and to a central point, will supply added protection.

Operating Procedures The first defense is a perimeter defense. There should, if possible, be only one entrance used into the building, with a guard stationed there at all times. All windows and doors should have alarm devices. Any attempt to get into the building by other than the main door should trigger an alarm to the guard and to a central point. The guard should inspect all packages to ensure against explosives or firearms being carried into the building.

Access to the computer facility should be limited to those whose presence is needed. The day of the computer as a show piece is gone. Visitors should be limited and always accompanied by a supervisor. In addition to the security equipment detailed under Site Construction, employees can wear color-coded badges. One color would enable the wearer to go into all parts of the data processing department, except the computer room. Another color would provide entry to the computer room. Despite card colors, moreover, face recognition or introduction by the supervisor of a new employee, helps control unwanted visitors. Also, a log should be kept of all visitors. Any visitor permitted to take anything from the computer room or tape vault should be required to sign a receipt.

The tape room should be locked and under the control of a tape librarian. A tape log should be maintained with a complete record of tape withdrawals, returns, times, purposes, and person involved. Access to this room should be severely limited. No one, and that includes cleaning personnel, should be allowed in the tape room without the express permission of the supervisor. If, for any purpose, someone other than the tape librarian is permitted entry, be sure he carries no magnetized material. He should be watched closely at all times during his stay in the tape room. Tapes are comparatively small and easily damaged. At a minimum all tapes should have identification data, date of creation, and a disposal date. Backup tapes for necessary programs and data should be maintained in a safe room, preferably in another building. As programs are changed or files updated the current program or file should be substituted for the outdated one. This is a comparatively inexpensive means of ensuring safety of programs and data.

Regardless of how good a security system is, undependable employees can negate it. Computer room employees should be checked carefully before employment. Furthermore, a buddy system should be used. There must never be only one person in the computer room.

Good internal control procedures are a key protection. Examples of such procedures follow. The run of a key program by an unauthorized employee might result in loss or embarrassment to the company. A changeable key word required before the program can be run will help make sure that there are no unauthorized runs. All error messages should be clear, and no computer run should be considered completed, unless there is a specific End of Job message.

A separate console in a locked room is a good means of monitoring all changes and instructions entering the computer, all uses, and all outgoing messages. If this is not possible, two-part console paper, with the carbon going directly into a locked container, provides some protection, though not as much.

Operating procedures, no matter how carefully devised, quickly become ineffective without good supervision. Good procedures should be established and employees should be trained to follow them. Even this is not enough. Continual inspections and audits should be carried out to ensure that these procedures are followed faithfully. People have a tendency to bypass safety devices or procedures they consider to be unnecessarily restrictive. It is only by following the above suggestions that a safe, well-run computer installation will result.

Data Protection If it doesn't matter who sees anything that comes out of a computer installation, the following suggestions need not be followed. The degree of protection depends upon the amount of secrecy needed. Overprotection of computer records can be a very costly matter. The computer manager normally cannot make the determination. His job is to give the risks, the possibilities of the data being stolen, his estimate of the possible consequences, and the costs of the protection. He should give these with his recommendations to management, which makes the final decision concerning the precautions to be taken.

Unless proper precautions are taken almost all input to or output from a computer can be read from outside the computer room without the knowledge or consent of those inside. Also, data transmitted over wire or by radio can be tapped. For complete safety the computer room should be enclosed with lead, and all outlets grounded. These are very expensive measures, and are not used in any but the most secret installations. Without them sensitive jobs should not be run on a fixed schedule. Running them mornings with a lot of outside noise will deter stealing of data.

Input/output gear should be located as close to the center of the computer room as possible. This will make reading them from outside more difficult. Either have no telephone in the computer room or unplug it when a sensitive job is run. Remove all unused wiring from the computer room. Pipes, heating ducts, etc., should be grounded as close to the computer room as possible.

Ability to read disks, tapes, platens, and core after sensitive jobs are run is possible. In order to prevent such readings after programs are run, at least three streams of random characters should be written over these devices. Waste material, such as carbon paper and typewriter ribbons, should be destroyed. Procedures should be designed to prevent anyone gaining access to this waste prior to disposal.

Growth in the use of telecommunications, on-line systems, time-sharing, and companies using remote terminals for access to the computer has raised an entire new crop of security problems. That anything going over a wire can be read is a good assumption. To preclude such reading, encrypting all messages and decoding them at the receipt point will help. However, any code can be broken. Multiconductor cable with more than one circuit used at the same time will make reading more difficult. A rather expensive means normally restricted to short-distance transmission is the use of dry air jackets around cables. Sensors note any penetration of the cable and trigger an alarm.

The ability of the computer to distinguish between different users of remote terminals and to limit their access to files accordingly is of paramount importance in today's on-line and time-sharing systems. Finger print and voice print recognition devices are not yet practicable. A feasible, sophisticated device is one which measures the hand and fingers of the user. This device is almost 100 per cent accurate, but is fairly costly.

Most systems depend upon key words, special numbers, and person-terminal coordination for recognition. These methods require programs and the ability to make unreadable the typewritten record of the key word or special number by an unauthorized person. Furthermore, these key words or numbers can be changed as often as necessary. The computer can contain a table listing the files the user is permitted to use. This will help protect the files of other users. Key words or numbers should never be given over the telephone; they are too vulnerable to outside reading.

As mentioned previously, no software system is 100 per cent safe. Assuming that all the methods discussed have been employed, a log of all users, their queries, and the files accessed should be kept where the user cannot control what goes into the log, nor read nor change what is in there. Regular and continual audit of this file should reveal any attempted accession of sensitive files before the accessor has accomplished his purpose.

Legal Protection With the growth of suits by users against manufacturers, software houses, and service bureaus, the computer manager must pay attention to this possibility. In dealing with a computer manufacturer thousands, perhaps millions, of dollars are at stake. Even though it is a "standard contract," get a lawyer who is experienced with computer contracts. Many of the caveats of these one-sided standard contracts may not be enforceable in court.

Don't believe the promises of a computer salesman. To bind the company the written word of an officer of the company may be necessary. If the manufacturer decides not to keep the promise of a salesman, all the potential buyer has is the promise of a former employee of the vendor. Don't depend upon memory. After every meeting prepare a memorandum for the file, with copies to the individuals involved. Include advertisements and brochures in this file. Such a file might be extremely helpful in case of a suit years later.

If you are in a software house or service bureau be careful of promises and assurances to customers. The honeymoon, where all errors or nonperformances were excused, is over. Failure to produce what is promised, when it is promised, and with the quality promised can result in a large suit. Even if you win the suit, the cost of defending it can be extremely high.

For internal operating purposes, when a person is hired or when a program is loaned or released for rental, insist upon a nondisclosure statement at the outset. Use an experienced lawyer in deciding how to protect software. Copyright, patent, and trade secret, or a combination thereof, are possible. Use a lawyer in determining whether to capitalize or treat as current operating expenses the considerable cost of software development. In order to protect yourself against derivative suits by stockholders, files should be kept. These files should give details and cost out possible alternatives that were considered in making decisions. Escape routes in case things go wrong also should be included. With such documentation, charges are reduced to how good the decision was, not (to the fact) that alternatives were not considered.

AMELIORATIVE MEASURES

Many of the preventive measures discussed previously also act as ameliorative measures, if the event they were designed to prevent occurs. For example, a fire protection system should lessen the effects of the fire, if one occurs. The measures treated in the previous section will not be repeated here. Instead, this section will be limited to additional measures and expansions of preventive steps.

The computers of a multicomputer company can be decentralized. If anything should put a computer installation out of operation, the complete data processing capability of the company will not be wiped out. Another possibility would be to have an unused but duplicate installation in a remote location. Few companies, however, could afford or should afford this expense.

Almost as much protection, but with far less cost, is the use of a backup facility. The agreement with the furnisher of the backup capability should be in writing. Knowledge that the same model of the computer is used is not enough. Extra or missing capabilities or different versions of operating systems may cause programs to fail when run on the backup computer. Periodically declare an emergency and run some jobs at the backup facility. You may find that despite the agreement and the complete compatibility of hardware and software, the backup computer is used 100 per cent of the time. There is no time to run your work. It will not cost very much to declare such emergencies. The knowledge that your backup plan works or adequate time to implement a new backup plan is worth a great deal more than the cost involved. In order for the backup plan to work, of course, an adequate supply of current programs and files should be maintained in a location other than your computer installation.

Although installation of fire- or heatproof safes will not prevent fire, they will lessen damage if a fire occurs. Safes will protect only to a limited degree. If the fire is not too bad, damage will be limited. Procedures should be established concerning actions employees are to take in case of an emergency. Periodic drills will make automatic following these procedures.

If you are using a time-sharing system send one of your tapes to the central location. Have your files dumped on your tape, ensuring that it is clearly marked as your property. If the time-sharing company goes bankrupt you will be able to recover both your tape and your data.

Business insurance is another ameliorative measure. Employees should be bonded if they are in a position to seize any assets of the company fraudulently. Fire insurance should be taken out, not only for hardware and the premises, but also for software and the additional expenses involved in continuing operations in a backup site until the computer facility is restored. Insurance covering errors or omissions is available also. For almost any of the risks detailed previously some form of insurance can be bought.

COUNTERMEASURES

A computer installation probably should not take every precaution discussed. Over-protection can be very expensive. Furthermore, the ultimate decision rests with top management, not with the computer manager.

What can the computer manager do? What should he do? He must recognize the potential dangers. After recognizing these dangers he should prepare a cost/value analysis. At least the following elements should be considered: hazard, degree of damage, probability of occurrence, consequences, possible dollar damages, measures recommended, cost comparison of probable damages and costs of measures recommended, alternative measures considered, and costs of alternative measures considered. Figure 1 is a structured format for making such analyses. A data processing manager completing this analysis will have quantified the major elements of hazards and countermeasures considered. He now is ready to make specific recommendations to top management.

Situation The company in Figure 1 is completely wedded to computers as a means of operation. All records are maintained on magnetic tape and disk. For audit purposes the backup documents are held in central files, which is adjacent to data processing. Input documents are punched or entered by a key to tape process. The cards are maintained in data processing until the annual audit. Upon release by auditing the cards are destroyed. Backup documents are kept in central files for three years before disposal.

The tapes and disks are kept in an unlocked, non-fireproof room in data

Figure 1 Cost/Value Analysis

Hazard	Cost of loss	Probability of occurrence	Preventive action	Annual cost of loss, col. 2 × col. 3	Annual cost of preventive action	Net savings col. 5 − col. 6
Catastrophic fire	$5,000,000	0.01%		$500		
Minor fire or malicious damage to tapes	200,000	0.1%		200		
Subtotal			Remote backup tapes	$700	$200	$500
Accidental damage:						
One tape	20	100 times a year		2,000		
Both tapes	1,000	5%		50		
Theft and fraud	500,000	1%		5,000		
Subtotal			Add tape librarian Install security procedures	7,050	6,000 2,000	1,050
Accidental damage to disk	1,000	5 times a year	Add tape librarian Copy disks on tape	5,000	Cost of tape librarian covered above	3,000
Total				2,750	$8,200	$4,350

Construction of a fireproof tape vault also was considered. This would have cost $20,000. Since it could take 100 years of probable loss to amortize the cost, this construction is not recommended.

processing. All backup tapes are held in the same room. There is no backup to data kept on disks. When these disks are removed they are kept in the tape room. There is no tape and disk librarian. When tapes and/or disks are needed for a computer run, the operator gets the appropriate tapes, disks, programs, and working tapes from the tape room. After the computer run the tapes and disks are filed in the tape room.

Problems If there were a serious fire which included data processing and central files, there would be no way of reconstructing accounts receivable, accounts payable, or other computer records.

- A minor fire in the tape room, sabotage by a disgruntled employee, or similar occurrences can wipe out the original and backup tapes and disks and all programs.
- Employees can take the wrong tapes or disks. In some cases they might write on these tapes and/or disks, destroying what was stored on them.
- The tapes are not protected from theft or fraudulent changes. For example, programs could be manipulated to indicate payments by customers when such payments never were made. A list of customers could be sold to competitors. These are only two of the possible fraudulent opportunities.

Consequences The company probably could not continue as a viable enterprise.

- It would be necessary to keypunch backup documents and programs. Remedial computer runs would be needed. It would be at least two months before data processing could operate effectively again.
- If both the original and the backup tapes were destroyed, repunching and remedial runs would be needed. If only the original tape were destroyed, a short computer run would correct the situation. If a disk were involved, keypunching and remedial computer runs would be necessary.
- A list of company customers and details of their purchases could be sold to competitors. The company could be cheated out of amounts due. Employees could be overpaid fraudulently. Thefts of merchandise could be covered up. These are only a few examples of the many opportunities for fraud.

There are many potential hazards to a computer installation. For each hazard there is a countermeasure, preventive, ameliorative, or both. It is extremely risky to fail to take appropriate countermeasures. The cost of taking all countermeasures is very high. The major problem is that of determining what measures are appropriate. The data processing manager's prime responsibility is to recognize all of the hazards that exist. Using a cost/value analysis he should make recommendations to top management concerning which measures are appropriate for that particular installation. Top management then has the tools with which to make the best decision for the company.

READING 22 DISCUSSION QUESTIONS

1 "There are many potential hazards to a computer installation. For each hazard there is a countermeasure, preventive, ameliorative, or both." Discuss five hazards and the appropriate countermeasures.
2 How may cost/value analyses of computer hazards be useful in determining preventive action?

Reading 23

Controlling the Costs of Data Services

Richard L. Nolan

Without exception, the companies that I have studied for the past four years have found it difficult to make their transfer-pricing, or "chargeout," systems for data processing services understandable to the managers who use them.

The root of this problem is not the inherent technical complexity of computer technology—it is a historical error made in the management of data processing. To date, we have designed our DP management systems around the *computer* instead of the *data*. Consequently, the chargeout systems have been designed to hold the manager who uses the data accountable for computer-related resources such as processing time, main memory time and space, and input/output accesses.

However, the user works with output units, such as invoices processed, inventory reports, and production schedules. Thus the user is forced to somehow translate input and processing charges into the information for which he or she receives value. Only then can he take appropriate control and be held accountable. In a sense, what is being asked of the user is analogous to asking a car buyer to make a decision on several automobiles by being given a bill of materials on the different types of cars. The car buyer makes the decision on information such as performance of a V-8 versus the economy of a six-cylinder engine; the convenience of an automatic versus manual transmission; economy, safety, and wear of radial versus belted tires, not on kilos of steel, cast iron, and rubber.

Take, for example, this all too common vignette. On July 1, the vice president of marketing had just received his third monthly bill for his department's use of the order entry system. The bill he received is shown in Figure 1.

Although he did not understand the detail of the bill (for example, he had no idea what CPU, kilobytes, and EXCP stand for), he felt that it was way too

Reprinted from the *Harvard Business Review,* July–August 1977. Copyright © 1977 by the president and fellows of Harvard College; all rights reserved. Mr. Nolan is Chairman of D. P. Management Corporation, Lexington, Ky.

Figure 1 Data processing services bill

Resource	Use	Charge per unit	Total
Elapsed time on computer (minutes)	243,000	$0.04	$ 9,720
CPU (seconds)	2,430,000	0.0167	40,500
Kilobytes (1K memory/minute)	14,515,000	0.0016	23,220
EXCP (I/O accesses)	105,000,000	0.0002	21,000
Total due			$94,440

much. In fact, the charge represented a good 25% of his budget. He also knew from the president's recent memorandum that he was now accountable for these expenses. So he picked up the telephone and made an appointment to talk with his newly appointed "data processing coordinator."

Management's experience with data processing had followed the pattern of many other companies. After starting out in the early 1960s by automating payroll, the company had experienced extremely rapid growth in its DP budget as applications were developed for almost all parts of the business. The order entry system was one of the early applications.

It was close to a disaster when the revised estimate of development costs skyrocketed from $100,000 to $275,000 with less than half of the originally promised capability. Nevertheless, the marketing department stuck with it, and the costs were treated as corporate overhead. The bugs were shaken out by 1967, and the system was gradually expanded to the point where the vice president of marketing said that the company couldn't carry on business without it.

A year ago, management had become concerned with ever-rising DP expenses and seemingly declining performance, as maintenance problems with existing applications seemed to have got out of hand. Therefore, the company centralized data processing under a new vice president of information services, and there was a general consensus that users should be held accountable for the services they were using. With the support of the president, the vice president of information services had his staff design a system for charging out all costs on the basis of resources used to support the various applications. He also established data-processing coordinators for each major user group.

It was in this context that the vice president of marketing opened the meeting with his data processing coordinator:

"Although I really don't understand this bill, it has to be too high. Order entry cost us less than $30,000 per month before the computer system was installed. Not only is the $94,400 too high, even taking inflation into account, but the cost has varied from $78,000 to $104,000 in the three short months that the chargeout system has been in effect. How is a manager supposed to plan in such a volatile environment?"

"You are absolutely right about the variance," the coordinator responded. "It is due partly to the volume of orders processed and due partly to the upgrade in the computer operating system software last month. We have also incurred technical difficulty in measuring kilobyte minutes in an MVS operating system environment. You see we have a 'meg' of main memory, but with virtual memory software we have a lot more. Our problem in charging equitably is one of . . ."

The vice president didn't understand this explanation and felt that he was getting the same waffle treatment that he had come to expect from data processing. Somewhat irritated, he said he didn't give a damn about the technical problems but wanted the bill to be reduced by 25%.

The coordinator reminded him that the information services division was only a service department and that it was the vice president's responsibility to provide the guidance for making such cuts. He then asked him what component of the bill he would like to attack: CPU seconds, elapsed time, kilobytes, or EXCPs?

At this point, the vice president of marketing became very angry. Shoving the coordinator out of the door with instructions not to come back, he got the president on the telephone: "I'm strapped. Data processing is charging me for services that are essential, and I can't do anything about the cost. When I try to get down to how to control the costs, all I get is technical gibberish . . ."

DESIGN FOR CHARGEOUTS

Data services have become much too important to companies to be left to technicians. Management must devote the time necessary to understand data processing's current and future impact on the business so that it can provide the guidance that both data processing and users need.

In a sense, the chargeout systems that I have studied have been attempts to provide this guidance. Unfortunately, many of them were built on shaky DP accounting systems and implemented without a clear understanding of what was expected from the user.

As a result, both DP management and users became frustrated. The extent and intensity of the frustration are reflected in the vignette. The vice president of marketing was confused about what actions he should take to be accountable, and what the control rationale was. Another dysfunctional result is that the user gets too involved in the operational details of data processing.

One manager told me, "I now demand internal reports from data processing to check up on just how well they are running their operation."

How can a company develop an effective chargeout system? Obviously, no one system can work for all companies, since the needs of companies vary tremendously. However, I think that one good approach to designing an effective system is to follow these seven steps:

1 Assess the overall status of data processing services within the company.
2 Sort out how data processing is organized.
3 Evaluate capacity of accounting systems to support a DP management control system.
4 Access current chargeout approach.
5 Develop chargeout system objectives and strategy.
6 Develop implementation goals and milestones.
7 Implement and review.

Let's look at each of these seven chargeout system steps in turn.

Assess Status of Data Services

The search for alternatives begins with a careful analysis of the characteristics of a company's industry and management philosophy. For example, managements of companies in high technology industries, such as electronics and aerospace, are more tolerant and understanding of technical complexities than managements of companies in service industries, such as insurance and banking. Also, managements of companies with sophisticated budgeting and financial controls are more receptive to similar systems for data processing. The general rule is that management control systems for data processing cannot be significantly more advanced than the management control systems used for the company as a whole.

Management's next task is to determine the status of its services. What I call the "stage process audit" is a useful way to structure this analysis.[1] Based upon the status of the applications portfolio, data processing organization, control mechanisms, and user awareness, an organization's data services can be thought of as being in one of four stages: initiation, contagion, control, or integration. Figure 2 shows the attributes for each of these stages. This detailed audit provides the foundation for tailoring the design of a control system.

A frequent mistake in designing an effective system is to impose sophisticated controls upon organizational units that are not "ready." The organizational unit is not ready if controls hinder its operation or if personnel cannot clearly see the relevance of the controls to their problems.

For example, one user in my study was charged for programming services that he did not fully understand because a new on-line system was being developed. Nevertheless, he was asked to make judgments on the resource commitments being made on the project, as well as to accept an accountability for those judgments, even though the development process was largely out of his hands.

[1]See my article, "Managing the Computer Resources: A Stage Hypothesis," *Communications of the ACM,* July 1973, p. 300.

Figure 2 Stage Process Audit Criteria

Criteria	Stage I: Initiation	Stage II: Contagion	Stage III: Control	Stage IV: Integration
DP organization				
Objective	Get first application on the computer	Broaden use of computer technology	Gain control of data processing activities	Integrate data processing into business
Staffing emphasis	Technical computer experts	User-oriented system analysts and programmers	Middle management	Balance of technical and management specializations
Structure	Embedded in low-functional area	Growth and multiple DP units created	Consolidation of DP activities into central organizational unit	Layering and "fitting" DP organization structure
Reporting level	To functional manager	To higher level functional manager	To senior management officer	VP level reporting to corporate top management
User awareness				
Senior management	Clerical staff reduction syndrome	Broader applications in operational areas	Crisis of expenditure growth Panic about penetration in business operations	Acceptance as a major business function Involvement in providing direction
User attitude	"Hands-off" Anxiety over implications	Superficially enthusiastic Insufficient involvement in applications design	Frustration from suddenly being held accountable for DP expenditures	Acceptance of accountability Involvement in application, budgeting design, and maintenance
Communication with DP	Informal Lack of under-standing	Oversell and unrealistic objectives and schedules Schism develops	Formal lines of communication Formal commitments Cumbersome	Acceptance and informed communication Application development partnership
Training	General orientation on "what is a computer"	Little user interest	Increase in user interest due to accountability	User seeks out training on application development and control

Planning and control				
Objective	Hold spending at initial commitment	Facilitate wider functional uses of computer	Formalize control and contain DP expenditures	Tailor planning and control to DP activities
Planning	Oriented toward computer implementation	Oriented toward application development	Oriented toward gaining central control	Established formal planning activity
Management control	Focus on computer operations budget	Lax to facilitate applica-tions development activity growth	Proliferation of formal controls	Balanced formal and informal controls
Project management	DP manager responsibility	Programmer's responsibility	Formalized system DP department responsibility	Formalized system tailored to project DP and user/manage-ment joint responsibility
Project approval and priority setting	DP manager responsibility	Multi-functional managers First in, first out	Steering committee	Steering committee Formal plan influence
DP standards	Low awareness of importance	Inattention	Importance recognized Activity aggressively implemented	Established standards activity Published policy manuals

Application portfolio				
Objective	Prove value of computer technology in organization	Apply computer technology to multi-functional areas	Moratorium on new applications Consolidate and gain control of existing applications	Exploit opportunities for integrative systems Cost-effective application of advanced technology
Application justification	Cost-savings	Informal user/manager approval	Hard cost savings Short-term payout	Benefit/cost analysis Senior management approval

Sort Out the Organization Structure

Although many companies for the most part have centralized their data processing, there are usually pockets of activities still embedded within the organization that have not been dislodged.

The question of what constitutes an effective organization is complicated by wide disagreement on which activities should be centralized even when they are only broadly categorized into systems development and operations. The majority of DP personnel I interviewed agreed that operations should be centralized, at least enough to support the specialists necessary to run and maintain the computer facility. However, proponents of minicomputers believe decentralization is preferable. The main disagreement concerns the location of systems development personnel, even though for the 18 research sites studied, 90% of the central DP departments had programmers and 60% had systems analysts—and over half of the user organizations had programmers and systems analysts.

Organizating data processing becomes even more complex and difficult when activities are sorted into maintenance, data entry, batch processing, online services and processing, and telecommunication facilities.

A study of an organization's structure will expose irrational locations for various data processing activities. The majority of these locations can probably be changed; others may have to be viewed as constraints in the short run.

Even when an irrational structure cannot be altered, the structure must be understood, because almost every control action taken for the central DP group will also affect the splinter groups.

For example, in one company I studied, the corporate data processing department decided to charge users the full cost of providing services. The divisional data processing department charged less than full costs because occupancy and employee benefits were excluded from the calculation of costs. The effect of the corporate decision was to shift users to the divisional data processing facility, even though the best interests of the company were not served. If these responses are anticipated, systems may be designed to avoid dysfunctional relationships between the central and splinter groups, as well as between corporate and divisional management.

Evaluate Capacity of Accounting System

Since accounting systems provide the foundation for management control, management control can only reflect the quality of the accounting system. As shown in Figure 3, a logical progression exists in the development of the accounting systems, from after-the-fact, object-of-expenditure control to budgetary control responsibility center, by program (or job), and by quantitative measure of output units.

Although all 18 companies studied had developed meaningful classifications for expenditures—that is charts of accounts—4 companies still had not integrated the DP chart of accounts into the company's general ledger system. In

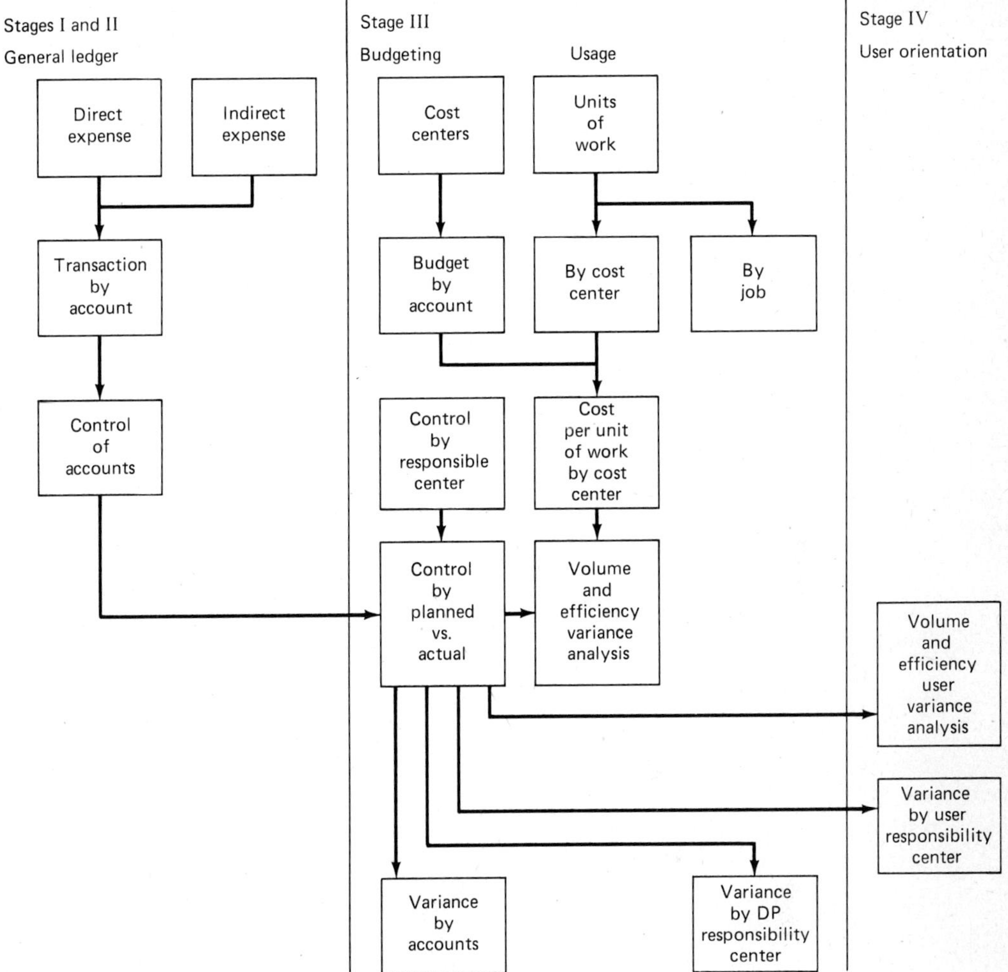

Figure 3 Evolution of accounting and control systems.

addition, the DP accounting systems were of varying quality, which influenced their reliability.

The development of data processing accounting systems is initially an accounting problem rather than a data processing problem because basic accounting concepts are most important. Unfortunately, this need for accounting skills does not seem to be fully recognized in the beginning. Over half of the companies studied reported that their technical personnel played the dominant role in designing the initial accounting systems. Systems analysts and programmers were usually assigned this task on the assumption that their technical skills were needed to measure computer system resource usage. Rather quickly, however, it became apparent that the real problems were accounting problems concerning responsibility centers, costing and allocating costs to responsibility centers. Accounting personnel then would be brought into the project.

Cost centers, too, seemed to have evolved from the existing structure of the data processing department rather than from an analysis of basic DP functions. Consequently, organizational changes often have a detrimental effect on control. In addition, costs are not consistently categorized by type—direct, indirect, and overhead.

These fundamental problems seriously hindered the effective design, implementation, and administration of the chargeout systems. Simply stated, you cannot build a sophisticated control system on a sandy foundation of weak accounting systems.

Assess Current Chargeout Approach

A useful chargeout system communicates to managers the consequences of their decisions concerning use of services. Cost responsibility will tend to motivate users to employ the resources more effectively and efficiently. Four criteria can be used for determining the usefulness of a chargeout system—understandability, controllability, accountability, and cost/benefit incidence. Figure 4 shows the criteria and questions for determining the maturity of the chargeout system.

As shown in Figure 4, chargeout systems initially are directed at high-level managers. Summary data processing bills are sent to divisional controllers without much information on the charges being conveyed to end users. With maturity, the chargeout systems become more sophisticated and permit detailed bills to be sent directly to low-level users. It is important that the chargeout system evolve through successive phases, so that users and DP managers can learn how to interpret and use the information. It is especially important that the means for accountability be coordinated with expectations for accountability.

After assessing the status of the existing chargeout system, management's next objective is to develop a strategy that will increase the maturity (and effectiveness) of the chargeout system at an appropriate pace for the major user groups. It is likely that several chargeout strategies may be required for the different user groups.

Develop Objectives and Strategy

In the companies I studied, objectives for the chargeout systems were rarely articulated. Or, if they were articulated, the objectives were often narrowly defined short-term goals. For example, eight of the companies stated that their chargeout system objective was to allocate data processing costs. No mention was made of providing the cost information to users that they needed to make effective decisions about services. In other words, using data accounting systems to allocate costs for financial reporting and budgeting purposes should not be confused with chargeout. Chargeout brings the user into the realm of control and accountability.

In my opinion, the absence of a clear statement of objectives or an

Figure 4 Criteria for Chargeout Systems

Understandability

To what extent can the manager associate chargeout costs to the activities necessary to carry out his or her tasks?

Attributes

High—Manager can associate costs with functions and determine variables accounting for costs.

Medium—Manager can roughly associate costs with functions, but cannot directly determine major variables accounting for costs.

Low—Manager cannot associate costs with functions.

Controllability

To what extent are charges under the control of the user?

Attributes

None—No control. The manager has no influence on acceptance or rejection of the charges. These decisions are made at a higher level.

Indirect—Through communication with others, such as divisional or departmental controllers that receive charges, the manager can influence the charges.

Direct/arbitrary—Charges are allocated directly to the manager, but his decision is to either accept or reject the application charges. Little information is provided on controllable versus noncontrollable data processing costs.

Direct/economic—Charges are directly charged in a manner that allows the manager to make decisions that actually reduce controllable data processing costs.

Accountability

Are costs and utilization of computer-based systems included in performance evaluation of the user?

Attributes

None—Not included in performance evaluation.

Indirect—Included indirectly in performance evaluation; costs can be related to user, but not done routinely.

Direct—Included directly in periodic user-performance evaluation.

Cost/benefit incidence

Does the user responsible for task accomplishment also receive the chargeout bill?

Attributes

Yes.
No.

excessively narrow statement was the single most troublesome factor inhibiting chargeout system effectiveness. Consequently, systems were not well thought out, but were designed to provide minimal information for accounting, or to support other management tools such as project management systems.

Chargeout objectives should be stated in terms of desirable results for user accountability. Examples of such objectives include:

- Make managers aware of the economic (full absorption) costs of data processing services provided to them.
- Make managers responsible for the economic costs of services they use.
- Motivate managers to make decisions about the use of data processing on the basis of the direct costs of providing the services.
- Charge costs in understandable volume units to facilitate data processing capacity planning.
- Charge costs in a manner to facilitate manager product (service) pricing.

Each of these examples specifies a particular result, and taken together they imply the design of a system much broader than one that simply charges for computer services. Alterations in organization structure, budgeting, and performance review and measurement are often necessary. Once management has articulated an appropriate set of objectives, it should formulate a strategy to achieve them that takes into account the necessary changes in organization and administrative practices.

Develop Implementation Goals

The stage audit I discussed earlier provides an idea of how advanced a company is in respect to data processing. It also specifies a long-term objective.

Keeping in mind that a great deal of difficult organizational changes are required to first synchronize the status of the applications portfolio, organization, control system, and user awareness, and second, to progress through the advanced stages, management can lay out short-run goals and a schedule for longer term goals. A common mistake is to go too fast or to attempt to leap-frog a stage. It is important to remember that learning at all levels within the organization is involved in progressing through the stages.

The more detailed analysis of the organization's chargeout status and specification of management control objectives provide the groundwork for establishing short-run and long-run goals. These goals should also be realistic in terms of schedule and sequence. In addition, they should be initially tailored to the individual user groups with the long-term goal of progressing toward a common chargeout system for the entire organization or, at least, a common chargeout system for each of the major divisions.

Implement and Review

The data processing department should never take it upon itself to implement a management control and chargeout strategy. Implementation of the strategy will have far-reaching effects on the overall management control system of the company, as well as immediate effects on users. It is clear that managers must be able to evaluate information system alternatives, since it is the development and operation of *their* applications that will determine what the costs will be. The chargeout system effectively brings the user into control by matching costs and benefits by responsibility center. Of course, there are complicating factors where applications serve several users in more than one responsibility center.

High-level steering committees play a crucial role in providing a forum for shaking down and ratifying a management control and chargeout strategy. Just as important as ratification is management's agreement on implementation goals and schedules. Organizational changes associated with a realistic strategy will inevitably result in some conflict and disagreement. To constructively negotiate through obstacles that arise, management needs to have a plan or road map on direction and destination.

The steering committee, or some type of quarterly review board, should ensure that the organization maintains progress. In addition to its role of approval and guidance, such a group provides a source of commitment that is necessary for successful management control programs.

THE FUTURE

The 18 companies that I studied are at the forefront of data processing. Their DP organization charts, trends, and plans provide a glimpse of future organization structures and control systems. The extensive incorporation of data-base technology is the most important trend, leading toward a structure that facilitates data-oriented management.[2]

For example, one of the more advanced companies had explained especially well the role of data-base technology in this orientation. The company used a facsimile of Figure 5 to compare the traditional computer-oriented accountability scheme with the data-oriented accountability scheme for two applications: an order entry system and an inventory control system. Traditionally, both the definition of data (inventory part numbers, reorder points, customers) and function (the way an order is processed) is contained in the application, using programming languages such as COBOL or PL/1. Chargeout is based on the computer-related resources used, and the user is held accountable for both data and function.

But data-base technology enables management to separate function from data. As a result, users can be held directly accountable for function, and data processing can be held directly accountable for management of the company's data resources.

This company envisions a chargeout system including both simplified user bills and data processing bills from users. In other words, data would be purchased from functional groups that originate them, as well as from outside sources. In responding to requests from users, data processing would provide value-added services by combining, processing, and distributing data. The users would be charged for the cost of the data plus the value-added services of

[2]See my article "Computer Data Base: The Future is Now," *Harvard Business Review,* September–October 1973, p. 98.

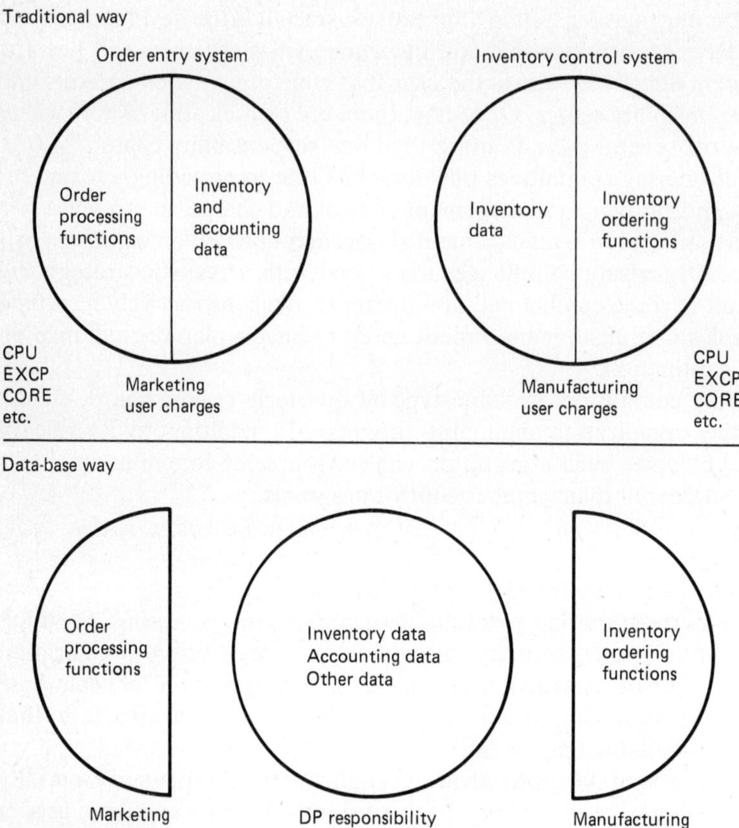

Figure 5 Comparison of traditional computer-oriented accountability with data-oriented accountability.

processing them. The value-added concept solves a basic problem of current chargeout systems; it provides a quid pro quo for those who bear the costs of collecting the data but who are not the end users.

The rapid development of data-base technology will most likely lead to specialized components for data management. Figure 6 shows the three main components: data, processing, and control.

To start with, current processing systems will be relieved of data management functions and will be designed to carry out value-added functions of combining, mutating, and distributing data. Both the data and processing systems will incorporate large-scale and mini/microcomputer technologies.

This division of functions will then lead to a separate control system to facilitate specialized management necessary to account, bill, schedule, monitor, and control the efficiency of the company's data processing installation. Although this control component is at present at a rudimentary state, one manufacturer has already entered the market and has delivered such systems to the Social Security Administration and the General Electric Company.

The impact of the evolving data processing installation is distinctly visible

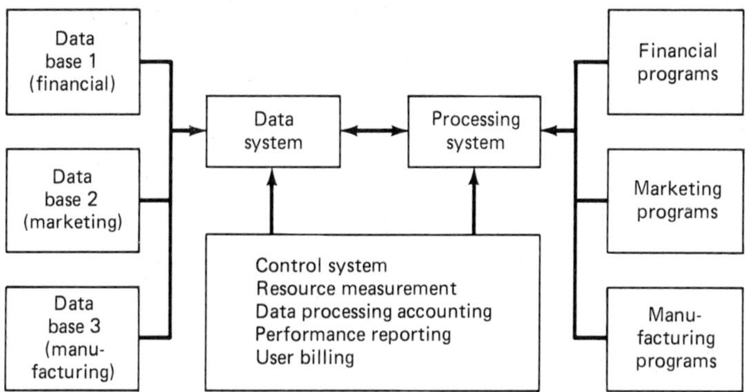

Figure 6 Components of future data services installation.

on several of the organization charts of the companies I studied. One of the first signs is the incorporation of data administration positions. Data administration separates the management of data from the development of user applications. Another sign is the emergence of the controller position. This position is created to recognize the need for more formal management of data processing, as well as to cope with the need for bringing about effective user accountability. Figure 7 shows my projected organization chart for the future data processing installation.

Figure 7 Future data services organization.

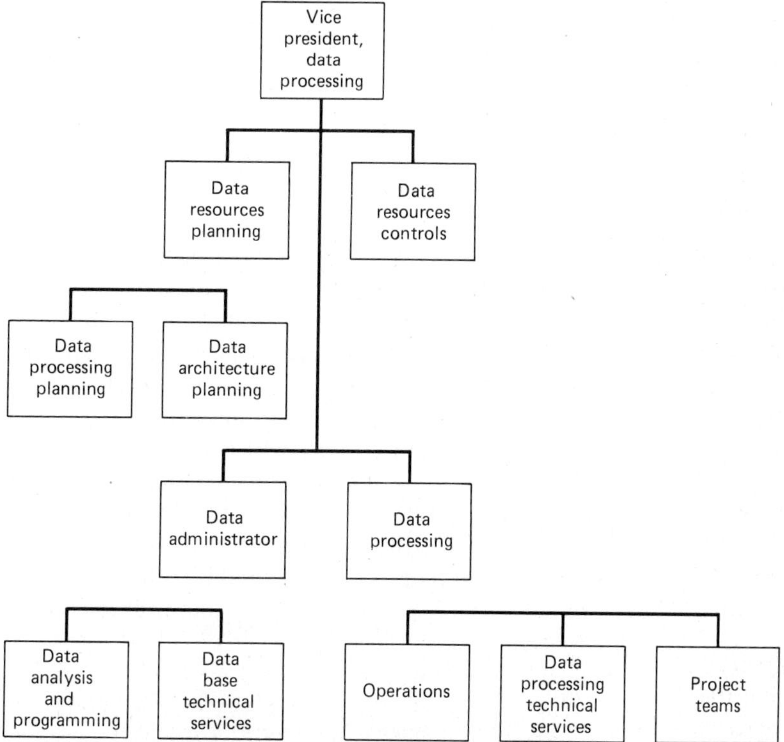

IN SUMMARY

The role and position of data processing has now taken sufficient form to mount effective management programs to fit it into the modern organization. It is clear that organizations progress through stages of maturity for data processing management and the next apparent stage is to establish three separate functions for this management.

In order for it to better control these functions, it is important that top management first understand the natural shift from computer management to data management. This shift cannot and will not take place overnight. It is, and for each organization will be, a gradual shift beginning with the incorporation of data-base technology and an elaboration of control systems.

Next, top management needs to realize that an effective chargeout system is essential if those who use data processing are to be in control and held accountable for the services they receive. It is the users that ultimately justify and obtain the potentially lucrative returns from the company's investment in data processing.

It is this simple fact that should determine top management's orientation and decisions concerning data processing.

READING 23 DISCUSSION QUESTIONS

1 What are the major ways of allocating computer costs to user departments? What are the advantages of these methods?
2 What trends are taking place which affect the control of computer costs within an organization?

Case F

Getting Control of the System

There is a story in the computer industry that sums up the reaction of many management-level officials to their data processing departments. It goes like this:

One evening a doctor, an engineer and a manager of data processing were discussing which of their respective professions might be the oldest. They agreed that the Bible would be a good reference work for the discussion.

The doctor began by pointing out that in Genesis 2:21 the Lord removed a rib from Adam and from that created woman. "Quite a feat of surgery," he said, and sat back satisfied that neither of the other two could top that story.

But the engineer quickly pointed out that in Genesis 1:6 God said: "Let there be a firmament in the midst of the waters." Creating this firmament must have been a great engineering feat, he claimed, particularly since there was no

Reprinted with the special permission of *Dun's Review*, July 1977. Copyright 1977, Dun and Bradstreet Publications Corporation.

mention of cost overruns. The doctor was forced to agree that the engineer had found an earlier reference to his profession.

THE TOPPER

The data-processing manager was not about to concede defeat, however. "After all," he said, "Genesis 1:2 says that 'the earth was without form, and void.' This shows that the Lord must have had a data processing department."

Whether the Lord's data-processing operation was a formless void or not, many managers today feel that their computer operations are typified by uncontrolled costs and uncontrolled personnel—in short, that their data processing operations are not amenable to normal business practices and operations.

And management is not happy. A recent study by the Chicago office of accountants Peat, Marwick, Mitchell & Co. showed that fewer than one-third of the respondents were satisfied with the service they were getting from their computer centers. Almost everyone felt that he did not have enough computer capacity and that he couldn't get the job done between 9 at night and 9 in the morning, when the reports were needed, reports Robert Forney, a PMM data-processing consultant.

"Most systems cost more and take longer to install than expected," adds Timothy Cronin, president of Inforex Corp., and the installations "don't always give the desired results." Cronin says that this is usually because "computer people tend to make users bend to fit the available technology, not the technology to fit the users." Furthermore, "There's more technology around now than can be used. We don't need more technology, but rather a change in attitude so that it can be used better."

Unfortunately, there is a communications gap in many business organizations today between what might be called "regular" management and the management of the data-processing operation, and the fault for this gap lies on both sides of the chasm. Because of the confusing jargon and the "computer mystique" that tries to claim that only the initiated are qualified to judge the operation, management has too often abdicated its responsibility for this vital resource and turned it over to a group of technocrats who often care less about the management objectives of a firm than they do about the technology they serve.

Horror stories abound on how computers have been misused—sometimes intentionally, sometimes not. Perhaps the greatest fraud to date was the Equity Funding scandal, in which management used its computer system to generate false insurance policies. In another case, an employee at the Union Dime Savings Bank of New York manipulated the firm's computerized records to embezzle thousands of dollars. And in a more bizarre case, an employee passed over for promotion in one firm was so jealous of the man brought into the job that he tried to sabotage the individual by entering data into the firm's computer designed to make the new boss look foolish.

EXPENSIVE MISTAKES

More important than such cases of deliberate misuse of computers are the times when the machines unintentionally fail to serve their purpose. Some of these experiences were extremely expensive.

For example, both TWA and United Air Lines had horrendous results with early ticketing and reservation systems. TWA spent a total of $26.5 million on a reservation system that it later had to abandon. The firm recovered some of the money in a lawsuit against the supplier, but the payment could not make up for the lost time and effort. In all, the airline spent five years trying to set up the system before scrapping it, and another two in litigation.

In the United case, the firm invested an estimated $39 million and several years of effort in its ticketing and reservation system before abandoning the project. Then the firm had to spend an additional $60 million to get a system that worked.

While all these problems have been developing, computer resources have been consuming larger and larger chunks of the corporate budget each year—often without plan or control. Computer users spent $30 billion for equipment, services and personnel during 1976; of that total, $12.6 billion went for hardware, $9.9 billion to pay the people who work with and program the systems and $7.5 billion for outside software and services. And by 1980, total spending on data processing is expected to leap 66%, to $50 billion, according to International Data Corp., a computer industry research firm.

But many organizations—albeit a minority—have shown that data processing, used and controlled effectively, can make substantial contributions to the management and profits of their firms.

For example, New York's Citibank—a pacesetter in the emerging field of distributed data processing—has used small computers to cut labor costs, and the savings have been dramatic—$80 million after taxes.

Computer operations themselves can be made more efficient—and they can be made to serve the real needs of a company—if management only learns how to express its desires better and if it regains the control over the computer that it has abdicated in the past.

To do this, management does *not* have to become immersed in bytes, bauds, transfer rates and memory sizes, but rather has to begin asking the right, business-oriented questions and insisting on answers couched in business language, not in the jargon of data processing.

WHERE WE ARE

Unfortunately, there are no magic formulas for judging the effectiveness of all data-processing operations. Each organization is different, and management must determine its own value system and measure the performance of its computer operations against that system. It is a painstaking effort. And to begin with, it is helpful to understand how management has let that operation exempt itself from normal business controls.

According to computer consultant Gopal Kapur, a major reason that top management has not paid the attention it should to the data-processing operations is the fact that, despite the overall growth of total spending on data processing, the operation does not consume a very high proportion of the revenues of any particular company. In most cases, he notes, the computer function takes less than 2% of the overall revenues of the firm—small potatoes when compared with sales and manufacturing.

But just looking at this cost is misleading, Kapur says, because data processing is almost the only function that can affect 100% of a firm's operations. For example, in a bank with six branches, if one branch manager is not performing well only his branch will be affected and the problem can be cleared up. However, if the data-processing operation for that bank is operating inefficiently, it will affect all of the branches.

Another important reason it is so difficult to evaluate computer operations is that there is no universal value system that can be applied to them. And this situation stems from the historical development of the computer, according to an internal IBM memo that the government has made public in its current antitrust suit against the firm.

"During the punch-card period, boxes (that is, individual machines) were priced and marketed on the concept of displaceable costs," the memo notes. This was a "discrete measurable value," since the cost of buying and operating the punch-card machines could be stacked against the cost of the firm's current administrative methods.

But at the dawn of the electronic data-processing era, pioneer users—insurance companies, large banks, the federal government and the defense industry—"in the main were not motivated by displaceable cost considerations." This was because the sheer volume of transactions these organizations had to handle, or the complexity of their computational requirements, were beyond the scope of punch-card technology.

With the development of more flexible and complex systems, many users "relegated cost-of-the-old-way versus cost-of-the-new to minor consideration," the memo adds. In addition, by 1959 the use of a computer had become a matter of prestige in large and medium-sized concerns, causing "a further depressing influence on displaceable cost as a criterion for placing an order." By the early 1960s—as demand for computers continued to outpace supply—these systems, "came to be regarded as *necessities,* not capital asset acquisitions to be painstakingly evaluated for their potential return on investment."

IBM's System/360 computer line—the first real family of computers—was introduced in the mid-1960s. It gave users improved functions at close to the same prices, IBM observed, rendering "totally unnecessary a comprehensive cost analysis as a criterion for placing an order. The reason for this was that a series of forerunners was in place. These had a perceived value that was not unquestioned, although rarely, if ever, quantified." And, according to IBM, users ordered System/360 equipment "on a value system *related to the perceived and unquantified value of predecessor systems.* (Not to displaceable cost in the traditional . . . connotation.)"

This method of valuing new computers solely on the basis of predecessor systems, and not on displaceable costs, began to be questioned during the 1970–71 recession. There was a reluctance to buy more equipment without some quantification of its value to the firm, but this quantification was difficult.

"The historical erosion of the displaceable cost, combined with the existence of a new breed of professional programmers interposed between top management and the in-house user of the output, rendered all but impossible the gaining of any insight on what the value in fact was, or if indeed any existed," IBM noted.

The memo mentioned many additional factors: "The complexity of the machines and operating systems . . . ; management's inability and lack of motivation to understand the system; a delayed awareness that hardware costs are moving down rapidly while people costs are moving up sharply; the natural instinct for self-preservation among (data-processing) professionals, who are hence reluctant to have management gain an understanding that could result in reducing or eliminating the professional's role, etc."

Thus the IBM executives, who probably know the market better than anyone else, concluded: "It is unlikely that significant progress will be made in establishing a realistic value system that would have applicability outside a single firm." And so it is up to the managers of each firm to develop techniques that can pin down the value of data processing to their organizations.

With no universal value system for judging the effectiveness of a company's computer, what can be done?

First, it is important to note that there are many tools to measure the performance of a particular computer. These range from hardware monitors attached to the system to software monitors that can be used on a computer while it is running other jobs. Each of these is invaluable to the manager of the data-processing center, and can be of value to his superiors.

These devices can record how much the central processor and peripheral units are in use at any given time, whether there are bottlenecks, and if so, where they are. From such readings, it is clear that computer equipment is not used as effectively as it might be. For example, a 1970 study on computer utilization by A. T. Kearney, Inc., showed that in some instances only 45% of the available computer time was used productively and that in many large installations the effective use was under 65%.

Among other things, the Kearney study noted one company in which the computer was manned round the clock and the rental of outside computer time had risen sharply; this was being used to justify a proposal to buy more computers. But an analysis of the actual output of the in-house machine "revealed very low utilization of the installed computer." Management then started to review several performance indicators on a monthly basis and to establish specific goals, whereupon "EDP personnel, working diligently to achieve these goals, discovered numerous ingenious ways to increase throughput and eliminate outside rental time. They successfully delayed acquisition of a new, larger computer for two years and created much better rapport and communications with management."

The key to success in this example was not the use of a measurement tool to find that the system was underutilized, but rather the involvement of management in setting up performance guidelines. Like the computer itself, the measurement devices are just a tool to to be used by management.

These tools are available from a wide variety of independent vendors and from the computer manufacturers. In fact, many of the latest computer systems have monitors built in. While these only give crude measures they provide more data about the performance of the equipment than many managers are receiving today.

BUSY DOING WHAT?

Despite the wide availability of these tools, it is surprising how rarely they are used. The Peat, Marwick study found that only 30% of the responding organizations were using quantified measures of computer performance. And only 25% had even attempted the trickier question of measuring the return from data-processing investments. The study showed, by the way, that there was a high correlation between those who were satisfied with their data-processing operation and those who used performance-evaluated techniques.

Computer performance evaluation tools can only tell how hard the computer is working—not *what* it is working on. It does an executive little good to know that the computer system is working 90%-to-100% of the time if he does not know what it is busy doing. The data-processing center could be busy producing unneeded and unwanted reports.

George Glaser, a well-known consultant and former president of the American Federation of Information Processing Societies, says that a better way to judge the effectiveness of a company's computer operation is to "ask the operating people what they think of it," since they are the ultimate users of the system. "If they all say nice things about the reports they get from DP and about its service, then probably the center is operating effectively," says Glaser. "If they don't like what they are getting, then the data processing is no good, no matter how expensive the equipment, how skilled the staff or how efficient DP is internally." There is probably no better way than this to judge the data-processing operation.

Another technique, suggested by consultant Kapur, is to require the data-processing department to report periodically on the status of the programs it is running, the reports that are being produced and the programs under development. Incredibly, he says, many firms do not even have a master list of all the programs being run by the data-processing department. Yet a look at a master list can sometimes be a real eye-opener for management. Often reports that have outlived their usefulness continue to be produced just because no one has taken the time or the effort to cancel them. Sometimes two separate reports serve essentially the same needs and could easily be combined into one. Along with the list of reports, there should also be a rundown on who receives the reports and what they use them for. There may be better ways to serve those same information needs.

Kapur and the other consultants feel that business must also begin to apply the same classical management tools to the data-processing department as are applied to the other segments of the corporation. They point out that a company would not consider building a multi-million dollar plant without a careful analysis of the projected return on investment. But rarely do managers require the same type of analysis of their computer operations.

In addition, rarely are alternatives explored when computer operations are considered. Usually, the computer department proposes an expanded system without any reference to the possibility of doing the job with ordinary accounting machines, or manually—leaving management with an all-or-nothing choice. Computer people have a stake in increasing the size and budget of their operations, and so they are not wont to propose manual solutions to problems as alternatives to the automated solution.

LONG-RANGE VIEW

In the long run, however, the real solution to the problems with data processing in many organizations will come as both managers in the traditional departments become more familiar with data processing and the computer-center manager become more familiar with the business objectives of a corporation. The current gap between the two groups is "about twenty years wide," Glaser says. "Twenty years from now, both sides will have matured and the technology will be better understood by managers and data-processing people will have a better understanding of business." The situation is already "improving a bit," he says, since many big shops have weeded out the poor managers on both sides.

Glaser notes that this entails a constant game of "catch up," since the technology is changing so fast. Often, just as an organization feels that it has control of data processing, whole new applications open up involving new problems and new learning curves for both sides.

But just how do companies close the communications gap between middle managers and the computer center?

The key phrase bandied about is "management involvement." But Glaser points out this is often used as an excuse by data-processing people, who often claim that the lack of "management involvement" is why projects fail. "It is a two-way street," Glaser believes; the data-processing department has to meet management halfway and itself become involved in company management. Companies need to set up programs so their line managers can gain some feel for how computers can be used effectively, and the firm needs to provide the personnel in the data processing with a greater understanding of the business.

This is nothing startlingly new. In fact, the phrase "management involvement" was used first in a pioneering report on computer use in business published by McKinsey & Co. in the early 1960s. What it takes is a real commitment on the part of management to get involved.

In the past, however, management has often been put off by computer programs. Often these involved one- and two-day seminars on data processing, what Kapur calls "music appreciation" courses. And as Dr. Jack Stone, another consultant who specializes in the training area, puts it: "The trainees quickly succumbed to the side effects, certainly in mind if not in body, of toxic injections of bits and bytes, DBMS and EXCPs, Hipos and OCRs."

TRAINING EXECUTIVES

A good way to train executives in a short time is to make the program "consistent with the executive's operating style," Stone says. He adds: "The successful executive is one who has an almost uncanny ability to grasp the essence of a business problem in very short order, evaluate the alternatives quickly and reach a decision promptly. The training program should therefore be workshop-oriented so the material is of immediate interest, the technical and management principles involved are concisely and simply presented . . . and the executive/student addresses and solves a set of problems that are directly relevant to current DP operations."

Aside from formal training programs for executives, Kapur recommends that line managers actually serve time early in their career in the data-processing department to give a feel for the possibilities—and the limitations—of computers.

Meetings between management and data-processing personnel are a must, most experts agree, particularly if a project is under development. And the user department should be involved from the beginning if the system being designed is to have any real chance of success.

Companies that use their data-processing operations effectively often establish "project management" teams comprised of personnel from both the computer center and the user department. The team and not the computer center then has responsibility for the system under development. The user members of the team are responsible for defining what they want the computer system to actually do for them, and the computer people for determining if what is wanted is actually feasible and at what cost.

Another technique is to model the data-processing department on the structure of the company. This results in user departments interacting with a specific group of people in the computer center. The computer people become more versed in the particular problems and needs of the user organization and they gain a better understanding how automation can meet those needs.

But for management to become involved, the DP department has to do things in return, Glaser says. The manager of the data-processing operation often has come up through the technical ranks of the company. He is familiar with the technology involved in computing, but less so with the actual business of the firm. Essentially many of these people are "a-corporate."

In one limited survey of twenty DP managers a few years ago, Richard L. Nolan of the Harvard Business School found that only two had held their present jobs for five years and that most of them "view their jobs and their career prospects in stoic and rather negative terms."

Writing in the *Harvard Business Review,* Nolan notes that the data-processing manager now has to manage quite a disparate group, ranging from clerical keypunch operators to some of the most specialized workers in the company—programmers and computer scientists. At the same time, the DP manager is responsible for a broad range of activities, from the most routine type of processing to experimental projects.

"Once it was possible to assume that a good EDP manager must first and foremost be an expert on computer technology. This assumption was valid enough during the 1960s, when many EDP departments were just getting off the ground. The EDP manager designed and programmed many systems himself," Nolan says.

"In the 1970s, however, most medium- and large-sized companies have long since automated their manual clerical systems," he notes. Newer, more sophisticated computer applications are being developed.

Because of this, the nature of the DP manager has had to change. He still needs a good understanding of the trends of computer technology, but he does not need the same level of expertise as his computer scientists. On the other hand, he must have a good understanding of his company and its competitive environment.

Thus, says Nolan, "to view the EDP manager's activities solely in terms of engineering computer technology is a narrow and grossly inadequate view of the environment of the 1970s." Unfortunately, this attitude is "too typical of senior managements. The result is costly—the computer resource is not used effectively and scarce managerial talent is squandered."

Nolan and others agree that top executives must begin to look on the DP manager as a manager and not a technician. Consultant Kapur says that computer personnel with a talent for management should be identified early and given management training courses. In addition, Kapur would have these people do tours of duty in departments outside the computer room.

In short, says Nolan, to end the waste—both in terms of dollars and missed opportunities—caused by the gap between management and data processing, "senior management and EDP management must jointly reassess the function, and focus on the management dimensions of the computer resource."

CASE F DISCUSSION QUESTIONS

1 "The current gap between computer managers and regular management is about 20 years wide—it will take that long for each to understand the other's problems." Discuss this statement.

2 What role should the chief executive play in the overall direction of the DP department? Which decisions should she or he reserve for herself/himself? Delegate to end users? To the DP department?

SUMMARY OF CHAPTER 7

Controlling a computer facility usually involves making efforts to (1) improve operating efficiency from failure to safeguard data integrity, system security, and personal privacy. A number of control steps and techniques have been discussed in this chapter.

Several controlling implications associated with the use of computer systems that are of concern to managers and auditors have also been presented in the preceding pages. We have seen, for example, that information produced by computer systems can help improve managerial control over business operations. But we have also seen that the introduction of a computer can have a significant effect on the internal control of the information system itself. In some cases, the control procedures that have replaced the numerous employee-oriented checks used in a manual system have been poorly designed. Several system failures resulting from poor internal controls were presented in the chapter. Of course, managers and auditors are concerned about these failures and are working to develop and preserve system-oriented controls and auditing procedures that will safeguard assets and maintain the integrity and security of the system.

Chapter 8

Computers in Not-for-Profit Organizations

Throughout this text, we have seen that over the past 25 years computers have had—as they continue to have—an ever-increasing impact on the activities performed by business organizations and on the tasks that managers perform within these organizations. Some of these impacts have been felt in other types of organizations. Initially, computers in these *nonbusiness* organizations have been used for traditional types of record keeping. For example, a local government often uses the computer to process utility billing operations; a college may use the computer to process student records; a library may use the computer to keep track of the issuing of books and the preparation of overdue fines. However, it has become apparent that in many of these *not-for-profit* organizations, the potentials for more sophisticated uses of the computer may well exceed those that exist in business and industry.

One objective of this book is to describe briefly some of the uses of computers in other social environments and in the *not-for-profit sector*. Thus, in the following pages of this chapter, we shall examine computer applications in such areas as government, law, health, education, the humanities, the fine arts, museums, and historical and archaeological research.[1]

[1]For a complete coverage of the impact of computers in these areas, see Donald H. Sanders, *Computers in Society,* 2d ed., McGraw-Hill Book Company, New York, 1977.

COMPUTERS IN THE FEDERAL GOVERNMENT

Existing broad social and political problems such as creeping urban decay, air and water pollution, and traffic congestion affect our everyday lives. In addition to attacking these problems, greater attention must also be given in the future to such social needs as more comprehensive health care, better transportation planning and improved public safety. Governmental agencies at all levels in our society are involved. But because of the interrelated (and interstate) nature of many of the existing social needs and because of the magnitude of the economic resources which must be made available to deal with many of the problems, citizens expect the federal government to provide direction and resources to effect many of the necessary improvements. In seeking solutions to difficult social problems, federal government administrators need timely, accurate, and relevant information.

Computers are used in the federal government for (1) *planning and decision making,* (2) *control,* and (3) *law enforcement purposes.* Let us look at applications in each of these usage categories.

Planning and Decision Making in the Federal Government

Governmental planners and decision makers have a mandate to efficiently use public funds and resources in ways that best serve the needs of society. Unfortunately, government policy makers have often been required to function in settings where the data available for public policy making are inadequate and/or inaccurate. Although the federal government has amassed and stored a vast body of statistical data, it is not yet able to satisfactorily measure "the human toll of illness, the pollution of the environment, the quality of our education, and the nature of the alienation expressed in burning and looting in the ghetto . . . and crime in the city streets."[2]

Since effective planning begins with an understanding of the existing situation, and since information detailing social conditions as they actually exist is not always available, it is not surprising that public planning in the past has failed to remedy many types of problems. With the development of new information systems, however, the hope of government planners is that they will have higher-quality information with which to (1) make better plans and decisions, (2) improve operating efficiency, and (3) better serve society. Some *examples of how computers are now being used for planning and decision-making purposes at the federal government level* are discussed below.

Environmental Planning *Technology assessment* is a relatively new phrase used in the federal government to refer to the evaluation of the consequences of technological change beyond short-term economic costs and benefits. Because many of the problems of environmental quality are the result of changes in

[2]Abe Gottlieb, "The Computer and the Job Undone," *Computers and Automation,* November 1970, p. 19.

technology, use of the technology-assessment concept has become increasingly important in environmental planning and in the protection of our natural resources. In 1970 the National Environmental Policy Act went into effect with the requirement that federal agencies include a detailed statement in every proposal for legislation (or other major federal action) that significantly affects the quality of the environment. The detailed statement should outline such points as (1) the environmental impact of the proposed action, (2) any adverse environmental effects that cannot be avoided, and (3) any irreversible and irretrievable commitments of resources that would be required in the proposed action. The result of this act will be to give greater future emphasis to the use of computers for ecological and environmental research.

But computer usage has already proved valuable in environmental planning. The Department of Health, Education and Welfare, for example, has sponsored the development and use of a highly sophisticated computer simulation to predict the life-sustaining ability of rivers. The simulation model consists of interrelated equations that represent oxygen supply and biochemical oxygen demand in a river. Up to 450 simultaneous first-order differential equations (and a 450 x 450 matrix) are required by the model. In addition to analyzing existing river conditions, the model can also be used by planners to gain insights into the cause-and-effect relationships of water pollution, so that preventive action can be taken to protect a river or so that corrective measures can be initiated to restore a polluted stream to a satisfactory condition. A nationwide system of computers is also helping the planners of the United States Geological Survey (an agency of the Department of the Interior) to find answers to water supply problems. What will be the result, for example, of major alterations of a river's flow pattern by an electric power company for generating purposes? What will be the effect on sewage and waste assimilation, on aquatic life, and on other current uses of the water? Computer simulation models are helping planners to arrive at answers to such questions.

Finally, in the air pollution fight, the Air Pollution Control Office of the Environmental Protection Agency is currently developing a National Aerometric Data Information Service. It is expected that an initial data base of 5 billion characters will be increased by 50 million characters of new data each year. This computer-based information will be used by Environmental Protection Agency planners and by the Council on Environmental Quality.[3]

Weather Forecasting A mathematical model has been in existence for years, with equations that describe how changes in such atmospheric variables as air pressure, temperature, humidity, and velocity of the air occur over time. Thomas Crowley has succinctly summarized the use of the computers in weather forecasting:

[3]For further information on this and other environmental planning projects, see R. P. Ouellette, R. S. Greeley, and J. W. Overby II, *Computer Techniques in Environmental Science,* Petrocelli/Charter Publishers, Inc., New York, 1975.

> At least as long ago as 1911, it was pointed out that the weather could be predicted by solving these equations. If the pressure, temperature, humidity, and velocity of the air are known for the same instant of time at many points around the world, the solution of the equations is mathematically quite straight-forward and accurately predicts what these quantities will be 1 hour, 1 day, or 1 week later. A network of weather stations around the world can make the measurements necessary to provide the initial conditions for these calculations, but it happens that a tremendous number of numerical calculations are required. Without a computer these computations required months of work, and there was obviously no point to predicting the weather if the weather was already over! . . .
>
> Immediately after it became clear that digital computers would vastly speed up such calculations, mathematicians and meteorologists intensified study of this method of prediction. Although the first results were crude, by 1962 a useful system was in routine operation.[4]

This early system used about 2,000 measurement reports to establish the initial conditions, and then a large computer of that day required 1 hour to make a 1-day prediction.

Although weather predictions still leave something to be desired, the accuracy of certain types of forecasts has been significantly improved by computer usage. Furthermore, the use of new supercomputers promises to improve the numerical prediction techniques.

Military Planning Computers are increasingly being used by military planners and decision makers. Complex worldwide military command and control systems have been developed for use by military commanders from the President on down. It is not difficult to envision, in the years to come,[5] a system which could receive and integrate information from battlefield computers, from intelligence agents, from spy satellites, and from other military and political sources to form an overall picture for top-level planners such as the President and the Joint Chiefs of Staff. Because of technology, military decisions formerly made in the field may increasingly involve decision makers at much higher levels. The United States military today has well over 20 telecommunication satellites positioned to transmit data to and from all points in the world.[6] Thus, the data transmission capability needed by future military systems should be available when needed.

At the present time, computers are being used by military planners to simulate wars—i.e., to sharpen analytical skills and gain experience in decision making through the use of "war games." In fact, Dr. Ruth Davis, Director of the National Bureau of Standards' Institute for Computer Sciences and Technology,

[4]Thomas H. Crowley, *Understanding Computers,* McGraw-Hill Book Company, New York, pp. 105–106, 1967.

[5]Alas, the assumption here is that people will continue to behave in the future as they have in the past.

[6]The number of communications satellites available to the world's civilian users is only about one-sixth the number employed by the United States military.

is of the opinion that the first battles of World War III may already have been fought with computers rather than cannons. In an address to an international meeting of computer professionals in Stockholm, Sweden, Dr. Davis said:

> World War I was fought with chemistry. World War II was fought with physics. World War III is being fought with computer science. The first battles of World War III may well have occurred when mathematical formulations of strategies and counter-strategies of realistic proportions were able to be tried out as war games on computers. With realistic wars fought in 20 minutes or 20 hours on computers, decisions to engage in such encounters (between large computer-using nations) have been nil.[7]

Congressional Data Systems Members of Congress are expected to perform in at least three capacities: as *lawmakers* deciding on important legislation, as *responsible representatives* of their states or districts, and as *public servants* who will try to assist their constituents on both important and trivial matters. To perform these roles, they need accurate, complete, and timely information. To illustrate, during the Ninetieth Congress over 29,000 bills and resolutions were introduced. Even though much substantive work is performed by the several working committees, each member of Congress must still do research, form opinions, and make decisions on dozens of bills each session. And, of course, the number of bills to be considered is increasing each year. It is not surprising, then, that representatives have voted on bills in the past without understanding all the implications of the legislation. In fact, "the problem of maintaining even the most rudimentary knowledge of the content and status of 'major' legislation continues to plague congressmen and staff aides."[8]

Control in the Federal Government

Obviously, computers are used by many federal government agencies for control purposes. The Internal Revenue Service, for example, uses multiple computers to monitor the returns of individual and corporate taxpayers. Filed reports of interest paid to individuals by organizations may be compared against interest income reported by the taxpayer. Without computers, such comparisons would probably not be possible. Computers may also be used by the IRS in randomly selecting and making preliminary audits of tax returns.

A *military application* of the use of computers for control and monitoring purposes is found in the air defense system for North America. Over a dozen computers at the nerve center of the North American Air Defense Command (located inside Cheyenne Mountain near Colorado Springs, Colorado) accept, store, and constantly update masses of data from worldwide radar installations, weather stations, and other intelligence sources. Every object produced by human beings that is in earth orbit is tracked. Radar sets scanning the Eurasian land mass feed data into the computer. If a rocket is launched, the computers are

[7]"Newsdata," *Computer Decisions,* October 1974, p. 8.

[8]Robert L. Chartrand, "Computer Support for Congress," *Journal of Systems Management,* July 1970, p. 8.

able to quickly calculate its trajectory. If an all-out nuclear strike were aimed at North America from Russian rocket sites, the warning time would be 15 to 25 minutes. (Time enough for the President to trigger a United States nuclear retaliation; but by the time United States rockets took off, few of us would be around to cheer or bewail this grim spectacle.)

Computers are also used for *environmental control* purposes. Agencies processing environmental data with the help of computers include the Air Pollution Control Office and the Water Quality Office of the Environmental Protection Agency, the National Center for Health Statistics, the U.S. Geological Survey, and the Department of Agriculture. Setting environmental quality standards is a function of several federal agencies. For example, the Federal Water Quality Act of 1965 requires the states to set acceptable quality standards on interstate streams or submit to federal agency guidelines, and the Air Pollution Control Office has issued Air Quality Criteria documents. Monitoring of environmental quality is, of course, necessary to determine appropriate standards and/or to check on whether established standards are being met. Staffed or unstaffed monitoring stations may be used to send data to centrally located computer systems. One monitoring example is the work being done by the Division of Motor Vehicle Pollution Control of the Air Pollution Control Office. Basic applications being handled by timeshared computers include calibration of emission-testing equipment, processing and storing emission data after testing, and analysis and interpretation of data for future testing and development purposes.

Computers in Federal Law Enforcement

The Federal Bureau of Investigation makes extensive use of computers. The FBI's computerized National Crime Information Center (NCIC) is an automated nationwide police information network. Online terminals installed at local police stations are connected to central police computers in the states and to the NCIC computers in Washington (the central state computers are, of course, also connected to the NCIC network). Electronic direct access to the arrest records of individual citizens is thus possible in a short period of time. Obtaining such information can help federal, state, and local law enforcement officers make decisions about arresting, searching, detaining, interrogating, and investigating those suspected of having committed crimes. The NCIC computers also store information on stolen property and wanted persons. One example of the use of the NCIC system was reported in the March 24, 1971, issue of *Computerworld.* A hitchhiker was arrested in Pineville, Kentucky, where he stopped to use the restroom at a state police post. A routine check to the NCIC quickly revealed that the hitchhiker was violating his parole in Lansing, Michigan.

In 1968, Congress passed the Omnibus Crime Control and Safe Streets Act that established the Law Enforcement Assistance Administration (LEAA) as an agency of the Department of Justice. This agency administers federal grants to state and local law enforcement organizations. Some of the LEAA grants have been used for acquisition of computers by local and state police forces.

In spite of the fact that the FBI's data bank and the state data-base systems help law enforcement agencies with fixed geographical jurisdictions cope with the activities of increasingly mobile criminals, we have already seen that many concerned citizens believe that the issues of *individual freedom* and the *right to privacy* are not being given proper consideration. For example, a few years ago LEAA launched Project SEARCH (System for Electronic Analysis and Retrieval of Criminal Histories), a $7-million research effort to produce a nationwide computer network of law enforcement agencies at the federal, state, and local levels for the purpose of providing for an interchange of criminal histories.

Understanding that such a system, if uncontrolled, could be used by police to store all types of information on all citizens, the SEARCH Project Group established a Privacy and Security Committee to recommend needed safeguards. The Committee was composed of a number of respected state law enforcement officers and administrators, including directors of important agencies in New York, Minnesota, and Connecticut.

COMPUTERS IN STATE AND LOCAL GOVERNMENTS

The 50 states, 3,000 counties, and 18,000 cities and towns in the United States all require processed data. Obviously, not all these governmental entities use computers; but in attempting to acquire better information in order to cope with growing urbanization, an increasing crime rate, larger populations, inadequate social welfare programs, etc., many state and local government units have turned to computer processing in recent years. In fact, state and local governments represent one of the fastest-growing markets for computer hardware and software. Computer installations in these sectors have more than doubled in the last four years; expansion has been particularly concentrated in the acquisition and use of online terminals, data-base systems, and direct-access storage devices.

Planning and Decision Making in State and Local Governments

The preliminary statements made earlier on planning and decision making at the federal level apply here: state, county, and city planners have often been required to function in settings where the data available for public policy making is inadequate and/or inaccurate. The hope of these administrators, however, is that new computer-based systems will provide them with higher-quality information with which to make better plans and decisions and improve operating efficiency. In the early 1970s, most states were "analyzing, defining, implementing or planning for a State Information System. These efforts range from centralization of hardware into a minimum number of installations, to genuine plans for the interchange of information among agencies."[9] Such state efforts are continuing at the present time, and many neighboring counties and cities are also

[9]Charles R. Rowan, "Information Systems Technology in State Government," *State Government,* p. 117, Spring 1971.

pooling resources to jointly acquire hardware and software for mutually beneficial planning and decision-making purposes. The following sections present a few examples of how computers are now being used for these purposes at the state and local government levels.

Legislative Data Systems A number of state legislatures—New York, Washington, Florida, Pennsylvania, Hawaii, and North Carolina, to name just a few—make effective use of computers to index, store, process, and retrieve statutory material, to draft bills, to prepare roll-call vote reports, to provide census population data for planning purposes, to address mailing labels, to monitor fiscal data, and to provide other information and services to lawmakers and their staffs. As long ago as 1965, for example, a computerized Legislative Index made it possible for Florida legislators to quickly determine the status of any piece of pending legislation in order to (1) answer an inquiry from a constituent, (2) follow the progress of their own bills and other bills that were of particular interest to them, (3) determine the actions (if any) taken by colleagues in supporting or opposing a particular bill, and (4) evaluate possible alternative plans, strategies and decisions. The Florida Legislative Index has also proved helpful to news reporters covering legislative activities.

Social Welfare Planning In social welfare agencies, as in other organizations, computer usage can be of value in administrative planning and decision making. For example, in the administration of one social welfare agency—Family Service of Metropolitan Detroit—computer-processed data have speeded up administrative analysis and improved program planning. Caseloads of social workers, median income of the families served, size and composition of families (presence of young children, aged dependents, etc.), family stress caused by such factors as separations, divorces, and unemployment—all this information is used by Detroit administrators to analyze the effects of possible changes in agency policies and services. Better internal information on existing welfare cases and caseloads, combined with external information on population growth and migration, can be used to plan future agency needs far enough in advance to prevent unexpected crises from developing. Also, "administrators of all social welfare agencies in a community, cooperating in the utilization of computer services, could determine areas of essential services and unnecessary duplication of effort."[10]

Urban Planning It is no secret that city planners are currently facing an explosion of urban problems. Traffic congestion, pollution of air and water, tensions within and between racial, ethnic, and economic groups, deteriorating public housing, services, and facilities—all these problems (and others) are facing many cities. Those planners who would try to alleviate such problems

[10]Theron K. Fuller, "Computer Utility in Social Work," *Social Casework,* December 1970, p. 607.

need improved information systems that will give them accurate, timely, and relevant information.

Attempts have been made to develop more comprehensive city-level information systems that would provide urban planners with this quality information. For example, the Urban Information Systems Inter-Agency Committee (USAC) was established in 1969 as a federal government entity jointly sponsored and funded by several departments and offices in the executive branch. Six cities were selected by USAC to develop pilot computerized information systems on a test basis and in such a way that the systems could be used by other cities. Two of the six cities, Charlotte, North Carolina, and Wichita Falls, Texas, were selected to do development work on fully integrated systems that would eventually incorporate public finance, public safety, human resource development, and physical and economic development subsystems.

Although the USAC efforts have met with varying degrees of success, less ambitious computer applications have been assisting urban planners for some time. *Traffic congestion* problems have been tackled by planners using computers to simulate traffic flow patterns. Variables such as the expected distribution of trips, the type of travel modes used, and the routes traveled are used to estimate the flow of persons and vehicles on transit facilities and roads. (The travel mode used and the route selected by the simulated traveler may, in turn, depend on such variables as travel time, cost, convenience, etc.) Simulation is used to plan proposed roads and to use existing roads in the most efficient way. Various alternative transportation systems can be evaluated through computer simulation. In evaluating alternative traffic systems, however, the planner must take into consideration the interactions which exist between transportation systems and other aspects of urban life. All too often in the past, traffic planners have begun road construction without considering recreational, housing, and other alternative land-use needs.

The need to consider alternative uses of land as a vital input of detailed traffic models has, in fact, resulted in the development of local and regional *land-use models.* Included in land-use simulation equations are future expectations as to population, employment, number of households, income, and distribution of available land for commercial and residential purposes. Given alternative zoning and economic development plans and different assumed growth rates, the land-use model may provide planners with data about expected income, employment, and population distributions. These data, in turn, can be used as input into traffic planning simulations. In the Washington metropolitan area, a computer land-use data system is used for planning purposes. This system receives data from continuously updated files and is of value to satellite governments as well as to Washington planners.

Control in State and Local Governments

From monitoring a city's power generating station to controlling a county sewage treatment plant, and from controlling traffic signals to monitoring statewide water projects, computers are being used to supervise countless activities at the state, county, and local levels. Such applications as tax collection and revenue control and control of inventories of government-owned property are quite common. But perhaps some of the most interesting applications are those found in the areas of *conservation* and *environmental control.*

California's multimillion-dollar State Water Project, for example, is designed to *conserve* water by moving it from surplus areas in northern California to needy areas in the south and west. Water is moved hundreds of miles through a network of canals, tunnels, gates, pipelines, pumping stations, and power plants. All these facilities are monitored and controlled by computers located at five remote control centers. In the event of emergency, a control center will quickly shut down the affected part of the system—e.g., should a canal be broken by an earthquake, check gates in the affected section would be closed immediately to prevent serious loss of water.

States and cities are also using computers to monitor, evaluate, and control the levels of *water and air pollution.* The Empire State System of New York collects water and air data from water and air monitoring stations located at critical sites around the state. Data from the stations are automatically forwarded to a central computer (each air monitoring station reports every 15 minutes, and each water station transmits once every hour). Upon receiving transmitted data, the computer edits the message, sends any necessary operating instructions to the station, compares edited information to acceptable environmental standards, and, if standards are not met, sends an appropriate alarm to either the Air Resources or Pure Waters Division of the Department of Environmental Conservation. Corrective action may then be taken. Once each day a complete system report is prepared.

COMPUTERS, LAWYERS, AND THE COURTS

In this section we will first consider the impact of computer usage on lawyers and on the techniques used by lawyers in preparing their cases. We will then briefly examine the possible influence of computers on court administration.

Computers and Lawyers

Although most law firms and lawyers have not yet shown much interest in computers, this neglect is likely to change. *One reason* is that others are using computers more, and lawyers will therefore encounter more legal problems in the future that are influenced by the use of computers. Clients and opponents will be using computers to process records, and these records may be entered as evidence in court cases. How reliable are they? Could they have been manipulated by a program patch to present an incorrect procedure? Lawyers may have to call computer experts to testify to the validity of computer-produced evidence in the future, just as they have had to use expert testimony from medical doctors and engineers in the past. And lawyers will thus be required to learn enough about computers to communicate with the experts testifying for or against their clients. As one law professor has advised other lawyers: "The expert on computer-controlled production comes in, and you ask him, 'How did the program and the machine work to produce this result?' If all he will say is 'This program califlams the whingdrop and reticulates the residual glob,' it is perfectly clear that you are going to have to study up somewhat, in order to make up your mind about what went on."[11]

Another reason that lawyers may show greater future interest in computers is that more electronic systems are being developed for use inside the legal profession. Keeping track of a lawyer's time for billing purposes; maintaining the accounting records of a law firm; performing estate planning computations; searching for, retrieving, and displaying information on legal precedents from legal data banks—applications such as these can all be performed from a timesharing terminal in a law office.

There are several organizations that offer a *legal information retrieval service* for subscribers. Data Corporation of Dayton, Ohio, for example, has entered into a retrieval system the millions of words representing the entire body of Ohio case law since 1910. The system supplies document, page, and line numbers in response to key words entered by users. Computerized legal search systems are also in use in many other states, including New York, New Jersey, Iowa, Kansas, Hawaii, Pennsylvania, and Massachusetts. On a broader scale, Law Research Service, Inc., a New York organization, has developed an international service designed to give lawyers instant referrals to legal precedents that relate to the specific cases they are preparing. Lawyers subscribing to the service are equipped with an online terminal and several hundred legal volumes that cover major legal areas from criminal law to labor relations at both state and federal government levels. The lawyers type in key words that describe important facts in the cases they are preparing, the central computer searches its online file for applicable precedents, and the lawyers receive information in the form of volume and page numbers of recent similar cases. The service can also be used when the lawyers are away from their offices. They could, for example, use a courthouse telephone to contact one of the 150 branches located in 39 states and Canada for a rapid listing of legal citations.

Before concluding this section, mention should also be made of the use of computers by the Senate committee lawyers who investigated the Watergate crimes. An online computer was used to allow investigators to make immediate comparisons of the often conflicting testimony given by different witnesses.

Computers and the Courts

Computers may prove to be very useful in court administration. The current backlog of pending cases in many of the nation's courts is thwarting justice and is, in fact, creating injustices. (A guilty person may remain unpunished because witnesses have forgotten details, moved away, or even died during the long delay period, and an innocent person accused of a crime who does not have the ability to raise bail may be kept in jail for many months before trial.)

In Philadelphia, where the case load has nearly doubled in the last 8 years, a

[11]Vaughn C. Ball, "The Impact of Data-processing Technology on the Legal Profession," *Computers and Automation,* April 1968, p. 44.

computer system is being used for court administration. Since it went into operation, the system has helped to significantly reduce the backlog of criminal and civil cases. Reports generated by the computer on a daily or weekly basis include trial calendars, defendant and witness subpoenas, notices to the prisoner facility 23 miles away to bring defendants to court, and details of courtroom availability. In civil cases, when "certificates of readiness" (stating that the case is ready for trial) are filed by both parties, the information is stored in the system. A daily trial listing is prepared and published in a Philadelphia legal newspaper each morning. Lawyers for the top 20 cases on the daily list must appear in a court call room. Delays due to attorney conflicts have been significantly reduced. Courts in Jackson County (Kansas City), Missouri, and Los Angeles County are among those that use computers for administrative purposes.

Another way that computers can increase court efficiency is by helping to improve *jury selection* procedures. Once a month in the District of Columbia, approximately 10,000 residents are qualified for jury duty by a computer. These citizens then become anonymous six-digit numbers stored in the computer at Superior Court. The tasks of selecting jurors, preparing summonses, and producing the related reports required by the courts are performed by the computer. From the time one is qualified for jury duty until one's name is printed on a summons, one remains a number in storage. About 1,000 of the 10,000 qualified citizens will be selected as jurors to try the monthly civil and criminal cases that come before the Washington courts.

COMPUTERS IN MEDICAL PLANNING AND DECISION MAKING

Applications of computers which have medical planning and decision-making implications include (1) *computer-assisted diagnosis and research,* (2) *medical history preparation and retrival,* (3) *study of drug side effects,* (4) *physiological simulations,* and (5) *menu planning.*

Computer-Assisted Diagnosis and Research

Some physicians are now using the computer as a *diagnostic tool* in hospitals and clinics. At a number of "multiphasic" screening centers around the country, for example, patients are given physical examinations consisting of a series of basic tests. An electrocardiogram, chest x-ray, and urine test, along with measurements of blood pressure, lung function, vision, hearing, intraocular pressure (a test for glaucoma), height, and weight, are among the items included in the examination. Data from the tests may be fed into the computer in a separate operation, or the testing equipment may be linked directly to the computer for an automatic transfer of results. Once the data are received, the computer can compare test measurements against the standards established in the program. Within a few minutes after the examination procedures are completed, the computer output is ready. The test results are reported, and if they fall outside prescribed limits, procedures that should be repeated and/or additional tests that should be conducted may be indicated. The computer may also be programmed to suggest tentative diagnoses to explain abnormal test results. The patient's physician, of course, is responsible for the final diagnosis.

One advantage of *computer-assisted physical examinations* is that they free doctors from routine testing procedures, conserve their time, and enable them to give more attention to patient diagnosis and treatment. Physicians in northern Florida are using a health center computer at the University of Florida for patient testing; the Kaiser Foundation Hospital in Oakland, California, is processing about 4,000 people per month through its 19-step physical examination; and Good Samaritan Hospital in Cincinnati has a successful multiphasic testing program.

Statistical techniques can also be used for diagnostic purposes. Upon receiving a listing of symptoms and findings from a doctor, the computer can check and compare these symptoms against a description of diseases that are known to cause them. The computer may be programmed to supply the doctor with a listing of the known diseases, the statistical probability of each disease being the cause of the reported symptoms, a listing of medical references to check, and other possible variables to look for before arriving at a diagnosis. By correlating symptoms against diseases, a computer might also be able to produce statistics that would reveal hitherto unsuspected relationships.

Another similar diagnostic approach involves the use of the *clinical algorithm.* The clinical algorithm, or *protocol,* is a step-by-step set of instructions to guide paramedical workers in the management of common complaints. Computers are not necessarily required to process the instructions, but they can be used to (1) analyze symptoms, (2) branch to various parts of the algorithm when certain symptoms or data items are present or absent, and (3) determine if specific therapy should be employed, if additional information should be collected, or if the case should be referred to an M.D. Of course, some doctors may not be happy about the fact that computers are being programmed and protocols are being used in ways that permit trained paramedical personnel to perform some of the diagnostic tasks and make some of the therapeutic decisions that were once handled exclusively by physicians. They may feel that "little by little, the specialness of the doctor is stripped away: his interviewing technique can be replaced by a branching electronic sequence, his diagnostic acumen is nothing more than a collection of thresholds and logic trees, his therapeutic decisions simply programmed probabilities."[12]

Computers are also being used for such diagnostic purposes as (1) displaying heart function on a CRT from motion-picture x-rays and calculating the volume and width of the patient's left ventricle—the heart's pump—and (2) analyzing the measurement of radioactive isotopes in any given portion of the body in order to detect the possible presence of a malignant growth (most malignant nodules in the thyroid gland, for example, do not absorb the radioactive iodine given to the patient, so that the absence of radioactive material would be considered suspicious).

[12]Jerry Avorn, M.D., "The Future of Doctoring," *Atlantic,* November 1974, p. 77.

Medical History Preparation and Retrieval

In developing a record of a patient's medical history, a usual practice is for the doctor (or nurse) to ask the patient a series of questions about past illnesses or health problems. In areas where heredity may be a factor, the patient is also asked questions about the health of blood relatives. This history taking is a time-consuming aspect of the patient-physician relationship. Computers can be used to reduce the time involved and to tailor the questions to the patient's situation.

At the Mayo Clinic in Minnesota, Dr. John Mayne has developed a system that displays medical history questions and multiple-response choices on the screen of a CRT terminal. The patient answers the questions by pointing to the appropriate response with a light pen—a device attached to the terminal that permits the computer to detect the response selected. Medidata Sciences, Inc., in Massachusetts, also uses an online visual display device to project questions for patient response. The patient answers by pressing one of the five buttons opposite the most appropriate answer to the question. The computer is programmed to follow certain question paths depending on the answers received. For example, if the question is "Do you smoke?" and the answer is yes, then several additional questions will be asked; if the answer is no, these questions will be omitted. After the patient has answered all relevant questions, the medical history can be printed out for the doctor's use, or it may be stored on magnetizable or microfilm media.

Once the patient's history and medical records are available in machine-accessible form, they may be retrieved by the physician as necessary for review and updating. Although medical records of most people are currently kept and manually maintained in file cabinets in a doctor's office, it is possible that in the future this record-keeping function will increasingly be handled by a computer data bank. When a patient moves (or changes doctors), personal health records may be transferred to a new data bank, alleviating the need for completing a new medical history. And, since the patient is often a poor transmitter of personal health data, the new doctor would probably have a more complete and accurate record available through a terminal than would otherwise be possible. Better information about patients should prove valuable in preventing potential health problems and diagnosing illnesses.

One example of a computer-maintained medical data bank is found in New York City. Records of about 20,000 children from low-income families are kept up to date by a computer at New York University. Data pertaining to the children can be retrieved by physicians using terminals located at Bellevue Hospital.

Study of Drug Side Effects

Even though a drug may be extensively tested prior to being placed on the market, it is possible that undetected side effects can occur. Combining the new drug with other medications and administering the drug to patients with illnesses or in conditions not encountered during the testing period can result in the appearance of side effects that were previously unsuspected. A computer system can be used to gather data on the experiences of many physicians with a particular drug over time. Shared drug experiences should give faster indications of the efficacy of a particular product and the possibility that the product was responsible for unfortunate results. Computer analyses could be made to reveal a relationship between the use of a drug and reported undesirable consequences. Knowledge of such a relationship would certainly be valuable to doctors in their planning and decision making. Perhaps the magnitude of a tragedy such as that which occurred a few years ago when a number of babies were born deformed because their mothers were given thalidomide during pregnancy could be reduced by the use of a data bank of shared drug experiences.

Physiological Simulations

Imagine a patient who suffers nausea, blockage of the bronchial tubes, and heart attacks several times daily. Such a "patient" is Sim One, a lifelike computer-controlled mannequin used by resident doctors at the University of Southern California to develop their skills in anesthesiology. Sim One has a heartbeat, pulse, blood pressure, and a breathing action; its eyes open and close and the pupils dilate and constrict; its jaw opens and closes; and its muscles twitch and flutter. These computer-controlled human reactions are used to simulate various conditions and emergencies that the student doctors may expect to encounter with real patients. An incorrect decision during a simulation can lead to the death of poor Sim One. If a student makes a mistake, the computer may flash a warning light. At the end of a training session, the computer prepares a printed critique of the student's efforts. The value of computer simulation in sharpening the skills and decision-making abilities of doctors has been demonstrated at USC.

Other physiological simulation systems include the MUMPS system at Massachusetts General Hospital and the system at the Royal College of Physicians and Surgeons of Canada. Each of these systems supplies student doctors with the symptoms of patients admitted to a hypothetical emergency ward. The student must make quick decisions and the computer responds as the patient would, and/or it reports the results of lab tests ordered by the student.

Menu Planning

Hospital dietitians are using computers to plan patient meals. At Georgia's Central State Hospital, for example, a computer-assisted menu-planning system is in operation. Menu items are now repeated less often, thereby giving patients greater variety in the foods they receive. The computer analyzes nutrient values of foods, prepares menus for 90-day time periods, and supplies day-by-day food requirements to purchasers in advance of needs (thus permitting the more efficient shopping that has helped cut food costs by 5 percent). Dietitians are able to modify the 90-day menu plan to take advantage of favorable food-buying opportunities. A nutritional analysis is run at the end of a 90-day period to verify that all meals met nutritional specifications and to provide information that could lead to better future planning.

HEALTH CONTROL

Control of (1) *the physiological status of patients,* (2) *blood bank inventories,* (3) *the dispensing of drugs in hospitals,* and (4) *laboratory tests* are among the many applications of computers in medicine.

Physiological Monitoring

Several real time computer systems are being used for patient monitoring. For example, patients who are critically ill, those that have just had major surgery, and those who have recently suffered heart attacks can be connected to computer-monitored sensing devices capable of immediately detecting dangerously abnormal conditions. If necessary, the system would, of course, flash a warning signal to doctors and nurses. Such body functions as heartbeat, blood pressure, respiratory rate, and temperature may be monitored. At the Pacific Medical Center in San Francisco, the body functions of patients in the cardiopulmonary intensive care unit are *continuously* checked; at Los Angeles County Hospital, patients suffering from circulatory shock are monitored about once every 5 minutes.

Blood Bank Inventory Control

A blood bank must meet the requests made upon it for blood, but it must also minimize waste of this very important medical resource. Demands for whole blood are unpredictable, but it cannot be stockpiled in large quantities because of a 21-day shelf life. Supplies of blood received from donors are also unpredictable. The blood type demanded by patients and supplied by donors is subject to variation. Determining proper inventories of blood to maintain at the bank and at hospitals is difficult, as is determining the needed ratio of whole blood to blood components. At the Milwaukee Blood Center, an average of 175 units per day are collected, a daily inventory of 1,500 units of whole blood and blood components is maintained, and about 1,000 clerical transactions are performed at the bank each day—e.g., adding to and subtracting from the inventory, shipping blood to hospitals, converting whole blood into blood components, etc. A computer system may be used (1) to handle these transactions, (2) to help control blood management, and (3) to speed the right blood to the right person at the right time.

Hospital Drug Control

Since the creation in 1971 of the Federal Bureau of Narcotics and Dangerous Drugs, hospitals have been required to maintain records on more than 300 drugs in order to comply with tougher federal drug-control laws. (This control requirement tripled the number of drugs on which records had to be kept.) Because hopsital personnel may dispense thousands of doses of medication to patients each day, the task of maintaining pharmacy records is substantial. Furthermore, time spent by nurses in filling out forms is time taken away from that which they can spend treating patients. Seven hospitals of the Franciscan Sisters of the Poor located in Ohio, Kentucky, and Kansas have joined together to develop a drug-reporting system to provide better control over the narcotic items dispensed. Each hospital has a data station linked directly to the central computer in Cincinnati. All information about patient medication is relayed to the computer for processing. Summary reports, including those required to comply with narcotic control laws, are prepared by the computer and sent back to the participating hospital. This system has reduced the paperwork load on nurses and has given better control information to local pharmacies. Other hospitals—e.g., Cleveland Metropolitan General Hospital—make use of computer programs that can signal to pharmacists whether or not newly prescribed drugs will be likely to react adversely with other medications the patient may be receiving, or if the new drugs are likely to cause an allergic reaction. If not challenged by the system, the prescription is filled and the computer prints out the label to be affixed to it.

Control of Laboratory Tests

Some of the more successful applications of computers in hospitals are found in the laboratory. Computer processing of data related to test ordering, specimen identification, and test result reporting is now common. (As we saw earlier in the chapter, multiphasic screening centers employ computers to control test procedures and report results.) From the doctor's initial request for a test to the printing of test results, a computer may be used to monitor each step in the process. Automated testing may lead to greater accuracy and faster reporting of findings. Also, the information reported may be in a more useful format—e.g., abnormal results may be emphasized for special attention and compared with normally expected readings for those in the patient's age and sex category.

HOSPITAL INFORMATION SYSTEMS

What is a hospital information system (HIS)? There seems to be no single definition that authorities in medicine, hospital administration, and information processing can agree upon. To some the words imply a *total information system* encompassing the entire informational needs of all hospital personnel; to others, they refer only to computer-based billing and accounting operations associated with hospital administration; and to still others a HIS is defined to be merely all the applications that are being processed on the computer at their particular hospital. For our purposes, a HIS may be defined as the processing procedures developed in a hospital and integrated as necessary for the purpose of providing physicians and hospital personnel with timely and effective information.

The extent to which systems integration is needed varies, of course, from one hospital to another. Some of the elements that have been included in the computer-based information systems of hospitals may be found in the following list. (Few, if any, hospitals have extensive applications in *all* these areas.)

1 *Clerical and accounting elements.* As noted at the beginning of the chapter, computers were first introduced into hospitals to perform accounting and record-keeping operations. Accumulating patient charges, keeping track of health insurance coverages, ordering and then controlling supplies and medicines, preparing patient bills, accounting and paying for services and supplies purchased, preparing personnel payrolls—these are but a few of the business-type applications that a hospital must process. And equipment is now available to support comprehensive financial management systems for smaller hospitals.

2 *Information retrieval elements.* Discussions of some information retrieval applications have been presented in earlier pages.

3 *Scheduling elements.* Computers are being used to schedule (*a*) appointments of patients in outpatient clinics, (*b*) the performance of tasks by service departments, and (*c*) the use of specialized hospital facilities and equipment.

4 *Medical planning, research, and control elements.* Many of these computer applications have been described in earlier pages. Control of laboratory tests represents the most popular current type of computer application in the planning, research, and control category.

5 *Peer review elements.* Federal government regulations that went into effect early in 1975 created Professional Standards Review organizations (PSRO) at the local levels to conduct peer reviews—i.e., to review such things as admissions (is the patient in the right place to receive the needed care?), bed utilization (did the patient spend an appropriate time in the hospital?), and care (did the patient get tests that were not needed, or was there a failure to administer needed tests?). The creation of PSROs has forced hospitals to use computers to provide the peer review data, just as the passage of Medicare legislation forced most hospitals to use computers or computer services for financial management processing.

PLANNING AND DECISION MAKING IN EDUCATION

Curriculum Planning

Research is being conducted into ways of using computers for curriculum planning. It is reasoned that if college students, for example, are given aptitude, interest, and achievement tests when they enter a school, it should then be possible to use this information to develop two- to four-year plans for the courses and number of sections needed to satisfy student goals. (Such plans, of course, would have a direct bearing on staffing needs and on the physical facilities required.) Researchers would, in effect, produce a plan that would be based on explicitly set and objectively measured educational goals of students. A thorough analysis of the concepts and tasks that would have to be measured in order to satisfy those goals would be required, and students would be expected to follow a specified educational path.

Although impressive efforts have been made by researchers in the curriculum planning area, their progress thus far has not been great. It is not surprising that this is the case. After all, some fields of study may not lend themselves to neatly programmed paths leading to clearly specified goals; some students may stray from the "ideal" path as they realize that their interests have changed; and a great deal more must be discovered about learning processes before effective predetermined curriculum plans and controls will be accepted by most educators.

Planning for Individual Instruction

Operating on the reasonable assumptions that (1) individual differences exist between students (interests, goals, learning abilities, etc.) and (2) programs tailored to the needs of individuals are educationally more effective than those aimed at "average" groups of students, some educational institutions are seeking to plan and implement more individualized programs of instruction. But as one educational researcher writes:

> Attempts at individualization in conventional classroom environments by the most imaginative of teachers is likely to lead to at best modest success and at worst nervous frustration. The major difficulty in such an undertaking . . . is the management of instruction for large numbers of students with widely varying competencies and needs.[13]

The computer is a tool that may assist teachers in managing individual instruction programs. *Computer-managed instruction* (CMI) is a name sometimes given to this use of the machines. A properly programmed computer may help teachers to (1) manage a student's schedule of activities as she progresses through a program of instruction, (2) periodically test the student's mastery of the material presented, and (3) determine an appropriate tutoring plan for students who are having difficulty with some phase of the program. Educational research centers at such schools as the University of Pittsburgh and Florida State University are working on CMI projects. At one elementary school participating in a University of Pittsburgh project, a computer is being used to make required day-to-day instructional plans and decisions. In the science curriculum, for example, a student may specify a particular subject he or she wishes to study. The computer may then be used to evaluate the student's background in order to determine any needed prerequisite lessons prior to beginning the study of the specified topic.

There have been some charges that using computers in the educational process will "dehumanize" instruction and make robots of students. There might be some validity to these charges if all students were required to spend the day in front of a computer terminal going through the same exercises and if the only or main source of curriculum content consisted of what a few educational programmers selected to put into the machines. Advocates of CMI maintain, however, that the computer is simply a supporting tool that relieves teachers of unnecessary tasks and helps them to individualize instruction. They point out that students can progress through the curriculum materials at their own pace and can skip certain elements if their educational backgrounds make this possible. How, they argue, can a more flexible curriculum be objectionable? Besides, they contend, most students would prefer attention from a machine to neglect from an overworked teacher. And how many times, they ask, have you, as a student, really been helped in a remedial or tutorial way by overworked

[13]Richard L. Ferguson, "Computer Assistance for Individualizing Instruction," *Computers and Automation,* March 1970, p. 27.

teachers? Skeptics about the use of computers in the classroom maintain, however, that the high cost of preparing computer-based instructional programs is bound to result in the use of prepared materials for much longer periods of time and at numerous schools. Thus, they maintain, materials are more likely to become obsolete, curriculum standardization is probably inevitable, and the autonomy of local schools will suffer. These arguments serve at least to illustrate one noncontroversial point: In education, as in other fields, computer usage may threaten to sweep aside current practices, may introduce new problems, and may create resistance to change.

Class Scheduling

Computers are speeding up the scheduling of classes every term in several schools. Improved class scheduling procedures may make it possible for school administrators to make better plans and decisions about the use of such resources as teachers, textbooks, and classroom space. Purdue University was one of the first institutions to experiment with using computers to fit thousands of students into hundreds of classes. The Purdue system will now handle "the scheduling of over 18,000 students in less than 6 hours of computer time and produce an assortment of classlists, enrollment reports, and other by-products. Now in an experimental state at Purdue is the computerized optimum scheduling of classes."[14]

CONTROL IN EDUCATION

Two control applications of computers in education are found in the areas of *testing* and *error analysis*.

Probably the most common *testing* application is the use of computers to score objective tests that students have answered on sheets which they mark with a special pencil. Computed measures such as arithmetic means and standard deviations can be used by teachers to compare class performance against norms or standards—a necessary step in educational control. In another area of testing—interactive computer-assisted testing—student progress can be quickly determined, students can get immediate feedback of their successes and mistakes, instructors can be relieved from having to grade the tests, and control information can be supplied to teachers, indicating activities where student performance is not up to expectations. To illustrate, at Dartmouth College randomized vocabulary tests in Latin may be taken by students. Sitting at an online terminal, students select the Latin lesson or lessons they wish to be checked on. The computer program may randomly select Latin words from the indicated lesson and the students must then respond with the English meanings. If the students miss on the first try, they are given one more chance before the

[14]Eric Weiss, ed., *Computer Usage/Applications,* McGraw-Hill Book Company, New York, 1970, pp. 224–225. See chap. 13, "Scheduling Classes for High Schools and Colleges," for a detailed technical discussion of computer scheduling.

correct response is supplied; if they have no idea what the correct response should be, they can type a question mark and the proper word will be presented. Of course, the computer is keeping track of the students' success (or lack of success) during the exercise. Because the Latin words are selected randomly from a lesson, it is not likely that students would ever get the same list of words twice.

The stored results of computer-assisted testing may also be used for error-analysis purposes. The types of errors being made by students during testing can be analyzed, and suggestions for eliminating detected deficiencies may be supplied to the student and/or to the teacher at the end of the session. Obviously, suggestions for improvement must take into account the resources of printed materials, audiovisual equipment, and computer hardware/software that are available in the school system.

COMPUTER-ASSISTED INSTRUCTION

What is *computer-assisted instruction* (CAI)? As is so often the case when coming to grips with computer-related terminology, one can find different definitions advanced by different authorities. In some definitions, the distinction between computer-managed instruction and CAI becomes blurred. In this text we refer to the former (CMI) as primarily an exchange of information between *teachers* and computers, while the latter phrase (CAI) is used to refer to situations where *students* and computers interact and where instruction takes place. As we saw earlier in the chapter, a CMI program may indicate to a teacher that a child needs remedial tutoring, and this makeup work may be completed using CAI, but the two phrases should not be confused. In short, then, we are using CAI to refer to a learning situation in which the student interacts with (and is guided by) a computer through a course of study aimed at achieving certain instructional goals.

In a typical CAI setting, the student sits at an online device (usually either a typewriter terminal or a visual display) and communicates with the program in the CPU. Interaction may take place in the following way: (1) the computer presents instructional information and questions; (2) the student studies the information or instructions presented, answers the questions, and, perhaps, asks questions of his own; and (3) the computer then accepts, analyzes, and provides immediate feedback to the student's responses, and it maintains records of his performance for evaluation purposes. Thus far, CAI development efforts have been concentrated in three areas—the *drill-and-practice, tutorial,* and *dialogue* areas.

COMPUTERS AND THE HUMANITIES

Art Authenticity

At New York's Metropolitan Museum of Art, Carl Dauterman, Associate Curator of Western European Decorative Arts, is using a computer to study the sets of coded marks found on Sèvres porcelain—an eighteenth-century French porcelain that is commonly forged. Pieces of genuine porcelain have coded sets of painted and incised marks that identify individual workers, dates, type of paste, etc. There can be 10 different painted and incised marks on a single piece of porcelain. The computer is used to compare and cross-correlate the combinations of painted and incised marks found on genuine articles. Thus, the computer correlations can serve as a warning flag against forged pieces by revealing how normal patterns of agreement among various markings are violated. One printout, for example, revealed 13 pieces of porcelain with suspicious markings.[15]

Authorship Identification

The Federalist Papers consist of 77 essays written to persuade New York citizens to ratify the United States Constitution. Although published anonymously, it is generally agreed that John Jay wrote 5 of the essays, Alexander Hamilton wrote 43, James Madison wrote 14, and Hamilton and Madison collaborated on 3. A quick tally (without a computer) tells us that the authorship of 12 essays has not been accounted for. There is no dispute that the author of each of the remaining essays was either Madison or Hamilton. In spite of the fact that after Hamilton's death Madison claimed to have written the 12 papers, scholars for years have been debating the validity of this claim. Since the writing styles of Hamilton and Madison were quite similar, it appeared that the issue would remain unresolved. However, Frederick Mosteller of Harvard and David Wallace of the University of Chicago have used a computer to determine that Madison was probably, as he claimed, the author of all 12 disputed essays. How was this done? Thank you for asking. The papers known to be written by Madison and Hamilton were first analyzed for stylistic differences. Statistical concepts were then employed to produce a test that would discriminate correctly between the writings of the two authors in all cases. (The test resulted in positive values being computed when Madison was known to be the author, while negative values resulted when Hamilton's papers were analyzed.) Since counts and calculations involving 100,000 words were involved, the study would have been virtually impossible without the use of a computer.

Computers have also been used in studies attempting to identify the authors of portions of the Old Testament of the Bible. The authorship of the Book of Isaiah, for example, has vexed scholars for centuries. The first 12 chapters are generally attributed to Isaiah; the authorship of the remaining 54 chapters is disputed. On the one hand, there are those scholars who believe that Isaiah wrote the entire work; on the other hand, there are many more who contend that after the first 12 chapters the book was written by a varying number (from two to four) of other anonymous prophets. In an attempt to shed some light on this emotionally charged controversy (disputants have long ago ceased to be on speaking terms), Y. T. Radday, Lecturer in Charge of Hebrew Studies at the

[15]For more details on this application, see *Computers and Their Potential Applications in Museums,* The Metropolitan Museum of Art, New York, 1968, pp. 177–194; also see "The Computer and the Art Historian," *Data Systems,* April 1969, pp. 26–28ff.

Israel Institute of Technology, has employed a computer in his authorship study. Although Radday was convinced at the beginning of his analysis that Isaiah had written the entire book, his final conclusion was that multiple authors were involved. The probability that the author of Chapters 1 to 35 wrote Chapters 40 to 66 was computed to be only 1/100,000.[16]

Literary Analysis

In addition to possibly identifying the author(s) of controversial literary works, computers may also be used for other language and literary analysis purposes. For example, there is sometimes a dispute over *when* a known author wrote a particular work. In one such case, Ernest Hemingway wrote to a journalist in 1951 that he was working on the story that was subsequently published in 1952 as *The Old Man and the Sea.* But Darrell Mansell, a Dartmouth English professor, was "convinced that Hemingway wrote the novel much earlier, in 1935 or 1936, put it away, then dusted it off in 1951 and claimed to be in the process of writing it." To test his hypothesis, Mansell used statistical techniques to compare passages from *The Old Man and the Sea* against four other Hemingway works whose dates of composition are fairly certain. The conclusion of this study supported the hypothesis: the resemblance between *The Old Man and the Sea* and a work that was written in 1936 was much greater than the resemblance between other works written at other times.

Language Translation

In 1954, a computer with a stored vocabulary totaling 250 words and six rules for determining word relationships in sentences was programmed to translate a few Russian sentences into English. This small demonstration program was widely publicized, and it was then commonly predicted that computers would be used extensively in the future to translate documents from one natural language into another. The reasoning was that since computers could hold a large number of, say, Russian-English synonyms in storage, and since grammar rules for the two languages could probably be programmed, there should be a substantial amount of machine translation in the future.

Relative to 1954, it is now "the future." Are computers being extensively used for language translation today? The answer is no. After about 20 years of effort, researchers have yet to achieve substantial progress. Late in 1970, Edmund Berkeley wrote that

> a definitive report by a committee of the National Research Council headed by John R. Pierce showed that after a very large investment in effort and money, the amount of progress had been very small, the demand for such translation was very low, the supply of human interpreters and translators was much more than adequate, and the surge of follow-the-crowd attention in this field was quite unjustified.[17]

[16]For further information on this interesting study, see Yehuda T. Radday, "Isaiah and the Computer: A Preliminary Report," *Computers and the Humanities,* vol. 5, 1970, pp. 64–73.

[17]Edmund C. Berkeley, "Starting before the Race Begins," *Computers and Automation,* December 1970, p. 6.

Why the lack of success? There are several reasons, but we need mention only two here. *First,* grammarians have not been very successful in determining all the appropriate rules of grammar for a specific natural language. And *second,* a good translation requires that the meanings of words (semantics) in a particular context be taken into consideration in making translation decisions.

Concordance Preparation

A concordance is an alphabetical listing of the principal words in one or more literary works with reference to the passages in which they occur. Computers have been widely used in the preparation of concordances and indexes. Concordance preparation, in fact, represents the greatest single use of computers in the field of literary scholarship.

There is, of course, nothing new about the preparation of concordances. Alexander Cruden, an Englishman, produced a concordance to the Bible in 1737 (after which he was confined in a madhouse for 10 weeks before he escaped); F. S. Ellis published a concordance to the poems of Shelley in 1892 after 6 years of work; and Lane Cooper, a Cornell University professor, published a concordance to the works of Wordsworth in 1911.

COMPUTERS IN THE FINE ARTS

The following eloquent comment on the importance of art is found in a computer publication:

> When human beings approach the meaning of art, when they attempt to define it in words, they must come near to the meaning of life and pull at the strings of philosophy. . . . Art is important to society because man's life should have meaning, not to someone else, but to himself. Individual men without meaning in their lives cannot produce a society or a civilization with meaning. Art is . . . important to man . . . because without art he cannot survive as a human being. Art is man's outward expression and impression and integration of himself with his universe.[18]

How, then, in a field that appeals to individual imagination and personal feelings, can there be a place for an "unfeeling" computer? To one group of artists, the answer is that there can be *no* place for an analytical machine in the realm of art; to another group, the answer is that computers can be used to *analyze existing art;* and to a third group, computers can be used to *help create meaningful new art.*[19]

Michael Noll has programmed a computer to generate *drawings* in the style of the Dutch painter Piet Mondrian. Mondrian's 1917 painting entitled

[18]C. B. S. Grant, "Computers Put Traditional Creative Arts Education on Verge of Collapse," *Data Processing Magazine,* October 1969, pp. 60–61.

[19]The third group would not necessarily disagree with the second. As might be expected, however, there is disagreement among artists about the computer's role in art. At an American Musicological Society national meeting in 1967, for example, there was a stormy session resulting in a widening gulf between scholars in the noncomputer group and those who have adopted the computer as a tool.

"Composition with Lines" consists of a large number of vertical and horizontal bars of varying length arranged in a more or less orderly manner. Noll's computer-produced drawing arranged similar bars in a random fashion. When 100 people were asked to compare copies of the Mondrian and the computer pictures and decide (1) which was artistically better and (2) which was produced by a machine, the results were interesting. Only 28 percent were able to correctly identify the Mondrian picture, and 59 percent preferred the computer picture.[20] Noll's use of computers has gone beyond imitation. Interesting works have been produced by specifying some form of order in the program and by then allowing the computer to incorporate random patterns. Thus the computer "creates" pictures which may amaze the artist programmer. Art students at the University of New Mexico are encouraged to take programming and computer graphics courses. Professor Charles Mattox believes that preparing a program helps students understand some of the factors involved in artistic creation because "they must concentrate on the form and other characteristics of the design, rather than on how well the design is drawn."[21]

COMPUTERS AND MUSEUMS

Museum personnel have been interested in using computers for *three principal purposes:* (1) to maintain regional or national data banks for storing and retrieving information of interest to participants, (2) to catalog and control the inventory of items in the collection of a large museum, and (3) to support their own particular research projects whenever appropriate. (We have already seen an example of this third purpose—the study of Sèvres porcelain—so we will not discuss this purpose further in the following paragraphs.) The first two purposes, of course, are closely related in that both are concerned with automated retrieval of information about museum holdings.

To achieve the *first* purpose listed above, several museum information systems have been developed. Over 20 art museums in New York, Washington, D.C., and other cities, for example, have joined together to form an information retrieval system known as the Museum Computer Network. And at the University of Oklahoma, a system has information stored on the holdings of over 30 museums in Oklahoma and Missouri. To avoid a proliferation of small museum networks, each of which would probably be unable to conveniently exchange data bank information with the others, the Smithsonian Institution sponsored a meeting in 1972 to discuss the requirements and capabilities of the retrieval systems in existence at that time. This meeting led to the formation of the Museum Data Bank Coordinating Committee (MDBCC)—an organization that gives advice and information on the use of computers for museum data storage and retrieval. The MDBCC has its office at the University of Arkansas

[20]See A. Michael Noll, "Human or Machine: A Subjective Comparison of Piet Mondrian's 'Composition with Lines' (1917) and a Computer-generated Picture," *The Psychological Record,* January 1966, pp. 1–10.

[21]News release, Department of Art, University of New Mexico, July 1971.

and is working on plans for the interchange of data between museum networks. Similarly, in England, an information retrieval group of the British Museums Association is working on the development of an integrated museum cataloging system—one that would meet the needs of that nation's science, history, and art institutions. Other computer data banks are serving museums in France and Germany.

Museum personnel at the Smithsonian Institution are interested in computers for the *second purpose* mentioned.The Smithsonian's Museum of Natural History has over 50 million specimens of fossils, flowers, fish, birds, etc. A million new specimens are being added each year. In one section alone, crustacean specimens in 500,000 bottles occupy more than 10 miles of shelves. Detailed information about the museum's holdings is of interest to researchers in colleges, hospitals, and other museums. To enable scientists to locate specimens (and information about the specimens) more quickly, the museum is developing an electronic data bank. Other large museums with vast holdings that are planning similar computer catalogs are the National Museum of Natural Sciences in Canada and the National Museum of Anthropology in Mexico.

COMPUTERS AND HISTORICAL RESEARCH[22]

A small but growing number of historians are using computers and statistical techniques to aid them in their research efforts. Quantitative historians typically gather and analyze masses of data found in such public documents as state, county, and city records, voting records of public officials, federal government census reports, etc. Studies dealing with economic history sometimes incorporate data from nongovernmental sources.

Some *examples of computerized historical research* follow.

1 William Aydelotte has correlated biographical data with the voting records of over 800 members of the British Parliament of 1841–1847. His findings "disproved several pet theories concerning English reformism in the 1840s, notably those of economic determinism, Tory paternalism, and aristocratic benevolence."[23] Thomas Alexander has, with the help of a computer, studied the roll-call voting patterns of members of Congress between 1836 and 1860. And Allan Bogue's analysis of roll-call voting in Congress during the Civil War showed that party loyalty served to control the strife between radical Republicans and New England moderates. Other analyses of voting records have been (and are being) conducted.

2 Theodore Rabb has made a study of English overseas investments between 1575 and 1630. A computer was used to process data on 5,000 individual investors and 3,000 Parliament members.

[22]For a summary of this topic, see Charles Tilly, "Computers in Historical Analysis," *Computers and the Humanities,* September–November 1978, pp. 323–335, and Joel H. Silbey, "Clio and Computers: Moving into Phase II, 1970–1972," *Computers and the Humanities,* November 1972, pp. 67–79.

[23]Robert P. Swierenga, "Clio and Computers: A Survey of Computerized Research in History," *Computers and the Humanities,* September 1970, p. 7.

3 Western historians have assumed that young single men were responsible for opening up the frontier between 1840 and 1860. Jack Eblen used census data from an 88-county sample to show that "frontier-opening" had been a family undertaking, although the men were somewhat younger than the national average age at the time.

4 Stephen Thernstrom has used census data, tax lists, marriage licenses, birth records, etc., to study social mobility patterns. A sample of 8,000 Boston residents was selected from the 1880 census, the 1910 marriage license records, and the 1930 birth records. By tracing these individuals through later public records, Thernstrom was able to generalize about social mobility among various ethnic and religious groups over a long time span.

COMPUTERS AND ARCHAEOLOGY

A number of statistical techniques and simulation methods have been developed by computer-using archaeologists and statisticians to analyze and classify archaeological data, and several computer data banks have been created for the storage and retrieval of archaeological information. Some *examples of computer usage in archaeology* follow.

1 George Cowgill of Brandeis University has studied the origin and growth of the pre-Aztec city of Teotihuacán in central Mexico. Using a computer programmed to sketch a map of the city on the basis of the site information presented, Cowgill has been able to show the types of neighborhoods that existed in a city that covered an area 8 or 9 miles square. For example, an *almena* is a ceramic roof decoration that was found in the upper-class neighborhoods. Since the computer can produce a map showing the number of *almenas* discovered on every site, it is thus possible to see that an elite neighborhood was located near the "main street." The computer mapping for various time periods shows that building density was high and that there was a high degree of planning.

2 Luraine Tansey of San Jose City College uses information contained in a computer data bank to classify and date pre-Columbian art found in Mexico and Central America.

3 Ray Winfield Smith has used a computer to solve the puzzle of 35,000 decorated blocks of stone found in Egypt. The blocks were originally thought to be the remains of a single temple, but after classifying the blocks the computer showed that there had been a large complex of temples and buildings stretching across the desert for over a mile.

4 James Strange of the University of South Florida is restoring an ancient synagogue in the village of Khirbet Shema that was destroyed around A.D. 417. The site is located 90 miles north of Jerusalem. When most of the dimensions of the building site were known, the computer was used to make engineering calculations to determine the missing structural parameters. The computer was also used to make drawings of what the building probably looked like.

REVIEW AND DISCUSSION QUESTIONS

1 Discuss and give examples of how computers have been used for planning and decision making at the federal government level.

2 (*a*) How can computers be used in environmental planning? (*b*) How can computers be used in forecasting the weather?

3 "Computers are increasingly being used by military planners." Discuss this statement.

4 (*a*) What is a legislative data bank? (*b*) For what purposes is such a data bank used?

5 How may computers be used in political campaigns?

6 (*a*) Give examples of ways in which computers are used by the federal government to perform the control function. (*b*) Give examples of state and local government control activities.

7 (*a*) How may computers be used for social welfare planning? (*b*) For urban planning?

8 How are computers being used by state and local governments for law enforcement purposes?

9 (*a*) How may computers affect the legal profession? (*b*) The courts?

10 Why is there an accelerating use of computers in health fields?

11 "Some physicians are now using the computer as a diagnostic tool in hospitals and clinics." Discuss this statement.

12 How can a computer be of value in physical examinations?

13 What benefits are being derived from computer-assisted research in medicine?

14 (*a*) How can a computer be used to take a medical history? (*b*) Would there be any advantages to a medical record data bank? (*c*) Would there be any possible disadvantages to such a data bank?

15 "A primary purpose of using computers in education should be to provide insight." Discuss this statement.

16 (*a*) How can computers be used in curriculum planning? (*b*) In planning for individual instruction?

17 (*a*) What is meant by computer-managed instruction? (*b*) What is meant by computer-assisted instruction?

18 "Using computers in education will dehumanize instruction and make robots of students." Evaluate this statement.

19 (a) How can computers be used in class scheduling? (*b*) In athletic planning?

20 Give examples of how computers have been used for authorship identification.

21 (*a*) Are computers being extensively used for language translation today? (*b*) Why?

22 Discuss computer applications in the fine arts.

23 "Museum personnel have been interested in using computers for three principal purposes." Identify and discuss these purposes.

24 Discuss ways in which computers have been applied in historical research.

25 How have computers been applied in archaeological research?

Chapter 8 Readings

INTRODUCTION TO READINGS 24 THROUGH 28

24 Nonprofit institutions have as much need for efficient information and control systems as for-profit organizations. In this article Regina Herzlinger analyzes the status of computer use in nonprofit institutions and suggests that *bad management has led to misuse or underuse of information and control systems.*

25 More complex computer uses within the United States government are explored in this article by Neal Gregory. He argues that "as Congress acquires *information literacy,* the prospects for a national information policy are certain to improve."

26 The potentials of using computers in the area of medical diagnosis, prognosis, and therapy are discussed by Harold M. Schoolman and Lionel M. Bernstein in this article. They describe how computers can and are being used to simulate the techniques of expert clinicians.

27 As labor-management programs within government have increased in size and number, they have become more structured and complex. In this article, Ronald A. Leahy of the U.S. Civil Service Commission describes the computer-assisted systems approach that has been developed to help resolve some of the problems of information delivery in the labor relations area.

Reading 24

Why Data Systems in Nonprofit Organizations Fail

Regina Herzlinger

The director of a large social service agency in a New England state was told at fiscal midyear that unexpectedly lower tax revenues had forced a 5% reduction in his budget (or about $100 million). The distribution of the cut among the different programs was left to his judgment, but he couldn't respond to the order in a reasonable manner because he lacked the resources that would have given him the needed information. The state's use of a line-item, object-of-expense budgeting and accounting system frustrated his efforts to learn how much money had been committed to different programs; the statistical system that was supposed to tell him how many people were served and how many services were

Reprinted from *Harvard Business Review,* January–February 1977. Copyright © 1976 by the president and fellows of Harvard College; all rights reserved. Professor Herzlinger is an associate professor of business administration at the Harvard Business School.

delivered wasn't working; and, to boot, the most recent cost data were four months out of date.

Lacking relevant information, he had to make a judgment solely on the basis of political considerations. He chose to cut the budgets of those programs affecting people with the least political influence—abandoned children and the mentally retarded.

The state of control and information systems in most nonprofit organizations is dismal. Despite billions of dollars spent to provide relevant, accurate, and timely data, few nonprofit organizations possess systems whose quality equals those found in large, profit-oriented corporations. Nonprofit organizations do not lack data; if anything, they enjoy an overabundance of numbers and statistics. Rather, they lack *systematically* provided information to help management do its job. Without good information, it is obviously difficult for managers to make reasoned and informed decisions, evaluate performance, motivate their employees, and protect the institution against fraud.

This problem is by no means confined to public agencies; it also crops up in private, nonprofit organizations.

Consider the case of one voluntary agency that delivered services ranging from medical care to adult education classes. Once boasting a healthy endowment and a substantial yield on its endowment, the agency had suffered through three consecutive years of increasing deficits and was suspended on the brink of bankruptcy.

Its director was a controversial person who had converted it from a stodgy, upper-class "charity" to a vital, exciting organization. Or so her supporters said. Her detractors, convinced that she was responsible for the precarious financial position, accused her of wasting money on frivolous, faddish activities that benefited neither their participants nor the organization's reputation.

Was she a superlative manager or an incompetent? The answer to that question was vital to the organization's future. But it couldn't be answered objectively; the agency's board simply had too little information with which to evaluate the quality of her management. The agency had no budget, no output data, and such a poor system of internal controls that even the number of members was in doubt.

Many nonprofit organizations are deficient in the routinized internal control that ensures the integrity of the accounting for expenditures and services. The welfare error rate is a familiar subject of newspaper stories. Often as high as 40%, the error rate consists of seemingly random underpayments and overpayments to welfare recipients. It is vivid evidence of a poor system of internal control.

A similar case is the Guaranteed Student Loan Program, administered by the Office of Education of HEW. Every one of the program's annual financial statements has received an "adverse" opinion from the General Accounting Office. This opinion is rendered, in part, because the program's managers do not know the magnitude of the loans they have insured and therefore can accurately account for neither the contingent reserves account on their balance sheet nor the loss expense account on their income statement. The loan volume outstanding is estimated at $7 billion to $8 billion—with an unknown amount in the range of $1 billion for which there are no proper accounting records. The possibilities for fraud in these cases are staggering.

The presence of a management information system does not guarantee its proper use, of course. Many hospitals, for example, identify their outpatient departments as "money losers," while in fact the outpatient department frequently substantially offsets the total operating costs of the hospital and may even contribute to covering the direct costs of its inpatient side.

The losing position of the outpatient department is merely an artifact of some states' medical aid systems, in which a ceiling is placed on the reimbursement a hospital receives per inpatient day, while reimbursement for the outpatient department is handled on a "cost or charges, whichever is lower" basis. To maximize reimbursement, a hospital will allocate as many "joint costs" as possible to the outpatient department and thereby create an accounting "loser." This system of cost accounting is perfectly sensible for purposes of reimbursement, but it creates an unfair basis for the evaluation of the manager of an outpatient department.

More serious are situations in which the data network leads to a totally inappropriate course of action. In the mid-1960s, the U.S. Department of Labor designed an elaborate information system for programs to train the hard-core unemployed and place them in useful employment. While the system measured many aspects of cost and output, one measure was of paramount importance: number of people placed in jobs. When Labor Department supervisors visited a local manpower office, they particularly wanted to know the number of placements the director had generated.

The directors of the local programs got the message. Soon they were ensuring a high placement rate through a practice known as "creaming"—that is, they skimmed the cream of the unemployed and accepted only persons who were temporarily unemployed and who had a high probability of appropriate placement. This strategy was obviously antithetical to the purpose of the national program.

In some far-removed location in a public agency or a private nonprofit organization, computing equipment frequently stands idle, away from prying eyes—another symptom of the problem. It is idle because the computer has not "worked out" for its intended purpose. Its intended purpose may have been based on a totally unrealistic notion of what an information system can do. When the inevitable failure occurs, the computer gets the blame, anthropomorphically, and ignominiously disappears.

Computer graveyards are most often found in large hospitals and welfare departments. They have mammoth data-processing requirements that supposedly can be met by buying large computers and "integrated" management information system packages. The systems will somehow solve all the organizations' information needs, from record keeping to planning and control reports. Since the human mechanisms for obtaining and "inputting" the data are weak, however, an integrated system never quite succeeds. Moreover, the technical problems of programming and operating such a system are sometimes beyond the capability of the organization and its system contractor.

AT THE ROOT OF THE PROBLEM

A major cause of the problem is the method of financing such organizations. Funding in block grants, which vary with neither volume nor quality of service and which are made before the work is done, does not reward effective and efficient performance and gives managers little incentive to encumber themselves with tighter controls.

The best way to change this attitude is to make the form of funding more like the financing mechanisms used in the private sector. Financing the *consumers* of services—rather than the *suppliers* of services—would impose the discipline of the marketplace on the organizations. Consumers, armed with purchasing power, could pick and choose among them.

Such a policy change, however, is unlikely to occur. Proposals for it have been aired since early in the twentieth century; the most recent one is Milton Friedman's plan for the use of vouchers in education. Although the federal government has experimented with vouchers in education and housing, it shows little sense of urgency about adopting these mechanisms. Even the laudable negative income tax idea—a voucher-like device which, among other benefits, would eliminate much of the paper pushing in welfare departments—is now languishing in academic journals.

Admittedly, nonprofit organizations are beset by demands for data from financial supporters and other parties. A typical hospital files financial and statistical reports with a number of insurance companies, the state in which it is located, the federal government, the planning agencies in its area, the licensing authorities, the certificate-of-need agency personnel, and the quality and utilization review administration—not to mention the financial statement it prepares, on a fund-accounting basis, for its own board of trustees. None of these statements duplicates another in content or format. School systems use an accounting system recommended by the U.S. Office of Education that has more than one million possible entries!

Obviously, many factors inhibiting improved information handling are beyond the control of a nonprofit organization. Yet the one factor accounting for most failures of information systems lies directly within the control of the organization: the characteristics and attitudes of top management.

Rarely does one hear the executives of a nonprofit organization described as being "good with numbers." More frequently, the accolades are "creative," "innovative," "caring," or "great scholars." Being good with numbers may actually do the managerial image a disservice, for it implies the absence of such qualitative skills as creativity, courage, and humanitarianism. Indeed, some managers of nonprofits view their lack of quantitative skills as a rather endearing imperfection—like having freckles.

Many of these managers were initially professionals who carry with them the culture and attitudes of the professional, including strong resistance to quantitative measures of their organizations' activities. They argue, sometimes persuasively, that professional work is too complex and diffuse in its impact to be easily accounted for and that naive attempts to account for its outcome might undermine the credibility and integrity of the work itself.

A case in point is the experience of the state of Michigan, which in 1969 began a program to collect data on the resources and achievements of its school systems. The purpose of the assessment was to link expenditures with results and presumably to hold school personnel responsible for their performance.

The project was greeted with such hostility that the department of education retreated from its original goals. The report on the third year of the project stressed that the assessment "is not to be viewed as an evaluation of Michigan schools. Instead it is to provide information on . . . student needs." The next year the department expanded its cautionary position, explaining that the program "does not indicate which schools or districts are most effective or efficient."[1]

Many professionals-turned-managers do not command the technical skills required for the design and implementation of a good information system. When I have taught accounting to top executives of large nonprofit organizations, they have often told me that until then they had never been able to understand their own financial statements.

A lack of technical skills and an institutionalized aversion to measurement, when combined with the traditional definition of the role of manager in these organizations, lead many managers of nonprofit institutions to abdicate the task of designing and implementing a sound information system to their staffs, particularly to their accountants. A manager will say, "I don't know much about these numbers, but my accountant is a genius." It is doubtful that the manager has the capability to judge an accountant's genius.

SOME SOLUTIONS

The problem of the multiplicity of external demand for data could be partly reduced through coordination of the agencies that fund a particular organizational entity in the design of the data system for monitoring the program. The many federal agencies that finance community health centers could, for example, design a single system that would meet not only their data needs but also those of the insurance companies and the state welfare departments involved.

We should not, however, be overly sanguine about the likelihood of this solution. Under the present structure of federal and most other government units, the different groups have no reason to coordinate. Moreover, organiza-

[1]Jerome T. Murphy and David K. Cohen, "Accountability in Education—the Michigan Experience," *The Public Interest,* Summer 1974, p. 62.

tions and benefactors fund programs for different reasons, and they are unlikely to agree on a common data set that meets all their needs. Finally, even if federal and state agencies could cooperate on information system design, their actions would still be subject to legislative review, which is not always intelligent or objective.

An approach different from most has been taken by the National Centers for Health Statistics and for Health Services Research and Development. They have designed a data system for planning and evaluating purposes. The network, now in its early stages of implementation, involves these steps:

- The federal level specifies a very small amount of information for each program to generate.
- State and local programs receive funding for experimentation with the installation of systems that meet their internal needs.
- The federal government reimburses the state and local bodies for providing the required data.

This approach has several admirable aspects: (*a*) the requirements for external data are kept to a minimum; (*b*) the operational programs are given the opportunity, and funding, to integrate the external data into a system that meets their needs; and (*c*) the users must pay for the data. The user payment feature is important and unusual, because the payment is direct and thus tends to make agencies asking for the data more sensitive to the financial impact of their requests.

Until the necessity and feasibility of approaches like that of the National Centers are recognized, nonprofit organizations must limp along individually as best they can. Much depends on the quality of their managers, who, as I pointed out earlier, are often long on professional training and experience but short on administrative skills and experience. The management component of most professional training is usually completely absent, limited to office practices such as billing, or covered through a quick survey course of administrative techniques—a week on accounting, a week on interpersonal behavior, and so on. This level of education is unlikely to develop people with the skills and attitudes of professional managers. Many professional schools, however, are beginning to offer their students appropriate managerial training courses.

Guidelines for Managers

Of course, the impact of that trend will not be felt for a while, so the main thrust of the improvement of information systems must lie with present managers. Here are some suggestions for improvement of the design, installation, and operation of information systems:

System Design The top manager who remains uninvolved in the design of the content of the system negates the reason for its existence. Participation in the system design process ensures that the system is relevant and responsive to management's needs.

It is also important to recognize that information systems must meet different needs (also, some questions can be answered on a totally ad hoc basis). The framework developed by Robert N. Anthony is very useful for classifying different types of information systems.[2] He distinguishes three managerial functions and delineates the characteristics of the different kinds of information systems needed to support these functions.

Measurement of output and efficiency in most nonprofit institutions is a big problem with a host of measurable attributes. Furthermore, since the output is generally not sold, it is impossible to measure it in financial terms by assigning it a market value. Some system designers go overboard in an attempt to solve the problem. A small nursing agency, for example, drew up a list of 103 finely grained output measures and 21 efficiency measures per nurse. To get an overall measure of effectiveness, the agency then adjusted and weighted these criteria in some arcane manner. Such efforts result in data of dubious validity. A balanced solution sets a standard of measurement without excessive elaboration.

An important component of the design phase is the stipulation of the means for implementing the system, including estimates of time required, cost involved, and milestones to be achieved. This step is frequently omitted or neglected because managers justify information systems on a "cost-saving" basis and fear that documentation of the costs of installing the system will belie their initial estimates.

Since most nonprofit organizations seriously underfund their information system activities, it is unrealistic and unnecessary to justify installation of a new design on a cost-saving basis. Rather, they should be justified on benefit/cost reasoning—that is, that the benefits of the system will exceed its cost. And the design phase should include meticulous documentation of these costs.

The design phase should also include designation of the organizational unit that will install and/or operate the system. Otherwise, such responsibility is diffused along the breadth of the organization. This leads to difficulties in assigning responsibility and authority.

Installation An important and frequently neglected precondition to success is adequate pretesting of the form and content of the system. The organization should not stint in the planning and financing of the pretesting phase.

Extensive training of those who will use and operate the system is a worthwhile investment. Because of the high rate of turnover at the top level of most nonprofit organizations, it is important to "institutionalize" the system through training.

Thorough documentation of all aspects of the form and content of the system is an essential part of the installation process, especially the preparation of manuals explaining how every item of input or output is to be measured. At a minimum, the organization should draw up a chart of the accounts used for

[2]See Robert N. Anthony, *Planning and Control Systems: A Framework for Analysis,* Division of Research, Harvard Business School, Boston, 1965, particularly the first three chapters.

reporting purposes and give a detailed explanation of how and when they are to be recognized. This is a tedious job, often neglected. Furthermore, some designers gain power from the absence of documentation, making them the only ones who know how to run the system.

Operation An information system used regularly by top management for making such key decisions as budget allocation will eventually overcome any initial flaws of design and installation. At the same time, it is important to designate an appropriate organizational unit for the routinized production of the information. If this unit is different from the one that designed the system, the people in the former unit will be less reluctant to modify the system. This policy of separation, however, may cost the organization much more money than having one unit responsible for the operation of the system as well as its design.

Most of the issues in the design and implementation of these information systems in nonprofit institutions are similar to those in profit-oriented organizations. If the condition of such systems in these two types of organizations were also the same, we would enjoy a much more efficient environment.

READING 24 DISCUSSION QUESTIONS

1 What are some of the reasons that data systems present special problems in *nonprofit* organizations?
2 What can be done by a manager in a nonprofit organization to prevent some of the difficulties described by Professor Herzlinger?

Reading 25

Congress—The Politics of Information

Neal Gregory

Last June, as the House of Representatives finally faced the issue of voting itself a pay raise, the press galleries were packed. Reporters came early and occupied every seat to watch the members of Congress agonize over a politically loaded amendment that would remove from the Legislative Appropriations Bill some one million dollars set aside to finance the salary increase. On the following day a single reporter was in the gallery as the lights of the electronic voting system tallied the votes of a bill appropriating $110 billion to run the nation's defense establishment for the coming year.

Which was the more important story? Which was the more important information that should be relayed to the nation?

Reprinted with permission. Copyright 1978 *Data Management Magazine,* Data Processing Management Association. All rights reserved. Mr. Gregory is staff director, Computer Policy Group, U.S. House of Representatives, Washington, D.C.

Defining Information

Each reporter who covers the Congress has his or her own definition of information, selecting which Capitol Hill drama to chronicle and how much detail to provide. The filtering process is controlled not only by the reporters but also by their editors, who are guided by constraints of a television time-slot or the news space available around the advertising on a printed page. Within the limits of staff and budget, the media must choose from a wide range of stages. These include the floor action of the House or the Senate or the activities of 23 standing House committees, five select committees and 152 subcommittees. In the Senate there are 15 standing committees, six select committees and more than 100 subcommittees. Although sentiment is against them, four joint committees still function—Printing, the Library, Economics and Taxation.

There are also assorted *ad hoc* committees and conference committees and the Democratic Caucus and the Republican Conference, as well as rural, urban, regional, women, blue collar, black or other special interest groups.

The media's problem is compounded for the citizen. Jurisdiction is the initial political hurdle for any trade association, professional society, industry group, member of Congress or individual voter who wants to define information policy or secure legislation affecting that policy (e.g., deregulate transmission facilities, fund libraries, improve access to scientific data or protect privacy). There is no committee on information, nor is there much feeling within Congress for information policy as an issue.

Lot of Talk

At the present time, information policy is a lot like the weather. There is a lot of talk, but very little is being done about it. Many of those talking about it, particularly those in Congress, are not even aware that their relatively small area of concern is part of a larger information picture.

The recent nine-volume Commerce Department study on "The Information Economy" concludes that 46 percent of the Gross National Product is derived from producing, processing and distributing information, with almost half the country's labor force involved in "information activity."

The principal author of the study, Marc U. Porat, defines information as "data that is organized and communicated." Joseph Becker, a librarian and engineer who formerly headed the American Society for Information Science, says the word means "facts about any subject." Paul Zurkowski, president of the Information Industry Association, says "it is concepts or ideas which enter a person's perception, are evaluated and assimilated, reinforce or change the individual's concept of reality and/or ability to act." If one accepts these sweeping definitions, then every single committee in both houses of Congress can claim a piece of the action.

Information policy as a subject of legislative inquiry is not unlike the jurisdictional maze of committees faced by proposals for dealing with the energy crisis: Gasoline taxes? Ways and Means. Coal mining and oil leases? Interior and Insular Affairs. Pipeline? Interstate and Foreign Commerce. American tankers? Merchant Marine and Fisheries. Solar research? Science and Technology. Mass transit? Banking, Finance and Urban Affairs. A new Energy Department? Government Operations.

These are some of the House committees involved. A similar situation exists in the Senate.

Three Phenomena

A relatively narrow definition of information policy was taken by the Ford Administration's Domestic Council Committee on the Right to Privacy. Its 1976 study suggests that public policy questions are being generated by three specific phenomena—by rapidly escalating advances in computer technology, by shifts in the nation's economy from a manufacturing to an information base and by citizen demands for clarification of their right to have and control information.

Quincy Rodgers, an attorney and principal author of the study, believes these questions are now converging along four vectors of information policy—privacy and freedom of information, the spread of computers, the communications infra-structure and improved utilization of scientific and technical information. If Congress accepted these categories, it ought to mean that committee jurisdictional problems would be eliminated. That would not be the case, however, even though each of the four areas is linked by questions of computer technology.

The most politically popular issue ought to be improved use of scientific and technical information (STI). With billions of dollars committed in space exploration, agricultural experiments and medical research over the years, there is a general consensus that we should spread the knowledge around. But the methods for accomplishing this are muddled by side issues ranging from copyright ambiguities to geographical jealousies to anti-communist sentiments.

Primary policy jurisdiction for STI lies with the Science and Technology Committee in the House and the Committee on Commerce, Science and Transportation in the Senate. But these committees in recent months have been tied up in the energy debate, opposing the President on the question of developing breeder reactors.

STI policy is directly related to research and development funds which are eagerly sought by practically every department of government and most of the nation's universities. The two appropriations committees become battlegrounds for funding, and there is frequently a duplication of effort. But more often than not, there is simply a lack of communication, an inability to obtain information because of conflicting agency policies on making data available to other agencies, to the public or to the scientific community. New advances in microform technology and digital bibliographical services have the potential of cutting through this academic and bureaucratic red tape, but funds for such electronic libraries represent a relatively new area of concern for most R & D personnel and a new consideration for Congress.

CDC Sale

Probably the most highly publicized STI event of the past year did not directly involve this sort of information policy decision, although computer technology was involved. The Control Data Corporation (CDC) was attempting to sell a sophisticated computer system to the Union of Soviet Socialist Republics. The machine's function would be to provide weather and climatic data as part of an international information link involving similar data-gathering computers in the United States and Australia.

Over 200 members of Congress from across the political spectrum signed a letter urging President Carter to veto any export license for the sale. CDC contended the computer was secure and that safeguards had been taken to guarantee that it could not be used for any military purpose, but the export license was not granted. It is highly doubtful that the decision was reached strictly on the merits of the case. Several commentators noted that antibusiness pressures from the left and anticommunist pressures from the right are an unbeatable combination.

Privacy

The issue of privacy also cuts across all political lines, but unlike many technical considerations involved in most information policy decisions, this is one issue most members of Congress feel they understand. There is an automatic conflict between the goals of keeping personal data secure while opening government activities to public scrutiny, and the issues cross many committee jurisdictions. There are now 90 pending bills that the Congressional Research Service of the Library of Congress has indexed under the term "Privacy." While most are awaiting action in the judiciary committees of the two houses, at least ten other committees are involved. Many of these bills are directed toward solving a problem unique to a particular occupational group, class of documents or specific government agency.

Bills defining private standards for medical records and the privileges of newsmen are in the Committee on Interstate and Foreign Commerce; rights of civil servants and regulations governing agricultural statistics are being considered by the Post Office and the Civil Service. Foreign surveillance prevention is pending in House International Relations Committee and the Senate Foreign Relations Committee. Privacy of tax records is the concern of the House Ways and Means Committee and the Senate Finance Committee. General policy on document security within the government is being considered by the House Government Operations Committee. Intelligence reorganization proposals were sent to both armed services committees, even though there are now new committees on intelligence in the House and the Senate.

Privacy Act of 1974

Congress has exempted itself from coverage of many laws, most notably the civil rights statutes; however, the Privacy Act, passed in 1975, has impacted relations of the legislative and executive branches. When the Act took effect, the

Veterans Administration told its Congressional liaison personnel they could no longer answer queries from Congress about hospital claims, compensation, GI Bill status, lost pension checks or the myriad other matters about which individual veterans typically write their Congressmen. The agency contended that such Congressional inquiries violated the veterans' privacy rights. The policy was quickly reversed with an interpretation that the individual who writes is in fact giving the senator or representative a limited power of attorney to intervene in that person's behalf.

Other agencies changed some of their routine responses to Congress. The Department of Agriculture, for instance, no longer supplies members of Congress with lists or computer tapes showing all the farmers in their states or Congressional districts.

The problem of unforeseen results from legislation is not new; the executive branch (and the courts) have frequently interpreted statutes in ways not dreamed of by the Congressional authors. Edward Wink of the University of Washington, in discussing the needs for improved information for Congress, pointed to the unforeseen effects of the Interstate Highway Act, which the public works committees considered strictly from the obvious needs for improved roads. No one considered pollution, damage to the environment, the energy crisis, the movement of jobs from the city or other societal impacts that have resulted from passage of the bill. Many of the privacy protection laws—those on the books and bills pending in committee—will have such unforeseen results; but the public endorses the concept of privacy, and there is no turning back on this issue.

Faster Than Response

Technological changes are escalating faster than the legislative process can respond in many areas. Probably in no area is this more true than in communications and computers. Two data processing devices can interact and share time and logic, communicating in the performance of a single job. It makes no difference if the machines are in the same room or an ocean apart, linked by telephone lines, satellites or microwave towers. With packet switching and other marvels of the laboratory, it makes little difference to the user of the end product which part of the apparatus is communicating and which is processing. Distinction between the two is becoming totally blurred except to certain segments of the industry. Anthony Oettinger, of the Program on Information Resources Policy, at Harvard University, contends that computation systems and communications systems are no longer separate at all. He has coined a new phrase, *compunications technology*.

"Messages are data," he says. "Pictures and sounds are data; and, as data, all are subject to processing by computer, and all are subject to digital transmission.

"A picture is the same as a thousand words."

But the picture is not always that clear in Congress.

The subcommittees on communications of the House and Senate have traditionally had a broadcast orientation. In the past, when a broadcaster was elected to Congress, he caused few ethical concerns by seeking a seat on the subcommittee. Press coverage of committee activities tended to focus on legislation affecting television programming. Indeed, the bill that allegedly cleared both houses in record time was legislation mandating television broadcasts of certain professional football games.

While TV policy is still a major focus for the subcommittees, most of their resources are devoted to much less glamorous matters.

Changing Lifestyles

The House subcommittee staff recently prepared a series of options papers, listing topics that will be facing the members—uses of the spectrum (citizens band radio, satellite communications, garage door openers, microwave ovens, all broadcasting and long distance telephone calls); safety, special and mobile radio; domestic common carrier policy; cable television regulation; international telecommunications; the impact of communications technology on the right to privacy, and structural and procedural options for regulation of telecommunications. Rep. Lionel van Deerlin, of California, chairman of the House subcommittee, has announced plans for a virtual rewriting of the Communications Act of 1934, a move that a Congressional economist feels would cause an impact on American lifestyles similar to that resulting from the railroad legislation of the last century.

Not only broadcasters, but other corporate interests are watching and waiting to see what the subcommittees will do. The new shared technology is pitting the communications industry, a highly regulated monopoly dominated by American Telephone and Telegraph Co., against an unregulated computer industry led by International Business Machines Corp.

While conducting hearings and analyzing the impact of pending legislative changes, the subcommittees also are overseeing telecommunications activities of the Executive Branch, particularly those under the new Assistant Secretary of Commerce for Communications and Information and those within the chief regulatory agency, the Federal Communications Commission (FCC). As the FCC reopens its computer inquiry and explores the relationship between the two technologies, its actions will have a profound influence on decisions facing Congress.

Impacting Policy

Indeed, the oversight role of congressional committees—looking into the way various agencies are spending the money and executing laws—can have a greater impact on information policy than new statutes. More and more, the information practices of each agency are coming in for additional scrutiny. A proposed new computer system may be the target or privacy may be the issue that triggers a complaint which causes some member of Congress to ask for an investigation by the General Accounting Office (GAO). But an information probe of an agency by a congressional committee staff is still a relatively new endeavor.

The House Ways and Means Oversight Subcommittee has been assigned jurisdiction over the Internal Revenue Service, whose computers process 152 million income tax returns each year, and over the Social Security Administration, which annually issues computer-written checks totaling 84 billion dollars. Yet no one on the subcommittee staff is familiar with automatic data processing operations or computer technology.

The problem is not unique, and the Committee on House Administration, through its Policy Group on Information and Computers, is attempting to remedy this through a series of seminars explaining the basic concepts of computers. The seminars are being offered to all congressional staffs in an effort to insure that those engaged in oversight will take a closer look at agency requests and explanations in the data processing area.

Earlier this year the Economic Development Administration (EDA) of the Department of Commerce announced target planning grants for its four-billion-dollar local public works program. But representatives from rural areas noticed a strange pattern to the grants which were listed on computer printouts. Rep. Charlie Rose, of North Carolina, asked permission of EDA for personnel from the House computer center to look into the data, the software and the procedures used in compiling the lists. The Congressional investigators discovered that almost all cities and towns with populations of under 2,500 showed a work force of "zero" and an unemployment rate of "zero." EDA officials said there was no error, but a "conscious choice from available options," because employment data was not readily available from the Bureau of Labor Statistics (BLS) for these small towns. Rose countered with language from the House-Senate Conference Committee Report directing EDA to accept data from local sources when information was not available from BLS. The agency responded that this would be too time-consuming and would defeat the purpose of the legislation, the rapid creation of jobs.

Examining Computers

Some 40 communities with high unemployment, who had erroneous data added to their applications for a grant, have filed suit against the Department of Commerce, asking the Federal Courts to enjoin officials from issuing any more funds until a new formula is drawn up. In Vermont, an out-of-court settlement was made to several towns who received grants of nearly $900,000. But the courts move slowly, even more slowly than the bureaucracy. By the time an injunction is issued, the money will have been disbursed and the question at issue will probably be declared moot. But the significance of this episode is that the Congress, for the first time, looked into the internal operations of an Executive Branch computer system to ascertain if the intent of Congress was being carried out. A precedent has been set. Perhaps some future appropriations bill will include an actual computer program providing for the distribution of funds, rather than just a formula left to bureaucratic interpretation.

The effectiveness of oversight varies from committee to committee, but the dominant watchdogs are the House Government Operations Committee and the Senate Governmental Affairs Committee. Their jurisdictions include "studying the operation of government activities at all levels with a view to determining its economy and efficiency." And no activity lends itself more readily to this mandate than the government's information systems.

Brooks Bill

The House has provided greater continuity in this area, chiefly because of Rep. Jack Brooks, of Texas. He has spent two decades insisting that the Executive Branch increase the effectiveness of its computer operations and tighten up on its systems procurement practices. His landmark legislation—the Brooks Bill of 1965—is still the Bible for Federal procurement officers and ADP managers. But at oversight hearings last year Brooks himself admitted that Federal agencies "have shown little willingness to comply voluntarily with the law." He castigated all three agencies that have enforcement responsibility for the Act—the Office of Management and Budget (OMB) "for failing to provide adequate policy direction," the General Services Administration (GSA) "for failing to administer the Act effectively," and the National Bureau of Standards "for failing to establish standards."

The original legislation was enacted when Brooks headed the Subcommittee on Government Activities. A recent article in a trade periodical theorized that, since he now is chairman of the full committee with jurisdiction over every operating facet of the entire government, he has little interest in agency usage of computers.

However, the question of computer policy is essential to government operations. Not only is computer use around four percent of the budget involved, but most agencies are locked into their computer systems, and, as a GAO report last year concluded: it would be "impractical, if not impossible, to accomplish their mission without computers."

As a result of the Brooks hearings and in response to other criticism, OMB is undertaking a Data Processing Reorganization Study with goals of

- Improving the delivery of governmental services through the effective application of computer and related telecommunications technology,
- Improving the acquisition, management and use of these resources, and
- Eliminating duplication and overlap in agency jurisdictions relative to computer issues.

The study could be enormously important, for decisions by the government, the largest user of computers in the world, will have a major impact on the industry and its policies. For the member of Congress, an improved DP operation will mean more accurate reports coming to them from the agencies and departments and fewer complaints coming from their constituents.

Diverse Role

The role of a senator or representative is diverse. He or she is a legislator, a would-be statesman, a politician, an overseer of the public purse, a spokesman for varying interests and an ombudsman, representing a half-million constituents or states varying in size from Delaware to California. It is in these many roles that they encounter the politics of information, but it is as the ombudsman that the problem focuses most clearly. When the constituent—a poor pensioner or a wealthy businessman—has a problem with a government agency, a problem involving a pending legislative vote, a lost check, a misinterpreted regulation or simply a request for information that went astray, a letter goes to the congressman.

Every month, the House Post Office alone handles 8.4 million pieces of mail. The letters have to be answered, and the Congress is turning to computerized word-processing systems to track the casework, to store reply paragraphs, to assist in filing and to retrieve information from assorted on-line data bases. The Senate provides each of its members with a terminal and access to a sophisticated correspondence production system featuring the latest micrographics technology. In the House, each member has the option of diverting up to $12,000 from his or her clerk-hire allowance to lease equipment and services from a variety of commercial vendors. In the two years this policy has been in effect, 210 of the members have acquired terminals and another 100 have contracted for off-line computer services.

The computer systems on Capitol Hill provide the usual behind-the-scenes housekeeping services such as payroll and personnel record-keeping and inventory control. But more sophisticated, highly visible operations such as electronic voting, legislative tracking and econometric modeling are making many representatives and senators and their staffs acutely aware of improvements in the legislative process that information technology is making possible.

There is still a long way to go. The latest GSA inventory for the Federal Government (May 31, 1977) lists 10,282 computers. On Capitol Hill there are nine—four in the House, three in the Senate and two in the Library of Congress, plus another dozen minicomputers devoted to electronic publishing. Combined government ADP budgets are in excess of four billion dollars. (The GAO, with a 1974 estimate which it called conservative, put the figure at $10 billion.) That portion of the Legislative Branch appropriation designated for computers and ADP personnel is under 35 million dollars. No one is advocating a massive increase in the spending earmarked for Capitol Hill computers; however, there is a massive gap in the information resources available to the two branches.

State of Use

A study for the Library of Congress by McKinsey and Company concluded that the present state of the art of computer systems in Congress "can best be described as ensnared in problems and issues the private sector resolved over a decade ago." The study cited a proliferation of hardware "owned by a number of competing parochial groups," parallel development of "jealously guarded applications similar in purpose but not compatible in concept, design or even language" and services "provided at no cost and treated as a 'free good.' "

There is duplication in services. To cite one example, the Information Systems Office of the Library of Congress provides an on-line Legislative Digest for each of the 26,000 bills and resolutions; the House Information Systems provides a Legislative Information System (formerly Bill Status System) with similar data. Even the payroll systems differ; Library employees are paid every two weeks, House and Senate employees, monthly. These systems grew up independently to serve different needs, and personalities in charge of various committees and offices took narrow views as information systems and services were designed and implemented. However, there are moves toward ending these duplications as working groups have been set up to plan a common program for computerized information needs of the Congress. Among the areas under consideration are legislative information systems, budget and fiscal systems, word processing technology, bill drafting and statutory retrieval, microform technology, hardware and software requirements, and video and audio technology.

The peculiarities of Congress as an institution add to the difficulties. The Constitution mandates the two bodies, and there are probably more differences—in style, rules of procedure, methods of operation and personalities of leadership—than there are similarities between the House and Senate. The smaller Senate chamber, with its members forced to seek re-election every six years, is slower to change; although it has just reorganized its committee structure in an effort to spread power around. The House in recent years has seen reformers make major rules changes, and others are imminent. With the entire body up for re-election every two years, the House acquires more new members, who bring with them innovative information ideas from their roles in business, the professions or academia.

This year saw the establishment of a Policy Group on Information and Computers to direct the House Information Systems and to plan and promote more effective use of technology by members and committees.

But many problems which appear simple in theory are complex in political reality. For instance, the leadership of the House is trying to come to grips with scheduling, a problem the computer has solved for most of the nation's community colleges. But the next week's floor agenda or hearings on an energy tax bill will not sort like the twice-weekly classes in Psychology 201. Scheduling a piece of legislation can be a key ingredient for its success or failure, and powerful chairmen do not like to give up their options. A change in signals from the White House, an impact statement by a government agency or a vote count by a knowledgeable lobbyist—even the whim of a chairman—can pull a bill off the calendar and set off a ripple effect on the plans and priorities of scores of legislators. Some 75 hearings could be underway on a given Wednesday morning, but no central authority has control of the meeting rooms.

House System

A new system called COMIS (Committee Information and Scheduling) recently became operational in the House. Designed along a matrix concept, it matches the 435 members of the House (plus the four non-voting delegates from the District of Columbia, Puerto Rico, Guam and the Virgin Islands) with their committee and subcommittee assignments. Any official scheduling a meeting can get an on-line picture of potential conflicts. This may be an incentive for chairmen to schedule early, but the system is entirely voluntary. Even though members are already listed elsewhere, one theoretically could add another meeting for the same hour, forcing a choice.

Time and space are clearly important to members of Congress. Their concerns in this area can be a major factor in focusing on some of the external questions of information policy.

Electronic voting in the House saves at least 20 minutes on each roll call over the old verbal aye-and-nay method; so far this year there have been 639 roll calls. New correspondence systems are saving staff time and freeing up space formerly allocated for filing cabinets; follow-up letters on legislative queries are easily generated. Electronic publishing systems are saving money and permitting members to see the results of a mark-up session immediately, rather than a day later when amendments have been incorporated into a bill through conventional hot-type printing. The computer can search the *United States Code,* the *Congressional Record* and the Federal Budget; legislative history and legal precedents are readily available on-line as decisions are being made. On the drawing boards are plans for a computerized network to provide improved communication links and expanded information data bases and video transmission via cable to all parts of Capitol Hill.

The cynics respond that there is no time saved with electronic voting; there are just more roll calls . . . people will be confused if detailed data from the Federal Budget is made too easily available . . . complete information on a subject may come in conflict with political reality . . . lack of information is a perfect excuse for some of the bad bills that become law.

But the majority of representatives and senators are opting for the new technology and asking more questions. As they learn about data bases in the Executive Branch, they will want access. They will be less likely to cosponsor a Consumer Communications Reform Bill advocated by the telephone company without also seeking the views of the computer industry. An electronic funds transfer policy for the banking industry may not receive their approval until they get assurances that the postal service will not be injured by their action.

As the Congress acquires "information literacy," the prospects for a national information policy are certain to improve.

READING 25 DISCUSSION QUESTIONS

1 What do you assess to be the major problems associated with the increased computer use by government agencies?
2 Neal Gregory suggests in the article that there is considerable duplication of data. What can be done to prevent this type of duplication?
3 What limits should be placed on government use of computers? Should each potential application be required to be justified by a cost/benefit analysis?

Reading 26

Computer Use in Diagnosis, Prognosis, and Therapy

Harold M. Schoolman
Lionel M. Bernstein

Diagnosis, prognosis, and therapy are three inextricably bound components of medical practice. We will review some of the major approaches of automated information management to these components. Computer systems for literature searches, hospital inventory control, housekeeping, billing, patient medication and procedure scheduling, patient monitoring, laboratory tests, diagnostic radiology, dosimetry in x-ray therapy, electrocardiogram interpretation, and so forth are well developed and widely used, but are not discussed.

Although diagnosis, prognosis, and therapy are better today than at any time in the past, there is now a greater dissatisfaction with them than ever before. We suggest that the problem results from faults in basic medical education. Our argument is that there are unrecognized and untaught distinctions among the acquisition of information, the synthesis of information (knowledge), the use of information for problem-solving (competence), and the performance of physicians in actual patient encounters.[1] Medical education has in the past, by concentrating on the first two steps, stopped short of its critical objective. Today "problem-solving" medical curricula are being developed. The problem-solving curriculum is usually described in terms of competence as measured by ability to solve test problems on paper rather than in actual performance, but there is no doubt that performance is the ultimate objective.

The goal is straightforward: to maximize the likelihood of "correct" decisions about diagnosis, prognosis, and therapy. The decisions depend on the physician's fund of information and ability to synthesize that information and appropriately apply it to problem-solving. The rapid growth of biomedical information has created an available body of knowledge (facts, concepts, and their interrelationships) far greater than any individual can assimilate. Even the most industrious and astute physician uses less than the total amount of potentially available relevant information and knowledge in making decisions. Computers, with their massive information-handling capabilities, are looked to as potential expanders of the physician's information and knowledge resources. It is in this restricted sense that the role of computerized medical information systems used in diagnosis, prognosis, and treatment will be reviewed by describing examples of some of the various approaches.

[1]J. R. Senior, *Toward the Measurement of Competence in Medicine* (Rittenhouse, Philadelphia, in press).

Reprinted with permission from *Science,* vol. 200, May 26, 1978. Copyright 1978 by the American Association for the Advancement of Science. The authors specialize in research and education at the National Library of Medicine, Bethesda, Maryland.

COMPUTER-BASED CONSULTATION

Bleich[2] has constructed a computer program to help physicians manage patients with electrolyte and acid-base disorders. The program directs a dialogue in which the physician (or other user) enters clinical and laboratory information. The data are checked for proper syntax, internal consistency, compatibility with life, and so on. On the basis of abnormalities detected, the program asks additional questions to further characterize the electrolyte and acid-base disturbance. During or at the completion of the dialogue, an evaluation note is produced. As might a consultant's note, the program evaluation provides a list of diagnostic possibilities, an explanation of underlying pathophysiology, therapeutic recommendations, precautionary measures, suggestions for further studies, and reference to the medical literature.

This program addresses an important area of medicine covering many patient encounters. The subject is one in which reliable laboratory tests provide much of the necessary information and about which considerable pathophysiologic understanding exists. Thus, the programming of definitive advice regarding decisions about individual patient care is greatly facilitated. To use the program successfully the physician must not only have identified the appropriateness of the subject for the patient but must also understand that the program does not take concomitant disorders into account. The system can readily accommodate additions or corrections, and its information data base has the authority of a consensus of a group of physicians and physiologists who have been in the forefront of research and clinical work in this subject. It provides information and is highly directive. The information provided significantly expands the working memory of facts and concepts.

The system is in wide use; although Bleich cautions[3] that "repeated usages cannot be taken as evidence of a positive contribution to patient care," it is probable that, in the area of electrolyte acid-base balance, wide use of the system would improve considerably the decision-making by physicians.

AUTOMATED MEDICAL RECORDS

The medical record has a critical function in all phases of patient management. It is used not only by doctors but also by nurses, pharmacists, therapists, laboratory workers, and accountants, among others. Indeed, it is the link of all activities impinging on patient management and the legal documentation of all transactions concerning the patient.

PROMIS (the Problem Oriented Medical Information System), developed by Weed[4] and his colleagues, is a computerized patient-management system that specifically addresses four major problems inherent in the traditional medical record. These are (i) the lack of coordination among health care providers, (ii)

[2]H. L. Bleich, *J. Clin. Invest.*, 48, 1689 (1969); *Am. J. Med.* 53, 285 (1972).
[3]Ibid., *N. Engl. J. Med.*, 284, 141 (1971).
[4]L. L. Weed, *Your Health Care and How to Manage It* (Essex, Essex Junction, Vt., 1976).

excessive reliance on memory by the providers of both knowledge of the patient and the medical literature, (iii) the lack of recorded rationality regarding observations and actions taken, and (iv) inadequate feedback loops for continual improvement of the practice of medicine. This system replaces paper records with the problem-oriented computer record using touch-sensitive terminal devices connected to a single minicomputer. Access to the electronic record is afforded to those involved in patient care.

Medical interactions are divided into four phases: (i) data base, (ii) problem formulation, (iii) initial and other plans, and (iv) progress notes. The data base is created by cumulating data entered for individual patients. Members of the hospital staff enter the patient's chief complaint and general physical characteristics into the system. The patient adds information on review of systems by answering yes-no and multiple-choice questions. Positive findings or responses are then reviewed by the physician, whose memory is aided by branched-logic displays, specific for each symptom or finding. The physician formulates the problem in any convenient manner. This absence of limitation allows a sign, symptom, disease complex, physiologic disorder, or abnormal x-ray finding to be identified as a problem without having to be restated in accordance with the requirement of many computer programs for a standardized language. Initial plans are entered by the physician for each identified problem. To help select among them, displays are again provided to aid in gathering data to rule out a specific cause of the problem, to gather information to assist in managing the problem, to order treatment, and so forth. The displays called up for each problem minimize the need for reliance on individual memory by providing up-to-date information from the medical literature. The developers of PROMIS believe it is this access to the medical literature coupled with instant access to specific patient data that facilitates integration and results in improved quality of care. "Progress notes" is the term applied to all subsequent notes after the initial plan whether from physicians, nurses, social workers, or others. Progress notes are entered in conjunction with data on each appropriate single identified problem. Data can be retrieved in many ways, such as on specific problems, chronologically, or in flow-sheet format. Drug orders, laboratory findings, and various aspects of the management of the patient can all be called onto the screen for immediate review.

The obvious and undeniable strength and advantage of PROMIS lies in the immediate availability of highly organized, reliable, complete records to all health care providers dealing with a patient. This alone must improve the performance of the individual health care providers as well as the coordination among the members of the health care delivery team. The organization provides a rational record relating the management action to the identified problems. The touch-sensitive input choices of displays minimize the "computer-terminal barrier." The system's potential cost-effectiveness ratio is markedly reduced by using it effectively to support many hospital subsystems. The management summaries provide a helpful tool to review the institution's or individual's activities and practices and can contribute to a medical management-education loop. The system is not specifically directive, but in practice, 99 percent of the time the physician chooses an alternative presented by the display. Whether this is a testimony to the accuracy and completeness of the displays or to a dependence of the user is not clear.

The PROMIS user draws on a library of 36,000 displays of information[5]. The creation and maintenance of such a volume of authoritative information covering most of medicine was and is a monumental task. The creators of PROMIS have suggested that the content of these displays could be created, maintained, audited, and validated by national groups of experts.

THE DUKE UNIVERSITY CARDIOVASCULAR INFORMATION SYSTEM

The purpose of diagnosis is to categorize a patient in a manner that allows the patient to be related to the physician's experience and knowledge. The physician making a diagnosis uses experience and knowledge of the disease to anticipate the course, predict the response to therapy, and influence management decisions. Deficiencies are that memory of personal experience is markedly biased by recent and dramatic events, and that the physician's knowledge is less than that potentially available.

Classification or diagnosis may suggest a homogeneous group acting in a similar manner. Often this is not the case. For example, patients with myocardial infarction may die within minutes or live for 50 years. To influence their decisions, physicians subclassify, hoping to identify one subgroup that would indeed be made up of those that live 50 years as distinct from those that die in 3 minutes. The number of subgroups the physician can carry in his head is small, however, and their characteristics inconstant. For the diagnosis of coronary artery disease, the Duke Medical Center group[6] estimates that at least 100 subgroups would have to be defined to achieve a reasonable likelihood that all members within each group would follow a similar course. Considering also the number of descriptors per group, the dimensionality goes well beyond the capability of the human brain. Thus, this is a problem in medicine with no solution other than by computerization.

Physicians at Duke University have developed a medical information system on the basis of their clinical experience with coronary artery disease that describes outcomes of patients with various sets of attributes[7]. The attributes (laboratory and physical findings, history, outcomes) of a large number of patients are stored in a computer, which accomplishes the entire classification process. When attributes of a new patient are entered, the computer selects the most closely matched subgroup. The courses and outcomes of all patients previously categorized in the same subgroup are displayed. The computer's

[5] *NCHSR Research Digest Series: Automation of the Problem-Oriented Medical Record* [Publ. (HRA) 77-3177, Department of Health, Education, and Welfare, Washington, D.C., 1977].

[6] R. A. Rosati, A. G. Wallace, E. A. Stead, Jr., *Arch. Intern. Med.*, 131, 285 (1973).

[7] Ibid.

memory is wholly accurate, is unbiased by recent or dramatic events, and is enhanced by the greater number of entries derived from the entire institution's rather than one physician's experience. Therefore, the physician's management decisions can be based on far more accurate and relevant information than could be possible without the computer.

The system covers an important although relatively narrow part of medicine for which there is considerable pathophysiologic understanding. Much of the total input is hard data. The system has the advantage of continuously adding to and modifying itself. Efforts are under way to expand participation to other institutions and thus, to demonstrate its transportability. It gains authority from the involvement of large numbers of physicians participating in the cardiology care activities of Duke University. There is relatively little controversial material on which individual and consensus judgments would differ. The system is designed for application of the accumulated data to have an impact on an individual unique decision with the specifically described characteristics. Therefore, the system will improve the decision-making process of both the average and the best physician.

The Duke classification system could be used to generate homogeneous groups for whom the results of clinical trials should prove more decisive than current methods of patient selection used in such trials. Since random assignment is not the method of treatment allocation (for example, coronary bypass surgery versus medical management), differences in outcomes in subgroups have not been determined to be truly characteristic of some unidentified bias in the decision-making process.

An interesting aspect of this system is that it continuously accumulates and refines data by means of which increasingly accurate estimates of risks for each intervention can be made. Thus, in part, it provides groundwork data that may be useful in the application of decision analysis to clinical decision-making.

DECISION ANALYSIS

The systems described thus far have not explicitly modeled the mechanisms of the decision-making process. Decision analysis is a formal discipline for making decisions that in many respects resembles the informal strategies of clinicians. Schwartz and co-workers[8] present several examples of its application to clinical problems. In the differentiation of essential hypertension from functional renal artery stenosis (a surgically correctable cause of hypertension) a qualitative approach is used. The model is presented as a decision tree with several pathways, along each of which are several nodes or decision points. Each intervention is a decision node. Other "chance" nodes are not under physician control. The tree is progressively built, from signs, symptoms, laboratory tests, and diagnostic and therapeutic interventions. The tree is constructed in sufficient detail to make the representation realistic, yet is constrained to

[8]W. B. Schwartz, A. G. Gorry, J. P. Kassirer, A. Essig, *Am. J. Med.*, 55, 459 (1973).

become not unmanageably large. It is acknowledged that individual physicians would differ as to the detail, but what is important is that the method forces an explicit examination and trimming of the tree by the physician. Thus, branches are pruned where both the probability and risks are low; not pruned where both are high; and assume individualized contours in intermediate combinations of probability and risk. The goal is, of course, to reach the best decision—which depends on the probabilities of various outcomes and the value judgments assigned to each outcome by the physician and the patient. But an equally important objective is to give the user far greater insight into the basis of his decisions and to force a continuing examination of his perspective and judgments.

Gorry *et al.*[9] have suggested that some clinical problems may be so complex that the qualitative approach is inadequate. For these situations, the procedure can be quantitated, but the calculations and representations require the aid of a computer. Such a prototypic computer program has been developed for the management of acute oliguric renal failure. This example uses disease lists, lists of attributes for each disease, and estimates of the likelihood of various potential consequences of tests and treatments. By use of the Bayesian approach, probabilities are calculated for each alternative at each decision point.

The computer program also stores large amounts of information which is available to the user. The computer's performance is, of course, consistent and separates probability estimates from value judgments. In operation, computer choices match very well those of the medical experts who created the system. It is suggested that the method may be profitably used to identify a best solution to various complex generic problems (for example, the role of gastroscopy in the management of gastric ulcer).

The methods have size limitations. Trimming the tree to retain manageability may necessitate choosing among incomplete sets of alternatives. The probabilities needed for various interventions are often not available from the literature and require use of subjective expert judgments. Gorry *et al* carefully acknowledged other current limitations such as a limited ability to deal with multiple diseases, inadequate dealing with the temporal changes of disease states, and the requirement of a constrained medical area.

SIMULATED CLINICAL COGNITION

Pauker *et al.*[10] have increased the complexity of computer use in simulating clinical decision-making. Techniques of "artificial intelligence" have been merged with the decision analysis approach to develop a computer program which takes the history of the "present illness" of patients with edema.

The concept of "intelligence" is that the computer is exhibiting behavior which would be termed intelligent if such behavior were that of a person. This

[9] A. G. Gorry, J. P. Kassirer, A. Essig, W. B. Schwartz, ibid., p. 473.

[10] S. G. Pauker, A. G. Gorry, J. P. Kassirer, W. B. Schwartz, ibid., 60, 981 (1976).

program is intelligent in that the computer pursues an inquiry in a manner that suggests it is trying to "understand" the illness well enough to formulate hypotheses to evaluate the clinical problem and suggest management. It does this by combining an information-gathering function with a stored information synthesis function. The latter requires no further input from the patient. The program components are (i) patient-specific data; (ii) a supervisory program that guides the computer in taking the history of the illness and generates hypotheses to be tested, accepted, or rejected; (iii) a short-term memory in which data about the patient interacts with general medical knowledge, which is, in turn, stored in (iv) an associative (long-term) memory. The long-term memory is a collection of frames each of which contains closely related facts about diseases, clinical states, or physiologic states; it consists of such information as signs, symptoms, laboratory data, and time courses, as well as rules for judging how closely a given patient's attributes match those of a frame. The frames are linked into a network by a variety of relationships (for example, "caused by" and "complicated by").

The long-term memory contains a mass of "dormant" frames of information. When some characteristics of a given frame in the long-term memory match some characteristics of the patient being explored, that frame is pulled into short-term memory (where it is then called "active") and comparisons are made between the frame's and the patient's data. As an active frame moves into short-term memory, its closely related frames (connected through a network) are pulled more closely to the short-term memory (and are thus semiactive); some of their characteristics then have greater opportunity to be compared with the characteristics of the patient. Frames that are pulled into short-term memory for comparison constitute hypotheses. Decisions are made by the program about the goodness of fit of the case to the hypothesis or on the need for more information. It measures the extent to which the frame accounts for all facts in the case, using weighted numerical scores (based on estimates of probabilities). If the hypothesis is not fully accepted, the program seeks more information by selecting questions whose answers have the greatest probability of giving useful definitive information. Cycles are repeated until the program has completed its diagnostic process.

The investigators believe that this procedure represents an important advance because it retrieves and applies knowledge when required, thus freeing the programmer from the impossible task of specifying all contingencies in advance, as would be required in branching flowchart approaches. The goal-directed character of the computer supervisory program allows (i) selection of the pertinent medical and real-world knowledge from the computer's memory and (ii) dynamic assembly of small problem-solving techniques to guide acquisition of additional information.

The investigators' assessment of their efforts identifies certain persistent limitations of the system. The most important are the limited ability to deal with a wide range of clinical problems rather than with constrained areas and the lack of capacity to deal with coexisting diseases or to fully use the temporal and changing aspects of the patient's history and course. Better methods are needed to aid the computer to focus rapidly on a narrow range of concern, a function now performed very well by the experienced physician.

INTERNIST: A PROBLEM SOLVER

INTERNIST is a computer-based diagnostic consultation system for problems in internal medicine.[11]

If a full range of diagnostic categories had to be specified in advance, the number required to arbitrarily classify patients has been estimated at the order of 10^{40}.[12] This is not because a large number of disease entities are known to a clinician (estimated from 2000 to 10,000), but rather because of the presentation of concurrent clinical problems (a dozen or more is not rare). Given what may appear to be an indiscriminate collection of data (signs, symptoms, laboratory results, for example), the clinician's first job is to decide what problems are to be dealt with. J. D. Meyers and his associates at the University of Pittsburgh have concentrated on a model of synthetic reasoning that simulates those aspects of an expert clinician's behavior concerned with formulating composite problem hypotheses.

The system is based on assigning rough estimates of likelihood of the association of a disease given a finding and a similar estimate of the likelihood of the finding given a disease. Thus, each disease entity has an associated list of manifestations known to occur in that disease and an estimate (on a scale of 1 to 5) of the frequency of occurrence of each in that disease. Similarly, for each manifestation there is a list of diseases in which it is known to occur and a weighting factor (0 to 5) for each. The weighting factor is not a simple estimate of frequency but rather an estimate of strength of association or likelihood that the manifestation and disease are causally related. This weight is called the "evoking strength." There is also recorded a hierarchy of disease categories, which has at the top level primarily organ systems (such as kidney disease, lung disease). Each of these may be subdivided any number of times until a specific disease entity is reached (chronic glomerulonephritis, carcinoma of the lung). Other accessible information in the data base includes causal, temporal, and other associations by which various disease entities are interrelated. The estimates developed for the knowledge base are based on general medical knowledge, a review of the literature, discussion and consultation with subject-matter experts, clinical case experience, trial use of the system, and a variety of other sources, all of which are funneled through and ultimately decided on by Meyers. This is a continuing process.

In the scoring process, the evoking strength is particularly useful in reducing the dimensions of concern, thus acting as a "constrictor." The evoking strength

[11] H. E. Pople, J. D. Meyers, R. A. Miller, in *Proceedings of the 4th International Joint Conference on Artificial Intelligence* (Tabilisi, U.S.S.R., 1975), pp. 848–855.

[12] H. E. Pople, in *Proceedings of the 5th International Joint Conference on Artificial Intelligence* (Cambridge, Mass., 1977), pp. 1030–1037.

and the importance of manifestations explained by a disease being tested are counted in its favor; frequency weights are counted against those diseases in which the manifestations are expected but not found in the problem case. The INTERNIST system uses constrictor concepts to delineate top-level structures of complex problems and considers within subproblems only those findings that are relevant. Multiple problems are addressed simultaneously, with the likelihood of each disease under consideration being indicated at each step. The system presents a running record of those findings not explained by the hypotheses being considered. To pursue the diagnosis, the program identifies additional manifestations (symptoms, findings, laboratory tests) about which it would like additional information in order to reach a more definitive conclusion. In so doing, it weighs the risks, hazards, discomforts, and other adverse aspects of gaining such information. It asks first for simple data that can be obtained without much cost. The program can reach conclusions about simple problems (a single disease) or complex mixes of diseases and their associated disease states.

It is estimated that the system now covers about two-thirds of internal medicine. When the test patient's problems are within the system, informal testing of the system's performance has been remarkable. Obviously, it cannot diagnose a disease not yet entered into its knowledge bank. The system mimicks the diagnostic behavior of the excellent clinician. It can partition manifestations into those associated with one or more disease states and leave unsettled and unexplained some manifestations (as is frequently done when the judgments are made by the expert clinician).

The system covers a broad area of medicine. It can deal effectively with areas where the pathophysiology is little understood and where much of the data is soft. New information is constantly added. It effectively uses a data base far greater than that retainable by any individual physician. The system retains the episodic peaks of excellence reached by the creator and by his colleagues at the time the information is entered and does not suffer from what Meyers calls the "fade-away" of information with the passage of time. In his view, the system can therefore do things he himself cannot.

The authority of the knowledge base derives from the input of a small group of physicians, and ultimately from the broad experience, competence, and synthesizing ability of one physician. The incredible complexity and ever-increasing volume of new medical information suggests that the ultimate development and maintenance of a complete knowledge base will involve developing some form of consensus by multiple experts in their respective subspecialty areas.

A MEDICAL INFORMATION BANK

Each of the medical information systems described so far intrudes into and participates directly in the interactions between the physician, the patient, patient data, and general medical knowledge as decisions are made. An alternate approach is to develop methods for making readily available the current state of that medical knowledge relevant to the specific decisions being made. Such an approach focuses on remedying existing deficits in the transfer of biomedical information and is directed toward extending and augmenting the physician's memory and capacity to synthesize the vast and ever-increasing medical literature, but it does not intervene directly in the decision-making process. Reliance is placed on the physician (or other health care provider) to use appropriately the knowledge provided in making decisions. An effort of this kind is not a substitute for the medical information systems described. Rather, it is a prototype method for developing authoritative knowledge bases.

Within the Lister Hill National Center for Biomedical Communications (the research and development arm of the National Library of Medicine) a program is aimed at developing, demonstrating, and evaluating a prototypic, computerized information transfer system. As a comprehensive bank of information, the system will (i) contain substantive anwers to questions posed by practitioners, (ii) provide answers that are current and are the consensus of a group of experts, (iii) be immediately responsive to inquiries, and (iv) provide data supporting the answers as well as citations to primary publications for more detailed study if desired. The diseases "viral hepatitis" have been selected to serve as the initial test model.

A data base suitable for automated search and retrieval techniques has been constructed. Knowledge pertaining to aspects of viral hepatitis important to the practitioner has been synthesized from the information contained in several outstanding review articles previously published by hepatitis experts.[13] Relevant information has been selected, placed in a highly organized hierarchical arrangement to permit easy retrieval, and encoded into a minicomputer. The data base is arranged by topic headings. For each heading there is an accompanying heading statement that synthesizes the state of knowledge about the subject. Data elements—paragraphs taken from previously published sources—support each heading and heading statement. Citations included within the data-element paragraphs are to the primary publications cited by the experts in their review articles to support their conclusions or general statements.

The synthesized statements offered by the information bank reflect a consensus of nationally recognized experts on the state of knowledge of the subject, and may convey substantive unanimous agreement, support for two or more mutually exclusive views, or indicate that information in a given area is simply lacking. By consensus, the same group of experts will maintain currency of the data bank by monitoring selected newly published material and revising as appropriate. A "computer-conferencing" network, linking the geographically dispersed experts with one another and with the staff of the National Library of

[13] J. W. Mosley and J. Galambos, in *Diseases of the Liver,* L. Schiff, Ed. (Lippincott, Philadelphia, ed. 4, 1975), pp. 500–593; National Academy of Sciences Symposium on Viral Hepatitis, *Am. J. Med. Sci.* 270 (Nos. 1 and 2) (1975).

Medicine, will serve as the principal medium of communication to facilitate monthly updating of the data base.

Planned access to the information bank may be available directly through a computer terminal or indirectly through a trained intermediary who can be reached on a toll-free telephone. Users may also have telephone access to programmed questions and answers or receive computer-generated printed material in hard copy or on microfiche. Other derived multimedia products would also be available.

DISCUSSION

The medical information systems described demonstrate important advances in the use of computers to help the physician make decisions. Computers clearly can function successfully as extenders of the physician's memory for information generally and for individual patient data, and they can greatly augment the information resources available to support decision-making. The approaches are in some ways complementary, in other ways overlapping; in no way can the sum of them be considered to address fully and successfully the recognized problems in the arenas of diagnostic, prognostic, and treatment decisions.

Four of the systems perform within narrow ranges of disease but in considerable detail. They are the electrolyte and acid-base disorders consultation system, the Duke coronary artery system, decision analysis, and the computer simulation of clinical cognition. In contrast, PROMIS and INTERNIST perform in less detail, but across broad areas of disease.

The electrolyte and acid-base disorders computer consultation system covers small substantive areas of medicine for which hard data provide much of the critical input and about which considerable pathophysiologic understanding exists. Because of their highly constrained nature, they can operate on the basis of a relatively small number of definitive diagnoses. Although this approach can be extended to some other constrained arenas of medicine, there are many substantive areas in which these criteria are not met. Such a system can be useful only after the physician recognizes that the patient's problem falls within its scope. These approaches cannot deal simultaneously with arrays of multiple disease categories as can the expert clinician, nor do they effectively deal with the temporal relationships of additional data.

Systems using decision analysis and computer simulation of clinical cognition share most of the characteristics described above. Although applied so far only in constrained areas, these approaches could be extended to all medical areas. They alone offer very explicit consideration of value judgments assigned to outcomes by both physicians and patients; all other systems rely upon implicit integration of both the physician's and the patient's value judgments in the decision.

Both PROMIS and INTERNIST cover broad areas of medicine, including those for which the pathophysiology is little understood and much of the data soft. As the scope increases, diagnostic and therapeutic directiveness decreases.

The breadth of coverage requires developing and maintaining an authoritative data base, which can best be accomplished through the collaboration of a large number of subject specialists. PROMIS deals with multiple disorders largely by treating them separately and sequentially. INTERNIST mimics an expert clinician and is the only one of these systems that handles symptoms and findings of multiple diseases simultaneously.

The medical information bank approach is a prototypic attempt to make readily available an authoritative statement of current medical knowledge relevant to specific decisions being made. The information can be used directly, or it can complement other computer approaches to medical decision-making.

Computers perform as instructed in support of the various systems described. The acid-base program assumes that each of its diagnoses is exclusive; it deals with management on this unitary basis by a completely preprogrammed management flow-sheet display. The computer problem is reduced to choosing the appropriate display. The computer problem for PROMIS is qualitatively the same, but now the choice is from a library of 36,000 displays. In the coronary artery system the displays are being revised constantly as new experience is gained. These revisions, made by the computer, provide directly authoritative information necessary to make decisions on subclassification (diagnosis), prognosis, and management for individual patients. Computer simulation of clinical cognition has introduced an important "synthesis" concept. Here the final displays do not exist in a preformed set but must be built up by appropriate combination of small modules. The computer problem is to select and apply knowledge from its stores when it is required, thus freeing the programmer from the impossible task of prior specification of all possible contingencies. This concept of synthesis is also employed in INTERNIST which combines it with elements of probabilistic computations and pathophysiologic flow charts to build and select displays. INTERNIST keeps track of and displays both explained and unexplained findings. The hepatitis data base uses the computer for simplifying text editing and updating and for convenience of storage, retrieval, and dissemination.

In this brief review of examples of some of the classes of computer systems being developed to support diagnosis, prognosis and therapy, there is evident a clear evolution of both an increasing sophistication of systems and a progressive recognition of the complexity of the problems. Also changing is the man-machine relationship. What may have been considered earlier as an adversary relationship is evolving through greater recognition and respect for the unique capabilities of each into a synergistic collaboration. Whatever the limitations of existing systems, the data justify an optimistic view of the future of this collaboration in medicine.

READING 26 DISCUSSION QUESTIONS

1 What are some of the major obstacles to using computers in the field of medicine?
2 Are there areas of medicine which definitely do *not* lend themselves to computerization?

3 Project ahead to the year 2000 and discuss the possible computer applications in the health field.

Reading 27

Labor Relations Information Delivery in the Public Sector

Ronald A. Leahy

Public sector labor-management relations practitioners have not escaped the deluge of information that has saturated virtually every aspect of modern personnel management in public service in the United States. During the past two decades, the Federal Government's labor relations program has been producing a burgeoning, complex mass of information in various forms—regulations, negotiated agreements, arbitration awards, and rulings of administrative bodies.

Moreover, State and local governments, numbering in the tens of thousands, have accumulated a store of data many times greater than that generated by the Federal sector.

At the same time, the labor relations data needs of elected officials, government agencies, and public labor organizations have not only expanded dramatically, but have become crucial to effective decisionmaking in agencies that negotiate or consult with labor organizations.

GROWTH IN PUBLIC EMPLOYEE REPRESENTATION

The magnitude of this groundswell becomes apparent when one considers the meteoric rise in labor organization representation of public employees in recent years. In the Federal Government, shortly after President Kennedy conferred formal status on labor-management relations in his 1962 Executive Order (No. 10988), fewer than 200,000 employees were represented by labor organizations. This number grew to 900,000 by 1970. Further expansion was stimulated by Executive Order 11491 (1970), which added new, intricate dimensions to the program; and by Executive Order 11636 (1971), which applied to employees in the Foreign Service.

By 1975, more than 1.2 million employees (a six-fold increase during just 12 years) were represented in some 4,000 local units, in more than 50 Federal agencies, nationwide and overseas.

At the same time, State and local governments experienced an equivalent growth in employee representation. The 1972 Census of Governments reports

Reprinted from *Civil Service Journal,* April–June 1977. Reprinted by permission from the Office of Personnel Management, Washington, D.C. Mr. Leahy is Assistant Director for Information Services, Office of Labor-Management Relations, U.S. Civil Service Commission.

that as of October 1972, 4,319,941 full-time State and local government employees (50.4 percent of all employees) were members of employee organizations. Of the 78,268 State and local governments, 10,737 engaged in collective negotiations and/or consultation and had 19,547 negotiated agreements. (For more information, see *Census of Governments,* U.S. Bureau of the Census, 1972, Vol. 3, Public Employment No. 3: Management-Labor Relations in State and Local Government, U.S. Government Printing Office, Washington, D.C., 1974.)

NEW DEMANDS ON PUBLIC MANAGERS

As these labor-management programs have expanded in size and number, they have become much more structured and complex. Consequently, public managers must meet extraordinary new demands. They must fairly apply wide-ranging merit system regulations. At the same time, they must meet the requirements of negotiated agreements that touch on nearly every facet of personnel policy and work conditions. Adding to the burden is the fact that these agreements are laden with provisions often subject to interpretation through arbitration or similar procedures.

But a computer-assisted system—Labor Agreement Information Retrieval System (LAIRS)—was developed recently at CSC that will help. It has improved the organization and delivery of labor relations information. Although the CSC staff devised LAIRS to satisfy the Federal Government's needs, the system also has some immediate applicability in State and local government labor relations. It could pave the way for development of similar intergovernmental systems.

It was in 1972 that the U.S. Civil Service Commission first recognized the intense need for a coordinated, Federal Government–wide method for accumulating, organizing, retrieving, and disseminating useful information from this vast mélange of intelligence. It was immediately evident that systems then in existence, relying principally on manual techniques, would be grossly inadequate both in the short and the long run.

LAIRS TAKES SHAPE

After nearly 2 years of concerted effort, closely orchestrated with agency management and labor organizations, the Commission in December 1974 announced the new LAIRS.

The Labor Agreement Information Retrieval System is a multifaceted service center providing current and historical information about the Federal labor relations program. The information takes the form of computer searches, microfiche of full text decisions, published analytical reports, current periodicals, and a variety of other audio-visual training aids.

The computer/microfiche file contains negotiated agreements, arbitration awards, and significant case decisions of the Federal Labor Relations Council, the Assistant Secretary of Labor for Labor-Management Relations, the Federal Service Impasses Panel, the Comptroller General, and the Federal Employee Appeals Authority. More than 10,000 documents are coded by subject matter for computerized indexing, and microfiche storage and retrieval.

The LAIRS system employs a nationwide timesharing system called INFONET, which provides the teleprocessing network for immediate (interactive) or overnight (batch) searching of the computer files through a keyboard terminal located at the U.S. Civil Service Commission in Washington, D.C. INFONET was conceived, designed, and implemented by Computer Sciences Corporation in response to timesharing requirements of both business and government data processing users.

The U.S. Civil Service Commission acquires INFONET services through the General Services Administration. The Commission's own data processing center provides file update service three times yearly and produces regular and ad hoc programmed reports.

Normally computer searches are couched in precise, uniform terms in combination to describe a special or unique information need. Requesters may choose from among hundreds of subject categories and thousands of subtopical variations in conjunction with frequency of occurrence, agency or labor union identifiers, number and occupation of affected employees, and geographic location of work unit, among numerous other options.

Often a requester needs a computer printout of all records on file in a predetermined sequence or format. Such requests are filled within a few days to a few weeks, depending on the complexity of the programming required, urgency of the need, cost considerations, and LAIRS staff time required.

HOW TO USE LAIRS

Although the system was established primarily to serve Federal agencies and certified labor organizations representing Federal Government employees, written requests for information are accepted from most other organizations and individuals. Regular users have a manual of instructions and forms for submitting requests. All other requesters are required to submit a written statement of the publication(s) or other information desired to: U.S. Civil Service Commission, Office of Labor-Management Relations, LAIRS Section, 1900 E. St. NW., Washington, D.C. 20415; or to one of the 10 regional offices of the U.S. Civil Service Commission located in major cities across the United States.

Nominal fees are charged for computer searches and for microfiche copies. For Federal agencies, this means that an interagency reimbursement is required. Other requesters are billed. For regular high-frequency users, a subscription arrangement is available that reduces costs and expedites transactions. A schedule of fees is provided upon written request.

Frequently, LAIRS publishes labor-management reports and surveys. These may be purchased from the National Technical Information Service

(NTIS) in papercopy or microfiche form. NTIS, part of the U.S. Department of Commerce, is a central source for the public sale of Government-sponsored research reports and other analyses prepared by Federal agencies. It is located at 5285 Port Royal Road, Springfield, Va. 22161. A public reference room, located at the U.S. Civil Service Commission in Washington, D.C., is also available for use by appointment. There is, of course, no fee charged for this service.

The LAIRS system is designed not only to serve the Federal labor-management information needs of today, but tomorrow as well. Expansion and contraction in the scope of negotiable topics can be quickly reflected in the data file. If future demand dictates a requirement for direct access to the computer file from multiple locations throughout the nation, the system has the inherent capacity to respond, without need to redesign programs or files.

READING 27 DISCUSSION QUESTIONS

1 Discuss some of the problems associated with operating an information retrieval system such as LAIRS.
2 What are the major advantages to various government units in having such labor relations data available?

Case G

Why Police States Love the Computer

Hugh Wiener

"Computers," said Herman Kahn late last year, "are obviously the supporting device for a totalitarian culture. I'm not saying it will happen, but it is an open issue."

You're a bit late, Mr. Kahn. It has already happened.

The largest single customer for computers in every country is the country's government. All governments use computers for social control. They differ only in the degree of control they exercise via the computer and the kinds of activities they control. Pioneered by the wealthy and technologically advanced democracies, the use of computer systems for police, political, health, medical, and economic administration is now a high priority for every dictatorship.

The problems raised by the use and abuse of information-processing systems are not restricted by national boundaries. The international flow of data, once a trickle, is rapidly becoming a torrent. Files on political activists, potential activists, and even socially concerned clergymen are being exchanged among the governments of Latin American regimes. Dossiers stored on the computers of

Reprinted with permission from *The Business and Society Review*, No. 22, Summer 1977. Copyright 1977, Warren, Gorham and Lamont Inc., 210 South Street, Boston, Massachusetts. All rights reserved. Mr. Wiener is the editor of *Computer Decisions*.

the FBI, State Department, and other agencies (many of whose files are already linked to state and local police files) are finding their way into the computers of foreign governments—sometimes accompanied by fingerprints or passport photographs.

Private institutions also have immense collections of data, and all the problems associated with dossiers in the hands of government agencies become more severe when private interests are involved. It is difficult to distinguish between data that may be used for commercial purposes and data used for repression. Private interests are so powerful in this area that any legal restrictions on the collection, storage, and sale of data by private concerns may eventually be overcome by the establishment of offshore data banks—data havens in a few countries that wish to profit from them.

The companies that manufacture computers are aware of the problems brought about by the misuse of their products. They know that their machines are used to enforce the social policies of reasonable and unreasonable governments alike. In particular, they know that their machines are sought by dictatorial regimes to aid in the roundup of political enemies and by megalomaniacal despots to plan and execute intrigues and wars. The knowledge of the computer companies is extensive and, in some cases, so specific that it borders on complicity.

The computer manufacturers know what they are involved in because large computers are not sold and abandoned. The companies induce customers to purchase computers by promising assistance and a continuing technical presence, which they provide. In fact, even if the computer manufacturers wished to maintain some distance between themselves and their customers, they would fail. Computers and the programs which make them work are so complex that no customer could use them effectively without help from the seller. The most carefully kept secrets of the U.S. government are stored on computers run with the active involvement of the manufacturers.

The level of detail known to a company which installs and services a computer includes knowledge of the kinds of jobs being done, but generally falls short of information about the exact data stored in the computer's memory. For example, a company that sells a computer to a social surveillance agency would know whether the machine will be used for the storage of files, or for computation, or for communications. It would know the size and form of each file and the total size of the data base, but it would not know who or what will be on file. It would know something of the complexity and type of calculations to be performed, but it would not know the details of the calculations. It would know the capacity of the system for sending messages, but it would not know the content of the messages.

SEE NO EVIL, COMPUTE NO EVIL

There is some question about who has responsibility for the way computers are used. The greatest burden must be borne by whoever uses the computer, of course. But there is also some responsibility borne by the government agencies which issue permits for the shipment and installation of computers abroad. The companies which provide data processing resources can be held responsible for their decision to sell or not sell the equipment. And after the machinery is installed, the companies have a responsibility to evaluate their commitments. Having learned the details of the way their computers are used, the manufacturers could cease providing the promised service.

These questions must be addressed most seriously by American computer companies, which dominate the world market for computers. In the non-Communist world, nearly all government computers are of American manufacture. Even the governments of nations with indigenous computer industries own and operate many computers of American manufacture.

Among the American companies one corporation clearly dominates the market for large systems: International Business Machines Corporation. IBM is believed to have between one-half and three-fourths of the large systems worldwide. By virtue of IBM's commitment to excellence, particularly in service and support, its products have become worldwide standards. The computers of many other nations—Japan, Germany, France, the United Kingdom, and the Eastern bloc—borrow heavily from IBM's designs, and their manufacturers mimic IBM's attitudes and policies. While IBM did not invent the computer, IBM did invent the computer industry.

This leadership makes IBM the place to begin questioning an industry that has given great record-keeping power to benign and demonic governments alike. And IBM's home country, the United States, is the leader of all the world's governments in matters involving computers. In particular, the most questionable use of computers involves the alliances between the U.S. government and Latin American dictatorships.

Similar situations exist outside Latin America, notably in Korea, Iran, and the Communist world. For example, Iran has an American electronics network called Ibex (a descendant of the McNamara Line across Vietnam), which is said to guard borders, monitor communications, and store the files of the Shah's secret police. The Korean CIA is believed to depend on American computers for its wide-ranging activities. The Eastern bloc, far behind the West in using computers, is said to envy and emulate the facilities of its more advanced competitors.

But Latin America has been a main focus of recent investigations into the ways computers are misused with the help of American funds and know-how. Chile, Argentina, Uruguay, and Brazil are in virtual states of siege. Persons suspected of harboring adversary political beliefs are systematically kidnapped, imprisoned, tortured, and killed—most often by agents of government. Persons believed to be associates of known political activists are similarly treated. Torture is commonplace, and computers are helping. In Chile, according to one refugee who had served in a high academic position, the government's computer systems store complete information about "the opposition, those considered leftists or suspects. The computer has all the facts." Reports of police roundups in Chile include descriptions of the processing of identification cards in ways that can only be explained by the presence of computers.

Last winter, the Chilean government wanted to buy a new information system for $5.5 million from Rockwell International. The U.S. government refused to issue an export permit, because it believed that the computer would be used to terrorize the Chilean populace further. Undaunted, the Chilean government decided to buy the computers directly and hire American consultants to turn the machines into a system capable of storing complete dossiers, including fingerprints, on every citizen of Chile. One executive of an American consulting firm has said that his company was asked to provide expertise, not equipment, to the Chilean government, thus circumventing export restrictions. His company, after thinking over the proposal, turned it down. But an official of the Chilean embassy confirms that this contract will be awarded after all—to a company that helped build the fingerprint system used by the FBI. The system, which will be operated by the Chilean government, could be functioning within a year.

Not all the computers used by the government of Chile are in the offices of governmental agencies. According to a former official of the Allende regime, there is a data-processing service called ECOM that does extensive work for Chile's secret police. The chairman of ECOM, which uses IBM and Burroughs computers, is an active general in the Chilean army. The president of ECOM is René Peralta, a former officer of the Chilean navy and a former director of computation at the University of Chile. The university also has a computer, and the National Council of Churches claims that the machine is being used by police agencies. IBM disputes the claim, but a company spokesman admits that his firm is aware that "the generals have taken over the university."

One man's ordeal in Uruguay indicates that dossiers kept on computers are exchanged among the governments of Latin America. The man entered Uruguay and was picked up by the police for questioning. His interrogators asked him about a Catholic priest they sought. The man was presented with a computer printout detailing the priest's career, including all the priest's known addresses, his salary at each, his telephone numbers, and his relationships with persons in Uruguay. What most amazed the interrogated man was that the sought-after priest had never been in Uruguay. The data on the computer printout had been supplied by the police of another country!

Brazil, the largest and wealthiest nation in South America, is also a leader in using computers. IBM has a factory there which makes large System/370 machines and ancillary equipment. It is believed that the police of Brazil use IBM computers to manage large collections of dossiers. Evidence of this practice comes from a document prepared by IBM.

The IBM paper, which came from a survey of IBM's customers conducted by its Rio Governo office in Rio de Janeiro, indicates that in December 1973 the police of the state of Rio de Janeiro (then called the state of Guanabara) were planning to install a pair of IBM 370/145 computers equipped with forty inquiry terminals. These terminals would be placed where they could be used to retrieve files instantly.

The report lists the uses to which the computers would be put. In addition to routine files—such as those containing lists of stolen vehicles, criminals' names and wanted persons—the computers would be used to store files of "political activists."

IBM has admitted, following publication of the document, that it is authentic. IBM claims that the system was never ordered, but refused to say whether Brazilian police have other, similar systems. At the time the system was sought by the Brazilians, American newspapers were carrying detailed reports of abduction and torture by the Brazilian secret police.

The police in Argentina have a system, built by an American company, which is the most advanced of its kind anywhere. The equipment sold under the trade name Digicom by E-Systems of Garland, Texas, is a radio communications system connecting police cars with computerized information at police headquarters in Buenos Aires. One of Digicom's many abilities is locating by triangulation the police cars which carry it. Another device being used by the police of Buenos Aires is called Wheelbarrow. Like Digicom it has a radio transmitter and receiver, and like Digicom it can be used to locate the vehicle bearing it. Unlike Digicom, it does not facilitate communications. Wheelbarrow is a self-locating bomb, triggered from police headquarters.

The problems caused by computers in the hands of dictators are compounded by the international flow of dossiers. One important agent for the transfer of police and other government files is Interpol, headquartered in St. Cloud, France, outside Paris. Interpol is a coordinating agency for the police of its 125-member nations. Each member maintains a national central bureau which serves as Interpol's local anchor. The U.S. bureau, for example, housed in the Treasury building in Washington, sorts out requests for information and sends them to the appropriate agencies. Among the agencies fulfilling Interpol requests are the FBI, which provides criminal records and fingerprints; the State Department, which provides passport information, including photographs; the Immigration and Naturalization Service; the Drug Enforcement Administration; the Bureau of Alcohol, Tobacco and Firearms of the Internal Revenue Service; the Postal Service; and local police agencies. In addition to information requests, Interpol may ask for services such as surveillance or detention.

The information on the requests made by Interpol members is sometimes sketchy. Because the United States examines each request and only provides data in response to those queries stemming from criminal charges, the Government Accounting Office believes that the American office of Interpol is not being misused. However, requests from foreign countries are also made directly to foreign offices of the FBI, Drug Enforcement Administration, and other U.S. agencies abroad. This less-regulated route is used very often.

These police channels are not the only links among the computers of various nations. Credit bureaus in the United States have extensive records on many foreigners, principally Canadians, and medical records travel along the same routes that tourists and immigrants do. In fact, the linkage of computers to remote sites is so easy today that, according to Congressman Barry Goldwater, Jr., fire marshals in Southern Sweden routinely use a data file in Cleveland to plan fire control strategies.

There has been no evidence that these files suffer widespread abuse. But there are also no laws or regulations to limit the flow of data. American and European nations, principally those which have enacted legislation to control data flow within their borders, have expressed concern that any efforts to control the misuse of computerized information will fail unless international conventions are established.

For the most part, the social problems posed by the widespread interchange of computerized records among nations are overshadowed by the problems of computer misuse within nations. But all the problems are growing rapidly throughout the world. While not as dramatic as the threats to human survival posed by shortages of food, energy, and housing, the threats to freedom and privacy may be more pernicious just because they are largely invisible.

CASE G DISCUSSION QUESTIONS

1 Discuss the use and abuse of computers in areas such as those described in the case.
2 What can be done—and by whom—to prevent the abuse of computers?
3 Limiting the use of computers in certain areas is one solution to resolving societal problems such as those discussed in the case. How realistic is this alternative?

SUMMARY OF CHAPTER 8

In this chapter, we have surveyed selected computer applications in not-for-profit organizations. We have seen that government planners at all levels have a mandate to efficiently use public funds and resources in ways that best serve the needs of society. High-quality information is needed by planners to achieve their objectives, and hundreds of computer applications have been developed to supply planners with better information. Federal government decision makers are actively using computers in such areas as environmental planning, weather forecasting, and military planning; state and municipal decision makers are concerned with such areas as social welfare planning and urban planning. Members of Congress and legislators are finding legislative data banks to be of value and are exploring the use of computers in political campaigns.

Millions of dollars have been channeled into the development and use of law enforcement computer systems. Many of these systems are tied together at the state levels, and the state systems are, in turn, linked to the FBI's NCIC system. Thus, a nationwide network of police data banks is now operational. Such a network helps law enforcement agencies with fixed geographical jurisdictions cope with the activities of increasingly mobile criminals, but there are many concerned citizens who believe that the issues of individual freedom and the right to privacy have not been given proper consideration as these interlocking data banks have been developed.

The use of computers in health fields is increasing rapidly. In the area of medical planning and decision making, for example, computers are now being used to assist doctors in diagnosing illnesses, and computer-assisted research is providing new insights into the way the body functions and into the causes and cures of disease. By placing the medical history of a patient in a data bank, one or more doctors can retrieve and update it as needed. Better information about a patient's medical background should enable doctors to do a more effective job of preventing potential health problems and detecting illnesses. Studies of drug addiction and drug side effects are being facilitated through computer usage, computer simulation is sharpening the skills and decision-making abilities of student doctors, and hospital menus are being planned with the help of machines.

Computers can bring to the educational process such attributes as patience, around-the-clock availability, and individualized and student-paced instruction programs. Thus, although progress to date in applying computers in the instructional process has been relatively slow, the future of the machines in education is assured. A primary purpose of using computers as an instructional tool should be to provide insight and not merely to compute numbers or process documents.

In educational planning and decision making, computers are being applied in the areas of curriculum planning and planning for individual instruction. *Computer-managed instruction* is the name given to the use of computers to assist teachers in the administration of individual instruction programs; *computer-assisted instruction* refers to situations where students themselves interact with computers and where instruction is presented or reinforced. Charges have been made that using computers in the educational process will "dehumanize" instruction and make robots of students. Perhaps these fears are exaggerated, but in education as in other fields, computer usage may sweep aside some current practices and introduce new problems. Such changes are likely to be resisted by some educators.

Control applications of computers in education are found in the areas of testing and error analysis. In some subjects, CAI methods are well suited for testing student progress. The simplest and most used form of CAI is the drill-and-practice approach; other forms are the tutorial and dialogue approaches. The advantages and problems of CAI are discussed in this chapter.

Computer simulations may be used as teaching aids. Students learn by making decisions and by learning of the consequences of those decisions. Theories can be put into practice and valuable experience can be gained in a safe and inexpensive way.

Although there are those scholars who argue that computers have no place in the humanities, the fact is that a small but growing number of humanists are finding the computer to be a useful tool in their work.

Computers have been used to aid experts in making judgments about the authenticity of art objects and the authorship of literary works; they have been used successfully to prepare a large number of concordances that are of value to literary scholars; they have been used to create new "art" and to analyze existing art; they have an unquestioned future in the developing museum information-retrieval systems; and they permit historians and archaelogists to manipulate masses of data to arrive at relationships and insights that might otherwise remain undetected.

Index